W9-BFF-467

ADDISON WESLEY

Math Makes Sense

Author Team

Jason Johnston
Bryn Keyes
Mary Doucette
Antonietta Lenjosek
Steve Thomas
Margaret Sinclair
Trevor Brown
Cathy Heideman
Don Jones
Michael Davis
Jennifer Paziuk
Sharon Jeroski
Ken Harper

PEARSON
Addison Wesley

Publishing Team
Lesley Haynes
Enid Haley
Lynne Gulliver
Ingrid D'Silva
Cristina Gulesiu
Stephanie Cox
Judy Wilson
Nicole Argyropoulos

Editorial Contributors
John Burnett
Jim Mennie
Janine Leblanc
Christina Yu

Publisher
Claire Burnett

Elementary Math Team Leader
Anne-Marie Scullion

Product Manager
Nishaant Sanghavi

Photo Research
Karen Hunter

Design
Word & Image Design Studio Inc.

ISBN 0-321-23536-3

Printed and bound in Canada.

5 -- TCP -- 09 08 07 06

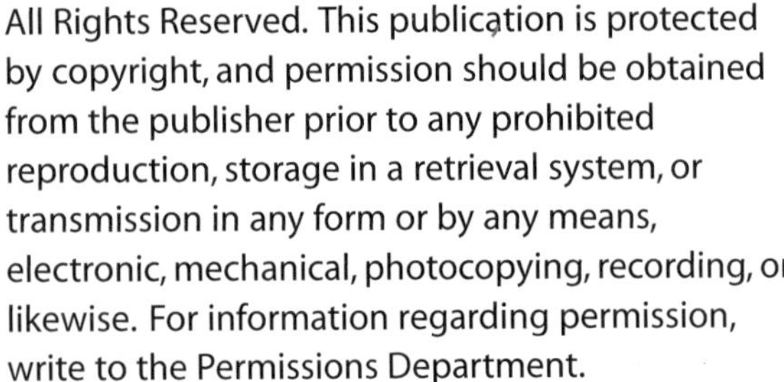

The publisher has taken every care to meet or exceed industry specifications for the manufacturing of textbooks. The spine and the endpapers of this sewn book have been reinforced with special fabric for extra binding strength. The cover is a premium, polymer-reinforced material designed to provide long life and withstand rugged use. Mylar gloss lamination has been applied for further durability.

Program Consultants and Advisers

Program Consultants

Craig Featherstone
Maggie Martin Connell
Trevor Brown

Assessment Consultant
Sharon Jeroski

Elementary Mathematics Adviser
John A. Van de Walle

Program Advisers

Pearson Education thanks its Program Advisers, who helped shape the vision for *Addison Wesley Mathematics Makes Sense* through discussions and reviews of prototype materials and manuscript.

Anthony Azzopardi
Sandra Ball
Victoria Barlow
Lorraine Baron
Bob Belcher
Judy Blake
Steve Cairns
Christina Chambers
Daryl M. J. Chichak
Lynda Colgan
Marg Craig
Elizabeth Fothergill
Jennifer Gardner
Florence Glanfield
Linden Gray
Pamela Hagen
Dennis Hamaguchi
Angie Harding
Andrea Helmer
Peggy Hill
Auriana Kowalchuk
Gordon Li
Werner Liedtke
Jodi Mackie
Lois Marchand
Becky Matthews
Betty Milne
Cathy Molinski
Cynthia Pratt Nicolson
Bill Nimigon
Stephen Parks
Eileen Phillips
Carole Saundry
Evelyn Sawicki
Leyton Schnellert
Shannon Sharp
Michelle Skene
Lynn Strangway
Laura Weatherhead
Mignonne Wood

Program Reviewers

Field Testers

Pearson Education would like to thank the teachers and students who field-tested *Addison Wesley Math Makes Sense 7* prior to publication. Their feedback and constructive recommendations have helped us to develop a quality mathematics program.

Aboriginal Content Reviewers

Early Childhood and School Services Division
Department of Education, Culture, and Employment
Government of Northwest Territories:

Steven Daniel, Coordinator, Mathematics, Science, and Secondary Education
Liz Fowler, Coordinator, Culture Based Education
Margaret Erasmus, Coordinator, Aboriginal Languages

Grade 7 Reviewers

Judy Blaney
OISE/University of Toronto, ON

Michaela Clancy
Simcoe Muskoka Catholic District School Board, ON

Tina Conlon
Niagara Catholic District School Board, ON

Kelly Denholme
School District #43 (Coquitlam), BC

Gwen Emery
Toronto District School Board, ON

Thomas Falkenberg
School District #44 (North Vancouver), BC

Norma Fraser
School District #83 (North Okanagan/Shuswap), BC

Rob D'Ilario
Niagara Catholic District School Board, ON

AJ Keene
Lakehead District School Board, ON

Linda LoFaro
Ottawa-Carleton Catholic School Board, ON

David MacLean
School District #43 (Coquitlam), BC

Becky Matthews
Victoria, BC

Jim McCann
Simcoe County District School Board, ON

Timothy T. Millan
Toronto District School Board, ON

Mark Moorhouse
Lakehead District School Board, ON

Walter Rogoza
Rainy River District School Board, ON

Wendy Swonnell
School District #61 (Greater Victoria), BC

James Tremblay
Durham Catholic District School Board, ON

Gregg Williamson
Hamilton-Wentworth District School Board, ON

Table of Contents

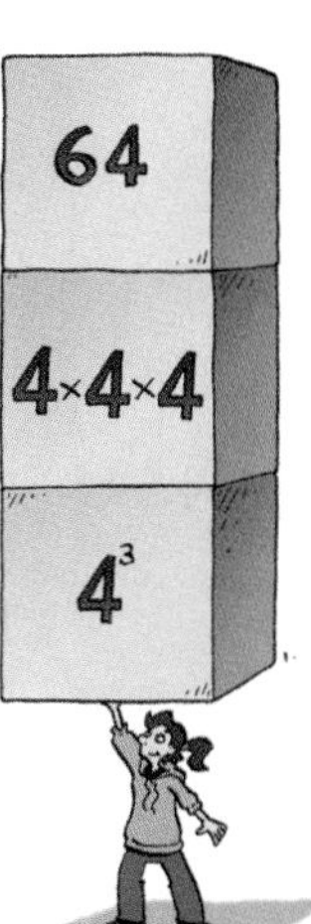

UNIT 3 Geometry and Measurement

Strand
- Geometry and Spatial Sense
- Measurement

UNIT 4 Fractions and Decimals

Strand
- Number Sense and Numeration

UNIT 5 Data Management

Strand • Data Management and Probability

UNIT 6 Measuring Perimeter and Area

Strand • Measurement • Patterning and Algebra

UNIT 7 Geometry

Strand • Geometry and Spatial Sense

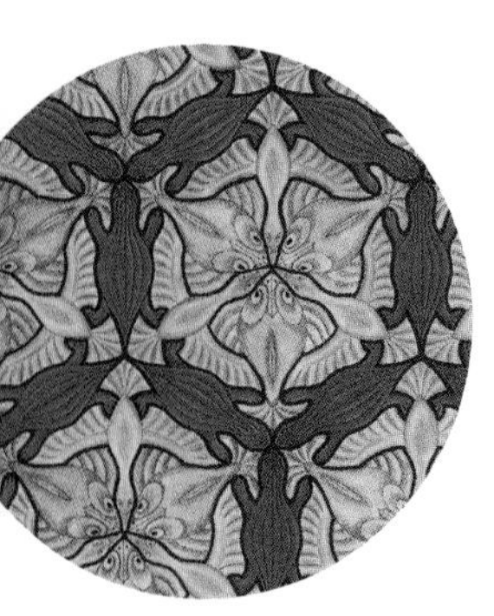

UNIT 8 Working with Percents

Strand • Number Sense and Numeration
• Data Management and Probability

GRAND SALE
You pay 75% of the original price!

UNIT 9 Integers

Strand • Number Sense and Numeration

UNIT 10 Patterning and Algebra

Strand • Patterning and Algebra

UNIT 11 Probability

Strand • Data Management and Probability

Welcome to
Addison Wesley Math Makes Sense 7

Math helps you understand your world.

This book will help you improve your problem-solving skills and show you how you can use your math now, and in your future career.

The opening pages of **each unit** are designed to help you prepare for success.

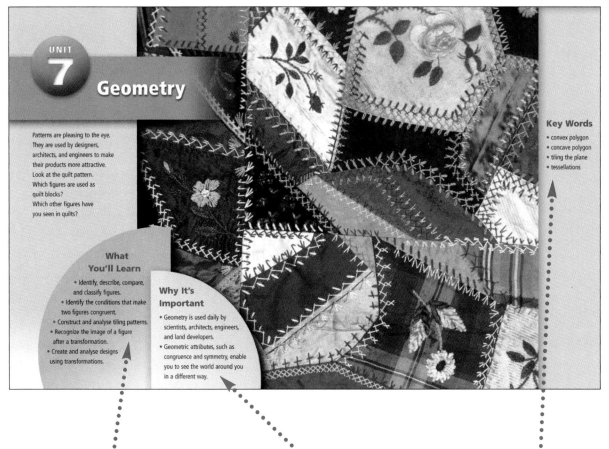

UNIT 7

Geometry

Patterns are pleasing to the eye. They are used by designers, architects, and engineers to make their products more attractive. Look at the quilt pattern. Which figures are used as quilt blocks? Which other figures have you seen in quilts?

What You'll Learn

- Identify, describe, compare, and classify figures.
- Identify the conditions that make two figures congruent.
- Construct and analyse tiling patterns.
- Recognize the image of a figure after a transformation.
- Create and analyse designs using transformations.

Why It's Important

- Geometry is used daily by scientists, architects, engineers, and land developers.
- Geometric attributes, such as congruence and symmetry, enable you to see the world around you in a different way.

Key Words

- convex polygon
- concave polygon
- tiling the plane
- tessellations

Find out **What You'll Learn** and **Why It's Important**. Check the list of **Key Words**.

Review some of the math concepts you've already met.

Study the **Example**.

Then try the **Check** questions to review your skills.

UNIT 6

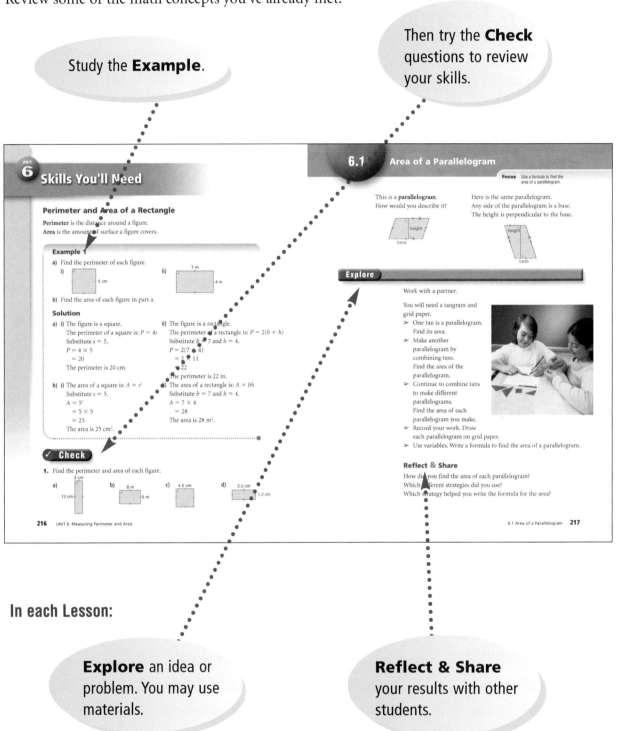

Skills You'll Need

Perimeter and Area of a Rectangle

Perimeter is the distance around a figure.
Area is the amount of surface a figure covers.

Example 1

a) Find the perimeter of each figure.
i) 5 cm
ii) 7 m, 4 m

b) Find the area of each figure in part a.

Solution

a) i) The figure is a square.
The perimeter of a square is: $P = 4s$
Substitute $s = 5$.
$P = 4 \times 5$
$= 20$
The perimeter is 20 cm.

ii) The figure is a rectangle.
The perimeter of a rectangle is: $P = 2(b + h)$
Substitute $b = 7$ and $h = 4$.
$P = 2(7 + 4)$
$= 2 \times 11$
$= 22$
The perimeter is 22 m.

b) i) The area of a square is: $A = s^2$
Substitute $s = 5$.
$A = 5^2$
$= 5 \times 5$
$= 25$
The area is 25 cm^2.

ii) The area of a rectangle is: $A = bh$
Substitute $b = 7$ and $h = 4$.
$A = 7 \times 4$
$= 28$
The area is 28 m^2.

✓ Check

1. Find the perimeter and area of each figure.
a) 3 cm, 12 cm
b) 8 m, 5 m
c) 4.5 cm
d) 3.0 cm, 1.2 cm

216 UNIT 6: Measuring Perimeter and Area

6.1 Area of a Parallelogram

Focus Use a formula to find the area of a parallelogram.

This is a **parallelogram**.
How would you describe it?

height
base

Here is the same parallelogram.
Any side of the parallelogram is a base.
The height is perpendicular to the base.

height
base

Explore

Work with a partner.

You will need a tangram and grid paper.

- One tan is a parallelogram. Find its area.
- Make another parallelogram by combining tans. Find the area of the parallelogram.
- Continue to combine tans to make different parallelograms. Find the area of each parallelogram you make.
- Record your work. Draw each parallelogram on grid paper.
- Use variables. Write a formula to find the area of a parallelogram.

Reflect & Share

How did you find the area of each parallelogram?
Which different strategies did you use?
Which strategy helped you write the formula for the area?

6.1 Area of a Parallelogram 217

In each Lesson:

Explore an idea or problem. You may use materials.

Reflect & Share your results with other students.

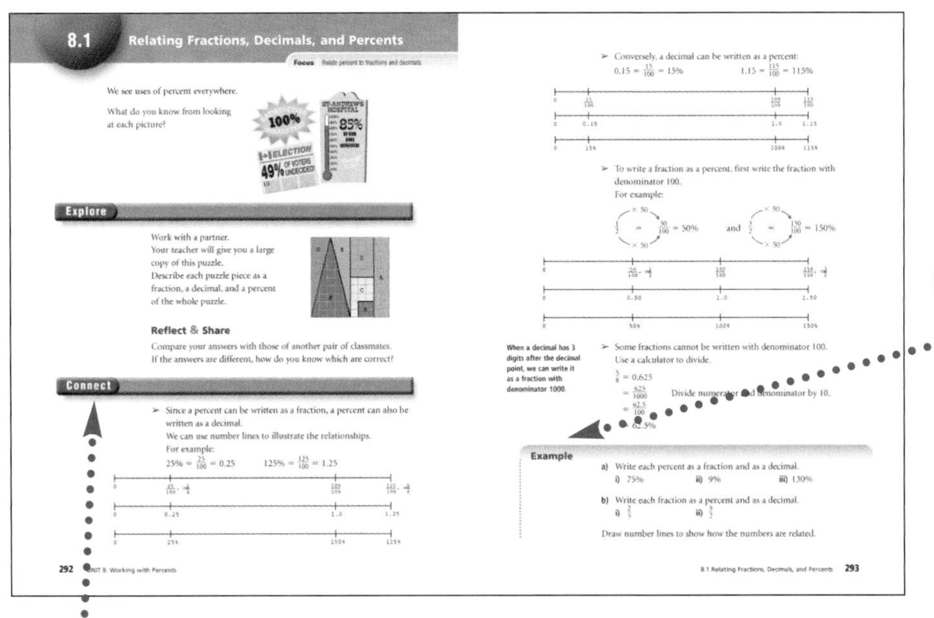

8.1 Relating Fractions, Decimals, and Percents

Focus: Relate percent to fractions and decimals.

We see uses of percent everywhere.

What do you know from looking at each picture?

Explore

Work with a partner.
Your teacher will give you a large copy of this puzzle.
Describe each puzzle piece as a fraction, a decimal, and a percent of the whole puzzle.

Reflect & Share

Compare your answers with those of another pair of classmates.
If the answers are different, how do you know which are correct?

Connect

➢ Since a percent can be written as a fraction, a percent can also be written as a decimal.
We can use number lines to illustrate the relationships.
For example:
$25\% = \frac{25}{100} = 0.25$ $\quad 125\% = \frac{125}{100} = 1.25$

➢ Conversely, a decimal can be written as a percent:
$0.15 = \frac{15}{100} = 15\%$ $\quad 1.15 = \frac{115}{100} = 115\%$

➢ To write a fraction as a percent, first write the fraction with denominator 100.
For example:
$\frac{1}{2} = \frac{50}{100} = 50\%$ and $\frac{3}{2} = \frac{150}{100} = 150\%$

When a decimal has 3 digits after the decimal point, we can write it as a fraction with denominator 1000.

➢ Some fractions cannot be written with denominator 100.
Use a calculator to divide.
$\frac{5}{8} = 0.625$
$= \frac{625}{1000}$ Divide numerator and denominator by 10.
$= \frac{62.5}{100}$
$= 62.5\%$

Example

a) Write each percent as a fraction and as a decimal.
i) 75% ii) 9% iii) 130%

b) Write each fraction as a percent and as a decimal.
i) $\frac{2}{5}$ ii) $\frac{5}{2}$

Draw number lines to show how the numbers are related.

292 UNIT 8: Working with Percents

8.1 Relating Fractions, Decimals, and Percents 293

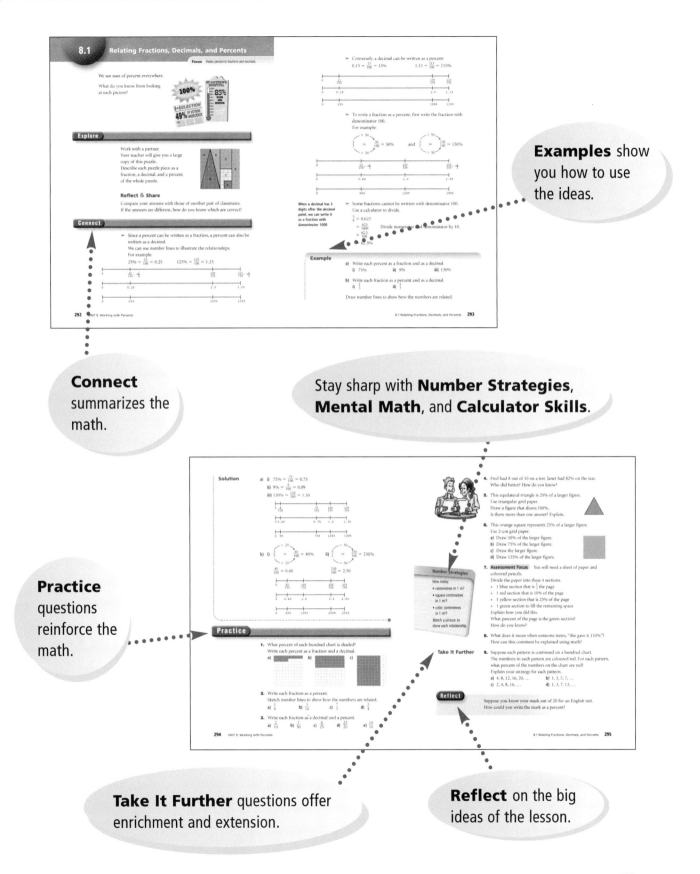

Examples show you how to use the ideas.

Connect summarizes the math.

Stay sharp with **Number Strategies**, **Mental Math**, and **Calculator Skills**.

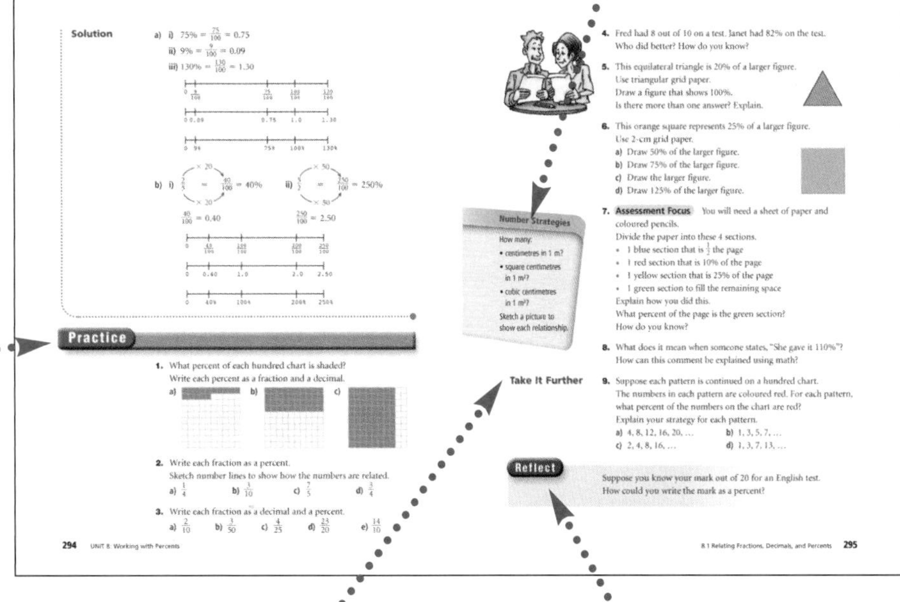

Solution

a) i) $75\% = \frac{75}{100} = 0.75$
ii) $9\% = \frac{9}{100} = 0.09$
iii) $130\% = \frac{130}{100} = 1.30$

b) i) $\frac{2}{5} = \frac{40}{100} = 40\%$ ii) $\frac{5}{2} = \frac{250}{100} = 250\%$
$\frac{40}{100} = 0.40$ $\quad \frac{250}{100} = 2.50$

Practice

1. What percent of each hundred chart is shaded?
Write each percent as a fraction and a decimal.
a) b) c)

2. Write each fraction as a percent.
Sketch number lines to show how the numbers are related.
a) $\frac{1}{4}$ b) $\frac{3}{10}$ c) $\frac{7}{5}$ d) $\frac{3}{4}$

3. Write each fraction as a decimal and a percent.
a) $\frac{2}{10}$ b) $\frac{3}{50}$ c) $\frac{4}{25}$ d) $\frac{23}{20}$ e) $\frac{14}{10}$

4. Fred had 8 out of 10 on a test. Janet had 82% on the test.
Who did better? How do you know?

5. This equilateral triangle is 20% of a larger figure.
Use triangular grid paper.
Draw a figure that shows 100%.
Is there more than one answer? Explain.

6. This orange square represents 25% of a larger figure.
Use 2-cm grid paper.
a) Draw 50% of the larger figure.
b) Draw 75% of the larger figure.
c) Draw the larger figure.
d) Draw 125% of the larger figure.

7. Assessment Focus You will need a sheet of paper and coloured pencils.
Divide the paper into these 4 sections.
- 1 blue section that is $\frac{1}{4}$ the page
- 1 red section that is 10% of the page
- 1 yellow section that is 25% of the page
- 1 green section to fill the remaining space

Explain how you did this.
What percent of the page is the green section?
How do you know?

Number Strategies
How many:
- centimetres in 1 m?
- square centimetres in 1 m²?
- cubic centimetres in 1 m³?

Sketch a picture to show each relationship.

8. What does it mean when someone states, "She gave it 110%"?
How can this comment be explained using math?

Take It Further

9. Suppose each pattern is continued on a hundred chart.
The numbers in each pattern are coloured red. For each pattern, what percent of the numbers on the chart are red?
Explain your strategy for each pattern.
a) 4, 8, 12, 16, 20, … b) 1, 3, 5, 7, …
c) 2, 4, 8, 16, … d) 1, 3, 7, 13, …

Reflect

Suppose you know your mark out of 20 for an English test.
How could you write the mark as a percent?

294 UNIT 8: Working with Percents

8.1 Relating Fractions, Decimals, and Percents 295

Practice questions reinforce the math.

Take It Further questions offer enrichment and extension.

Reflect on the big ideas of the lesson.

Use the **Mid-Unit Review** to refresh your memory of key concepts.

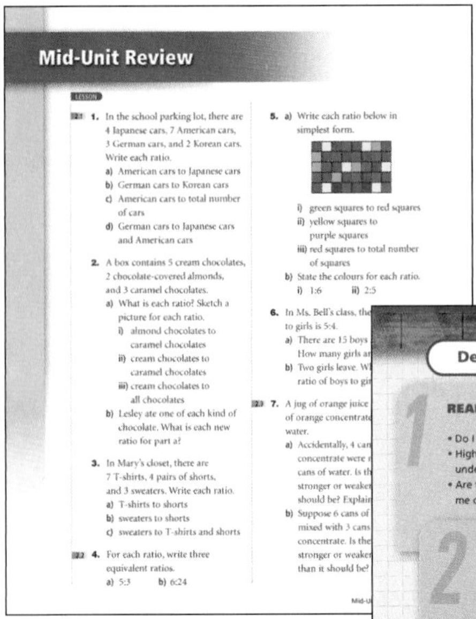

Mid-Unit Review

LESSON

1. In the school parking lot, there are 4 Japanese cars, 7 American cars, 3 German cars, and 2 Korean cars. Write each ratio.
   a) American cars to Japanese cars
   b) German cars to Korean cars
   c) American cars to total number of cars
   d) German cars to Japanese cars and American cars
2. A box contains 5 cream chocolates, 2 chocolate-covered almonds, and 3 caramel chocolates.
   a) What is each ratio? Sketch a picture for each ratio.
      i) almond chocolates to caramel chocolates
      ii) cream chocolates to caramel chocolates
      iii) cream chocolates to all chocolates
   b) Lesley ate one of each kind of chocolate. What is each new ratio for part a?
3. In Mary's closet, there are 7 T-shirts, 4 pairs of shorts, and 3 sweaters. Write each ratio.
   a) T-shirts to shorts
   b) sweaters to shorts
   c) sweaters to T-shirts and shorts
4. For each ratio, write three equivalent ratios.
   a) 5:3 b) 6:24
5. a) Write each ratio below in simplest form.
      i) green squares to red squares
      ii) yellow squares to purple squares
      iii) red squares to total number of squares
   b) State the colours for each ratio.
      i) 1:6 ii) 2:5
6. In Ms. Bell's class, the ... to girls is 5:4.
   a) There are 15 boys ... How many girls ar...
   b) Two girls leave. W... ratio of boys to gi...
7. A jug of orange juice ... of orange concentrat... water.
   a) Accidentally, 4 can... concentrate were ... cans of water. Is th... stronger or weake... should be? Explai...
   b) Suppose 6 cans of ... mixed with 3 cans ... concentrate. Is the... stronger or weake... than it should be?

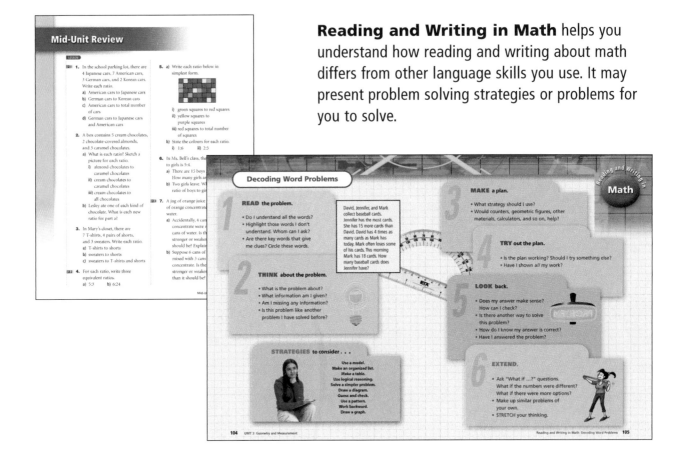

Reading and Writing in Math helps you understand how reading and writing about math differs from other language skills you use. It may present problem solving strategies or problems for you to solve.

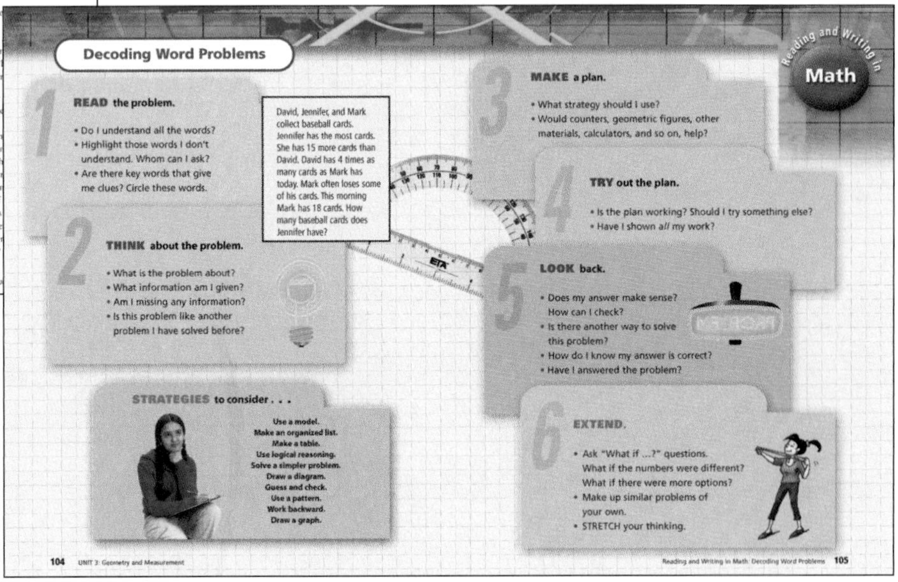

Decoding Word Problems

Reading and Writing in Math

1 **READ** the problem.
- Do I understand all the words?
- Highlight those words I don't understand. Whom can I ask?
- Are there key words that give me clues? Circle these words.

David, Jennifer, and Mark collect baseball cards. Jennifer has the most cards. She has 15 more cards than David. David has 4 times as many cards as Mark has today. Mark often loses some of his cards. This morning Mark has 18 cards. How many baseball cards does Jennifer have?

2 **THINK** about the problem.
- What is the problem about?
- What information am I given?
- Am I missing any information?
- Is this problem like another problem I have solved before?

3 **MAKE** a plan.
- What strategy should I use?
- Would counters, geometric figures, other materials, calculators, and so on, help?

4 **TRY** out the plan.
- Is the plan working? Should I try something else?
- Have I shown *all* my work?

5 **LOOK** back.
- Does my answer make sense? How can I check?
- Is there another way to solve this problem?
- How do I know my answer is correct?
- Have I answered the problem?

STRATEGIES to consider . . .

Use a model.
Make an organized list.
Make a table.
Use logical reasoning.
Solve a simpler problem.
Draw a diagram.
Guess and check.
Use a pattern.
Work backward.
Draw a graph.

6 **EXTEND.**
- Ask "What if ...?" questions. What if the numbers were different? What if there were more options?
- Make up similar problems of your own.
- STRETCH your thinking.

104 UNIT 3: Geometry and Measurement

Reading and Writing in Math: Decoding Word Problems 105

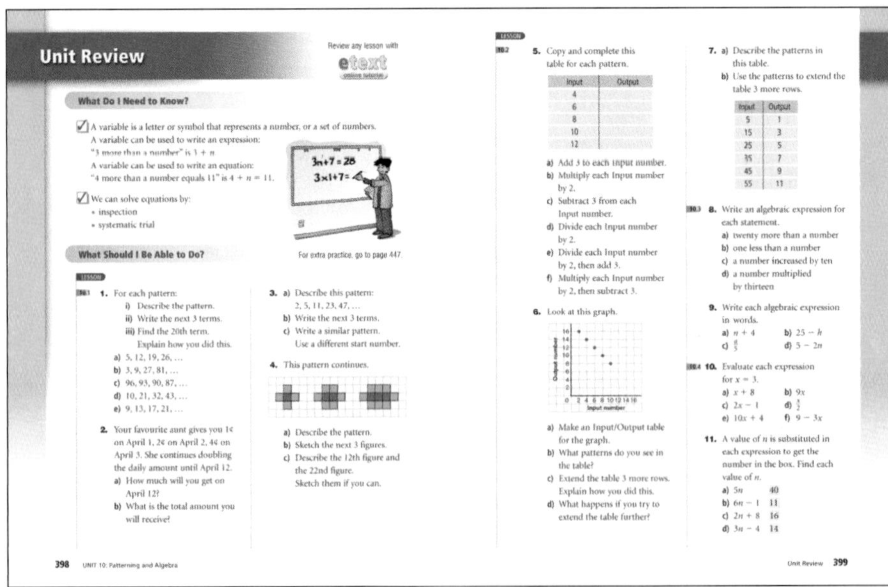

Unit Review

Review any lesson with etext

What Do I Need to Know?

✓ A variable is a letter or symbol that represents a number, or a set of numbers.
A variable can be used to write an expression:
"3 more than a number" is $3 + n$
A variable can be used to write an equation:
"4 more than a number equals 11" is $4 + n = 11$.

✓ We can solve equations by:
- inspection
- systematic trial

For extra practice, go to page 447.

What Should I Be Able to Do?

398 UNIT 10: Patterning and Algebra

Unit Review 399

What Do I Need to Know? summarizes key ideas from the unit.

What Should I Be Able to Do? allows you to find out if you are ready to move on. The on-line tutorial **etext** provides additional support.

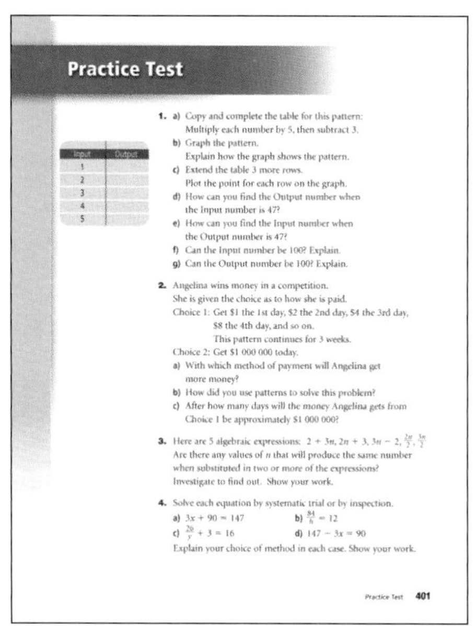

Practice Test

Input	Output
1	
2	
3	
4	
5	

1. a) Copy and complete the table for this pattern:
   Multiply each number by 5, then subtract 3.
   b) Graph the pattern.
   Explain how the graph shows the pattern.
   c) Extend the table 3 more rows.
   Plot the point for each row on the graph.
   d) How can you find the Output number when the Input number is 47?
   e) How can you find the Input number when the Output number is 47?
   f) Can the Input number be 100? Explain.
   g) Can the Output number be 100? Explain.
2. Angelina wins money in a competition.
   She is given the choice as to how she is paid.
   Choice 1: Get $1 the 1st day, $2 the 2nd day, $4 the 3rd day, $8 the 4th day, and so on.
   This pattern continues for 3 weeks.
   Choice 2: Get $1 000 000 today.
   a) With which method of payment will Angelina get more money?
   b) How did you use patterns to solve this problem?
   c) After how many days will the money Angelina gets from Choice 1 be approximately $1 000 000?
3. Here are 5 algebraic expressions: $2 + 3n$, $2n + 3$, $3n - 2$, $\frac{2n}{2}$, $\frac{3n}{2}$
   Are there any values of n that will produce the same number when substituted in two or more of the expressions?
   Investigate to find out. Show your work.
4. Solve each equation by systematic trial or by inspection.
   a) $3x + 90 = 147$ b) $\frac{84}{h} = 12$
   c) $\frac{26}{y} + 3 = 16$ d) $147 - 3x = 90$
   Explain your choice of method in each case. Show your work.

Practice Test 401

The **Practice Test** models the kind of test your teacher might give.

The **Unit Problem** presents problems to solve, or a project to do, using the math of the unit.

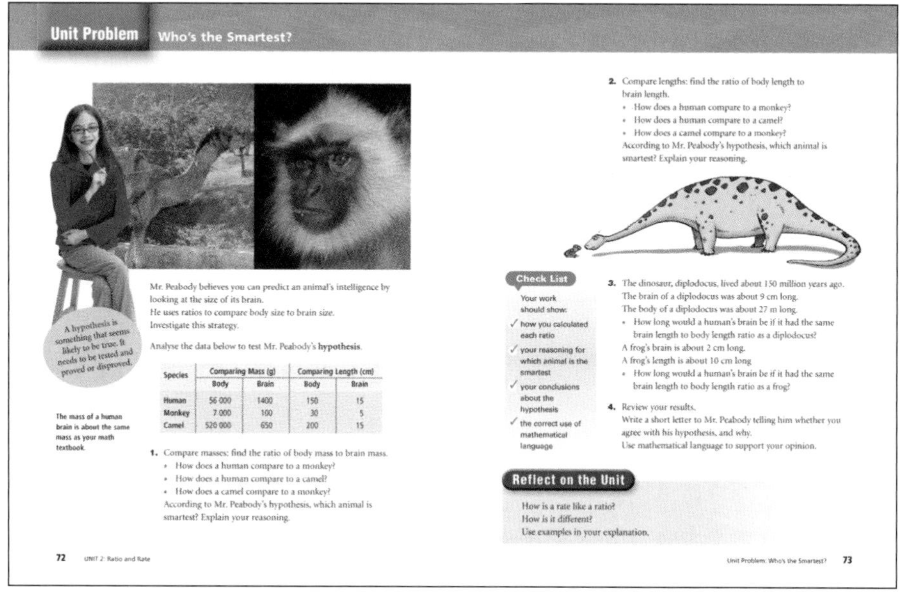

Unit Problem Who's the Smartest?

A hypothesis is something that seems likely to be true. It needs to be tested and proved or disproved.

Mr. Peabody believes you can predict an animal's intelligence by looking at the size of its brain.
He uses ratios to compare body size to brain size.
Investigate this strategy.

Analyse the data below to test Mr. Peabody's **hypothesis**.

Species	Comparing Mass (g)		Comparing Length (cm)	
	Body	Brain	Body	Brain
Human	56 000	1400	150	15
Monkey	7 000	100	30	5
Camel	520 000	650	200	15

The mass of a human brain is about the same mass as your math textbook.

1. Compare masses: find the ratio of body mass to brain mass.
   - How does a human compare to a monkey?
   - How does a human compare to a camel?
   - How does a camel compare to a monkey?
   According to Mr. Peabody's hypothesis, which animal is smartest? Explain your reasoning.

72 UNIT 2: Ratio and Rate

2. Compare lengths: find the ratio of body length to brain length.
   - How does a human compare to a monkey?
   - How does a human compare to a camel?
   - How does a camel compare to a monkey?
   According to Mr. Peabody's hypothesis, which animal is smartest? Explain your reasoning.

Check List

Your work should show:
- ✓ how you calculated each ratio
- ✓ your reasoning for which animal is the smartest
- ✓ your conclusions about the hypothesis
- ✓ the correct use of mathematical language

3. The dinosaur, diplodocus, lived about 150 million years ago.
   The brain of a diplodocus was about 9 cm long.
   The body of a diplodocus was about 27 m long.
   - How long would a human's brain be if it had the same brain length to body length ratio as a diplodocus?
   A frog's brain is about 2 cm long.
   A frog's length is about 10 cm long
   - How long would a human's brain be if it had the same brain length to body length ratio as a frog?
4. Review your results.
   Write a short letter to Mr. Peabody telling him whether you agree with his hypothesis, and why.
   Use mathematical language to support your opinion.

Reflect on the Unit

How is a rate like a ratio?
How is it different?
Use examples in your explanation.

Unit Problem: Who's the Smartest? 73

Keep your skills sharp with **Cumulative Review** and **Extra Practice.**

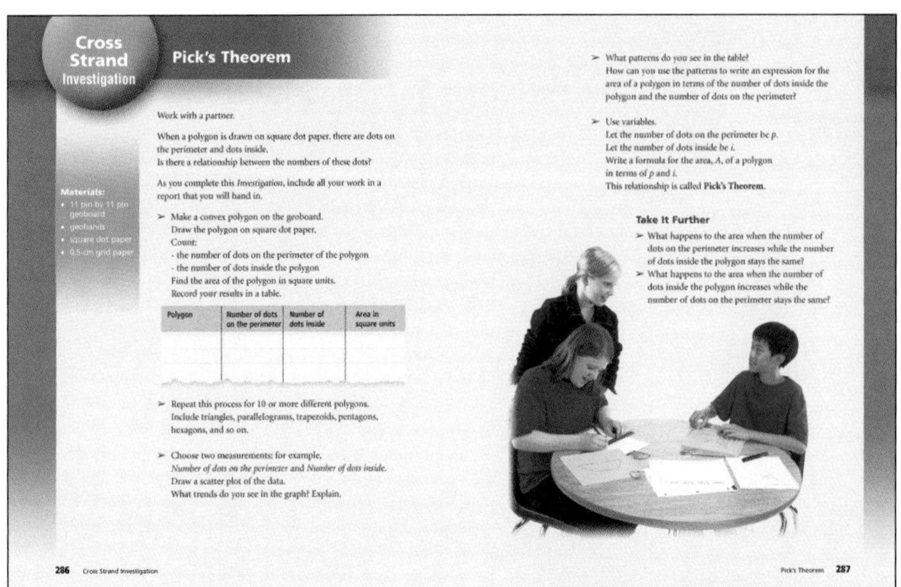

Cross Strand Investigation

Pick's Theorem

Materials:
- 11 pin by 11 pin geoboard
- geobands
- square dot paper
- 0.5-cm grid paper

Work with a partner.

When a polygon is drawn on square dot paper, there are dots on the perimeter and dots inside.
Is there a relationship between the numbers of these dots?

As you complete this *Investigation*, include all your work in a report that you will hand in.

➢ Make a convex polygon on the geoboard.
Draw the polygon on square dot paper.
Count:
- the number of dots on the perimeter of the polygon
- the number of dots inside the polygon
Find the area of the polygon in square units.
Record your results in a table.

Polygon	Number of dots on the perimeter	Number of dots inside	Area in square units

➢ Repeat this process for 10 or more different polygons.
Include triangles, parallelograms, trapezoids, pentagons, hexagons, and so on.

➢ Choose two measurements: for example,
Number of dots on the perimeter and *Number of dots inside*.
Draw a scatter plot of the data.
What trends do you see in the graph? Explain.

➢ What patterns do you see in the table?
How can you use the patterns to write an expression for the area of a polygon in terms of the number of dots inside the polygon and the number of dots on the perimeter?

➢ Use variables.
Let the number of dots on the perimeter be p.
Let the number of dots inside be i.
Write a formula for the area, A, of a polygon in terms of p and i.
This relationship is called **Pick's Theorem.**

Take It Further

➢ What happens to the area when the number of dots on the perimeter increases while the number of dots inside the polygon stays the same?
➢ What happens to the area when the number of dots inside the polygon increases while the number of dots on the perimeter stays the same?

286 Cross Strand Investigation

Pick's Theorem 287

Explore some interesting math when you do the **Cross Strand Investigations**.

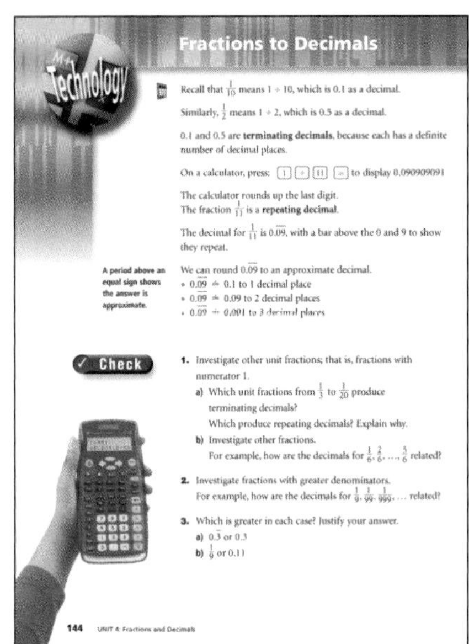

Technology

Fractions to Decimals

Recall that $\frac{1}{10}$ means 1 ÷ 10, which is 0.1 as a decimal.

Similarly, $\frac{1}{2}$ means 1 ÷ 2, which is 0.5 as a decimal.

0.1 and 0.5 are **terminating decimals**, because each has a definite number of decimal places.

On a calculator, press: 1 ÷ 11 = to display 0.090909091

The calculator rounds up the last digit.
The fraction $\frac{1}{11}$ is a **repeating decimal**.

The decimal for $\frac{1}{11}$ is $0.\overline{09}$, with a bar above the 0 and 9 to show they repeat.

A period above an equal sign shows the answer is approximate.

We can round $0.\overline{09}$ to an approximate decimal.
- $0.\overline{09} \doteq 0.1$ to 1 decimal place
- $0.\overline{09} \doteq 0.09$ to 2 decimal places
- $0.\overline{09} \doteq 0.091$ to 3 decimal places

✓ Check

1. Investigate other unit fractions; that is, fractions with numerator 1.
   a) Which unit fractions from $\frac{1}{3}$ to $\frac{1}{20}$ produce terminating decimals?
   Which produce repeating decimals? Explain why.
   b) Investigate other fractions.
   For example, how are the decimals for $\frac{1}{6}, \frac{2}{6}, \ldots, \frac{5}{6}$ related?
2. Investigate fractions with greater denominators.
   For example, how are the decimals for $\frac{1}{9}, \frac{1}{99}, \frac{1}{999}, \ldots$ related?
3. Which is greater in each case? Justify your answer.
   a) $0.\overline{3}$ or 0.3
   b) $\frac{1}{9}$ or 0.11

144 UNIT 4: Fractions and Decimals

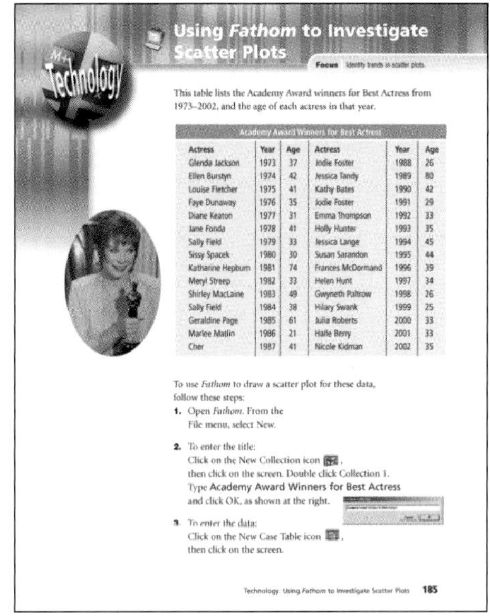

Technology

Using *Fathom* to Investigate Scatter Plots

Focus Identify trends in scatter plots.

This table lists the Academy Award winners for Best Actress from 1973–2002, and the age of each actress in that year.

Academy Award Winners for Best Actress

Actress	Year	Age	Actress	Year	Age
Glenda Jackson	1973	37	Jodie Foster	1988	26
Ellen Burstyn	1974	42	Jessica Tandy	1989	80
Louise Fletcher	1975	41	Kathy Bates	1990	42
Faye Dunaway	1976	35	Jodie Foster	1991	29
Diane Keaton	1977	31	Emma Thompson	1992	33
Jane Fonda	1978	41	Holly Hunter	1993	35
Sally Field	1979	33	Jessica Lange	1994	45
Sissy Spacek	1980	30	Susan Sarandon	1995	44
Katharine Hepburn	1981	74	Frances McDormand	1996	39
Meryl Streep	1982	33	Helen Hunt	1997	34
Shirley MacLaine	1983	49	Gwyneth Paltrow	1998	26
Sally Field	1984	38	Hilary Swank	1999	25
Geraldine Page	1985	61	Julia Roberts	2000	33
Marlee Matlin	1986	21	Halle Berry	2001	33
Cher	1987	41	Nicole Kidman	2002	35

To use *Fathom* to draw a scatter plot for these data, follow these steps:

1. Open *Fathom*. From the File menu, select New.
2. To enter the title:
   Click on the New Collection icon,
   then click on the screen. Double click Collection 1.
   Type Academy Award Winners for Best Actress
   and click OK, as shown at the right.
3. To enter the data:
   Click on the New Case Table icon,
   then click on the screen.

Technology: Using *Fathom* to Investigate Scatter Plots 185

Icons remind you to use **technology**.
Follow the step-by-step instructions for using a computer or calculator to do math.

Game

Trapezoid Challenge

HOW TO PLAY THE GAME:

1. Roll 3 number cubes to get the height and lengths of the 2 parallel sides of a trapezoid.
2. Use the geoboard to make a trapezoid with those dimensions.
   Choose which number represents which dimension.
3. The area of the trapezoid is your score for the round.
4. Take turns.
   The winner is the first person to reach 50 points.

YOU WILL NEED
11 by 11 geoboard; geobands; 3 number cubes labelled 1 to 6; dot paper

NUMBER OF PLAYERS
3 or 4

GOAL OF THE GAME
To get 50 points

What strategies did you use to try to win?
Does it matter which of the 3 numbers you use for the height? Explain.

Variation: Record each trapezoid on grid paper. No two trapezoids can be the same. If you cannot create a different trapezoid, you forfeit your turn.

238 UNIT 6: Measuring Perimeter and Area

Play a **Game** with your classmates or at home to reinforce your skills.

The World of Work describes how people use mathematics in their careers.

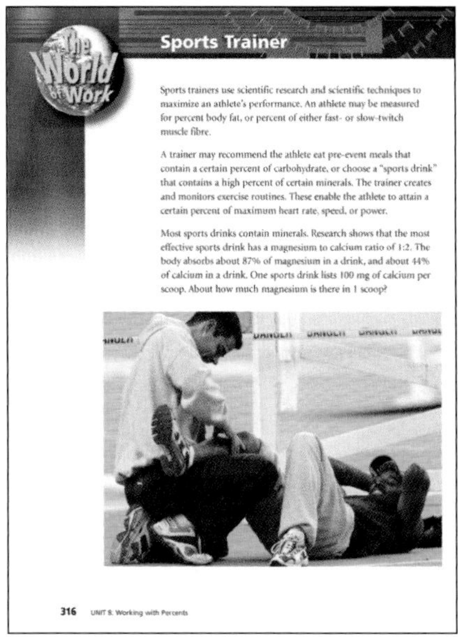

The World of Work

Sports Trainer

Sports trainers use scientific research and scientific techniques to maximize an athlete's performance. An athlete may be measured for percent body fat, or percent of either fast- or slow-twitch muscle fibre.

A trainer may recommend the athlete eat pre-event meals that contain a certain percent of carbohydrate, or choose a "sports drink" that contains a high percent of certain minerals. The trainer creates and monitors exercise routines. These enable the athlete to attain a certain percent of maximum heart rate, speed, or power.

Most sports drinks contain minerals. Research shows that the most effective sports drink has a magnesium to calcium ratio of 1:2. The body absorbs about 87% of magnesium in a drink, and about 44% of calcium in a drink. One sports drink lists 100 mg of calcium per scoop. About how much magnesium is there in 1 scoop?

316 UNIT 8: Working with Percents

The **Illustrated Glossary** is a dictionary of important math words.

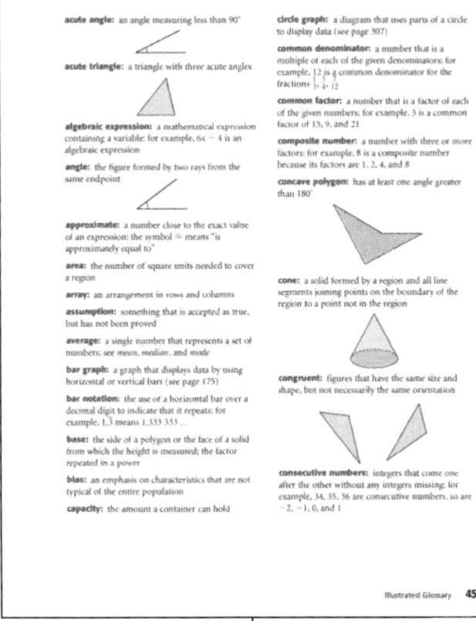

Illustrated Glossary

acute angle: an angle measuring less than 90°

acute triangle: a triangle with three acute angles

algebraic expression: a mathematical expression containing a variable: for example, 6x − 4 is an algebraic expression

angle: the figure formed by two rays from the same endpoint

approximate: a number close to the exact value of an expression; the symbol ≐ means "is approximately equal to"

area: the number of square units needed to cover a region

array: an arrangement in rows and columns

assumption: something that is accepted as true, but has not been proved

average: a single number that represents a set of numbers; see *mean*, *median*, and *mode*

bar graph: a graph that displays data by using horizontal or vertical bars (see page 175)

bar notation: the use of a horizontal bar over a decimal digit to indicate that it repeats; for example, $1.\overline{3}$ means 1.333 333 ...

base: the side of a polygon or the face of a solid from which the height is measured; the factor repeated in a power

bias: an emphasis on characteristics that are not typical of the entire population

capacity: the amount a container can hold

circle graph: a diagram that uses parts of a circle to display data (see page 307)

common denominator: a number that is a multiple of each of the given denominators; for example, 12 is a common denominator for the fractions $\frac{1}{3}, \frac{5}{4}, \frac{7}{12}$

common factor: a number that is a factor of each of the given numbers; for example, 3 is a common factor of 15, 9, and 21

composite number: a number with three or more factors; for example, 8 is a composite number because its factors are 1, 2, 4, and 8

concave polygon: has at least one angle greater than 180°

cone: a solid formed by a region and all line segments joining points on the boundary of the region to a point not in the region

congruent: figures that have the same size and shape, but not necessarily the same orientation

consecutive numbers: integers that come one after the other without any integers missing; for example, 34, 35, 36 are consecutive numbers, so are −2, −1, 0, and 1

Illustrated Glossary 451

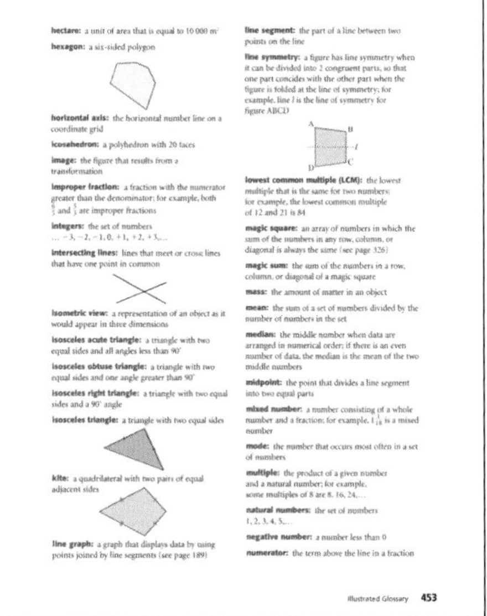

digit: any of the symbols used to write numerals; for example, in the base-ten system the digits are 0, 1, 2, 3, 4, 5, 6, 7, 8, and 9

dimensions: measurements, such as length, width, and height

dodecahedron: a polyhedron with 12 faces

equation: a mathematical statement that two expressions are equal

equilateral triangle: a triangle with three equal sides

equivalent: having the same value; for example, $\frac{2}{3}$ and $\frac{6}{9}$ are equivalent fractions; 2:3 and 6:9 are equivalent ratios

estimate: a reasoned guess that is close to the actual value, without calculating it exactly

evaluate: to substitute a value for each variable in an expression

even number: a number that has 2 as a factor; for example, 2, 4, 6

event: any set of outcomes of an experiment

experimental probability: the probability of an event calculated from experimental results; another name for the *relative frequency* of an outcome

exponent: a number, shown in a smaller size and raised, that tells how many times the number before it is used as a factor; for example, 2 is the exponent in 6^2

expression: a mathematical phrase made up of numbers and/or variables connected by operations

factor: to factor means to write as a product; for example, 20 = 2 × 2 × 5

formula: a rule that is expressed as an equation

fraction: an indicated quotient of two quantities

fraction strips: strips of paper used to model fractions (see page 121)

frequency: the number of times a particular number occurs in a set of data

frustum: part of a cone or pyramid that remains when a cut is made parallel to the base, and the top of the cone or pyramid is removed (see page 90)

greatest common factor (GCF): the greatest number that divides into each number in a set; for example, 5 is the greatest common factor of 10 and 15

452 Illustrated Glossary

hectare: a unit of area that is equal to 10 000 m²

hexagon: a six-sided polygon

horizontal axis: the horizontal number line on a coordinate grid

icosahedron: a polyhedron with 20 faces

image: the figure that results from a transformation

improper fraction: a fraction with the numerator greater than the denominator; for example, both $\frac{6}{5}$ and $\frac{5}{3}$ are improper fractions

integers: the set of numbers ... −3, −2, −1, 0, +1, +2, +3,...

intersecting lines: lines that meet or cross; lines that have one point in common

isometric view: a representation of an object as it would appear in three dimensions

isosceles acute triangle: a triangle with two equal sides and all angles less than 90°

isosceles obtuse triangle: a triangle with two equal sides and one angle greater than 90°

isosceles right triangle: a triangle with two equal sides and a 90° angle

isosceles triangle: a triangle with two equal sides

kite: a quadrilateral with two pairs of equal adjacent sides

line graph: a graph that displays data by using points joined by line segments (see page 189)

line segment: the part of a line between two points on the line

line symmetry: a figure has line symmetry when it can be divided into 2 congruent parts, so that one part coincides with the other part when the figure is folded at the line of symmetry; for example, line *l* is the line of symmetry for figure ABCD

lowest common multiple (LCM): the lowest multiple that is the same for two numbers; for example, the lowest common multiple of 12 and 21 is 84

magic square: an array of numbers in which the sum of the numbers in any row, column, or diagonal is always the same (see page 326)

magic sum: the sum of the numbers in a row, column, or diagonal of a magic square

mass: the amount of matter in an object

mean: the sum of a set of numbers divided by the number of numbers in the set

median: the middle number when data are arranged in numerical order; if there is an even number of data, the median is the mean of the two middle numbers

midpoint: the point that divides a line segment into two equal parts

mixed number: a number consisting of a whole number and a fraction; for example, $1\frac{1}{18}$ is a mixed number

mode: the number that occurs most often in a set of numbers

multiple: the product of a given number and a natural number; for example, some multiples of 8 are 8, 16, 24,...

natural numbers: the set of numbers 1, 2, 3, 4, 5,...

negative number: a number less than 0

numerator: the term above the line in a fraction

Illustrated Glossary 453

Cross Strand Investigation

Making a Booklet

Materials:
- sheets of newsprint measuring 25 inches by 38 inches

Work with a partner.

A book is made up of **signatures**. A signature has 16 or 32 pages. A signature is a sheet of paper printed on both sides, in a special arrangement. The sheet is measured in inches. The dimensions for the sheet in this *Investigation* are 25 inches by 38 inches. This is approximately 64 cm by 97 cm.
This sheet of paper is then folded into sections of 16 or 32 pages. When the sheet of paper is folded and cut in some places, the pages read in the correct numerical order.

As you complete this *Investigation*, include all your work in a report that you will hand in.

Part 1

Here are both sides of a 16-page signature.
The pages are from 1 to 16.

		13	4

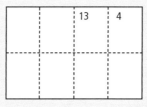

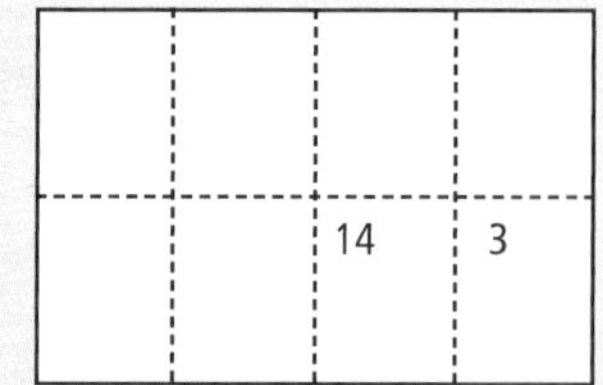

There are patterns in the numbers on a signature. These patterns help the printer decide which page numbers go on each side of a sheet when it goes on press.

Your challenge will be to find the patterns in the numbers on a signature. How would knowing these patterns help you create a book with more than 32 pages?

➢ How many folds are needed to make a 16-page signature? Fold a 25-inch by 38-inch piece of paper in half, several times, to find out.

Write the page numbers consecutively on the pages.
Open the sheet of paper.
Where are all the even numbers?
Where are all the odd numbers?
What else do you notice about the page numbers?
What patterns do you see in the page numbers?

- ➢ The 2nd signature has pages 17 to 32.
  Draw a sketch. Show both sides of this signature with page numbers in place.
- ➢ Look for patterns in the numbers.
  How do these patterns compare with those in the 1st signature?

Part 2

Here are both sides of a 32-page signature.

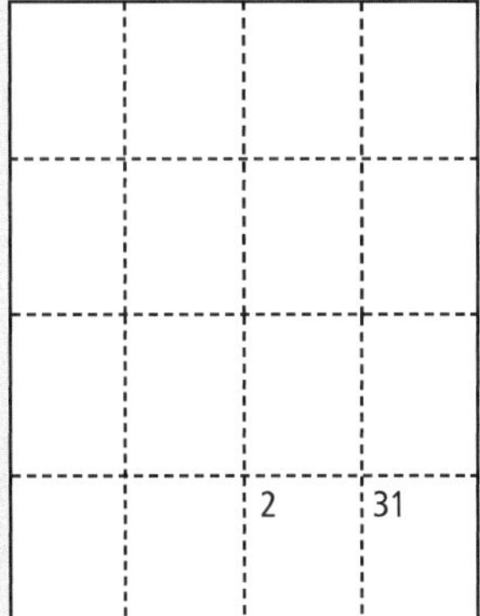

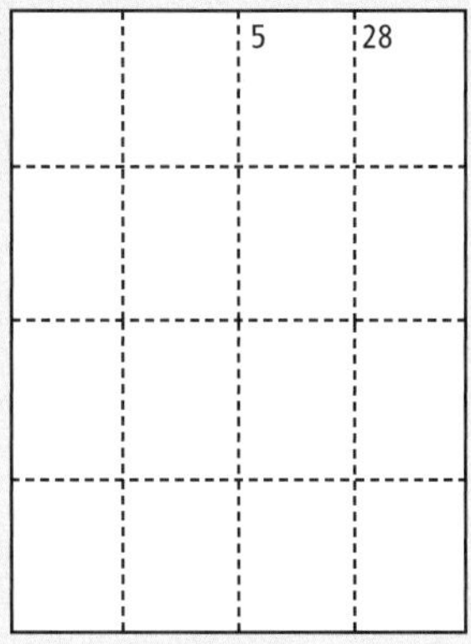

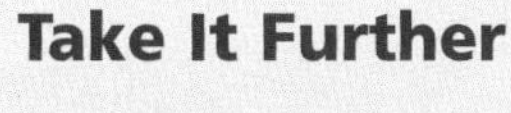

- ➢ Repeat the steps in *Part 1* for this 32-page signature.
  Describe all the patterns you discover.
- ➢ Find some books in the school or class library.
  Calculate how many signatures each book might have.

Take It Further

Suppose you have to create a 64-page signature.
How can you use the number patterns in *Parts 1* and *2* to help you create a 64-page signature?

UNIT 1

Patterns in Whole Numbers

There are many patterns you can see in nature. You can use numbers to describe many of these patterns.

At the end of this unit, you will investigate a famous set of numbers, the Fibonacci Numbers. You will explore these numbers, and find how they can be used to describe the breeding of animals, such as rabbits.

Think about the different patterns you learned in earlier grades. Give an example of each type of pattern.

What You'll Learn

- Use mental math, paper and pencil, calculators, and estimation to solve problems.
- Justify your choice of method for calculations.
- Find factors and multiples of numbers.
- Find the greatest common factor and lowest common multiple of two numbers.
- Identify prime and composite numbers.
- Use exponents to represent repeated multiplication.
- Identify and extend number patterns.
- Choose and justify strategies for solving problems.

Why It's Important

- You need to know an appropriate and efficient method for calculations.
- You need to be able to find common denominators for fraction calculations.

Key Words

- factor
- prime number
- composite number
- greatest common factor (GCF)
- multiple
- lowest common multiple (LCM)
- square number
- square root
- exponent form
- base
- exponent
- power
- cube number
- perfect square
- perfect cube

Skills You'll Need

Rounding

The place-value chart below shows the number 1 234 567.

Millions	Hundred thousands	Ten thousands	Thousands	Hundreds	Tens	Ones
1	2	3	4	5	6	7

To round:
Look at the digit to the right of the place to which you are rounding.
Is this digit 5 or greater?
If it is, add 1 to the place digit.
If it is not, leave the place digit as it is.
Change all the digits to the right of the place digit to 0.

Example 1

a) Round 425 to the nearest ten.

b) Round to the nearest thousand.
i) 2471 **ii)** 13 999

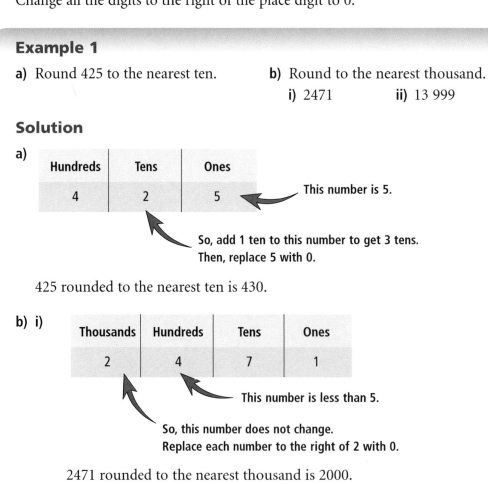

Solution

a)

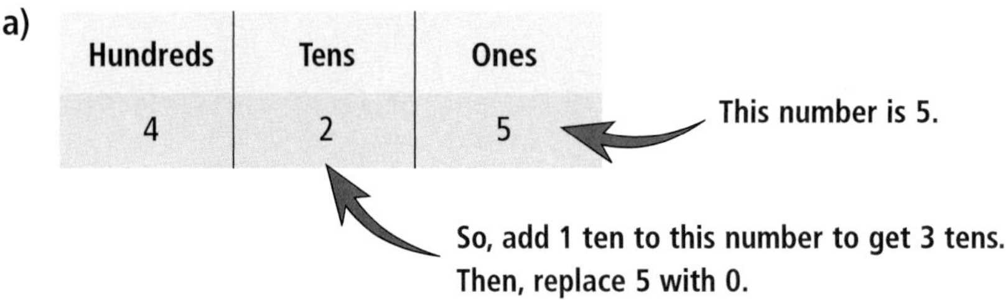

Hundreds	Tens	Ones
4	2	5

This number is 5.
So, add 1 ten to this number to get 3 tens.
Then, replace 5 with 0.

425 rounded to the nearest ten is 430.

b) i)

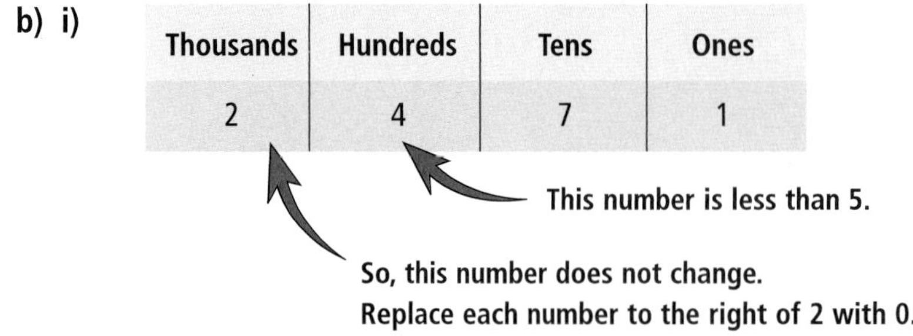

Thousands	Hundreds	Tens	Ones
2	4	7	1

This number is less than 5.
So, this number does not change.
Replace each number to the right of 2 with 0.

2471 rounded to the nearest thousand is 2000.

ii)

Ten thousands	Thousands	Hundreds	Tens	Ones
1	3	9	9	9

This number is greater than 5.

So, add 1 thousand to this number to get 4 thousands.
Replace each number to the right of 4 with 0.

13 999 rounded to the nearest thousand is 14 000.

✓ Check

1. Round to the nearest ten.

a) 36 **b)** 42 **c)** 75 **d)** 361

2. Round to the nearest hundred.

a) 311 **b)** 789 **c)** 625 **d)** 2356

Multiplying by 10, 100, 1000

To multiply a whole number:
– by 10, write 0 after the number.
– by 100, write 00 after the number.
– by 1000, write 000 after the number.

Example 2

Multiply.

a) 32×10 **b)** 478×100 **c)** 51×1000

d) 32×20 **e)** 47×300

Solution

a) $32 \times 10 = 320$ **b)** $478 \times 100 = 47\,800$ **c)** $51 \times 1000 = 51\,000$

d) $32 \times 20 = 32 \times 2 \times 10$
$= 64 \times 10$
$= 640$

e) $47 \times 300 = 47 \times 3 \times 100$
$= 141 \times 100$
$= 14\,100$

✓ Check

3. Find.

a) 3×10 **b)** 1000×5 **c)** 131×10 **d)** 100×63

4. Use a place-value chart. Explain why we can write zeros after a number when we multiply by 10, 100, or 1000.

5. Multiply.

a) 50×72 **b)** 18×600 **c)** 4000×33

Mental Math

Example 3

Use mental math.

a) 53×6 **b)** $308 + 56 - 6$ **c)** $197 + 452$

Solution

a) 53×6

Think:

$50 \times 6 + 3 \times 6$
$= 300 + 18$
$= 318$

b) $308 + 56 - 6$

Think:

$56 - 6 = 50$
Then: $308 + 50 = 358$

c) $197 + 452$

$197 = 200 - 3$
Then: $200 + 452 - 3 = 652 - 3$ Count back to subtract.
$= 649$

✓ Check

6. Use mental math.

a) $4 + 17$ **b)** $9 + 8$ **c)** $12 + 6$
d) $20 + 6$ **e)** $40 + 30$ **f)** $17 - 2$
g) $22 - 4$ **h)** $70 - 20$ **i)** $20 - 15$

7. Use mental math. Explain your strategy.

a) $28 + 13 + 12$ **b)** $2 \times 29 \times 5$ **c)** $98 + 327$
d) $4 \times 981 \times 25$ **e)** 99×21 **f)** 62×8

Divisibility Rules

A number is divisible by:

- 2 if the number is even
- 3 if the sum of its digits is divisible by 3
- 4 if the number represented by the last 2 digits is divisible by 4
- 5 if the last digit is 0 or 5
- 6 if the number is divisible by 2 and 3
- 8 if the number represented by the last 3 digits is divisible by 8
- 9 if the sum of the digits is divisible by 9
- 10 if the last digit is 0

Example 4

Which of these numbers is 1792 divisible by?

a) 2 **b)** 3 **c)** 4 **d)** 5 **e)** 6

Solution

a) 1792 is divisible by 2 because 1792 is an even number.

b) $1 + 7 + 9 + 2 = 19$

19 is not divisible by 3, so 1792 is not divisible by 3.

c) The last 2 digits are 92.

$92 \div 4 = 23$

Since the last 2 digits are divisible by 4, 1792 is divisible by 4.

d) 1792 is not divisible by 5 because the last digit is not 0 or 5.

e) Since 1792 is not divisible by 3, 1792 is also not divisible by 6.

✓ Check

8. Which numbers are divisible by 3?

a) 490 **b)** 492 **c)** 12 345

9. Write 4 other numbers greater than 400 that are divisible by 3.

10. Which numbers are divisible by 6?

a) 870 **b)** 232 **c)** 681

11. Which numbers from 1 to 10 is:

a) 660 divisible by? **b)** 1001 divisible by?

1.1 Numbers All Around Us

Focus Justify the choice of strategy when solving problems.

We use numbers to understand and describe our world.

December 6, 1917

Two Ships Collide as Halifax Reels

HALIFAX, NS -- Tragedy struck the Halifax harbour shortly after 9:00 yesterday morning when an unmarked munitions vessel collided with another ship and exploded.

To avoid German U-boat attacks the Mont-Blanc was not flying any warning flags, despite carrying 2600 tons of military explosives.

The Halifax Explosion

Did You Know?

At the time of the explosion, the Mont-Blanc was carrying
- 226 797 kg of TNT
- 2 146 830 kg of picric acid
- 56 301 kg of guncotton
- 223 188 kg of benzol

— all highly explosive and dangerous chemicals.

The 1917 explosion was 1/7 the strength of the atomic bomb dropped on Hiroshima.

Saturday, August 23, 2003

Southern BC Fires Approach City

KELOWNA, BC – Police with bullhorns ordered a staggering 20,000 Kelowna residents to evacuate their homes as fast-moving wildfires moved closer.

Thick smoke choked Kelowna's 100,000 residents and at times clouded the view of nearby Okanagan Lake.

The fire prompted the closure of Route 97, between Okanagan Falls and Penticton, and brought the total number of evacuees driven out by the fire to 30,000.

More than 3,000 firefighters from British Columbia and elsewhere in Canada are battling over 825 fires in the province.

Explore

January, 1998

Five Day Ice Storm Cripples Quebec and Eastern Ontario

The 1998 Ice Storm

Did You Know?
- The ice storm of 1998 was Canada's most expensive natural disaster, and cost approximately $1.6 billion, including $500 million in private property damage.
- When the ice storm ended on Jan 10, 23,000 hydro poles and 80 km of power lines were destroyed on the south shore of Montreal.
- A wooden hydro pole costs $3000.
- Hydro towers are built to withstand 15 mm of freezing rain. Montreal received over 100 mm during the storm.

Work on your own.
Read the articles above and at the left.

➢ Which numbers do you think are exact?
Which numbers are estimates? Explain your thinking.

➢ Use the numbers in the articles.
Write a problem you would solve each way:
- using mental math
- by estimating
- using pencil and paper
- using a calculator

➢ Solve your problem.

➢ Trade problems with a classmate.
Solve your classmate's problem.

Reflect & Share

Compare the strategies you used to solve the problems.
- Explain why some strategies work while others may not.
- Is one strategy more effective? Why?

Connect

- When the numbers are easy to handle, use mental math.
- When the problem has too many steps, use a paper and pencil.
- When an approximate answer is appropriate and to check reasonableness, estimate.
- When a more accurate answer is needed and the numbers are large, use a calculator.

Example

The population of Canada was 30 750 000 in July 2000. Statistics Canada (Stats Can) data show that there were 6367 telephones per 10 000 people in that year.

a) About how many telephones were there in Canada in 2000?
b) Find the exact number of telephones in Canada in 2000.
c) How did Stats Can know there were 6367 phones per 10 000 people? Explain how this answer affects the answer to part b.

Solution

a) Estimate.
Round 30 750 000 to the nearest ten million: 30 000 000
Round 6367 to the nearest thousand: 6000
10 000 people use about 6000 phones.
10 000 000 people use about 6000×1000, or 6 000 000 phones.
30 000 000 people use about $6\ 000\ 000 \times 3$, or
18 000 000 phones.
There were about 18 million phones in Canada in 2000.

b) Find how many groups of 10 000 people there are in 30 750 000.
That is, $30\ 750\ 000 \div 10\ 000 = 3075$
For each group of 10 000 people, there were 6367 phones.
The number of phones: $3075 \times 6367 = 19\ 578\ 525$
So, there were 19 578 525 phones in Canada in 2000.

c) Stats Can conducted a survey of about 40 000 people.
It asked how many phones each person had.
Stats Can then calculated how many phones per 10 000 people.

To find out exactly how many phones there are in Canada, Stats Can would have to survey the entire population. This is impractical. So, the number of phones in part b is an estimate.

Practice

1. Solve without a calculator.

a) 72 + 43	b) 123 + 85	c) 672 + 189
d) 97 − 24	e) 195 − 71	f) 821 − 485
g) 65 × 100	h) 14 × 75	i) 83 × 25
j) 780 ÷ 10	k) 724 ÷ 4	l) 245 ÷ 7

2. Use pencil and paper to find each answer.

a) 6825 + 127	b) 7928 − 815	c) 3614 − 278
d) 138 × 21	e) 651 ÷ 21	f) 6045 ÷ 15

3. Estimate each answer. Explain the strategy you used each time.

a) 103 + 89	b) 123 − 19
c) 72 × 9	d) 418 ÷ 71

Mental Math

Multiply.

3.6 × 1000	3.6 × 100
3.6 × 10	3.6 × 1
3.6 × 0.1	3.6 × 0.01

What patterns do you see in the questions and the answers?

Questions 4 to 7 pose problems about the 1997 Red River Flood in Manitoba. Use mental math, estimation, pencil and paper, or a calculator. Justify your strategy.

4. The 1997 Red River Flood caused over $815 036 000 in damages.
   a) Write this amount in words.
   b) How close to $1 billion were the damages?

5. Pauline Thiessen and fellow volunteers made an average of 10 000 sandwiches every day for 2 weeks to feed the flood relief workers. How many sandwiches did they make?

6. Winnipeg used 6.5 million sandbags to hold back the flood. Each sandbag was about 10 cm thick. About how high would a stack of 6.5 million sandbags be in centimetres? Metres? Kilometres?

7. To help with the flood relief, Joe Morena of St. Viateur Bagels in Montreal trucked 300 dozen of his famous bagels to Manitoba.
   a) How many bagels did he send?
   b) Joe sells bagels for $4.80 a dozen.
   What was the value of his donation?

8. The Monarch butterfly migrates from Toronto to El Rosario, Mexico. This is a distance of 3300 km.
   A monarch butterfly can fly at an average speed of 15 km/h.
   How long does the migration flight take?

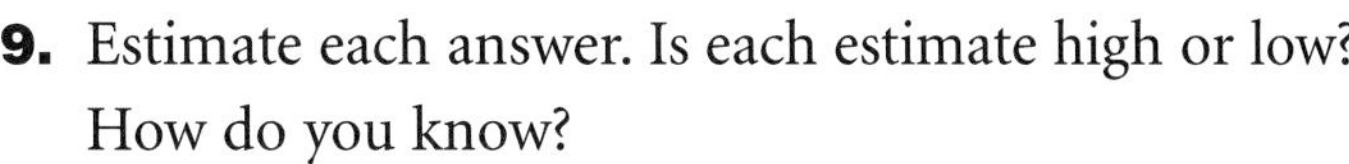

9. Estimate each answer. Is each estimate high or low?
How do you know?
a) $583 + 702$ **b)** $3815 - 576$ **c)** $821 \div 193$ **d)** $695 \div 310$

For questions 10 and 11: Make up a problem using the given data. Have a classmate solve your problems.

10. Sunil earns \$7 per hour. He works 4 h per day during the week and 6 h per day on the weekends.

11. In October 1954, Hurricane Hazel blew through Toronto, Ontario. Winds reached 124 km/h, 111 mm of rain fell in 12 h, and over 210 mm of rain fell over 2 days.

12. **Assessment Focus** The table shows the populations of some Canadian provinces in 1999.

Province	Population
NF and Labrador	541 000
PEI	138 000
Nova Scotia	939 800
New Brunswick	755 000
Ontario	11 513 800

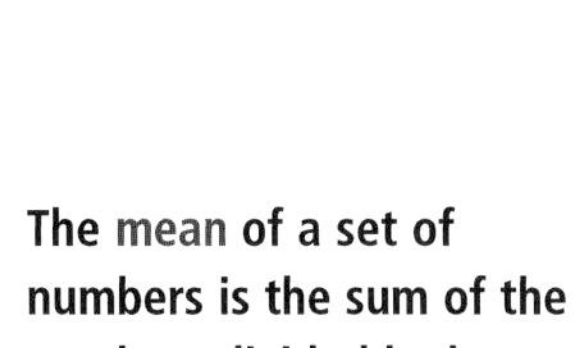

The mean of a set of numbers is the sum of the numbers divided by how many numbers there are.

a) Do you think these numbers are exact? Explain.
b) Find the total population of the 4 Atlantic provinces.
c) Find the mean population of the Atlantic provinces.
d) Approximately how many times as many people are in Ontario as are in the Atlantic provinces?
e) Make up your own problem about these data. Solve it.

Take It Further

13. Find 2 whole numbers that:
a) have a sum of 10 and a product of 24
b) have a difference of 4 and a product of 77
c) have a sum of 77 when added to 3
Which of parts a to c have more than one answer? Explain.

Reflect

Write an example of a problem you would solve:
- by estimation
- by using a calculator

Justify your choice.

1.2 Factors and Multiples

Focus Generate factors and multiples of given numbers.

Just as numbers can describe our world, we can use numbers to describe other numbers. We can describe a number by its factors, by the number of its factors, and by the sum of its factors.

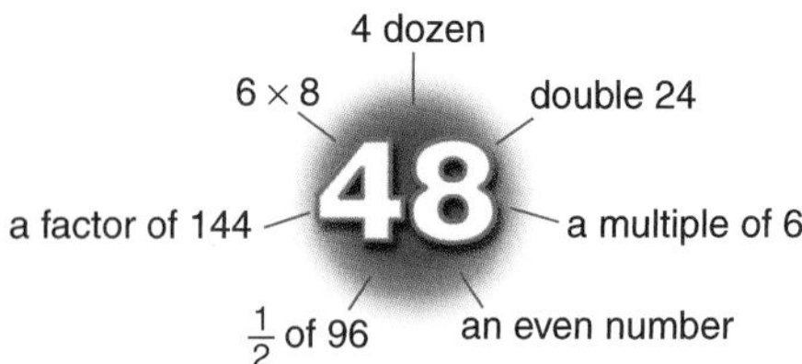

Explore

Work with a partner.

➢ Analyse the numbers in the circles.

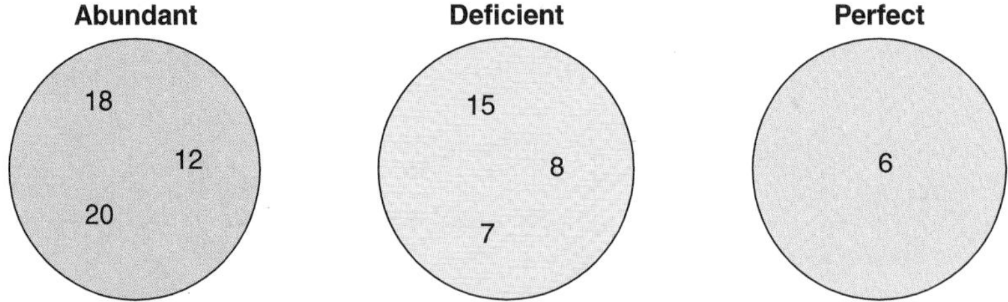

Use a table to record the factors of each number.
Cross out the number itself.
Find the sum of the remaining factors.

Number	Factors	Sum of Factors

➢ Look for patterns among your results.
Why do you think a number is called "Abundant," "Deficient," or "Perfect"?

➢ Copy the 3 circles. Based on your ideas, place each number from 2 to 30 in the appropriate circle. What do you notice?

➢ Use your observations to predict where 36 and 56 belong.
Check your predictions.

Reflect & Share

Share your results with another pair of students.
What relationships did you see?
How did you describe each type of number?

Connect

➢ Recall that a factor is a number that divides exactly into another number.
For example, 1, 2, 3, and 6 are the factors of 6.
Each number divides into 6 with no remainder.

A **prime number** has only 2 factors, itself and 1.
2, 3, and 5 are prime numbers.
All prime numbers are deficient.

A **composite number** has more than 2 factors.
8 is a composite number because its factors are 1, 2, 4, and 8.
Composite numbers can be deficient, abundant, or perfect.

1 has only one factor, so 1 is neither prime nor composite.

When we find the factors that are the same for 2 numbers, we find **common factors**.

Example 1

Show the factors of 12 and 30 in a Venn diagram.
What is the **greatest common factor** (**GCF**) of 12 and 30?

Solution

Use the divisibility rules.

Find pairs of numbers that divide into 12 exactly.

$12 \div 1 = 12$	1 and 12 are factors.
$12 \div 2 = 6$	2 and 6 are factors.
$12 \div 3 = 4$	3 and 4 are factors.

Stop at 3 because the next number, 4, is already a factor.
The factors of 12 are 1, 2, 3, 4, 6, and 12.

Find the factors of 30.

$30 \div 1 = 30$	1 and 30 are factors.
$30 \div 2 = 15$	2 and 15 are factors.
$30 \div 3 = 10$	3 and 10 are factors.
$30 \div 5 = 6$	5 and 6 are factors.

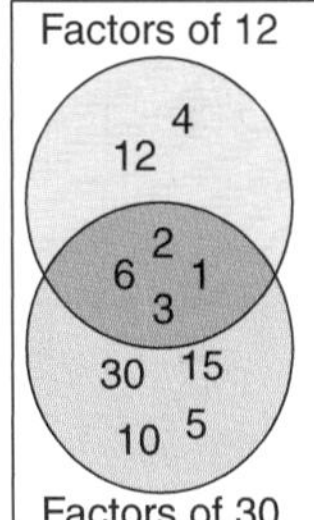

Mark the factors on the Venn diagram.
Place the common factors in the overlapping region.
The GCF of 12 and 30 is 6.

➢ The **multiples** of a number are found by multiplying the number by 1, by 2, by 3, by 4, and so on, or by skip counting.
When we find multiples that are the same for 2 numbers, we find **common multiples.**
We can use a 100 chart to find multiples and common multiples.

Example 2

a) Use a 100 chart to find the common multiples of 12 and 21.
b) Find the **lowest common multiple** (**LCM**) of 12 and 21.

Solution

a)

1	2	3	4	5	6	7	8	9	10
11	12	13	14	15	16	17	18	19	20
21	22	23	24	25	26	27	28	29	30
31	32	33	34	35	36	37	38	39	40
41	42	43	44	45	46	47	48	49	50
51	52	53	54	55	56	57	58	59	60
61	62	63	64	65	66	67	68	69	70
71	72	73	74	75	76	77	78	79	80
81	82	83	84	85	86	87	88	89	90
91	92	93	94	95	96	97	98	99	100

The multiples of 12 are blue.
The multiples of 21 are shaded green.
The common multiple is blue and shaded green.

b) Multiples of 12 are 12, 24, 36, 48, 60, 72, **84**, 96, …
Multiples of 21 are 21, 42, 63, **84**, …
The LCM is 84.

Practice

1. List 4 multiples of each number.
a) 5 **b)** 7 **c)** 8

2. Find the factors of each number. Explain how you did it.
a) 18 **b)** 20 **c)** 28 **d)** 36 **e)** 37 **f)** 45

3. Find the factors of each number.
a) 50 **b)** 51 **c)** 67 **d)** 75 **e)** 84 **f)** 120

Number Strategies

Three CDs cost $12.99, $8.18, and $7.88 (tax included).

Approximately how much change should there be from $40.00?

4. Is each number prime or composite? How do you know?
   a) 18 b) 13 c) 9 d) 19 e) 61 f) 2

5. Find the GCF of each pair of numbers.
   Which strategy did you use?
   a) 10, 5 b) 12, 8 c) 15, 25 d) 9, 12 e) 18, 15

6. Use a 100 chart. Find the LCM of each pair of numbers.
   a) 3, 4 b) 2, 5 c) 12, 18 d) 10, 25 e) 27, 18

7. Can a pair of numbers have:
   a) more than one common multiple?
   b) more than one common factor?
   Use a diagram to explain your thinking.

8. Julia and Sandhu bought packages of granola bars.
   a) Julia had 15 bars in total. Sandhu had 12 bars in total.
      How many bars could there be in one package?
   b) What if Julia had 24 bars and Sandhu had 18 bars?
      How many bars could there be in one package?
   Draw a diagram to explain your thinking.

9. **Assessment Focus** Kevin, Alison, and Fred work part-time. Kevin works every second day. Alison works every third day. Fred works every fourth day. Today they all worked together. When will they work together again?
   Explain how you know.

10. The numbers 4 and 16 could be called "near-perfect".
    Why do you think this name is appropriate?
    Find another example of a near-perfect number.
    What strategy did you use?

Reflect

What is the difference between a factor and a multiple?
Is a factor ever a multiple? Is a multiple ever a factor?
Use diagrams, pictures, or a 100 chart to explain.

The Factor Game

Game

YOU WILL NEED

One gameboard;
2 coloured markers

NUMBER OF PLAYERS

2

GOAL OF THE GAME

To circle factors of a number

HOW TO PLAY THE GAME:

1. Roll a number cube. The person with the greater number goes first.
2. Player A circles a number on the game board and scores that number. Player B uses a different colour to circle all the factors of that number not already circled. She scores the sum of the numbers she circles.

For example, suppose Player A circles 18.
Player B circles 1, 2, 3, 6, and 9 (18 is already circled)
to score $1 + 2 + 3 + 6 + 9 = 21$ points

3. Player B circles a new number.
Player A circles all the factors of that number not already circled. Record the scores.

1	2	3	4	5	6	7	8
9	10	11	12	13	14	15	16
17	18	19	20	21	22	23	24
25	26	27	28	29	30	31	32
33	34	35	36	37	38	39	40
41	42	43	44	45	46	47	48
49	50	51	52	53	54	55	56
57	58	59	60	61	62	63	64

4. Continue playing. If a player chooses a number with no factors left to circle, the number is crossed out. The player loses her or his turn, and scores no points.

For example, if player A circled 16, but 1, 2, 4, and 8 have already been circled, he would lose his turn and score no points.

5. The game continues until all numbers have been circled or crossed out. The player with the higher score wins.

What is the best first move? What is the worst first move? Why? How does this game involve factors, multiples, and prime numbers?

1.3 Squares and Square Roots

Focus Find the squares and square roots of whole numbers.

Explore

Work with a partner.
This chart shows the number of factors of each whole number.

																							X						X
																							X						X
											X						X		X				X				X		X
											X				X		X		X				X				X		X
					X		X		X		X		X	X	X		X		X	X	X		X		X	X	X		X
			X		X		X	X	X		X		X	X	X		X		X	X	X		X	X	X	X	X		X
	X	X	X	X	X	X	X	X	X	X	X	X	X	X	X	X	X	X	X	X	X	X	X	X	X	X	X	X	X
X	X	X	X	X	X	X	X	X	X	X	X	X	X	X	X	X	X	X	X	X	X	X	X	X	X	X	X	X	X
1	2	3	4	5	6	7	8	9	10	11	12	13	14	15	16	17	18	19	20	21	22	23	24	25	26	27	28	29	30

Look for patterns and relationships in this chart.
Find the factors of the numbers with two factors.
What do you notice?
Describe the numbers with four or more factors.
Describe the numbers that have an odd number of factors.

Reflect & Share

One way to describe a number with an odd number of factors is to call it a **square number**.
Why do you think this name is used?
Draw pictures to support your explanation.

Connect

The factors of a composite number occur in pairs.
For example, $48 \div 2 = 24$ 2 and 24 are factors of 48.
When the quotient is equal to the divisor, the dividend is a square number.
For example, $49 \div 7 = 7$, so 49 is a square number.

dividend **divisor** **quotient**

We can get 49 by multiplying the whole number, 7, by itself.

$49 = 7 \times 7$

We write: $7 \times 7 = 7^2$

We say: 7 squared

- One way to model a square number is to draw a square.
  This square has area 9 square units.
  The side length is $\sqrt{9}$, or 3 units.
  We say: A **square root** of 9 is 3.

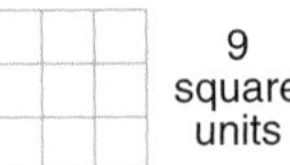

Other inverse operations are addition and subtraction, multiplication and division

- When we multiply a number by itself, we square the number.
  Squaring and taking a square root are inverse operations.
  That is, they undo each other.

  $7 \times 7 = 49$
  so, $7^2 = 49$

  $\sqrt{49} = \sqrt{7^2}$
  $= 7$

Example 1

Find the square of each number.

a) 5 **b)** 15 **c)** 32

Solution

a) $5^2 = 5 \times 5$
$= 25$

b) $15^2 = 15 \times 15$
$= 225$

c) $32^2 = 32 \times 32$
$= 1024$
Use a calculator.

Example 2

Draw a diagram to find a square root of each number.

a) 16 **b)** 36

Solution

a) On grid paper, draw a square with area 16 square units.
The side length of the square is 4 units.
So, $\sqrt{16} = 4$

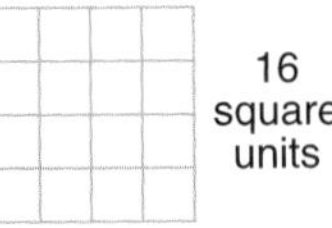

b) On grid paper, draw a square with area 36 square units.
The side length of the square is 6 units.
So, $\sqrt{36} = 6$

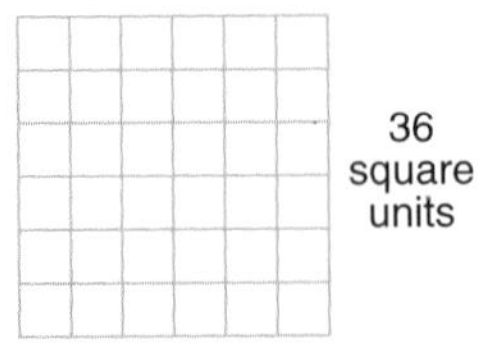

Practice

1. Find.

   a) 8^2 b) 16^2 c) 1^2 d) 29^2

2. Find the square of each number.

   a) 4 b) 17 c) 13 d) 52

3. a) Find the square of each number.

   i) 1 ii) 10 iii) 100 iv) 1000

   b) Use the results of part a. Predict the square of each number.

   i) 10 000 ii) 1 000 000

Number Strategies

Chris had saved $145.98 by June. He spent $2.25 in July, $4.50 in August, and $9.00 in September. If Chris' spending pattern continues, when will he have less than $5.00?

4. Use grid paper. Find a square root of each number.

   a) 16 b) 4 c) 900 d) 144

5. Calculate the side length of a square with each area.

   a) 100 m^2 b) 64 cm^2 c) 81 m^2

6. Order from least to greatest.

   a) $\sqrt{36}$, 36, 4, $\sqrt{9}$ b) $\sqrt{400}$, $\sqrt{100}$, 19, 15

7. Which whole numbers have squares between 50 and 200?

8. **Assessment Focus** Which whole numbers have square roots between 1 and 20? How do you know?

9. A large square room has an area of 144 m^2.

   a) Find the length of a side of the room.

   b) How much baseboard is needed to go around the room?

   c) Each piece of baseboard is 2.5 m long. How many pieces of baseboard are needed?

10. A garden has an area of 400 m^2.
    The garden is divided into 16 congruent square plots.
    What is the side length of each plot?

Reflect

How can you find the perimeter of a square when you know its area? Use an example to explain.

Mid-Unit Review

LESSON

1.1 **1.** The table shows the most common surnames for adults in the United Kingdom.

Surname	Number
Smith	538 369
Jones	402 489
Williams	279 150

a) Approximately how many adults have one of these three names?
To which place value did you estimate? Explain your choice.

b) Exactly how many more Smiths are there than Jones? Explain.

c) Write your own problem about these data. Solve your problem. Justify your strategy.

2. In one week, Joe worked 23 h cutting grass. He was paid \$9/h. From this money, Joe bought 5 tickets for a football game, at \$15 per ticket, and 2 DVDs for \$21 each, including tax. How much money did Joe have left?

1.2 **3.** Find all the factors of each number.

a) 35 **b)** 24

4. Find 2 factors of each number.

a) 6 **b)** 10
c) 14 **d)** 15
e) 9 **f)** 21

5. Organize the first 8 multiples of 6 and 8 in a Venn diagram.

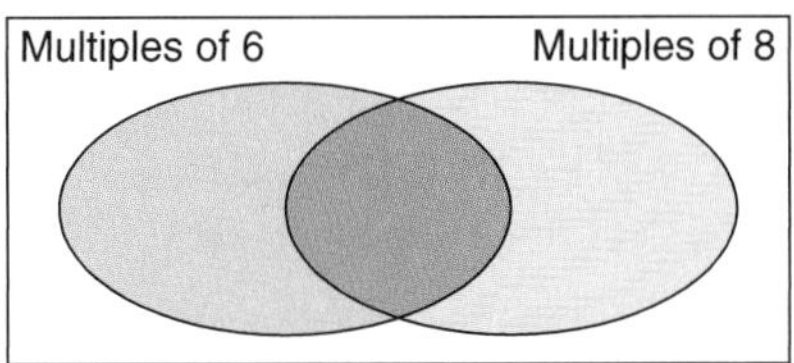

6. For the numbers 15 and 6, find:

a) the GCF **b)** the LCM

7. a) Why is 7 a prime number?
b) Why is 8 not a prime number?

1.3 **8.** Can three consecutive whole numbers all be primes? Justify your answer.

9. A square patio has an area of 81 m^2. How long is each side?

10. Find.

a) $\sqrt{49}$ **b)** 8^2
c) $\sqrt{100}$ **d)** the square of 9

11. Find two squares with a sum of 100.

12. Write 100 as a square number and as a square root of a number.

13. Explain why:
$\sqrt{1} = 1$

1.4 Exponents

Focus Use exponents to represent repeated multiplication.

Explore

Work with a small group.
You will need 65 interlocking cubes.
The edge length of each cube is 1 unit.
The volume of each cube is 1 cubic unit.

- How many different ways can you make a larger cube?
- What is the volume of each larger cube you make?
  What is its edge length?
- Use factors to write the volume of each cube.
- Record your results in a table.

Number of Cubes	Volume (cubic units)	Edge Length (units)	Volume As a Product
1	1	1	$1 \times 1 \times 1$

Reflect & Share

Observe how the volume grows. Describe the growth using pictures or numbers. What other patterns do you see in the table?
Use these patterns to help you write the volumes of the next 3 cubes in the pattern.

Connect

When numbers are repeated in multiplication, we can write them in **exponent form.**

For example, we can write $2 \times 2 \times 2 \times 2$ as 2^4.
2 is the **base.**
4 is the **exponent.**
2^4 is the **power.**

2^4 — base, exponent, power

We say: 2 to the power of 4, or
2 to the 4th
2^4 is a power of 2.

If we graph the power against the exponent, we see how quickly the power gets very large.

Exponent	Power
1	$2^1 = 2$
2	$2^2 = 4$
3	$2^3 = 8$
4	$2^4 = 16$
5	$2^5 = 32$

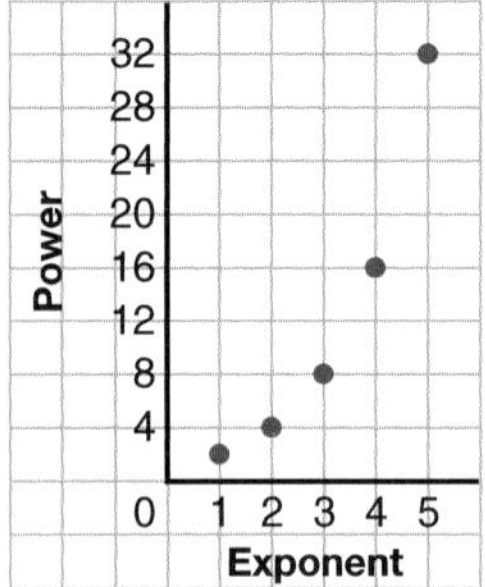

Square numbers and cube numbers are special powers.

➢ A power with exponent 2 is a **square number**.
The area of a square is side length $\times$ side length.
This square has side length 4 cm.
Area $= 4$ cm $\times$ 4 cm
$= 16$ cm^2

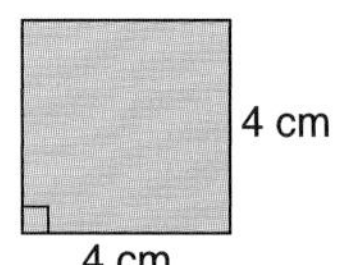

Here are 3 ways to write 16:
Standard form: 16
Expanded form: 4×4
Exponent form: 4^2
4^2 is a power of 4.
16 is called a **perfect square**.

➢ A power with exponent 3 is a **cube number**.
The volume of a cube is edge length $\times$ edge length $\times$ edge length.
This cube has edge length 4 cm.
Volume $= 4$ cm $\times$ 4 cm $\times$ 4 cm
$= 64$ cm^3

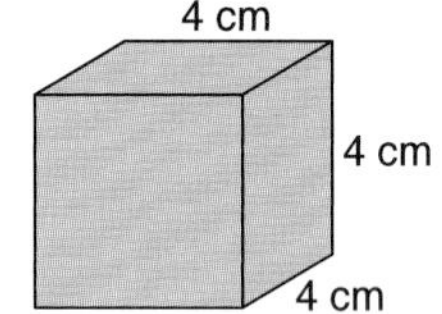

Here are 3 ways to write 64:
Standard form: 64
Expanded form: $4 \times 4 \times 4$
Exponent form: 4^3
4^3 is a power of 4.
64 is called a **perfect cube**.

Example 1

Write in exponent form.

a) 6×6 b) $5 \times 5 \times 5$ c) 32

Solution

a) $6 \times 6 = 6^2$ b) $5 \times 5 \times 5 = 5^3$

c) $32 = 2 \times 2 \times 2 \times 2 \times 2 = 2^5$

Example 2

Write in expanded form and standard form.

a) 3^5 b) 7^4

Solution

a) 3^5
$= 3 \times 3 \times 3 \times 3 \times 3$
$= 243$

b) 7^4
$= 7 \times 7 \times 7 \times 7$
$= 2401$

A calculator can be used to simplify a power such as 3^5.
For a scientific calculator, the keystrokes are:

[3] [^] [5] [ENTER] or [3] [y^x] [5] [ENTER] to display 243

For a non-scientific calculator, use repeated multiplication.
The keystrokes are:

[3] [×] [=] [=] [=] [=] to display 243

Practice

1. Write the base of each power.

a) 2^4 b) 3^2 c) 7^3 d) 10^5 e) 6^9 f) 8^3

2. Write the exponent of each power.

a) 2^5 b) 3^2 c) 7^1 d) 9^5 e) 8^{10} f) 10^4

3. Write in expanded form.

a) 2^4 b) 10^3 c) 6^5 d) 4^2 e) 2^1 f) 5^4

4. Write in exponent form.

a) $3 \times 3 \times 3 \times 3$ b) $2 \times 2 \times 2$ c) $5 \times 5 \times 5 \times 5 \times 5 \times 5$

d) $10 \times 10 \times 10$ e) 79×79 f) $2 \times 2 \times 2 \times 2 \times 2 \times 2 \times 2 \times 2$

Calculator Skills

A case of 24 cans of pop costs $7.49 at a local grocery store. A variety store charges customers $1.25 for 1 can. How much more money is the variety store making?

5. Write in exponent form, then in standard form.

a) 5×5 b) $3 \times 3 \times 3 \times 3$
c) $10 \times 10 \times 10 \times 10 \times 10$ d) $2 \times 2 \times 2$
e) $9 \times 9 \times 9$ f) $2 \times 2 \times 2 \times 2 \times 2 \times 2 \times 2$

6. Write in standard form.

a) 2^4 b) 10^3 c) 3^5 d) 7^3 e) 2^8 f) 4^1

7. Write as a power of 10. How did you do it?

a) 100 b) 10 000 c) 100 000
d) 10 e) 1000 f) 1 000 000

8. Write as a power of 2. Explain your method.

a) 4 b) 16 c) 64 d) 256 e) 32 f) 2

9. What patterns do you see in the pairs of numbers? Which is the greater number in each pair? Explain how you know.

a) 2^3 or 3^2 b) 2^5 or 5^2 c) 3^4 or 4^3 d) 5^4 or 4^5

10. Write these numbers in order from least to greatest: 3^5, 5^2, 3^4, 6^3. How did you do this?

11. Simplify.

a) 3^{12} b) 7^3 c) 5^6 d) 4^8 e) 9^8 f) 2^{23}

12. Assessment Focus

a) Express each number in exponent form in as many different ways as you can.
   i) 16 ii) 81 iii) 64
b) Find other numbers that can be written in exponent form, in more than one way. Show your work.

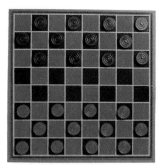

13. Write in exponent form:

a) the number of small squares on a checkerboard
b) the area of a square with side length 5 units
c) the volume of a cube with edge length 9 units

Reflect

When you see a number, how can you find out if it is a perfect square, or a perfect cube, or neither? Give examples.

Hospital Administrator

The administrator of a busy hospital makes hundreds of decisions every day, many of which involve whole number computations and conversions. Should she purchase more 'standard' 24-tray carts for the orderlies to deliver meals to the new 84-bed hospital wing? The administrator calculates she would need four of these carts to take enough meals to the new wing. In the cart supplier's catalogue, there are also 32-tray carts which are more expensive, but priced within budget. Only three of the 32-tray carts would deliver all the meals, and they would cost less than four of the standard carts.

When the orderlies look at the catalogue picture of the 32-tray cart, they tell the administrator that the cart is too low. It is tiring and slower to bend so far down, so they wouldn't use the lowest eight tray bins. So, it's back to the calculator for the administrator. Which cart would *you* choose now? Give reasons for your answer.

Your World

Carpet and tile prices are given per square unit. A paint can label tells the area the paint will cover in square units. Wallpaper is sold in rolls with area in square units.

1.5 Number Patterns

Focus Describe, extend, and explain patterns.

Explore

Work on your own.
Blaise Pascal lived in France in the 17th century.
He was 13 years old when he constructed the triangle below.
This triangle is called Pascal's Triangle.

1	row 1
1 1	row 2
1 2 1	row 3
1 3 3 1	row 4
1 4 6 4 1	row 5
1 5 10 10 5 1	row 6

➢ What patterns do you see in the triangle?
➢ What symmetry do you see in the triangle?

Reflect & Share

Compare your patterns with those of a classmate.
Together, write about three different patterns you see in the triangle.

Connect

Here are some of the patterns in Pascal's Triangle.

➢ Each row begins and ends with 1.
After the second row, each number is the sum of the 2 numbers above it.
To write row 7:
Start with 1.
Add: $1 + 5 = 6$
Add: $5 + 10 = 15$
Add: $10 + 10 = 20$, and so on

	Sum
1	1
1 1	2
1 2 1	4
1 3 3 1	8
1 4 6 4 1	16
1 + 5 + 10 + 10 + 5 + 1	32
1 6 15 20 15 6 1	64

➢ The sum of the numbers in each row is shown above, and in the table on the next page.
From the 2nd row on, the sums can be written as powers.

Row	2	3	4	5	6	7
Sum in standard form	2	4	8	16	32	64
Sum in exponent from	2^1	2^2	2^3	2^4	2^5	2^6

We can use this table to predict the sum of the numbers in any row. All sums are powers of 2.
The exponent is 1 less than the row number.
So, the 10th row has sum: $2^9 = 512$
And the 19th row has sum: $2^{18} = 262\ 144$

➢ The 3rd numbers in each row have this pattern: 1, 3, 6, 10, 15, ...
To get each term in the pattern, we add 1 more than we added before. We can use this to extend the pattern.
The 5th term: 15
The 6th term: $15 + 6 = 21$
The 7th term: $21 + 7 = 28$, and so on

Example

Describe each pattern in words. Write the next 3 terms.

a) 4, 9, 14, 19, … **b)** 1, 3, 9, 27, … **c)** 1, 3, 7, 13, 21, …

Solution

a) 4, 9, 14, 19, …
Start at 4.
Add 5 to get the next number.
The next 3 terms are 24, 29, 34.

b) 1, 3, 9, 27, …
Start at 1.
Multiply by 3 to get the next number.
The next 3 terms are 81, 243, 729.

c) 1, 3, 7, 13, 21, …
Start at 1.
Add 2.
Increase the number added by 2 each time.
The next 3 terms are 31, 43, 57.

Practice

1. Write the next 3 terms in each pattern.
   a) 7, 9, 11, 13, …
   b) 1, 5, 25, 125, …
   c) 4, 7, 10, 13, …
   d) 1, 10, 100, 1000, …
   e) 20, 19, 18, 17, …
   f) 79, 77, 75, 73, …

2. Write the next 3 terms in each pattern.
   a) 3, 4, 6, 9, …
   b) 1, 4, 9, 16, …
   c) 101, 111, 121, 131, …
   d) 1, 12, 123, 1234, …
   e) 1, 4, 16, 64, …
   f) 256, 128, 64, 32, …

3. Describe each pattern in words.
   Write the next 3 terms.
   a) 200, 199, 201, 198, …
   b) 4, 7, 12, 19, …
   c) 100, 99, 97, 94, …
   d) 2, 6, 12, 20, …
   e) 50, 48, 44, 38, …
   f) 2, 6, 18, 54, …

4. Create your own number pattern. Trade patterns with a classmate. Describe your classmate's pattern.
   Write the next 3 terms.

5. a) Copy this pattern. Find each product.

99 × 11 = □	99 × 111 = □	…
99 × 22 = □	99 × 222 = □	…
99 × 33 = □	99 × 333 = □	…
⋮	⋮	

   b) Extend this pattern sideways and down.
   Predict the next 6 terms in each row and column.
   c) Check your predictions with a calculator.

Number Strategies

One can of pop contains 355 mL. About how many 2-L pop bottles can be filled with one case of 24 cans of pop?

6. This pattern shows the first 3 triangular numbers.

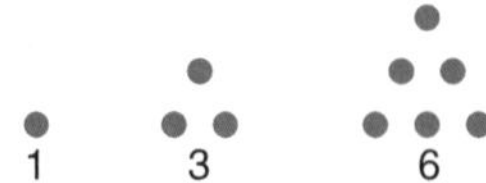

   a) Draw the next 3 terms in the pattern.
   b) List the first 6 triangular numbers.
   c) Find the next 2 triangular numbers without drawing pictures.
   Explain how you did this.

d) Add consecutive triangular numbers;
that is, Term 1 + Term 2; Term 2 + Term 3; and so on.
What pattern do you see?
Write the next 3 terms in this pattern.

e) Subtract consecutive triangular numbers;
that is, Term 2 − Term 1; Term 3 − Term 2; and so on.
What pattern do you see?
Write the next 3 terms in this pattern.

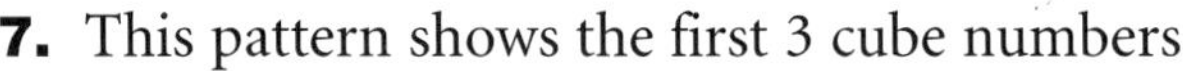

7. This pattern shows the first 3 cube numbers.

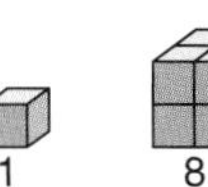

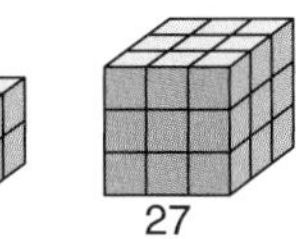

a) Sketch the next 3 cube numbers in the pattern.
Use interlocking cubes if they help.

b) Write the next 3 cube numbers without drawing pictures.
Explain how you did this.

8. Assessment Focus

a) Write the first 10 powers of 2; that is, 2^1 to 2^{10}, in standard form.

b) What pattern do you see in the units digits?

c) How can you use this pattern to find the units digit of 2^{40}?

d) Investigate powers of other numbers.
Look for patterns in the units digits.
Explain how you can use these patterns to find units digits for powers too large to display on the calculator.

Take It Further

9. Some sequences of numbers may represent different patterns.
Extend each pattern in as many different ways as you can.
Write the pattern rule for each pattern.

a) 1, 2, 4, … **b)** 1, 4, 9, … **c)** 5, 25, …

Reflect

Choose 3 different types of patterns from this section.
Describe each pattern.
Explain how you can use the pattern to predict the next term.

Using Different Strategies

Problem

There are 8 people at a party.
Each person shakes hands with everyone else.
How many handshakes are there?

Think of a strategy

Strategy 1: **Draw a diagram and count.**

Draw 8 dots. Join every dot to every other dot.
Count the line segments.

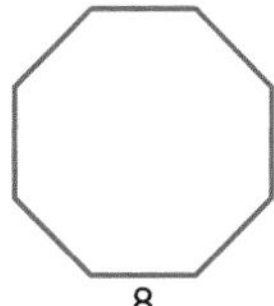

Number of line segments
= 8 + 5 + 5 + 4 + 3 + 2 + 1
= 28

There are 28 handshakes.

Strategy 2: **Solve simpler problems, then look for a pattern.**

2 people	3 people	4 people	5 people
1 handshake	3 handshakes	6 handshakes	10 handshakes

Make a table.
Each time you add a person, you add one more handshake than the time before.
So, 6 people: 10 + 5, or 15 handshakes
7 people: 15 + 6, or 21 handshakes
8 people: 21 + 7, or 28 handshakes

Number of People	Number of Handshakes	
2	1	
3	3	+2
4	6	+3
5	10	+4

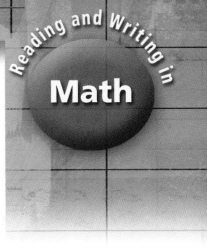

Strategy 3: **Use reasoning.**

Each of 8 people shakes hands with 7 other people.
That is, 8×7, or 56 handshakes
But we have counted each handshake twice.
We have said that A shaking hands with B is different from B shaking hands with A.
So, we divide by 2: $\frac{56}{2} = 28$
There are 28 handshakes.

Look back

- Look at the numbers of handshakes for 2 to 8 people. Where have you seen this pattern before?
- What if there were 9 people at the party? How many handshakes would there be? How do you know?

Problems

Solve each problem. Try to use more than one strategy.

1. A ball is dropped from a height of 16 m. Each time it hits the ground, the ball bounces to one-half its previous height. The ball is caught when its greatest height for that bounce is 1 m. How far has the ball travelled?

2. A rectangular garden is 100 m long and 44 m wide. A fence encloses the garden. The fence posts are 2 m apart. How many posts are needed?

3. Here is a 5 by 5 square. How many squares of each different size can you find in this large square?

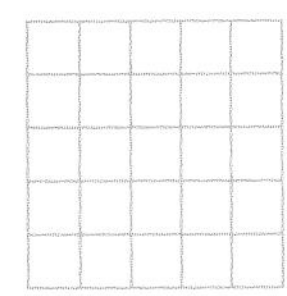

Reflect

Why might you want to solve a problem more than one way?

Unit Review

Review any lesson with

What Do I Need to Know?

✓ A *factor* of a number divides into the number exactly; that is, there is no remainder.
For example, $6 \div 2 = 3$, so 2 is a factor of 6.

✓ A *prime number* has only 2 factors, itself and 1.
For example, the only factors of 17 are 17 and 1, so 17 is a prime number.

✓ A *composite number* has more than 2 factors.
For example, 12 has factors 1, 2, 3, 4, 6, and 12, so 12 is a composite number.

✓ A *square number*, or *perfect square*, has an odd number of factors.
It can also written as a power with exponent 2.
For example, the factors of 9 are 1, 3, and 9, so 9 is a perfect square.
We write $9 = 3^2$.

✓ A *square root* of a number is a factor that is squared to get the number.
For example, 9 is a square root of 81 because $9^2 = 81$.
We write $\sqrt{81} = 9$.

✓ When a number is written in *exponent form*, it is written as a *power*.
For example, for the power 5^3:
5 is the *base*.
3 is the *exponent*.
$5 \times 5 \times 5$ is the *expanded form*.
125 is the *standard form*.

✓ A *cube number*, or *perfect cube*, is a power with exponent 3.
For example, $1^3 = 1$, $2^3 = 8$, $3^3 = 27$, $4^3 = 64$,
so 1, 8, 27, and 64 are perfect cubes.

What Should I Be Able to Do?

For extra practice, go to page 438.

LESSON

1.1 **1.** Find each answer.
Use pencil and paper.
a) 3621 + 8921
b) 5123 − 4123
c) 35 × 12
d) 125 × 27
e) 815 + 642 − 85
f) 1638 ÷ 21

2. This table shows the highest all-time scorers at the end of the 2000–2001 NBA season.

Kareem Abdul-Jabbar	38 387
Karl Malone	32 919
Wilt Chamberlain	31 419
Michael Jordan	29 277

a) What is the total number of points?
b) Write a problem about these data. Solve your problem. Justify the strategy you used.

3. a) Write the number 300 as the sum of 2 or more consecutive whole numbers. Find as many ways to do this as you can.
b) What patterns do you see in the numbers added?
c) Suppose you started with another 3-digit number. Will you see similar patterns? Investigate to find out.

4. Solve each problem. State any assumption you made.
a) Armin's house is 3 km from a mall. He walks 1 km in 15 min. How long does it take Armin to walk to the mall?
b) Tana makes $15, $21, and $19 for baby-sitting one weekend. How much will Tana make in a month?

5. The table shows the ticket prices and number of tickets sold for a popular movie.

	Ticket Price ($)	Number of Tickets Sold
Adults	12	125
Seniors	10	34
Youths	8	61

Calculate the total cost of the ticket sales.

1.2 **6.** Find all the factors of each number.
a) 36 **b)** 50
c) 75 **d)** 77

7. Find the first 10 multiples of each number.
a) 9 **b)** 7
c) 12 **d)** 15

8. For the numbers 18 and 60, find:
a) the GCF **b)** the LCM
Draw a Venn diagram to illustrate part a.

LESSON

9. How many prime numbers are even?
Justify your answer.

1.3 10. Find a square root of each number.
a) 121 b) 169 c) 225

11. Find each square root.
Draw a picture if it helps.
a) $\sqrt{25}$ b) $\sqrt{100}$ c) $\sqrt{81}$

12. Calculate the area of a square with each side length.
a) 7 cm b) 17 cm c) 93 m

13. The area of a square is 81 m^2.
What is the perimeter of the square? How do you know?

14. Raquel cooks 8-cm square hamburgers on a grill.
The grill is a rectangle with dimensions 40 cm by 40 cm.
How many hamburgers can be grilled at one time?
Justify your answer.

1.4 15. Copy and complete this table.

	Exponent Form	Base	Exponent	Expanded Form	Standard Form
a)	3^4				
b)	2^5				
c)	10^7				
d)		5	4		
e)				4×4×4×4	

1.5 16. A perfume formula requires 4 g of an essential oil per bottle.
a) How many grams are needed for 2500 bottles?
b) Write this number in exponent form.

17. Write these numbers in order from greatest to least.
3^4, 4^4, 5^3, 2^6

18. a) Write the next 3 terms in each pattern.
i) 3, 5, 6, 8, 9, …
ii) 1, 2, 4, 8, …
iii) 1, 4, 9, 16, …
iv) 3, 4, 6, 9, …
b) Describe each pattern in part a.

19. a) Copy and complete this pattern.
$1^2 + 2^2 = \square$
$2^2 + 3^2 = \square$
$3^2 + 4^2 = \square$
$4^2 + 5^2 = \square$
b) Write the next two rows in the pattern.
c) Describe the pattern.

20. $1^2 = 1$
$1^2 + 2^2 = 5$
$1^2 + 2^2 + 3^2 = 14$
$1^2 + 2^2 + 3^2 + 4^2 = 30$
a) Write the next two lines in the pattern.
b) What pattern do you see?

Practice Test

1. Estimate. Describe your strategy.

a) $624 + 1353$ **b)** $897 \div 23$ **c)** 752×36

2. Use mental math to evaluate $2 \times 395 \times 5$. Explain your strategy.

3. Use a Venn diagram to show the factors of 48 and 18. Circle the GCF.

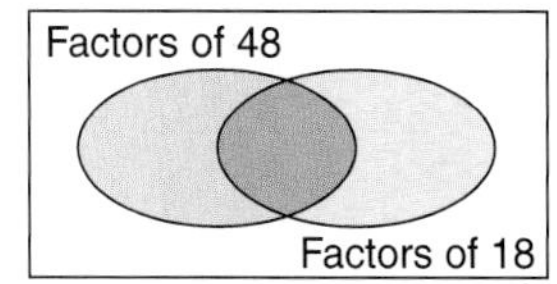

4. Use patterns to find the first 6 common multiples of 15 and 6.

5. Use the clues below to find the mystery number. Explain your strategy and reasoning.

Clue 1: I am a 2-digit number.
Clue 2: I am less than 9^2.
Clue 3: I have 26 and 6 as factors.

6. Sharma plays basketball every third day of the month. She baby-sits her little brother every seventh day of the month. How many times in a month will Sharma have a conflict between basketball and baby-sitting? Explain your thinking.

7. Write these numbers in order from least to greatest.

a) $5^2, 2^5, \sqrt{25}, 10^2, 3^3$ **b)** $10 \times 10 \times 10, 2^3, \sqrt{400}, 3^2, 17$

8. The perimeter of a square is 32 cm. What is the area of the square? Explain your thinking. Include a diagram.

9. Write the next 3 terms in each pattern. Describe each pattern.

a) 1, 3, 6, 10, … **b)** 23, 25, 27, … **c)** 100, 81, 64, 49, …

10. Write the number 35 as:

a) the sum of 3 squares
b) the difference between 2 squares
c) the sum of a prime number and a square

Unit Problem Fibonacci Numbers

One of greatest mathematicians of the Middle Ages was an Italian, Leonardo Fibonacci.

Fibonacci is remembered for this problem:

A pair of rabbits is placed in a large pen.
When the rabbits are two months old, they produce another pair of rabbits.
Every month after that, they produce another pair of rabbits.
Each new pair of rabbits does the same.
None of the rabbits dies.
How many rabbits are there at the beginning of each month?

This table shows the rabbits at the beginning of the first 5 months.

Beginning of Month	Number of Pairs	Number of Rabbits
1	1	
2	1	
3	2	
4	3	
5	5	

1. a) Continue the pattern for two more months.
Use different colours to show the new rabbits.

b) Write the number of pairs of rabbits at the beginning of each month, for the first 7 months.
These are the Fibonacci numbers.
What pattern do you see?
Explain how to find the next number in the pattern.

2. The Fibonacci sequence appears in the family tree of the drone, or male bee.
The drone has a mother, but no father.
Female bees are worker bees or queens.
They have a mother and a father.
The family tree of a male bee back to its grandparents is shown on the next page.

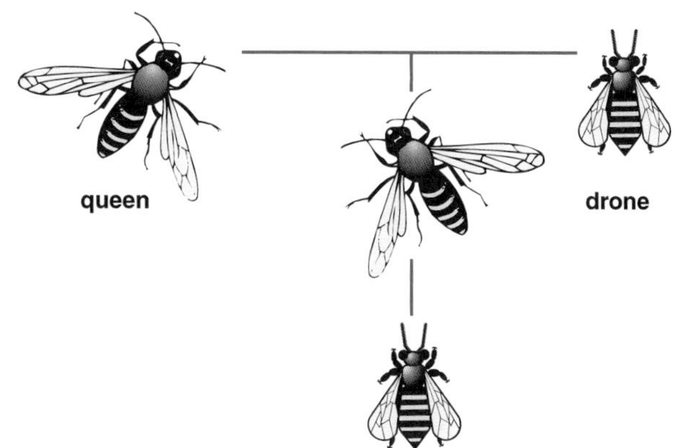

a) Copy the diagram. Trace the male bee's ancestors back 5 more generations.
b) Explain how you can use this pattern to find the Fibonacci numbers.

There are many patterns you can find in the Fibonacci sequence.

3. Write the first 15 Fibonacci numbers.
a) What type of number is every third number?
b) Which number is a factor of every fourth number?
c) Which number is a factor of every fifth number?

4. Add the squares of the:
2nd and 3rd terms
3rd and 4th terms
4th and 5th terms
What do you notice?
Write the next two lines of this pattern.

5. Research Fibonacci numbers. Make a poster to show your work.

Check List

Your work should show:

✓ how you used patterns to find your answers
✓ all diagrams and charts, clearly presented
✓ a clear explanation of your results
✓ your understanding of Fibonacci numbers

Reflect on the Unit

What have you learned about whole numbers?
What have you learned about number patterns?
Write about some of the things you have learned.

UNIT 2 Ratio and Rate

The animal kingdom provides much interesting information. We use information to make comparisons. What comparisons can you make from these facts?

A sea otter eats about $\frac{1}{3}$ of its body mass a day.

A Great Dane can eat up to 4 kg of food a day.

A cheetah can reach a top speed of 110 km/h.

A human can run at 18 km/h.

The heart of a blue whale is the size of a small car.

One in 5000 North Atlantic lobsters is born bright blue.

What You'll Learn

- Understand what a ratio is.
- Find equivalent ratios.
- Compare ratios and use them to solve problems.
- Understand what a rate is.
- Find unit rates.
- Compare rates and use them to solve problems.

Why It's Important

You use ratios and rates to compare numbers and quantities; and to compare prices when you shop.

Key Words

- ratio
- part-to-whole ratio
- part-to-part ratio
- terms of a ratio
- equivalent ratios
- simplest form
- rate
- unit rate
- average speed

UNIT 2

Skills You'll Need

Greatest Common Factor

Recall that the greatest common factor (GCF) of a set of numbers is the greatest number that will divide exactly into the given numbers.
For example, 6 is the greatest common factor of 18 and 24.

Example 1

Find the GCF of 24 and 30.

Solution

Draw a factor tree for each number.

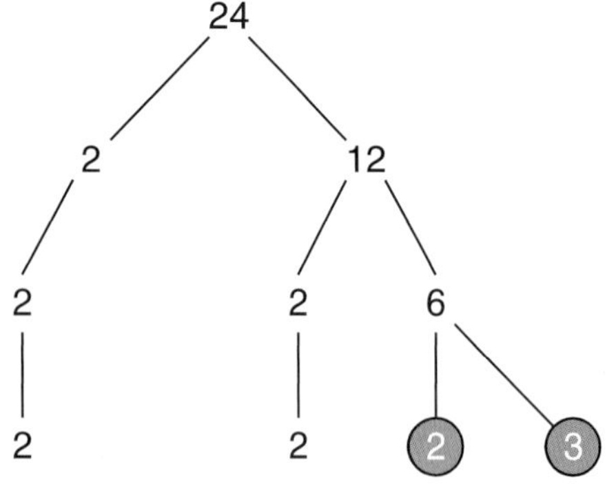

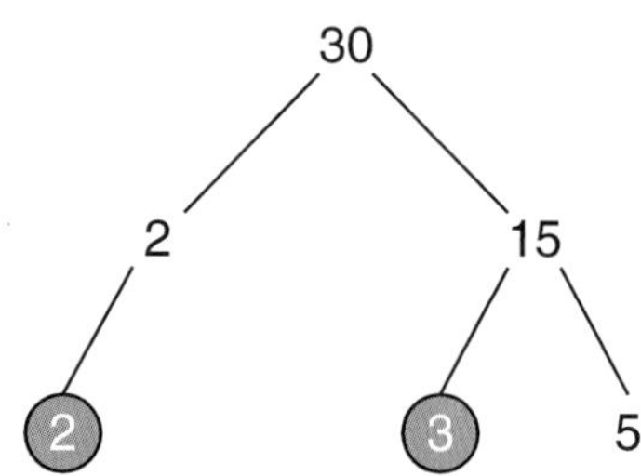

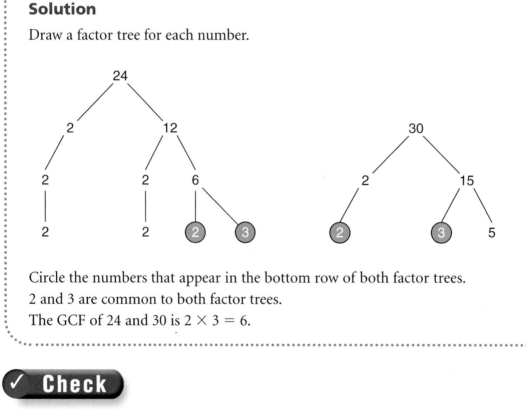

Circle the numbers that appear in the bottom row of both factor trees.
2 and 3 are common to both factor trees.
The GCF of 24 and 30 is $2 \times 3 = 6$.

✓ **Check**

1. Find the GCF of the numbers in each set.

a) 30, 75 **b)** 27, 63 **c)** 42, 56 **d)** 12, 18, 42

Lowest Common Multiple

Recall that the lowest common multiple (LCM) of a set of numbers is the least number that is a multiple of each number in the set. This also means that each number in the set is a factor of the lowest common multiple.

Example 2

Find the LCM of 18 and 32.

Solution

Draw a factor tree for each number.

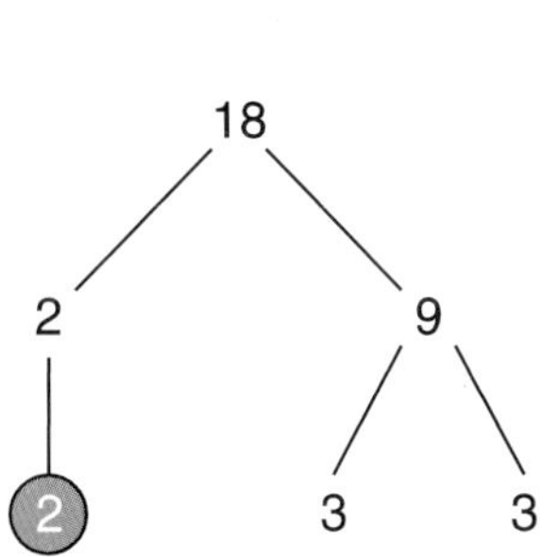

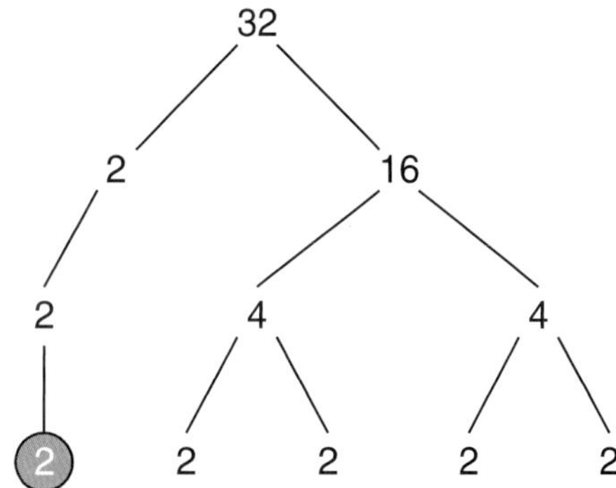

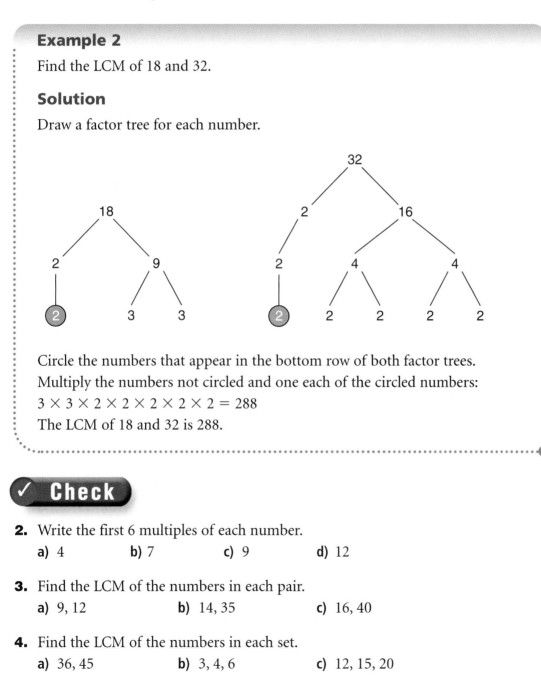

Circle the numbers that appear in the bottom row of both factor trees.
Multiply the numbers not circled and one each of the circled numbers:
$3 \times 3 \times 2 \times 2 \times 2 \times 2 \times 2 = 288$
The LCM of 18 and 32 is 288.

✓ Check

2. Write the first 6 multiples of each number.
a) 4 **b)** 7 **c)** 9 **d)** 12

3. Find the LCM of the numbers in each pair.
a) 9, 12 **b)** 14, 35 **c)** 16, 40

4. Find the LCM of the numbers in each set.
a) 36, 45 **b)** 3, 4, 6 **c)** 12, 15, 20

Converting among Metric Units

100 cm = 1 m　　1000 m = 1 km

1000 g = 1 kg　　1000 mL = 1 L

- To convert centimetres to metres, divide by 100.
- To convert:
  metres to kilometres
  grams to kilograms
  millilitres to litres
  } Divide by 1000.

Divide to convert to a larger unit.

- To convert metres to centimetres, multiply by 100.
- To convert:
  kilometres to metres
  kilograms to grams
  litres to millilitres
  } Multiply by 1000.

Multiply to convert to a smaller unit.

Example 3

Convert.

a) 650 cm to metres　　**b)** 82 km to metres

c) 2.4 kg to grams　　**d)** 2840 mL to litres

Solution

a) $650 \text{ cm} = \frac{650}{100} \text{ m}$
$= 6.5 \text{ m}$

b) $82 \text{ km} = 82 \times 1000 \text{ m}$
$= 82\,000 \text{ m}$

c) $2.4 \text{ kg} = 2.4 \times 1000 \text{ g}$
$= 2400 \text{ g}$

d) $2840 \text{ mL} = \frac{2840}{1000} \text{ L}$
$= 2.84 \text{ L}$

✓ Check

5. Convert.

a) 1280 cm to metres　　**b)** 680 m to kilometres

c) 2454 g to kilograms　　**d)** 1987 mL to litres

e) 8.2 m to centimetres　　**f)** 1.25 km to metres

g) 0.45 kg to grams　　**h)** 2.3 L to millilitres

2.1 What Is a Ratio?

Focus Use models and diagrams to investigate ratios.

There are different ways to compare numbers.
Look at these advertisements.

How are the numbers in each advertisement compared?
Which advertisement is most effective? Explain.

Explore

Work with a partner.

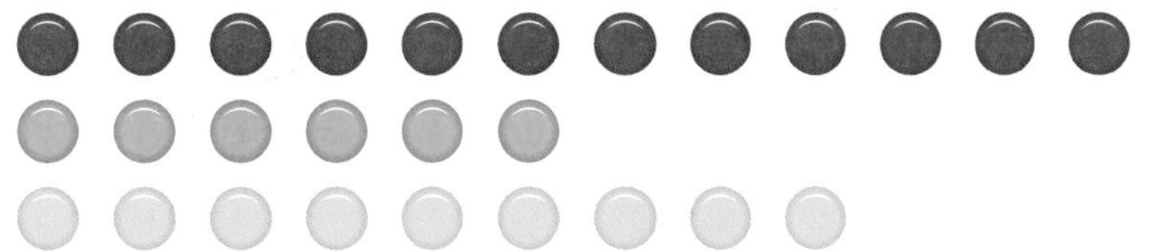

How can you compare the number of blue counters to the number of yellow counters?
How many different ways can you compare the counters?
Write each way you find.

Reflect & Share

Share your list with another pair of classmates.
Add any new comparisons to your list.
Talk about the different ways you compared the counters.

Connect

Here is a collection of models.

This is a **part-to-whole** ratio.

- We can use a **ratio** to compare one part of the collection to the whole collection.
  There are 9 cars compared to 13 models.
  The ratio of cars to models is written as 9 to 13 or 9:13.

This is a **part-to-part** ratio.

- We can use a ratio to compare one part of the collection to another part.
  There are 9 cars compared to 4 planes.
  The ratio of cars to planes is written as 9 to 4 or 9:4.
  9 and **4** are called the **terms** of the ratio.
  9 is the first term and 4 is the second term.

Example

At a class party, there are 16 boys, 15 girls, and 4 adults.
What is each ratio?

a) boys to girls **b)** girls to adults
c) adults to total number of people at the party

Solution

a) There are 16 boys and 15 girls.
So, the ratio of boys to girls is 16:15.

b) There are 15 girls and 4 adults.
So, the ratio of girls to adults is 15:4.

c) The total number of people is 16 + 15 + 4 = 35.
So, the ratio of adults to total number of people is 4:35.

Practice

1. Look at the crayons below. Write each ratio.
   a) red crayons to the total number of crayons
   b) yellow to the total number of crayons
   c) blue crayons to green crayons

2. Use words, numbers, or pictures.
   Write a ratio to compare the items in each sentence.
   a) A student had 9 green counters and 7 red counters on his desk.
   b) In a dance team, there were 8 girls and 3 boys.
   c) The teacher had 2 fiction and 5 non-fiction books on her desk.

3. The ratio of T-shirts to shorts in Frank's closet is 5:2.
   Write the ratio of T-shirts to the total number of garments.

4. a) What is the ratio of boys to girls in your class?
   b) What is the ratio of girls to boys?
   c) What is the ratio of boys to the total number of students in your class?
   d) What if two boys leave the room?
   What is the ratio in part c now?

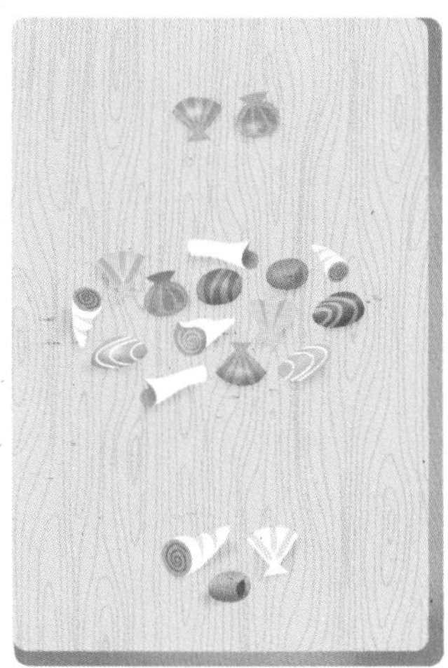

5. a) Draw two different diagrams to show the ratio 3:5.

   b) Draw a diagram to show the ratio 7:1.

6. Maria shares some seashells with Jeff.
   Maria says, "Two for you, three for me, two for you, three for me …"
   Tonya watches.
   At the end, she says, "So Jeff got $\frac{2}{3}$ of the shells."
   Do you agree with Tonya? Give reasons for your answer.

Number Strategies

What is the sum of all the prime numbers between 1 and 30?

7. A box contains 8 red, 5 green, 2 brown, 3 purple, 1 blue, and 6 yellow candles.
   a) Write each ratio.
      i) red:purple ii) green:blue
      iii) purple:green iv) brown and yellow:total candles
   b) What if 3 red, 2 green, and 4 yellow candles were burned? Write the new ratios for part a.

8. **Assessment Focus** Patrick plans to make salad. The recipe calls for 3 cups of cooked macaroni, 3 cups of sliced oranges, 2 cups of chopped apple, 1 cup of chopped celery, and 2 cups of mayonnaise.
   a) What is the total amount of ingredients?
   b) What is the ratio of oranges to apples? Mayonnaise to macaroni?
   c) What is the ratio of apples and oranges to the total amount of ingredients?
   d) Patrick makes a mistake. He uses 2 cups of oranges instead of 3. What are the new ratios in parts b and c?
   e) Write your own ratio problem about this salad. Solve your problem.

Take It Further

9. a) Create four different ratios using these figures.

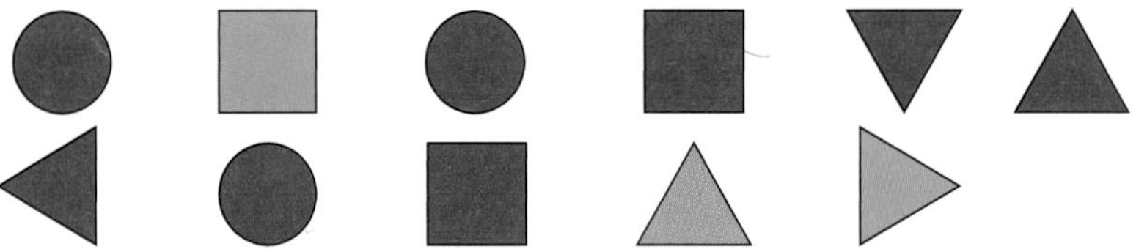

   b) How can you change one figure to create ratios of 2:5 and 7:3? Explain.

Reflect

Look in newspapers and magazines for examples of ratios.
Cut out the examples. Paste them in your notebook.
Explain how the ratios are used.
What information can you get from them?

2.2 Equivalent Ratios

Focus Write equivalent ratios.

Explore

Work on your own.
Which cards have the same ratio of pepperoni pieces to pizzas?

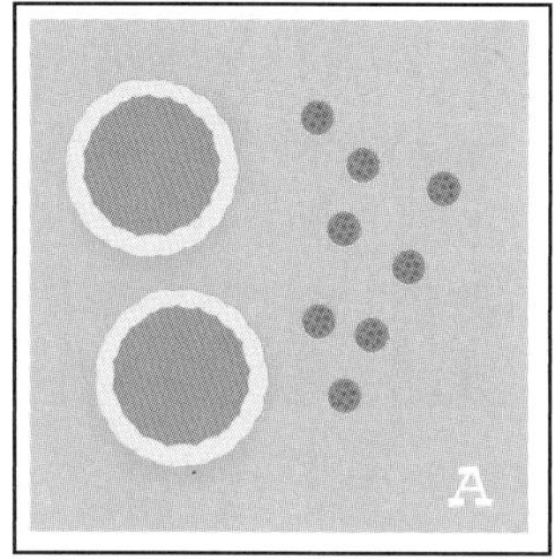

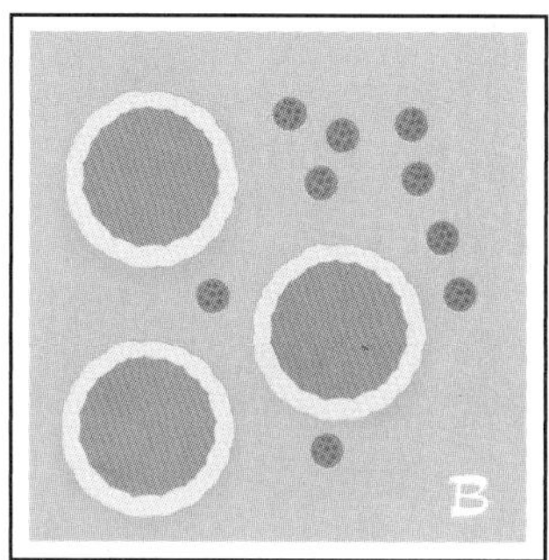

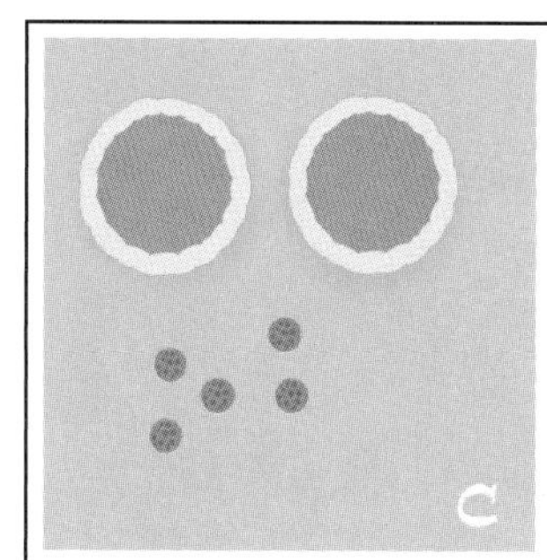

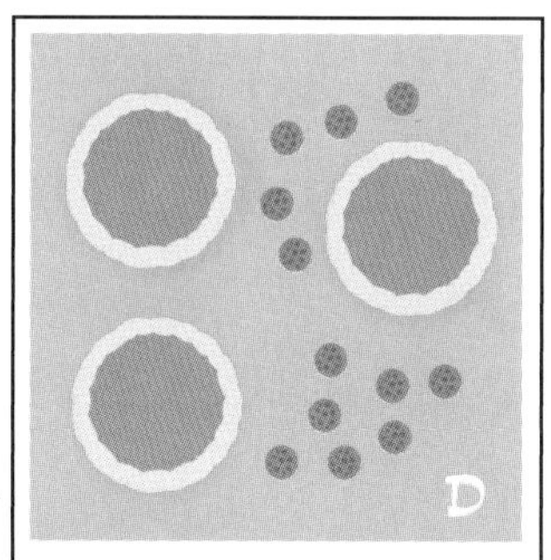

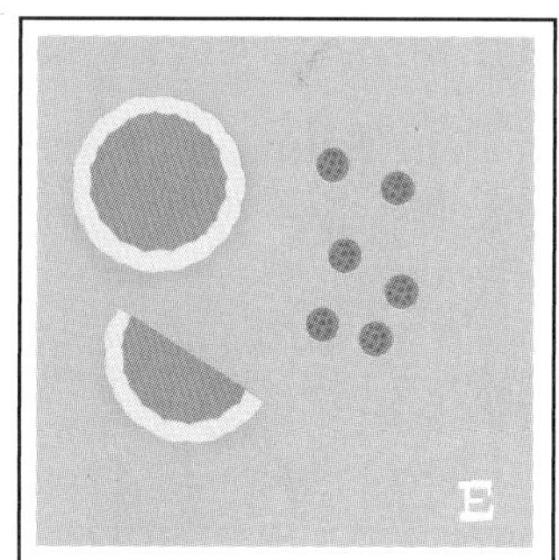

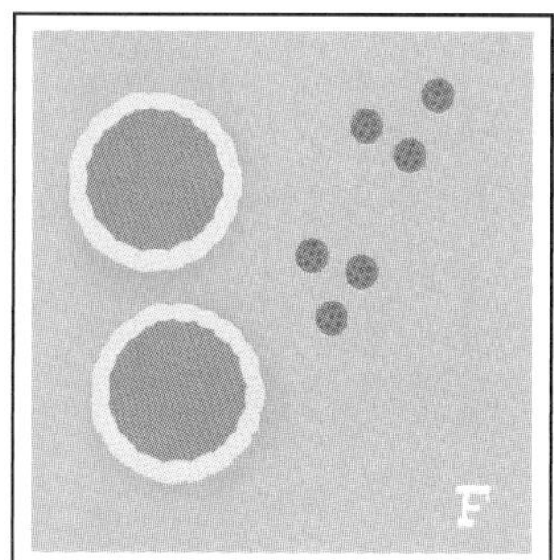

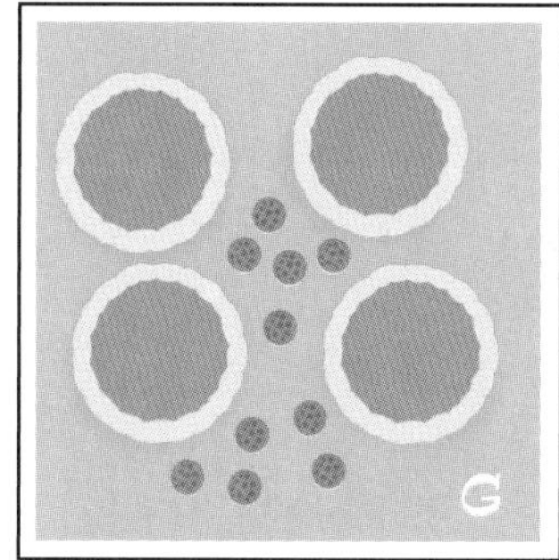

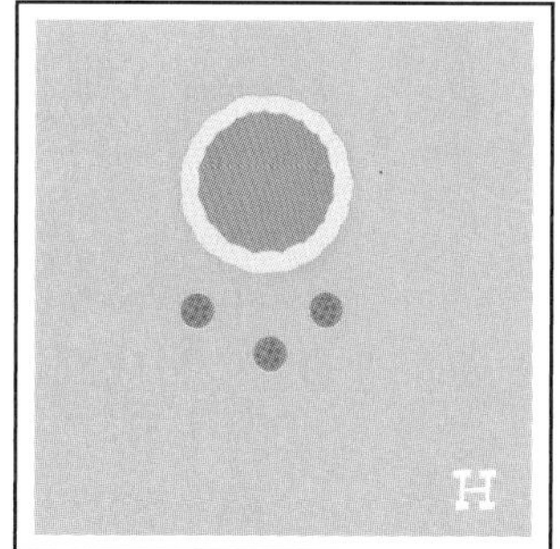

Reflect & Share

Share your answers with a classmate.
Why do you think your answers are correct?
What patterns do you see?

Connect

A ratio of 4:3 means that, for every 4 triangles, there are 3 squares.

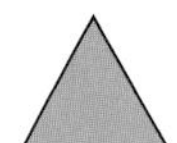 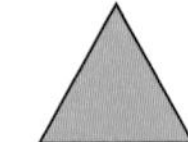 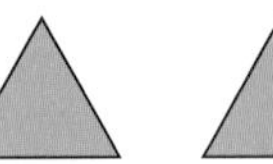 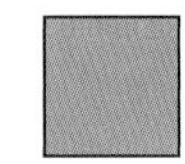  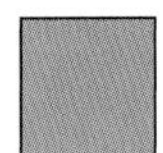

A ratio of 8:6 means that, for every 8 triangles, there are 6 squares.

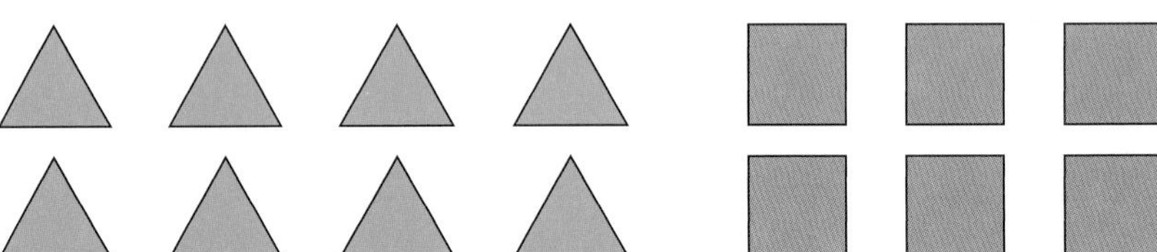

The ratios 8:6 and 4:3 are called **equivalent ratios.**
Equivalent ratios are equal. 8:6 = 4:3

➢ An equivalent ratio can be formed by multiplying or dividing the terms of a ratio by the same number.

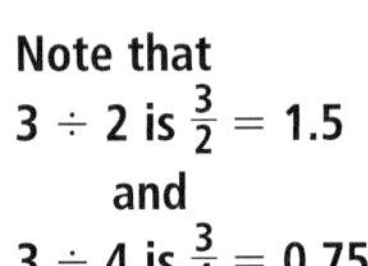

Note that
$3 \div 2$ is $\frac{3}{2} = 1.5$
and
$3 \div 4$ is $\frac{3}{4} = 0.75$

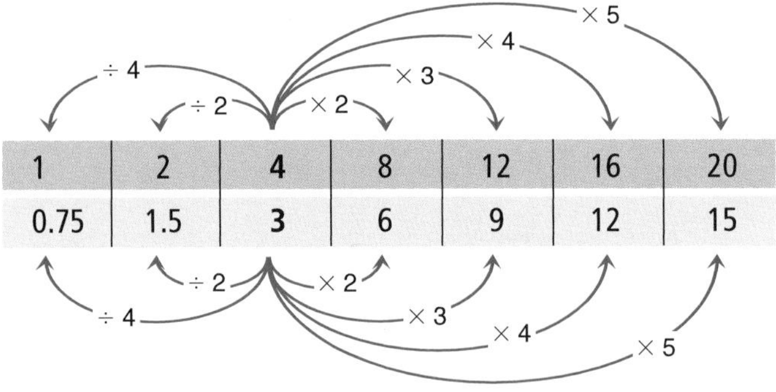

1	2	4	8	12	16	20
0.75	1.5	3	6	9	12	15

The equivalent ratios are:
1:0.75; 2:1.5; 4:3; 8:6; 12:9; 16:12; 20:15

➢ The equivalent ratios can be shown on a grid.

1st term	1	2	4	8	12	16	20
2nd term	0.75	1.5	3	6	9	12	15

The points representing the ratios lie on a straight line.

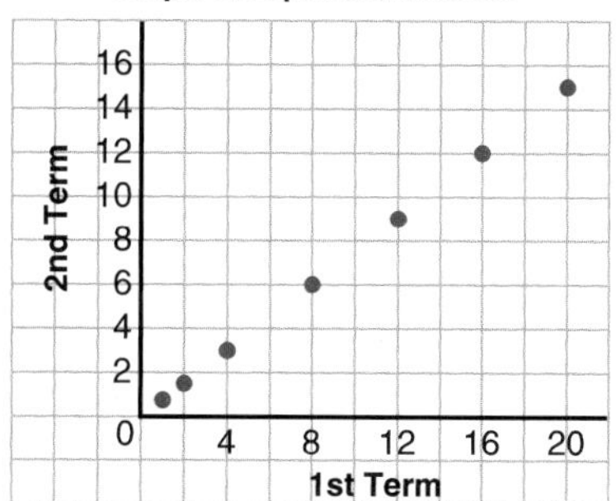

A ratio is in simplest form when its terms have no common factors.

➢ When we divide the terms in a ratio by their greatest common factor, we write the ratio in **simplest form**.

To write 24:16 in simplest form:

$$24:16 \qquad \text{The GCF is 8. Divide by 8.}$$
$$= (24 \div 8):(16 \div 8)$$
$$= 3:2$$

So, 24:16 and 3:2 are equivalent ratios.

The ratio 3:2 is in simplest form.

Example

Construction kits come in different sizes.
The Regular Kit contains 120 long rods, 80 short rods, and 40 connectors.

a) What other kits could be created with the same ratio of rods and connectors?

b) One kit has 10 connectors. How many short and long rods does it have?

Solution

a) Use a table to find equivalent ratios.
Label each new kit.

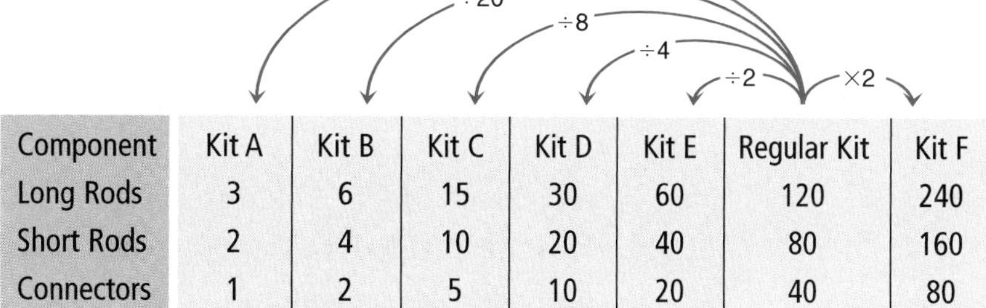

Component	Kit A	Kit B	Kit C	Kit D	Kit E	Regular Kit	Kit F
Long Rods	3	6	15	30	60	120	240
Short Rods	2	4	10	20	40	80	160
Connectors	1	2	5	10	20	40	80

b) Use the table in part a.
The kit with 10 connectors is Kit D.
It has 20 short rods and 30 long rods.

Practice

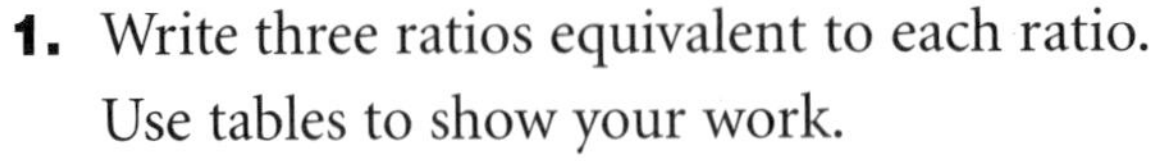

Number Strategies

Find the greatest common factor of the numbers in each set.

- 16, 40, 24
- 33, 77, 88
- 45, 75, 30
- 150, 75, 225

1. Write three ratios equivalent to each ratio.
Use tables to show your work.
a) 3:4 **b)** 14:4

2. Rewrite each sentence as a ratio statement in simplest form.
a) In a class, there are 15 girls and 12 boys.
b) In a parking lot, there were 4 American cars and 12 Japanese cars.
c) A paint mixture is made up of 6 L of blue paint and 2 L of white paint.
d) A stamp collection contains 12 Canadian stamps and 24 American stamps.

3. Name the pairs of equivalent ratios:
2:3, 9:12, 8:5, 1:2, 2:1, 16:10, 3:6, 6:9, 5:8, 3:4
Tell how you know they are equivalent.

4. In a class library, 3 out of 4 books are non-fiction.
The rest are fiction.
a) How many non-fiction books could there be?
How many fiction books?
b) How many different answers can you find for part a?
Which answers are reasonable? Explain.

5. The official Canadian flag has a length to width ratio of 2:1.
Doreen has a sheet of paper that measures 30 cm by 20 cm.
What are the length and width of the largest Canadian flag Doreen can draw? Sketch a picture of the flag.

6. **Assessment Focus** Use red, blue, and green counters.
Make a set of counters with these two ratios:
red:blue = 5:6 blue:green = 3:4
How many different ways can you do this?
Record each way you find.

Reflect

Choose a ratio. Use pictures, numbers, or words to show how to find two equivalent ratios.

2.3 Comparing Ratios

Focus Use equivalent ratios to compare ratios.

Explore

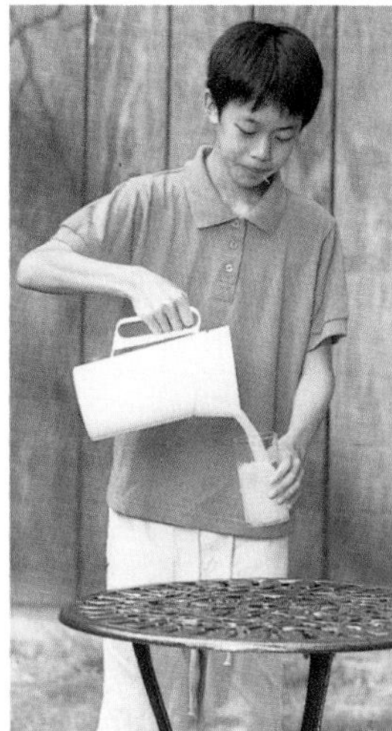

Work with a partner.

Recipe A for punch calls for 2 cans of concentrate and 3 cans of water.

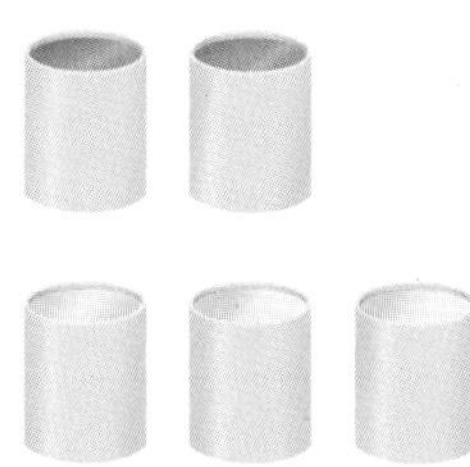

Recipe B for punch calls for 3 cans of concentrate and 4 cans of water.

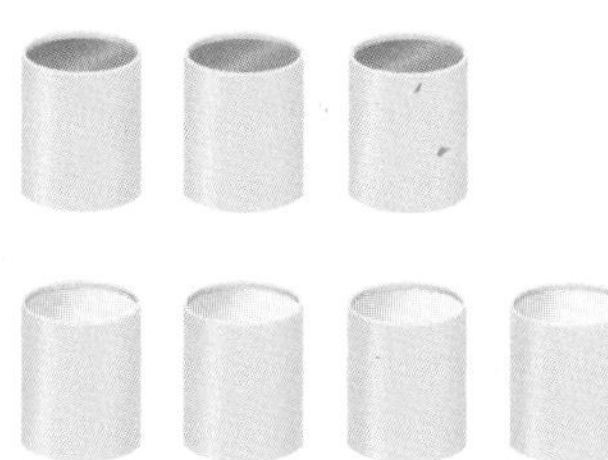

In which recipe is the punch stronger?
Or are the drinks the same?
Explain how you know.

Reflect & Share

Compare your answer with that of another pair of classmates.
Compare strategies.
If your answers are the same, which strategy do you prefer? Would there be a situation when the other strategy would be better? Explain.
If your answers are different, find out which is correct.

Connect

Erica makes her coffee with 2 scoops of coffee to 5 cups of water.

Jim makes his coffee with 3 scoops of coffee to 7 cups of water.

Here are two ways to find out which coffee is stronger.

➢ Find how much water is used for 1 scoop of coffee.

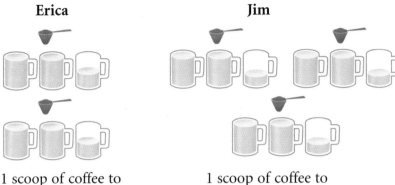

Erica	**Jim**
1 scoop of coffee to $2\frac{1}{2}$ cups of water.	1 scoop of coffee to $2\frac{1}{3}$ cups of water.

Since $2\frac{1}{3}$ is less than $2\frac{1}{2}$,
Jim uses less water to 1 scoop of coffee.
So, Jim's coffee is stronger.

➢ Find how much coffee is used for the same amount of water.
Write each mixture as a ratio.
Write each ratio with the same second term,
then compare the first terms.
Use equivalent ratios.

Erica

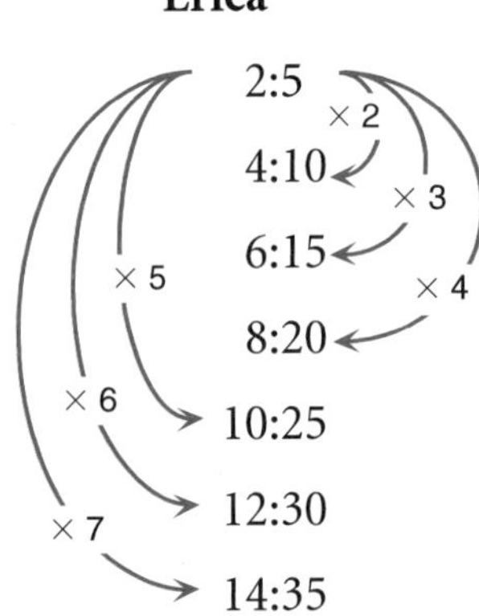

Jim

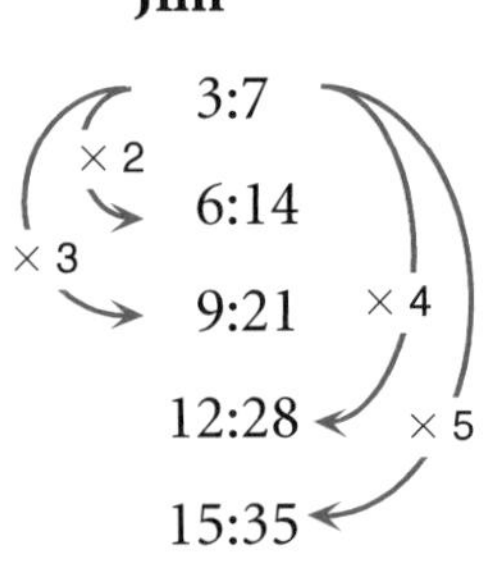

Since 2:5 = 14:35,
Erica uses 14 scoops of
coffee to 35 cups of water.

Since 3:7 = 15:35,
Jim uses 15 scoops of
coffee to 35 cups of water.

Jim uses more coffee. So, Jim's coffee is stronger.
Notice that, as we multiply to get equivalent ratios,
we get multiples of the terms of the ratios.
That is, the first terms in Erica's equivalent ratios are multiples of 2;
the second terms are multiples of 5.

A quicker way to write each ratio with the same second term is to find the lowest common multiple of the second terms.
That is, the lowest common multiple of 5 and 7 is 35.

Example

At the outdoor centre, there were the same numbers of boys and girls. Five out of every 8 boys wanted to kayak. Two out of every 3 girls wanted to kayak. Do more boys than girls want to kayak? Explain.

Solution

Five out of every 8 boys want to kayak.
This is a ratio of 5:8.
Two out of every 3 girls want to kayak.
This is a ratio of 2:3.
To compare the ratios, write them with the second terms the same.
The lowest common multiple of 8 and 3 is 24.
Multiply to make the second term of each ratio 24.

Boys	**Girls**
5:8	2:3
$= (5 \times 3):(8 \times 3)$	$= (2 \times 8):(3 \times 8)$
= 15:24	= 16:24
15 out of 24 boys want to kayak	16 out of 24 girls want to kayak

Since 16 is greater than 15, more girls want to kayak.

Practice

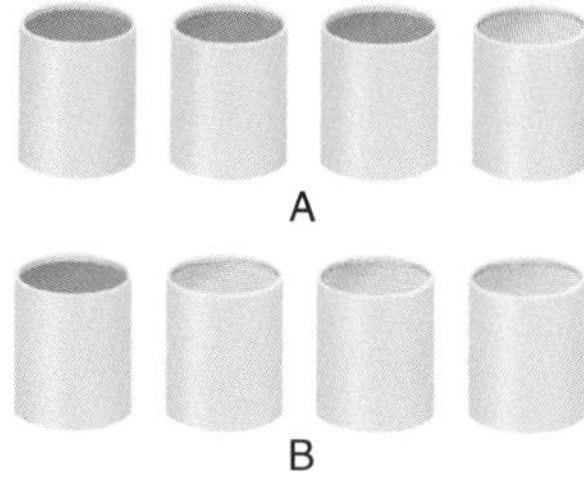

1. The concentrate and water in each picture are mixed.
Which mixture is stronger: A or B?
Draw a picture to show your answer.

2. Two boxes contain pictures of hockey and basketball players.
In one box, the ratio of hockey players to basketball players is 4:3.
In the other box, the ratio is 3:2.
The boxes contain the same number of pictures.

a) What could the total number of pictures be?

b) Which box contains more pictures of hockey players?
Draw a picture to show your answer.

Number Strategies

There are 10 coins that total $0.60.
What are the coins?

3. In a basketball game, Alison made 6 of 13 free shots. Madhu made 5 of 9 free shots. Who played better? Explain.

4. The principal is deciding which shade of blue to have the classrooms painted. One shade of blue requires 3 cans of white paint mixed with 4 cans of blue paint. Another shade of blue requires 5 cans of white paint mixed with 7 cans of blue paint.

a) Which mixture will give the darker shade of blue? Explain.

b) Which mixture will require more white paint?

5. Look at the two mixtures.

a) What is the ratio of concentrate to water in A and in B?

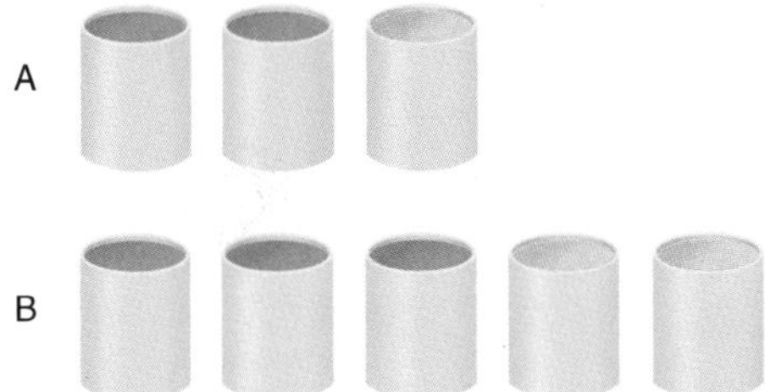

b) Explain how you could add concentrate or water to make both ratios the same.
Draw a picture to show your answer.

6. **Assessment Focus** The ratio of fiction to non-fiction books in Ms. Arbuckle's class library is 7:5.
The ratio of fiction to non-fiction books in Mr. Albright's class library is 4:3.
Each classroom has 30 non-fiction books.

a) Which room has more fiction books? How many more?

b) Mr. Albright added two non-fiction books to his class library. Does this make the ratio the same in both classes? Explain.

7. At Ria's party, there were 2 pizzas for every 3 people.
At Amin's party, there were 5 pizzas for every 7 people.
At which party did each person get more pizza? Explain.

Reflect

In one store, the ratio of DVDs to videos is 7:5.
In another store, the ratio of DVDs to videos is 4:3.
Explain why you cannot say which store has more DVDs.

Mid-Unit Review

LESSON

2.1 **1.** In the school parking lot, there are 4 Japanese cars, 7 American cars, 3 German cars, and 2 Korean cars. Write each ratio.

a) American cars to Japanese cars

b) German cars to Korean cars

c) American cars to total number of cars

d) German cars to Japanese cars and American cars

2. A box contains 5 cream chocolates, 2 chocolate-covered almonds, and 3 caramel chocolates.

a) What is each ratio? Sketch a picture for each ratio.

i) almond chocolates to caramel chocolates

ii) cream chocolates to caramel chocolates

iii) cream chocolates to all chocolates

b) Lesley ate one of each kind of chocolate. What is each new ratio for part a?

3. In Mary's closet, there are 7 T-shirts, 4 pairs of shorts, and 3 sweaters. Write each ratio.

a) T-shirts to shorts

b) sweaters to shorts

c) sweaters to T-shirts and shorts

2.2 **4.** For each ratio, write three equivalent ratios.

a) 5:3 **b)** 6:24

5. a) Write each ratio below in simplest form.

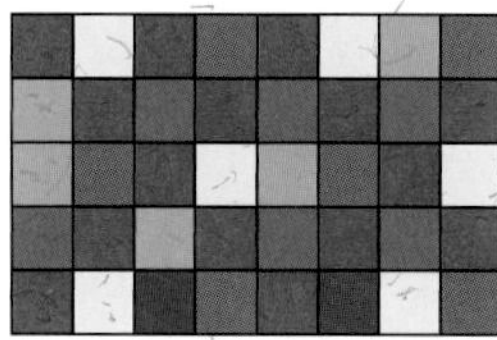

i) green squares to red squares

ii) yellow squares to purple squares

iii) red squares to total number of squares

b) State the colours for each ratio.

i) 1:6 **ii)** 2:5

6. In Ms. Bell's class, the ratio of boys to girls is 5:4.

a) There are 15 boys in the class. How many girls are there?

b) Two girls leave. What is the new ratio of boys to girls?

2.3 **7.** A jug of orange juice requires 3 cans of orange concentrate and 5 cans of water.

a) Accidentally, 4 cans of concentrate were mixed with 5 cans of water. Is the mixture stronger or weaker than it should be? Explain.

b) Suppose 6 cans of water were mixed with 3 cans of concentrate. Is the mixture stronger or weaker than it should be? Explain.

2.4 Applications of Ratios

Focus Use ratios to solve problems.

Explore

Work on your own.
In the book *Gulliver's Travels*, Gulliver meets little people who are only 15 cm tall, and giants who are 18 m tall.
Gulliver is 1.80 m tall.
How many times as big as a little person is Gulliver?
How many times as big as Gulliver is a giant?
Write these comparisons as ratios.

Reflect & Share

Compare your answers with those of a classmate.
Work together to find the ratio of the height of the giants to the height of the little people.
How many times as big as a little person is a giant?

Connect

You can use diagrams and tables to model and solve ratio problems.

Example 1

Jolene makes a scale drawing of her home.
She uses a scale of 5 cm to represent 1.5 m.

a) What is the ratio of a length in the drawing to the actual length? What does this ratio mean?

b) Jolene measures her bedroom on the drawing. It is 16 cm long. What is the actual length of Jolene's bedroom?

c) The house measures 18 m by 12 m. What are the dimensions of the scale drawing?

Solution

a) Length in the drawing:actual length

= 5 cm:1.50 m

= 5 cm:150 cm

= (5 cm ÷ 5 cm):(150 cm ÷ 5 cm)

= 1:30

When you write ratios of measurements, the units must be the same. Multiply 1.50 m by 100 to change metres to centimetres.

Each 1 cm in the drawing represents 30 cm in the home.

b) Draw a diagram.

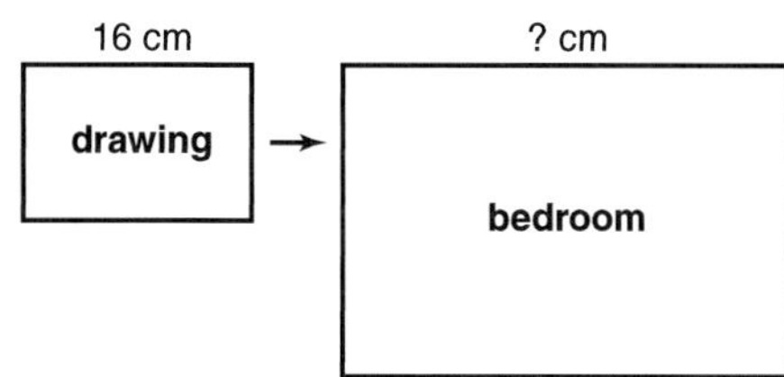

The length in the drawing is 16 cm.
Each 1 cm in the drawing represents 30 cm in the bedroom.
So, the length of the bedroom is 16×30 cm $= 480$ cm
$= 4.8$ m

c) Draw a diagram.

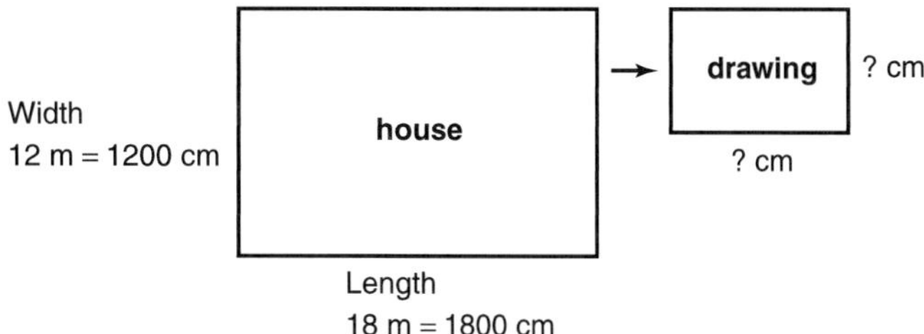

1 cm in the drawing represents 30 cm in the house.
Divide each measurement in the house to find the measurement on the drawing.

Length in the drawing $= \frac{1800 \text{ cm}}{30}$
$= 60$ cm

Width in the drawing $= \frac{1200 \text{ cm}}{30}$
$= 40$ cm

The dimensions of the scale drawing are 60 cm by 40 cm.

Example 2

Wallpaper paste can be made by mixing flour and water.
The table shows the volume of water to be mixed with flour to make different quantities of paste.

Water (mL)	16	32	48
Flour (mL)	3	6	9

a) What is the ratio of the volume of water to the volume of flour?

b) How much water is required for 15 mL of flour?

Solution

a) Volume of water:volume of flour = 16:3

b) Use a pattern to continue the table in part a.
For the water, the pattern rule is: Start at 16, then add 16.
The next three terms are 64, 80, 96.
For the flour, the pattern rule is: Start at 3, then add 3.
The next three terms are 12, 15, 18.
Extend the table to include these numbers.

Water (mL)	16	32	48	64	80	96
Flour (mL)	3	6	9	12	15	18

From the table, 80 mL of water are needed for 15 mL of flour.

Practice

Mental Math

Find all the factors of each number.

7, 15, 27, 36, 48, 51

1. This table shows the quantities of concentrate and water needed to make punch.

Orange concentrate (cans)	2	4	6		
Cranberry concentrate (cans)	1	2	3		
Water (cans)	3	6	9		
Punch (L)	1.5	3	4.5		

a) What are the next two numbers in each row of the table?
b) What is the ratio of cranberry concentrate to water?
c) Suppose you use 10 cans of orange concentrate.
How much punch would you get?
d) Suppose you use 12 cans of concentrate in total.
How much punch would you get?
e) How much of each ingredient would you need to make 15 L of punch? Explain your reasoning.

Remember to convert the units so you work with all measurements in the same units.

2. Jenny makes models of Canadian Coast Guard ships.
She uses a scale of 3 cm to 1.5 m.
a) What is the ratio of a length on the model to a length on the ship?
b) The Terry Fox ship is 88 m long. How long is the model?
c) The model of the Otter Bay is 27 cm long.
What is the actual length of the Otter Bay?
Draw diagrams to show your answers.

3. A set designer builds a model of the stage and the different pieces of furniture on it. He uses a scale of 5 cm to 1 m.
   a) What is the ratio of a length on the model to a length on the stage?
   b) The length of a table is 1.4 m. What is the length of the model?
   c) The height of the model of a lamp is 3 cm. What is the actual height of the lamp?
   d) The height of the model of an ornament is 0.5 cm. What is the actual height of the ornament? How did you find out?

   Draw diagrams to show your answers.

Social Studies

A scale on a provincial map is 1:1 500 000. This means that 1 cm on the map represents 1 500 000 cm on the ground, which is $\frac{1\,500\,000}{100}$ m, or 15 000 m on the ground.
And, 15 000 m is $\frac{15\,000}{1000}$ km, or 15 km.
So, a scale of 1:1 500 000 is 1 cm to 15 km.

4. Janice builds a model using a scale of 2 cm to represent 3 m. Her friend William says she is using a ratio of 2:3. Is William correct? Explain.

5. This table shows the quantities of salt and water needed to make salt solutions.

Water (L)	2	4	6	8
Salt (g)	18	36	54	72

   a) How much salt would be needed for 7 L of water?
   b) How much water would be needed for 90 g of salt?

6. **Assessment Focus** Aston challenges his father to a 100-m race. Aston runs 4 m for every 5 m his father runs.
   a) Who wins the race? Draw a diagram to show your answer.
   b) How far will Aston have run when his father crosses the finish line?
   c) Aston asks to race again but wants to be given a head start. How much of a start should Aston's father give him to make it a close race? Explain your answer.

Reflect

Make up your own ratio problem.
Solve your problem. Show your work.

2.5 What Is a Rate?

Focus Investigate rates.

Explore

Work with a partner.
You will need a stopwatch.
One person is the "blinker." The other person is the timekeeper.
The blinker blinks as many times as possible.
Count the number of times the blinker blinks in 20 s.
Reverse roles.
Count the number of times the blinker blinks in 30 s.

➢ Who was the faster blinker?
  How do you know?
➢ Estimate how many times each person would blink in 1 h.
  What assumptions do you make?
  Are these assumptions reasonable?

Reflect & Share

Compare your results with those of another pair of classmates.
How can you decide who is the fastest blinker?

Connect

When we compare two different things, we have a **rate**.
Here are some rates.

- We need 5 sandwiches for every 2 people.
- Oranges are on sale at $1.49 for 12.
- Gina earns $4.75 per hour for baby-sitting.
- There are 500 sheets on one roll of paper towels.

The last two rates above are **unit rates**.
Each rate compares a quantity to 1 unit.

Jamal skipped rope 80 times in 1 min.
We say that Jamal's rate of skipping is 80 skips per minute.
We write this as 80 skips/min.

To find unit rates, we can use diagrams, tables, and graphs.

Example 1

The doctor took Marjorie's pulse. He counted 25 beats in 20 s. What was Marjorie's heart rate in beats per minute?

Solution

Draw a diagram.
There are 25 beats in 20 s.
There are 60 s in 1 min.
We multiply 20 s by 3 to get 60 s.
So, multiply the number of beats in 20 s by 3 to get the number of beats per minute.

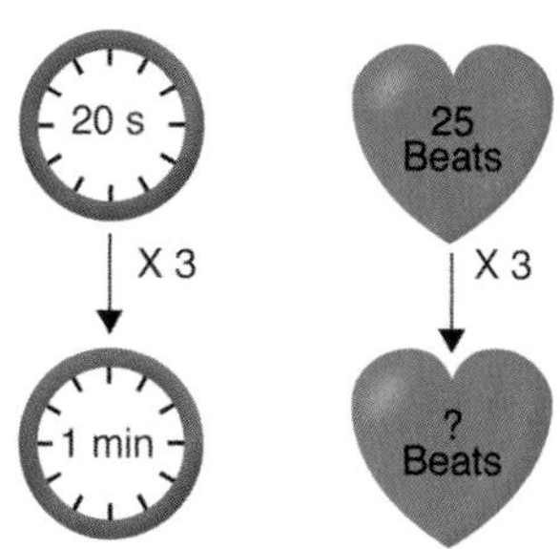

25 beats $\times$ 3 = 75 beats

Marjorie's heart rate is 75 beats/min.

Example 2

A printing press prints 120 sheets in 3 min.

a) Express the printing as a rate.
b) How many sheets are printed in 1 h?
c) How long will it take to print 1000 sheets?

Solution

a) Draw a diagram.
The press prints 120 sheets in 3 min.
So, in 1 min, the press prints:
120 sheets $\div$ 3 = 40 sheets
The rate of printing is 40 sheets/min.

120
Sheets
in
3 min
÷ 3
÷ 3
?
Sheets
in
1 min

b) In 1 min, the press prints 40 sheets.
One hour is 60 min.
So, in 60 min, the press prints:
60 $\times$ 40 sheets = 2400 sheets
The press prints 2400 sheets in 1 h.

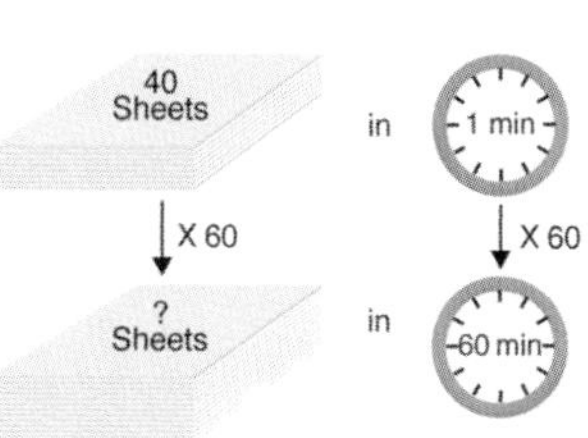

c) *Method 1*
In 1 min, the press prints 40 sheets.
So, in 5 min, the press prints: 5 $\times$ 40 = 200 sheets
Make a table. Every 5 min, 200 more sheets are printed.
Extend the table until you get 1000 sheets.

Time (min)	5	10	15	20	25
Sheets printed	200	400	600	800	1000

Method 2

The press prints 40 sheets in 1 min.
Think: What do we multiply 40 by to get 1000?
Use division: $1000 \div 40 = 25$
So, $40 \times 25 = 1000$
We multiply the time by the same number.
$1 \text{ min} \times 25 = 25 \text{ min}$
The press takes 25 min to print 1000 sheets.

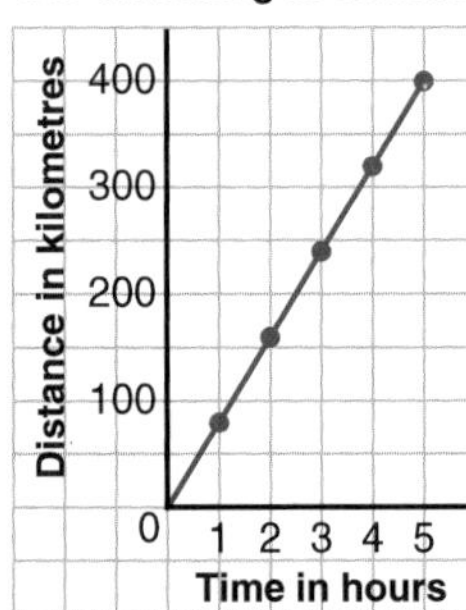

The rate at which a car travels is its **average speed**.
When a car travels at an average speed of 80 km/h, it travels:

80 km in 1 h
160 km in 2 h
240 km in 3 h
320 km in 4 h
400 km in 5 h … and so on

We can show this motion on a graph.
An average speed of 80 km/h is a unit rate.

Practice

1. Express as a unit rate.
- **a)** Morag typed 60 words in one minute.
- **b)** Peter swam 25 m in one minute.
- **c)** Abdu read 20 pages in one hour.

2. Express as a unit rate.
- **a)** June cycled 30 km in 2 h.
- **b)** An elephant travelled 18 km in 30 min.
- **c)** A plane flew 150 km in 15 min.

3. Before running in a 100-m race, Gaalen's heart rate was 70 beats/min. Which do you think is more likely after the race: 60 beats/min or 120 beats/min? Explain.

Mental Math

Find a square root of each number.

49, 25, 81, 16, 64, 144, 4, 121

4. Ribbon costs $1.44 for 3 m.
   a) What is the cost per metre?
   b) How much would 5 m of ribbon cost?
   c) How much ribbon could you buy for $12?

5. The graph shows the distance travelled by a cyclist in 3 h.
   a) How far did the cyclist travel in 1 h?
   b) What is the average speed of the cyclist? How do you know?

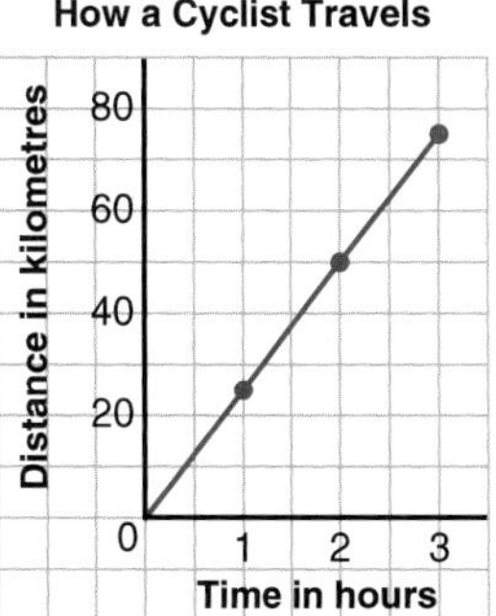

In England, the currency is pennies and pounds. There are 100 pennies in one pound, £1.

6. James and Lucinda came to Canada on holiday from England. The rate of exchange for their money was $2.50 Can to £1.
   a) How many Canadian dollars would James get for £20?
   b) What is the value in English pounds of a gift Lucinda bought for $30 Can?

7. When a person runs a long-distance race, she thinks of the time she takes to run 1 km (min/km), rather than the distance run in 1 min (km/min).
   On a training run, Judy took 3 h 20 min to run 25 km.
   What was Judy's rate in minutes per kilometre?

8. **Assessment Focus** Scott trained for the marathon.
   On day 1, he took 70 min to run 10 km.
   On day 10, he took 2 h 40 min to run 20 km.
   On day 20, he took 4 h 15 min to run 30 km.
   a) What was Scott's running rate, in minutes per kilometre, for each day?
      i) Day 1 ii) Day 10 iii) Day 20
   b) What do you think Scott's running rate, in minutes per kilometre, might be for the 44 km of the marathon?
      How long do you think it will take him? Explain.

Reflect

Look through newspapers and magazines to find three different examples of rates. Explain how the rates are used.

Organizing a Math Notebook

1

You must include the date for each new note taken or activity performed.

2

You must include a title for each new note or activity.

3

All dates and titles must be underlined with a ruler.

4

All tables must be neat.
Use a ruler to draw a table.

For example:

Section 2.5, question 8.

April 13, 2005

Day	Time (min)	Distance (km)	Rate (min/km)
1			

5

Your daily work must be legible, complete, and well-organized.

Reading and Writing in

Math

6

You must make corrections where necessary.

7

To organize a math problem:

- Restate the problem in your own words.
  For example, "This problem is about..."

- Think about a strategy you will use
  and tell about it.
  For example, "The strategy I will use
  is...________ because..."

- Solve the problem. Show all your work.

- State the answer to your problem, and explain how you
  know it is reasonable and correct.
  For example, "I found the answer to be...
  I know my answer is reasonable because...
  I know my answer is correct because..."

- Extend your thinking. Make up a similar problem by
  asking "What if?" questions.
  For example, "What if all the numbers in this question
  were doubled? How would the answer change?"

Race Engineer

The equivalent of the 100-m sprint in the world of cars is the $\frac{1}{4}$-mile drag race. One-quarter of one mile is about 400 m. The race engineers (men and women who help design, build, and tune the cars) are an important part of the racing team. Theirs is a world filled with gear ratios, cylinder compression ratios, fuel mixture ratios, acceleration, and speed. It's a constant cycle of theory, real-world application, testing, and evaluating. And, sometimes, all these take place during a few hours between race runs! Helping the dragster team driver get to the finish line $\frac{1}{1000}$ th of a second faster than a previous run could mean the difference between winning and losing the race.

In October, 2003, a top fuel dragster recorded a new "fastest time" of 4.441 s for the $\frac{1}{4}$-mile drag race. But another car and driver continued to hold the record for the fastest recorded speed achieved during a race—an incredible 536 km/h! Why do you suppose the second car doesn't hold the record for fastest time?

Unit Review

Review any lesson with

What Do I Need to Know?

✓ A ratio is a comparison of quantities.
For example, 3 dogs to 7 cats is 3:7.

✓ An equivalent ratio can be formed by multiplying or dividing the terms of a ratio by the same number.

For example:

5:8	and	36:30
$= (5 \times 3):(8 \times 3)$		$= (36 \div 6):(30 \div 6)$
$=$ 15:24		$=$ 6:5
5:8 and 15:24 are equivalent ratios.		36:30 and 6:5 are equivalent ratios.

✓ Two ratios can be compared when the second terms are the same.
For example, Scott's scoring record was 16:5.
Brittany's scoring record was 10:3.
To find who had the better record, use equivalent ratios to make the second term of each ratio 15.

Scott	**Brittany**
16:5	10:3
$= (16 \times 3):(5 \times 3)$	$= (10 \times 5):(3 \times 5)$
$=$ 48:15	$=$ 50:15

Brittany had the better record.

✓ A rate is a comparison of two quantities with different units.
For example:
Heart rate is measured in beats per minute (beats/min).
Average speed is measured in kilometres per hour (km/h).
Fuel consumption of an aircraft is measured in litres per hour (L/h).

What Should I Be Able to Do?

For extra practice, go to page 439.

LESSON

2.1 **1.** On a school trip, there are 9 boys, 10 girls, and 4 adults.
Write each ratio.
a) girls to boys
b) boys and girls to adults
c) adults to boys and girls

2.2 **2.** Write four ratios to describe the coloured squares.

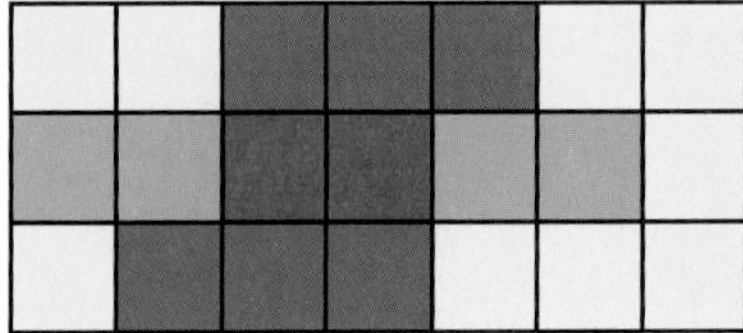

3. Explain two different ways to get ratios equivalent to 25:10.

4. Jake has to draw a flag with a length to width ratio of 3 to 2. What is the largest flag Jake can draw on a 25-cm by 20-cm sheet of paper?

2.3 **5.** The ratio of computers to students in Ms. Beveridge's class is 2:3. The ratio of computers to students in Mr. Walker's class is 3:5. Each class has the same number of students.
Which room has more computers? Explain.

2.4 **6.** Ali builds model planes. He uses a scale of 8 cm to represent 1.8 m.
a) What is the ratio of a length on the model to the actual length on the plane?
b) A plane has a length of 72 m. What is the length of the model?
c) A model has a length of 60 cm. What is the actual length of the plane?

Draw pictures to show your answers.

7. Red and white paint is mixed in the ratio of 3 to 2.
a) How many cans of red paint would be needed with 6 cans of white paint?
b) How many cans of each colour are needed to make 20 cans of mixture?

2.5 **8.** Express as a unit rate.
a) A bus travelled 120 km in 3 h.
b) An athlete ran 1500 m in 6 min.
c) A student earned $16 for 2 h work.

9. A lion can run 550 m in 25 s.
A zebra can run 270 m in 15 s.
a) Which animal is faster?
b) What is the ratio of their average speeds?

Practice Test

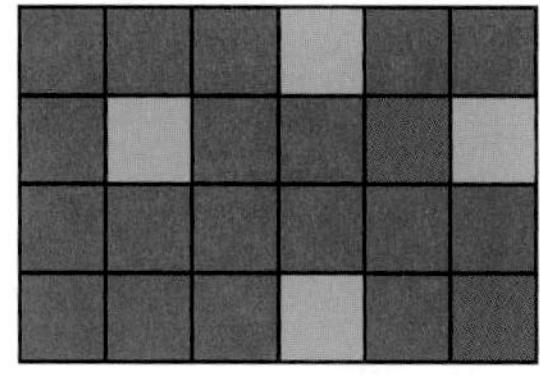

1. a) Write each ratio in simplest form.
   i) red squares to blue squares
   ii) blue squares to green squares
   iii) red squares and blue squares to total numbers of squares

   b) Suppose the grid is increased to a rectangle measuring 9 units by 4 units. The ratios of the colours remain the same. How many red squares will there be in the new rectangle?

2. In the league, the Leos play 8 games. Their win to loss ratio is 5:3. The Tigers play 11 games. Their win to loss ratio is 7:4.
   a) Which team has the better record? Explain.
   b) Suppose the Leos win their next game and the Tigers lose theirs. Which team would have the better record? Explain.

3. Hessa is building a scale model of a park. She uses a scale of 12 cm to represent 1.5 m.
   a) The actual length of the bridge is 20 m. What is the length of the model bridge?
   b) In the model, the height of the climbing frame is 10 cm. What is the actual height of the frame?

4. Look at this graph.
   a) What is the speed of each car?
   b) How far apart are the cars after 4 s?

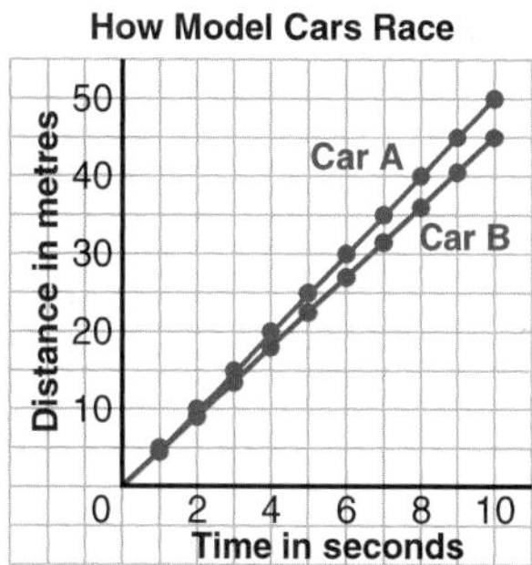

5. Trevor's mark on a math test was 10 out of 15. Anne's mark on another test was 15 out of 20. Trevor said, "Each of us got 5 wrong. So, our marks are equal." Do you agree? Give reasons for your answer.

Unit Problem Who's the Smartest?

Mr. Peabody believes you can predict an animal's intelligence by looking at the size of its brain.
He uses ratios to compare body size to brain size.
Investigate this strategy.

A **hypothesis** is something that seems likely to be true. It needs to be tested and proved or disproved.

Analyse the data below to test Mr. Peabody's **hypothesis**.

Species	Comparing Mass (g)		Comparing Length (cm)	
	Body	Brain	Body	Brain
Human	56 000	1400	150	15
Monkey	7 000	100	30	5
Camel	520 000	650	200	15

The mass of a human brain is about the same mass as your math textbook.

1. Compare masses: find the ratio of body mass to brain mass.
- How does a human compare to a monkey?
- How does a human compare to a camel?
- How does a camel compare to a monkey?

According to Mr. Peabody's hypothesis, which animal is smartest? Explain your reasoning.

2. Compare lengths: find the ratio of body length to brain length.
   - How does a human compare to a monkey?
   - How does a human compare to a camel?
   - How does a camel compare to a monkey?

   According to Mr. Peabody's hypothesis, which animal is smartest? Explain your reasoning.

Check List

Your work should show:

✓ how you calculated each ratio

✓ your reasoning for which animal is the smartest

✓ your conclusions about the hypothesis

✓ the correct use of mathematical language

3. The dinosaur, diplodocus, lived about 150 million years ago.
   The brain of a diplodocus was about 9 cm long.
   The body of a diplodocus was about 27 m long.
   - How long would a human's brain be if it had the same brain length to body length ratio as a diplodocus?

   A frog's brain is about 2 cm long.
   A frog's length is about 10 cm long
   - How long would a human's brain be if it had the same brain length to body length ratio as a frog?

4. Review your results.
   Write a short letter to Mr. Peabody telling him whether you agree with his hypothesis, and why.
   Use mathematical language to support your opinion.

Reflect on the Unit

How is a rate like a ratio?
How is it different?
Use examples in your explanation.

UNIT 3

Geometry and Measurement

Most products are packaged in boxes or cans.
How is a package made?
How do you think the manufacturer chooses the shape and style of package? What things need to be considered?

Look at the packages on this page.
Choose one package.
Why do you think the manufacturer chose that form of packaging?

What You'll Learn

- Recognize different views of an object.
- Sketch different views of an object.
- Sketch an object.
- Build an object from a net.
- Develop and use a formula for the surface area of a rectangular prism.
- Develop and use a formula for the volume of a rectangular prism.

Why It's Important

- Drawing a picture is one way to help solve a problem or explain a solution.
- Calculating the volume and surface area of a prism is an extension of the measuring you did in earlier grades.

Key Words

- polyhedron (polyhedra)
- prism
- pyramid
- regular polyhedron
- cube
- tetrahedron
- isometric
- pictorial diagram
- icosahedron
- octahedron
- dodecahedron
- frustum
- variable
- surface area

UNIT 3

Skills You'll Need

Identifying Polyhedra

A **polyhedron** is a solid with faces that are polygons.
Two faces meet at an edge.
Three or more edges meet at a vertex.

A **prism** has 2 congruent bases, and is named for its bases.
Its other faces are parallelograms.

A pentagonal prism

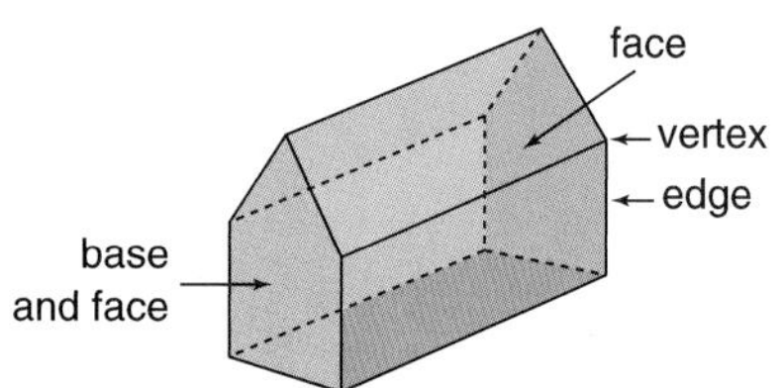

A triangular prism

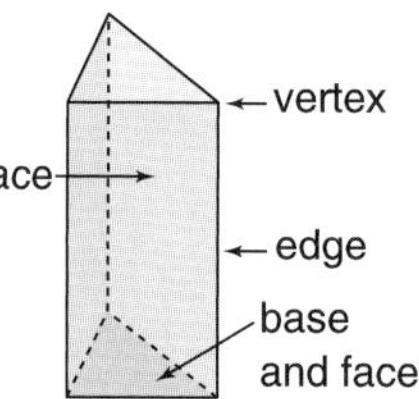

A **pyramid** has 1 base and is named for that base.
Its other faces are triangles.

A square pyramid

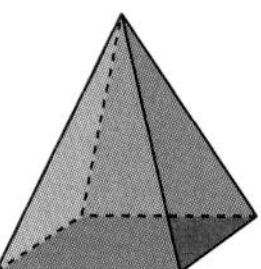

A hexagonal pyramid

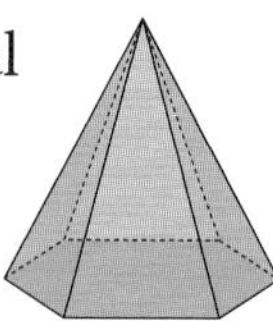

A **regular polyhedron** has all faces congruent.
The same number of faces meet at each vertex.
The same number of edges meet at each vertex.

A **cube** is a regular rectangular prism.

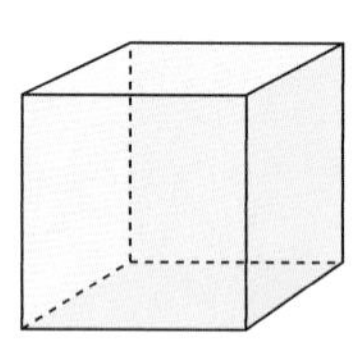

A **regular tetrahedron** is a regular triangular pyramid.

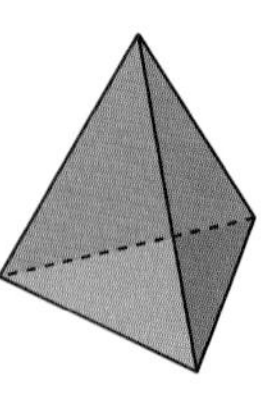

Use the pictures of the solids above. Use the solids if you have them.

1. **a)** How are the solids alike? How are they different?

b) Name a real-life object that has the shape of each solid.

Using Isometric Dot Paper to Draw a Cube

To draw this cube:

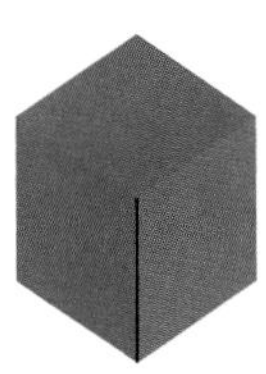

Join 2 dots for one vertical edge.

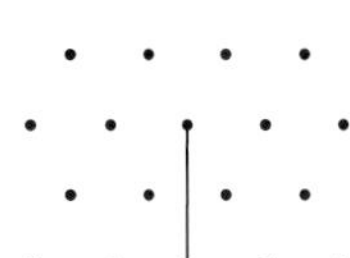

Join pairs of dots diagonally for the front horizontal edges, top and bottom.

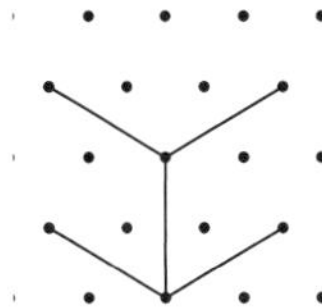

Join the dots for the other 2 vertical edges.

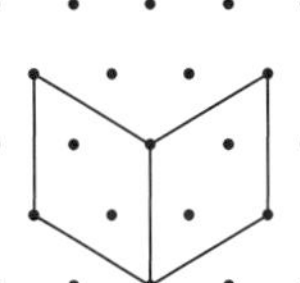

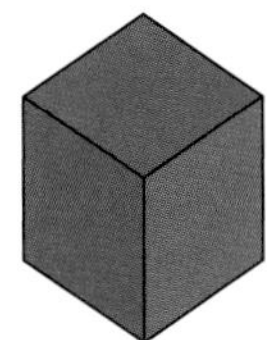

Complete the cube.
Join dots diagonally for the back horizontal edges at the top.

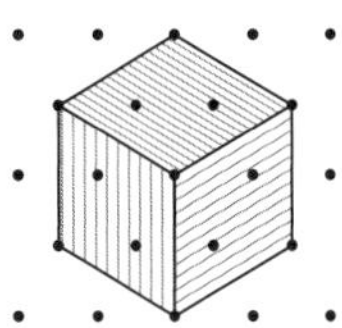

Shade visible faces differently to get a three-dimensional (3-D) look.

Isometric means "equal measure." On isometric dot paper, the line segments joining 2 adjacent dots in any direction are equal.

✓ Check

2. Use isometric dot paper. Draw each object. Use linking cubes when they help.

a)

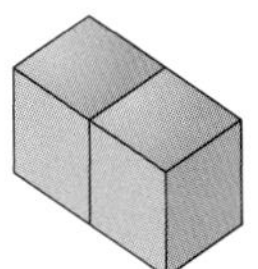

b)

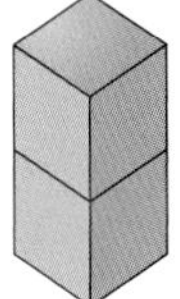

c)

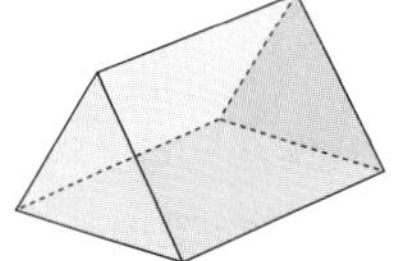

3.1 Sketching Views of Solids

Focus Recognize and sketch different views of objects.

Which objects do you see in this picture?

Choose an object. What does it look like from the top? From the side? From the back?

Explore

Work on your own.
Choose a classroom object.

Sketch the object from every view possible. Label each view.
Use dot paper or grid paper if it helps.
Describe each sketch.

Reflect & Share

Trade sketches with a classmate.
Try to identify the object your classmate drew.

Connect

We can use square dot paper to draw each view of the object at the left.
We ignore the holes in each face.

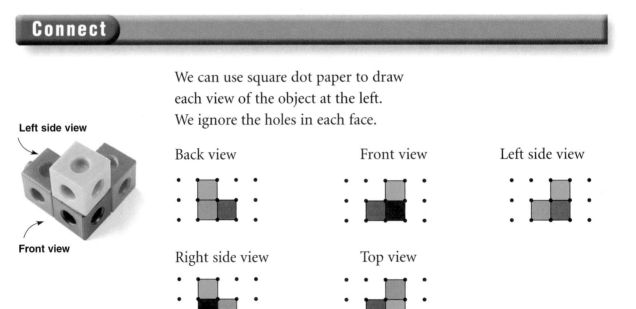

Back view

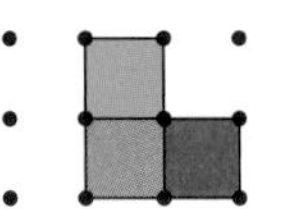

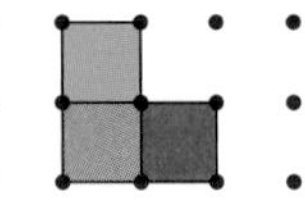

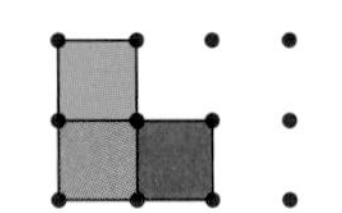

Front view

Left side view

Right side view

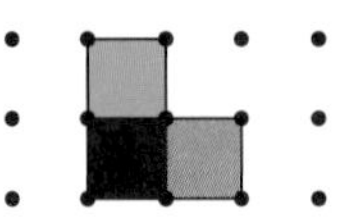

Top view

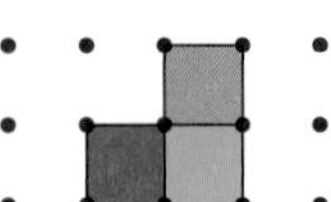

Example

A triangular prism fits on top of a rectangular prism. The bases of the triangular prism are right isosceles triangles. The rectangular prism has two square faces. Sketch the front, back, side, and top views.

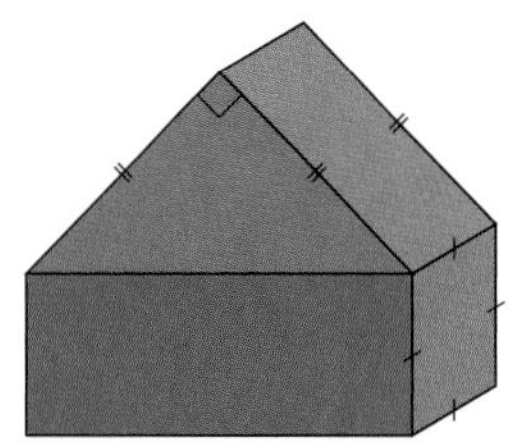

A right isosceles triangle has a 90° angle and two equal sides.

Solution

The front view and back view are the same. Sketch a right isosceles triangle on top of a rectangle.

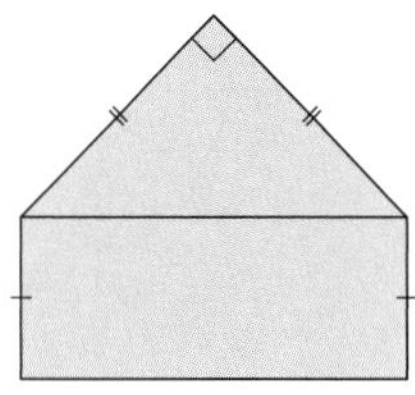

Front view

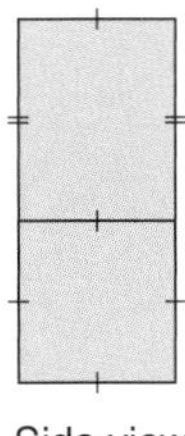

Side view

The two side views are the same. The side face of the triangular prism is a rectangle. Sketch a rectangle on top of a square.

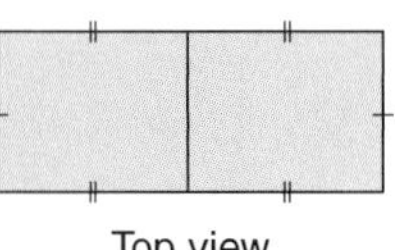

Top view

The top view is two congruent rectangles.

Practice

Use linking cubes when they help.

1. Many signs are views of objects.
Identify the view (front, back, side, or top) and the object on each sign.

a) Child care **b)** Airport transportation **c)** Fully accessible

2. Use linking cubes. Make each object A to E. Figures J to Q are views of objects A to E. Match each view (J to Q) to each object (A to E), in as many ways as you can.

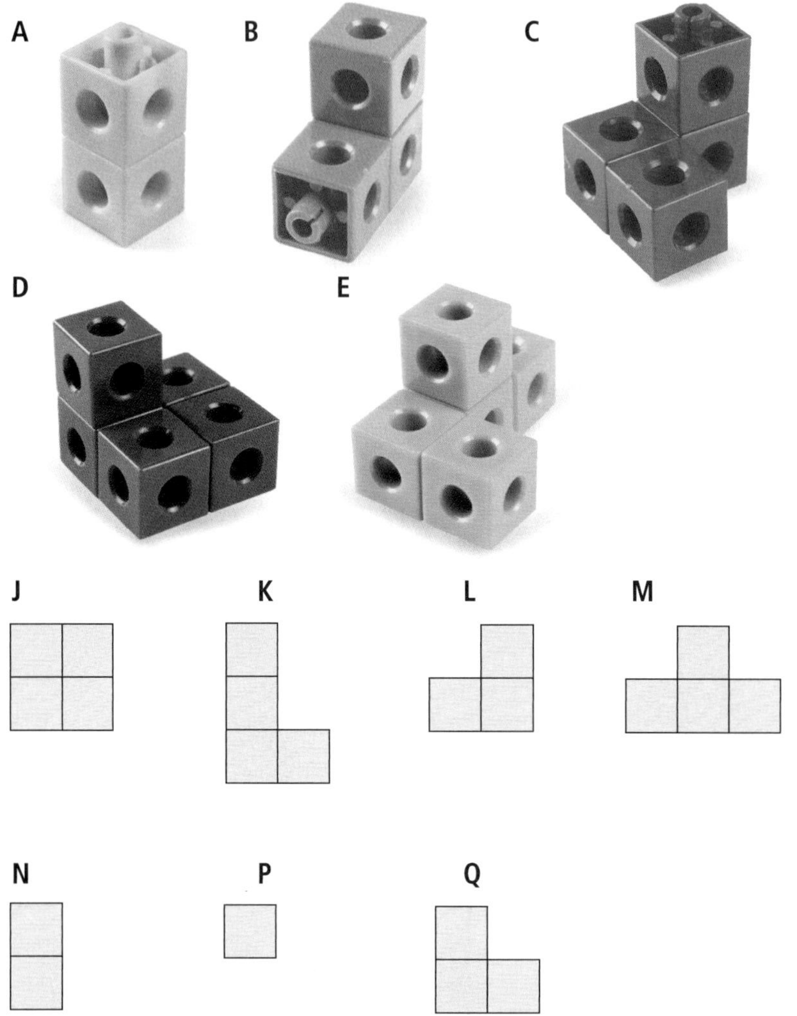

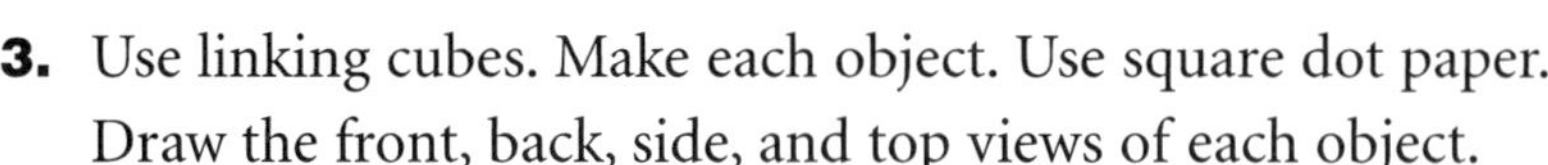

3. Use linking cubes. Make each object. Use square dot paper. Draw the front, back, side, and top views of each object.

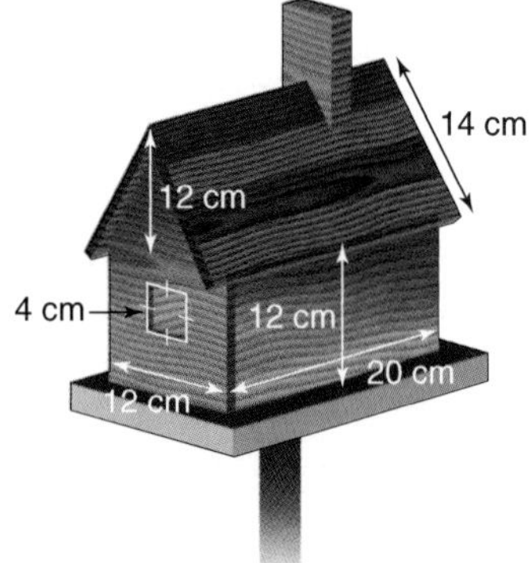

4. Sketch the top, front, side, and back views of the birdhouse at the left. Label each view.

5. Design a road safety or information sign for each situation. Tell which view you used. Explain how each sign shows the information.
   a) playground ahead
   b) tennis court
   c) skateboarding allowed
   d) no flash cameras allowed

6. Find each object in the classroom.
   Sketch the front, back, top, and side views of each object.
   a) filing cabinet
   b) vase
   c) teacher's desk

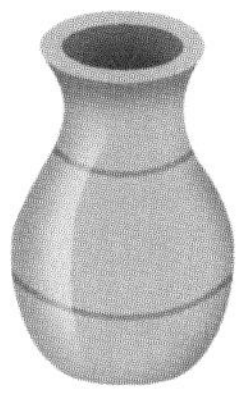

Mental Math

How many:
- days in a year?
- months in a year?
- days in a week?
- hours in a day?
- minutes in an hour?
- seconds in a minute?

7. **Assessment Focus** Use 4 linking cubes. Make as many different objects as possible. Draw the front, back, top, and side views for each object. Label each view. Use your sketches to explain how you know all the objects you made are different.

8. All 5 views of a cube are the same.
   Use the solids in the classroom.
   a) Are there any other prisms with all views the same? Explain.
   b) Which solid has 4 views the same?
   c) Which solid has only 3 views the same?
   d) Which solid has no views the same?
   If you cannot name a solid for parts b to d, use linking cubes to make a solid.

9. Here is one view of an object.
   Sketch a possible different view of the object.
   a)
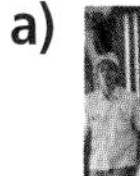

   b)

   c)

Reflect

Choose an object. How many views do you need to sketch, so someone else can identify it? Explain. Sketch the views you describe.

Using a Computer to Draw Views of Solids

Focus Use technology to sketch views of objects.

Software, such as *The Geometer's Sketchpad*, can be used to draw different views of solids.

Follow these steps.

1. Open *The Geometer's Sketchpad.*

To make a "dot paper" screen:

2. From the **Edit** menu, choose **Preferences.**
   Select the Units tab. Check the Distance units are cm.
   Click **OK.**

3. From the **Graph** menu, choose **Define Coordinate System.**
   Click on a point where the grid lines intersect.
   The grid is now highlighted in pink.

4. From the **Display** menu, choose **Line Width**, then **Dotted.**
   There are dots at the grid intersections.
   Click anywhere on the screen other than the dots.
   The dots are no longer highlighted. Hold down the shift key.
   Click on each numbered axis and the two red dots.
   Release the shift key.
   The axes and the dots are now highlighted.

5. From the **Display** menu, choose **Hide Objects.**
   The axes and dots disappear.
   The screen now appears like a piece of dot paper.
   From the **Graph** menu, choose **Snap Points.**

Make this object with linking cubes.
Follow the steps below to create
views of this object.

Front view

6. From the **Toolbox** menu, choose **A** (Text Tool).
   Move the cursor to the screen and a finger appears.
   Click and drag to make a box at the top left.
   Inside the box, type: Front View

7. From the **Toolbox** menu, choose (Straightedge Tool).

   Move to a dot on the screen below the title.
   Click and drag to draw a line segment.
   Release the mouse button.
   Continue to draw line segments to draw the front view.
   Click to select each line segment.
   From the **Display** menu, choose **Line Width**, then **Dashed.**
   This draws the line segments as broken lines.

8. From the **Toolbox** menu, click on (Selection Arrow Tool).

   Click to select the four corners of the top square, in clockwise order.
   From the **Construct** menu, choose **Quadrilateral Interior.**
   From the **Display** menu, choose **Color**, then choose blue.

9. Repeat *Step 8* to make the bottom squares red and green.

10. Repeat *Step 6* to *9* to draw and label the left side view and the back view.

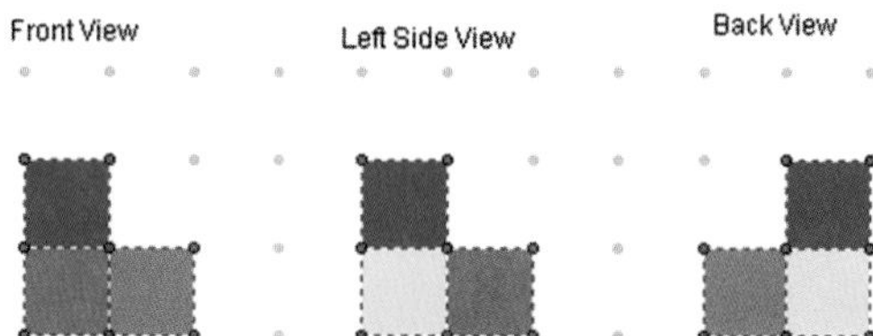

11. Draw the top view and right side view.

1. Open a new sketch. Draw different views of objects from *Section 3.1, Practice* question 3. Compare the hand-drawn views with the computer-drawn views.

3.2 Sketching Solids

Focus Sketch pictures of objects from models and drawings.

Explore

Work with a partner.
You will need isometric dot paper and 4 linking cubes.
Make an object so its front, top, and side views are all different.
Draw the object on isometric dot paper so all 4 cubes are visible.

Reflect & Share

Trade isometric drawings with another pair of classmates.
Make your classmates' object.
Was it easy to make the object? Explain.
Compare objects. If they are different, find out why.

Connect

An object has 3 dimensions: length, height, and width or depth.
A drawing is a picture of an object on paper.
It has 2 dimensions: length and width.

➢ We use isometric dot paper to show the 3 dimensions of an object. Parallel edges on an object are drawn as parallel line segments. An object made with 5 linking cubes is shown at the left.

When we draw the object from the front or the top, we see only 4 cubes.

Front view

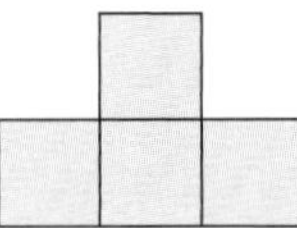

Top view

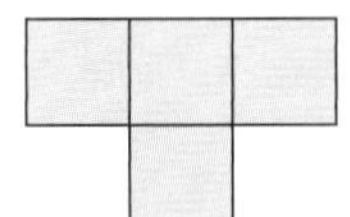

Place the object so that all 5 cubes are seen.

Draw the edges in this order:

- vertical edges (red)
- horizontal edges that appear to go down to the right (blue)
- horizontal edges that appear to go up to the right (green)

Shade faces to produce a 3-D effect.

Number Strategies

Simplify.
Use order of operations.

- $17 - 7 \times 2 + 3$
- $15 - 6 \div 2$
- $14 \div 2 \times 3$
- $8 \times 2 + 21 - 6$
- $15 + 3 \times 5$

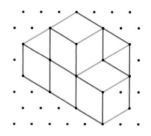

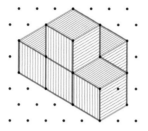

➢ We can use translations to draw a **pictorial diagram**.
A pictorial diagram shows the shape of an object in 2 dimensions.
It gives the impression of 3 dimensions.
To sketch the rectangular prism above right:

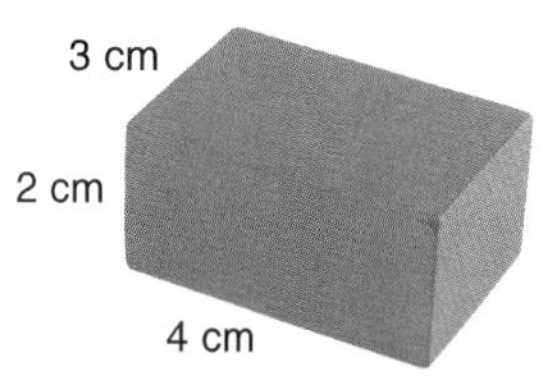

Draw a rectangle 4 cm by 2 cm.

Draw another rectangle that is the image of the first rectangle after a translation up and to the right.

Join corresponding vertices for a sketch of a rectangular prism.
Label the dimensions.

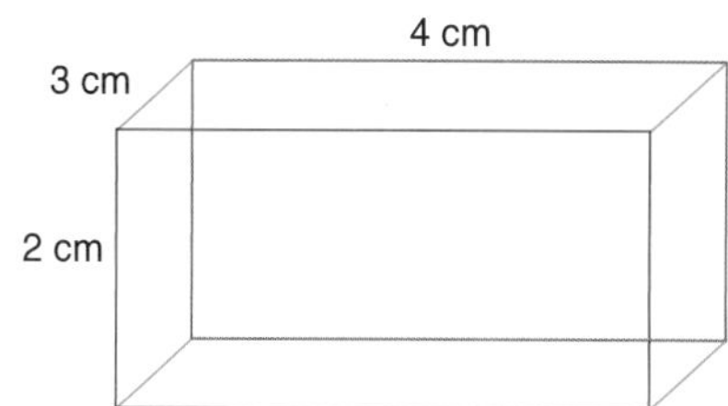

Note that the depth of the prism is 3 cm but, on the drawing, this distance is less than 3 cm. In a pictorial drawing, the depth of an object is drawn to a smaller scale than the length and width. This gives the appearance of 3 dimensions.

We can use similar ideas to sketch a 3-D picture of any object.

Example

Sketch this mug.

Solution

The mug is an open cylinder with a handle.
Draw an oval for the circular top.
Draw vertical lines for the curved surface (blue).
Draw half an oval for the circular base (red).
Draw 2 overlapping curves for the handle (green).

In a pictorial drawing, a circle is drawn as an oval.

Practice

Art

When you view an IMAX film, you "see" it in 3-D. The scenes are filmed from two slightly different angles. This imitates how our eyes view the world. Both films are projected onto the screen to give you the feeling of depth.

Use linking cubes when they help.

1. Make each object. Draw it on isometric dot paper.

a)

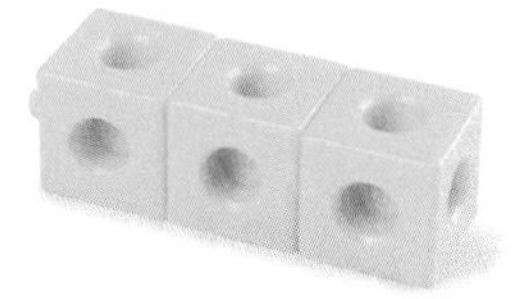

b)

2. Turn each object in question 1.
Draw it a different way on isometric dot paper.

3. Use linking cubes. Make each object.
Draw it on plain paper or isometric dot paper.

a)

b)

4. Here are different views of an object made with linking cubes.

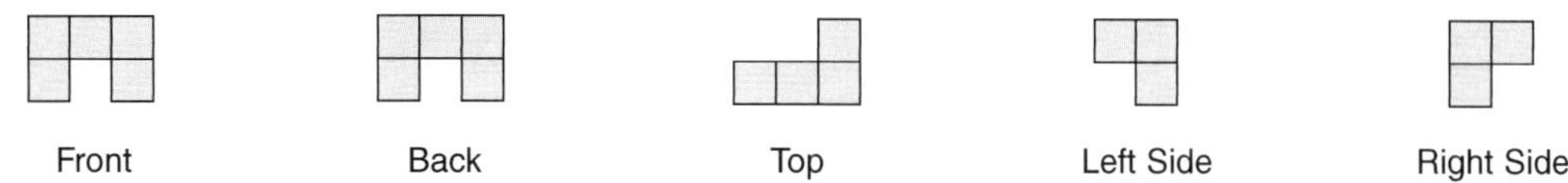

Make the object.
Draw it on isometric dot paper or plain paper.

5. Sketch a 3-D picture of each object on plain paper.

a) b) c)

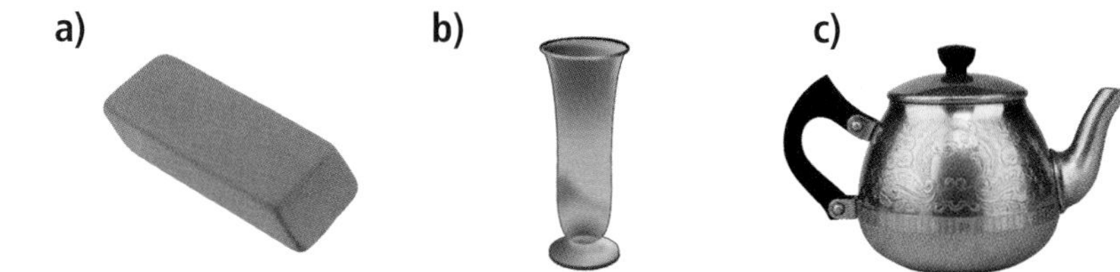

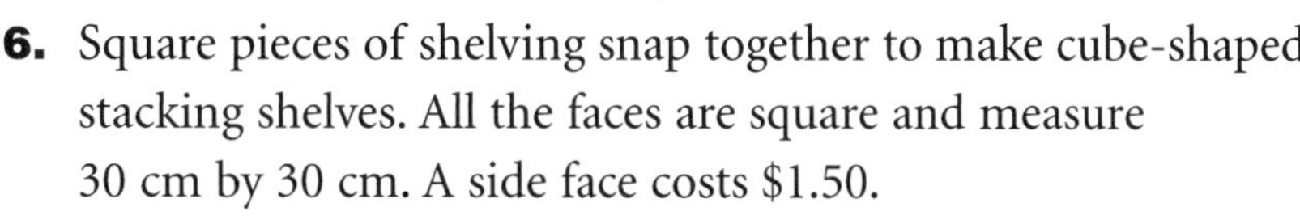

6. Square pieces of shelving snap together to make cube-shaped stacking shelves. All the faces are square and measure 30 cm by 30 cm. A side face costs $1.50.
A top or bottom face costs $1.30. The back face costs $1.10.
Kate built shelves using 9 side faces, 6 back faces, and 9 top/bottom faces.
   a) Use linking cubes to build a possible design.
   b) Draw a picture of your design on isometric dot paper.
   c) How much did the shelving cost?
   d) Is it possible to have the same number of cubes but use fewer pieces? Explain.
   e) If your answer to part d is yes, what is the new cost of shelving? Explain.

7. **Assessment Focus** Use 5 linking cubes. Make a solid.
   a) Sketch the solid on isometric dot paper.
   b) Sketch a 3-D picture of the solid on plain paper.
   c) How is sketching a solid on isometric paper different from sketching it on plain paper? How are the methods alike? Use your sketches to explain.

Reflect

How do you draw an object to show its 3 dimensions?
Use words and pictures to explain.

Forensic Graphics Specialist

A forensic investigator collects information from a crime scene to find out who was involved and exactly what happened. The forensic investigator also presents evidence in court as required by law.

The forensic graphics specialist visits the crime scene to take photographs and measurements. She may research to compose technical drawings to help with the investigation. When she prepares these drawings, the graphics specialist pays attention to shading and relative line thickness. It is important that she does not present optical illusions such as an object appearing to be "inside out."

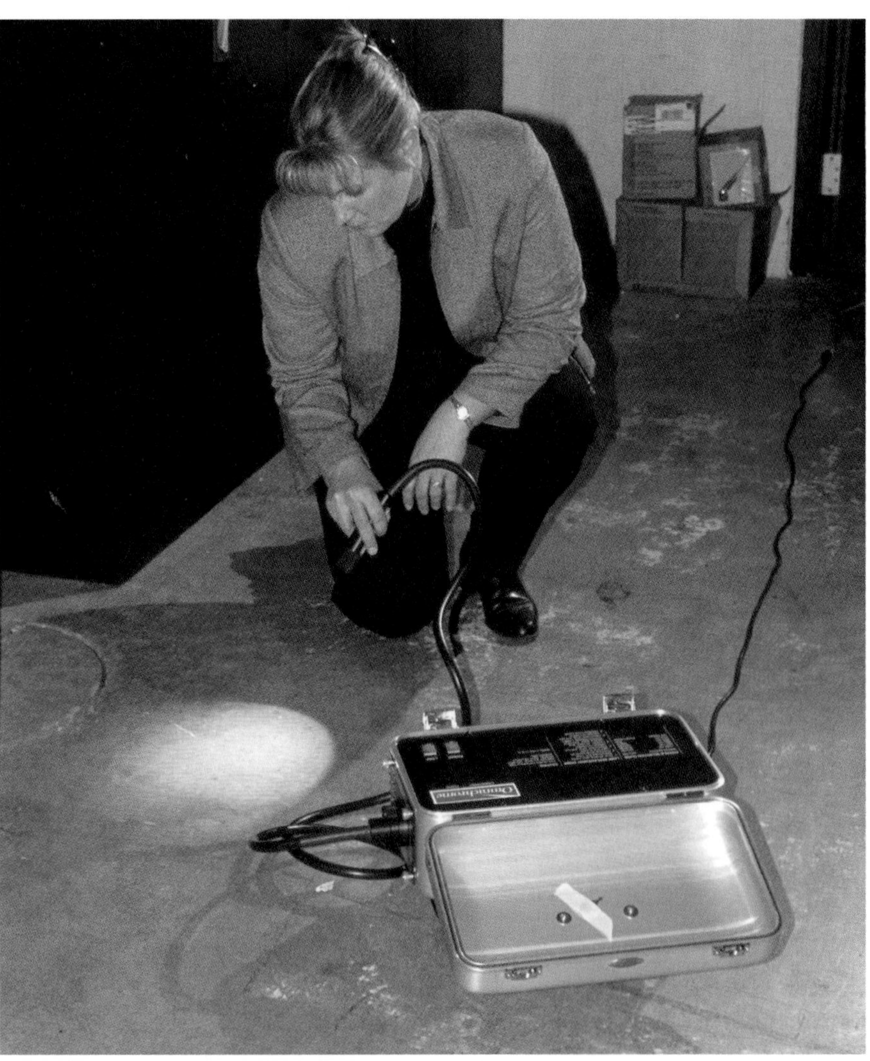

3.3 Building Objects from Nets

Focus Build objects from nets.

In earlier grades, you designed nets for prisms and pyramids.
Now, you will fold nets to make prisms, pyramids, and other polyhedra.

Explore

Work with a partner.
You will need scissors and tape.
Your teacher will give you large copies of the nets below.

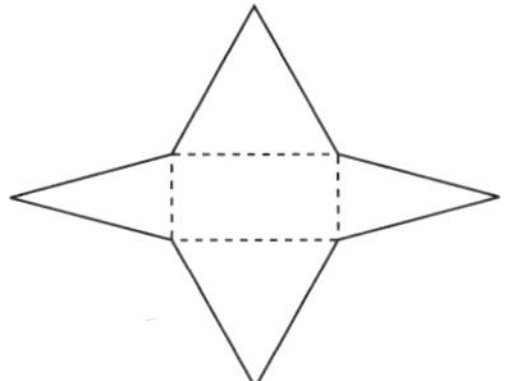

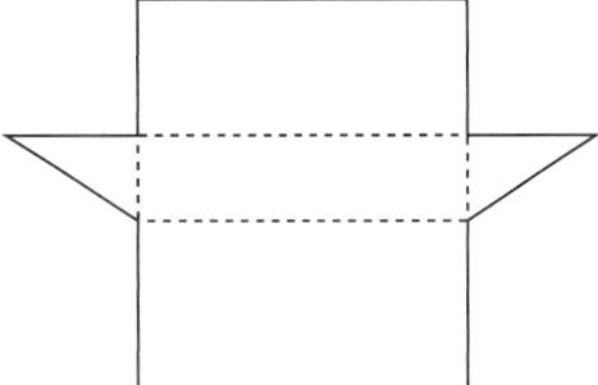

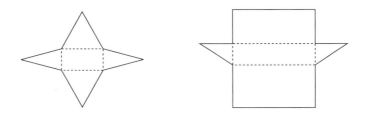

- ➢ Identify the polyhedron for each net above.
- ➢ Use a copy of each net.
  Cut it out. Fold, then tape it to make a polyhedron.
- ➢ Identify congruent faces on each polyhedron.

Reflect & Share

Look at each polyhedron from the top, front, back, and sides.
Which views are the same? Explain.

Connect

There are 5 regular polyhedra.
You reviewed 2 of them, the cube and the tetrahedron, in *Skills You'll Need*, page 76.

One regular polyhedron is an **icosahedron**.
Here is a net for one-half of an icosahedron.

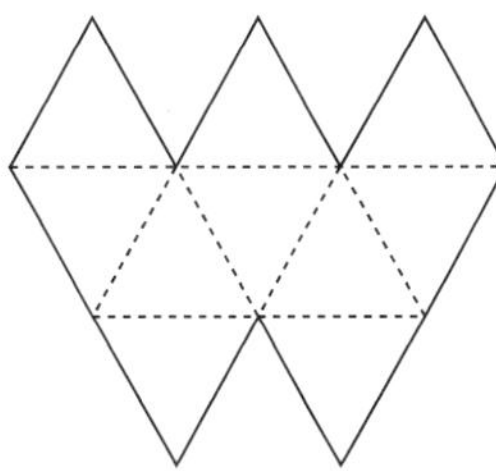

This net can be cut out and folded.
The net has 10 congruent triangles.

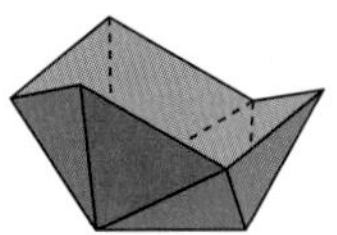

Two of these pieces are taped together to make an icosahedron.

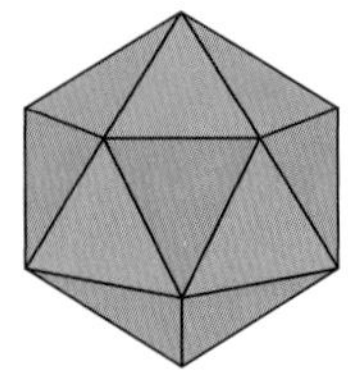

An icosahedron has 20 congruent faces.
Each face is an equilateral triangle.
In the *Practice* questions, you will make the other 2 regular polyhedra.

A regular **octahedron** A regular **dodecahedron**

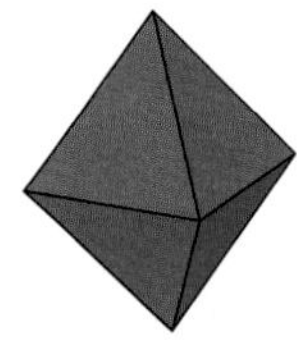

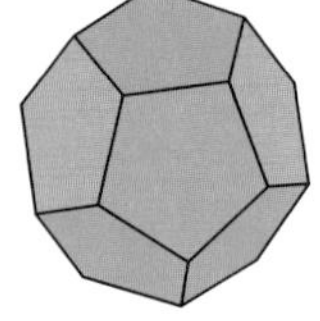

In previous grades, you designed and sketched nets of prisms and pyramids.
In the *Example* that follows, and in *Practice* questions, you will investigate nets for other objects.

Example

Fold this net to make an object.
Describe the object.

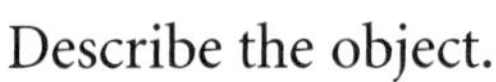

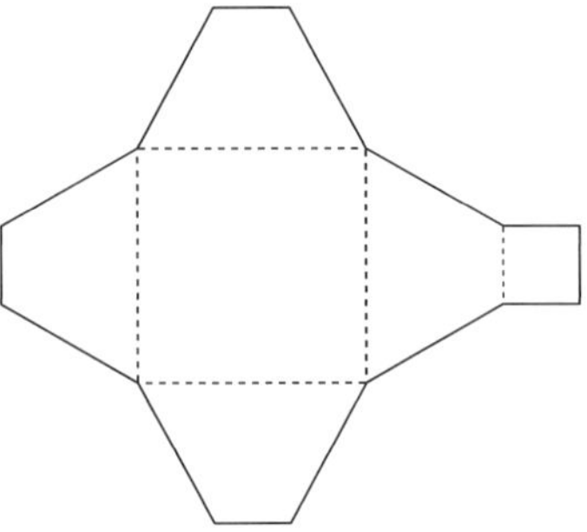

Solution

The net is folded along the broken line segments. Each edge touches another edge. The edges are taped.

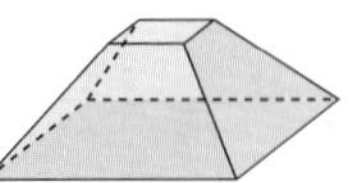

The object looks like the bottom of a pyramid;
that is, a pyramid with the top part removed.
The object is called a **frustum** of a pyramid.

The object has 2 non-congruent square faces, and 4 congruent trapezoid faces. The 2 square faces are parallel.

Practice

Your teacher will give you a large copy of each net.

1. Fold this net to make a polyhedron.
   a) Identify the polyhedron.
   b) Describe the polyhedron.

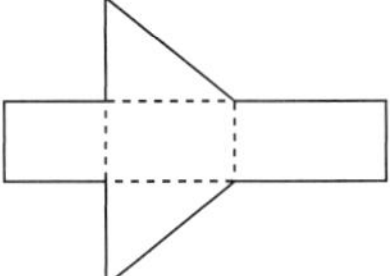

2. Fold this net.
   a) Is the object a polyhedron?
   If so, what are the attributes that make it a polyhedron?
   b) Identify parallel faces and perpendicular faces.

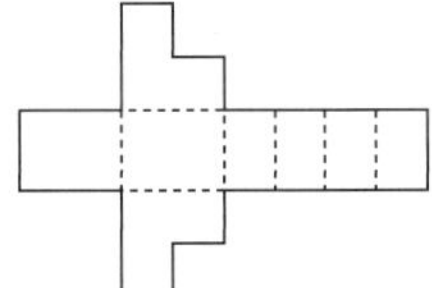

Calculator Skills

Find three prime numbers that have a sum of 43 and a product of 1085.

3. Fold two of these nets to make two square pyramids with no base.
Tape the two pyramids together at their missing bases.
You have made a regular octahedron.
   a) Why does it have this name?
   b) Describe the octahedron.
   How do you know it is regular?

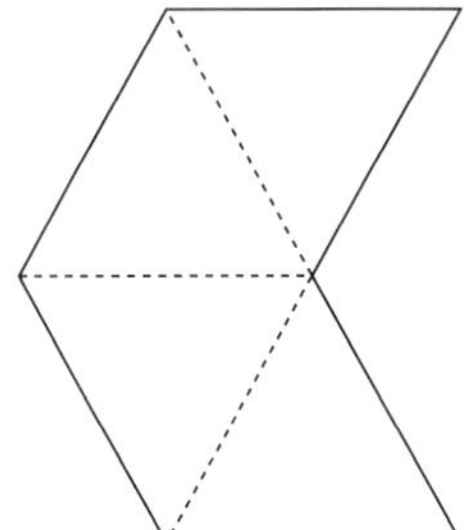

4. Fold each net. Describe each object.
How are the objects the same? How are they different?

a)

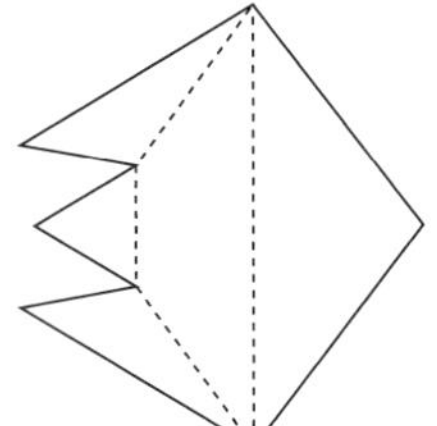

b)

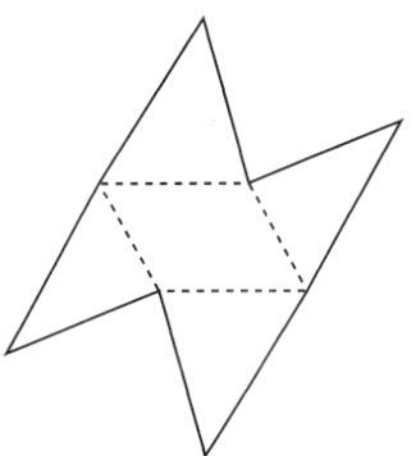

5. Fold two of these nets. Put the open parts together. Tape the pieces to make a regular dodecahedron. Describe the dodecahedron.

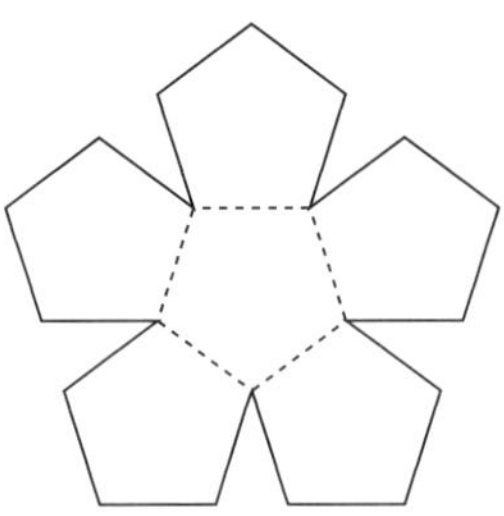

6. A soccer ball is not a sphere. It is a polyhedron.
Look at a soccer ball.
Explain which polygons are joined to make the ball.
How are the polygons joined?

7. **Assessment Focus** Fold the net shown.

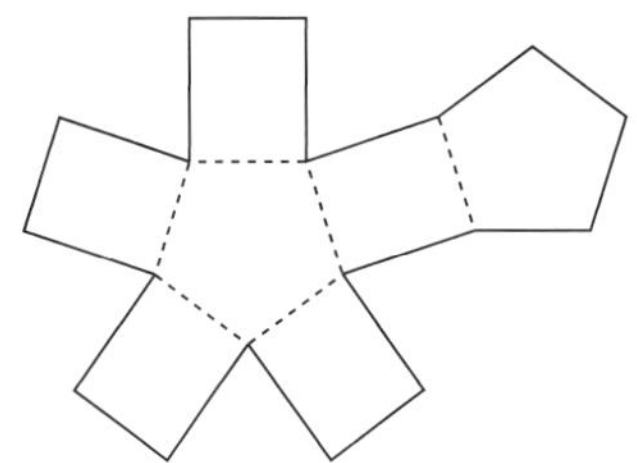

a) Describe the object formed.
b) Name the object. Justify your answer.

8. All the nets you have used fold to make objects.
Which features must be true for this to happen?

Take It Further

9. Use isometric dot paper or plain paper.
Draw the object that has this net. Explain your thinking.

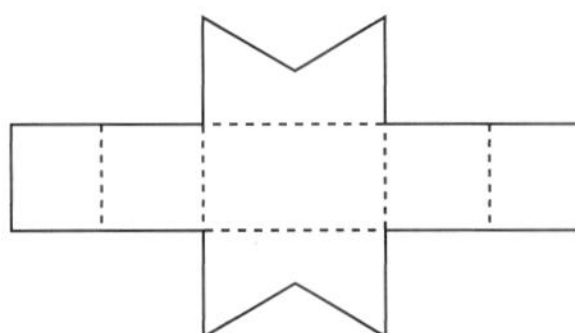

Reflect

Choose a product that has a package in the shape of a polyhedron.
Sketch the package. Include appropriate dimensions.
Cut along the edges to make the net.
Why do you think the manufacturer used this shape for the package?
Can you find a better shape for the packaging? Explain.

Mid-Unit Review

LESSON

3.1 **1.** Sketch the front, back, top, and side views of each object. Label each view.

a) Television

b) Baseball mitt

c) Chair

3.2 **2.** Make each object.
Sketch a 3-D view of the object on isometric dot paper.

a)

b)

3. Sketch a 3-D view of each object on plain paper.

a)

b)

4. Suppose you had to construct an object from linking cubes. Which would you prefer to use: a drawing of the object on isometric dot paper, or 5 different views on plain paper? Justify your choice. Use diagrams to support your choice.

3.3 **5.** Use a large copy of this net.
Fold the net to make an object.
Name the object. List its attributes.

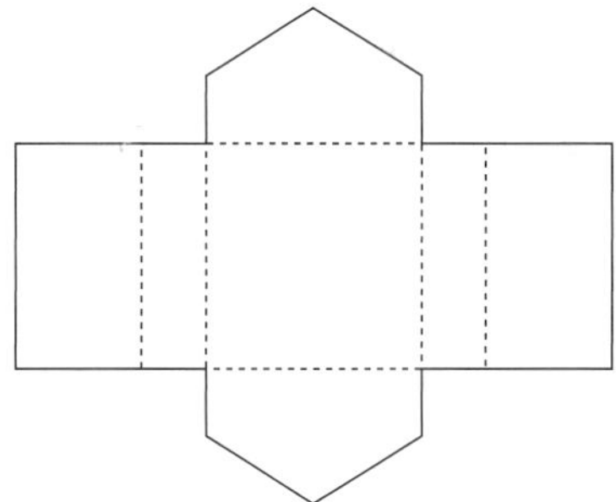

6. Which polyhedra could have each view shown below?
Find as many polyhedra as you can for each view.

a)

b)

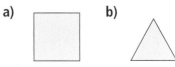

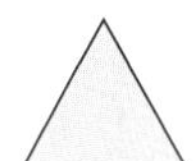

3.4 Using Variables in Measurement Formulas

Focus Use measurement formulas to introduce the concept of a variable.

Explore

Work with a partner.

➢ Find the area of each rectangle below, in square units.

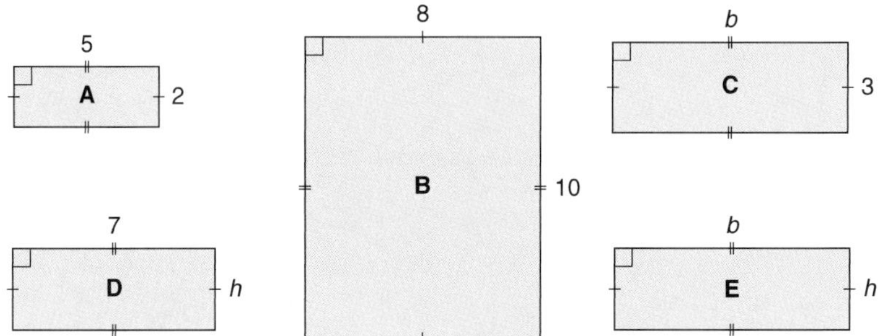

➢ Find the perimeter of each rectangle above, in units.

Reflect & Share

Compare your results with those of another pair of classmates.
How did you find the area when you did not know:

- the base?
- the height?
- the base and height?

How did you find the perimeter in each case?

Connect

When we do not know the dimensions of a figure, we use letters to represent them.
For a rectangle, we use b to represent the length of the base, and h to represent the height.

One way to find the area of a rectangle is to use a formula.
The formula for the area of a rectangle is:

$A = \text{base} \times \text{height}$

Then $A = b \times h$

We write $A = b \times h$ as $A = bh$.

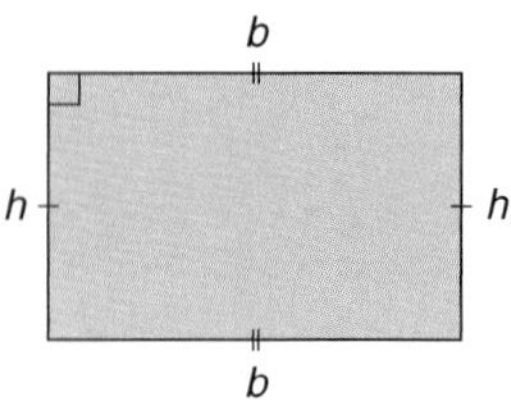

The formula for the perimeter of a rectangle is:
$P = 2 \times (\text{base} + \text{height})$
Then $P = 2 \times (b + h)$
We write $P = 2 \times (b + h)$ as $P = 2(b + h)$.

The letters we use to represent the base and height are called **variables**. Variables in a formula can represent different numbers. When we know the values of the variables, we **substitute** for the variables. That is, we replace each variable with a number.

A square is a rectangle with all sides equal.
The formula for the area of a square is:
$A = \text{side length} \times \text{side length}$
Use the variable s for the side length.
Then, $A = s \times s$
or $A = s^2$

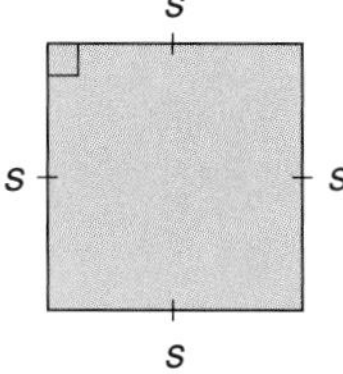

We use exponents to represent repeated multiplication.

The formula for the perimeter of a square is:
$P = 4 \times \text{side length}$
or $P = 4 \times s$

We write $P = 4 \times s$ as $P = 4s$.

Example

A rectangle has base 15 cm and height 3 cm. Use formulas to find its area and perimeter.

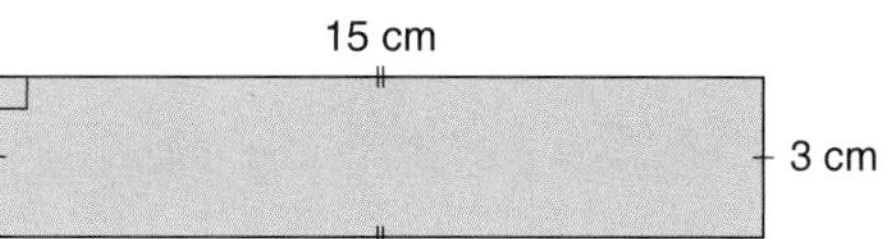

Solution

Area, $A = bh$
$b = 15$ and $h = 3$
Substitute for b and h in the formula.
$A = 15 \times 3$
$A = 45$
The area is 45 cm².

Perimeter, $P = 2(b + h)$
Substitute for b and h.
$P = 2(15 + 3)$
$P = 2(18)$
$P = 36$
The perimeter is 36 cm.

Use order of operations. Do the operation in brackets first. Then multiply.

Practice

1. Use the formula: $P = 4s$
   Find the perimeter of the square with each side length.
   a) 5 cm b) 9 cm c) 2 cm d) 8 cm

2. Use the formula for the area of a rectangle: $A = bh$
   Find the area of each rectangle.
   a) base: 6 cm; height: 3 cm b) base: 11 cm; height: 2 cm

3. a) For each rectangle, what is the value of b and the value of h?
   i) 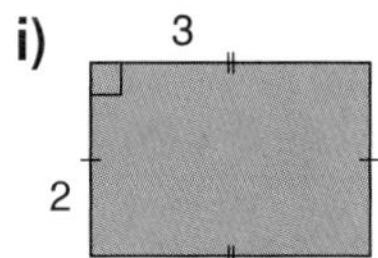

   ii) 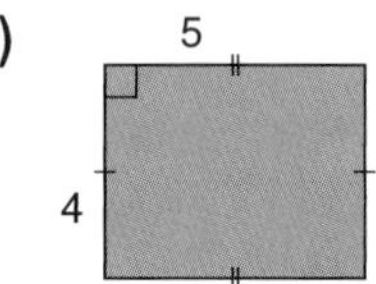

   iii) 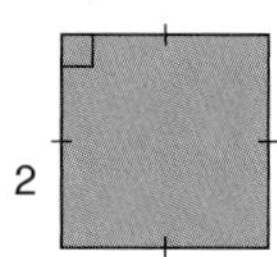

   b) Use your answers to part a to explain why we call b and h variables.
   c) What is true about b and h in part a, iii?

Number Strategies

Find the LCM and GCF of 10, 15, and 25.

4. Find the area and perimeter of each rectangle.
   a) base: 12 cm; height: 4 cm b) base: 10.5 cm; height: 3.0 cm

5. Find the perimeter and area of each square.
   a) side length: 2.8 cm b) side length: 3.1 cm

6. **Assessment Focus**
   Here is another formula for the perimeter of a rectangle:
   $P = 2b + 2h$
   Write this formula in words.
   Explain why there are two formulas for the perimeter of a rectangle.

Take It Further

7. a) How could you use the formula for the perimeter of a rectangle to get the formula for the perimeter of a square?
   b) How could you use the formula for the area of a rectangle to get the formula for the area of a square?

Reflect

What is a variable?
Why do we use variables to write measurement formulas?

3.5 Surface Area of a Rectangular Prism

Focus Use a formula to calculate the surface area of a rectangular prism.

Explore

Work in a group.
You will need several different empty cereal boxes, scissors, and a ruler.

- ➢ Cut along the edges of a box to make a net. What is the area of the surface of the box?
- ➢ Repeat the activity above for 2 other boxes.
- ➢ Write a formula to find the area of the surface of a rectangular prism.

Reflect & Share

Compare your formula with that of another group.
Did you write the same formula?
If not, do both formulas work? Explain.

Connect

Here is a rectangular prism, and its net.

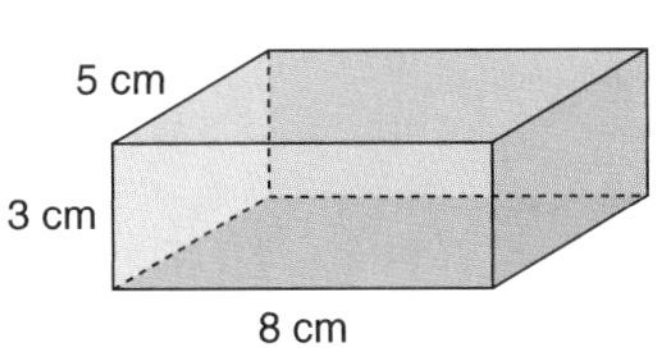

8
Area = 8 × 3
3 3
Area = 3 × 5
5
Area = 8 × 5
Area = 3 × 5
5
3 Area = 8 × 3 3
5 Area = 8 × 5 5
8

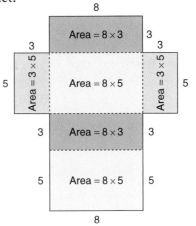

In the net, there are 3 pairs of congruent rectangles.
The area of the net is the sum of the areas of the rectangles.

Use order of operations, with brackets first.

The area of the net $= 2(8 \times 3) + 2(8 \times 5) + 2(3 \times 5)$
$= 2(24) + 2(40) + 2(15)$ Multiply.
$= 48 + 80 + 30$ Add.
$= 158$

The area of the net is 158 cm^2.
We say that the **surface area** of the rectangular prism is 158 cm^2.

We can use the net of a rectangular prism to write a formula for its surface area.
We use a variable to label each dimension.
The prism has length l, width w, and height h.

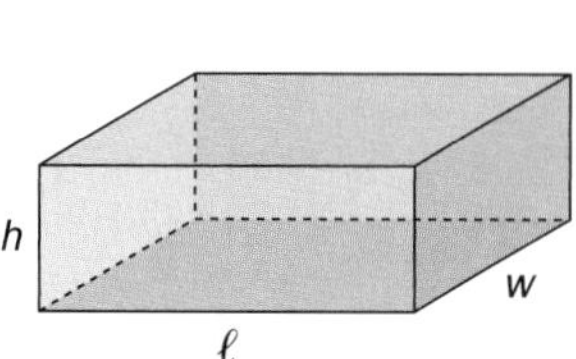

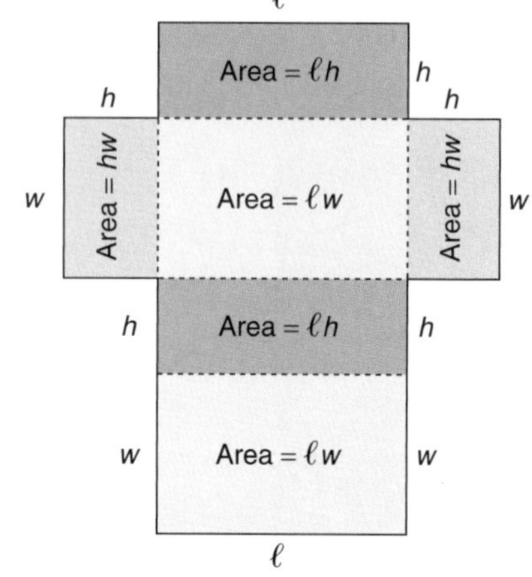

In the net, there are 3 pairs of congruent rectangles.
The surface area of the prism is the sum of the areas of the rectangles.

Remember that lw means $l \times w$.

The surface area of the prism $= 2lh + 2lw + 2hw$
We write: $SA = 2lh + 2lw + 2hw$

We can use this formula to find the surface area of a rectangular prism, without drawing a net first.

Example

Find the surface area of this rectangular prism.

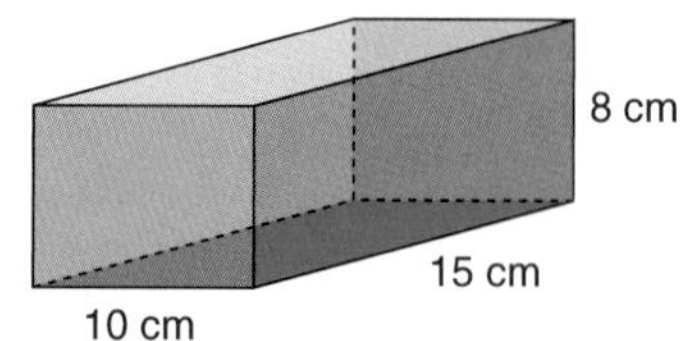

Solution

Use the formula:
$SA = 2lh + 2lw + 2hw$
Substitute: $l = 15$, $h = 8$, and $w = 10$

$$\begin{aligned} SA &= 2(15 \times 8) + 2(15 \times 10) + 2(8 \times 10) \\ &= 2(120) + 2(150) + 2(80) \\ &= 240 + 300 + 160 \\ &= 700 \end{aligned}$$

The surface area of the rectangular prism is 700 cm^2.

Practice

Visualize the net. How does that help to find the surface area?

1. Find the surface area of each rectangular prism.

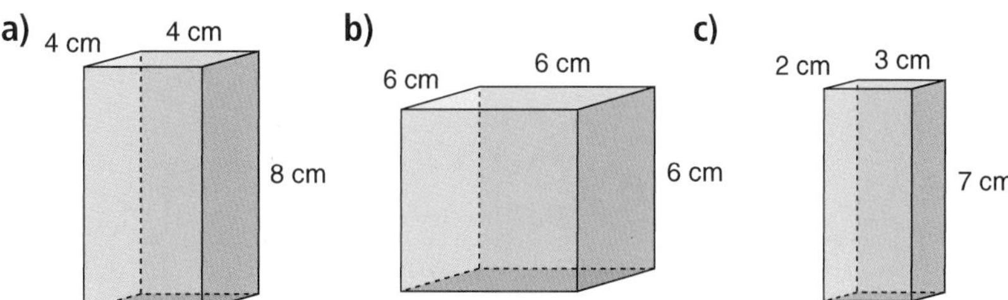

2. Use isometric dot paper or plain paper.
   Sketch a rectangular prism with these dimensions:
   6 cm by 3 cm by 2 cm.
   Find the surface area of the prism.

3. Find the surface area of each rectangular prism.

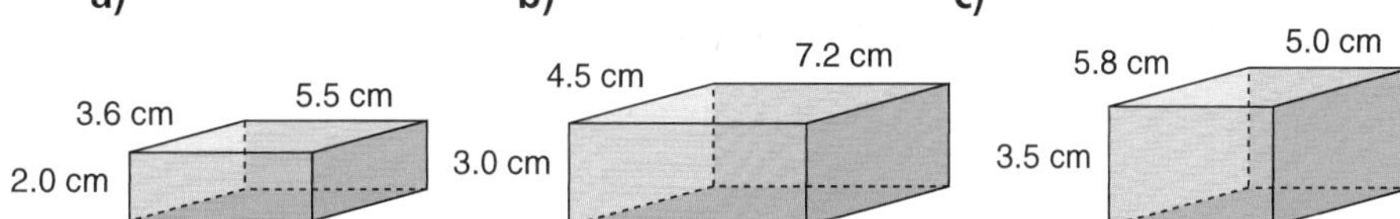

Mental Math

Estimate each product.
What strategies did you use?

Order the products from least to greatest.

- 24.8 × 3.2
- 35.2 × 2.8
- 13.2 × 5.7
- 5.5 × 15.5

4. Use linking cubes.
   a) Find the surface area of a cube with edge length 1 unit.
   b) What if the edge length is doubled?
      What happens to the surface area?
      Make a new cube to find out.
   c) What if the edge length is tripled?
      What happens to the surface area?
      Make a new cube to find out.
   d) Predict the surface area of a cube with edge length 4 units.
      Explain your prediction. Make a new cube to check.

5. a) Find a rectangular prism in the classroom.
      Measure its length, width, and height.
      Find its surface area.
   b) Suppose each dimension of the prism is halved.
      What happens to the surface area? Explain.

6. Tanya paints the walls of her family room.
   The room measures 3 m by 4 m by 7 m.
   The walls need 2 coats of paint. A 4-L can of paint covers 40 m^2.
   a) How much paint should Tanya buy?
   b) What assumptions do you make? Explain.

7. **Assessment Focus** Sketch a rectangular prism. Label its dimensions. What do you think happens to the surface area of a prism when its length is doubled? Its length is halved? Investigate to find out. Show your thinking.

8. Each object has the shape of a rectangular prism, but one face or parts of faces are missing. Find each surface area.

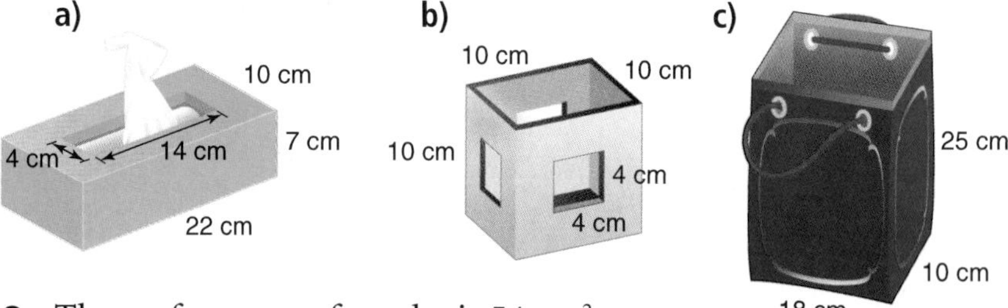

9. The surface area of a cube is 54 cm^2.
   a) What is the area of one face of the cube?
   b) What is the length of one edge of the cube?

Take It Further

10. A 400-g cereal box measures 20 cm by 7 cm by 31 cm.
    A 750-g cereal box measures 24 cm by 9 cm by 33 cm.
    a) Find the surface area of each box.
    b) What is an approximate ratio of surface areas?
       What is an approximate ratio of masses?
    c) Compare the ratios in part b.
       Do you expect the ratios to be equal? Explain.

11. A rectangular prism has a square base with area 4 m^2.
    The surface area of the prism is 48 m^2.
    What are the dimensions of the prism?

12. A rectangular prism has faces with these areas: 12 cm^2, 24 cm^2, and 18 cm^2. What are the dimensions of the prism? Explain.

Reflect

Explain how to find the surface area of a rectangular prism using a formula. Include an example in your explanation.

3.6 Volume of a Rectangular Prism

Focus Use a formula to calculate the volume of a rectangular prism.

Explore

Work in a group.
You will need several empty cereal boxes and a ruler.

- ➢ Find the volumes of 3 cereal boxes.
- ➢ Write a formula you can use to find the volume of a rectangular prism.
- ➢ Measure a 4th cereal box. Substitute its dimensions in your formula to check that your formula is correct.

Reflect & Share

Compare the formulas for the volume of a rectangular prism and the area of a rectangle. What do you notice? Explain.

Connect

Recall that the volume of a rectangular prism is:
Volume = base area $\times$ height

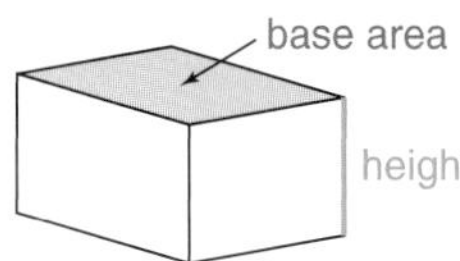

The base of a rectangular prism can be any face of the prism.

The base of the prism is a rectangle.
Label the length l and the width w.
Then, the area of the base is $l \times w$, or lw.

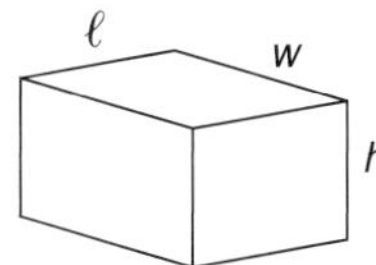

The height is measured from the base to the opposite face. The height is perpendicular to the base.

Label the height h.
Volume = base area $\times$ height

$$V = lw \times h$$

$$V = lwh$$

The volume of a rectangular prism is: $V = lwh$

If we let A represent the area of the base, then $A = lw$.

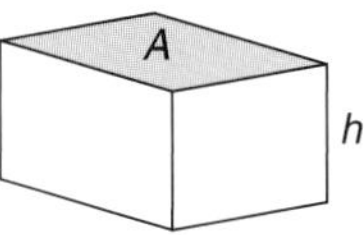

Another way to write the volume is: $V = A \times h$, or $V = Ah$

Example

A deck of 54 cards fits in a box with dimensions 6.5 cm by 9.0 cm by 1.6 cm. What is the volume of the box? Give the answer to the nearest cubic centimetre.

Solution

Recall that, when the dimensions are measured in centimetres (cm), the volume is measured in cubic centimetres (cm³).

Draw a diagram.
The box is a rectangular prism.
Label each dimension.

9.0 cm
6.5 cm
1.6 cm

Use the formula: $V = lwh$
Substitute: $l = 9.0$, $w = 6.5$, and $h = 1.6$
$V = 9.0 \times 6.5 \times 1.6$ Use a calculator.
$= 93.6$
The volume is 93.6 cm^3, or about 94 cm^3.

Practice

Use a calculator when it helps.

1. For each rectangular prism: find the area of its base, then find its volume.

a)

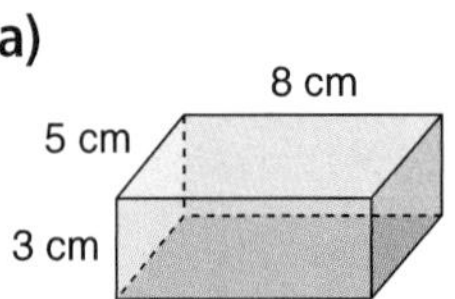

b)

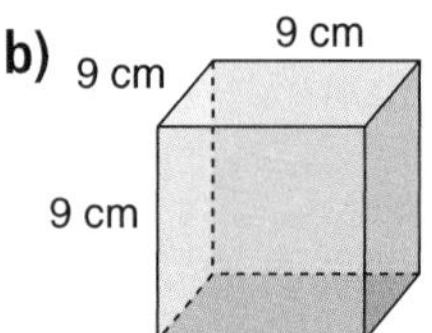

c)

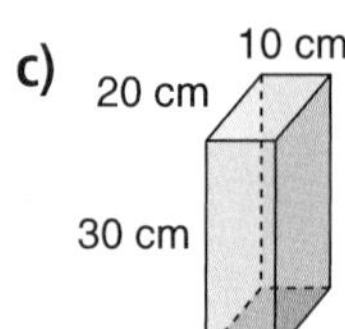

2. Find the volume of each rectangular prism.

a) **b)** **c)**

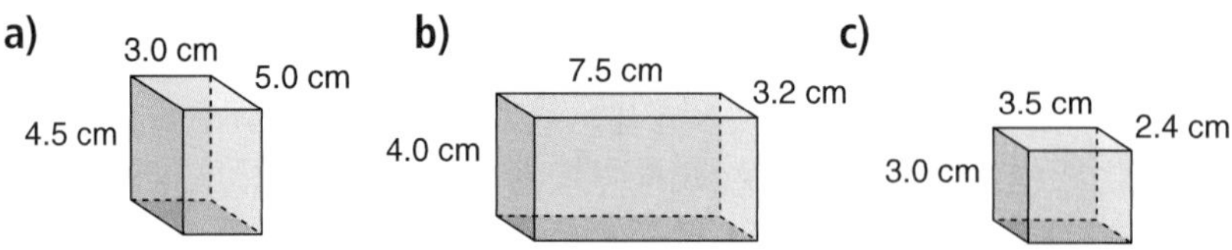

3. Use linking cubes.
Make all possible rectangular prisms with volume 36 $units^3$.
Sketch each prism you make.
Label each prism with its dimensions in units.
How do you know you have found all possible prisms?

4. Philip made fudge that filled a 20-cm by 21-cm by 3-cm pan.

a) What is the volume of the fudge?

b) Philip shares the fudge with his classmates. There are 30 people in the class. How much fudge will each person get?

c) How should Philip cut the fudge so each person gets the same size piece? Sketch the cuts he should make.

d) What are the dimensions of each piece of fudge?

5. Sketch a rectangular prism. Label its dimensions.
What do you think happens to the volume of the prism when:

a) its length is doubled?

b) its length and width are doubled?

c) its length, width, and height are doubled?

Investigate to find out. Show your work.
Will the results be true for all rectangular prisms?
How do you know?

Mental Math

Estimate each quotient.
What strategies did you use?

Order the quotients from least to greatest.

- $3572 \div 71$
- $4675 \div 58$
- $5007 \div 43$
- $6729 \div 95$

6. How can you double the volume of a rectangular prism?
Does its surface area double, too? Explain.

7. **Assessment Focus** Use linking cubes.

a) How many rectangular prisms can you make with 2 cubes? 3 cubes? 4 cubes? 5 cubes? 6 cubes? and so on, up to 20 cubes?

b) How many cubes do you need to make exactly 1 prism? Exactly 2 prisms? Exactly 3 prisms? Exactly 4 prisms?

c) What patterns do you see in your answers to part b?

8. **a)** Sketch 3 different rectangular prisms with volume 24 cm^3.

b) Which prism has the greatest surface area? The least surface area?

c) Try to find a prism with a greater surface area. Describe the shape of this prism.

d) Try to find a prism with a lesser surface area. Describe the shape of this prism.

Reflect

Suppose you know the volume of a rectangular prism.
How can you find its dimensions? Use words and pictures to explain.

Decoding Word Problems

1

READ the problem.

- Do I understand all the words?
- Highlight those words I don't understand. Whom can I ask?
- Are there key words that give me clues? Circle these words.

David, Jennifer, and Mark collect baseball cards. Jennifer has the most cards. She has 15 more cards than David. David has 4 times as many cards as Mark has today. Mark often loses some of his cards. This morning Mark has 18 cards. How many baseball cards does Jennifer have?

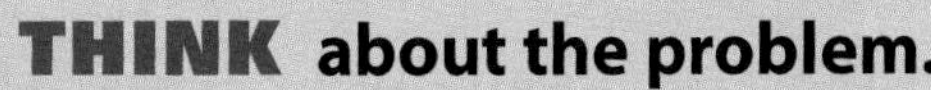

2

THINK about the problem.

- What is the problem about?
- What information am I given?
- Am I missing any information?
- Is this problem like another problem I have solved before?

STRATEGIES to consider . . .

Use a model.
Make an organized list.
Make a table.
Use logical reasoning.
Solve a simpler problem.
Draw a diagram.
Guess and check.
Use a pattern.
Work backward.
Draw a graph.

3 MAKE a plan.

- What strategy should I use?
- Would counters, geometric figures, other materials, calculators, and so on, help?

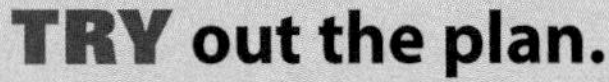

4 TRY out the plan.

- Is the plan working? Should I try something else?
- Have I shown *all* my work?

5 LOOK back.

- Does my answer make sense? How can I check?
- Is there another way to solve this problem?
- How do I know my answer is correct?
- Have I answered the problem?

6 EXTEND.

- Ask "What if ...?" questions. What if the numbers were different? What if there were more options?
- Make up similar problems of your own.
- STRETCH your thinking.

Unit Review

Review any lesson with

What Do I Need to Know?

☑ Perimeter of a rectangle:
$P = 2(b + h)$

☑ Area of a rectangle:
$A = bh$

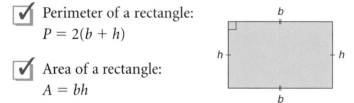

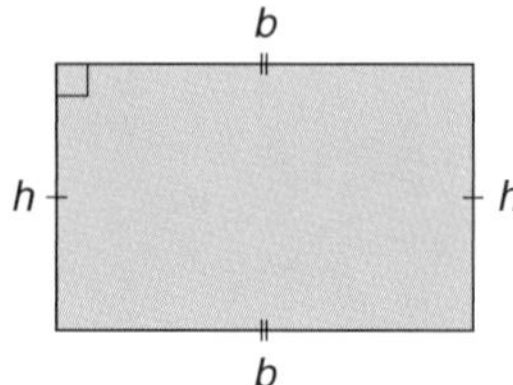

☑ Perimeter of a square:
$P = 4s$

☑ Area of a square:
$A = s^2$

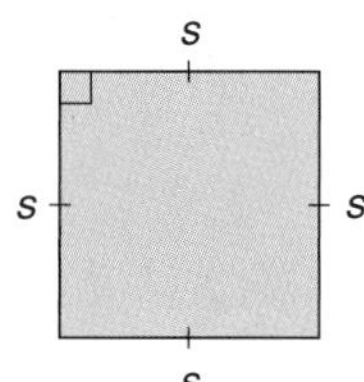

☑ Volume of a cube:
$V = c^3$

☑ Surface area of a cube:
$SA = 6c^2$

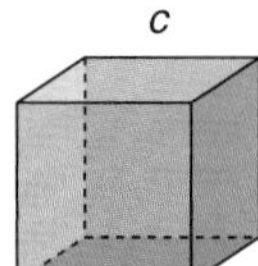

☑ Surface area of a rectangular prism:
$SA = 2lh + 2lw + 2hw$

☑ Volume of a rectangular prism:
$V = lwh$
or $V = Ah$, where $A = lw$

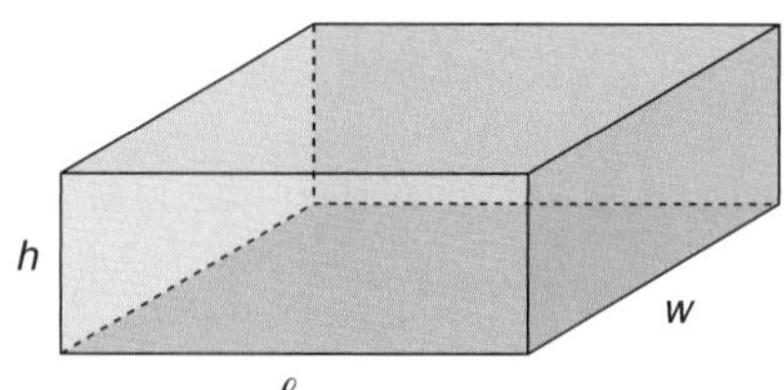

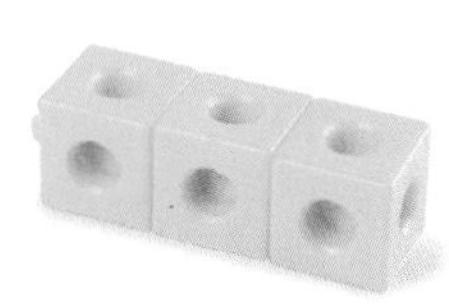

What Should I Be Able to Do?

For extra practice, go to page 440.

LESSON

3.1 **1.** Sketch the front, back, side, and top views of each object. Use square dot paper, plain paper, or *The Geometer's Sketchpad*.

a)

b)

c)

3.2 **2.** **a)** Identify the view and the objects on each sign.

i) Railway Crossing Ahead

ii) Fishing Area

b) Design a new sign from a different view. Sketch your design.

3.3 **3.** This is a net for an octahedron.

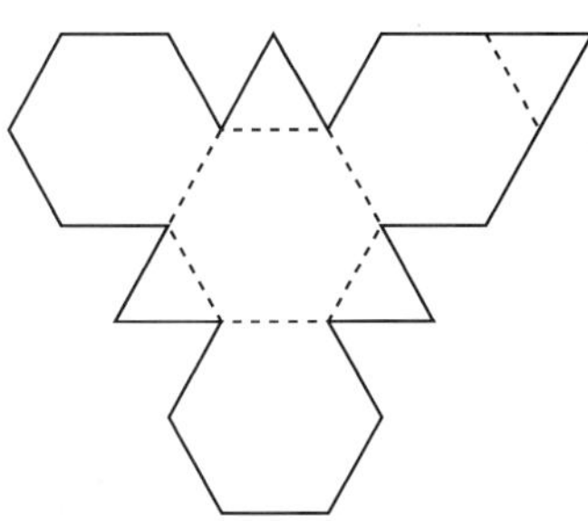

a) Fold a large copy of the net. Describe the object. Why do you think it is called an octahedron?

b) How is the object you built different from a regular octahedron?

3.4 **4.** Find the area of each figure.

a) a square with side length 7 cm

b) a rectangle with base 12 m and height 3 m

5. A cube has edge length *c*.

a) Write a formula for the surface area of the cube.

b) Use the formula to find the surface area when *c* is 4 cm.

6. A children's play area is 90 m long and 44 m wide. A fence will enclose the area.

a) How much fencing is needed?

b) Fencing comes in 12-m bundles. Each bundle costs $35. How much will the fence cost? Justify your answer.

LESSON

3.5 **7.** Find the surface area and volume
3.6 of each rectangular prism.

a)

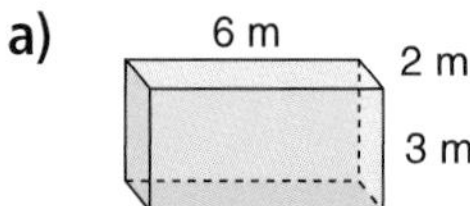

b)

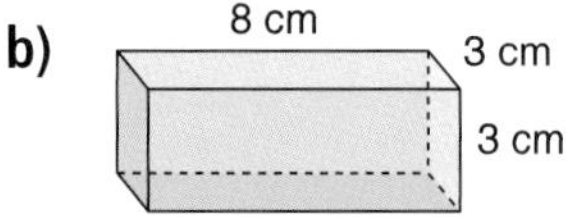

c)

50 cm
50 cm
50 cm

8. Elizabeth pastes wallpaper on 3 walls of her bedroom. She paints the 4th wall. This is one of the smaller walls. The dimensions of the room are 3 m by 5 m by 6 m. A roll of wallpaper covers about 5 m^2. A 4-L can of paint covers about 40 m^2.

a) How much wallpaper and paint should Elizabeth buy?

b) What assumptions do you make?

9. The surface area and volume of a cube have the same numerical value. Find the dimensions of this cube. How many answers can you find?

10. Sketch all possible rectangular prisms with a volume of 28 m^3. Each edge length is a whole number of metres. Label each prism with its dimensions. Calculate the surface area of each prism.

11. In *Gulliver's Travels* by Jonathan Swift, Gulliver visits a land where each of his dimensions is 12 times as large as that of the inhabitants.

a) Assume you can be modelled as a rectangular prism. Measure your height, width, and thickness.

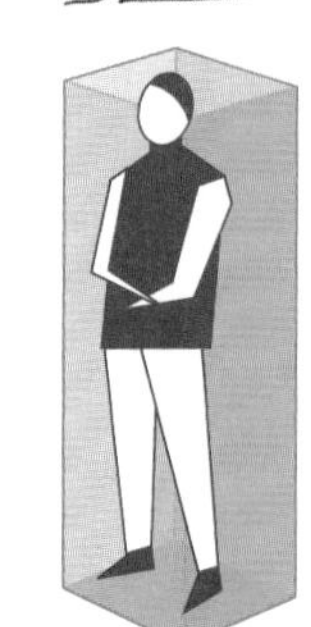

b) Suppose you were one of the inhabitants. What would Gulliver's dimensions be?

c) Use your dimensions. Calculate your surface area and volume.

d) Calculate Gulliver's surface area and volume.

12. The volume, *V*, and base area, *A*, of a rectangular prism are given. Find the height of each prism. Sketch the prism. What are possible dimensions for the prism? Explain.

a) $V = 18$ m^3, $A = 6$ m^2

b) $V = 60$ cm^3, $A = 15$ cm^2

13. Samya is making candles. She uses a 1-L milk carton as a mould. Its base is a 7-cm square. Samya pours 500 mL of wax into the carton. Recall that 1 mL = 1 cm^3. Approximately how tall will the candle be? Justify your answer.

Practice Test

1. Build the letter H with linking cubes.
Draw the front, back, side, and top views.

2. Fold a copy of this net.

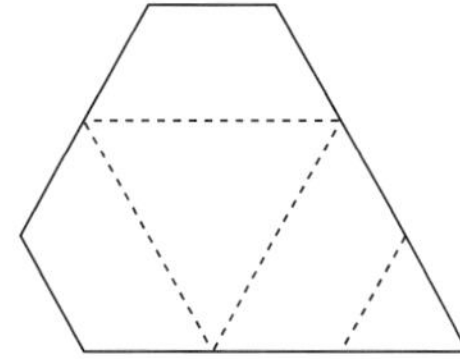

a) Describe the object.
What name could you give it?
Justify your answer.

b) Sketch the object.

3. Find the surface area and volume of this rectangular prism.

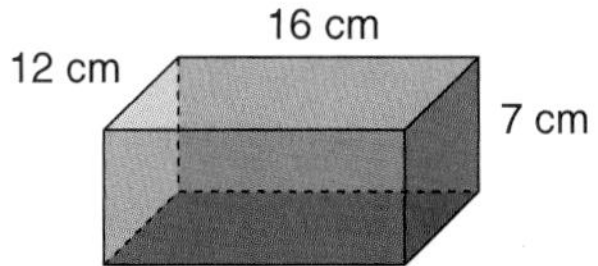

4. Each edge length of a rectangular prism is 7 cm.

a) Sketch the prism.

b) Use formulas to find its volume and surface area.

5. Here are the dimensions of two designs for a sandbox for the primary playground. Each sandbox is a rectangular prism.
One design is 3 m by 3 m by 30 cm.
A second design is 3.25 m by 3.25 m by 25 cm.

a) Sketch each sandbox. Include its dimensions.

b) Compare the designs. For each design, calculate the area of material needed to build it and the volume of sand it will hold.

c) Which sandbox should be built? Justify your answer.

6. Think about the nets you have folded and the solids you have made.
Suppose you are a tent manufacturer.
Which net would you use to make a tent?
Explain why it would be a good tent design.

Unit Problem Making Food for a Bake Sale

Suppose you are planning to sell baked goods at the local charity bake sale.
You have to decide the selling price for your baked goods.
You want to make sure that the price covers the cost of the ingredients and the packaging.

Decide on the baked goods you will sell.
For example, here is a recipe for Rice Krispies Treats.

Rice Krispies Treats

50 mL margarine
250 g marshmallows
1.5 L Rice Krispies

Melt the margarine.
Add marshmallows and stir until melted.
Remove from heat.
Add Rice Krispies.
Stir until the Rice Krispies are coated.
Press mixture into greased 32-cm by 23-cm pan.
When mixture is cool, cut into squares.

Use this recipe or find your own recipe for treats.
How many batches of treats will you make?
Calculate how much of each ingredient you need.
Use grocery flyers to find how much the ingredients will cost.

1. Calculate the cost of 1 batch of treats.

2. How many treats will you sell in 1 package?
Design a box as the package for your treats.
Decide if the box is open and covered with plastic wrap, or if the box is closed.
Draw a 3-D picture of your box.
Sketch a net for your box.

3. Calculate the surface area and volume of your box.
Suppose the cost of cardboard is 50¢/m^2.
How many boxes can you make from 1 m^2 of cardboard?
How much does each box cost?
What other costs are incurred to make the boxes?
What assumptions do you make?

4. Draw the top, front, back, and side views of your box.

5. How much will you sell 1 box of treats for?
Justify your answer.
Show how the selling price of the treats covers the cost of all the things you bought.

Check List

Your work should show:

- ✓ all calculations in detail
- ✓ all sketches clearly labelled
- ✓ a clear explanation of your results
- ✓ how you decided the selling price of 1 box of treats

Reflect on the Unit

Write a paragraph to tell what you have learned about polyhedra in this unit. Try to include something from each lesson in the unit.

Cross Strand Investigation

Ratios in Scale Drawings

Materials:
- 1-cm grid paper
  2-cm grid paper
  0.5-cm grid paper
- a ruler

Work with a partner.

A **scale drawing** is larger or smaller than the original drawing or object, but has the same shape. The scale of the drawing is the ratio of a length on the scale drawing to the same length on the original drawing or object.

Polygons that have the same shape but different sizes are **similar**.

As you complete this *Investigation*, include all your work in a report that you will hand in.

Part 1

How are the ratios of corresponding sides in similar polygons related?

➢ Use grid paper.
Draw a polygon with vertices where the grid lines meet.
Trade drawings with your partner.

- Draw a similar polygon that is larger or smaller than the polygon drawn by your partner. You can use the same sheet of grid paper or a sheet with different grid dimensions. Your drawing is a scale drawing of the polygon.
- Measure and record the lengths of the sides of the two polygons.
- Compare the lengths of corresponding sides of the two polygons. What are the ratios? Are the ratios the same for each pair? Explain.
- Predict the ratio of the perimeters of the polygons. Check your prediction.
- Compare your findings with those of your partner. Explain any differences.

Part 2

How are the ratios of corresponding sides related to the ratios of the areas of the polygons?

- Draw a polygon with vertices where grid lines meet. Draw a similar polygon that is larger. What is the ratio of the corresponding sides?
- Predict the ratio of the area of the original polygon to the area of the second polygon. Explain your reasoning for making this prediction.
- Find the area of each polygon. What is the ratio of the two areas?
- How does your prediction compare to your findings? Explain any differences.
- How is the ratio of the corresponding sides of the polygons related to the ratio of the areas of the polygons?

Take It Further

- Suppose you have to enlarge a polygon so that its area is doubled. Should you double the length of each side? Explain. Use an example in your explanation.
- Suppose you have to enlarge a polygon so that its area is four times its original area. How would you do that?
- What patterns do you see? How could you use these patterns to enlarge a polygon even more?

UNIT

4 Fractions and Decimals

Many newspapers and magazines sell advertising space. Why do small companies run small advertisements?

Selling advertising space is a good way to raise funds. Students at Garden Avenue School plan to sell advertising space in their yearbook.

How can fractions and decimals be used in advertising space and advertising rates?

What You'll Learn

- Add and subtract fractions.
- Multiply a fraction by a whole number.
- Compare and order decimals.
- Multiply and divide decimals.
- Use order of operations with decimals.
- Solve problems using fractions and decimals.

Why It's Important

- You use fractions when you share or divide.
- You use decimals when you shop and when you measure.

Key Words

- fraction strips
- equivalent fractions
- related denominators
- unrelated denominators
- common denominator
- lowest common denominator
- unit fraction
- terminating decimal
- repeating decimal

UNIT 4

Skills You'll Need

Adding and Subtracting Fractions with Pattern Blocks

Let the yellow hexagon represent 1:

Then the red trapezoid represents $\frac{1}{2}$:

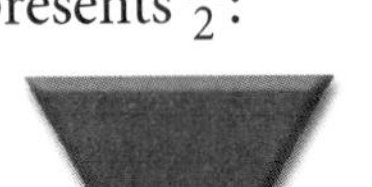

the blue rhombus represents $\frac{1}{3}$:

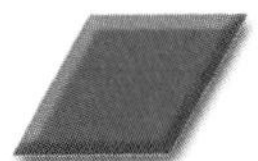

and the green triangle represents $\frac{1}{6}$:

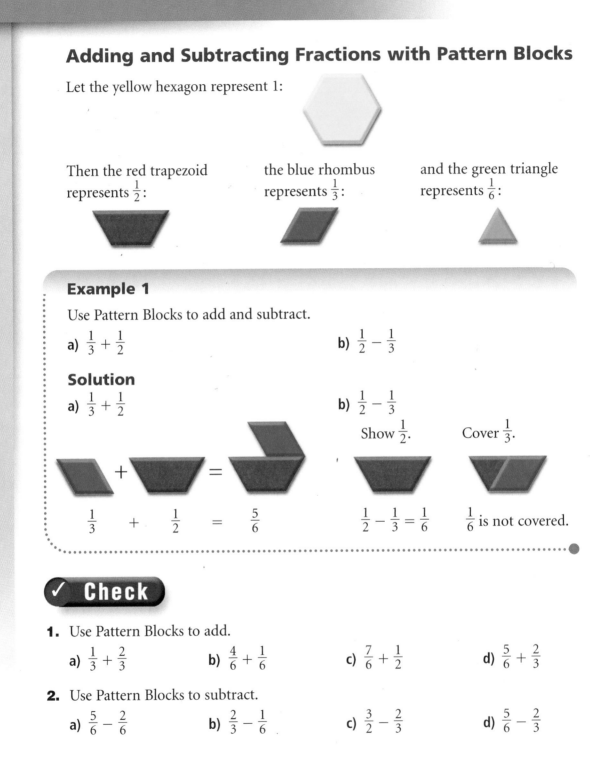

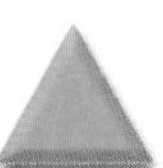

Example 1

Use Pattern Blocks to add and subtract.

a) $\frac{1}{3} + \frac{1}{2}$

b) $\frac{1}{2} - \frac{1}{3}$

Solution

a) $\frac{1}{3} + \frac{1}{2}$

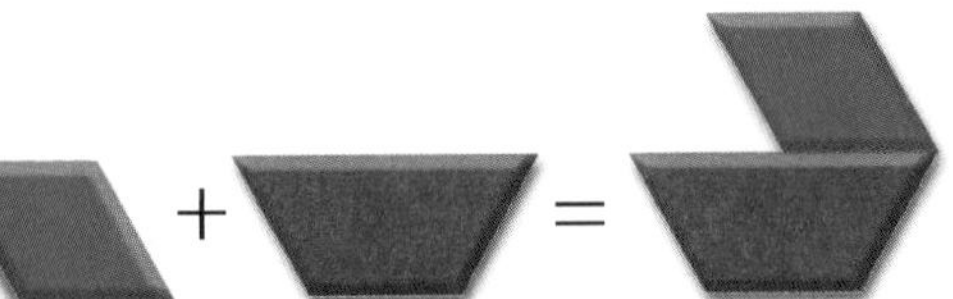

$\frac{1}{3} + \frac{1}{2} = \frac{5}{6}$

b) $\frac{1}{2} - \frac{1}{3}$

Show $\frac{1}{2}$.

Cover $\frac{1}{3}$.

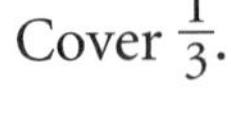

$\frac{1}{2} - \frac{1}{3} = \frac{1}{6}$

$\frac{1}{6}$ is not covered.

✓ Check

1. Use Pattern Blocks to add.

a) $\frac{1}{3} + \frac{2}{3}$ b) $\frac{4}{6} + \frac{1}{6}$ c) $\frac{7}{6} + \frac{1}{2}$ d) $\frac{5}{6} + \frac{2}{3}$

2. Use Pattern Blocks to subtract.

a) $\frac{5}{6} - \frac{2}{6}$ b) $\frac{2}{3} - \frac{1}{6}$ c) $\frac{3}{2} - \frac{2}{3}$ d) $\frac{5}{6} - \frac{2}{3}$

Multiplying by 0.1, 0.01, and 0.001

We can use patterns to multiply by 0.1, 0.01, and 0.001.
We can show products on a place-value chart.

	Thousands	Hundreds	Tens	Ones	•	Tenths	Hundredths	Thousandths
24 × 100	2	4	0	0	•			
24 × 10		2	4	0	•			
24 × 1			2	4	•			
24 × 0.1				2	•	4		
24 × 0.01				0	•	2	4	
24 × 0.001				0	•	0	2	4

On the chart:

- To multiply by 0.1, move each digit 1 place to the right.
- To multiply by 0.01, move each digit 2 places to the right.
- To multiply by 0.001, move each digit 3 places to the right.

To get the product:

- Move the decimal point 1 place to the left.
- Move the decimal point 2 places to the left.
- Move the decimal point 3 places to the left.

Example 2

Multiply.

a) 372 × 0.1 **b)** 56 × 0.01 **c)** 41 × 0.001

Solution

Mark the decimal point in the whole number.

a) 372. × 0.1 = 37.2 — The decimal point moves 1 place to the left.

b) 56. × 0.01 = 0.56 — The decimal point moves 2 places to the left.

c) 41. × 0.001 = 0.041 — Write zeros as placeholders. Then move the decimal point 3 places to the left.

✓ Check

3. Multiply.

a) 5 × 0.1 **b)** 98 × 0.1 **c)** 124 × 0.1

d) 326 × 0.01 **e)** 72 × 0.01 **f)** 6 × 0.01

g) 56 × 0.001 **h)** 276 × 0.001 **i)** 8 × 0.001

Operations with Decimals

Example 3

Evaluate.

a) 82.34 + 4.7 **b)** 79.1 − 43.8 **c)** 426.31 × 2 **d)** 9.47 ÷ 2

Solution

a) 82.34 + 4.7

Estimate: 80 + 5 = 85

Add the hundredths.

Add the tenths: 10 tenths = 1 whole

Add the ones. Add the tens.

$$\begin{array}{r} \overset{1}{8}2.34 \\ +\ 4.7 \\ \hline 87.04 \end{array}$$

b) 79.1 − 43.8

Estimate: 80 − 40 = 40

To subtract the tenths, trade 1 whole for 10 tenths.

Subtract the ones. Subtract the tens.

$$\begin{array}{r} 7\overset{8}{\not{9}}.\overset{11}{\not{1}} \\ -\ 43.8 \\ \hline 35.3 \end{array}$$

c) 426.31 × 2

Estimate: 400 × 2 = 800

Ignore the decimal point.

Multiply as you would with whole numbers.

Place the decimal point in the answer by estimation:

426.31 × 2 is about 400 × 2 = 800

So, 426.31 × 2 = 852.62

$$\begin{array}{r} 426.31 \\ \times \quad\ 2 \\ \hline 852.62 \end{array}$$

d) 9.47 ÷ 2

Use short division.

Estimate: 10 ÷ 2 = 5

Divide 9 ones by 2. There is 1 whole left.

Trade 1 whole for 10 tenths.

Divide 14 tenths by 2.

Divide 7 hundredths by 2. There is 1 hundredth left.

Trade 1 hundredth for 10 thousandths. Divide 10 thousandths by 2.

So, 9.47 ÷ 2 = 4.735

$$\begin{array}{r|l} 2 & 9.{}^{1}47{}^{1}0 \\ & 4.\ 73\ 5 \end{array}$$

✓ Check

4. Evaluate.

a) 12.3 + 3.5 **b)** 21.41 − 13.8 **c)** 31.47 × 4 **d)** 7.44 ÷ 2

e) 182.34 × 7 **f)** 52.103 + 71.81 **g)** 49.35 ÷ 3 **h)** 138.97 × 6

Comparing and Ordering Decimals

Here are two ways to order these decimals from least to greatest: 1.84, 2.10, 1.80, 1.89

➢ Use a number line.

Mark each decimal on a number line in hundredths from 1.75 to 2.15.
1.84 is between 1.80 and 1.85, but closer to 1.85.
1.89 is between 1.85 and 1.90, but closer to 1.90.

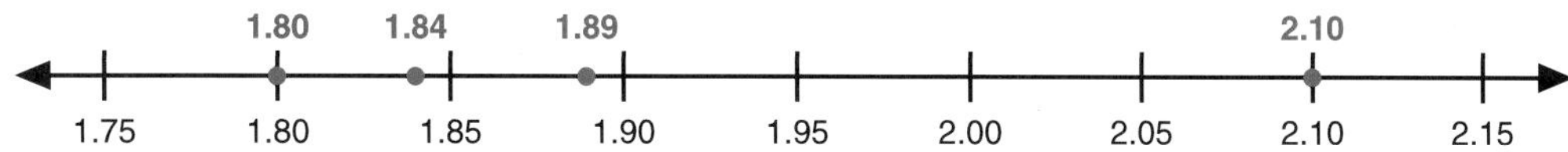

➢ Use place value.

1.84, 2.10, **1**.80, **1**.89
In the ones place, the least digit is 1.
Three decimals have 1 as a ones digit.
Compare these 3 decimals: 1.8**4**, 1.8**0**, 1.8**9**
In the tenths place, each decimal has the digit 8.
So, look in the hundredths place:
The least hundredths digit is 0; so, 1.80 is the least decimal.
The next hundredths digit is 4; so, 1.84 is the next largest decimal.
The next hundredths digit is 9; so, 1.89 is the next largest decimal.

So, from least to greatest: 1.80, 1.84, 1.89, 2.10

Example 4

Compare each pair of decimals. Place > or < between each pair.

a) 0.5 and 0.08

b) 47.305 and 47.5

Solution

a) 0.**5** and 0.**0**8
Both decimals have 0 ones.
In the tenths place, $5 > 0$
So, $0.5 > 0.08$

b) 47.**3**05 and 47.**5**
Both decimals have 4 tens and 7 ones.
In the tenths place, $3 < 5$
So, $47.305 < 47.5$

✓ Check

5. Order the numbers in each set from least to greatest.

a) 7.32, 4.116, 3.79, 4.12, 3.1

b) 4.4, 0.62, 2.591, 0.65, 4.15

c) 1.25, 3.62, 1.43, 2.81, 2.55

d) 3.669, 1.752, 3.68, 2.67, 1.8

4.1 Combining Fractions

Focus Find equivalent fractions and add fractions.

We can use an area model to show fractions of one whole.

Explore

Work with a partner.
Your teacher will give you a copy of the map.
The map shows a section of land owned by 8 families.

- What fraction of the land did each family own?
  What strategies did you use?

Four families sold land to the other 4 families.

- Use the clues below to draw the new map.
- Write addition equations, such as $\frac{1}{2} + \frac{1}{4} = \frac{3}{4}$, to keep track of the land sales.

1: When all the sales were finished, four families owned all the land – Smith, Perry, Haynes, and Chan.
2: Each owner can walk on her or his land without having to cross someone else's property.
3: Smith now owns $\frac{1}{2}$ of the land.
4: Perry kept $\frac{1}{2}$ of her land, and sold the other half to Chan.
5: Haynes bought land from two other people. He now owns $\frac{3}{16}$ of the land.
6 : Chan now owns the same amount of land as Haynes.

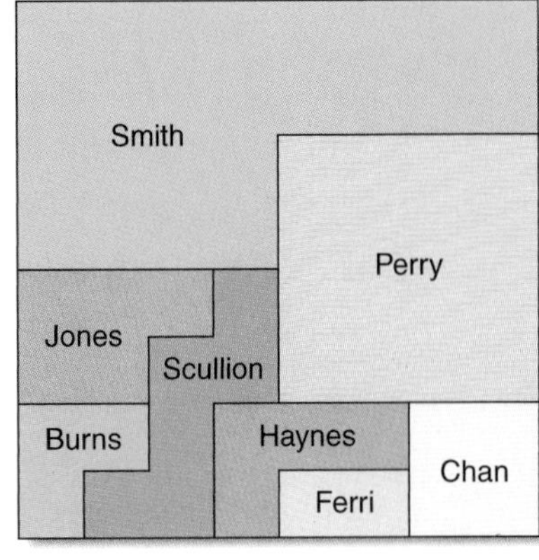

Reflect & Share

Did you find any equivalent fractions? How do you know?
Which clues helped you most to draw the new map?
Explain how they helped.

Connect

This circle shows equivalent fractions.

The circle also shows:
$\frac{1}{2} + \frac{2}{5} + \frac{1}{10} = 1$

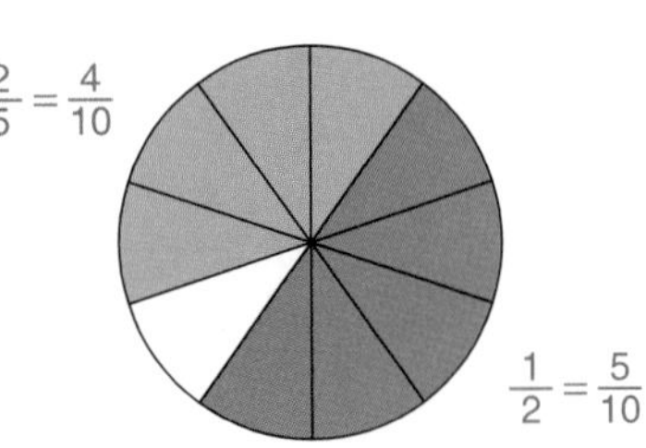

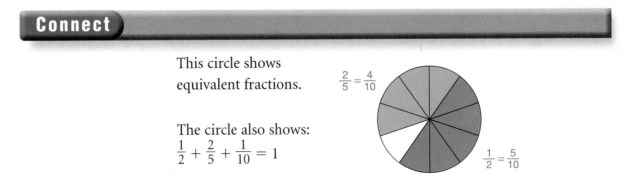

1

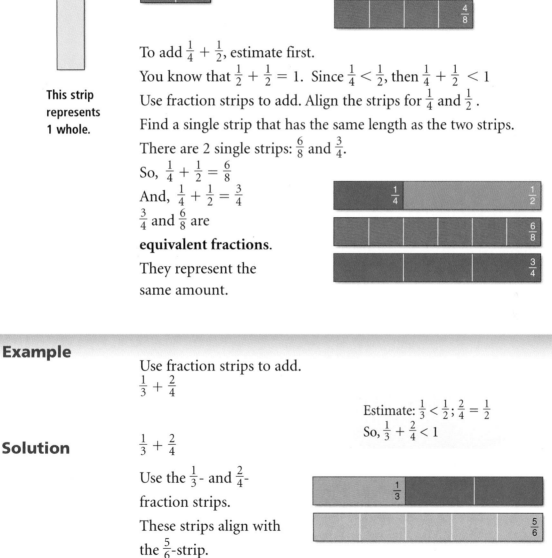

This strip represents 1 whole.

You can model fractions with strips of paper called **fraction strips**.

Here are more fraction strips and some equivalent fractions they show.

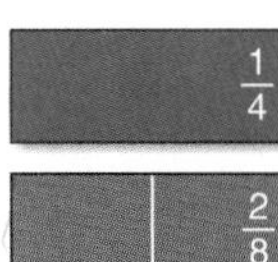

$\frac{1}{4} = \frac{2}{8}$

$\frac{1}{2} = \frac{2}{4} = \frac{4}{8}$

To add $\frac{1}{4} + \frac{1}{2}$, estimate first.
You know that $\frac{1}{2} + \frac{1}{2} = 1$. Since $\frac{1}{4} < \frac{1}{2}$, then $\frac{1}{4} + \frac{1}{2} < 1$
Use fraction strips to add. Align the strips for $\frac{1}{4}$ and $\frac{1}{2}$.
Find a single strip that has the same length as the two strips.
There are 2 single strips: $\frac{6}{8}$ and $\frac{3}{4}$.
So, $\frac{1}{4} + \frac{1}{2} = \frac{6}{8}$
And, $\frac{1}{4} + \frac{1}{2} = \frac{3}{4}$
$\frac{3}{4}$ and $\frac{6}{8}$ are **equivalent fractions**.
They represent the same amount.

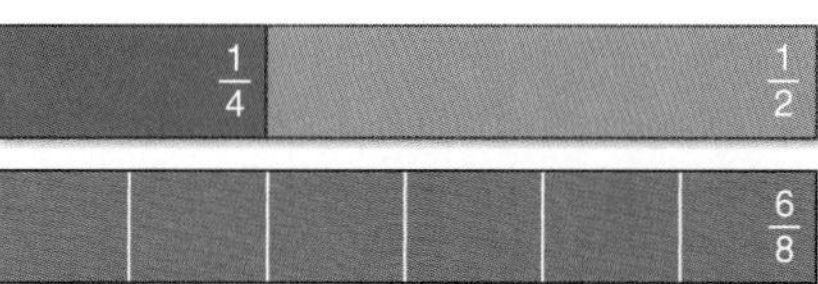

Example

Use fraction strips to add.
$\frac{1}{3} + \frac{2}{4}$

Solution

Estimate: $\frac{1}{3} < \frac{1}{2}$; $\frac{2}{4} = \frac{1}{2}$
So, $\frac{1}{3} + \frac{2}{4} < 1$

$\frac{1}{3} + \frac{2}{4}$

Use the $\frac{1}{3}$- and $\frac{2}{4}$-fraction strips.
These strips align with the $\frac{5}{6}$-strip.
$\frac{1}{3} + \frac{2}{4} = \frac{5}{6}$

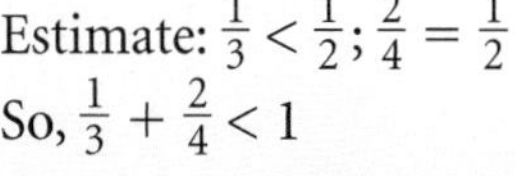

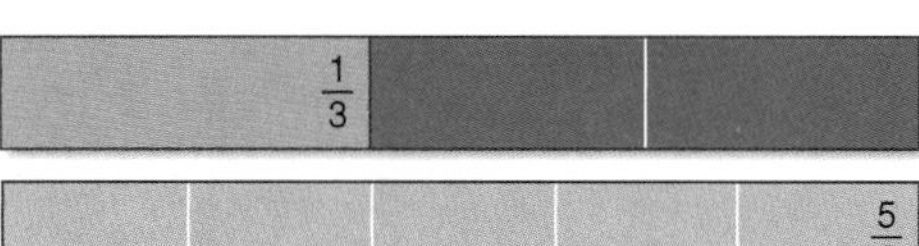

Practice

Use models.

1. Which fraction is greater? How do you know?

a) $\frac{2}{3}, \frac{2}{5}$ **b)** $\frac{3}{4}, \frac{2}{3}$ **c)** $\frac{5}{8}, \frac{3}{5}$ **d)** $\frac{3}{4}, \frac{5}{6}$

2. a) Add.

i) $\frac{1}{5} + \frac{1}{5}$ **ii)** $\frac{2}{3} + \frac{1}{3}$ **iii)** $\frac{4}{10} + \frac{3}{10}$ **iv)** $\frac{1}{4} + \frac{2}{4}$

b) Look at your work in part a.
How else could you add fractions with the same denominator?

3. Add. Estimate first.

a) $\frac{1}{5} + \frac{1}{10}$ **b)** $\frac{1}{2} + \frac{1}{3}$ **c)** $\frac{1}{6} + \frac{1}{3}$ **d)** $\frac{1}{4} + \frac{1}{8}$

4. Add. Estimate first.

a) $\frac{2}{4} + \frac{3}{8}$ **b)** $\frac{2}{3} + \frac{1}{6}$ **c)** $\frac{2}{5} + \frac{2}{10}$ **d)** $\frac{3}{6} + \frac{4}{8}$

5. Find 2 fractions that have a sum of 1.
Try to do this as many ways as you can.

6. Meena's family had a pizza for dinner. The pizza was cut into 8 equal pieces. Meena ate 1 piece, her brother ate 2 pieces, and her mother ate 3 pieces.

a) What fraction of the pizza did Meena eat? Her brother eat? Her mother eat?

b) Which person's fraction can you write in more than one way? Explain.

c) What fraction of the pizza was eaten? What fraction was left?

7. Find the missing number that makes both sides equal.

a) $\frac{1}{5} + \frac{1}{2} = \frac{\square}{10}$ **b)** $\frac{\square}{10} + \frac{2}{5} = \frac{6}{10}$ **c)** $\frac{1}{2} + \frac{3}{\square} = \frac{7}{8}$

8. Assessment Focus Boris added 2 fractions. Their sum was $\frac{5}{6}$.
Which 2 fractions might Boris have added?
Find as many pairs of fractions as you can.

Number Strategies

A loonie has a diameter of about 25 mm. About how many loonies, laid side by side, would there be in 1 km?

Reflect

Write 4 equivalent fractions.
How are these fractions the same? How are they different? Explain.

Join the Dots

YOU WILL NEED

Square dot paper

NUMBER OF PLAYERS

2 or more

GOAL OF THE GAME

To write the greatest number of equivalent fractions

HOW TO PLAY THE GAME:

1. Use dot paper. Mark an array of 49 dots.

2. Take turns to join 2 dots.
3. The player who completes a square claims that square by writing her initials in it.
4. Continue playing until all squares are claimed.
5. Each player writes the squares he has as a fraction of the whole.
6. The winner is the player who can write the greatest number of equivalent fractions for her share.

What if you used a square array of 81 dots. How would this affect the game?

4.2 Adding Fractions Using Models

Focus Add fractions using circles or fraction strips.

Explore

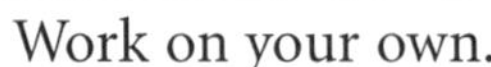

Work on your own.

Baljit trains for cross-country one hour a day.
One day, she ran for $\frac{1}{3}$ of the time, walked for 25 minutes, then got a second wind and ran for the rest of the time.

How long did Baljit run altogether?
What fraction of the hour is this?

- Use fractions to write an addition equation to show how Baljit spent her hour. Baljit never runs for the whole hour.
- Write another possible training schedule for Baljit.
  Share it with a classmate.
- Write an additon equation for your classmate's training schedule.

Reflect & Share

Compare your equations with your classmate's equation.
Were the equations the same? Explain.
When might a clock be a good model for thinking about adding fractions?
When is a clock not a good model?

Connect

There are many models that help us add fractions.

- We could use clocks to model halves, thirds, fourths, sixths, and twelfths.

$$\frac{1}{2} + \frac{1}{3} + \frac{1}{12} = \frac{11}{12}$$

Circle models are useful when the sum is less than 1.

- When the sum is greater than 1, we could use fraction strips and a number line.

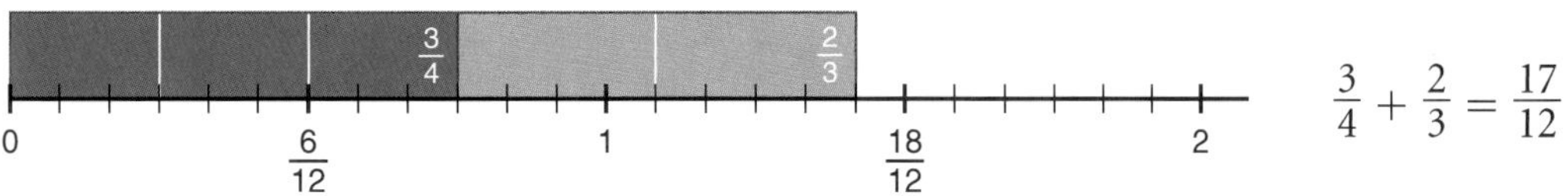

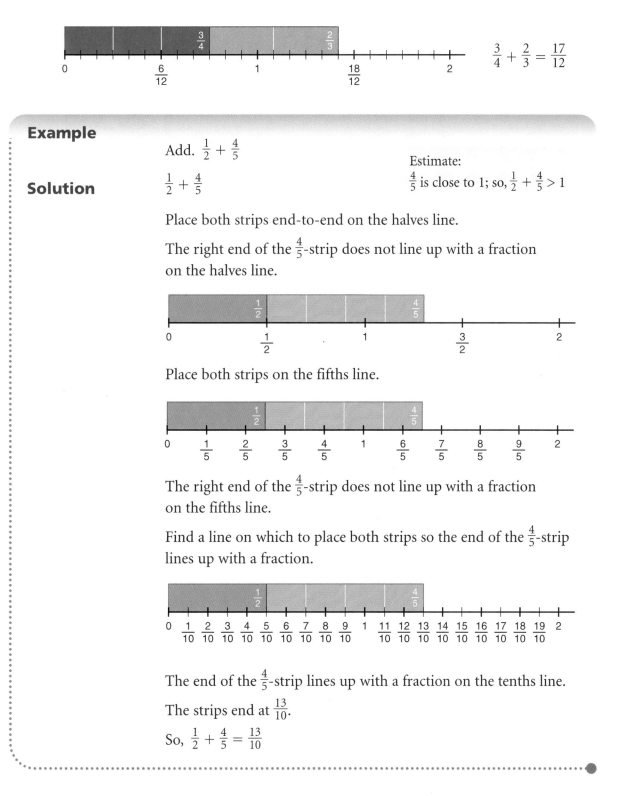

$\frac{3}{4} + \frac{2}{3} = \frac{17}{12}$

Example

Add. $\frac{1}{2} + \frac{4}{5}$

Solution

$\frac{1}{2} + \frac{4}{5}$

Estimate:
$\frac{4}{5}$ is close to 1; so, $\frac{1}{2} + \frac{4}{5} > 1$

Place both strips end-to-end on the halves line.

The right end of the $\frac{4}{5}$-strip does not line up with a fraction on the halves line.

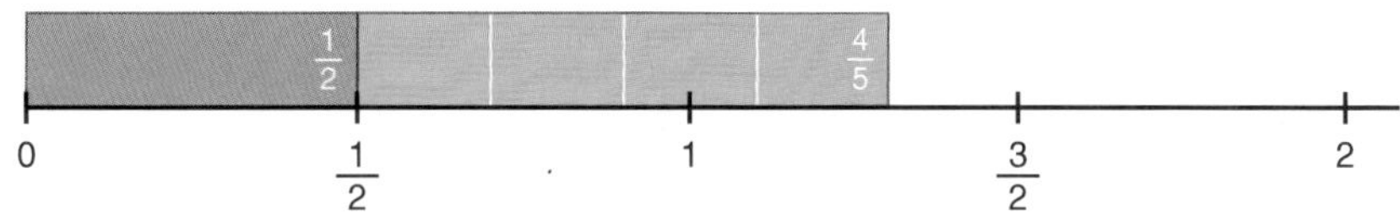

Place both strips on the fifths line.

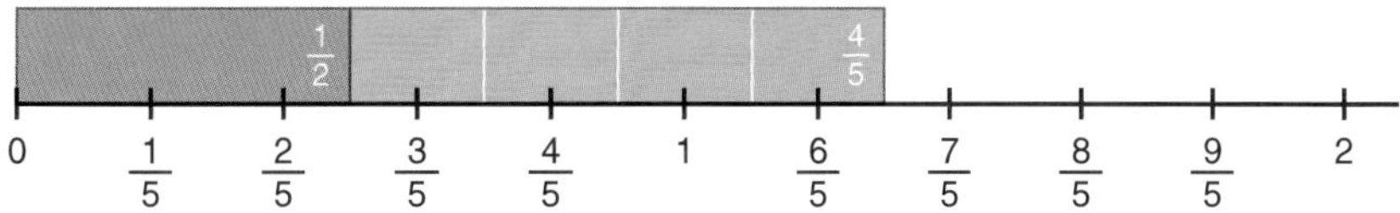

The right end of the $\frac{4}{5}$-strip does not line up with a fraction on the fifths line.

Find a line on which to place both strips so the end of the $\frac{4}{5}$-strip lines up with a fraction.

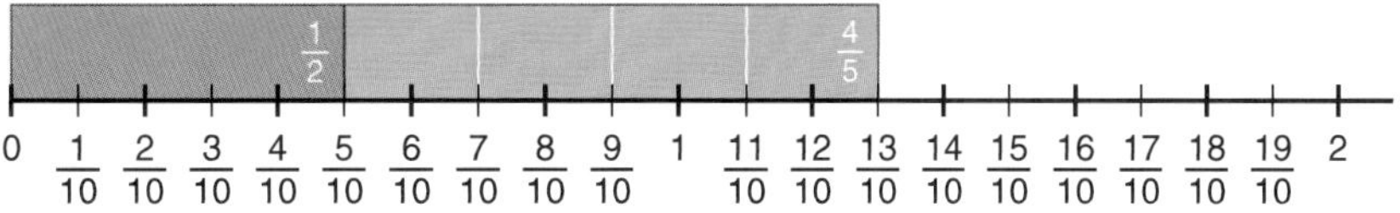

The end of the $\frac{4}{5}$-strip lines up with a fraction on the tenths line.

The strips end at $\frac{13}{10}$.

So, $\frac{1}{2} + \frac{4}{5} = \frac{13}{10}$

Practice

Use models.

1. Write 2 equivalent fractions for each fraction shown.

a) 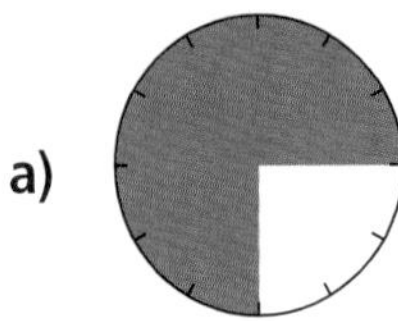

b) 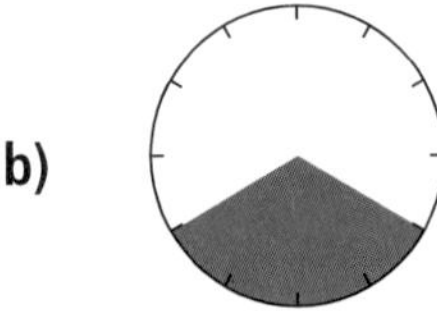

2. Add.

a) $\frac{2}{4} + \frac{3}{4}$ **b)** $\frac{8}{10} + \frac{9}{10}$ **c)** $\frac{3}{5} + \frac{4}{5}$ **d)** $\frac{7}{8} + \frac{7}{8}$

3. Find 2 fractions with a sum of $\frac{3}{2}$.
Try to do this as many ways as you can.
Record each way you find.

4. Add. Estimate first.

a) $\frac{7}{8} + \frac{1}{2}$ **b)** $\frac{7}{10} + \frac{3}{5}$ **c)** $\frac{1}{2} + \frac{3}{4}$ **d)** $\frac{5}{6} + \frac{2}{3}$

Calculator Skills

How many days are there in one million seconds?

5. Add. Estimate first.

a) $\frac{3}{8} + \frac{3}{4}$ **b)** $\frac{4}{4} + \frac{1}{2}$ **c)** $\frac{2}{2} + \frac{4}{6}$ **d)** $\frac{1}{2} + \frac{9}{10}$

6. Use your answers to questions 4 and 5.

a) Look at the denominators in each part, and the number line you used to get the answer. What patterns do you see?

b) The denominators in each part of questions 4 and 5 are **related denominators**.
Why do you think they have this name?

7. Add.

a) $\frac{1}{2} + \frac{2}{3}$ **b)** $\frac{1}{2} + \frac{2}{5}$ **c)** $\frac{1}{3} + \frac{3}{4}$ **d)** $\frac{2}{2} + \frac{3}{5}$

8. Look at your answers to question 7.

a) Look at the denominators in each part, and the number line you used to get the answer. What patterns do you see?

b) The denominators in each part of question 7 are called **unrelated denominators**.
Why do you think they have this name?

c) When you add 2 fractions with unrelated denominators, how do you decide which number line to use?

9. One day Ryan ran for 30 min, rested for 20 min, and then ran for another 45 min. Use fractions of one hour. Write an addition equation that represents his training session.

10. A jug holds 2 cups of liquid. A recipe for punch is $\frac{1}{2}$ cup of orange juice, $\frac{1}{4}$ cup of raspberry juice, $\frac{3}{8}$ cup of grapefruit juice, and $\frac{5}{8}$ cup of lemonade. Is the jug big enough for the punch? Explain.

11. **Assessment Focus** Use any of the digits 1, 2, 3, 4, 5, 6 only once. Copy and complete. Replace each □ with a number.

$$\frac{\square}{\square} + \frac{\square}{\square}$$

a) Find as many sums as you can that are between 1 and 2.
b) Find the least sum that is greater than 1.
Show your work.

12. Abey and Anoki are eating chocolate bars. The bars are the same size. Abey has $\frac{3}{4}$ left. Anoki has $\frac{7}{8}$ left. How much chocolate is left altogether?

Take It Further

13. A pitcher of juice is half empty. After $\frac{1}{2}$ cup of juice is added, the pitcher is $\frac{3}{4}$ full. How much juice does the pitcher hold when it is full? Show your thinking.

14. Which number line would you need to add each pair of fractions? Explain.

a) $\frac{1}{3} + \frac{1}{8}$ **b)** $\frac{1}{3} + \frac{1}{5}$ **c)** $\frac{1}{4} + \frac{1}{5}$ **d)** $\frac{1}{4} + \frac{1}{6}$

Reflect

Which strategies do you use to add 2 fractions? Include 3 different examples in your answer.

4.3 Adding Fractions

Focus Add fractions using symbols.

In *Section 4.2*, you used models to add fractions.
A clock model only works with certain fractions.
You may not always have suitable fraction strips.

We need a new strategy we can use to add fractions without using a model.

Explore

Work with a partner.

A cookie recipe calls for $\frac{3}{8}$ cup of brown sugar and $\frac{1}{3}$ cup of white sugar.
How much sugar is needed altogether?
How can you find out?
Show your work.

Reflect & Share

Describe your strategy.
Will your strategy work with all fractions?

Test it with $\frac{4}{5} + \frac{2}{3}$.

Use models to justify your strategy.

Connect

We can use equivalent fractions to add $\frac{1}{4} + \frac{1}{3}$.

Use equivalent fractions that have the same denominators.
12 is a multiple of 3 and 4.
12 is a **common denominator**.

$\frac{1}{4} = \frac{3}{12}$ and $\frac{1}{3} = \frac{4}{12}$

So, $\frac{1}{4} + \frac{1}{3} = \frac{3}{12} + \frac{4}{12}$

$= \frac{7}{12}$

Both fractions are written with the same denominator.

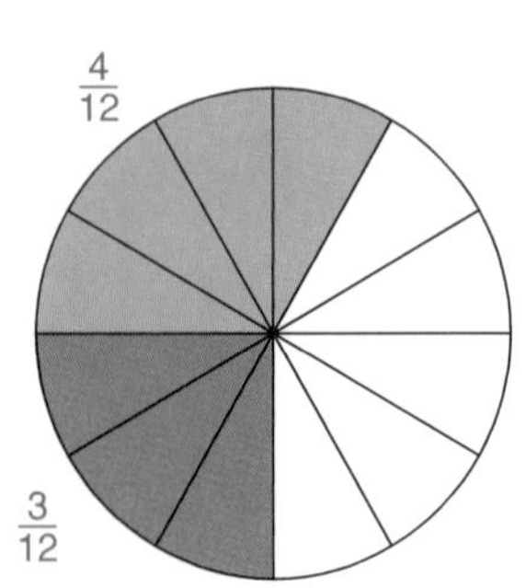

A fraction is in simplest form when the numerator and denominator have no common factors.

Look at the pattern in the equivalent fractions below.

$$\frac{1}{4} \overset{\times 3}{=} \frac{3}{12} \qquad \frac{1}{3} \overset{\times 4}{=} \frac{4}{12}$$

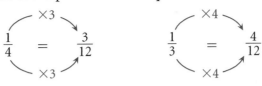

So, to get an equivalent fraction, multiply numerator and denominator by the same number.

We may also get equivalent fractions by dividing.

For example, $\frac{8}{10}$ can be written $\frac{8 \div 2}{10 \div 2} = \frac{4}{5}$

This fraction is in simplest form.

Example 1

Add. $\frac{5}{6} + \frac{2}{9}$

Solution

Estimate:
$\frac{5}{6}$ is close to 1; $\frac{2}{9} < \frac{1}{2}$
So, $\frac{5}{6} + \frac{2}{9}$ is less than $1\frac{1}{2}$.

$\frac{5}{6} + \frac{2}{9}$

The common denominator is a multiple of 6 and 9.

List the multiples of 6: 6, 12, **18**, 24, …

List the multiples of 9: 9, **18**, 27, 36, …

18 is the lowest common multiple of 6 and 9.

So, choose 18 as the common denominator.

$$\frac{5}{6} \overset{\times 3}{=} \frac{15}{18} \qquad \frac{2}{9} \overset{\times 2}{=} \frac{4}{18}$$

We say that 18 is the lowest common denominator.

$$\frac{5}{6} + \frac{2}{9} = \frac{15}{18} + \frac{4}{18}$$
$$= \frac{19}{18}$$

We can write $\frac{19}{18}$ as a mixed number: $1\frac{1}{18}$

Example 2

Add. $\frac{1}{2} + \frac{2}{3} + \frac{3}{4}$

Solution

Estimate:
$\frac{2}{3} > \frac{1}{2}$ and $\frac{3}{4} > \frac{1}{2}$
So, $\frac{1}{2} + \frac{2}{3} + \frac{3}{4}$ is greater than $1\frac{1}{2}$.

$\frac{1}{2} + \frac{2}{3} + \frac{3}{4}$

2 is a multiple of 4.

So, the common denominator is a multiple of 3 and 4.

List the multiples of 3: 3, 6, 9, **12**, 15, 18, …

List the multiples of 4: 4, 8, **12**, 16, 20, 24, …

12 is the lowest common multiple of 3 and 4.

So, 12 is the lowest common denominator.

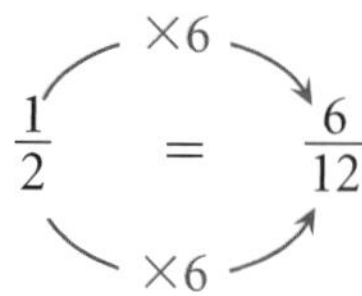

$\frac{1}{2} \xrightarrow{\times 6} \frac{6}{12}$ $\qquad \frac{2}{3} \xrightarrow{\times 4} \frac{8}{12}$ $\qquad \frac{3}{4} \xrightarrow{\times 3} \frac{9}{12}$

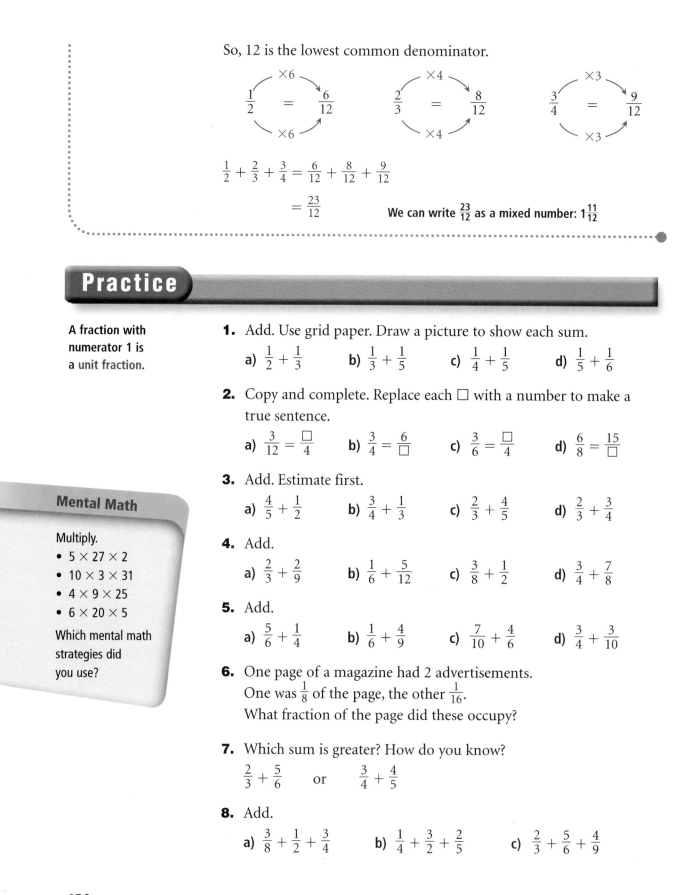

$$\frac{1}{2} + \frac{2}{3} + \frac{3}{4} = \frac{6}{12} + \frac{8}{12} + \frac{9}{12}$$

$$= \frac{23}{12}$$

We can write $\frac{23}{12}$ as a mixed number: $1\frac{11}{12}$

Practice

A fraction with numerator 1 is a unit fraction.

1. Add. Use grid paper. Draw a picture to show each sum.

a) $\frac{1}{2} + \frac{1}{3}$ **b)** $\frac{1}{3} + \frac{1}{5}$ **c)** $\frac{1}{4} + \frac{1}{5}$ **d)** $\frac{1}{5} + \frac{1}{6}$

2. Copy and complete. Replace each □ with a number to make a true sentence.

a) $\frac{3}{12} = \frac{\square}{4}$ **b)** $\frac{3}{4} = \frac{6}{\square}$ **c)** $\frac{3}{6} = \frac{\square}{4}$ **d)** $\frac{6}{8} = \frac{15}{\square}$

3. Add. Estimate first.

a) $\frac{4}{5} + \frac{1}{2}$ **b)** $\frac{3}{4} + \frac{1}{3}$ **c)** $\frac{2}{3} + \frac{4}{5}$ **d)** $\frac{2}{3} + \frac{3}{4}$

Mental Math

Multiply.

- $5 \times 27 \times 2$
- $10 \times 3 \times 31$
- $4 \times 9 \times 25$
- $6 \times 20 \times 5$

Which mental math strategies did you use?

4. Add.

a) $\frac{2}{3} + \frac{2}{9}$ **b)** $\frac{1}{6} + \frac{5}{12}$ **c)** $\frac{3}{8} + \frac{1}{2}$ **d)** $\frac{3}{4} + \frac{7}{8}$

5. Add.

a) $\frac{5}{6} + \frac{1}{4}$ **b)** $\frac{1}{6} + \frac{4}{9}$ **c)** $\frac{7}{10} + \frac{4}{6}$ **d)** $\frac{3}{4} + \frac{3}{10}$

6. One page of a magazine had 2 advertisements.
One was $\frac{1}{8}$ of the page, the other $\frac{1}{16}$.
What fraction of the page did these occupy?

7. Which sum is greater? How do you know?

$\frac{2}{3} + \frac{5}{6}$ or $\frac{3}{4} + \frac{4}{5}$

8. Add.

a) $\frac{3}{8} + \frac{1}{2} + \frac{3}{4}$ **b)** $\frac{1}{4} + \frac{3}{2} + \frac{2}{5}$ **c)** $\frac{2}{3} + \frac{5}{6} + \frac{4}{9}$

To add 2 mixed numbers:
Add the whole numbers.
Add the fractions.
Write the sum as a mixed number.

9. Add.

a) $1\frac{1}{6} + 2\frac{1}{2}$ **b)** $3\frac{1}{3} + 1\frac{1}{2}$ **c)** $4\frac{1}{6} + 2\frac{3}{8}$

10. A recipe for punch calls for $2\frac{2}{3}$ cups of fruit concentrate and $6\frac{3}{4}$ cups of water.
How many cups of punch will the recipe make?

11. **Assessment Focus** Three people shared a pie.
Which statement is true? Can both statements be true?
Use diagrams to show your thinking.

a) Edna ate $\frac{1}{10}$, Farrah ate $\frac{3}{5}$, and Fran ate $\frac{1}{2}$.

b) Edna ate $\frac{3}{10}$, Farrah ate $\frac{1}{5}$, and Fran ate $\frac{1}{2}$.

Take It Further

12. $\frac{1}{2} + \frac{1}{3} + \frac{1}{6} = 1$

Find 3 other fractions with different denominators that add to 1.
Explain your strategy.

13. Copy this sum. Replace □ with the correct digit.

$2\frac{1}{4} + 1\frac{\square}{3} = 3\frac{7}{12}$

Explain your strategy.

Reflect

When you add fractions, and the denominators are different, how do you add?
Give 2 different examples. Use pictures to show your thinking.

4.4 Subtracting Fractions Using Models

Focus Subtract fractions using fraction strips and number lines.

Explore

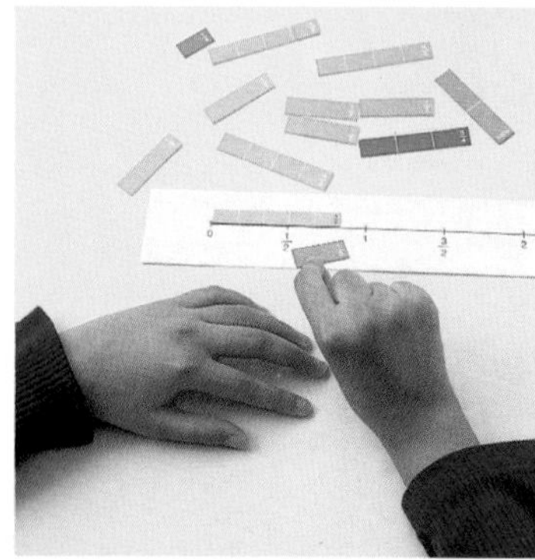

Work with a partner.
You will need fraction strips and number lines.

Find 2 fractions with a difference of $\frac{1}{2}$.

How many different pairs of fractions can you find?
Record each pair.

Reflect & Share

Discuss with your partner.
How are your strategies for subtracting fractions the same as your strategies for adding fractions? How are they different?

Connect

To subtract $\frac{3}{5} - \frac{1}{2}$, think addition: What do we add to $\frac{1}{2}$ to get $\frac{3}{5}$?
Try the fifths number line.
Place the $\frac{1}{2}$-strip with its right end at $\frac{3}{5}$.

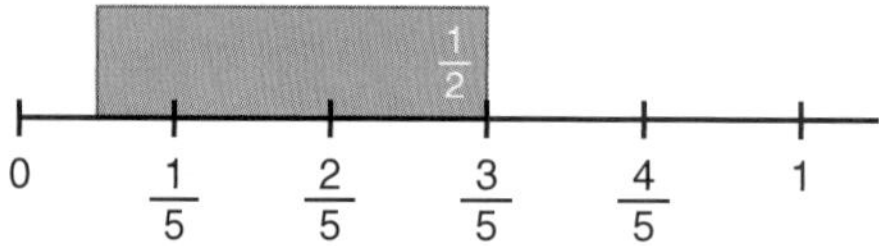

Estimate:
$\frac{3}{5} < 1$; so, $\frac{3}{5} - \frac{1}{2} < \frac{1}{2}$

Equivalent fractions:
$\frac{3}{5} = \frac{6}{10}$
$\frac{1}{2} = \frac{5}{10}$

The left end of the strip does not line up with a fraction on the line.
Use a number line that has equivalent fractions for halves and fifths.
Put the $\frac{1}{2}$-strip on the tenths number line, with its right end at $\frac{6}{10}$.

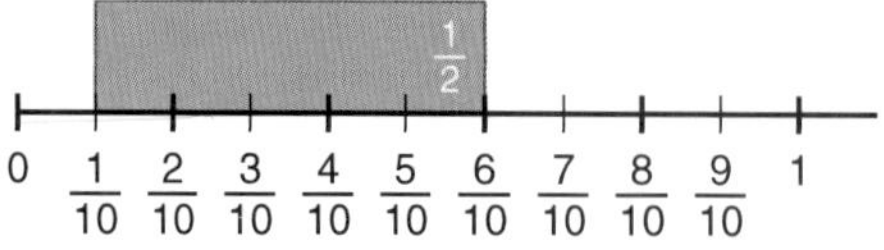

The left end of the strip is at $\frac{1}{10}$.

So, $\frac{3}{5} - \frac{1}{2} = \frac{1}{10}$

Example

Use fraction strips and number lines to subtract.

a) $\frac{6}{5} - \frac{4}{5}$ **b)** $\frac{5}{8} - \frac{1}{4}$

Solution

a) $\frac{6}{5} - \frac{4}{5}$

Estimate:
$\frac{6}{5} > 1, \frac{4}{5} < 1;$
so, $\frac{6}{5} - \frac{4}{5} < 1$

Think addition.
What do we add to $\frac{4}{5}$ to get $\frac{6}{5}$?
Use the fifths number line because both denominators are 5.
Place the $\frac{4}{5}$-strip on the fifths number line with its right end at $\frac{6}{5}$.

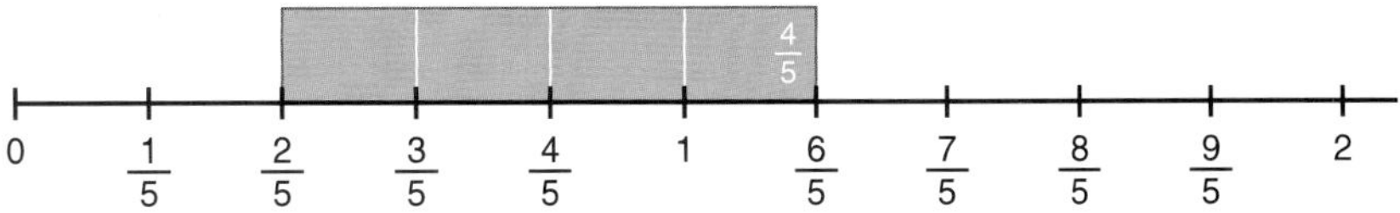

The left end of the strip is at $\frac{2}{5}$.

So, $\frac{6}{5} - \frac{4}{5} = \frac{2}{5}$

b) $\frac{5}{8} - \frac{1}{4}$

Estimate:
$\frac{5}{8}$ is between $\frac{1}{2}$ and 1,
$\frac{1}{4} < \frac{1}{2}$; so, $\frac{5}{8} - \frac{1}{4} < \frac{1}{2}$

Think addition.
What do we add to $\frac{1}{4}$ to get $\frac{5}{8}$?

Use a number line that shows equivalent fractions for eighths and fourths.
That is, use the eighths number line.
Place the $\frac{1}{4}$-strip on the eighths number line with its right end at $\frac{5}{8}$.

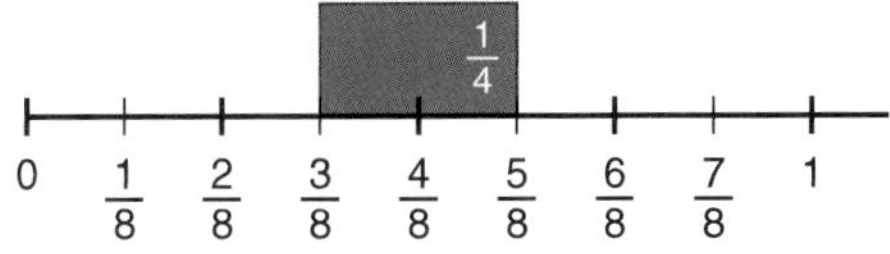

The left end of the strip is at $\frac{3}{8}$.

So, $\frac{5}{8} - \frac{1}{4} = \frac{3}{8}$

Practice

Use models.

1. Subtract.

a) $\frac{3}{4} - \frac{2}{4}$ b) $\frac{4}{5} - \frac{1}{5}$ c) $\frac{2}{3} - \frac{1}{3}$ d) $\frac{5}{8} - \frac{3}{8}$

2. a) Write a rule you could use to subtract fractions with like denominators without using number lines or fraction strips.

b) Write 3 subtraction questions with like denominators. Use your rule to subtract the fractions. Use fraction strips and number lines to check your answers.

3. Write the subtraction equation that each number line and fraction strip represent.

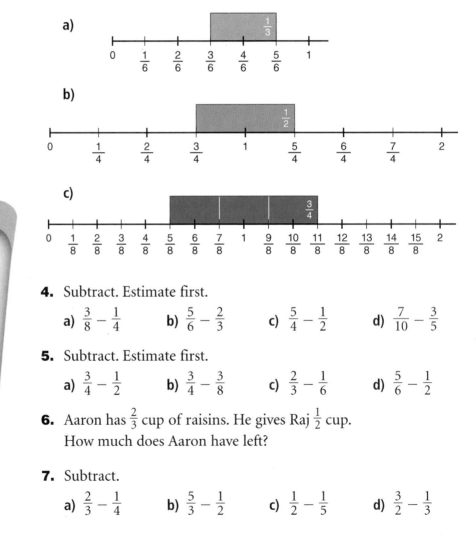

a)

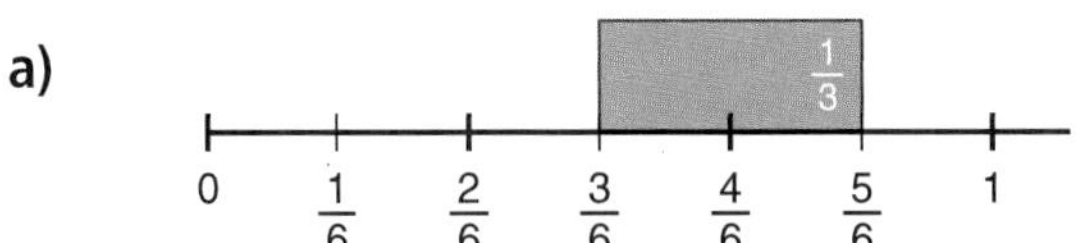

b)

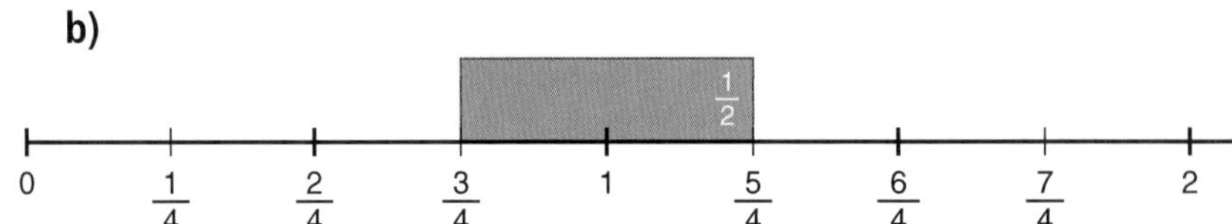

c)

4. Subtract. Estimate first.

a) $\frac{3}{8} - \frac{1}{4}$ b) $\frac{5}{6} - \frac{2}{3}$ c) $\frac{5}{4} - \frac{1}{2}$ d) $\frac{7}{10} - \frac{3}{5}$

5. Subtract. Estimate first.

a) $\frac{3}{4} - \frac{1}{2}$ b) $\frac{3}{4} - \frac{3}{8}$ c) $\frac{2}{3} - \frac{1}{6}$ d) $\frac{5}{6} - \frac{1}{2}$

6. Aaron has $\frac{2}{3}$ cup of raisins. He gives Raj $\frac{1}{2}$ cup. How much does Aaron have left?

7. Subtract.

a) $\frac{2}{3} - \frac{1}{4}$ b) $\frac{5}{3} - \frac{1}{2}$ c) $\frac{1}{2} - \frac{1}{5}$ d) $\frac{3}{2} - \frac{1}{3}$

Number Strategies

Find:

- 8 tenths less than 22.23
- 9 hundredths more than 94.43
- 36 hundredths more than 48.425
- 36 thousandths more than 48.425

8. Subtract.

a) $\frac{11}{8} - \frac{3}{4}$ b) $\frac{3}{2} - \frac{2}{3}$ c) $\frac{9}{5} - \frac{3}{2}$ d) $\frac{5}{3} - \frac{5}{6}$

9. Subtract.

a) $2 - \frac{1}{2}$ b) $1 - \frac{3}{5}$ c) $2 - \frac{5}{4}$ d) $1 - \frac{2}{3}$

10. A cookie recipe calls for $\frac{3}{4}$ cup of chocolate chips.
Spencer has $\frac{2}{3}$ cup. Does he have enough?
If your answer is yes, explain.
If your answer is no, how much more does Spencer need?

11. Copy and replace each □ with a number, to make each statement correct.
Try to do this more than one way.

a) $\frac{3}{4} - \frac{\square}{\square} = \frac{1}{4}$ b) $\frac{\square}{\square} - \frac{1}{5} = \frac{3}{5}$ c) $\frac{\square}{6} - \frac{2}{\square} = \frac{1}{6}$

12. **Assessment Focus** Kelly had $\frac{3}{4}$ of a tank of gas at the beginning of the week.
At the end of the week, Kelly had $\frac{1}{8}$ of a tank left.

a) Did Kelly use more or less than $\frac{1}{2}$ of a tank? Explain.

b) How much more or less than $\frac{1}{2}$ of a tank did Kelly use?

13. a) Which of these differences is greater than $\frac{1}{2}$?
How do you know?

i) $\frac{5}{6} - \frac{2}{3}$ ii) $\frac{5}{6} - \frac{1}{2}$ iii) $\frac{5}{6} - \frac{1}{6}$

b) Explain how you found your answers to part a.
Which other way can you find the fractions with a difference greater than $\frac{1}{2}$? Explain.

Reflect

Which pairs of fractions can you *not* subtract using the number lines and fraction strips you have? Give 3 examples.

4.5 Subtracting Fractions

Focus Subtract fractions using symbols.

Addition and subtraction are related operations.
You can use what you know about adding fractions to subtract them.

Explore

Work with a partner.
Use any of the digits 1, 2, 3, 4, 5, 6 only once.
Copy and complete. Replace each □ with a number.

$$\frac{\square}{\square} - \frac{\square}{\square}$$

Find the least difference greater than 0.
Which strategies did you use?

Reflect & Share

Compare your least difference with that of another pair of classmates.
Are the differences the same?
If your answer is no, what is the least difference?

Connect

To subtract $\frac{3}{4} - \frac{1}{6}$, estimate first.
$\frac{3}{4}$ is between $\frac{1}{2}$ and 1, and $\frac{1}{6} < \frac{1}{4}$.
So, $\frac{3}{4} - \frac{1}{6}$ is about $\frac{1}{2}$.
Use equivalent fractions to subtract.
Express $\frac{3}{4}$ and $\frac{1}{6}$ with a common denominator.
Find the lowest common denominator.
List the multiples of 4: 4, 8, **12**, 16, 20, …
List the multiples of 6: 6, **12**, 18, 24, 30, …
The lowest common denominator is 12.

$$\frac{3}{4} \overset{\times 3}{=} \frac{9}{12} \qquad \frac{1}{6} \overset{\times 2}{=} \frac{2}{12}$$

$$\begin{aligned}\frac{3}{4} - \frac{1}{6} &= \frac{9}{12} - \frac{2}{12} \\ &= \frac{7}{12}\end{aligned}$$

Think: 9 twelfths minus 2 twelfths is 7 twelfths.

Example

Subtract.

a) $\frac{3}{4} - \frac{5}{8}$ b) $\frac{3}{2} - \frac{2}{5}$

Solution

a) $\frac{3}{4} - \frac{5}{8}$

Since 8 is a multiple of 4, use 8 as the lowest common denominator.

Estimate:
Both $\frac{3}{4}$ and $\frac{5}{8}$ are between $\frac{1}{2}$ and 1; so, $\frac{3}{4} - \frac{5}{8} < \frac{1}{2}$

$$\frac{3}{4} \overset{\times 2}{=} \frac{6}{8}$$

$$\frac{3}{4} - \frac{5}{8} = \frac{6}{8} - \frac{5}{8}$$
$$= \frac{1}{8}$$

b) $\frac{3}{2} - \frac{2}{5}$

Estimate:
$\frac{2}{5} < \frac{1}{2}$; so, $\frac{3}{2} - \frac{2}{5} > 1$

List the multiples of 2:
2, 4, 6, 8, **10**, 12, …
List the multiples of 5:
5, **10**, 15, 20, …
The lowest common denominator is 10.
Write each fraction with a denominator of 10.

$$\frac{3}{2} \overset{\times 5}{=} \frac{15}{10} \qquad \frac{2}{5} \overset{\times 2}{=} \frac{4}{10}$$

$$\frac{3}{2} - \frac{2}{5} = \frac{15}{10} - \frac{4}{10}$$
$$= \frac{11}{10}$$

We can write $\frac{11}{10}$ as the mixed number $1\frac{1}{10}$.

Practice

1. Subtract.

a) $\frac{4}{5} - \frac{2}{5}$ b) $\frac{2}{3} - \frac{1}{3}$ c) $\frac{7}{9} - \frac{4}{9}$ d) $\frac{5}{7} - \frac{3}{7}$

2. Subtract. Estimate first.

a) $\frac{5}{8} - \frac{1}{2}$ b) $\frac{4}{9} - \frac{1}{3}$ c) $\frac{3}{2} - \frac{4}{10}$ d) $\frac{5}{3} - \frac{5}{6}$

3. Subtract.

a) $\frac{5}{6} - \frac{2}{9}$ b) $\frac{5}{6} - \frac{2}{4}$ c) $\frac{5}{8} - \frac{3}{12}$ d) $\frac{7}{10} - \frac{4}{15}$

4. Subtract. Estimate first.

a) $\frac{3}{4} - \frac{2}{3}$ b) $\frac{5}{2} - \frac{3}{4}$ c) $\frac{4}{5} - \frac{2}{3}$ d) $\frac{5}{4} - \frac{4}{5}$

5. Subtract.

a) $\frac{4}{6} - \frac{1}{2}$ b) $\frac{5}{3} - \frac{3}{4}$ c) $\frac{7}{2} - \frac{3}{2}$ d) $\frac{5}{6} - \frac{3}{4}$

To subtract 2 mixed numbers: Subtract the whole numbers. Subtract the fractions. Write the difference as a mixed number.

6. Subtract.

a) $5\frac{5}{7} - 1\frac{2}{7}$ b) $3\frac{4}{9} - 2\frac{1}{6}$ c) $4\frac{3}{10} - 2\frac{1}{5}$ d) $4\frac{3}{5} - 2\frac{1}{2}$

7. **Assessment Focus** Terri biked $2\frac{1}{4}$ h on Sunday.
Terri increased the time she biked by $\frac{1}{4}$ h every day.
Sam biked $\frac{1}{2}$ h on Sunday.
Sam increased the time he biked by $\frac{1}{2}$ h every day.

a) Who will bike longer the next Saturday? Explain.
b) For how much longer will this person bike?
c) What did you need to know about fractions to answer these questions?

8. A recipe calls for $\frac{3}{4}$ cup of walnuts and $\frac{2}{3}$ cup of pecans. Which type of nut is used more in the recipe? How much more?

9. Write as many different subtraction questions as you can where the answer is $\frac{3}{4}$.

10. The difference of 2 fractions is $\frac{1}{2}$.
The lesser fraction is between 0 and $\frac{1}{4}$.
What do you know about the other fraction?

Calculator Skills

Suppose the [8] key on your calculator is broken. How would you use your calculator to find each answer?

- 18 + 27
- 118 – 85
- 18 × 27
- 225 ÷ 8

Reflect

When you subtract fractions, and the denominators are different, how do you subtract? Give 2 different examples.
Explain your steps.

Shade One

YOU WILL NEED

One gameboard;
coloured markers;
1 set of 42 fraction cards

NUMBER OF PLAYERS

2 or more

GOAL OF THE GAME

To shade 1 whole on each fraction strip

HOW TO PLAY THE GAME:

1. Each player chooses a different colour marker.
2. Place the set of fraction cards face down.
3. Player A turns over a card. This is his *target fraction.*
4. Player A could shade the target fraction on one fraction strip, or share the fraction among several fraction strips. However, the total fraction shaded must equal the target fraction.

For example: If your target fraction is $\frac{3}{4}$, you could shade from 0 to $\frac{3}{4}$ on the fourths strip, or 0 to $\frac{6}{8}$ on the eighths strip. Or you could shade several fractions that add up to $\frac{3}{4}$. For example, you could shade $\frac{3}{12}$, $\frac{2}{8}$, and $\frac{1}{4}$; or you could shade $\frac{2}{5}$, $\frac{1}{10}$, and $\frac{1}{4}$.

5. Player B turns over the next fraction card. He repeats *Step 4* for his fraction.
6. Play continues with players taking turns to shade the target fraction. If there is not enough of a fraction strip left, and it is impossible to shade the target fraction, that player forfeits his turn. When a player is not able to shade any more fractions, the game is over.
7. The player who shades to complete 1 whole gets 1 point.
8. The person with the most points wins.

Mid-Unit Review

LESSON

4.1 **1.** Add. Use fraction strips to help you.

a) $\frac{2}{3} + \frac{1}{6}$ b) $\frac{2}{4} + \frac{1}{3}$

c) $\frac{2}{8} + \frac{2}{4}$ d) $\frac{2}{10} + \frac{3}{5}$

4.2 **2.** We know that $\frac{1}{2} + \frac{4}{5} = \frac{13}{10}$.
Use this result to find each sum.

a) $1\frac{1}{2} + \frac{4}{5}$ b) $5\frac{1}{2} + 2\frac{4}{5}$

3. Use models to add.

a) $\frac{4}{5} + \frac{3}{5}$ b) $\frac{2}{3} + \frac{1}{2}$

c) $\frac{1}{2} + \frac{5}{6}$ d) $\frac{3}{2} + \frac{1}{3}$

4.3 **4.** Add. Estimate first.

a) $\frac{3}{4} + \frac{5}{6}$ b) $\frac{3}{2} + \frac{2}{3}$

c) $\frac{7}{10} + \frac{2}{5}$ d) $\frac{5}{9} + \frac{5}{6}$

5. Add.

a) $\frac{2}{5} + \frac{3}{2} + \frac{3}{10}$

b) $\frac{3}{8} + \frac{3}{4} + \frac{1}{2}$

c) $\frac{1}{3} + \frac{5}{6} + \frac{2}{9}$

6. Add.

a) $2\frac{1}{3} + 3\frac{1}{3}$

b) $2\frac{1}{4} + 1\frac{1}{3}$

c) $1\frac{3}{4} + 3\frac{3}{8}$

4.4 **7.** Use models to subtract.

a) $\frac{7}{8} - \frac{3}{4}$ b) $\frac{3}{2} - \frac{3}{5}$

c) $\frac{4}{3} - \frac{5}{6}$ d) $\frac{11}{6} - \frac{2}{3}$

8. Peter put $\frac{4}{5}$ cup of chocolate chips into his cookie batter. Samantha put $\frac{7}{8}$ cup into hers. Whose batter contains more chips? How do you know?

9. Alex delivered flyers to $\frac{1}{4}$ of her route on Saturday morning. She delivered to $\frac{2}{3}$ of the route on Saturday afternoon, and the remainder on Sunday.

a) What fraction of her route did Alex deliver on Saturday?

b) What fraction did she deliver on Sunday?

4.5 **10.** Subtract. Estimate first.

a) $\frac{3}{2} - \frac{1}{5}$ b) $\frac{7}{6} - \frac{2}{3}$

c) $\frac{11}{6} - \frac{3}{4}$ d) $\frac{13}{10} - \frac{3}{5}$

11. We know that $\frac{9}{8} - \frac{1}{4} = \frac{7}{8}$.
Use this result to find each difference.
Explain how you did this.

a) $\frac{12}{8} - \frac{1}{4}$ b) $\frac{5}{8} - \frac{1}{4}$

12. Subtract.

a) $3\frac{5}{8} - 2\frac{3}{8}$ b) $2\frac{1}{2} - 1\frac{1}{4}$

4.6 Exploring Repeated Addition

Focus Multiply a fraction by a whole number.

How many ways can you find this sum?

$2 + 2 + 2 + 2 + 2 + 2 + 2 + 2 + 2$

You can use the same strategies in *Explore*.

Explore

Work with a partner.
Jan takes $\frac{3}{4}$ h to walk to her music lesson.
Jan has a music lesson once a week, for 9 weeks.
How much time does Jan spend walking to her music lessons?

Reflect & Share

Compare your strategy for solving the problem with that of another pair of classmates.
Did you get the same answers?
If not, who is correct? Explain.

Connect

$\frac{1}{5} + \frac{1}{5} + \frac{1}{5} + \frac{1}{5} = \frac{4}{5}$

All the fractions added are $\frac{1}{5}$.
Repeated addition can be written as multiplication.

$\frac{1}{5} + \frac{1}{5} + \frac{1}{5} + \frac{1}{5} = 4 \times \frac{1}{5} = \frac{4}{5}$

We can show this as a picture.

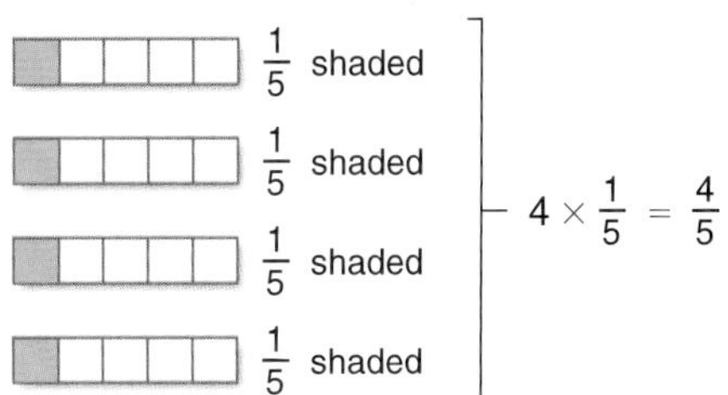

Similarly: $\frac{3}{4} + \frac{3}{4} + \frac{3}{4} + \frac{3}{4} + \frac{3}{4}$
$= 5 \times \frac{3}{4}$
$= \frac{15}{4}$

We can show this as a picture.

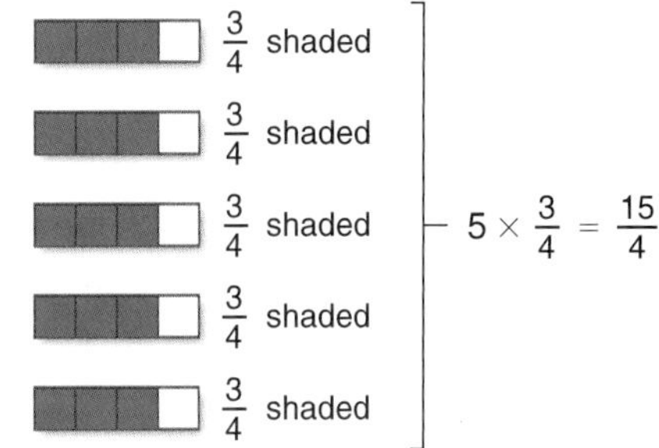

Example 1

Use multiplication to find this sum.

$\frac{3}{8}+\frac{3}{8}+\frac{3}{8}+\frac{3}{8}+\frac{3}{8}+\frac{3}{8}+\frac{3}{8}+\frac{3}{8}+\frac{3}{8}$

Solution

$$\begin{aligned}\frac{3}{8}+\frac{3}{8}+\frac{3}{8}+\frac{3}{8}+\frac{3}{8}+\frac{3}{8}+\frac{3}{8}+\frac{3}{8}+\frac{3}{8} &= 9 \times \frac{3}{8}\\ &= \frac{27}{8}\end{aligned}$$

Think: 9 times 3 eighths is 27 eighths.

Example 2

Multiply.

a) $\frac{3}{5} \times 5$

b) $7 \times \frac{5}{6}$

Solution

a) $\frac{3}{5} \times 5 = \frac{15}{5}$
$= 3$

Think: $\frac{15}{5}$ means $15 \div 5$, which is 3.

b) $7 \times \frac{5}{6} = \frac{35}{6}$

Think: 7 times 5 sixths is 35 sixths.

Practice

1. Write each repeated addition as a multiplication question.

a) $\frac{1}{4}+\frac{1}{4}+\frac{1}{4}$

b) $\frac{2}{7}+\frac{2}{7}+\frac{2}{7}+\frac{2}{7}+\frac{2}{7}$

c) $\frac{3}{10}+\frac{3}{10}+\frac{3}{10}+\frac{3}{10}$

2. Write each multiplication question as repeated addition. Draw a picture to show each answer.

a) $5 \times \frac{1}{8}$ **b)** $\frac{2}{5} \times 3$ **c)** $4 \times \frac{5}{12}$

3. Multiply. Draw a picture to show each answer.

a) $3 \times \frac{4}{7}$ **b)** $5 \times \frac{1}{12}$ **c)** $\frac{2}{15} \times 10$

d) $4 \times \frac{9}{4}$ **e)** $\frac{2}{5} \times 7$ **f)** $9 \times \frac{1}{2}$

4. Multiply.

a) $3 \times \frac{4}{5}$ b) $5 \times \frac{7}{10}$ c) $\frac{5}{6} \times 6$

d) $\frac{1}{2} \times 5$ e) $12 \times \frac{7}{12}$ f) $\frac{2}{3} \times 9$

5. It takes $\frac{2}{3}$ h to pick all the apples on one tree at Springwater Farms. There are 24 trees.
How long will it take to pick all the apples?
Show your work.

Number Strategies

Calculate each answer.

$6000 \div 10$	6000×0.1
$600 \div 10$	600×0.1
$60 \div 10$	60×0.1
$6 \div 10$	6×0.1

What patterns do you see in the questions and answers?

6. a) Draw a picture to show each product. What is each answer?

i) $4 \times \frac{3}{10}$ ii) $3 \times \frac{4}{10}$

b) How are the questions in part a related?
Write 2 more questions like these.
Find each product. What do you notice?

7. A cookie recipe calls for $\frac{3}{4}$ cup of oatmeal.
How much oatmeal is needed to make 3 batches of cookies?

8. **Assessment Focus**

a) Draw a picture to show $5 \times \frac{1}{2}$.

b) What meaning can you give to $\frac{1}{2} \times 5$?
Draw a picture to show your thinking.

Take It Further

9. Jacob takes $\frac{3}{4}$ h to fill one shelf at the supermarket.
Henry can fill the shelves in half Jacob's time.
There are 15 shelves. Henry and Jacob work together.
How long will it take to fill the shelves? Justify your answer.

Reflect

Draw a picture to show why $4 \times \frac{2}{5}$ is the same as $\frac{2}{5} + \frac{2}{5} + \frac{2}{5} + \frac{2}{5}$.
Explain your picture.
Draw a different picture to show the same answer.

Fractions to Decimals

Recall that $\frac{1}{10}$ means $1 \div 10$, which is 0.1 as a decimal.

Similarly, $\frac{1}{2}$ means $1 \div 2$, which is 0.5 as a decimal.

0.1 and 0.5 are **terminating decimals**, because each has a definite number of decimal places.

On a calculator, press: [1] [÷] [11] [=] to display 0.090909091

The calculator rounds up the last digit.
The fraction $\frac{1}{11}$ is a **repeating decimal**.

The decimal for $\frac{1}{11}$ is $0.\overline{09}$, with a bar above the 0 and 9 to show they repeat.

A period above an equal sign shows the answer is approximate.

We can round $0.\overline{09}$ to an approximate decimal.

- $0.\overline{09} \doteq 0.1$ to 1 decimal place
- $0.\overline{09} \doteq 0.09$ to 2 decimal places
- $0.\overline{09} \doteq 0.091$ to 3 decimal places

1. Investigate other unit fractions; that is, fractions with numerator 1.

a) Which unit fractions from $\frac{1}{3}$ to $\frac{1}{20}$ produce terminating decimals?
Which produce repeating decimals? Explain why.

b) Investigate other fractions.
For example, how are the decimals for $\frac{1}{6}, \frac{2}{6}, \ldots, \frac{5}{6}$ related?

2. Investigate fractions with greater denominators.
For example, how are the decimals for $\frac{1}{9}, \frac{1}{99}, \frac{1}{999}, \ldots$ related?

3. Which is greater in each case? Justify your answer.

a) $0.\overline{3}$ or 0.3

b) $\frac{1}{9}$ or 0.11

4.7 Multiplying Decimals

Focus Multiply decimals with tenths.

To multiply 2 whole numbers, we can use Base Ten Blocks.
This picture shows the product

$20 \times 16 = 100 + 100 + 60 + 60$
$= 320$

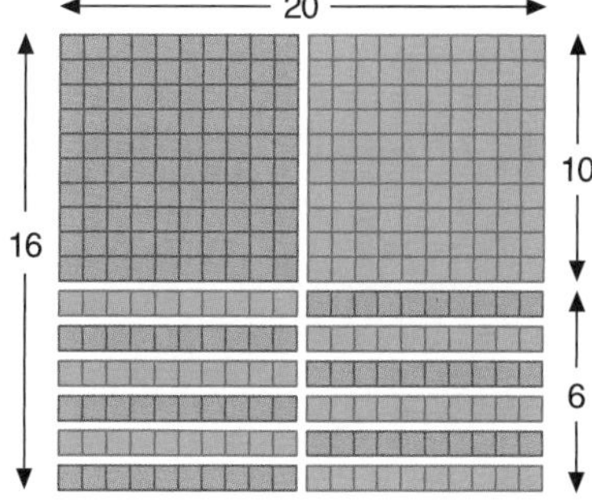

We can also use Base Ten Blocks to multiply a decimal and a whole number.

The flat represents 1.

The rod represents 0.1.

The small cube represents 0.01.

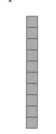

This picture shows the product

$2 \times 1.6 = 1 + 1 + 0.6 + 0.6$
$= 3.2$

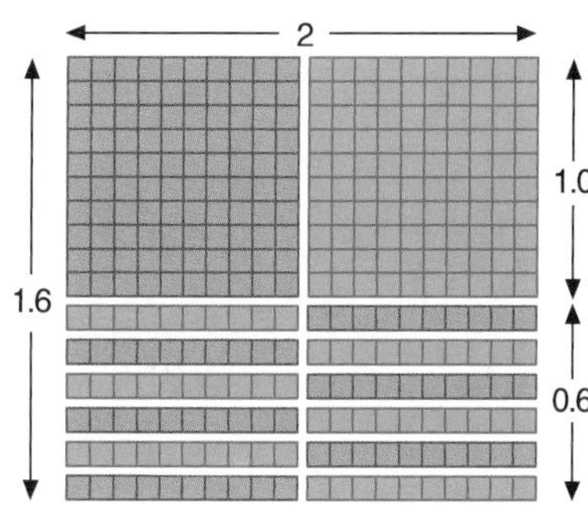

In *Explore*, you will use Base Ten Blocks to multiply 2 decimals.

Explore

Work with a partner.
A rectangular tabletop measures 2.4 m by 1.8 m.
Use Base Ten Blocks to find the area of the tabletop.
Record your work on grid paper.

Reflect & Share

Compare your answer with that of another pair of classmates.
Did you draw the same picture? Explain.
Did you get the same area? Explain.

Connect

A rectangular park measures 1.7 km by 2.5 km.

Here are 2 ways to find the area of the park.

➢ Use Base Ten Blocks.

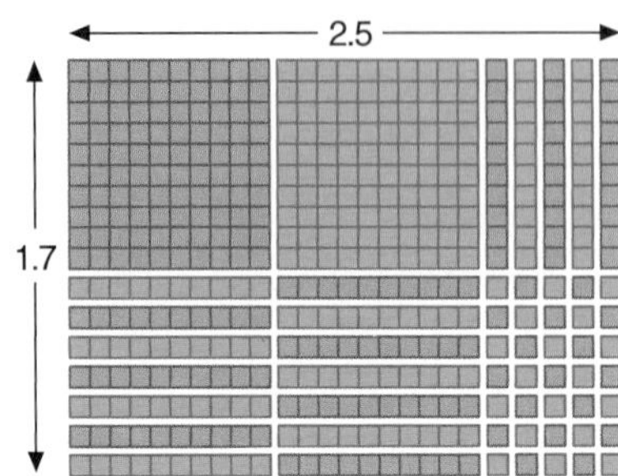

There are 2 flats: $2 \times 1 = 2$

There are 19 rods: $19 \times 0.1 = 1.9$

There are 35 small cubes: $35 \times 0.01 = 0.35$

The total area is $2 + 1.9 + 0.35 = 4.25$

The area of the park is 4.25 km^2.

➢ Use the method for multiplying 2 whole numbers.

The area, in square kilometres, is 1.7×2.5.

Multiply: 17×25

$$\begin{array}{r} 17 \\ \times\ 25 \\ \hline 85 \\ 340 \\ \hline 425 \end{array}$$

Estimate to place the decimal point in the answer.

1.7×2.5 is about $2 \times 3 = 6$

So, the product is 4.25.

The area of the park is 4.25 km^2.

Example 1

Multiply. 5.8×9.7

Solution

5.8×9.7

Multiply: 58×97

$$\begin{array}{r} 58 \\ \times\ 97 \\ \hline 406 \\ 5220 \\ \hline 5626 \end{array}$$

Estimate to place the decimal point.

5.8×9.7 is about $6 \times 10 = 60$.

So, the product is 56.26.

Example 2

Multiply.

a) 0.9×6.8 b) 0.5×0.4

Solution

a) 0.9×6.8

Multiply: 9×68

$$\begin{array}{r} 68 \\ \times\ 9 \\ \hline 612 \end{array}$$

Estimate to place the decimal point.

0.9×6.8 is about $1 \times 7 = 7$.

So, the product is 6.12.

b) 0.5×0.4

Multiply: $5 \times 4 = 20$

Estimate to place the decimal point.

0.5×0.4 is about $1 \times 0.4 = 0.4$.

So, the product is 0.20.

Practice

1. Write a multiplication equation for each picture.
   Each small square represents 0.01.

   a) 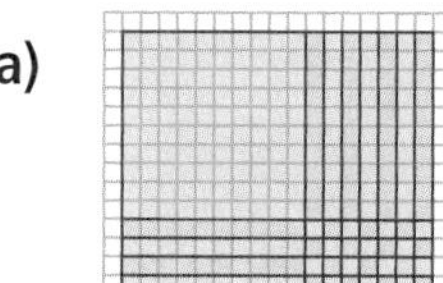

   b) 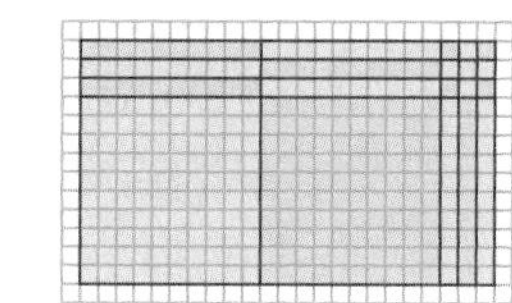

2. Use Base Ten Blocks to find each product.
   a) 2.6×1.5 b) 1.4×2.8 c) 2.7×1.6

3. Use Base Ten Blocks to find each product.
   Record your work on grid paper.
   a) 2.3×0.4 b) 0.6×1.9 c) 0.8×0.7

4. Multiply: 36×24
   Use this to find each product. Explain your work.
   a) 36×2.4 b) 3.6×24 c) 3.6×2.4

5. Multiply.
   a) 4.2×3.7 b) 8.9×0.3 c) 0.6×0.9

6. Carla drives 7.6 km to work. She drives the same distance home. How many kilometres does Carla drive in a 5-day workweek?

7. A rectangular plot of land measures 30.5 m by 5.3 m. What is the area of the plot?

8. a) Multiply.
   i) 6.3×1.8 ii) 4.2×0.7 iii) 0.8×0.5
   b) Look at the questions and products in part a. What patterns do you see in the numbers of decimal places in the question and the product? How could you use this pattern to place the decimal point in a product without estimating?

Calculator Skills

Which is greater in each pair?

0.3 or $\frac{1}{3}$ 0.4 or $\frac{1}{4}$

0.7 or $\frac{2}{3}$ 0.09 or $\frac{1}{11}$

Justify your answer.

9. The product of 2 decimals is 0.36. What might the decimals be? Find as many answers as possible.

10. Recall that dividing by 10 is the same as multiplying by 0.1. Multiply to find:
   a) $\frac{1}{10}$ of 25.2   b) $\frac{2}{10}$ of 37.3   c) $\frac{6}{10}$ of 58.7

11. **Assessment Focus** An area rug is rectangular. Its dimensions are 3.4 m by 2.7 m. Show different strategies you can use to find the area of the rug. Which strategy is best? Justify your answer.

12. a) Find each product.
   i) 4.8×5.3 ii) 4.8×0.6 iii) 0.4×0.6
   b) When you multiply 2 decimals, how does the product compare with the numbers you multiplied? Explain your reasoning.

Take It Further

13. Explain why the sum of the number of digits to the right of the decimal point in the factors of a product equals the number of digits to the right of the decimal point in the product.

Reflect

When you multiply 2 decimals, how do you know where to place the decimal point in the product? Use examples to explain.

4.8 Dividing Decimals

Focus Divide decimals with tenths.

Recall that we can use the same Base Ten Blocks to multiply:

$14 \times 18 = 252$ and $1.4 \times 1.8 = 2.52$

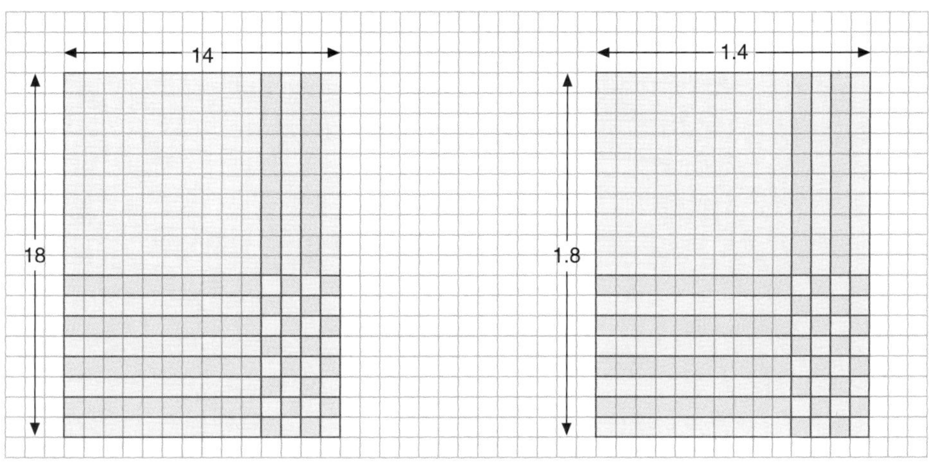

The only difference is the values we assign to the flat, the rod, and the small cube.

In a similar way, we can divide 2 decimals by thinking about whole numbers instead.

So, $252 \div 18 = 14$ and $2.52 \div 1.8 = 1.4$

To divide 2 decimals, ignore the decimal points.
Divide as you would whole numbers, then estimate to place the decimal point in the answer.

Explore

Work with a partner.
Mark bought 19.5 m of fabric to make costumes for a play.
Each costume needs 2.6 m of fabric.
How many costumes can Mark make?
How much material is left over?
Show your work.

Reflect & Share

How did you use division of whole numbers to find your answer?

Connect

Jan bought 18.9 m of framing to make picture frames.
Each picture needs 1.8 m of frame.
How many frames can Jan make?
How much framing material is left over?

When you divide 2 numbers, the answer is the quotient.

To divide: 18.9 ÷ 1.8, ignore the decimal points.
Find 189 ÷ 18, then estimate.

$$\begin{array}{r} 10.5 \\ 18\overline{)189.0} \\ \underline{180} \\ 9\,0 \\ \underline{9\,0} \\ 0 \end{array}$$

189 ÷ 18 = 10.5
Estimate to place the decimal point correctly.
18.9 ÷ 1.8 is about 20 ÷ 2, which is 10.
So, 18.9 ÷ 1.8 is 10.5.

Jan can make 10 frames.
10 frames use 10 × 1.8 m = 18 m.
So, the framing material left is 18.9 m – 18 m = 0.9 m.

Sometimes when we divide 2 decimals, the quotient is not a terminating decimal.

Example

Divide.

a) 12.5 ÷ 0.6

b) 25.2 ÷ 4.7

Solution

a) 12.5 ÷ 0.6

$$6\,\underline{|125.{}^{5}0{}^{2}0{}^{2}0}$$
$$20.\,8\;3\;3$$

Think: Use short division to find 125 ÷ 6.

If we continue to divide, the 3 in the quotient repeats.
So, 125 ÷ 6 = $20.8\overline{3}$
To estimate: 12.5 ÷ 0.6 is about 13 ÷ 1 = 13.
So, the quotient is $20.8\overline{3}$.

b) 25.2 ÷ 4.7 **Think:** Use long division to find 252 ÷ 47.

```
      5.36
47)252.00
   235
    17 0
    14 1
     2 90
     2 82
        8
```

There is 1 decimal place in each number in the question. Continue to divide until there are 2 decimal places in the quotient. That is, calculate the quotient to 1 more decimal place than in the question. Then, round the quotient to 1 decimal place.

Round the quotient to 5.4.
To estimate: 25.2 ÷ 4.7 is about 25 ÷ 5 = 5.
So, the quotient is approximately 5.4.

Practice

1. Look at each division equation on the left.
Use it to write each quotient on the right.

a)	234 ÷ 13 = 18	23.4 ÷ 1.3
b)	133 ÷ 7 = 19	13.3 ÷ 7
c)	714 ÷ 34 = 21	71.4 ÷ 3.4
d)	450 ÷ 18 = 25	4.5 ÷ 1.8
e)	51 ÷ 17 = 3	5.1 ÷ 1.7

Number Strategies

A rectangular prism has dimensions 6 cm by 4 cm by 8 cm. Find the surface area and volume of this rectangular prism.

2. Choose the correct quotient for each division question.
Explain how you know.

Question	Possible Quotients		
a) 5.95 ÷ 3.5	17	1.7	0.17
b) 195.3 ÷ 6.2	315	31.5	3.15
c) 31.32 ÷ 1.8	174	17.4	1.74
d) 1.44 ÷ 0.12	12	1.2	0.12

3. Divide.

a) 8.7 ÷ 0.3 **b)** 2.24 ÷ 0.7 **c)** 10.3 ÷ 0.6

4. Divide.

a) 10.92 ÷ 0.6 **b)** 30.42 ÷ 1.3 **c)** 18.56 ÷ 5.8

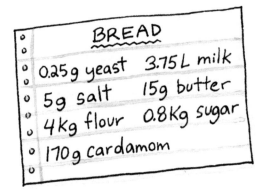

Measurement

The prefixes in units of length less than 1 m show fractions or decimals of 1 m.

One decimetre is $\frac{1}{10}$ or 0.1 m.

One centimetre is $\frac{1}{100}$ or 0.01 m.

One millimetre is $\frac{1}{1000}$ or 0.001 m.

One micrometre is $\frac{1}{1\,000\,000}$ or 0.000 001 m.

5. Divide. Round the quotient to the nearest tenth.

a) 172.5 ÷ 2.6 **b)** 21.68 ÷ 3.4 **c)** 92.8 ÷ 8.2

6. Divide. Round to the nearest tenth where necessary.

a) 7.3 ÷ 0.4 **b)** 1.98 ÷ 1.3 **c)** 426.8 ÷ 3.7

7. The quotient of 2 decimals is 0.12. What might the decimals be? Write as many different possible decimal pairs as you can.

8. **Assessment Focus** Alex finds a remnant of landscaping fabric at a garden store.
The fabric is the standard width, with length 9.7 m.
Alex needs twelve 0.85-m pieces for a garden patio.

a) Will Alex have more fabric than she needs? If so, how much more?

b) Will Alex need more fabric? If so, how much more?

9. The area of a rectangular lawn is 120.4 m^2.
The width is 5.6 m. What is the length?

10. The question 237 ÷ 7 does not have an exact quotient.
The first five digits of the quotient are 33857. The decimal point has been omitted. Use only this information and estimation.
Write an approximate quotient for each question.
Justify each answer.

a) 237 ÷ 0.7 **b)** 2.37 ÷ 7 **c)** 23.7 ÷ 7 **d)** 2370 ÷ 70

BREAD

0.25g yeast 3.75L milk
5g salt 15g butter
4Kg flour 0.8Kg sugar
170g cardamom

11. Here is a recipe for bread.
Sam wants to make one-half the amount.
Find how much of each ingredient Sam needs.

12. Jack has 2.5 L of juice.
Each day, he drinks 0.4 L.
How many days will it take Jack to drink the juice?
Justify your answer.

Reflect

Explain how you decide where to place the decimal point when you divide 2 decimals. Use an example in your explanation.

Advertising Sales Representative

Magazines and newspapers make money by selling advertising space.

The advertising sales representative contacts companies whose products might be of interest to readers. She offers to sell them various sizes of advertisement space at different rates. When talking about ads smaller than a full page, the sales rep uses fractions to describe them. It's much simpler to talk about a $\frac{2}{3}$-page ad instead of a 0.666 667 page ad!

The sales rep tries to sell combinations of ads that can fill pages, with no space left over. A sales rep has sold two $\frac{1}{4}$-page ads and one $\frac{1}{6}$-page ad. She wants to know the possible combinations of ad sizes she can sell to fill the page. What might they be?

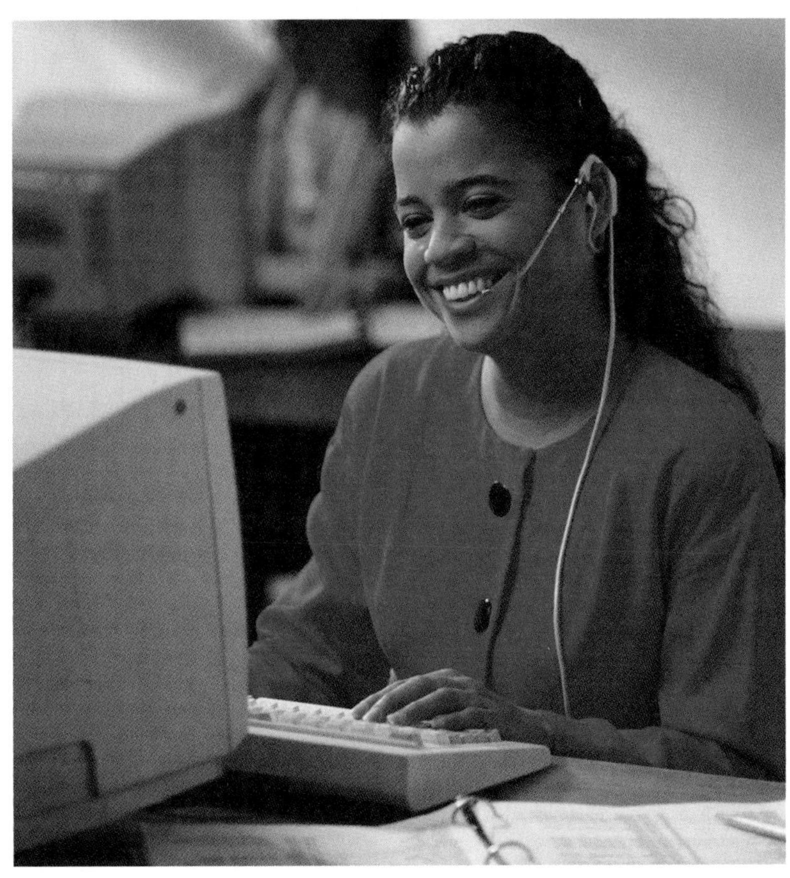

4.9 Order of Operations with Decimals

Focus Use the order of operations to evaluate expressions.

We use a base ten, or decimal, number system.
Every whole number is also a decimal.
So, we use the same order of operations for decimals as for whole numbers.

Explore

Work on your own.
Evaluate this expression: $6 \times (15.9 + 36.4) \div 4$
Explain each step.

Reflect & Share

Compare your solution and answer with that of a classmate.
If your answers are different, who has the correct answer?

Connect

Here is the order of operations.

- Do the operations in brackets first.
- Then divide and multiply, in order, from left to right.
- Then add and subtract, in order, from left to right.

Example

Evaluate. $12.4 - (4.7 + 1) + 2.4 \times 3 - 4.8 \div 2$

Solution

$12.4 - (4.7 + 1) + 2.4 \times 3 - 4.8 \div 2$ **Calculate in brackets.**

$= 12.4 - 5.7 + 2.4 \times 3 - 4.8 \div 2$ **Multiply and divide from left to right.**

$= 12.4 - 5.7 + 7.2 - 2.4$ **Add and subtract from left to right.**

$= 6.7 + 7.2 - 2.4$

$= 13.9 - 2.4$

$= 11.5$

Practice

1. Evaluate.
   a) $3.4 + 4 \times 7$ b) $14 - 2.2 \times 5$ c) $8 - 3.6 \div 2$

2. Evaluate.
   a) $7.4 - 3 + 2.3 \times 4$
   b) $4.6 + 5.1 - 3.2 \div 2$
   c) $16.4 - (10.8 - 3.1)$
   d) $23 \times 6.2 + 4$
   e) $81.2 - (35.8 + 2.1)$
   f) $85.7 \div 0.4 \times 7$

3. Evaluate.
   a) $46.78 - 6.1 \times 2.3$
   b) $75.06 \times (3.45 - 1.2)$
   c) $(98.5 + 7) \div 2.5$
   d) $9.0023 \times 5.1 - 4.32 \times 6$
   e) $8.3 + 46.2 \div 1.4$
   f) $70.56 - 32.8 \div 4.1$

Number Sense

A number cube has faces labelled 1 to 6.

The cube is rolled 75 times.

About how many times will the number 3 show?

4. Evaluate.
   a) $3.2 + 5.6 \times 7.2 \div 2.4 - 9.3$
   b) $8.5 \times 7 - 6.3 \div 9 + 10.6$
   c) $1.35 + (5 \times 4.9 \div 0.7) - 2.7 \times 2.1$
   d) $(4.7 - 3.1) \times 5 - 7.5 \div 2.5$

5. Evaluate.
   a) $164.5 \div 7 \times 10 + 7.2$
   b) $73.8 \times (3.2 + 6.8) - 14.1 \div 0.2$

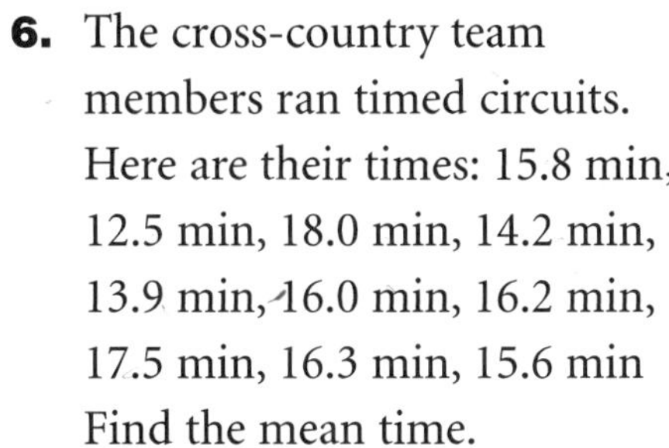

6. The cross-country team members ran timed circuits. Here are their times: 15.8 min, 12.5 min, 18.0 min, 14.2 min, 13.9 min, 16.0 min, 16.2 min, 17.5 min, 16.3 min, 15.6 min
   Find the mean time.

The mean time is the sum of the times divided by the number of times.

7. **Assessment Focus**
   Evaluate. Show all steps.
   $0.38 + 16.2 \times (2.1 + 4) + 21 \div 3.5$

Reflect

Explain why the brackets are unnecessary in this expression:
$(4.2 \times 3.8) - (15.25 \div 6.1)$
Find the answer. Show each step.

Writing a Math Journal Entry

1 THINK about what you did in math.

- Which materials did you use?
- Which problem did you solve?
  How did you solve it?
- What did you learn?
- What are you confused about?
- What vocabulary did you use?
- What was challenging? What was easy?

2 TALK about what you did in math.

- Work with a partner or in a group.
- Share your ideas. Listen to the ideas of others.
- What information did your partner or group share that was new?
- Ask your partner or group members about any issue that was confusing … what did they say?

3 BRAINSTORM all your ideas.

- Make dot jots of the things you discussed and thought about.
  Don't leave anything out … you can edit it later.
- Think about how you can support your written work.
  Use graphs, tables, numbers, symbols, diagrams, and so on.

Reading and Writing in

Math

4 WRITE your ideas.

- Put your thoughts into words.
  Be sure you follow a logical order.
- Think about what you write. Are you using math language? Underline this language.

5 READ your ideas out loud.

- Listen for missing words.
- Be sure your thoughts are in a logical order.
- Add anything that is missing.
- What is unclear? Why? What would help?
- Add graphs, tables, and so on, that will help explain your written work.

6 READ your work to your partner or group.

- Listen to your partner's or group members' ideas.
- Discuss: What was done well?
  What part was not clear?
  What would help improve the journal entry?

7 REVISE and REWRITE.

- Make the changes that are necessary.
- Rewrite on a new piece of paper if necessary.

Unit Review

Review any lesson with

What Do I Need to Know?

Adding and Subtracting Fractions

There are 4 types of fraction questions. Look at the denominators.

✓ **Same denominators**

For example, $\frac{5}{6}$ and $\frac{2}{6}$

$\frac{5}{6} + \frac{2}{6} = \frac{7}{6}$ $\frac{5}{6} - \frac{2}{6} = \frac{3}{6}$

✓ **Related denominators**

For example, $\frac{1}{6}$ and $\frac{1}{12}$

12 is a multiple of 6, so the lowest common denominator is 12.

$\frac{1}{6} = \frac{2}{12}$

$\frac{1}{6} + \frac{1}{12} = \frac{2}{12} + \frac{1}{12} = \frac{3}{12}$ $\frac{1}{6} - \frac{1}{12} = \frac{2}{12} - \frac{1}{12} = \frac{1}{12}$

✓ **Partially related denominators**

For example, $\frac{1}{6}$ and $\frac{1}{9}$

6 and 9 have the common factor, 3.

So, list multiples to find the lowest common denominator.

Multiples of 6: 6, 12, **18**, 24, 30, …

Multiples of 9: 9, **18**, 27, 36, …

The lowest common denominator is 18.

$\frac{1}{6} = \frac{3}{18}$; $\frac{1}{9} = \frac{2}{18}$; $\frac{1}{6} + \frac{1}{9} = \frac{3}{18} + \frac{2}{18} = \frac{5}{18}$; $\frac{1}{6} - \frac{1}{9} = \frac{3}{18} - \frac{2}{18} = \frac{1}{18}$

✓ **Unrelated denominators**

For example, $\frac{1}{5}$ and $\frac{1}{6}$

5 and 6 have no common factors, so the lowest common denominator is their product: $5 \times 6 = 30$

$\frac{1}{5} = \frac{6}{30}$; $\frac{1}{6} = \frac{5}{30}$; $\frac{1}{5} + \frac{1}{6} = \frac{6}{30} + \frac{5}{30} = \frac{11}{30}$; $\frac{1}{5} - \frac{1}{6} = \frac{6}{30} - \frac{5}{30} = \frac{1}{30}$

Multiplying a Fraction by a Whole Number

✓ This is the same as repeatedly adding the same fraction.

$4 \times \frac{3}{5} = \frac{3}{5} + \frac{3}{5} + \frac{3}{5} + \frac{3}{5} = \frac{12}{5}$

What Should I Be Able to Do?

For extra practice, go to page 441.

LESSON

4.1 **1.** Which fraction is greater? How do you know?

a) $\frac{2}{5}, \frac{2}{6}$ b) $\frac{3}{10}, \frac{1}{2}$
c) $\frac{4}{8}, \frac{3}{6}$ d) $\frac{7}{2}, \frac{7}{3}$

2. Add.

a) $\frac{2}{3} + \frac{1}{6}$ b) $\frac{3}{4} + \frac{2}{8}$
c) $\frac{1}{4} + \frac{3}{6}$ d) $\frac{1}{10} + \frac{3}{5}$

3. Find 2 fractions that add to $\frac{5}{8}$. Find as many pairs of fractions as you can.

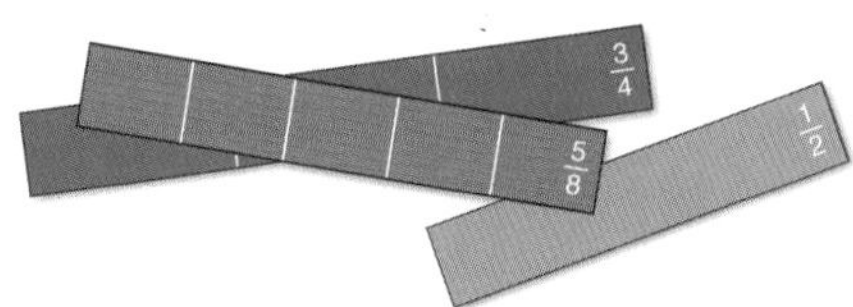

4.2 **4.** Add.

a) $\frac{2}{3} + \frac{5}{6}$ b) $\frac{1}{2} + \frac{3}{4}$
c) $\frac{1}{2} + \frac{9}{10}$ d) $\frac{8}{8} + \frac{1}{4}$

5. Adam eats $\frac{3}{10}$ of a pizza. Julie eats $\frac{2}{5}$ of the pizza.

a) How much of the pizza is eaten?
b) How much is left?

4.3 **6.** Add. Draw a picture to show each sum.

a) $\frac{1}{3} + \frac{2}{5}$ b) $\frac{1}{2} + \frac{3}{8}$
c) $\frac{2}{3} + \frac{3}{10}$ d) $\frac{3}{5} + \frac{1}{4}$

7. Add.

a) $\frac{2}{5} + \frac{5}{6}$ b) $\frac{1}{4} + \frac{2}{5}$
c) $\frac{3}{10} + \frac{5}{6}$ d) $\frac{3}{8} + \frac{2}{3}$

8. Add.

a) $6\frac{1}{3} + 2\frac{1}{3}$ b) $1\frac{5}{12} + 2\frac{1}{6}$
c) $2\frac{3}{10} + 3\frac{1}{5}$ d) $5\frac{1}{4} + 2\frac{2}{5}$

9. Add.

a) $\frac{2}{3} + \frac{3}{4} + \frac{3}{8}$
b) $\frac{5}{2} + \frac{1}{3} + \frac{2}{5}$
c) $\frac{7}{10} + \frac{3}{4} + \frac{5}{8}$

4.4 **10.** Subtract.

a) $\frac{1}{2} - \frac{1}{3}$ b) $\frac{7}{10} - \frac{2}{5}$
c) $\frac{3}{4} - \frac{1}{8}$ d) $\frac{5}{6} - \frac{1}{3}$

11. Find 2 fractions with a difference of $\frac{1}{4}$. Find as many pairs of fractions as you can. Remember to use fractions with different denominators.

4.5 **12.** Ali drank $\frac{3}{4}$ cup of water. Brad drank $\frac{2}{3}$ cup of water.

a) Who drank more water?
b) How much more water did he drink?

13. Subtract.

a) $\frac{9}{10} - \frac{2}{5}$ b) $\frac{7}{3} - \frac{5}{6}$

c) $\frac{8}{5} - \frac{1}{4}$ d) $\frac{9}{4} - \frac{2}{3}$

14. Subtract.

a) $3\frac{3}{4} - 2\frac{1}{8}$ b) $4\frac{4}{5} - 2\frac{2}{3}$

c) $9\frac{1}{2} - 3\frac{1}{3}$ d) $6\frac{3}{4} - 6\frac{1}{5}$

4.6 **15.** Multiply. Draw a picture to show each answer.

a) $\frac{1}{4} \times 7$ b) $8 \times \frac{3}{8}$

c) $6 \times \frac{7}{10}$ d) $\frac{4}{5} \times 5$

16. Sasha had 16 tomatoes in his vegetable garden. He gave: Samira $\frac{1}{8}$ of the tomatoes; Sielen $\frac{1}{8}$ of the tomatoes; and Amina $\frac{1}{4}$ of the tomatoes.

a) What fraction of the tomatoes did Sasha have left?

b) How many tomatoes did Sasha have left?

17. Orit spends $\frac{1}{4}$ of her day at school, $\frac{1}{12}$ of her day playing soccer, and $\frac{1}{3}$ of her day sleeping.
How many hours are left in Orit's day?

4.7 **18.** A rectangular park has dimensions 2.8 km by 1.9 km. What is the area of the park?

4.8 **19.** Nuri has 10.8 L of water. He pours 1.5 L into each of several plastic bottles.

a) How many bottles can Nuri fill?

b) How much water is left over?

20. Delia works at the library after school. She earns \$7.50/h. She usually works 15 h a week.

a) What does Delia earn in a week?
Use estimation to check your answer.

b) One week Delia only works $\frac{1}{2}$ the hours she usually works. What are her earnings that week?

4.9 **21.** Mr. Statler took his class to the local library 4 times last year. One student had a pedometer. She measured the trip as 1.7 km each way.
How far did the students walk back and forth to the library during the year?

22. Evaluate.

a) $5.3 + 5.1 \div 3$

b) $12.6 \times (1.5 + 2.5)$

c) $68.9 - 32.7 \times 2$

23. Evaluate.

a) $5.9 + 3.7 \times 2.8 - 1.5 \div 0.5$

b) $3.4 \times 1.9 \div 1.7 + 7.2 \div 1.2$

Practice Test

1. Add or subtract.

a) $\frac{5}{4} + \frac{3}{8}$ **b)** $\frac{3}{2} - \frac{3}{5}$ **c)** $\frac{11}{12} - \frac{2}{3}$ **d)** $\frac{4}{9} + \frac{7}{6}$

2. a) Find three pairs of fractions that have a sum of $\frac{3}{5}$.

b) Find three pairs of fractions that have a difference of $\frac{1}{5}$.

3. Add or subtract.

a) $6\frac{3}{8} - 2\frac{1}{5}$ **b)** $4\frac{1}{4} + 2\frac{2}{3}$

4. Lana does yard work. The table shows the approximate time for each job.

Job	Time
Mow small lawn	$\frac{1}{2}$ h
Mow large lawn	$\frac{3}{4}$ h
Mow lawn/tidy yard	$1\frac{1}{2}$ h
Plant annuals	$2\frac{1}{2}$ h

For one Saturday, Lana has these jobs:
– mow 3 small lawns
– mow 1 large lawn
– mow lawn/tidy yard in 2 places
– plant annuals in 1 place

Lana needs travel time between jobs, and a break for lunch. Do you think she will be able to do all the jobs? Justify your answer.

5. a) Evaluate.

i) $\frac{3}{4} + \frac{3}{4} + \frac{3}{4} + \frac{3}{4} + \frac{3}{4} + \frac{3}{4}$ **ii)** $7 \times \frac{2}{3}$ **iii)** $\frac{7}{8} \times 8$

b) Convert each answer in part a to a decimal.

c) Order the decimals from least to greatest.

6. A 6-kg bag of fertilizer covers a rectangular area of 2.5 m by 5.0 m.

a) How many bags of fertilizer are needed for a rectangular lawn measuring 7.5 m by 10.2 m?

b) A 6-kg bag of fertilizer costs $15.50. How much does it cost to fertilize the lawn?

7. Evaluate. Explain each step.

$12.4 \times (2.9 + 4.6) + 23.7 \div 2.4$

Unit Problem Publishing a Book

The students at Garden Avenue School are preparing a special book for the school's 100th anniversary. They finance the book by selling advertising space to sponsors.

The students sold the following space:

Full page	$\frac{1}{2}$ page	$\frac{1}{3}$ page	$\frac{1}{4}$ page	$\frac{1}{6}$ page	$\frac{1}{8}$ page
1	1	1	3	4	5

All the advertisements are to fit at the back of the book.

Sam asks: "How many pages do we need for the advertisements?"
Mara asks: "Will the advertisements fill the pages?"
Kathleen asks: "Is there more than one way to arrange these advertisements?"
Can you think of other questions students might ask?

1. Find the total advertising space needed.

2. Sketch the pages to find how the advertisements can be placed. Use grid paper if it helps.

3. Compare your group's sketch with those of other groups. When you made your sketch, what decisions did you make about the shape of each advertisement? Did other groups make the same decisions? Explain.

4. What are the fewest pages needed to display the advertisements? Will there be room for any other advertisements? Explain.

5. What else might students need to consider as they prepare the layout for the book?

Here are the fees for the advertisements.

Size	Full page	$\frac{1}{2}$ page	$\frac{1}{3}$ page	$\frac{1}{4}$ page	$\frac{1}{6}$ page	$\frac{1}{8}$ page
Cost ($)	500	360	250	200	150	100

6. How much money will students get from the advertisers?

7. Students will do the layout on computer. The cost to copy and bind 500 books is $4750. Use the income from question 6.
   a) What do the students have to charge per book so they do not incur a loss? Justify your answer.
   b) The students cannot print fewer than 500 books. What if they can sell only 350 books? What do the students have to charge per book so they do not incur a loss? Justify your answer.
   c) What if the students decide to charge $5 per book? How many books do the students need to sell so they do not incur a loss? Justify your answer.

Check List

Your work should show:

- ✓ all calculations in detail
- ✓ diagrams of the layout for the advertisements
- ✓ a clear explanation of how you prepared the layout
- ✓ a clear explanation of how students do not incur losses

Reflect on the Unit

Choose one operation with fractions and a different operation with decimals. Write an example that illustrates how to carry out each operation.

Units 1–4 Cumulative Review

UNIT

1

1. Find the number that is:

- a factor of 1000
- not a factor of 100
- a multiple of 5
- has fewer than 3 digits

Explain how you found the number.

2. A rectangular pen is built with 60 m of fencing.
The length of each side of the pen is a whole number of metres.

a) Which dimensions are possible? Make an organized list of your answers.

b) What are the dimensions of the pen with the greatest area? Explain.

3. The number 49 is a perfect square. It can be written as 7^2.
Some numbers that are not perfect squares can be written as the sum of a perfect square and a prime number.
For example: $21 = 4^2 + 5$

a) Find all the numbers between 40 and 50 that can be written this way.

b) Which numbers in part a can be written more than one way? Show each new way.

4. Write the next 3 terms in each pattern. Describe each pattern.

a) 49, 36, 25, 16, . . .

b) 3, 7, 15, 31, . . .

c) 6, 36, 216, 1296, . . .

2

5. Write each ratio in simplest form.

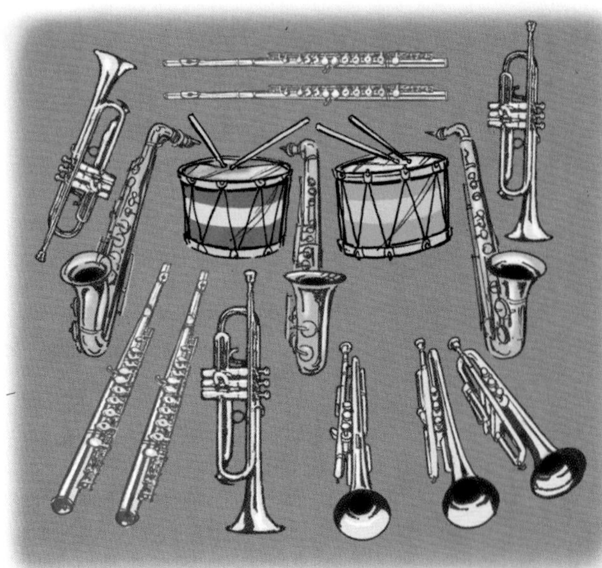

a) saxophones to trumpets

b) drums to flutes

c) saxophones to total number of instruments

6. The ratio of the number of hits to the times at bat for three baseball players is:
Irina, 3:5; Juana, 2:3; Carla, 3:4

a) Who has the best record?

b) Who had the least success?

Explain your answers.

7. The ratio of boys to girls in the sailing club is 4:5.

a) There are 15 girls in the club. How many boys are in the club?

b) What if 3 boys leave the club? What is the new ratio of girls to boys?

UNIT

3 **8.** Identify the view (front, back, side, or top) and the object on each sign. Then draw a different view of that object.

a) Post office

b) Picnic area

c) Microwave oven

9. Find the surface area of each rectangular prism.

a)

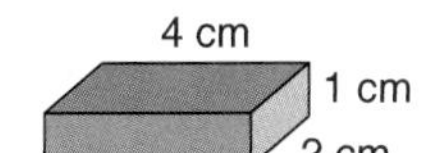

b)

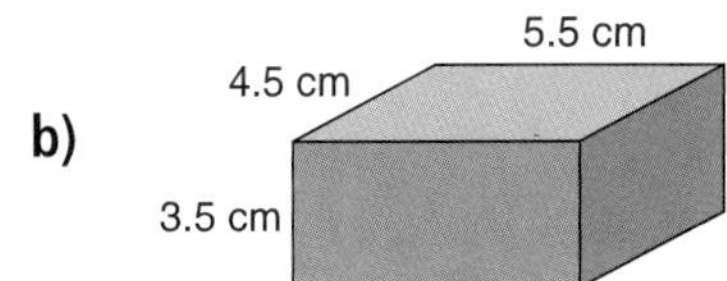

c)

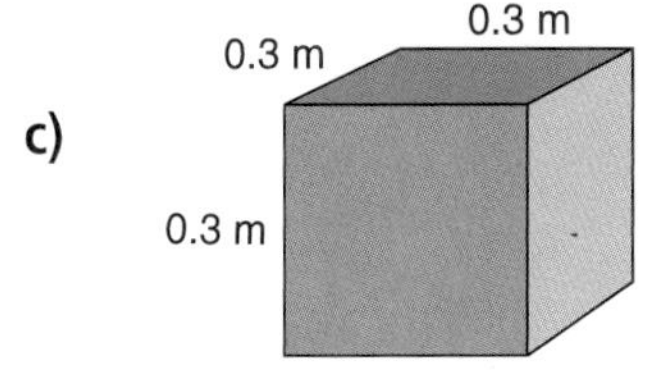

10. Use a large copy of this net.

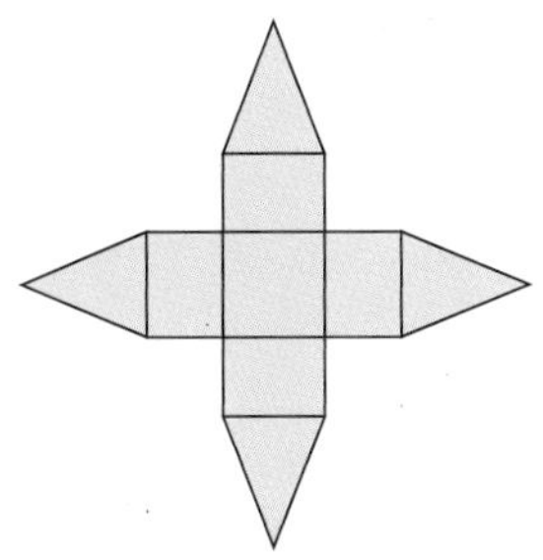

a) Fold the net to make an object.

b) Sketch the front, back, side, and top view of the object.

4 **11.** Use fraction strips, number lines, or another model to add or subtract.

a) $\frac{3}{8} + \frac{3}{2}$ b) $\frac{2}{3} + \frac{1}{4}$

c) $\frac{7}{5} - \frac{1}{2}$ d) $\frac{11}{6} - \frac{4}{3}$

12. Skylar and Riley work together on a project.
Skylar does $\frac{3}{10}$ of the work.
Riley does $\frac{2}{5}$ of the work.

a) Who does more work? How much more does this person do?

b) What fraction of the project has yet to be done?

13. Multiply. Draw a picture to show each answer.

a) $4 \times \frac{5}{8}$ b) $\frac{3}{5} \times 5$

c) $3 \times \frac{3}{10}$ d) $5 \times \frac{5}{4}$

14. Multiply.
Record your work on grid paper.

a) 3.5×2.1 b) 0.8×1.2

15. The area of a rectangle is $7.35\ m^2$.
The width is 2.1 m.
What is the length?

16. Evaluate.

a) $1.25 + 3.6 \times 2.4 \div 1.2$

b) $10.5 \div 1.5 - 2.8 \times 0.3$

c) $10.1 - 4.5 \div 0.5 + 7.5$

d) $(10.1 - 4.5) \div (0.5 + 7.5)$

Why are the answers to parts c and d different?

UNIT

5 Data Management

David and his friend surveyed their classmates. They wanted to find out which outdoor winter activities the students participated in. They recorded the results in a tally chart.

Outdoor Winter Activities

Activity	Tally
Skating	𝍸 𝍸 𝍸 𝍸 ||||
Skiing	𝍸 𝍸 𝍸
Snowboarding	𝍸 𝍸 ||
Tobogganing	𝍸 𝍸 𝍸 𝍸 𝍸 𝍸

- What survey question might the students have asked to get the data in the chart?
- How could you graph the data?
- Which graph is most suitable for the data?

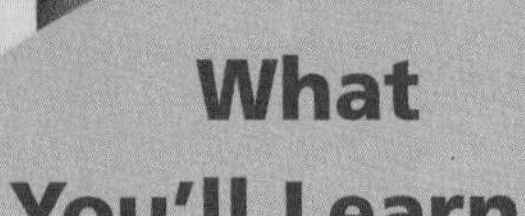

What You'll Learn

- Collect and organize data on tally charts and stem-and-leaf plots.
- Display data on frequency tables, bar graphs, pictographs, line graphs, and circle graphs.
- Describe and evaluate data presented on charts, tables, and graphs, and solve related problems.
- Use databases and spreadsheets.
- Calculate and use mean, median, and mode.
- Identify and describe trends in graphs.
- Use technology to draw graphs.

Why It's Important

- You see data and their interpretations in newspapers, magazines, and on TV. You need to understand how to interpret these data.

Key Words

- mean
- median
- mode
- primary data
- secondary data
- biased
- database
- fields
- Statistics Canada (Stats Can)
- frequency table
- stem-and-leaf plot
- cluster
- trend
- line graph
- spreadsheet

UNIT 5

Skills You'll Need

Calculating Mean, Median, and Mode

For any set of numbers:

- The **mean** is the sum of all the numbers divided by the number of numbers.
- The **median** is the middle number when the numbers are arranged in order. When there is an even number of numbers, the median is the mean of the two middle numbers. Half the numbers are above the median and half are below.
- The **mode** is the number that occurs most often. There may be more than one mode. There may be no mode.

Example

Calculate the mean, median, and mode of these numbers:
7, 13, 10, 12, 14, 8, 9, 7, 11, 6

Solution

There are 10 numbers in the set.

- For the mean, add the numbers, then divide by 10.

$$\text{Mean: } \frac{7 + 13 + 10 + 12 + 14 + 8 + 9 + 7 + 11 + 6}{10} = \frac{97}{10} = 9.7$$

- For the median, arrange the numbers in order, beginning with the least number. The median is the middle number. Since there are 10 numbers, the median is the mean of the two middle numbers. For 10 numbers in order, the first middle number is $\frac{10}{2} = 5$, or the 5th number. The next middle number is the 6th number.

  6, 7, 7, 8, 9, 10, 11, 12, 13, 14

  Median: $\frac{9 + 10}{2} = \frac{19}{2}$, or 9.5

- The mode is the number that occurs most often. The mode is 7.

✓ Check

1. Calculate the mean, median, and mode for the numbers in each set.

a) 3, 9, 5, 8, 2, 0, 9, 5

b) 25, 24, 55, 30, 44, 21, 17, 19, 21

c) 14, 18, 16, 12, 11, 16

d) 76, 81, 50, 64, 67, 69, 72, 94, 81, 76

5.1 Collecting Data

Focus Analyse data collection and possible bias.

Electronic games are popular among Grade 7 students.
Which electronic game do you think Grade 7 students in your class like to play?
How could you find out?

Explore

Work in a group.
Which electronic game is most popular in your class?
Conduct a survey to find out.
What survey question will you ask? Record your results.

Reflect & Share

Compare your results with those of another group.
How did the survey question affect the results?

Connect

Mia wanted to find out the favourite singer of her classmates.
She conducted a survey. She asked this question:

"Who is your favourite singer: Bryan Adams ____, Susan Aglukark ____, Celine Dion ____, Sam Roberts ____, Shania Twain ____, or Other ____?"

Mia recorded the results in a tally chart.

Singer	Number of Students
Bryan Adams	~~||||~~
Susan Aglukark	~~||||~~
Celine Dion	~~||||~~ //
Sam Roberts	///
Shania Twain	//
Other	~~||||~~ ~~||||~~ /

Mia concluded that Celine Dion was the most popular singer of those named.
However, if all the votes in the "Other" category were for the same person, then that person would be the most popular.

The word "data" is plural. So, we say "The data are ..." A single piece of information is called "datum."

Since Mia collected the data herself, they are called **primary data**.
Data that are found from the library or using the Internet are called **secondary data**.

It is important that a survey is conducted and data are collected in a fair way. Sometimes, the way a question is asked or written might persuade a person to answer a certain way. This type of question is **biased**. A survey question must be unbiased. That is, the question must not lead a person toward a particular answer.

Example

How is each survey question biased?
Rewrite the question so it is unbiased.

a) "Many students are bored at the end of August.
Should the school year be longer?
Yes _______ No _______"

b) "Some people get sick after visiting patients in a hospital.
Do you think patients in a hospital should have visitors?
Yes _______ No _______ No Opinion _______"

Solution

a) The question includes a statement about how some students feel.
This may encourage more people to answer "Yes."
An unbiased survey question is:
"The school year is 10 months long. Should it be longer?
Yes ________ No _______"

b) The question includes a statement that may encourage people to answer "No."
An unbiased survey question is:
"Should patients in a hospital have visitors?
Yes _______ No ________ No Opinion _______"

Practice

1. Are primary data or secondary data collected in each situation?
How do you know?
a) Elly used an encyclopedia to find the area of each continent.
b) Jason read the thermometer to find the outside temperature.
c) Jane looked in the newspaper to see which NHL team won the game.

2. Would you use primary or secondary data in each case? Explain.
   a) To find the favourite car model in Canada
   b) To find the favourite juice of Grade 7 students in your school
   c) To find the favourite song of Grade 7 students in Ontario
   d) To find the most popular type of transport used by students in your school

3. Biased data are unreliable. Yet, sometimes people use biased data. Why do people use biased data?

4. Think of a survey you could conduct in your school.
   a) Write a biased survey question.
   b) Write an unbiased survey question.

5. Comment on each survey question.
   If it is biased, write an unbiased question.
   a) "Sugar is bad for your teeth. Should children eat candy?
      Yes _______ No _______ No Opinion _______"
   b) "Children prefer snowboarding to skiing.
      Which do you think is more fun?
      Snowboarding _______ Skiing _______"

Number Strategies

How are these two patterns related?

- 0.75, 1.5, 3, 6, . . .
- 96, 192, 384, 768, . . .

6. **Assessment Focus** Suppose a person intends to open a shoe store in the local mall.
   The person is unsure of the style or make of shoes to stock.
   What questions should the person ask to make the best decision?
   Explain what role a survey might play in the decision.

7. a) Predict the favourite hobby or pastime of your classmates.
   b) Write a survey question you could ask to find out.
      Explain how you know your question is unbiased.
   c) Conduct the survey. Tally the results.
   d) How did your prediction compare with your results?

Reflect

Why is it important that a survey question is unbiased?

Using Databases to Find Data

Focus Search databases for information.

A **database** is an organized collection of data.
Examples of databases include a telephone book, a dictionary, an encyclopedia, or a library catalogue.

A database is organized into **fields**. Each field contains specific information. In a library database, a book may be stored with information in each of these fields: title, author, publisher, subject, ISBN (international standard book number), or Dewey decimal number.

Statistics Canada (Stats Can) is the federal government department that collects, analyses, and stores data about Canada and Canadians. Two of its Internet databases are **CANSIM** (**Can**adian **S**ocio-economic **I**nformation **M**anagement System) and **E-STAT**.

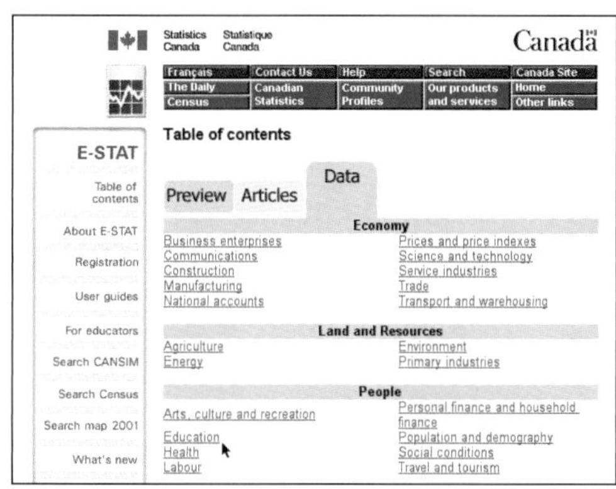

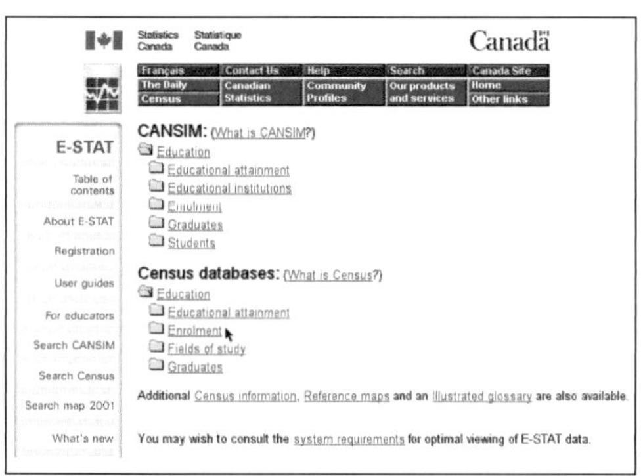

Stats Can charges a fee for some of its data on CANSIM, but all data are transferred to E-STAT once a year in the summer.
E-STAT is a free database for teachers and students. Your teacher will give you the website addresses for these databases.

To use E-STAT to find data on school attendance for 15- to 24-year-olds, follow these steps:

1. Open the E-STAT Website.
   You may be asked for your username and password. Ask your teacher for these.

2. Click the "Data" tab. Click "Education," as shown above left.

3. Under Census databases, click "Enrolment," as shown below left.

4. Under 2001 Census of Population (Provinces, Census Divisions, Municipalities), click "2001 School Attendance, Education, Field of Study, Highest Level of Schooling and Earnings," as shown below left.

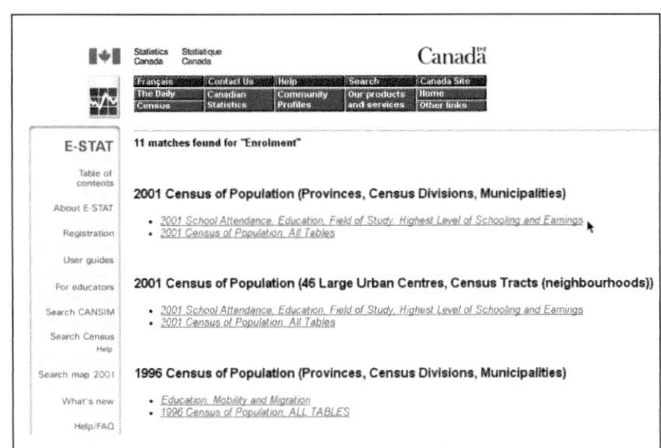

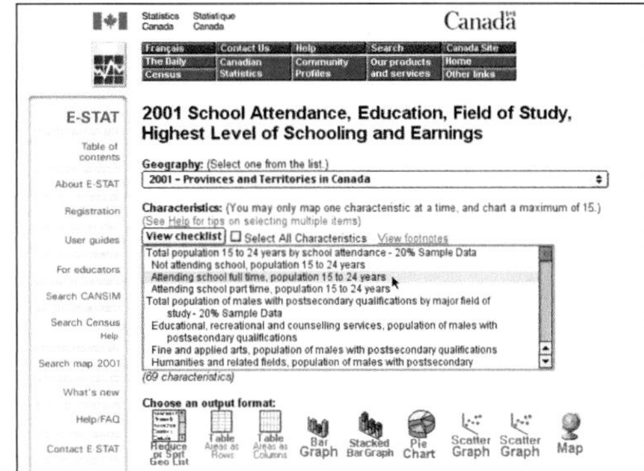

5. Click "Attending school, full time, population 15 to 24 years," as shown above right.

6. Choose an output format. For data in a table arranged in rows, click "Table Areas as Rows," as shown below left. The data are displayed as shown below right.

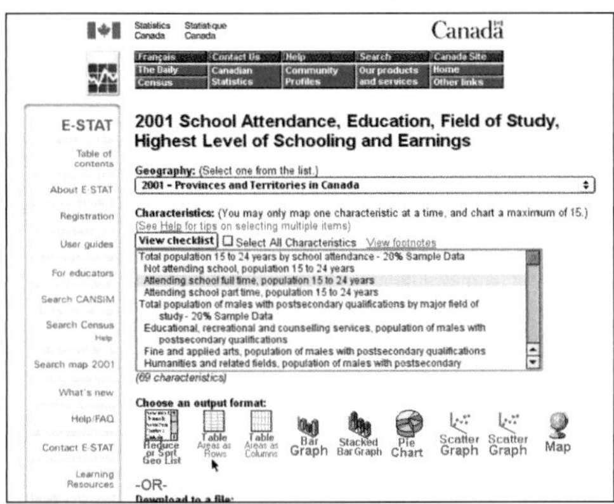

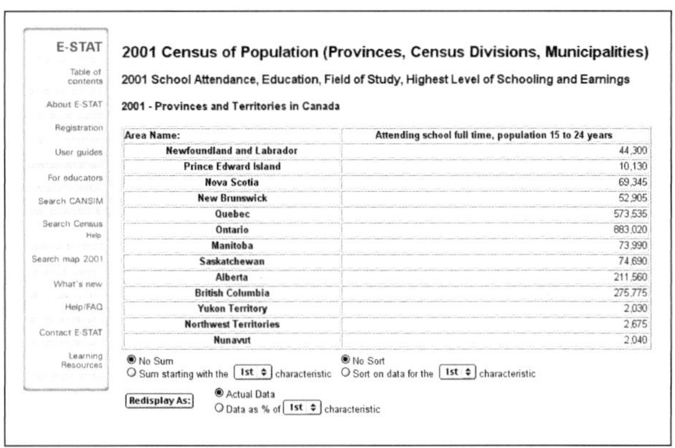
2001 Census of Population (Provinces, Census Divisions, Municipalities)

2001 School Attendance, Education, Field of Study, Highest Level of Schooling and Earnings

2001 - Provinces and Territories in Canada

Area Name:	Attending school full time, population 15 to 24 years
Newfoundland and Labrador	44 300
Prince Edward Island	10 130
Nova Scotia	69 345
New Brunswick	52 905
Quebec	573 535
Ontario	883 020
Manitoba	73 990
Saskatchewan	74 690
Alberta	211 560
British Columbia	275 775
Yukon Territory	2 030
Northwest Territories	2 675
Nunavut	2 040

1. Use E-STAT or another database.
Research one of the topics below. Print your data.
Be sure to state your source.
   - The number of Canadians who had a particular type of occupation at the time of the 1911 Census
   - The top 10 movies of the year
   - The top 10 music CDs of the year
   - A topic of your choice

   Write 3 things you know from looking at the data.

5.2 Recording Data

Focus Record data in tables, bar graphs, and pictographs.

Explore

Work on your own.
Use a novel you are currently reading.
Open it to any page.

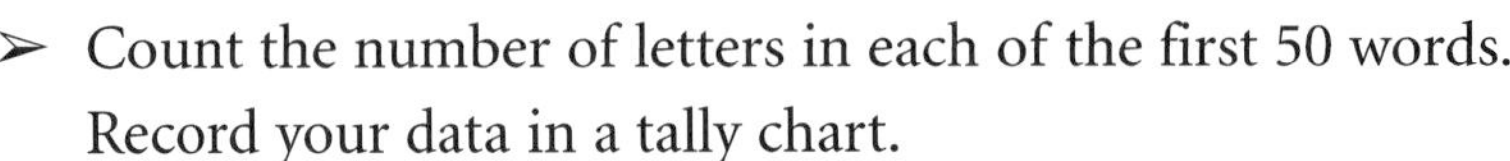

➢ Count the number of letters in each of the first 50 words.
Record your data in a tally chart.

Number of Letters	Tally of Number of Words
1	
2	
3	
4	

➢ Graph your data. Justify your choice of graph.
➢ Which is the most common length of word?
➢ Who might be interested in these data?

Reflect & Share

Compare your most common length of word with that of a classmate. Should the lengths be the same? Explain.

Connect

Data can be organized in a tally chart or **frequency table**.
A frequency table is a tally chart with an extra column.

Andrew recorded the different birds that visited his feeder one morning.

Birds at the Feeder		
Bird	Tally	Frequency
Blue jay	𝍸	5
Cardinal	////	4
Sparrow	𝍸 𝍸 𝍸 //	17
Robin	𝍸 𝍸 /	11
Chickadee	𝍸 //	7

To fill in the *Frequency* column, Andrew counted the tallies for each bird.
He graphed the data using a pictograph.
Andrew chose a key of 1 symbol represents 2 birds.

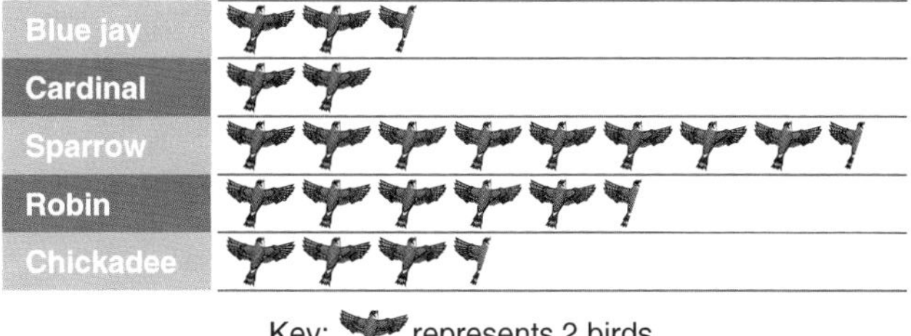

Example

a) Construct a bar graph of Andrew's data.

b) Compare the graph and tally chart.
How are they alike?

Solution

a) Construct a bar graph, below left.
One square represents 2 birds.

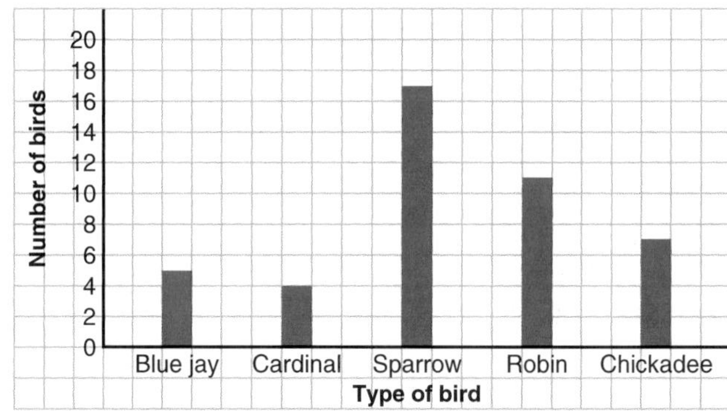

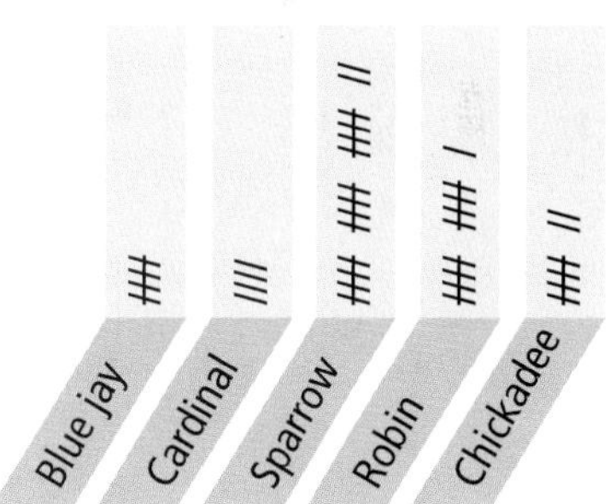

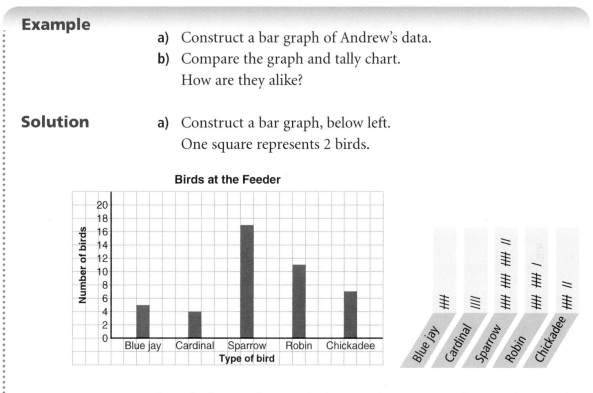

b) The longest bar on the bar graph represents the same bird as the longest row on the tally chart.
When we rotate the *Tally* column $\frac{1}{4}$ turn counterclockwise, above right, its shape matches that of the bar graph, above left.

Practice

Favourite Canadian Hockey Team		
Hockey Team	**Tally**	**Frequency**
Calgary Flames	𝍸 ///	
Edmonton Oilers	𝍸 /	
Montreal Canadiens	𝍸	
Ottawa Senators	𝍸	
Toronto Maple Leafs	𝍸 𝍸	
Vancouver Canucks	𝍸 /	

Rolling a Number Cube		
Number	**Tally**	**Frequency**
1		
2		
3		

1. The table shows the favourite Canadian hockey teams of some Grade 7 students at Hamilton Junior High School.

a) Write the frequency of each team.

b) How many students were surveyed?

c) Which team is the most popular among the sample? The least popular? Give some possible reasons for these results.

2. Work with a partner. You will need a number cube labelled 1 to 6.

a) Roll the number cube 50 times. Make a table. Record the frequency of each number.

b) Predict the results if you were to roll the number cube 50 more times. Justify your answer.

c) Compare your results with those of another pair of students. If they are different, explain why.

d) Graph your data. Justify your choice of graph.

3. This pictograph displays the results of a survey.

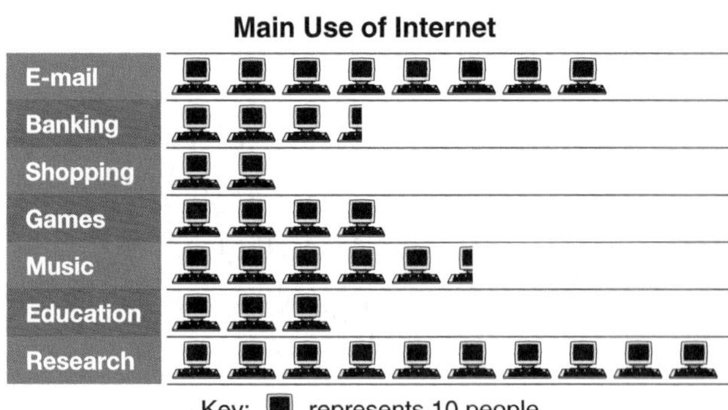

a) What do you think the survey question was? Explain.

b) How many people were surveyed?

c) How would the pictograph change if 💻 represented 1 person? 50 people?

d) Draw a bar graph to display these data.

e) Is a bar graph better than a pictograph to display the data? Explain.

f) Write a question you could answer using the pictograph or bar graph. Answer the question.

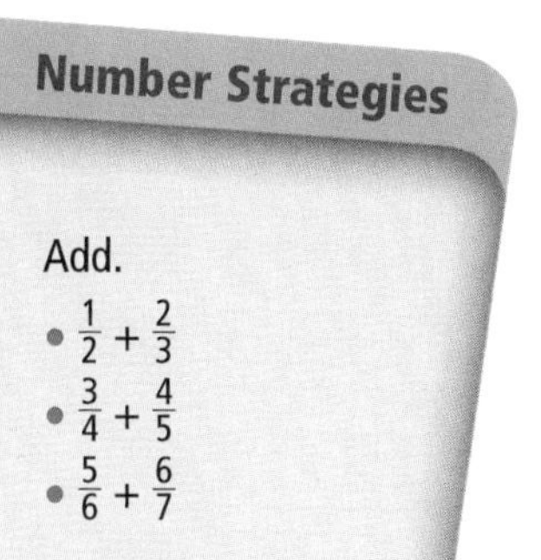

4. This is a double-bar graph.

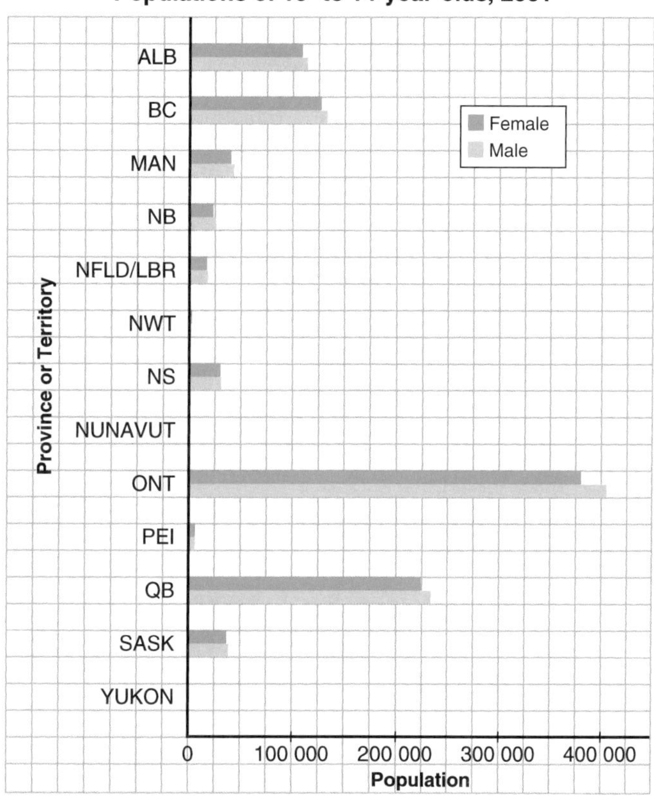

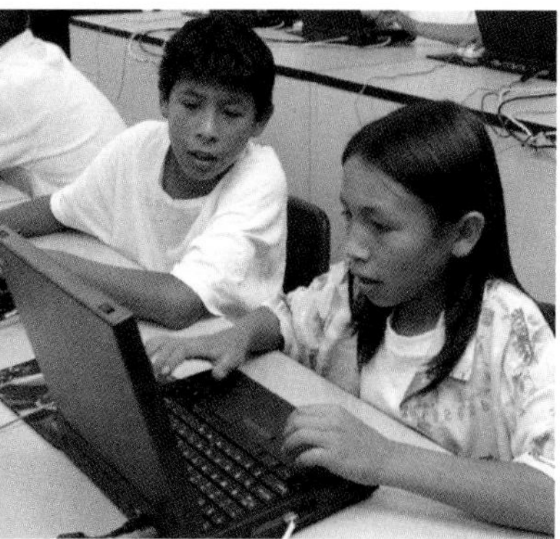

a) How is this bar graph different from the others in this lesson?

b) How does the female population compare with the male population?

c) Which province(s) have approximately the same number of 10- to 14-year-old females as males?

d) Here are the data for the 3 territories.

	Nunavut	Northwest Territories	Yukon
Females	1550	1725	1090
Males	1685	1785	1225

Why are there no bars on the graph for Nunavut and Yukon?

e) Could you use a pictograph to display the data in the double-bar graph? Explain.

5. Use an atlas or an almanac.
   a) Choose 5 cities in Canada.
   b) Choose a recent year.
   Find the population of each city in that year.
   c) Record the data in a table.
   d) Graph the data. Justify your choice of graph.
   e) What do you know from looking at the data?

6. **Assessment Focus**
   a) Suppose you want to find out how your classmates spend their money. Write a question you could use to survey your classmates.
   b) Conduct the survey. Record the data in a frequency table.
   c) Graph the data. Justify your choice of graph.
   d) What do most of your classmates spend their money on?
   e) Use the graph to write 3 other things you know about how your classmates spend their money.

Spelling Mistakes

4 7 9 2 1 0 6 5 8 10 7
3 2 12 8 11 3 4 8 4 5
8 15 9 6 2 1 0 17 19
16 3 11 5 10 7 3 7 1 9
10 3 5 8 6 13 8 2 4 6
18 19 5 20 0 1 8 10 3

The interval is 3 because the numbers of mistakes are counted in groups of 3.

7. Two classes of Grade 7 students took a spelling test. The number of words each student misspelled is recorded at the left.

Number of Mistakes	Tally	Frequency
0 – 2		
3 – 5		

   a) Copy the frequency table. Continue the pattern of the intervals in the 1st column to 18–20.
   Complete the 2nd and 3rd columns in the frequency table.
   b) Graph the data.

Reflect

When is a pictograph more appropriate than a bar graph?
When is a bar graph more appropriate than a pictograph?
Give examples.

5.3 Stem-and-Leaf Plots

Focus Display data on a stem-and-leaf plot.

The data, and **stem-and-leaf plot**,
show science test scores for a Grade 7 class.
How are the two displays related?
What can you see in the stem-and-leaf plot that you cannot see in the chart?

Science Test Scores

64	75	89	99	58	53	69
66	72	81	88	67	75	86
52	97	77	75	57	61	85
94	72	81	65	78	81	93

Science Test Scores

Stem	Leaf
5	2 3 7 8
6	1 4 5 6 7 9
7	2 2 5 5 5 7 8
8	1 1 1 5 6 8 9
9	3 4 7 9

This is a stem-and-leaf plot.

Explore

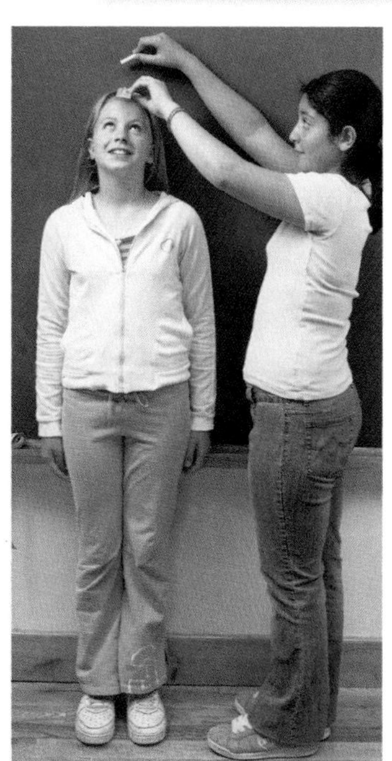

Work with a partner.
You will need a metre stick or a tape measure.
Measure each other's height in centimetres.
Write it on the board.
Use the data for the whole class.
Draw a stem-and-leaf plot to show the heights, in centimetres, of your classmates.

- ➢ Are any students the same height?
- ➢ Which is the shortest height? The tallest?
- ➢ What is the median height?
- ➢ What is the mode height?
- ➢ What else do you know from looking at the stem-and-leaf plot?

Reflect & Share

Compare your stem-and-leaf plot with that of another pair of classmates. Do your plots match?
If you answer no, how are they different?

Connect

Here are the numbers of books students in one Grade 7 class read in one year.
Each number is the number of books one student read.

Books Read in One Year

23	19	43	12	16	18	31	17
15	23	27	18	13	16	24	10
16	15	29	25	33	42	20	24
17	38	36	11	26	31	32	19

We can make a stem-and-leaf plot from these data.

- The least number of books is 10. The greatest number is 43. Students read between 10 and 43 books.
  Write the tens digits 1 to 4 in a column.
  These are the **stems.**

Books Read in One Year

Stem	Leaf
1	0 1 2 3 5 5 6 6 6 7 7 8 8 9 9
2	0 3 3 4 4 5 6 7 9
3	1 1 2 3 6 8
4	2 3

In a stem-and-leaf plot, the leaves are always numbers from 0 to 9.

- Start with the least number, 10.
  Write 0 as the **leaf** next to the stem, 1.
  Continue with the next greatest number, 11.
  Write 1 as the next leaf.
  Continue in this way.
  Record all the leaves in order from the least number to the greatest number.
- Write a title for the plot.

Example

Here are the heights, in centimetres, of the members of St. Mark's junior football team.

a) What is the range of the heights of the football players?
b) Draw a stem-and-leaf plot for the data.
c) What is the median height?
d) What is the mode height?

Heights of Football Players in Centimetres

147	153	162	171	159	168	145	183	164
187	153	164	148	164	167	187	179	
148	190	188	173	155	177	176	189	192

Solution

a) The least height is 145 cm.
The greatest height is 192 cm.
The range is 192 cm – 145 cm = 47 cm.

b) Each number has 3 digits, so the stem will be the hundreds and tens digits.
The leaf will be the ones digit.
The stems are from 14 to 19.
Start with the least number, 145.
Write the leaf, 5, next to the stem, 14.
Continue to write the leaves, from the least number to the greatest number.

Heights of Football Players in Centimetres

Stem	Leaf
14	5 7 8 8
15	3 3 5 9
16	2 4 4 4 7 8
17	1 3 6 7 9
18	3 7 7 8 9
19	0 2

c) There are 26 numbers.
This is an even number.
The median is the mean of the two middle numbers when the numbers are arranged in order.
For 26 numbers in order, the first middle number is $\frac{26}{2} = 13$,
or the 13th number.
The next middle number is the 14th number.
Count the leaves, beginning at 5.
The 13th and 14th numbers are 167 and 168.

Heights of Football Players in Centimetres

Stem	Leaf
14	5 7 8 8
15	3 3 5 9
16	2 4 4 4 **7 8**
17	1 3 6 7 9
18	3 7 7 8 9
19	0 2

The median is: $\frac{167 + 168}{2} = 167.5$
The median height is 167.5 cm.

d) The mode is the number that occurs most often.
Leaf 4 occurs three times next to stem 16.
The mode is 164 cm.

The *Example* shows that, when the data are displayed in a stem-and-leaf plot, the range, the median, and the mode can be found from the plot.
When you organize data in a stem-and-leaf plot, the original data are visible. A frequency table only shows how many numbers are in each group, and not what the numbers are.

Practice

Hours Worked by Part-Time Staff at a Video Store in One Month

Stem	Leaf
9	1 6 9
10	2 5 6 8
11	0 3 4 4 4 7
12	0 1 2 2 5 6 6 8 9
13	2 3 5 6 7 7 7 7 8 9 9

1. a) What does this stem-and-leaf plot show?
b) How many part-time employees work at the video store?
c) What is the least number of hours worked? The greatest number of hours worked?
d) What is the range of hours worked?
e) What is the median number of hours worked?
f) What is the mode number of hours worked?

2. The masses of parcels, in kilograms, are given.

Masses in Kilograms

28	32	40	36	31
40	48	35	38	34
43	35	41	36	52
37	47	29	42	35
33	39	32	48	37
38	30	35	44	54

a) Display the data in a stem-and-leaf plot.
b) Find the greatest mass. The least mass.
c) What is the range of masses?
d) What is the median mass?
e) What is the mode mass?

3. Which type of data cannot be shown in a stem-and-leaf plot? Explain.

4. Work with a partner. Use a metre stick to measure each other's stride, to the nearest centimetre. Record the measures on the board. Use the measures for the whole class.
a) Make a stem-and-leaf plot.
b) What did you find out about the strides of your classmates? Write down as much as you can.

5. A food manufacturer claims:
"We guarantee an average of 50 g of peanuts per bag."
In 6 months, Devon found the masses of peanuts, in grams, in 24 bags. Look at the data.

Masses of Peanuts in Grams

50.1, 49.9, 49.0, 48.9,
50.8, 50.3, 51.3, 49.8,
48.8, 49.0, 50.3, 51.2,
49.4, 49.0, 48.1, 49.6,
49.8, 51.3, 50.5, 50.7,
48.7, 51.0, 49.3, 52.5

a) Is the food manufacturer's claim true?
b) How could you use a stem-and-leaf plot to justify your answer?

Calculator Skills

Find two numbers with a difference of 2.75 and a product of 60.125.

6. **Assessment Focus**
   a) Collect data on the points scored by a basketball team in its last 15 games. The points could be from games played by your school team or a professional team.
   b) Make a stem-and-leaf plot.
   c) Write 3 things you know from looking at the plot.

Reflect

Explain why it is easier to read data in a stem-and-leaf plot than data in a table.

The World of Work

Meteorologist

A meteorologist is often a specialist. She uses data collection tools suitable for the weather condition being studied. The data collected are pooled nationally and internationally, and studied by a variety of meteorologists and others in related fields. The information and analysis produce severe weather alerts, which can save thousands of lives.

We may not experience surviving a tornado or a hurricane. But there are other weather conditions that are just as destructive.
On January 6, 1998, a severe ice-storm hit Quebec, eastern Ontario, and northeastern U.S. Many people called it the largest ecological disaster in the history of Quebec. On February 6, 1998, Quebec was restored to some normalcy.

When was the last time you heard a "severe weather warning"?
Was the prediction correct?
What kinds of data management tools might have been used to predict this event?

Mid-Unit Review

LESSON

5.1 **1.** A survey was conducted to decide if a new hockey arena should be built. The question was, "We have one hockey arena that is always in use. Do we need a new hockey arena?
Yes _____ No _____"

a) Is the question biased? Explain.

b) If your answer to part a is yes, rewrite the question so it is not biased.

5.2 **2.** The pictograph shows the types of movies rented from a video store in one day.

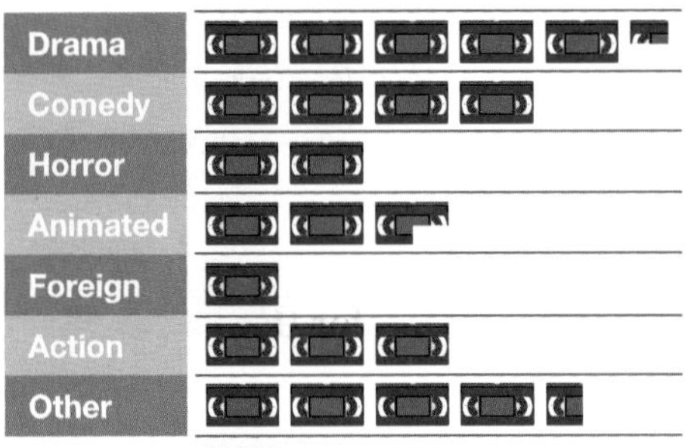

a) Record the data in a frequency table.

b) Construct a bar graph.

c) Write a question you could answer from the bar graph or pictograph.
Answer the question.

d) What else do you know from the graphs?

3. Use an atlas or other database.

a) Choose 5 countries other than Canada.

b) Find the area of each country and Canada.

c) Record the data in a table.

d) Graph the data.

e) How does each country's area compare with Canada's area?

f) What else do you know from the table or graph?

5.3 **4.** Here are the history test scores for students in Ms. Epstein's class.

History Test Scores

56	87	98	34	66	75	50
69	70	83	99	55	83	56
62	90	47	92	75	85	68
98	78	62	51	59	75	81
58	79	80	94	92	63	71

a) Draw a stem-and-leaf plot to represent the data.

b) What is the range of the scores?

c) The pass mark is 50.
How many students did not pass the test?

d) Students who scored below 60 had to rewrite the test.
How many students rewrote the test?

e) Find the median score.

f) Find the mode score.

Using *Fathom* to Investigate Scatter Plots

Focus Identify trends in scatter plots.

This table lists the Academy Award winners for Best Actress from 1973–2002, and the age of each actress in that year.

Academy Award Winners for Best Actress

Actress	Year	Age	Actress	Year	Age
Glenda Jackson	1973	37	Jodie Foster	1988	26
Ellen Burstyn	1974	42	Jessica Tandy	1989	80
Louise Fletcher	1975	41	Kathy Bates	1990	42
Faye Dunaway	1976	35	Jodie Foster	1991	29
Diane Keaton	1977	31	Emma Thompson	1992	33
Jane Fonda	1978	41	Holly Hunter	1993	35
Sally Field	1979	33	Jessica Lange	1994	45
Sissy Spacek	1980	30	Susan Sarandon	1995	44
Katharine Hepburn	1981	74	Frances McDormand	1996	39
Meryl Streep	1982	33	Helen Hunt	1997	34
Shirley MacLaine	1983	49	Gwyneth Paltrow	1998	26
Sally Field	1984	38	Hilary Swank	1999	25
Geraldine Page	1985	61	Julia Roberts	2000	33
Marlee Matlin	1986	21	Halle Berry	2001	33
Cher	1987	41	Nicole Kidman	2002	35

To use *Fathom* to draw a scatter plot for these data, follow these steps:

1. Open *Fathom*. From the File menu, select New.
2. To enter the title:
   Click on the New Collection icon, then click on the screen. Double click Collection 1.
   Type Academy Award Winners for Best Actress
   and click OK, as shown at the right.
3. To enter the data:
   Click on the New Case Table icon, then click on the screen.

Click on <new>; type Year, then press Enter. A new column appears to the right with the heading <new>. Click on the word <new>, type Age, then press Enter. Under the headings *Year* and *Age*, input the data from the table on page 185.

4. To graph the data:
Click on the New Graph icon ,
then click on the screen. Two axes appear.
Click on the column heading,
Year, and drag it to the horizontal axis.
Click on the column heading,
Age, and drag it to the vertical axis.
Fathom creates a scatter plot,
as shown at the right.

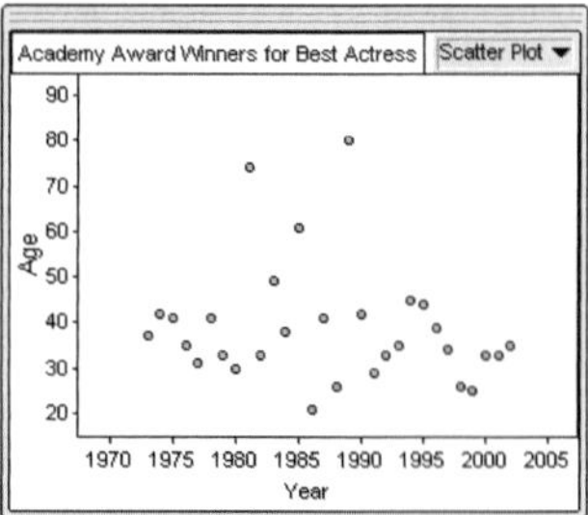

The range of the data is: 80 – 21, or 59 years.
However, most of the data are located between 31 and 42 years.
The data form a **cluster** between these ages.
This means that, from 1973 to 2002, most winners were between 31 and 42 years old.
There are two large sections without points — between 49 and 61 years, and between 61 and 74 years. These represent gaps in the data. From 1973 to 2002, none of the winners were between 49 and 61 years old, or between 61 and 74 years old.
From the scatter plot, we can see that there is no pattern or **trend** in the data.

Here is another example of data in a scatter plot:
Emidio works part-time as a waiter in a restaurant. The table and scatter plot on page 187 show the hours he worked each week for 12 weeks, and his earnings, in dollars, for each week.

From the scatter plot, the points show an **upward trend** from left to right. Emidio's earnings increase as time increases.
That is, the more hours per week Emidio works, the more he earns.

Emidio's Weekly Earnings

	Time_in_hours	Earnings_in_dollars
1	2	30
2	3	40
3	3	45
4	4	41
5	4	48
6	4	45
7	5	66
8	5	53
9	5	59
10	6	83
11	6	71
12	7	77

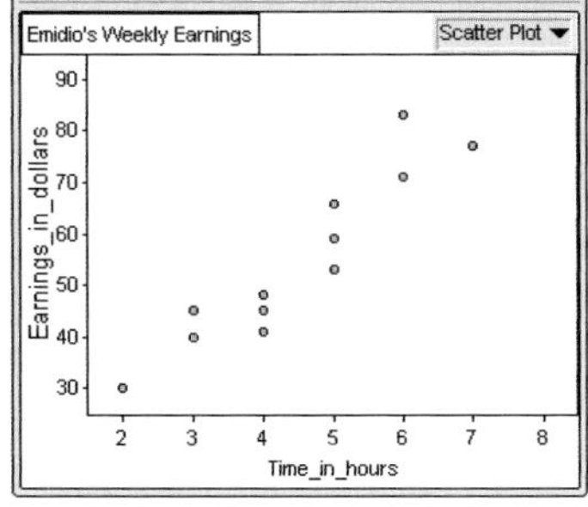

Here is a third example of data in a scatter plot:
Water is draining out of a swimming pool. The table and scatter plot show the volume of water, in litres, remaining in the pool at one-hour intervals.

Pool Water Draining

	Time_in_hours	Volume_in_litres
1	0	5200
2	1	4700
3	2	3900
4	3	3300
5	4	2600
6	5	2100
7	6	1100

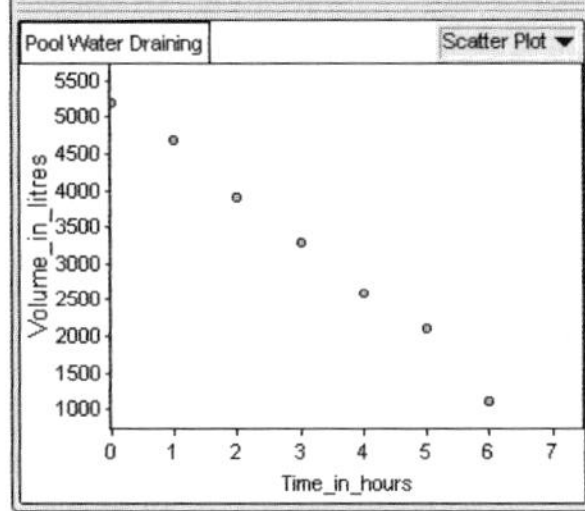

From the scatter plot, the points show a **downward trend** from left to right.
The volume of water in the pool decreases as time increases.
That is, the more hours the pool drains, the less water there is in it.

✓ Check

Time	Speed (km/h)
12 noon	0
12:30	70
1:00	85
1:30	100
2:00	100
2:30	100
3:00	0
3:30	0
4:00	100
4:30	65
5:00	0

1. Emily drove from Toronto to Cornwall.
She left Toronto at 12 noon and arrived in Cornwall at 5 p.m.
The table at the left shows the speed of the car recorded at different times during her trip.
Use *Fathom* to draw a scatter plot to represent the data.
Describe any trends.
What do you know from looking at the graph?

Reflect

Describe 3 different types of scatter plots.
Provide an example for each type.

5.4 Line Graphs

Focus Display data using line graphs and describe trends.

Explore

Work with a partner.
Madhu measured the mass of her pet guinea pig every 5 months, until it was 25 months old.
The data are shown at the left.

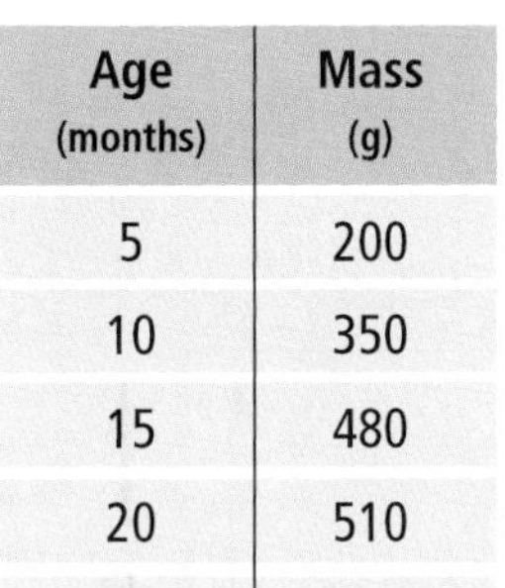

Age (months)	Mass (g)
5	200
10	350
15	480
20	510
25	520

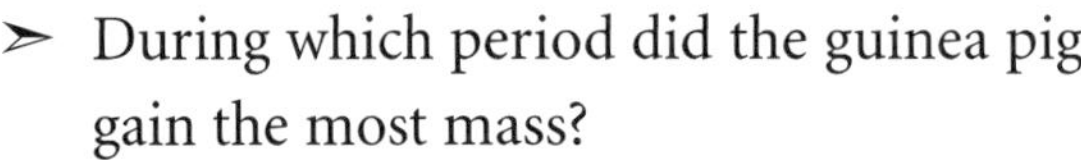

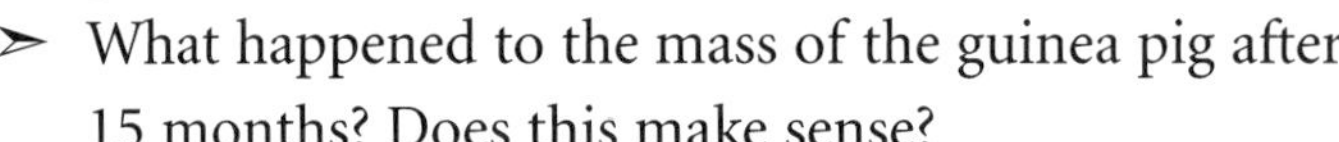

➢ One person draws a bar graph.
The other person draws a line graph.

➢ During which period did the guinea pig gain the most mass?

➢ What happened to the mass of the guinea pig after 15 months? Does this make sense?

➢ Predict the mass of the guinea pig at 30 months.

Reflect & Share

Discuss with your partner which graph is better for displaying the data. Justify your answer.
Estimate the mass of the guinea pig at 18 months.
Which graph is better to make this estimate? Explain.

Connect

A **line graph** displays data that change over time.
The line graph on page 189 shows how Leah's height changes as she gets older.
From 2 to 13 years, each line segment goes up to the right.
This shows that Leah's height increases.
From 13 to 16 years, the line segments still go up to the right, but they are not as steep.
This shows that Leah's height increases, but at a slower rate than before.
From 16 years on, the line segments are horizontal.
This shows that Leah's height has stopped increasing.
She has stopped growing taller.

This symbol on the vertical axis means that the numbers from 0 to 60 are not shown.

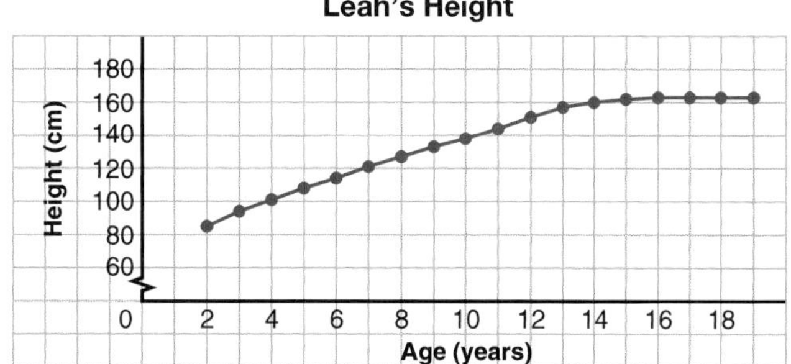

We can use this line graph to find values between data points. At $11\frac{1}{2}$ years, Leah was about 148 cm tall.

Example

a) Draw a line graph to display these data.

b) Use the graph. Describe any trends in Canada's population.

c) Use the graph. During which period did Canada's population increase the most? The least? How can you tell?

d) Estimate Canada's population in 2011. Explain how you used the graph to do this. What assumption did you make?

Canada's Population (to the nearest million)

Years	Number (millions)
1901	5
1911	7
1921	9
1931	10
1941	12
1951	14
1961	18
1971	22
1981	25
1991	28
2001	31

Solution

a) **Step 1.** Draw axes on grid paper. The horizontal axis represents time, in years. Use 1 square for each 10-year interval, starting in 1901. The vertical axis represents population, in millions. The greatest population to be graphed is 31 million. Make 35 the greatest number on the vertical scale. Use 1 square for every 5 million, starting at 0.

Step 2. Plot a point on the grid for each pair of entries in the table. Use a ruler to join adjacent points.

Step 3. Label the axes. Give the graph a title.

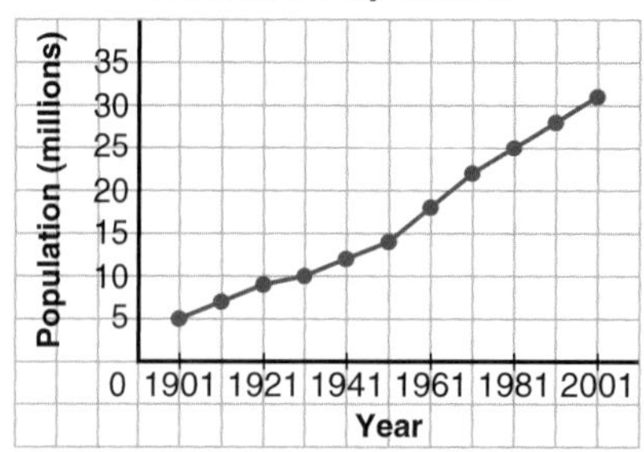

b) The graph goes up to the right.
This means that Canada's population increased from 1901 to 2001. In general, the line segments from 1951 to 2001 are steeper than the segments from 1901 to 1951.
This means that the population was increasing at a faster rate in the 2nd half of the century.

c) The period in which the line segment is the steepest represents the greatest increase in population. This happened from 1951 to 1971. From 1921 to 1931, the line segment is the least steep. This is when Canada's population had the least increase.

d) To predict Canada's population in 2011, extend the last line segment to 2011. From 2011 on the horizontal axis, draw a vertical line to the graph. From the graph, draw a horizontal line to the vertical axis. This line meets the axis at about 34 million. The population of Canada in 2011 will be approximately 34 million.
We assume that Canada's population will continue to grow at the same rate as it did from 1991 to 2001.

Canada's Population

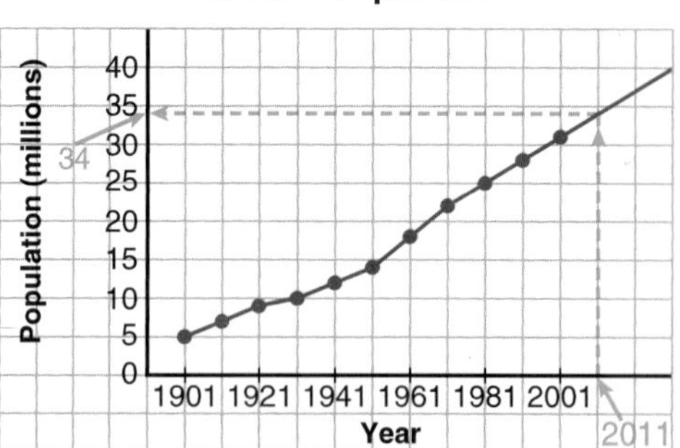

Practice

Calculator Skills

Three consecutive 2-digit numbers have a product of 551 286.

What is the sum of the three numbers?

1. a) What does this line graph show?
   b) About how tall was Nathan at each age?
      i) 8 years
      ii) 12 years
      iii) 15 years
   c) During which year did Nathan grow the most? The least? How does the graph show this?
   d) Predict Nathan's height at 18 years. Explain your reasoning.
   e) Predict Nathan's height at 50 years. Explain.

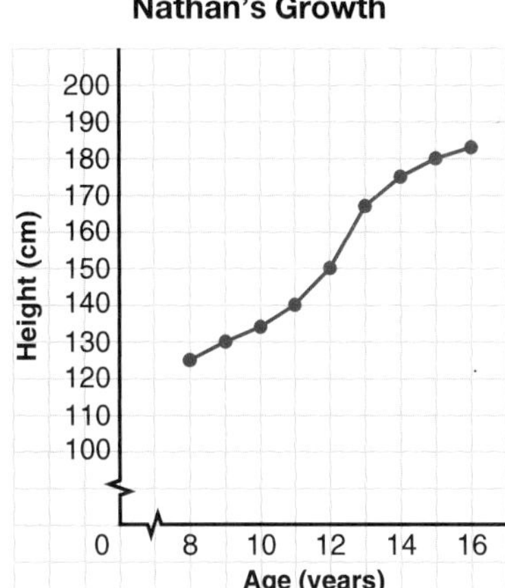

Average Monthly Rainfall (cm)		
Month	Vancouver	Ottawa
January	14.0	1.5
February	12.0	1.6
March	9.6	3.2
April	5.8	5.8
May	4.9	7.5
June	4.7	7.7
July	2.6	8.8
August	3.5	9.2
September	5.4	8.3
October	11.7	7.0
November	13.8	6.3
December	16.4	3.3

2. a) What does this table show?
   b) Draw a line graph for each city on the same grid.
   c) Describe the trends in rainfall for the two cities. How do the line graphs illustrate these trends?
   d) In which month(s) do the line graphs cross? What does this mean?
   e) What is the average annual rainfall for each city?

3. a) Research your region on one of these topics:
      i) the average precipitation for each month
      ii) the maximum temperature for the first day of each month
      iii) the average temperature for each month
   b) Organize the data in a table. Draw a line graph.
   c) Repeat part a for a city or region in a different part of Canada.
   d) Draw a line graph to display these data on the same grid as in part b.
   e) How are the line graphs alike? How are they different?
   f) Write all that you know from looking at the graphs.

Stopping Distance for a Car		
Speed (km/h)	Dry Pavement (m)	Wet Pavement (m)
0	0	0
10	3	6
20	7	11
30	12	17
40	16	26
50	23	38
60	30	50
70	38	64
80	49	78
90	60	97
100	72	120

4. **a)** What does stopping distance depend on?

b) On the same grid, draw a line graph for dry pavement and for wet pavement.

c) Why are line graphs suitable for these data?

d) Describe the trends in the graphs.

e) A car travels at 75 km/h on dry pavement. What is its stopping distance?

f) A car takes 30 m to stop on wet pavement. How fast was it travelling?

g) Write a question you could answer using the graph but not the table. Explain why you need the graph instead of the table.

5. **Assessment Focus** Nina owns a shoe store. These tables show data about the shoe store.

i)

Yearly Sales	
Year	Sales ($)
1997	579 000
1998	621 000
1999	598 000
2000	634 000
2001	657 000
2002	642 000
2003	675 000

ii)

Sizes of Shoes Sold in May	
Size	Number of Pairs Sold
6	60
7	239
8	217
9	156
10	61
11	43
12	36

a) Which data would be best represented with a line graph? Explain.

b) Draw a line graph for the table you chose in part a.

c) Describe the trends in the data.

d) Which type of graph would be suitable for the other table? Explain. Graph the data from the other table.

e) What do you know from looking at each graph?

Reflect

Why is a line graph the best type of graph to use to make predictions?

Technology

Using Spreadsheets to Record and Graph Data

Focus Display data on graphs using spreadsheets.

Spreadsheet software, such as *AppleWorks*, can be used to record, then graph, data.
This table shows the favourite sports of Grade 7 students in Mona's school.
To graph these data using *AppleWorks*, follow these steps:
Open *AppleWorks*. Choose Spreadsheet.
Enter the data into rows and columns in the spreadsheet.

Favourite Sports

Sport	Number of Students
Baseball	20
Soccer	15
Hockey	18
Football	10
Basketball	12

To create a bar graph

1. Highlight the data. Include the column heads, but do not include the table title.

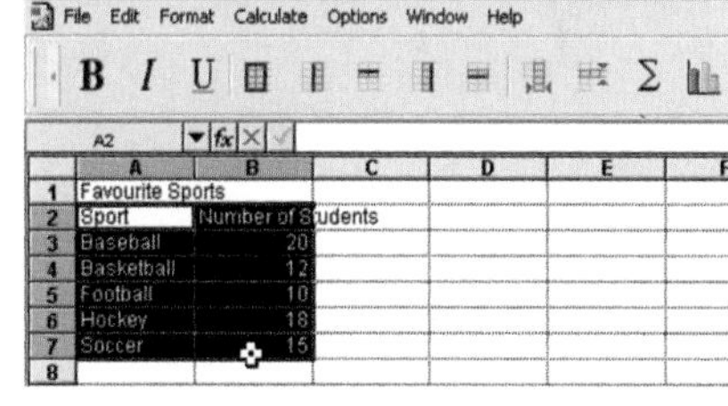

2. Click the graph icon on the tool bar. A Chart Options dialogue box appears.
Choose Bar, then click OK, as shown below left.

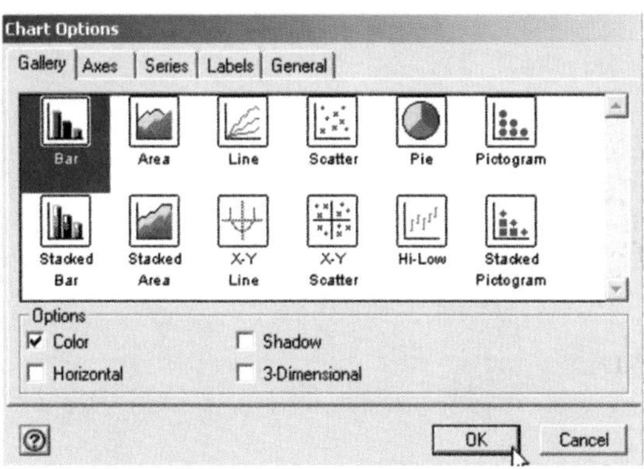

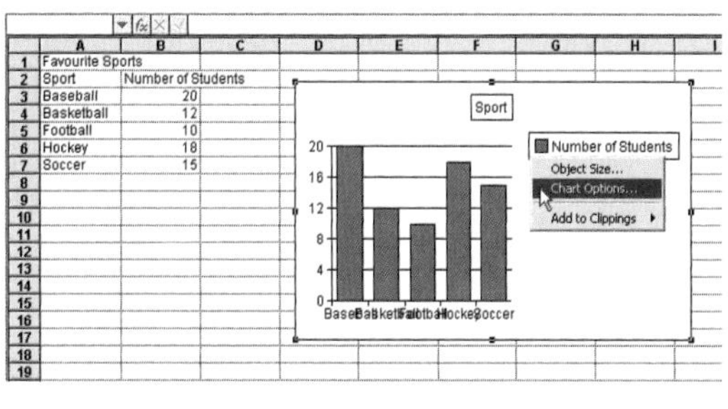

3. The software creates a legend, which is not needed for a bar graph. To remove the legend, right-click the graph. Choose Chart Options, as shown above right. Select the Labels tab. Click the box next to Show Legend to remove the check mark.

4. In the Title box, type **Favourite Sports**, as shown below left. To insert labels, click the Axes tab. Select X axis. Type **Sport**. Select Y axis. Type **Number of Students**, as shown below right. Then click OK.

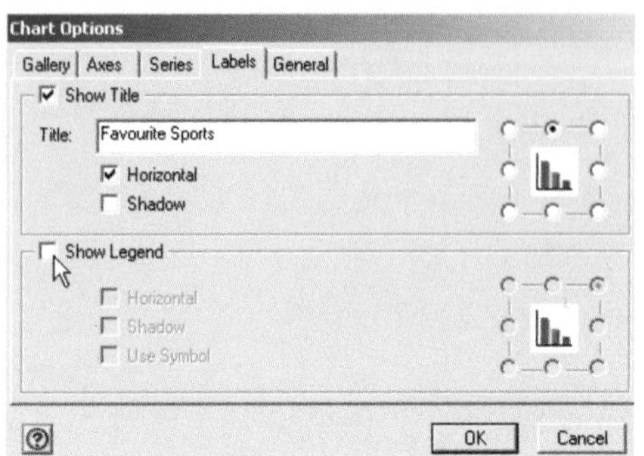

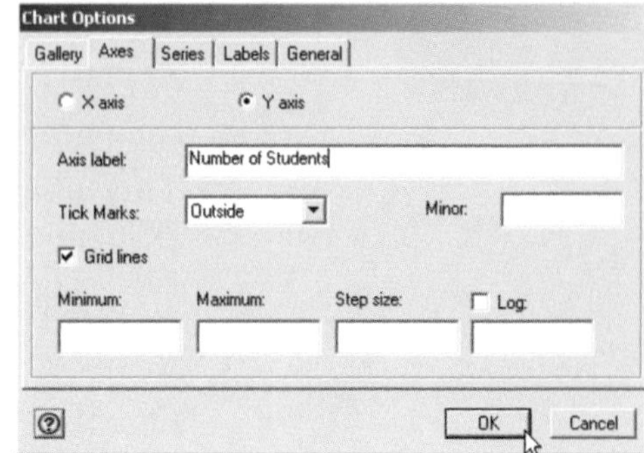

Your graph should look like the one below.

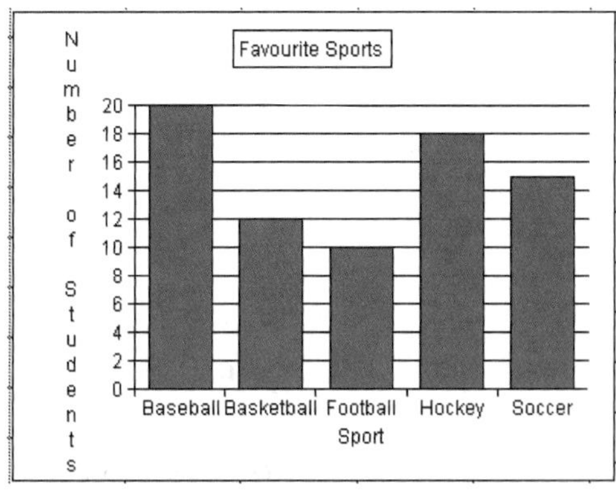

To create a circle graph

1. Use the data on page 193.
   Highlight the data as shown below left.
   Do not include the column heads or title.

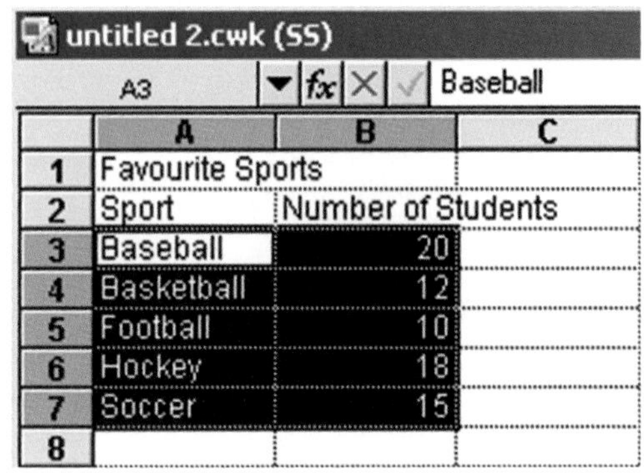

untitled 2.cwk (SS)

A3 Baseball

	A	B	C
1	Favourite Sports		
2	Sport	Number of Students	
3	Baseball	20	
4	Basketball	12	
5	Football	10	
6	Hockey	18	
7	Soccer	15	
8			

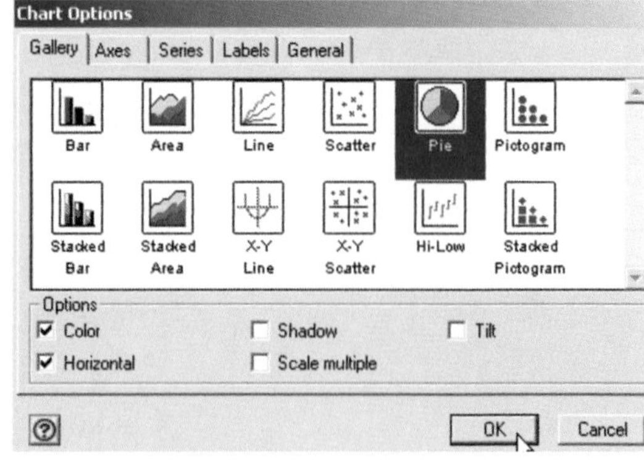

A spreadsheet program uses the term "pie" for a circle graph.

2. Click the graph icon on the tool bar.
A Chart Options dialogue box appears.
Choose Pie, then click OK, as shown bottom right, page 194.
The circle graph shows a legend at the right.
The legend shows what sport each sector represents.

3. To add a title, right-click the graph. Choose Chart Options.
Select the Labels tab. In the Title box, type Favourite Sports, as shown below left. Then click OK.
Your graph should look like the one below right.

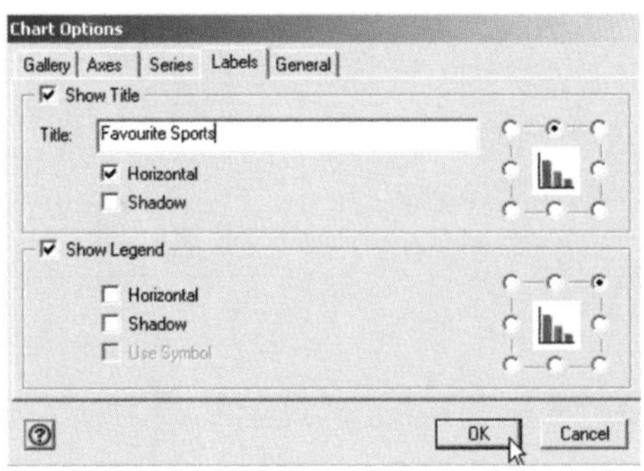

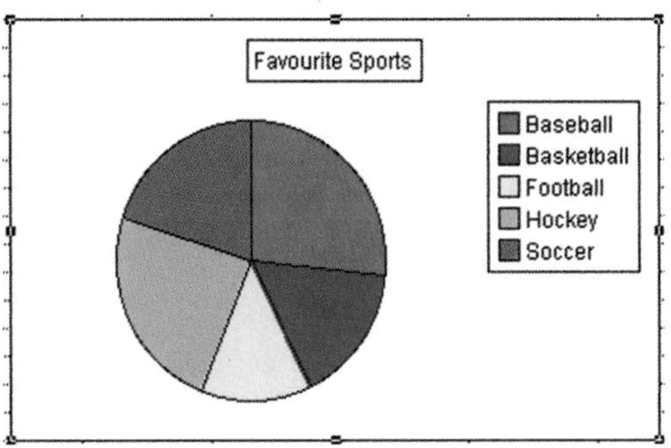

To create a line graph

Average Annual Income of Canadian Women	
Year	Income ($)
1989	28 219
1990	29 050
1991	29 654
1992	30 903
1993	30 466
1994	30 274
1995	30 959
1996	30 606
1997	30 484
1998	32 553
1999	32 026

These data came from the Statistics Canada website.

1. Enter the data into rows and columns in the spreadsheet.

2. Highlight the data.
Include the column heads, but do not include the table title.

3. Click the graph icon on the tool bar.
A Chart Options dialogue box appears.
Choose X-Y Line, then click OK, as shown below.

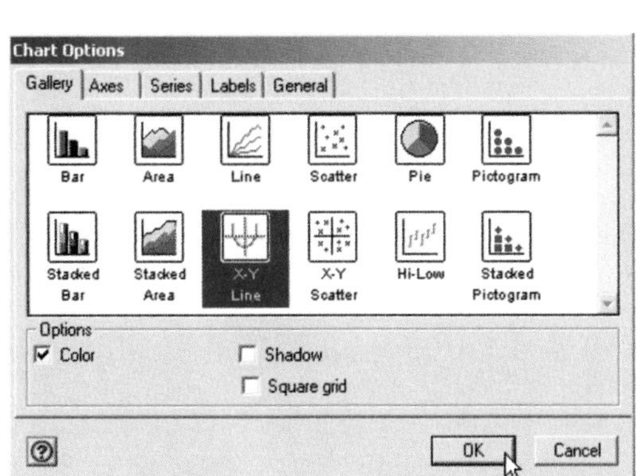

4. The software creates a legend, which is not needed for a line graph. To remove the legend, right-click the graph. Choose Chart Options. Select the Labels tab.
Click the box next to Show Legend to remove the check mark.
In the Title box, type Average Annual Income of Canadian Women. Then click OK.
Your graph should look like the one below.
   - What trend does the graph show? Explain.
   - How often did the average income increase? Decrease? How can you tell this from the graph?
   - When did the average annual income have the greatest increase? Greatest decrease?
   - Write what else you know from the graph.

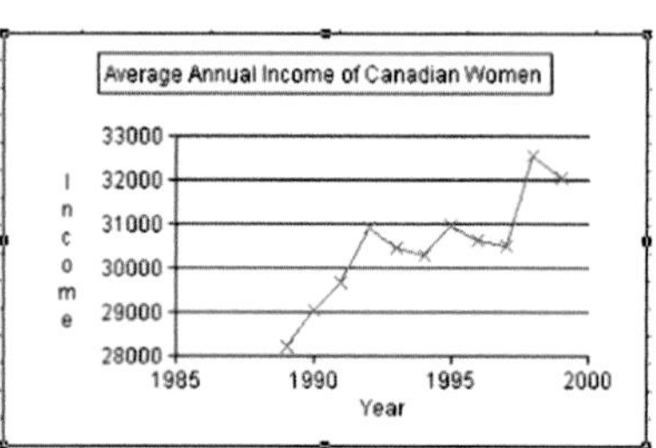

1. Think about where you met your best friend.
The table at the right lists the places where some Canadians met their best friends.
   a) Use a spreadsheet to draw a bar graph and a circle graph.
   b) Which graph represents the data better? Explain.

Place	Number
School	5700
Work	4100
Club or organization	1400
Religious organization	700
Home/neighbourhood	4300
Through family	1200
Through friend	1100
Other	600

Average Value of $1U.S.	
Year	Value in Canadian Dollars
1997	1.385
1998	1.484
1999	1.486
2000	1.485

2. Use a spreadsheet to draw a line graph for the data in the table at the left.
   a) What trend does the graph show?
   b) Predict the average value, in Canadian dollars, of $1U.S. in 2002 and in 2003.
   What assumptions did you make?
   c) Research to find the average value, in Canadian dollars, of $1U.S. in 2002 and 2003.
   Where could you get this information?
   How accurate was your prediction?

3. The data below are from the Statistics Canada website.
   a) Use a spreadsheet.
      Create a graph to display the data.
   b) Which type of graph best represents the data? Explain.
   c) Which type of graph could not be used to represent the data? Explain.

Average Hours of Television Viewing per Week, Fall 2001

Province	Adolescents 12–17 years
Newfoundland/Labrador	15.8
Prince Edward Island	12.4
Nova Scotia	14.1
New Brunswick	14.1
Quebec	14.5
Ontario	12.8
Manitoba	12.8
Saskatchewan	12.5
Alberta	13.3
British Columbia	10.9

Your World

Newspapers often publish survey results. The headlines may be misleading.

Try to find headlines like these. Cut them out. Explain why they are misleading.

Why would newspapers do this?

5.5 Applications of Mean, Median, and Mode

Focus Understand which measure of central tendency best describes a set of data.

Explore

Work on your own.
Record on the board how many siblings you have.
Use the class data.
Find the mean, the median, and the mode.
Find the range.

The mean, median, and mode are measures of central tendency. Each measure is an average.

Reflect & Share

With a classmate, discuss which measure of central tendency best describes the average number of siblings.

Connect

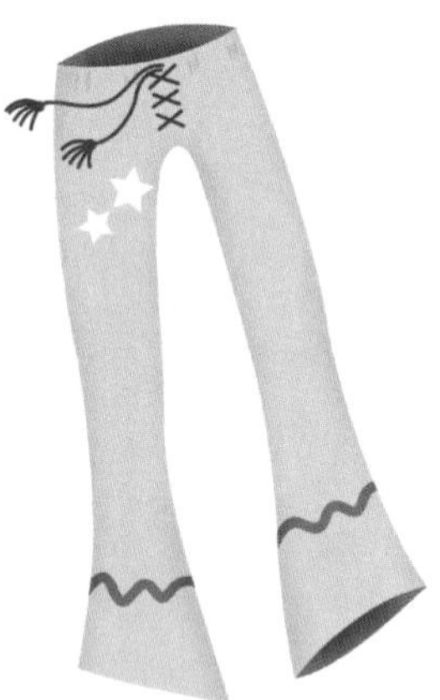

A clothing store sold jeans in these sizes in one day:
28 30 28 26 30 32 28 32 26 28 34 38 36 30 34 32 30

To calculate the mean jeans size sold, add the sizes, then divide by the number of jeans sold.

$$\text{Mean} = \frac{28 + 30 + 28 + 26 + 30 + 32 + 28 + 32 + 26 + 28 + 34 + 38 + 36 + 30 + 34 + 32 + 30}{17}$$
$$= \frac{522}{17}$$
$$\doteq 30.7$$

The mean size is approximately 30.7.

When there is an odd number of data, to find the middle number: Add 1 to the number of data, then divide by 2. This gives the position of the middle number.

For example:

$\frac{17 + 1}{2} = \frac{18}{2} = 9$;

the middle number is 9th.

To calculate the median, order the jeans sold from least size to greatest size. The middle number is the median.
There are 17 numbers. The middle number is 9th.
26, 26, 28, 28, 28, 28, 30, 30, 30, 30, 32, 32, 32, 34, 34, 36, 38
The median size is 30.

The mode is the number that occurs most often.
There are two numbers that occur most often.
They are 28 and 30. So, the mode sizes are 28 and 30.

In this situation, the mean, 30.7, is of little use.
The mean does not represent a size.

The median, 30, shows about one-half of the customers bought jeans of size 30 or smaller, and about one-half of the customers bought jeans of size 30 or larger.

The modes, 28 and 30, tell which sizes are purchased more often.
The mode is most useful to the storeowner.
He may use the mode to order extra stock of the most popular sizes.

Example

A bookstore has 15 books in its young adult section. There are 5 different prices.
This table shows the number of books at each price.

a) Find the mean, median, and mode prices.
b) Which measure best represents the average price of a young adult book?
c) What is the range of the prices?

Young Adult Books

Price ($)	Number of Books
8.99	3
9.99	5
13.99	5
32.99	1
37.99	1

Solution

a) Mean price:

- Multiply each price by the total number of books at that price, then add the prices.

$(8.99 \times 3) + (9.99 \times 5) + (13.99 \times 5) + 32.99 + 37.99 = 217.85$

- Divide the total price by the total number of books: 15

$\frac{217.85}{15} \doteq 14.52$

The mean price per book is approximately $14.52.

Median price:
There are 15 books.
The table shows the books in order from least price to greatest price.
The median price is the 8th price. The 8th price is $9.99.
The median price is $9.99.

Mode price:
There are two mode prices. They are $9.99 and $13.99.

b) The mean price is not charged for any of the books.
Only two books cost more than the mean of $14.52.

There are two mode prices.
One mode, $9.99, is the same as the median price.

One-half the books cost less than the median price.
One-half cost more.
So, the median price, $9.99, best represents the average cost of a young adult book at the store.

c) For the range, subtract the lowest price from the highest:
37.99 − 8.99 = 29.00
The range of prices is $29.00.

Practice

1. Here are Ira's practice times, in seconds, for the 100-m backstroke: 122, 118, 123, 119, 118, 120, 118, 121, 119

a) Find the mean, median, and mode of these data.
b) Of the mean, median, and mode, which do you think best describes Ira's race time? Explain.
c) What is the range of these data?

2. Caitlin received these test marks in each subject.

a) Find the mean, median, and mode for each subject.
b) Explain what information each measure of central tendency gives.
c) Which subject is Caitlin best at? Worst at? Explain your reasoning.

Caitlin's Marks							
Math	85	69	92	55	68	75	78
Spelling	72	81	50	69	81	96	92
History	68	74	82	80	76	67	74

3. The table shows the tips earned by five waiters and waitresses during two weeks in December.

a) Calculate the mean, median, and mode tips for each week.
b) Calculate the mean, median, and mode tips for the two-week period.
c) Compare your answers in parts a and b.
Which are the same? Which are different? Explain why.
d) Which measure of central tendency best represents the tips earned during the two weeks? Explain.

Weekly Tips Earned ($)		
Waiter	Week 1	Week 2
James	1150	600
Kyrra	700	725
Tamara	800	775
Jacob	875	860
George	600	1165

4. Jamal was training for a 400-m race.
His times, in seconds, for the first five races were:
120, 118, 138, 124, 118
   a) Find the median and mode times.
   b) Jamal wants his median time after 6 races to be 121 s.
   What time must he get in his 6th race? Explain.

5. Find 5 numbers that have a mean of 24 and a median of 25.
Justify your answer.
How many different sets of 5 numbers can you find?
Show that each set has the mean and median stated.

6. A quality control inspector randomly selects boxes of crackers from the production line. She measures their masses. On one day she selects 30 boxes. The inspector records these data:
   - 12 boxes: 405 g each
   - 4 boxes: 395 g each
   - 8 boxes: 390 g each
   - 4 boxes: 385 g each
   - 2 boxes: 380 g each

   a) Which expression can be used to calculate the mean mass?
   Use it to find the mean mass.
      i) $\frac{(405 \times 12 + 395 \times 4 + 390 \times 8 + 385 \times 4 + 380 \times 2)}{30}$
      ii) $405 \times 12 + 395 \times 4 + 390 \times 8 + 385 \times 4 + 380 \times 2 \div 30$
   b) For the shipment of crackers to be acceptable, the mean mass must be at least 395 g. Is this shipment acceptable? Explain.

7. **Assessment Focus**
Use these data: 28, 30, 30, 31, 32, 33, 34, 35, 37, 38, 39, 41
   a) Find the mean, median, and mode.
   b) What happens to the mean, median, and mode in each case?
      i) Each number is increased by 10.
      ii) Each number is doubled.
   Explain the results.

Number Strategies

Use only the digits 0, 2, 3, and a decimal point. Use each digit only once each time.

Make as many numbers with 2 digits as possible.

Find the sum of the numbers.

Reflect

Use your answers from *Practice*. Describe a situation for each case.

a) The mean is the best measure of central tendency.
b) The median is the best measure of central tendency.
c) The mode is the best measure of central tendency.

5.6 Evaluating Data Analysis

Focus Examine how data can be misleading.

Explore

Work on your own.
What do the two graphs below show?
How are the graphs similar? How are they different?
Explain.

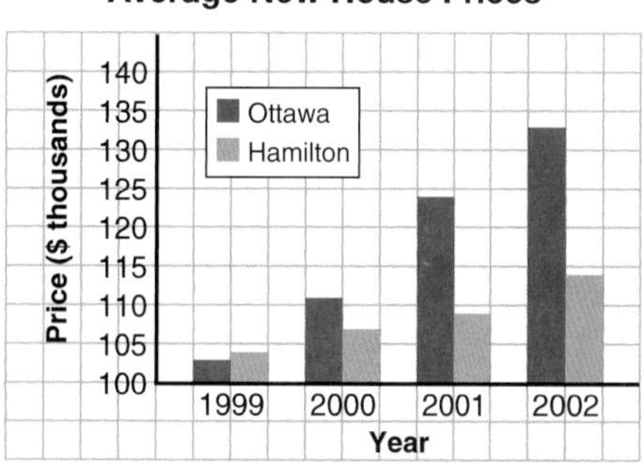

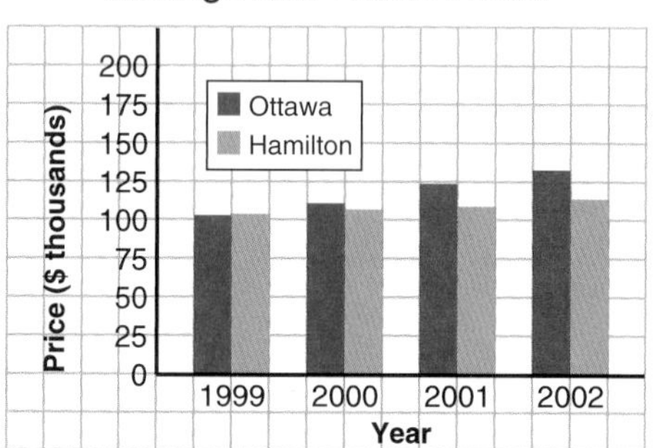

Reflect & Share

Discuss with a classmate:
What impression does each graph give? Explain.
Who may want to use each type of graph?

Connect

Sometimes, graphs are used to distort information and to mislead.
Look at these graphs.

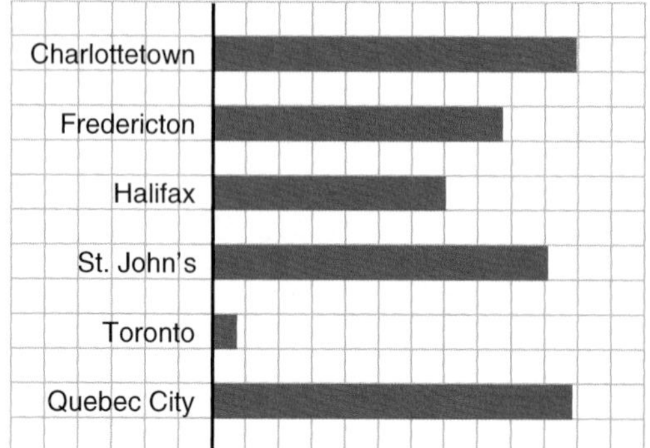

This bar graph is misleading.
It suggests that Quebec City has more than 10 times as much snow as Toronto.
This graph has no measurements of the depth of snow.

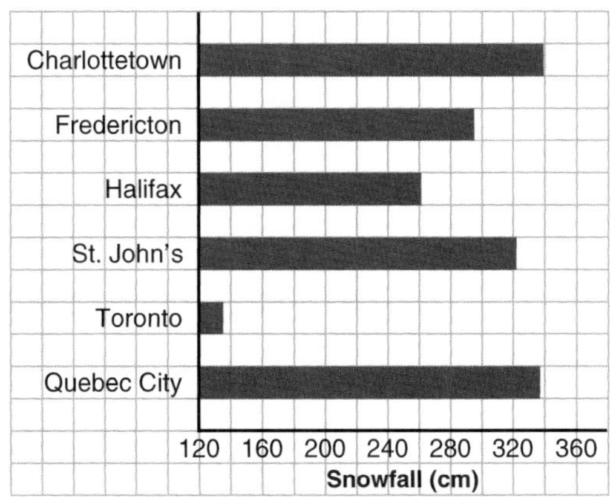

Visually, this graph suggests the same information as the first graph. However, the horizontal scale is labelled with the snowfall.

The scale shows that Toronto has about 135 cm of snow and Quebec City has about 335 cm.

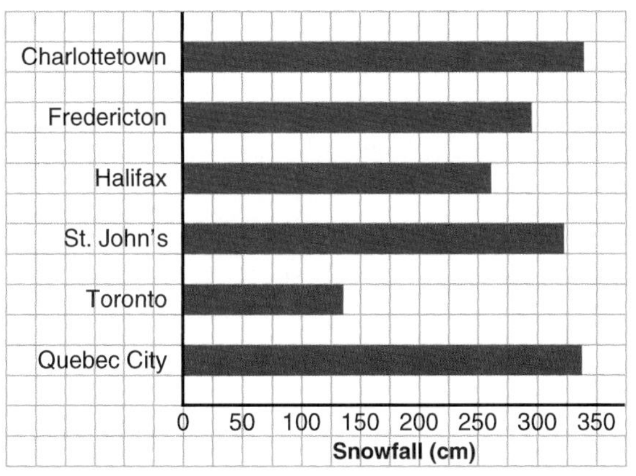

This graph accurately shows the data. The horizontal scale starts at 0.
The lengths of the bars are shown in the correct ratio. Quebec City has between 2 and 3 times as much snow as Toronto.

Example

This line graph is used to suggest that salaries have doubled in 6 years.

a) Why is this graph misleading?

b) Redraw the graph to show accurately how salaries have changed in 6 years.

Solution

a) Use the vertical scale.
The salary in year 1 is about $34 500.
The salary in year 6 is about $35 750.
The increase in salary is: $35 750 − $34 500 = $1250
The salaries have increased by only $1250 in 6 years.

b) Make a table from the line graph.
Estimate each salary.

Year	Salary ($)
1	34 500
2	34 600
3	35 250
4	35 000
5	35 300
6	35 750

Draw a graph.
Start the vertical scale at $0.
Use a scale of 1 square to represent $5000.

Salary Increases

Salary ($): 0, 10 000, 20 000, 30 000, 40 000
Year: 1, 2, 3, 4, 5, 6

Practice

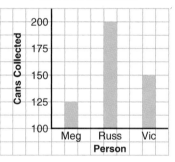

1. Which graph is misleading? Explain why it is misleading.

Food Drive Results

Cans Collected: 0, 50, 100, 150, 200
Person: Meg, Russ, Vic

Food Drive Results

Cans Collected: 100, 125, 150, 175, 200
Person: Meg, Russ, Vic

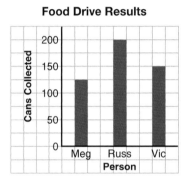

2. The two graphs display the Read Books Company's profits for a four-month period.

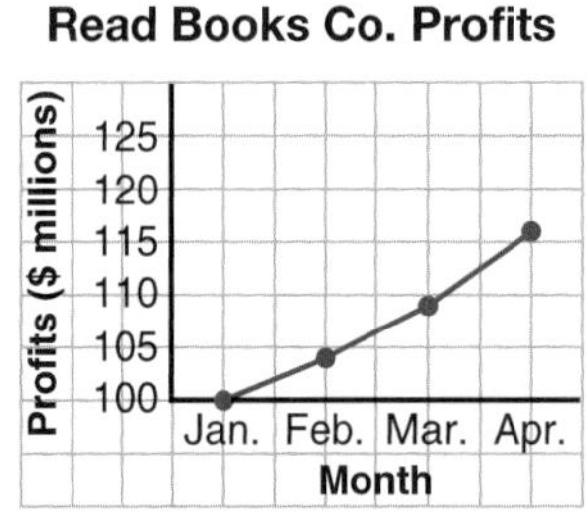

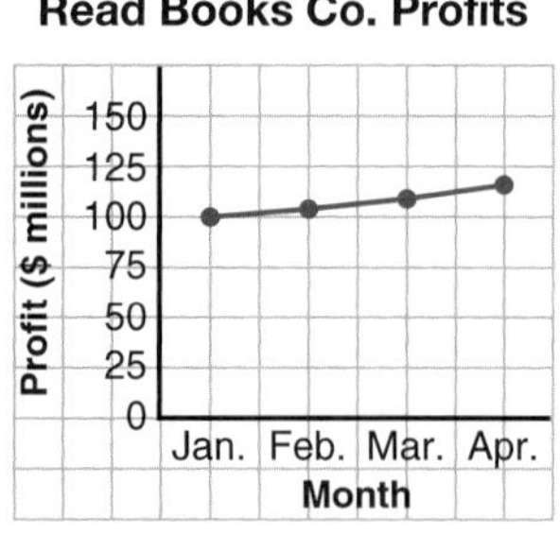

a) Which graph might the president of the company choose to report profits to the shareholders? Why?

b) Which graph might the rival company use to compare profits? Why?

c) Predict the company's profit for May.
What assumptions do you make?

3. Why do some graphs display data in a misleading way? Describe how a graph might be drawn to misrepresent data.

4. A graph similar to this is part of an advertisement for a truck manufacturer.
With the graph, Manufacturer A says that more than 98 out of 100 of its trucks sold in the last 10 years are still on the road.

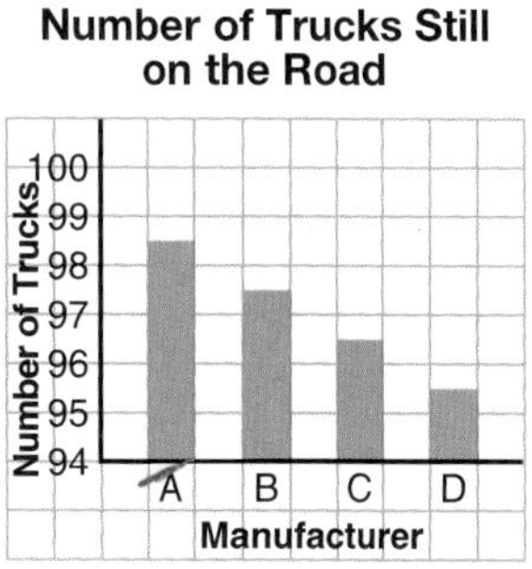

Number of Trucks Still on the Road

Number of Trucks: 94, 95, 96, 97, 98, 99, 100

Manufacturer: A, B, C, D

a) What impression does this graph give?
b) How many trucks, out of 100, are still on the road for Manufacturer B? C? D?
c) Do you think Manufacturer A's trucks are more dependable than the other manufacturers' trucks? Explain.
d) Redraw the graph to give an accurate representation of the data.

Mental Math

Estimate each product.

- 3.9 × 4.1
- 0.5 × 10.2
- 1.1 × 11.1
- 20.5 × 0.9

Board of Directors' Expenses	
Quarter	Amount ($)
1st	85 000
2nd	104 000
3rd	125 000
4th	155 000

5. Draw a graph to display the data at the left in each way:
a) The directors want the expenses to look low.
b) The shareholders want to show the expenses are too high.
c) Draw an accurate representation of the data.
For each graph you draw, explain how it shows what you intended.

6. **Assessment Focus**
Use newspapers, magazines, or the Internet.
Find a graph that creates a false impression.
a) Describe how the graph creates a false impression.
b) Why might the misleading graph be used?
c) How could the graph be changed to present the data more accurately?
d) Use your suggestions in part c to draw an accurate graph.

Reflect

Describe two ways in which a graph may be misleading.

Making a Study Sheet

1

Be sure that you know exactly what will be covered on the test or quiz. Ask your teacher if you are not sure. Highlight these areas in your notebook.

2

List the math vocabulary you will need. Write definitions and provide examples if you need to.

Congruent figures have exactly the same size and shape. Corresponding angles have the same measure. Corresponding sides have the same length.

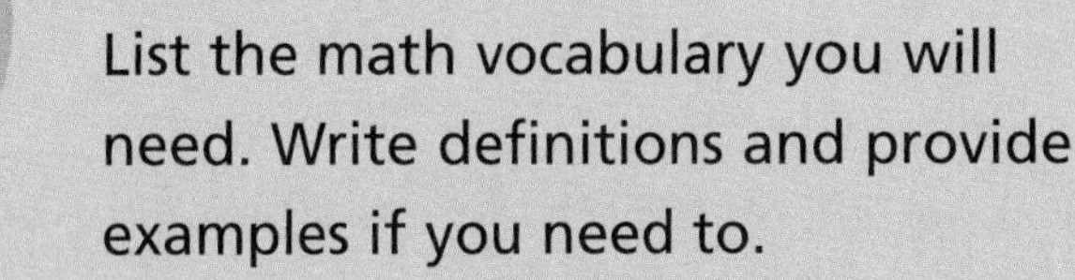

3

Colour code any formulas you will need.

Area of rectangle = Length × Width
Area of triangle = $\frac{1}{2}$ × Base × Height

4

Use pictures to help you remember.

Polygon: A closed figure formed by three or more line segments

YES: 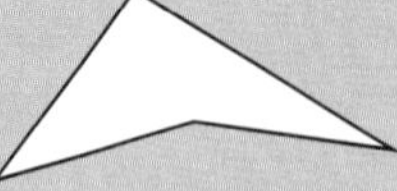 *NO:*

Reading and Writing in

Math

5

Copy out a sample problem. Include all necessary examples and discussion.

Sample Problem: *You have a choice of recess times:*

- *You may have 30 min a day for the next two weeks,*

OR

- *You may have 1 min of recess the 1st day, 2 min the 2nd day, 4 min the 3rd day, 8 min the 4th day, and so on, for the next two weeks. Which choice would give you more recess time in the 2 weeks? Explain your answer.*

Solution

This problem is about finding out which recess choice is better. The strategy I will use is to make a table.

Day	1	2	3
Choice 1 (min)	30	30	30
Total time (min)	30	60	90
Choice 2 (min)	1	2	4
Total time (min)	1	3	7

6

Use word association and patterns to help you remember.

A hexagon has six sides. (Both have an X.)

Octagon -- Octapus (Both have 8 sides/arms.)

Unit Review

Review any lesson with

What Do I Need to Know?

- ✓ **Primary data** are data you collect.
- ✓ **Secondary data** are found from databases on the Internet, or a library, or other sources.
- ✓ In a set of data:

  The **mean** is the sum of numbers divided by the number of numbers in the set.

  The **median** is the middle number, when there is an odd number of data in the set. When there is an even number of data, the median is the mean of the two middle numbers.

  The **mode** is the number that occurs most often. A set of data can have no mode, one mode, or more than one mode.

What Should I Be Able to Do?

For extra practice, go to page 442.

LESSON

5.1

1. A recreation group wants to find out the favourite summer activity of teenagers in the town.

a) Write an unbiased survey question.

b) Write a biased survey question. Explain how it is biased.

5.2
5.5

2. The data in this table are from Statistics Canada.

Average Weekly Earnings in 2001

Job	Earnings ($)
Forestry	831
Mining	1153
Utilities	1000
Construction	800
Real Estate	612
Education	696
Health Care	584
Transportation	742

a) What do the data show?
b) Draw a graph to display the data.
c) Explain your choice of graph. Could another type of graph have been used? Why?
d) Which job has the highest weekly earnings? The lowest weekly earnings? How is this shown in your graph?
e) How can the data be used to find the average annual earnings? The average monthly earnings? How might the graph be used to find these?
f) Which average: mean, median, or mode, do you think is shown in the table? Explain your answer.

5.5 **3.** Jacob collected the data in the table below. The table lists 5 TV shows that air on Sunday evenings. The survey question was "Which of these shows is your favourite?
Everyone Loves Jordan___, Girl Meets World___, Lost in Time___, Metro PD___, Reality Shock___"

TV Show	Tally	Frequency
Everyone Loves Jordan	~~////~~ ~~////~~ ~~////~~ //	
Girl Meets World	~~////~~ ~~////~~	
Lost in Time	~~////~~ ////	
Metro PD	////	
Reality Shock	~~////~~ ~~////~~ ~~////~~ ~~////~~	

a) Write the frequency of each response.
b) How many people did Jacob survey?
c) Suppose you were a TV producer and had to take one show off the air. Which show would it be? Explain.
d) Suppose you were an advertiser. Which show would you advertise with? Why?
e) Display the data using:
   i) a pictograph
   ii) a bar graph

5.3 5.5 **4.** A quality control inspector measures the masses of boxes of raisins. He wants to know if the average mass of a box of raisins is 100 g.
He randomly chooses boxes from the production department.
The masses, in grams, are recorded below.

Masses of Boxes of Raisins in Grams
99.1, 101.7, 99.8, 98.9, 100.8, 100.3, 98.3, 100.0, 97.8, 97.6, 98.5, 101.7, 100.2, 100.2, 99.4, 100.3, 98.8, 102.0, 100.3, 98.0, 99.4, 99.0, 98.1, 101.8, 99.8, 101.3, 100.5, 100.7, 98.7, 100.3, 99.3, 102.5

a) Draw a stem-and-leaf plot.
b) What can you tell from the plot that you could not easily see from the data?
c) Will this shipment be approved? Explain.
d) What is the median?
e) What is the mode?

f) Would the shipment be approved if the mode was used? If the median was used? Explain.

5.4
5.5 **5.** The mean monthly rainfalls for Calgary and Charlottetown are given.

Mean Monthly Rainfall (cm)		
Month	**Calgary**	**Charlottetown**
January	1.2	9.8
February	1.0	8.2
March	1.5	7.6
April	2.5	7.5
May	5.3	8.0
June	7.7	7.9
July	7.0	7.4
August	4.9	9.0
September	4.8	9.2
October	1.6	9.9
November	1.2	11.5
December	1.3	10.0

a) Draw a line graph for each city on the same grid.
b) Describe each graph. Are there any trends? Explain.
c) Do the line graphs cross? What does this mean?
d) Determine the mean annual rainfall for each city. Explain your steps.
e) Determine the median monthly rainfall for each city.
f) What else do you know from the table or the graph?

5.5 **6.** In each case, which is most useful: the mean, median, or mode? Justify your answer.

a) A storeowner wants to know which sweater sizes he should order. Last week he sold 5 small, 15 medium, 6 large, and 2 X-large sweaters.
b) Five of Robbie's friends said their weekly allowances are: \$5, \$8, \$10, \$6, and \$5. Robbie wants to convince his parents to increase his allowance.
c) Tina wants to know if her math mark was in the top half or bottom half of the class.

5.5
5.6 **7.** A small engineering company has an owner and 5 employees. This table shows their salaries.

Company Salaries	
Position	**Annual Salary ($)**
Owner	130 000
Manager	90 000
2 Engineers	50 000
Receptionist	28 000
Secretary	28 000

Which measure of central tendency would you use to describe the average annual salary in each case?

a) You want to attract a new employee.
b) You want to suggest the company does not pay its employees well.

Practice Test

1. a) Explain the difference between primary and secondary data.
   b) State if primary data or secondary data are used in each case. Justify your answers.
      i) Anna searched the Internet to find the top ten movies of the year.
      ii) Rory phoned his friends to ask if they were coming to his party.

800-m Race Times
3:25, 3:07, 1:55, 3:11
2:41, 2:47, 3:04, 1:58
2:35, 3:25, 3:08, 2:53
2:29, 3:15, 2:55, 2:28
3:14, 2:47, 3:07, 2:39
2:39, 2:43, 3:19, 2:54
3:11, 2:59, 2:42, 2:57

2. Here are the times, in minutes and seconds, of 28 people who competed in an 800-m race.
   a) Display the data in a stem-and-leaf plot.
   b) What is the range of times for the race?
   c) Find the median time.
   d) Is there a mode time? If so, what is it? If not, explain how you know.

3. Parham received these marks on 7 math tests:
   91, 75, 95, 80, 83, 86, 68
   What mark will he need on his next test in each case?
   Justify each answer.
   a) The mean of his 8 tests is 84.
   b) The mode of his 8 tests is 86.
   c) The median of his 8 tests is 84.

Country of Origin for Visitors to Canada

Country	Number of Visitors
Japan	500 000
France	400 000
Germany	400 000
Australia	175 000
United Kingdom	850 000
Mexico	150 000
Hong Kong	125 000

4. a) Graph the data at the left. Explain your choice of graph.
   b) In the year 2000, approximately 15 000 000 people visited Canada from the U.S.
      Suppose you want to add these data to your graph in part a. How would your graph change?
   c) Redraw the graph in part a.
      Include the data from part b.
   d) Compare the two graphs.
      Which graph gives you more information?
      Justify your answer.

Unit Problem Organizing a Winter Carnival

Your help is needed to organize a school Winter Carnival Day. Think about:

- the classes or grades that should participate
- which activities students would enjoy
- which snacks and drinks should be offered

You will collect, display, and analyse data.

Part 1

Brainstorm with your classmates. Keep a record of the ideas. Here are some topics you may want to discuss:

- Who will participate in Winter Carnival Day? Is it possible for all students in every grade in your school to participate? Are there special considerations for different age groups?
- What type of indoor and outdoor sports, games, and crafts do you think students in your school would enjoy?
- What types of snacks and drinks should be offered? How much will this cost?

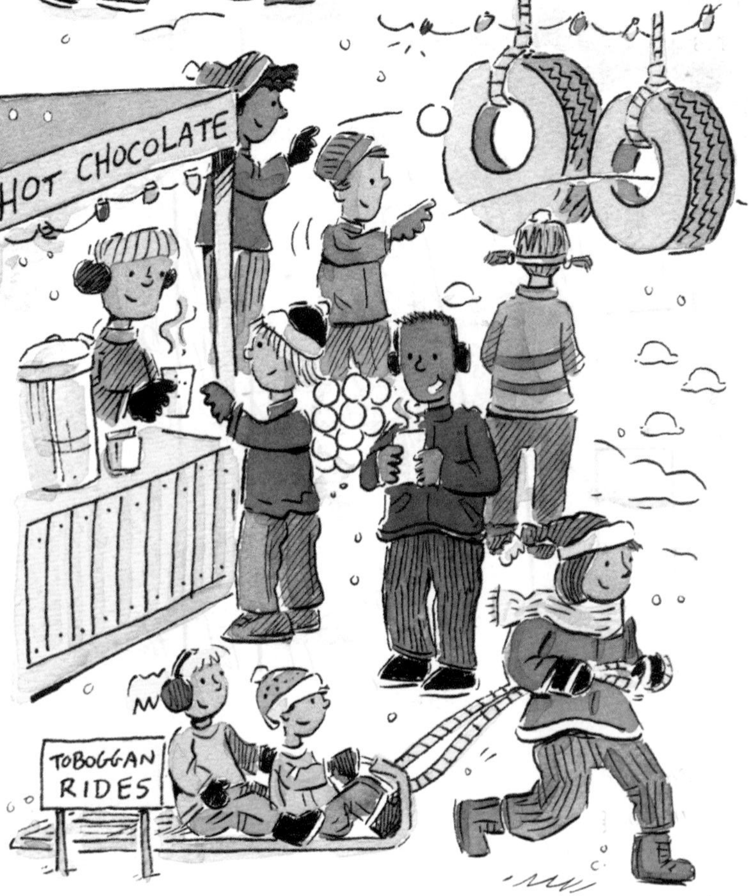

After brainstorming, break into five groups. Each group will be responsible for collecting data and reporting on one of the following topics:

- Indoor sports
- Outdoor sports
- Games
- Crafts
- Snacks and drinks

Part 2

Your group will collect, display, and analyse data related to your task.

- Write a survey question or questions related to your task. Explain how bias can be avoided when writing the question.
- Conduct the survey.
- Display the collected data in different ways. Justify your displays.
- Analyse the data. What decisions can be made about Winter Carnival Day from your results?
- Prepare a report of your findings.

Check List

Your work should include:

✓ your survey question and data collection plan

✓ at least two displays of your data

✓ justification for the procedures and displays you chose

✓ your analysis and recommendations

Part 3

Present the results of your group work to the rest of the class.

Reflect on the Unit

Describe the different types of graphs you drew.
What can you tell about the data from each type of graph?
Use examples to explain.

UNIT 6

Measuring Perimeter and Area

You see geometric figures all around you.

Look at these pictures.
Identify a figure.
What would you need to know to find the area of that figure?
What would you need to know to find the perimeter of the figure?

What You'll Learn

- Use formulas to find the areas of a parallelogram, a triangle, and a trapezoid.
- Find the area and perimeter of an irregular figure.

Why It's Important

- The ability to measure is a life skill. You measure to find how much paint you need for a wall; how much fencing you need for a garden; how much material you need for drapes; and so on.

Key Words

- perimeter
- area
- parallelogram
- triangle
- trapezoid

UNIT 6

Skills You'll Need

Perimeter and Area of a Rectangle

Perimeter is the distance around a figure.
Area is the amount of surface a figure covers.

Example 1

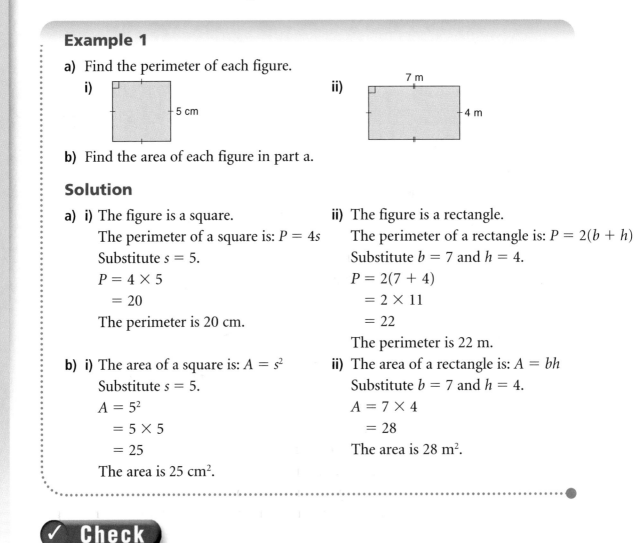

a) Find the perimeter of each figure.

i)

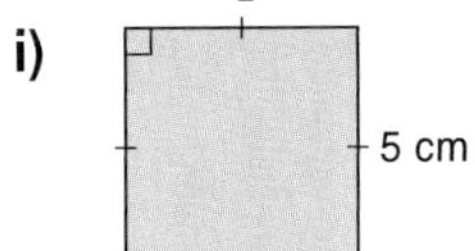

ii)

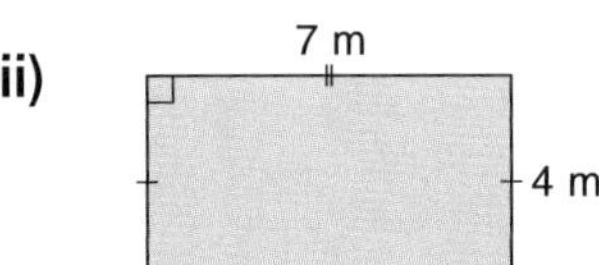

b) Find the area of each figure in part a.

Solution

a) i) The figure is a square.
The perimeter of a square is: $P = 4s$
Substitute $s = 5$.
$P = 4 \times 5$
$= 20$
The perimeter is 20 cm.

ii) The figure is a rectangle.
The perimeter of a rectangle is: $P = 2(b + h)$
Substitute $b = 7$ and $h = 4$.
$P = 2(7 + 4)$
$= 2 \times 11$
$= 22$
The perimeter is 22 m.

b) i) The area of a square is: $A = s^2$
Substitute $s = 5$.
$A = 5^2$
$= 5 \times 5$
$= 25$
The area is 25 cm^2.

ii) The area of a rectangle is: $A = bh$
Substitute $b = 7$ and $h = 4$.
$A = 7 \times 4$
$= 28$
The area is 28 m^2.

✓ Check

1. Find the perimeter and area of each figure.

a)

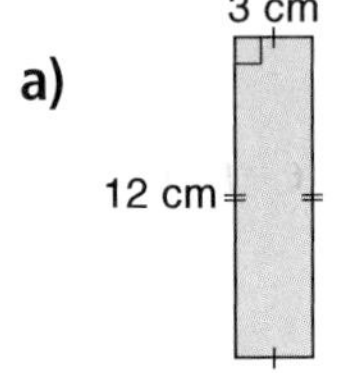

b)

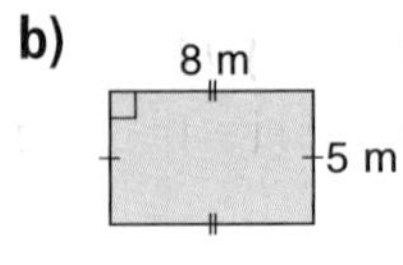

c)

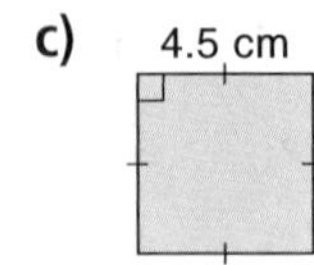

d)

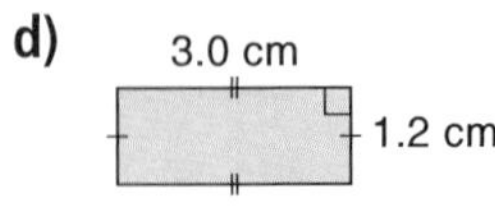

6.1 Area of a Parallelogram

Focus Use a formula to find the area of a parallelogram.

This is a **parallelogram**.
How would you describe it?

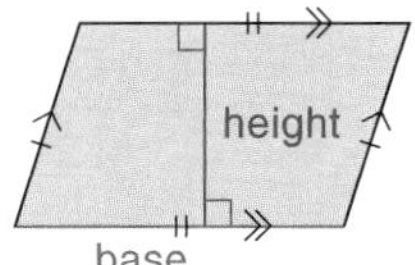

Here is the same parallelogram.
Any side of the parallelogram is a base.
The height is perpendicular to the base.

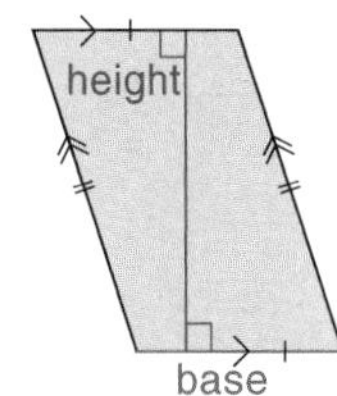

Explore

Work with a partner.

You will need a tangram and grid paper.

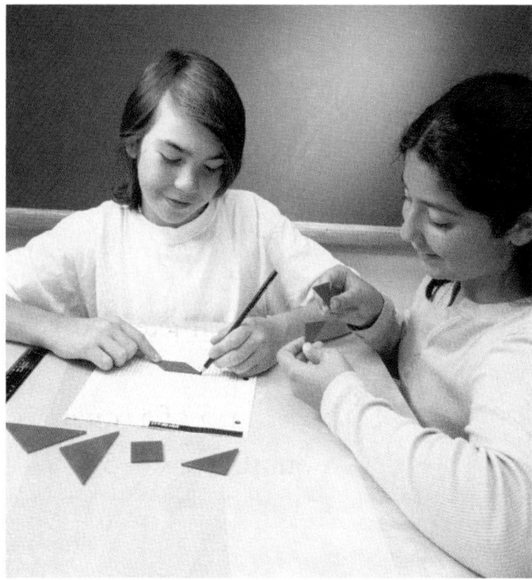

- One tan is a parallelogram. Find its area.
- Make another parallelogram by combining tans. Find the area of the parallelogram.
- Continue to combine tans to make different parallelograms. Find the area of each parallelogram you make.
- Record your work. Draw each parallelogram on grid paper.
- Use variables. Write a formula to find the area of a parallelogram.

Reflect & Share

How did you find the area of each parallelogram?
Which different strategies did you use?
Which strategy helped you write the formula for the area?

Connect

Recall that both a rectangle and a square are parallelograms.

Any parallelogram that is not a rectangle can be "cut" and rearranged to form a rectangle.

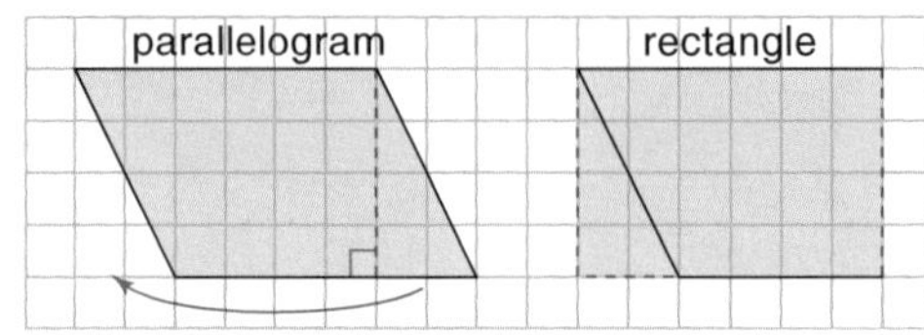

The parallelogram and the rectangle have the same area.
The area of a parallelogram is equal to the area of a rectangle with the same height and base.
To find the area of a parallelogram, multiply the base by the height.

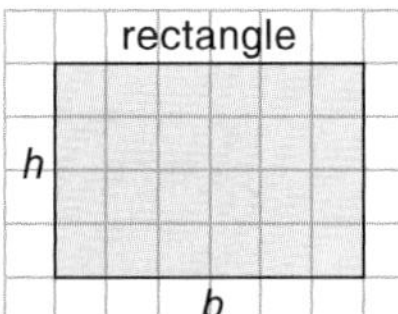

parallelogram, h, b

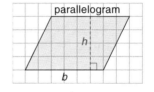

b represents the base.
h represents the height.

Area of rectangle:
$A = bh$

Area of parallelogram:
$A = bh$

Example

Calculate the area of each parallelogram.

a)

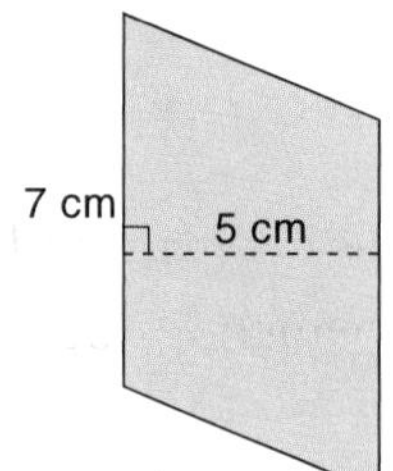

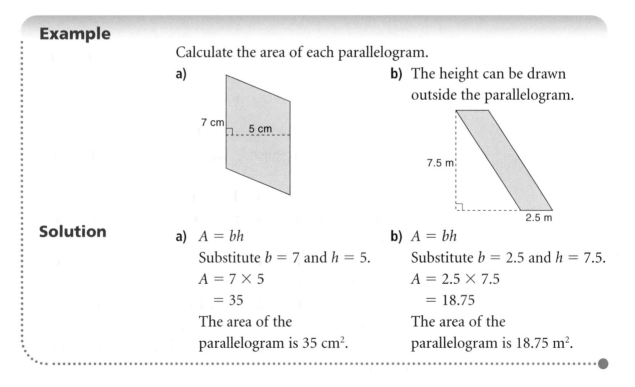

b) The height can be drawn outside the parallelogram.

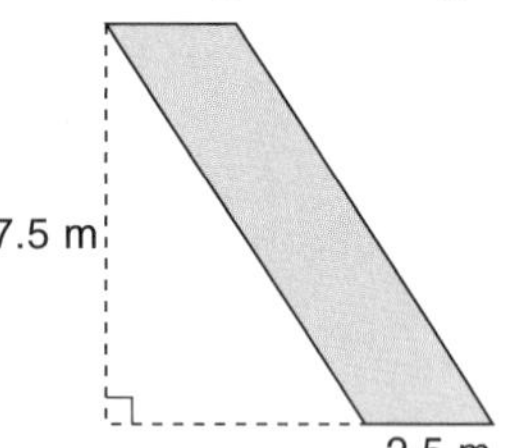

Solution

a) $A = bh$
Substitute $b = 7$ and $h = 5$.
$A = 7 \times 5$
$= 35$
The area of the parallelogram is 35 cm^2.

b) $A = bh$
Substitute $b = 2.5$ and $h = 7.5$.
$A = 2.5 \times 7.5$
$= 18.75$
The area of the parallelogram is 18.75 m^2.

Practice

Recall that you can use a protractor to draw the height perpendicular to the base.

1. Identify one base and height of each parallelogram.

a)

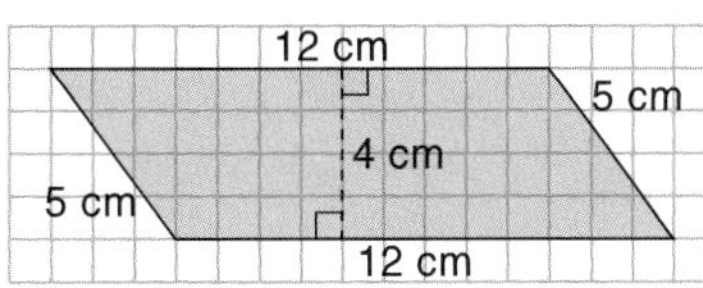

b)

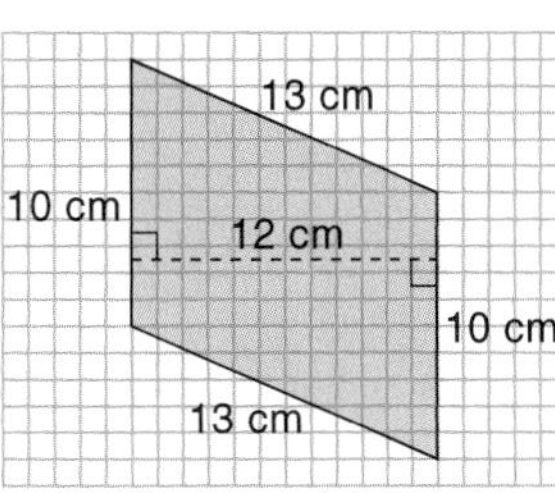

The base of a parallelogram is not always horizontal.

c)

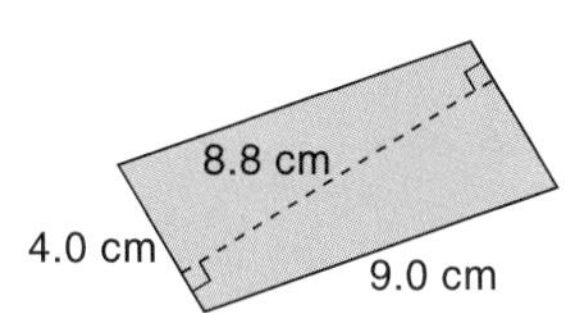

d)

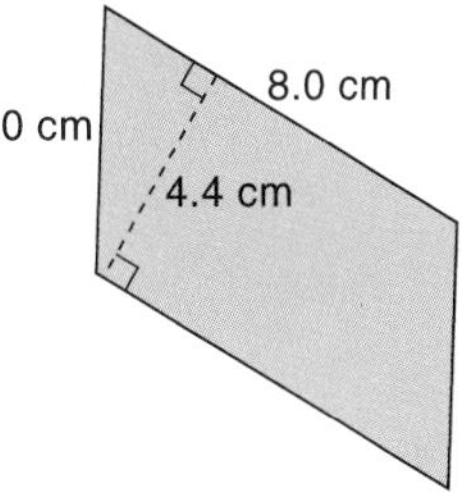

2. Find the area of each parallelogram in question 1.

3. **a)** On 1-cm grid paper, draw 3 different parallelograms with each base and height.

i) base: 3 cm; height: 5 cm **ii)** base: 3.5 cm; height: 7.0 cm

b) Find the area of each parallelogram you drew in part a. What do you notice?

4. On 1-cm grid paper, draw as many different parallelograms as you can with each area.

a) 10 cm^2 **b)** 18 cm^2 **c)** 28 cm^2

5. **Assessment Focus** Use 1-cm grid paper.
Draw a parallelogram, which is not a rectangle, with base 6 cm and height 4 cm.

a) What is the area of the parallelogram?

b) Change the base to draw a parallelogram with twice the area. What is the base?

c) Change the height to draw a parallelogram with twice the area. What is the height?

d) Change the base and height to draw a parallelogram with twice the area.
How many different pairs of base and height can you find?

Show your work.

Mental Math

It is Wednesday, January 14. Kim and Sun-Yi are working together.

Kim works every Wednesday. Sun-Yi works every 5th day.

When will Kim and Sun-Yi next work together?

6. The area of each parallelogram is given.
Find each unknown measure.

a) the height **b)** the base **c)** the height

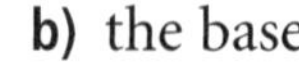

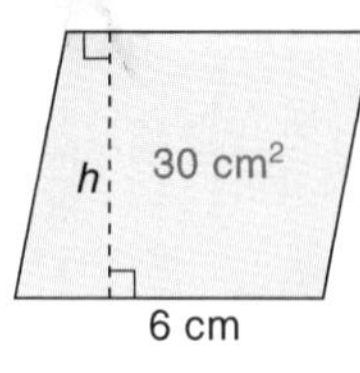

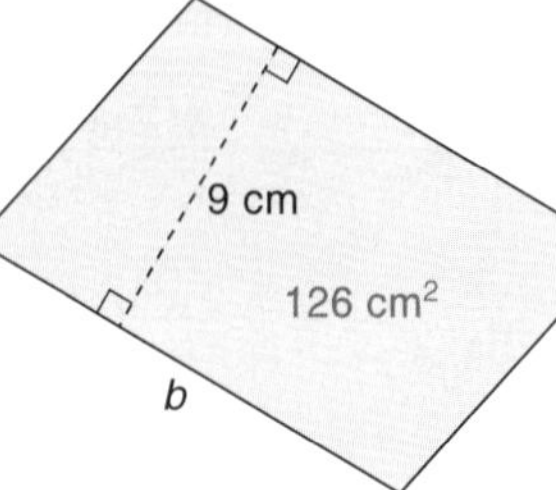

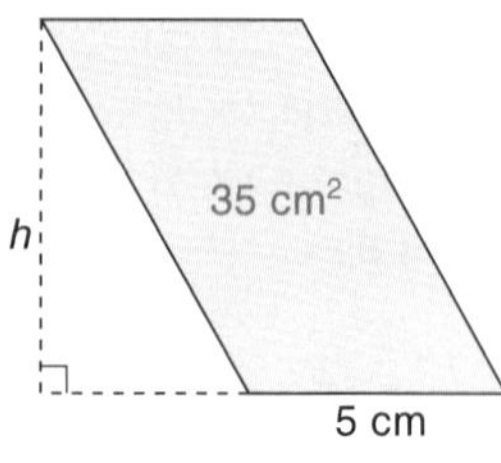

7. Use 1-cm grid paper.
Draw a rectangle with the same area as each parallelogram in question 6.
How many different ways can you do this?

8. Sasha is buying paint for a design on a wall.
Here is part of the design.
Sasha says figure B will need more paint than figure A.
Do you agree? Explain.

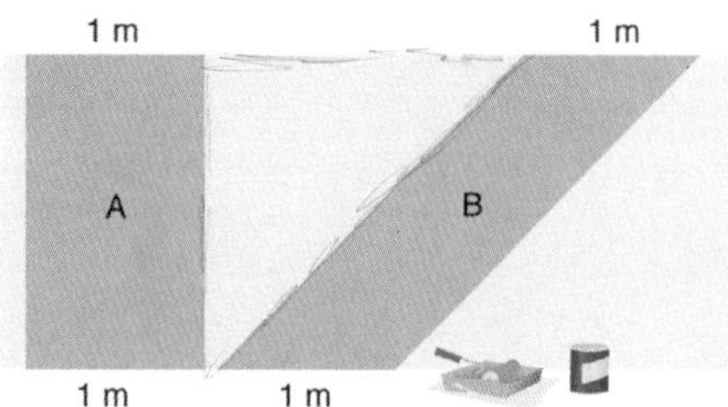

9. You will need 1-cm grid paper, ruler, and tracing paper.
Draw a parallelogram with base 10 cm and height 6 cm.
Draw a diagonal to make two triangles.

a) What do you notice about the two triangles?
How can you check your observation?

b) What is the area of the parallelogram?

c) What is the area of each triangle? How do you know?

Take It Further

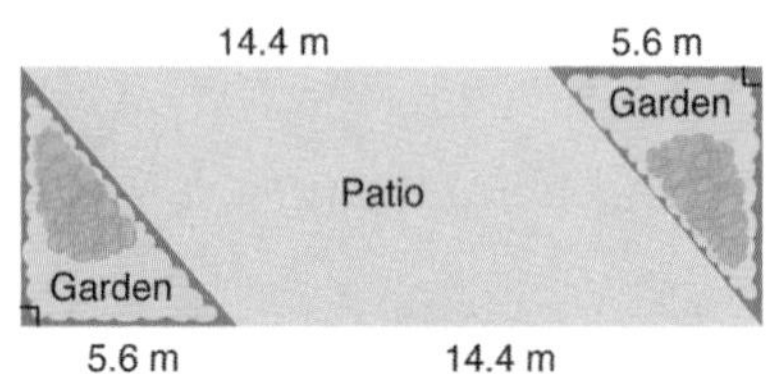

10. A restaurant owner built a patio in front of his store to attract more customers.

a) What is the area of the patio?

b) What is the total area of the patio and gardens?

c) How can you find the area of the gardens?

Show your work.

Reflect

What do you need to know to find the area of a parallelogram?
Use an example to explain.

6.2 Area of a Triangle

Focus Use a formula to find the area of a triangle.

Explore

Work with a partner.
You will need a ruler and 1-cm grid paper.
Draw each triangle below on 1-cm grid paper.

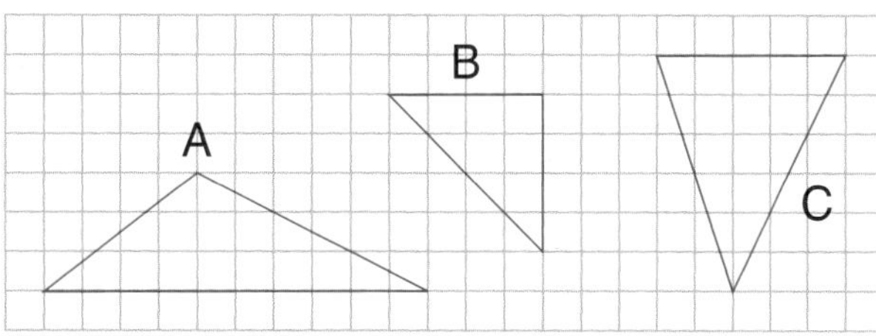

- How many different ways can you find the area of each triangle? What strategies did you use?
- Use what you know about parallelograms. Find the area of each triangle.
- Use variables. Write a formula to find the area of a triangle.

Reflect & Share

How did you use a parallelogram to find the area of a triangle?
Compare your formula with that of another pair of classmates.
If the formulas are different, can both of them be used to find the area of a triangle? Explain.

Connect

When we draw a diagonal in a parallelogram, we make 2 congruent triangles.
Congruent triangles have the same area.
So, the area of one triangle is $\frac{1}{2}$ the area of the parallelogram.

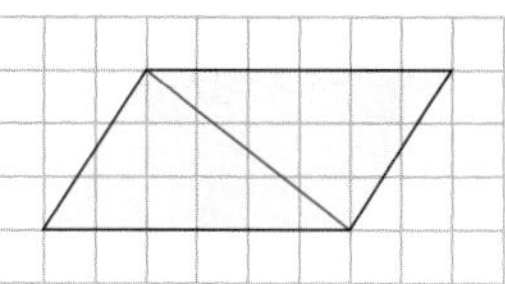

To find the area of this triangle:

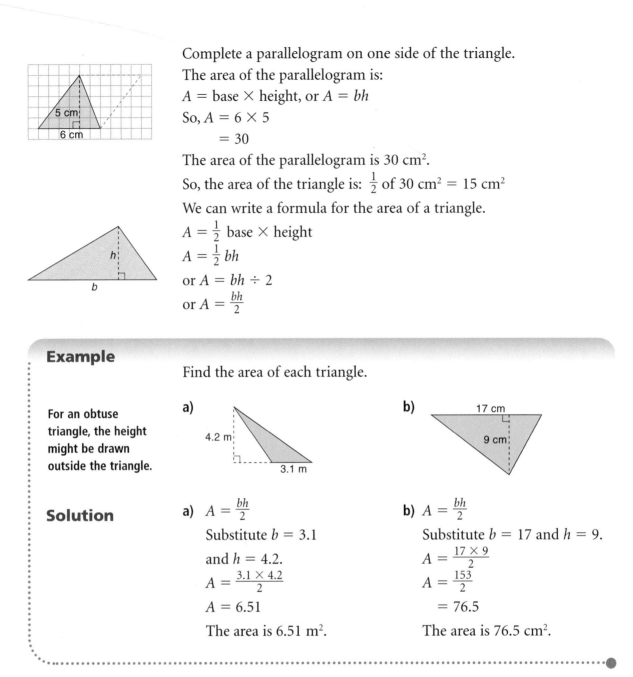

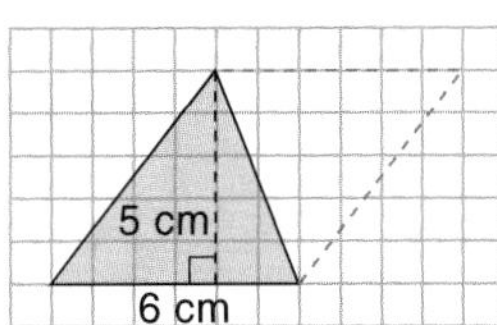

Complete a parallelogram on one side of the triangle.
The area of the parallelogram is:
$A = \text{base} \times \text{height}$, or $A = bh$
So, $A = 6 \times 5$
$= 30$
The area of the parallelogram is 30 cm^2.
So, the area of the triangle is: $\frac{1}{2}$ of 30 cm^2 = 15 cm^2
We can write a formula for the area of a triangle.

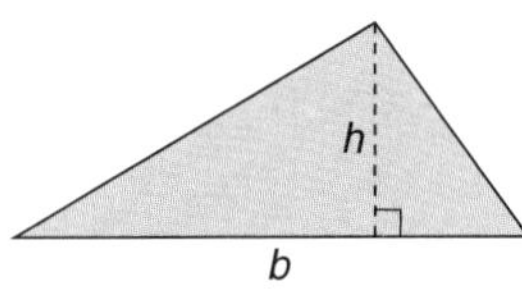

$A = \frac{1}{2}\text{ base} \times \text{height}$
$A = \frac{1}{2}bh$
or $A = bh \div 2$
or $A = \frac{bh}{2}$

Example

Find the area of each triangle.

For an obtuse triangle, the height might be drawn outside the triangle.

a)
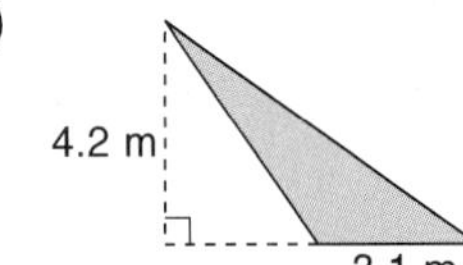

b)
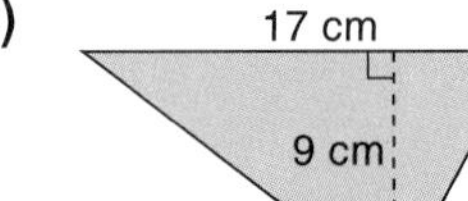

Solution

a) $A = \frac{bh}{2}$
Substitute $b = 3.1$ and $h = 4.2$.
$A = \frac{3.1 \times 4.2}{2}$
$A = 6.51$
The area is 6.51 m^2.

b) $A = \frac{bh}{2}$
Substitute $b = 17$ and $h = 9$.
$A = \frac{17 \times 9}{2}$
$A = \frac{153}{2}$
$= 76.5$
The area is 76.5 cm^2.

Practice

1. Identify one base and height of each triangle.

a)
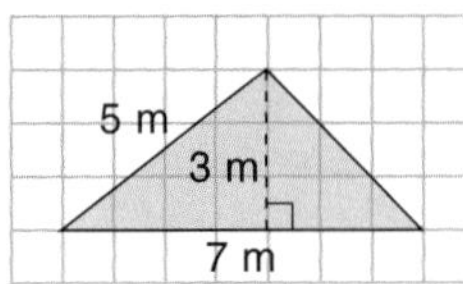

b)
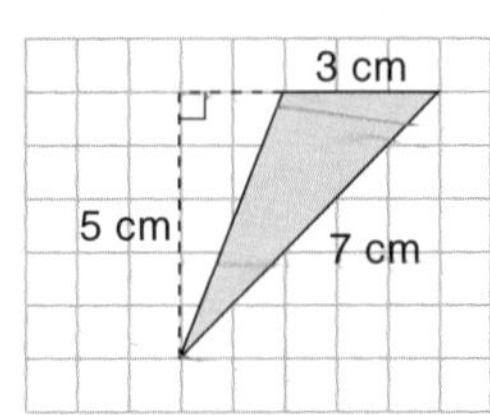

In a right triangle, one base and height are two sides of the triangle.

c)

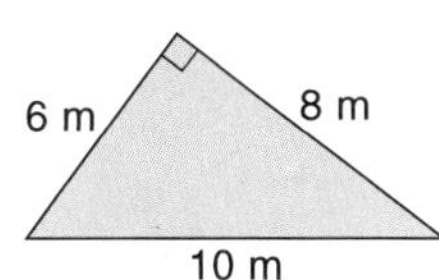

d)

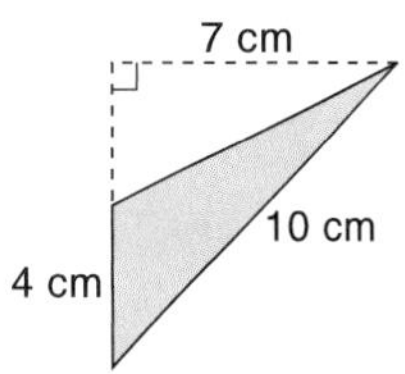

2. Find the area of each triangle in question 1.

3. **a)** On 1-cm grid paper, draw 3 different triangles with each base and height.

i) base: 4 cm; height: 3 cm **ii)** base: 7.5 cm; height: 6.5 cm

b) Find the area of each triangle you drew in part a.
What do you notice?

4. On 1-cm grid paper, draw two different triangles with each area.

a) 16 cm^2 **b)** 8 cm^2 **c)** 10 cm^2

5. Use 1-cm grid paper.

a) Draw a triangle with area 12 cm^2.

b) Investigate the different ways you can draw a triangle that has:

i) double the area **ii)** one-half the area

Write a report of your findings.

6. Use 1-cm grid paper.

a) Draw different triangles with base 4 cm and height 6 cm.

b) Find the area of each triangle you draw.

c) Measure the side lengths of each triangle you draw.

How do you know all the triangles are different?

Calculator Skills

Which is the best deal?
How do you know?
250 g cheese for \$2.99
400 g cheese for \$4.99
600 g cheese for \$6.79

7. The area of each triangle is given. Find each unknown measure.

a) the base

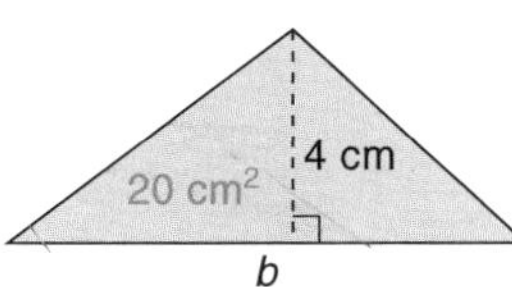

b) the height

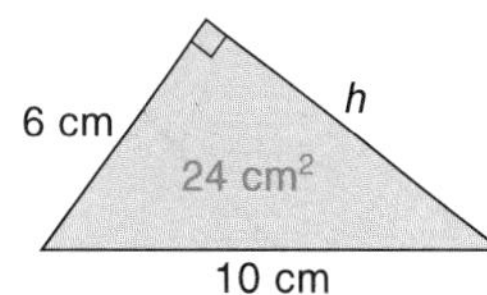

c) the base

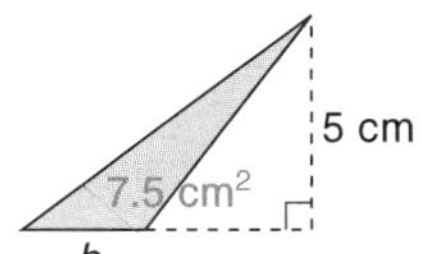

d) the height

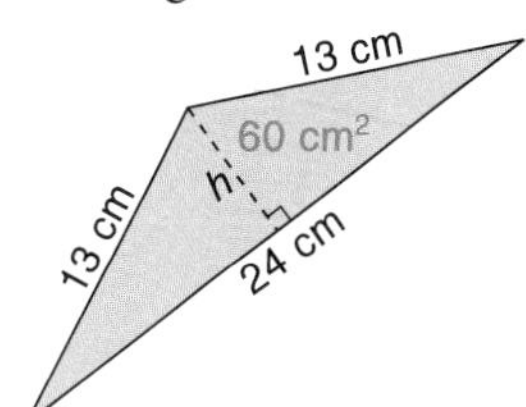

Your World

You use rulers and protractors to measure in the classroom.
Which measuring instruments do you have at home?
What do these instruments measure?
List all the instruments you can find.
Give an example of what each one measures.

8. When you know the area of a triangle, and its base, how can you find its height? Use an example to explain.

9. **Assessment Focus** The owner of a house paints this attic wall. There is a small rectangular window in the wall. One litre of paint covers 6.5 m^2.

a) What is the area that is to be painted?

b) The paint comes in 1-L cans. How many cans does the owner need? Explain your answer.

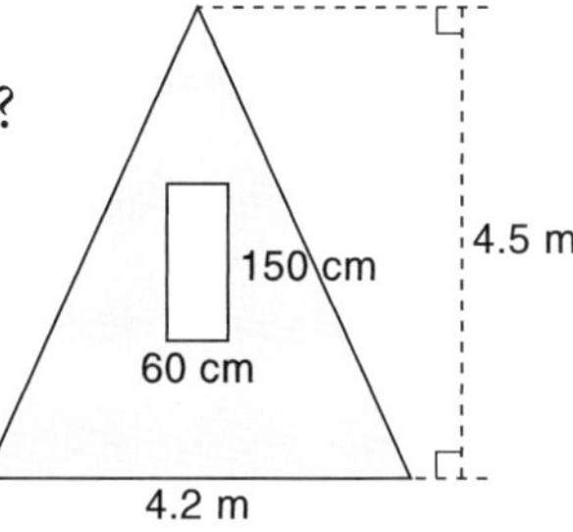

Take It Further

10. A local park has a pavilion to provide shelter. The pavilion has a roof the shape of a rectangular pyramid.

a) What is the total area of all four parts of the roof?

b) One sheet of plywood is 240 cm by 120 cm. It costs $24.95. What is the least number of sheets of plywood needed to cover the roof? What is the cost? Explain how you got your answer.

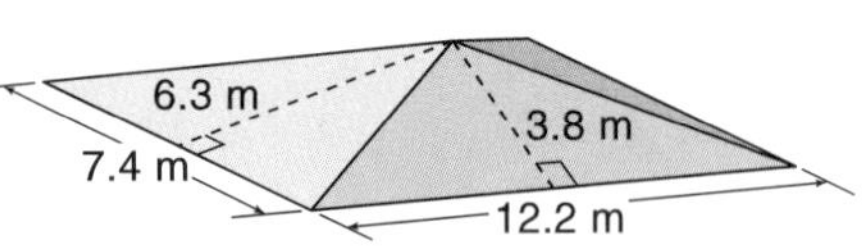

Reflect

A triangle and a parallelogram have the same base and height. How are the areas of the triangle and parallelogram related? Use an example to explain.

Mid-Unit Review

LESSON

6.1

1. Find the perimeter and area of each figure.

a)

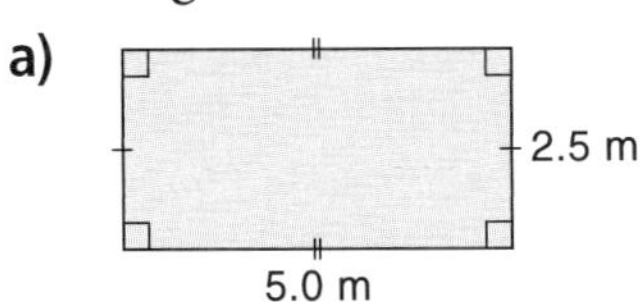

b)

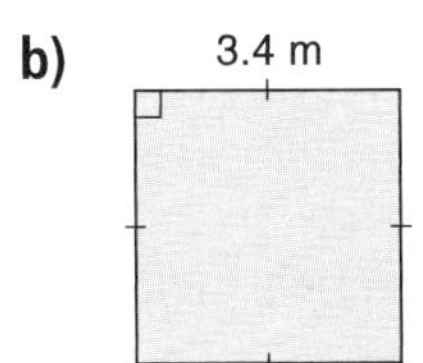

2. Find the area of each parallelogram.

a)

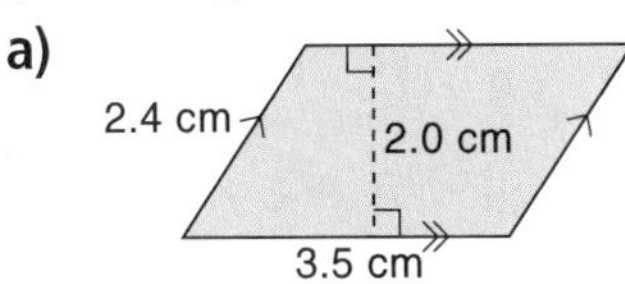

b)

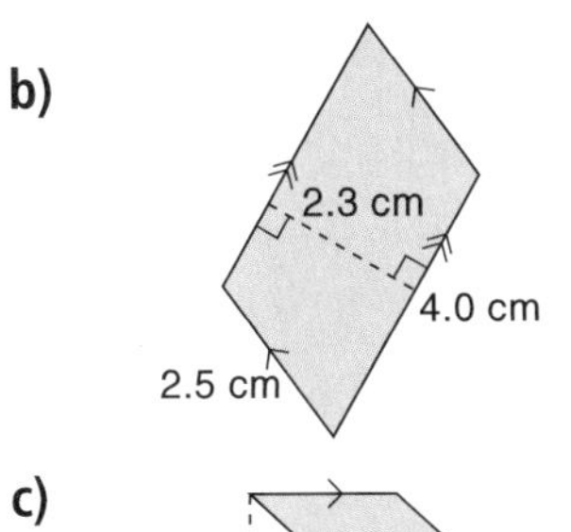

c)

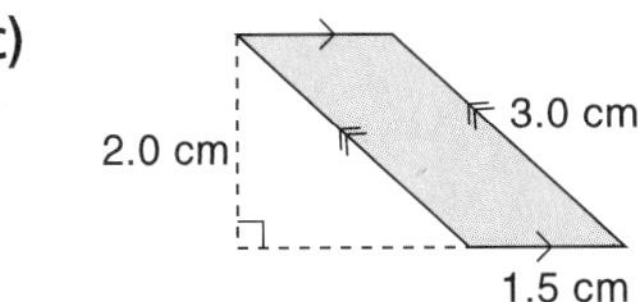

3. A parallelogram has height 45 cm and base 60 cm.

a) Find its area.

b) What is the base and height of a parallelogram with twice the area?

c) What is the base and height of a parallelogram with one-half the area?

6.2

4. Find the area of each triangle.

a)

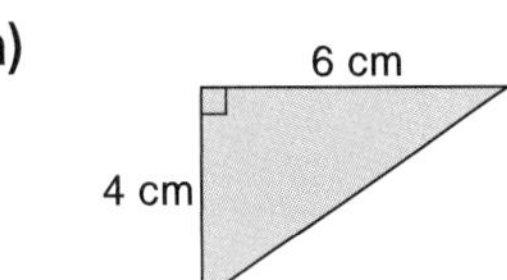

b)

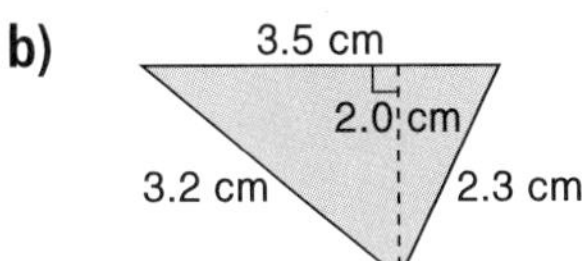

c)

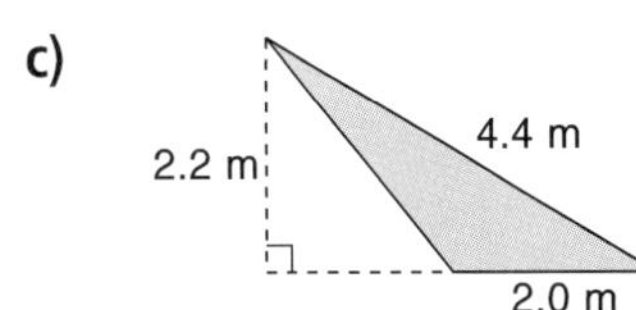

5. Po Ling is planning to pour a concrete patio beside her house. It has the shape of a triangle. The contractor charges $125.00 for each square metre of concrete poured.

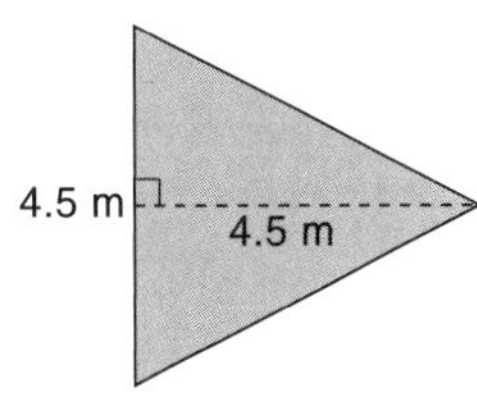

What will the contractor charge for the concrete?

6.3 Area and Perimeter of a Trapezoid

Focus Use a formula to find the area of a trapezoid.

This is a **trapezoid**.
How would you describe it?

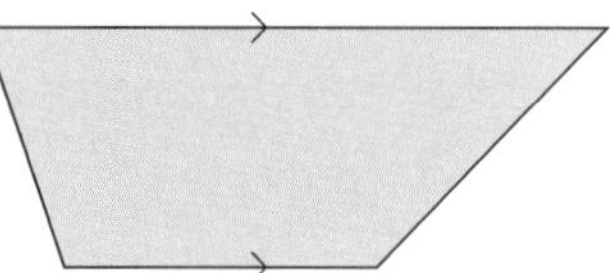

Recall that a rectangle, a square, and a parallelogram are trapezoids, too.

Explore

Work with a partner.
You will need scissors.
Your teacher will give you a copy of the figures below.

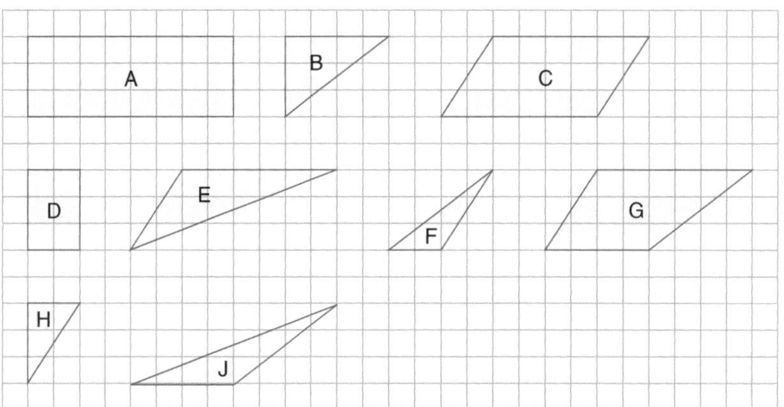

- ➢ Find the area of each figure.
- ➢ Cut out the figures.
- ➢ Identify the trapezoid that is not a parallelogram.
- ➢ How many different ways can you use the figures to find the area of the trapezoid?
- ➢ For each way you find, write a formula in words for the area of a trapezoid.
- ➢ Find the perimeter of the trapezoid.

Reflect & Share

How did you use what you know about the areas of a triangle, a rectangle, and a parallelogram to find the area of a trapezoid?

Connect

We can find the area of a trapezoid by dividing it into other figures.
Here are 3 ways to find the area of this trapezoid.

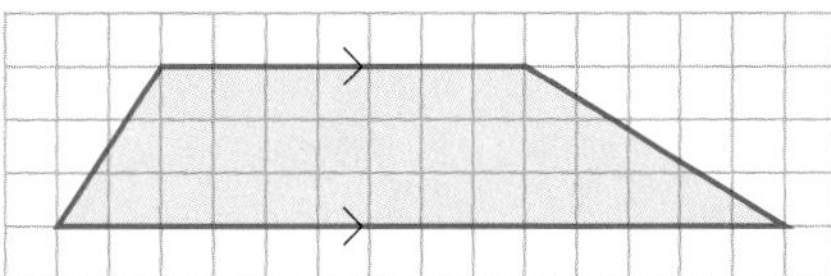

- Make 2 triangles and a rectangle.

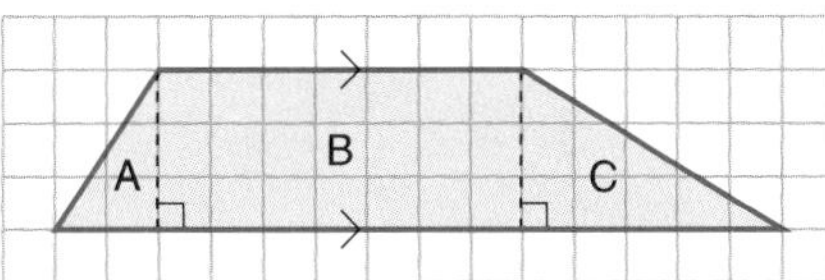

Area of trapezoid = area of triangle A + area of rectangle B + area of triangle C

- Make 1 triangle and a parallelogram.

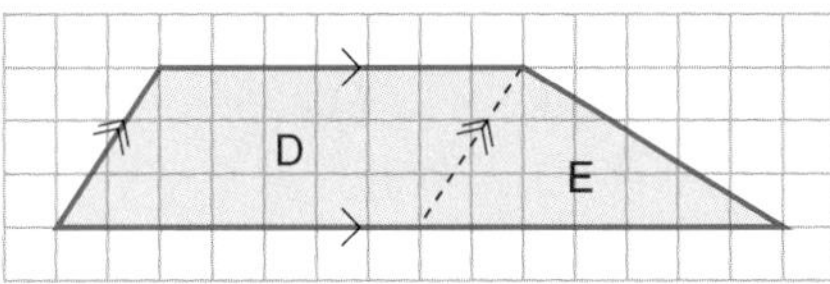

Area of trapezoid = area of parallelogram D + area of triangle E

- Make 2 triangles.

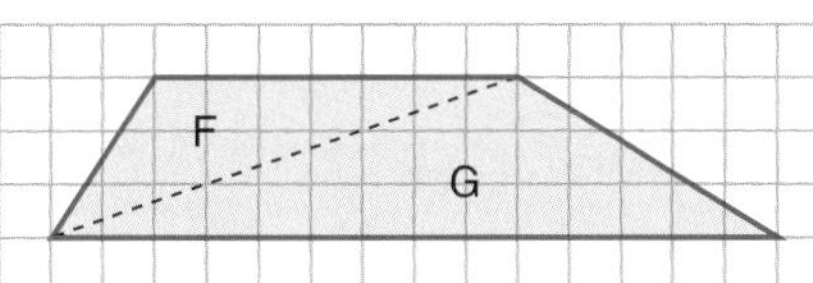

Area of trapezoid = area of triangle F + area of triangle G

Example

a) Estimate the area of this trapezoid.

b) Calculate the area to check your estimate.

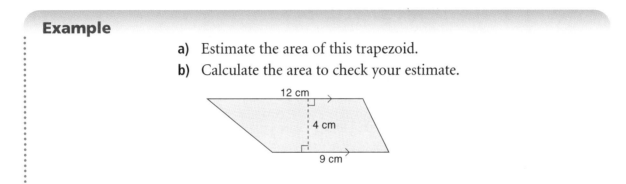

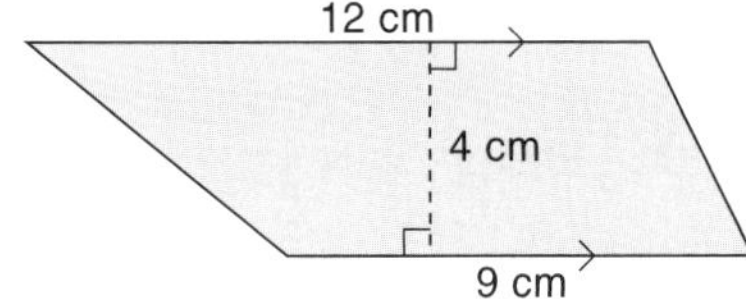

Solution

a) Sketch a rectangle with width 4 cm and length between 9 cm and 12 cm, maybe 10 cm. The area of the rectangle is an estimate of the area of the trapezoid.

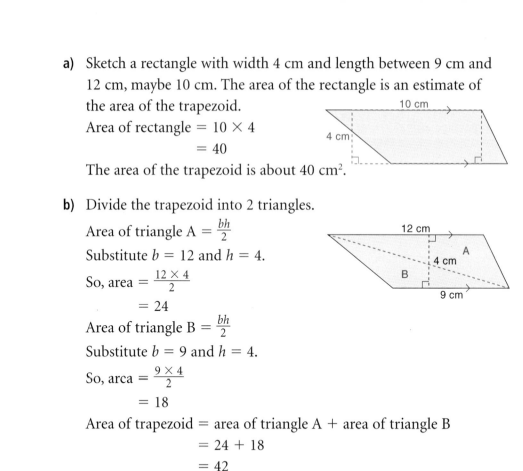

Area of rectangle $= 10 \times 4$

$= 40$

The area of the trapezoid is about 40 cm^2.

b) Divide the trapezoid into 2 triangles.

Area of triangle A $= \frac{bh}{2}$

Substitute $b = 12$ and $h = 4$.

So, area $= \frac{12 \times 4}{2}$

$= 24$

Area of triangle B $= \frac{bh}{2}$

Substitute $b = 9$ and $h = 4$.

So, area $= \frac{9 \times 4}{2}$

$= 18$

Area of trapezoid = area of triangle A + area of triangle B

$= 24 + 18$

$= 42$

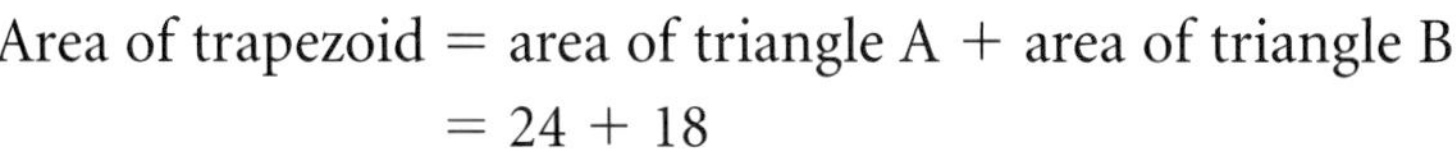

The area of the trapezoid is 42 cm^2.

Practice

1. Find the area of each trapezoid by dividing it into 2 triangles.

a)

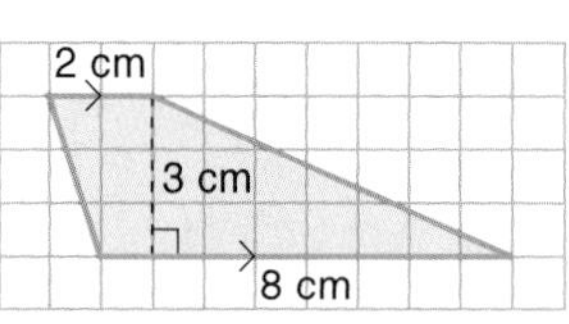

b)

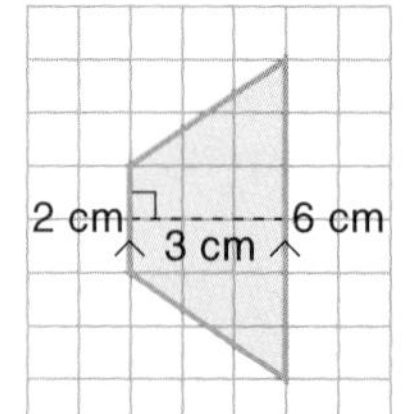

c)

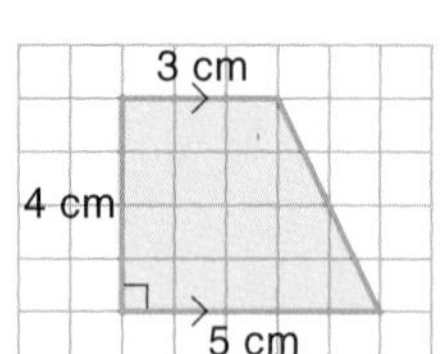

2. Find the area of each trapezoid by dividing it into 1 or 2 triangles and a rectangle.

a)

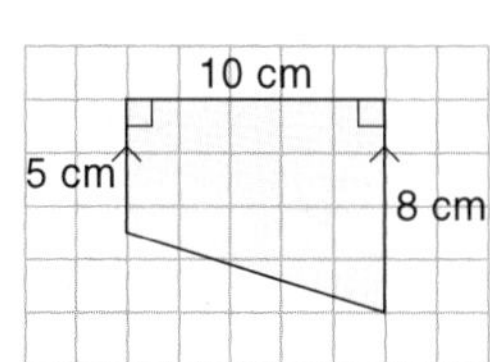

b)

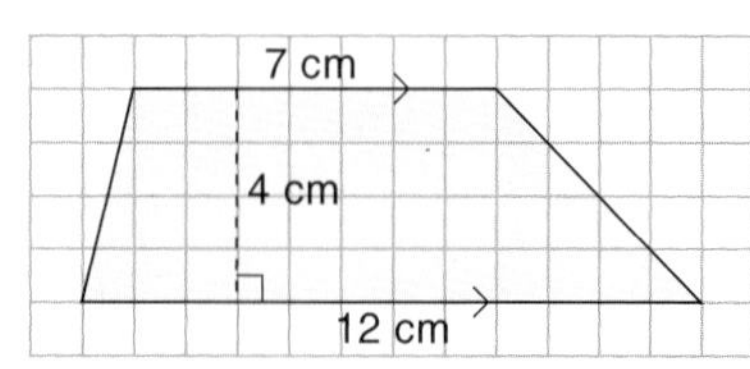

Calculator Skills

Predict each product.
Check your prediction.

What patterns do you see in the answers?

- 9 × 9
- 99 × 99
- 999 × 999
- 9999 × 9999

Use the pattern to predict the product of 99 999 × 99 999.

3. Find the area of each trapezoid.

a)

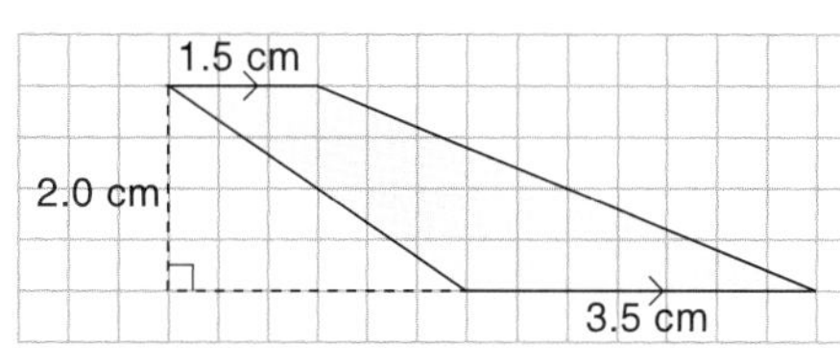

b)

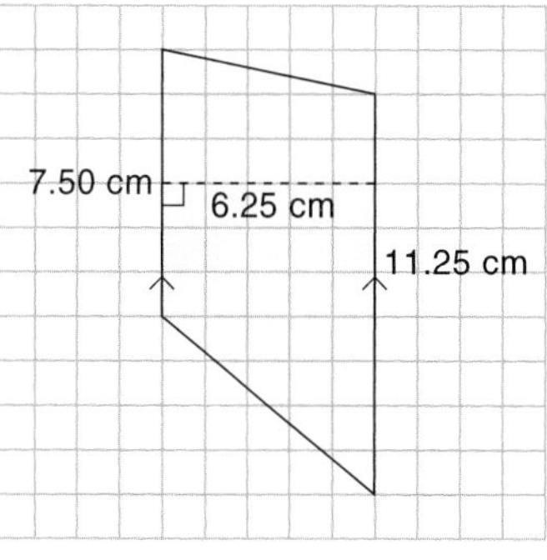

4. Find the area and perimeter of each trapezoid.

a)

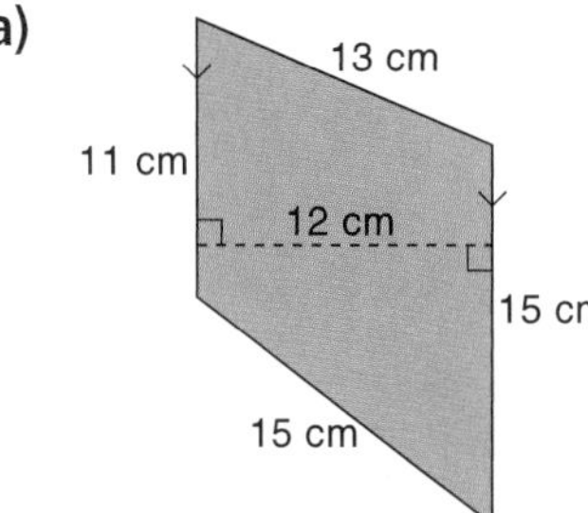

b)

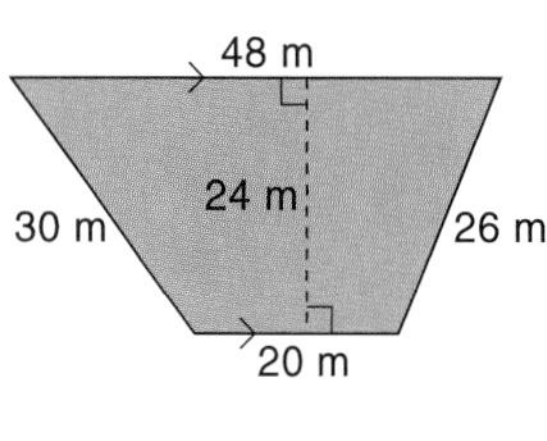

5. a) Estimate the area of each trapezoid.
Check your answer by calculating the area.

i)

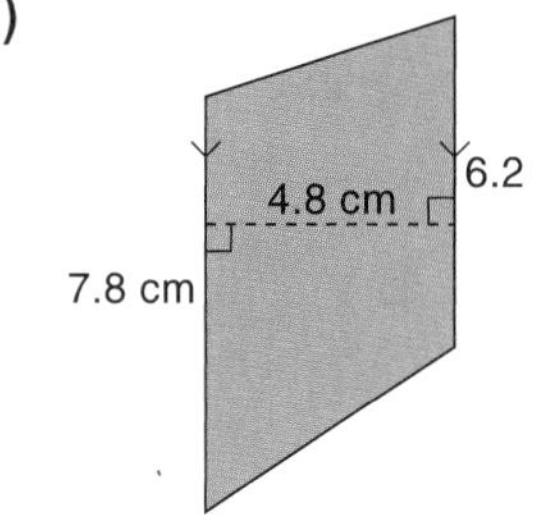

ii)

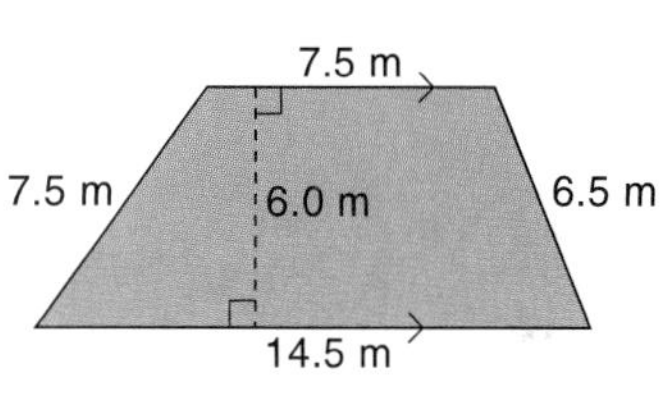

b) Can you find the perimeter of each trapezoid in part a?
Explain.

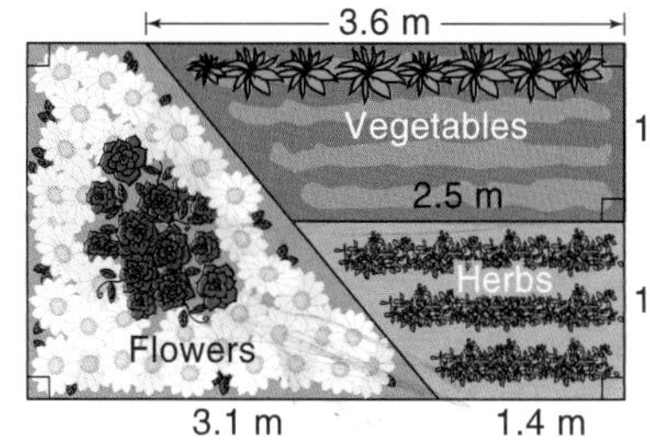

6. a) What is the area of each part of this garden?

b) Find the area of the whole garden two different ways.

7. Suppose you have a piece of string, 4 pushpins, a ruler, and grid paper.

a) Describe how to make a trapezoid with perimeter 20 cm.
Use your strategy to make the trapezoid.

b) Draw the trapezoid on grid paper.

c) Find the approximate area of the trapezoid.

8. Assessment Focus Two congruent trapezoids join to form a parallelogram.

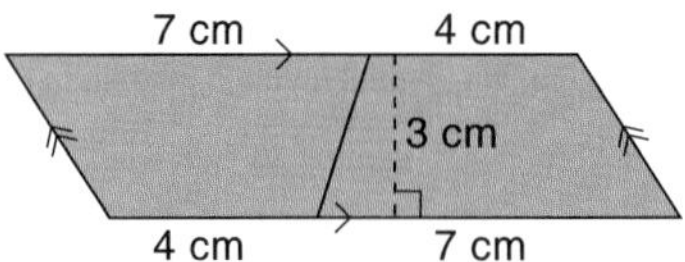

a) How can you use the area of the parallelogram to find the area of each trapezoid?

b) Use grid paper. Draw a trapezoid. Use the area of a parallelogram to find the area of your trapezoid.

Show your work.

Take It Further

9. A patio is made with congruent brick tiles.

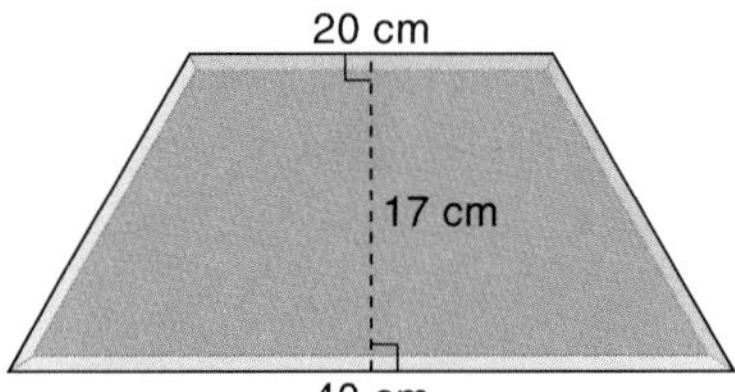

Each tile is a trapezoid.

a) What is the area of the top face of each tile?

b) Use red Pattern Blocks on triangular grid paper.
Sketch a patio that uses these trapezoid tiles.
How many tiles are in your patio?

c) What is the area of your patio?

d) When a patio is built, there is a 3-mm space between tiles for the grout.
Would your completed patio be larger or smaller than the area you calculated in part c? Explain.
How much larger or smaller would it be?

10. Use any of the methods you know to find the area of a trapezoid. Use variables. Write a formula for the area of a trapezoid.

Reflect

How can you use the strategies for finding the area of a trapezoid to find the areas of a square, rectangle, and parallelogram?
Use examples to explain.

Measuring for Construction

Before construction begins on a shopping mall, the site is precisely measured in different ways for different reasons. Measuring does not stop once construction begins. Initial measurements are checked and rechecked because estimates and plans sometimes change as the project continues.

The first "measurers" on the site are members of a survey team. The first thing they do is to verify the perimeter and area with an older, existing plan. In some cases, the last survey for the site might have been carried out 200 years before.

Most surveyors today have new, technology-based surveying tools. However, the team might use a transit (an angle-measuring device based on a telescope) and stadia (a graduated measuring rod). These measuring devices have been in use since the early 19th century. The survey team may have aerial or satellite photographs, EDM (Electronic Distance Measuring) equipment based on microwaves or lasers, or GPS (Global Positioning System) equipment.

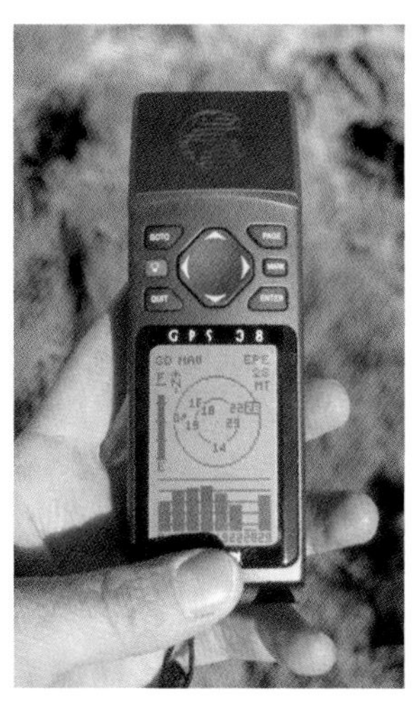

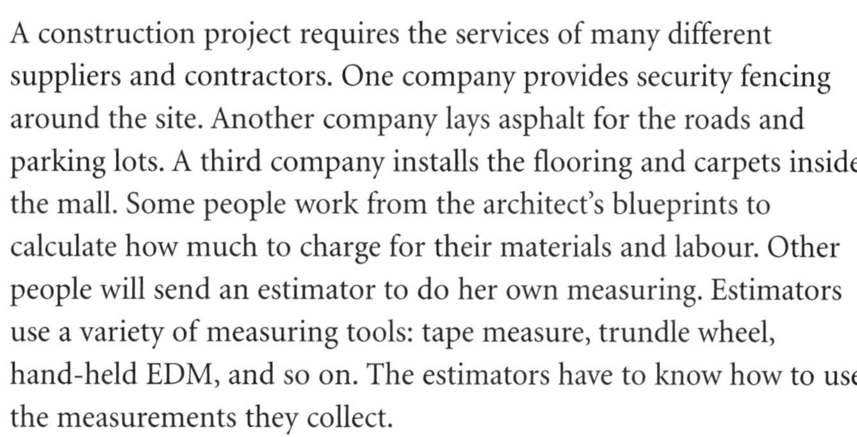

A construction project requires the services of many different suppliers and contractors. One company provides security fencing around the site. Another company lays asphalt for the roads and parking lots. A third company installs the flooring and carpets inside the mall. Some people work from the architect's blueprints to calculate how much to charge for their materials and labour. Other people will send an estimator to do her own measuring. Estimators use a variety of measuring tools: tape measure, trundle wheel, hand-held EDM, and so on. The estimators have to know how to use the measurements they collect.

Recently, a company introduced a digital measuring device. This device is wheeled around the perimeter of the region to calculate the area of the region. Why might this seem to be an impossible calculation? Can you explain how it might work?

Interpreting a Problem

Problem

How many different trapezoids can you draw with area 24 cm^2?

Interpret the problem

A trapezoid has at least 1 pair of parallel sides.
A trapezoid could have 2 pairs of parallel sides.
It would then be a rectangle or a parallelogram.

Solve the problem

Solution 1

To draw a rectangle with area 24 cm^2, find two factors of 24.
The factors in each pair are the base and the height of the rectangle:
$1 \times 24, 2 \times 12, 3 \times 8, 4 \times 6$
Each of these rectangles has area 24 cm^2.

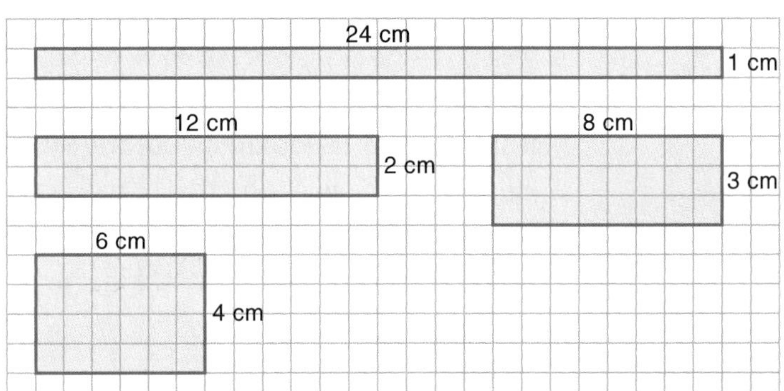

Solution 2

To draw a parallelogram with area 24 cm^2,
use the factors in *Solution 1*.
The factors in each pair are the base and the height
of the parallelogram.
Each of these parallelograms has area 24 cm^2.

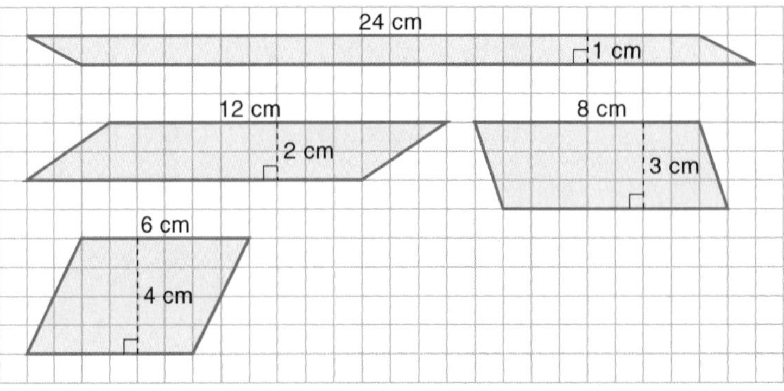

Solution 3 To draw a trapezoid (that is not a parallelogram) with area 24 cm^2:
Two congruent trapezoids join to form a parallelogram. If each trapezoid has area 24 cm^2, then the parallelogram has area 48 cm^2.

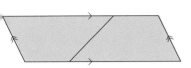

Work backward.
Draw a parallelogram with area 48 cm^2.
Divide it into 2 congruent trapezoids.
A parallelogram with area 48 cm^2 can have base 12 cm and height 4 cm.
Choose a length for one base of the trapezoid, less than 12 cm.
Choose 10 cm. Mark a point on the top side of the parallelogram 10 cm from the left vertex.
Mark a point on the bottom side of the parallelogram 10 cm from the right vertex.
Join these points to form two congruent trapezoids.
So, one trapezoid with area 24 cm^2 looks like this:

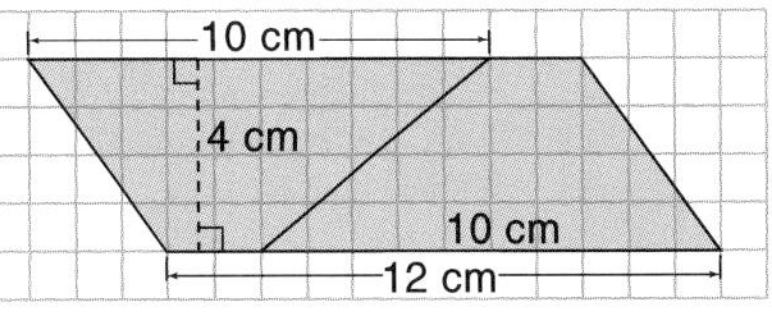

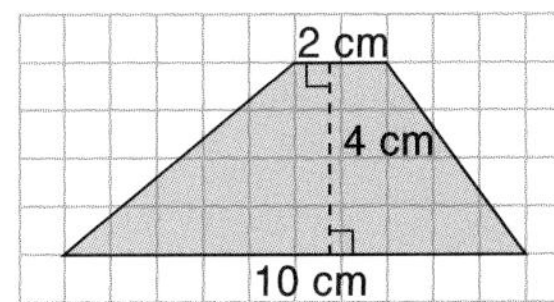

Look back

- What if we had chosen a parallelogram with base 8 cm and height 4 cm?
  What could the trapezoid look like?
- What if we had chosen 5 cm for one base of the trapezoid?
  What would the trapezoid look like?

Problems

1. Draw 3 different trapezoids with area 30 cm^2.

2. Think of other methods to find the area of a trapezoid.
Use a different method to draw a trapezoid with area 20 cm^2.

Choose an area for a trapezoid. Explain how to draw a trapezoid with that area. Include a diagram.

6.4 Measuring Irregular Figures

Focus Find the area and perimeter of an irregular figure.

In *Section 6.3*, you calculated the area of a trapezoid by dividing it into other figures.

You can use a similar strategy to find the areas of other irregular figures.

Explore

Work with a partner.
A garden in a backyard has this plan.

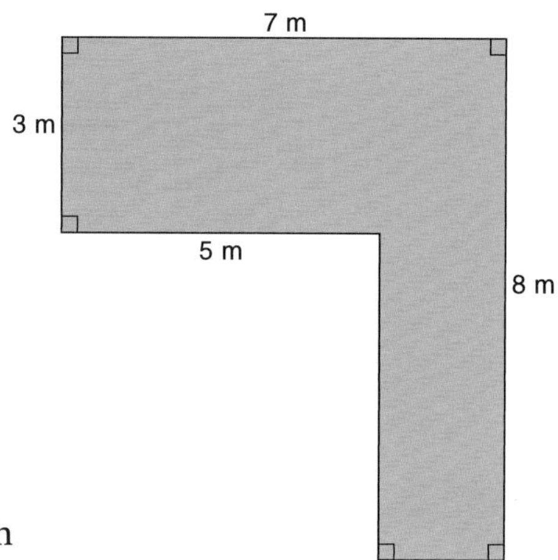

How many different ways can you find the area of the garden?
What is its perimeter?

Reflect & Share

Compare your strategies with those of another pair of students.
What other strategies could you have used?

Connect

Here are two ways to find the area of this irregular figure.

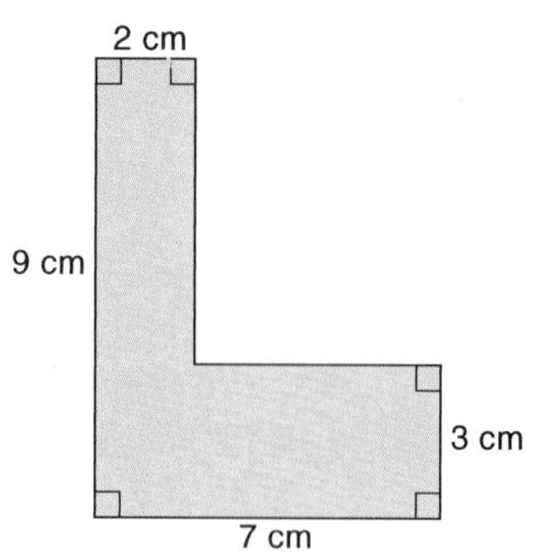

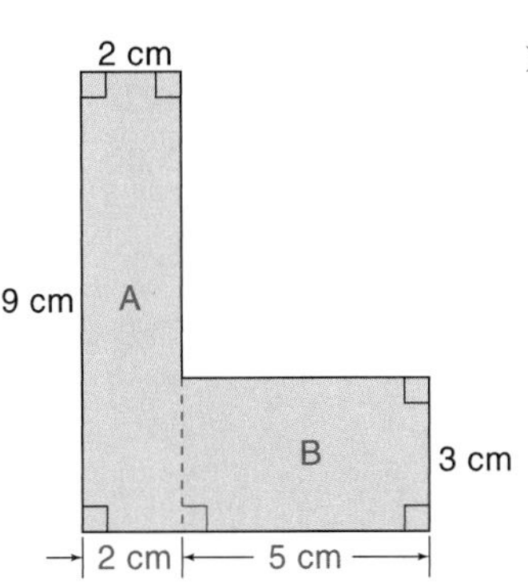

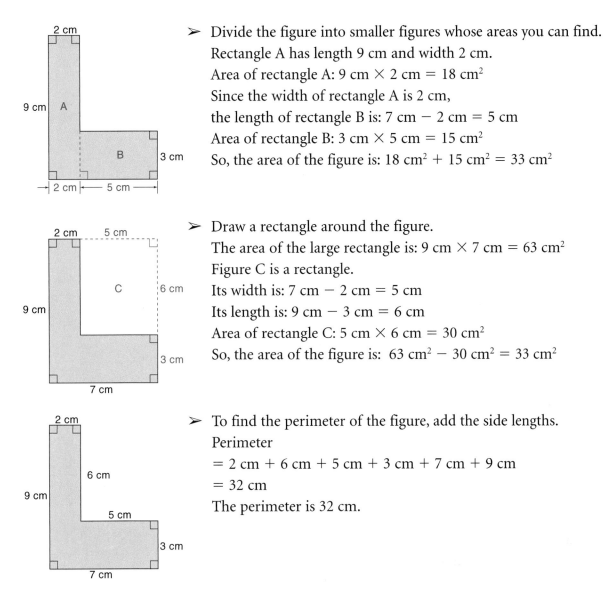

➢ Divide the figure into smaller figures whose areas you can find.
Rectangle A has length 9 cm and width 2 cm.
Area of rectangle A: 9 cm × 2 cm = 18 cm^2
Since the width of rectangle A is 2 cm,
the length of rectangle B is: 7 cm − 2 cm = 5 cm
Area of rectangle B: 3 cm × 5 cm = 15 cm^2
So, the area of the figure is: 18 cm^2 + 15 cm^2 = 33 cm^2

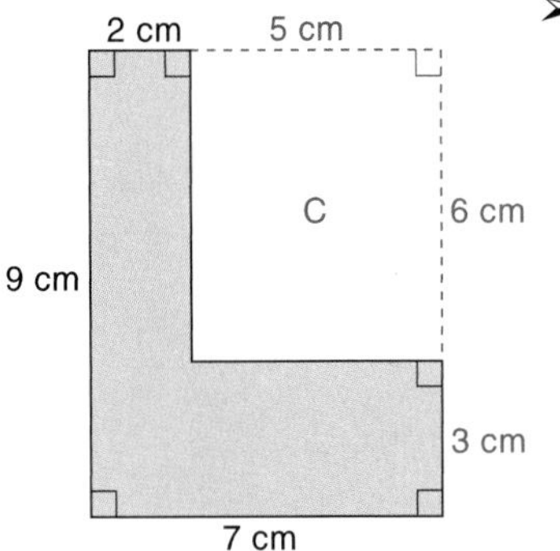

➢ Draw a rectangle around the figure.
The area of the large rectangle is: 9 cm × 7 cm = 63 cm^2
Figure C is a rectangle.
Its width is: 7 cm − 2 cm = 5 cm
Its length is: 9 cm − 3 cm = 6 cm
Area of rectangle C: 5 cm × 6 cm = 30 cm^2
So, the area of the figure is: 63 cm^2 − 30 cm^2 = 33 cm^2

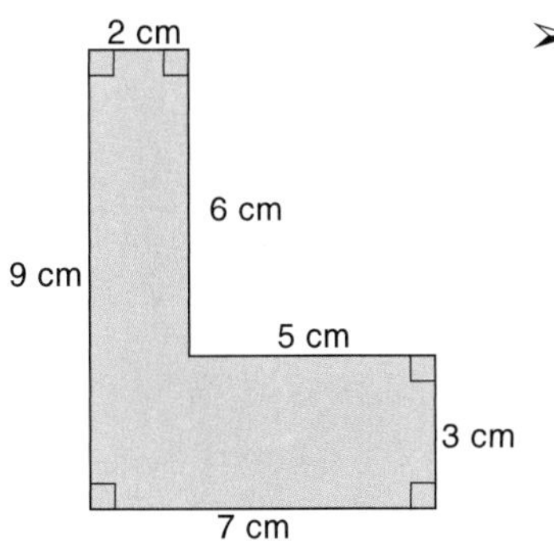

➢ To find the perimeter of the figure, add the side lengths.
Perimeter
= 2 cm + 6 cm + 5 cm + 3 cm + 7 cm + 9 cm
= 32 cm
The perimeter is 32 cm.

Example

Here is a plan of the back wall of a barn.

a) What is the area of the wall?

b) One can of paint covers 40 m^2.
How many cans are needed to paint this wall?

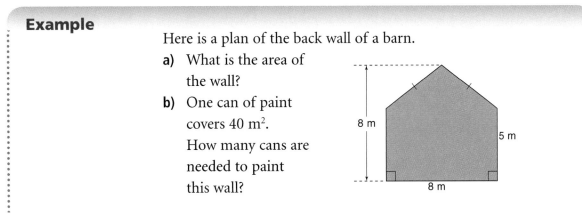

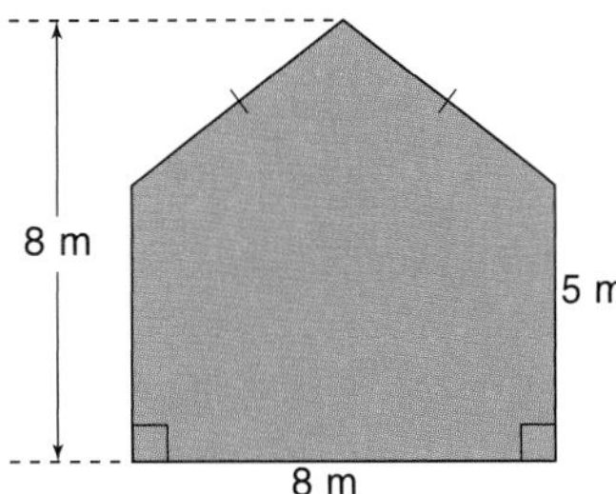

Solution

The wall is a rectangle with an isosceles triangle above it.

a) For the triangle:

The base, b, is 8 m.

The height, h, is 8 m $-$ 5 m $=$ 3 m.

Area $= \frac{bh}{2}$

Substitute $b = 8$ and $h = 3$.

Area $= \frac{8 \times 3}{2}$

$= 12$

For the rectangle:

Area $= bh$

Substitute $b = 8$ and $h = 5$.

Area $= 8 \times 5$

$= 40$

Area of wall $= 40\text{ m}^2 + 12\text{ m}^2$

$= 52\text{ m}^2$

The area of the wall is 52 m^2.

b) The area of the wall is 52 m^2.

One can of paint covers 40 m^2.

One can is not enough.

Two cans of paint are needed.

Practice

1. A living room in a home has the shape, below left.
What is the area of the living room?

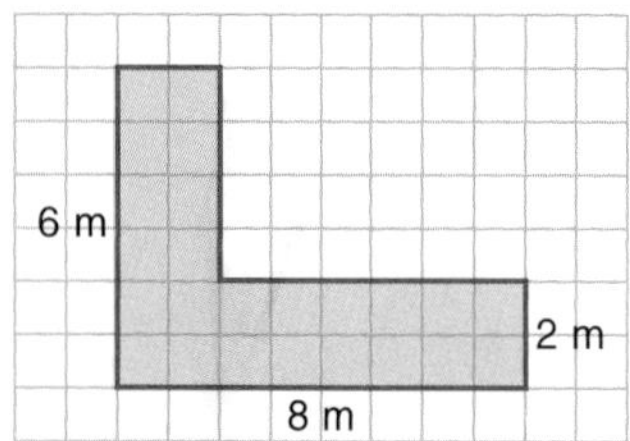

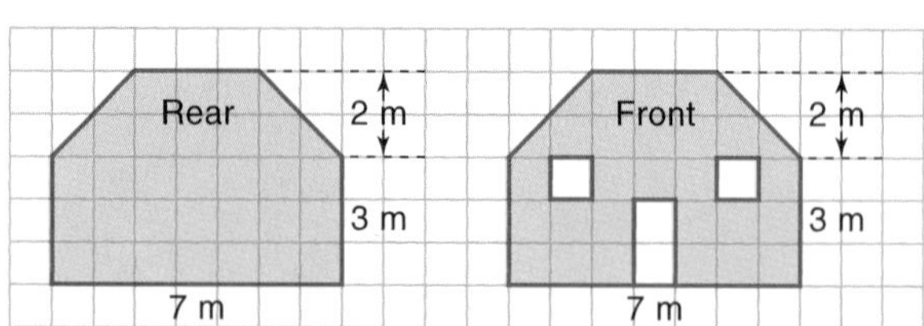

2. The rear and front walls of a shed are shown, above middle and right.

a) Find the area of the rear wall.

b) Find the area of the front wall, excluding the windows and door.

Number Strategies

Which is the next number in each pattern?
Write each pattern rule.

3, 9, 27, 81, ___

12, 14, 18, 26, ___

52, 28, 16, 10, ___

5, 14, 41, 122, ___

3. The diagram shows the basement floor of a home.

a) Estimate the area and perimeter of the floor.

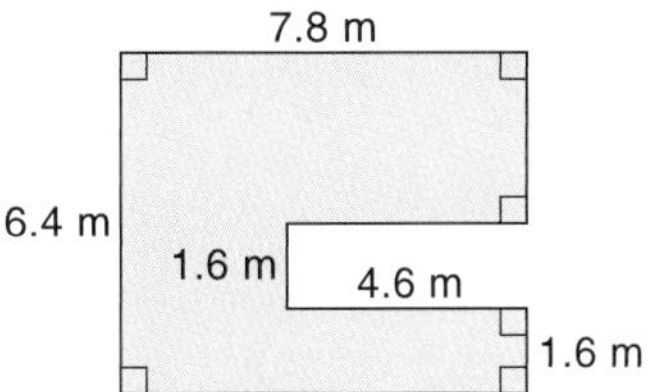

b) Calculate the area and perimeter of the floor.

c) Compare your estimates with your calculations. Was your estimate reasonable? Explain.

4. This diagram shows a plan of a parking lot.

a) Estimate the area and perimeter of the lot.

b) Calculate the area and perimeter of the lot.

c) How could you use the grid to verify your answers?

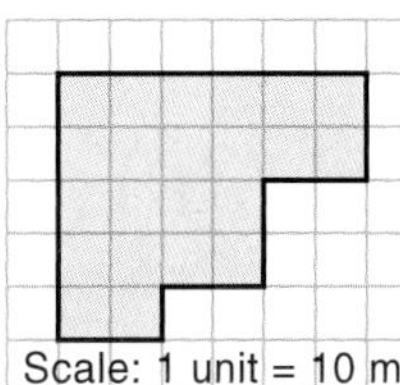

5. A backyard is a rectangle 15 m long by 10 m wide. In one corner, there is a rectangular garden 5 m by 3 m.

a) Use grid paper. Draw a diagram of the backyard.

b) Calculate the area of the backyard, excluding the garden.

c) What if the garden was in a different place in the yard? Would the answer to part b be different? Explain.

6. **Assessment Focus** An L-shaped swimming pool has area 30 m^2. Each rectangular arm has width 3 m.

a) Use grid paper. Draw 3 different pools.

b) Find the perimeter of each pool you drew. What do you notice about the perimeters?

c) What if the width of each arm was 5 m? What effect does this have? Explain.

Reflect

There are different ways to find the area of an irregular figure.
Which way do you prefer to use?
Use an example to explain your reasoning.

Game

Trapezoid Challenge

YOU WILL NEED

11 by 11 geoboard; geobands; 3 number cubes labelled 1 to 6; dot paper

NUMBER OF PLAYERS

3 or 4

GOAL OF THE GAME

To get 50 points

HOW TO PLAY THE GAME:

1. Roll 3 number cubes to get the height and lengths of the 2 parallel sides of a trapezoid.

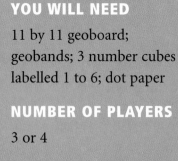

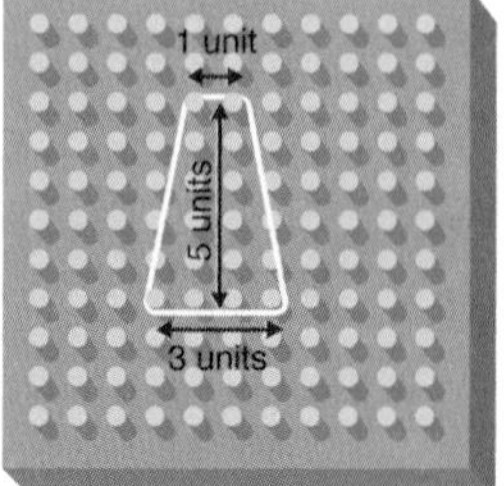

2. Use the geoboard to make a trapezoid with those dimensions.
   Choose which number represents which dimension.

3. The area of the trapezoid is your score for the round.

4. Take turns.
   The winner is the first person to reach 50 points.

What strategies did you use to try to win? Does it matter which of the 3 numbers you use for the height? Explain.

Variation: Record each trapezoid on grid paper.
No two trapezoids can be the same. If you cannot create a different trapezoid, you forfeit your turn.

Unit Review

Review any lesson with

What Do I Need to Know?

- ✓ The *perimeter* of a figure is found by adding the lengths of its sides.

- ✓ **Area of a Parallelogram**
  $A = bh$

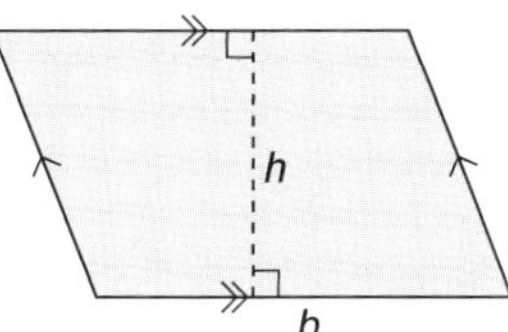

- ✓ **Area of a Triangle**
  $A = \frac{bh}{2}$

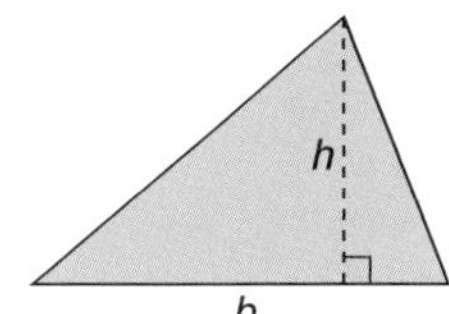

- ✓ **Area of a Trapezoid**
  Divide the trapezoid into:
  - Two triangles
  - A parallelogram and a triangle
  - A rectangle and 2 triangles

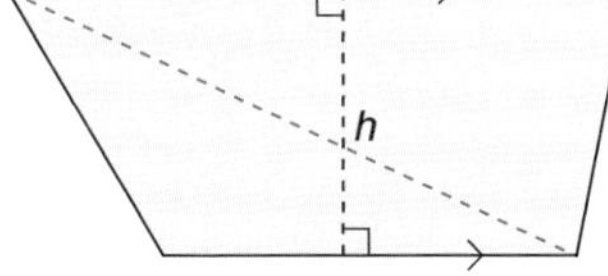

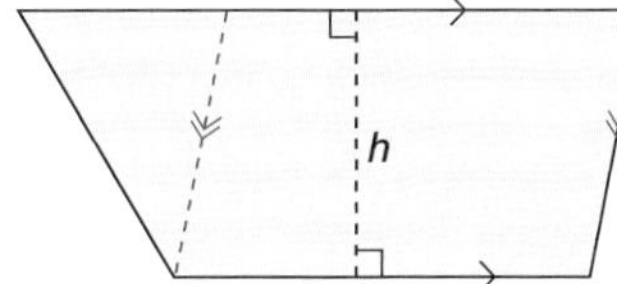

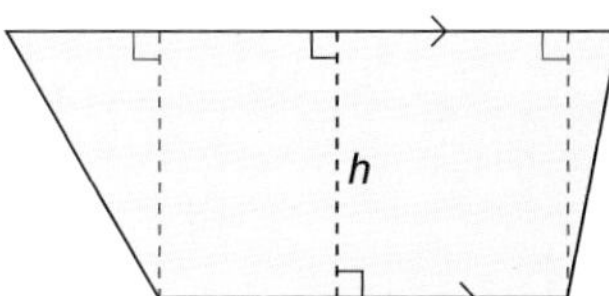

- ✓ **Area of an Irregular Figure**
  - Divide the figure into figures whose area you can find, then add the areas.
  - Or, draw a rectangle around the figure; subtract the areas of the newly formed figures from the area of the rectangle.

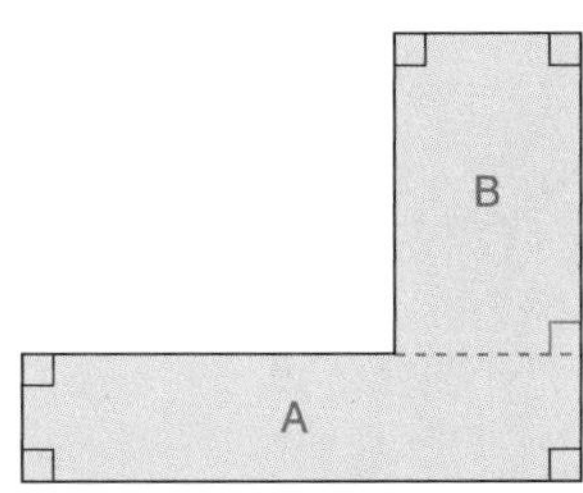

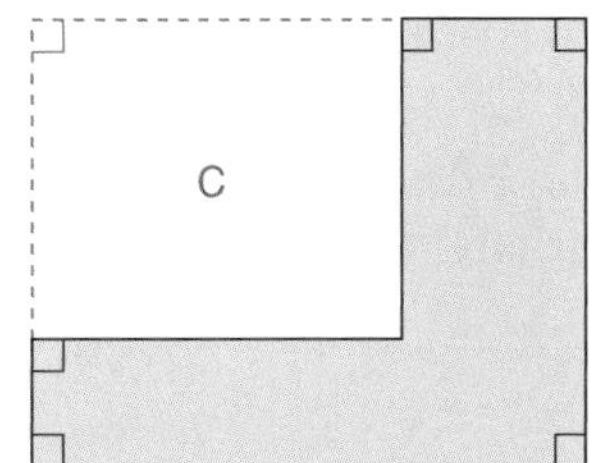

For extra practice, go to page 443.

LESSON

6.1
6.2

1. Find the area of each figure.
Explain your strategy.

a)

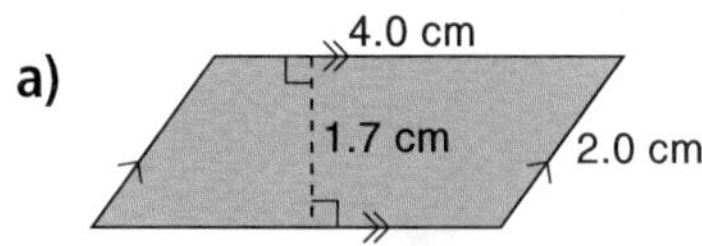

b)

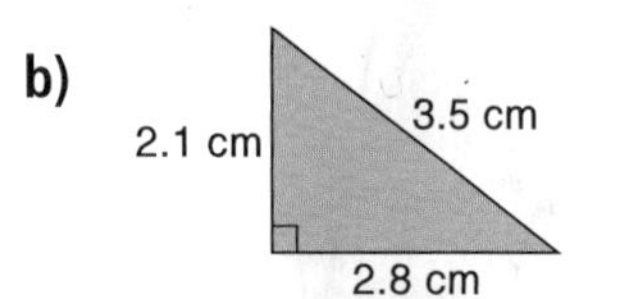

c)

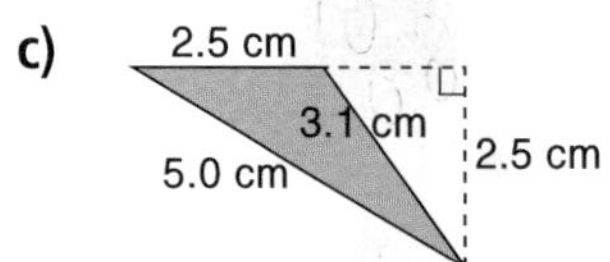

d)

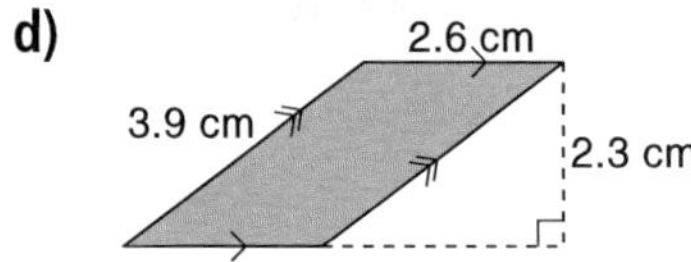

6.3

2. Estimate the area of each trapezoid.
Then, calculate the area to check if your estimate was reasonable.

a)

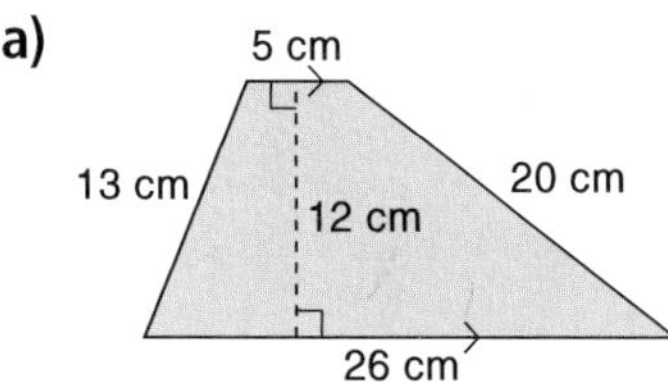

b)

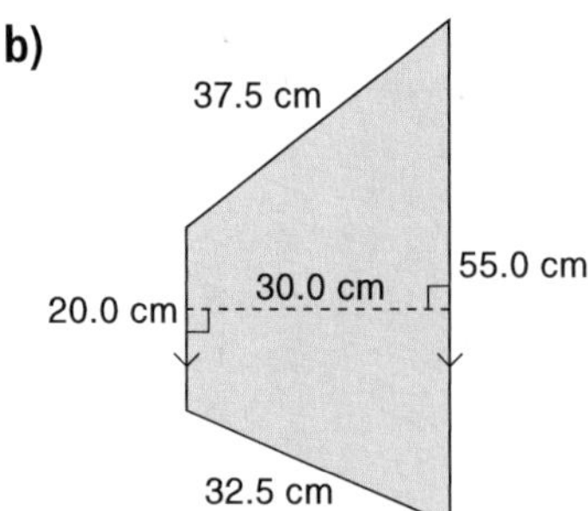

3. Estimate the perimeter of each trapezoid in question 2. Then, calculate the perimeter to check.

4. The area of this trapezoid is approximately 150 cm^2.

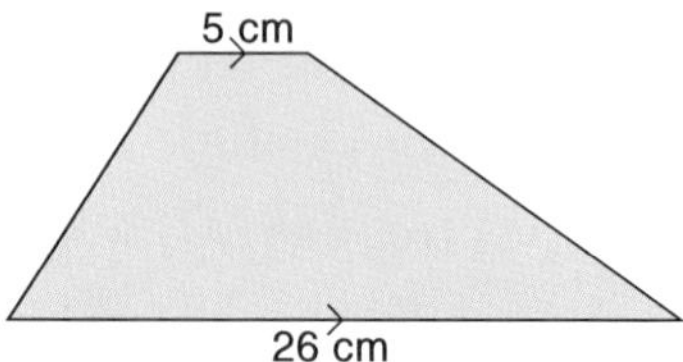

Estimate its height.
Show your work.

6.4

5. Find the perimeter and area of each figure.

a)

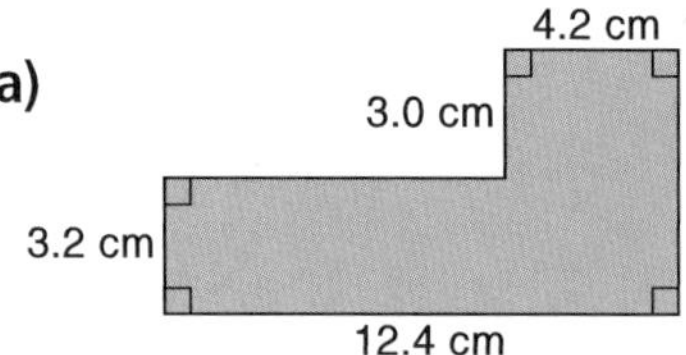

b)

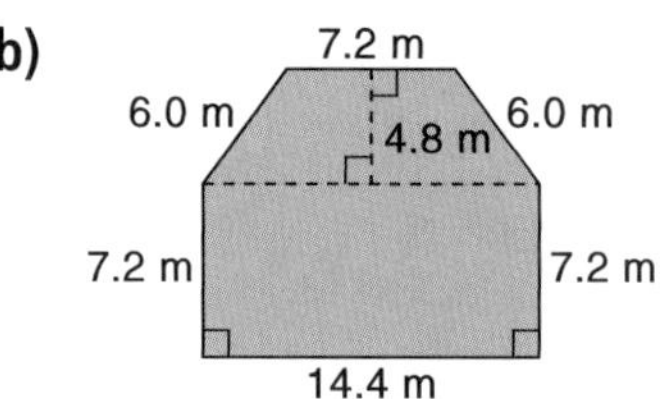

6. A school playground has a paved surface and a grass surface.

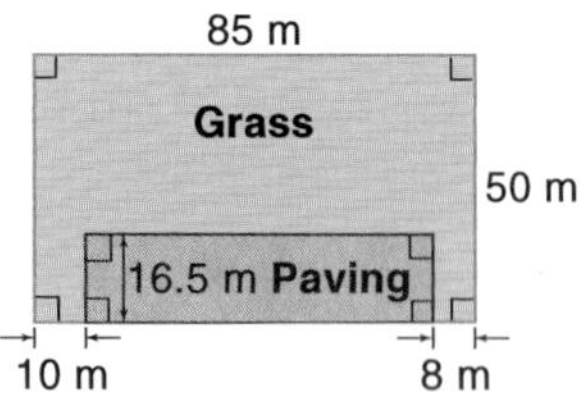

a) What is the area of the paved surface?

b) Fencing costs \$35.50/m.
How much would it cost to fence the grass area?

Practice Test

1. Find the area and perimeter of each figure.
Explain your strategies.

a)

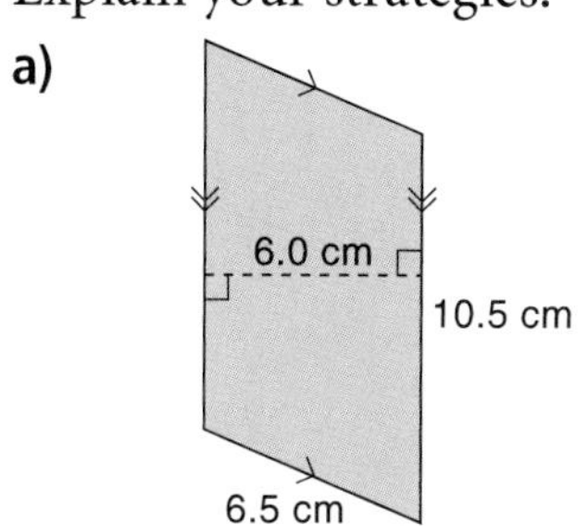

b)

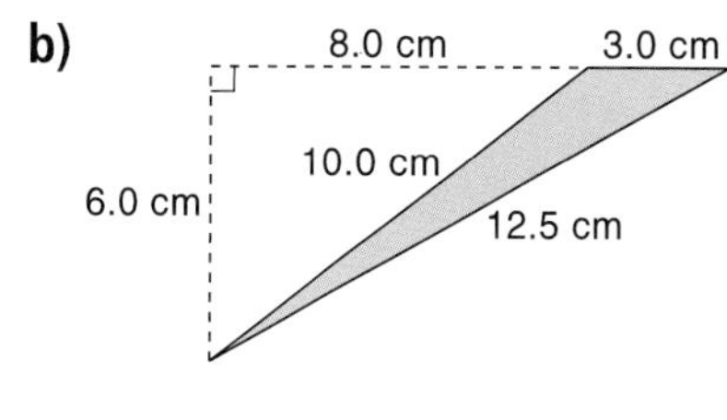

c)

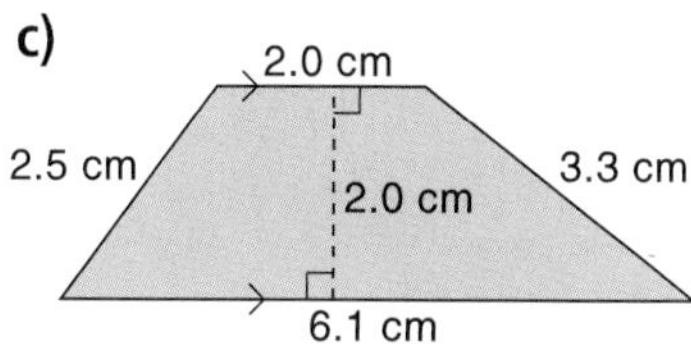

d)

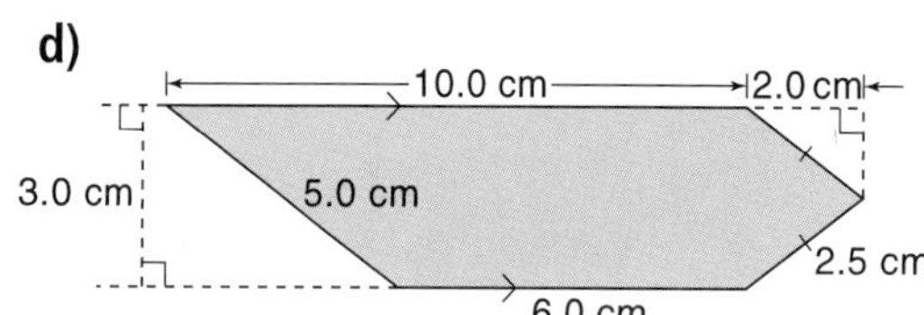

2. How does the area of a triangle change in each case?
   a) Its height is doubled.
   b) Its base is halved.
   c) Its height is doubled and its base is halved.

   Explain how you know.

3. Use 1-cm grid paper.
Draw an irregular figure with area 64 cm^2.
Label all the dimensions of the figure.
Find the perimeter of the figure.

4. A design has a series of trapezoids.
For each trapezoid, one parallel side is always 1.5 m shorter than the other parallel side.
The height of each trapezoid is 6.0 m.
   a) What is the area of the 6th trapezoid in the design?
   b) How long is the design with 6 trapezoids?

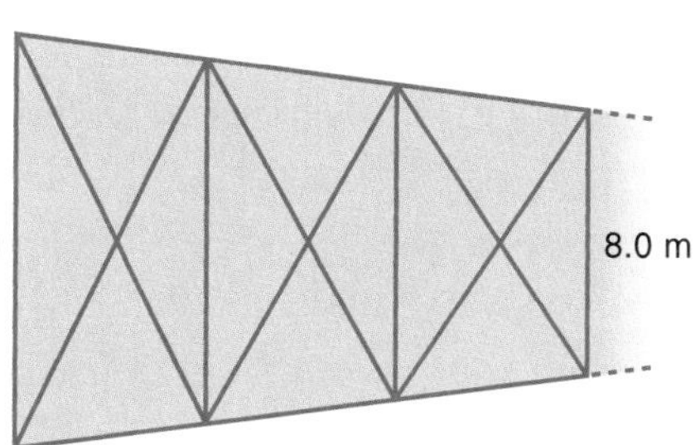

Unit Problem Designing a Patio

The owners of a large shopping centre want to build a patio in front of the main entrance to attract more customers. Your task is to design the tiled surface of the patio.
You must use tiles with these shapes: triangle, parallelogram, rectangle, trapezoid

The patio has the shape shown at the right. Each square on this plan has side length 10 cm.

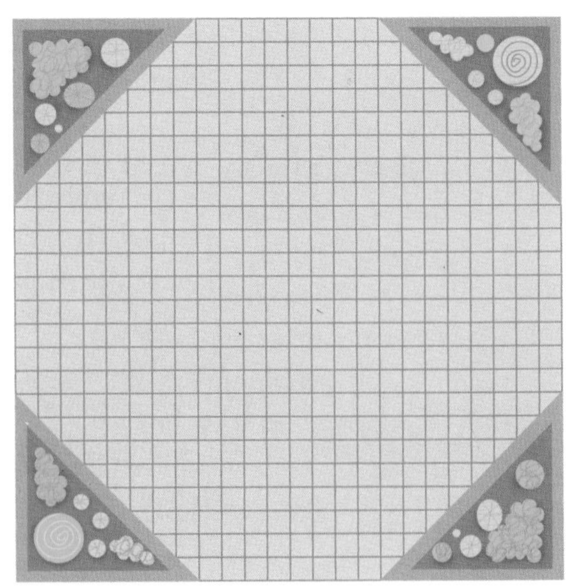

- You must include at least:
  3 triangles with different areas
  3 parallelograms with different areas
  3 rectangles with different areas
  3 trapezoids (that are not parallelograms) with different areas
- Use a formula to find the area of each tile.

Your teacher will give you a grid to draw your design.
Complete the design.
Colour the design if it helps to show the different figures.

Check List

Your work should show:

- ✓ the area of each different figure you used
- ✓ the formulas you used to calculate the areas
- ✓ a diagram of your design on grid paper
- ✓ an explanation of how you created the design

Reflect on the Unit

What do you need to know to find the area of a parallelogram, a triangle, and a trapezoid? Explain.
Include a diagram and an example to show how you found each area.

UNIT 7

Geometry

Patterns are pleasing to the eye. They are used by designers, architects, and engineers to make their products more attractive. Look at the quilt pattern. Which figures are used as quilt blocks? Which other figures have you seen in quilts?

What You'll Learn

- Identify, describe, compare, and classify figures.
- Identify the conditions that make two figures congruent.
- Construct and analyse tiling patterns.
- Recognize the image of a figure after a transformation.
- Create and analyse designs using transformations.

Why It's Important

- Geometry is used daily by scientists, architects, engineers, and land developers.
- Geometric attributes, such as congruence and symmetry, enable you to see the world around you in a different way.

Key Words

- convex polygon
- concave polygon
- tiling the plane
- tessellations

UNIT 7

Skills You'll Need

Classifying Triangles

Here are two ways to classify triangles.

- By side length

An equilateral triangle has all sides equal.

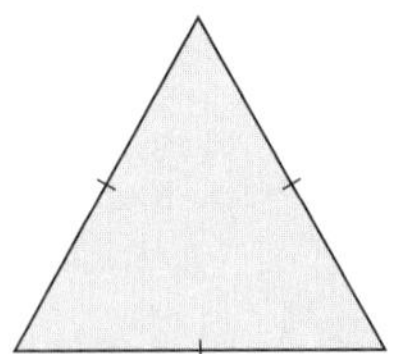

An isosceles triangle has 2 sides equal.

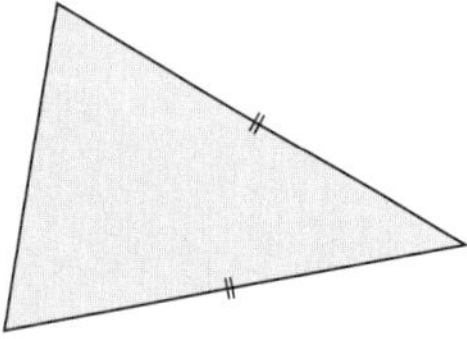

A scalene triangle has all sides different.

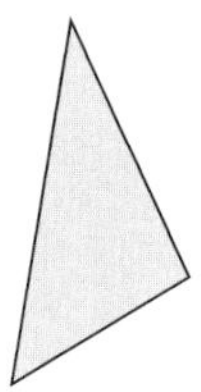

- By angle measure

An acute triangle has all angles less than 90°.

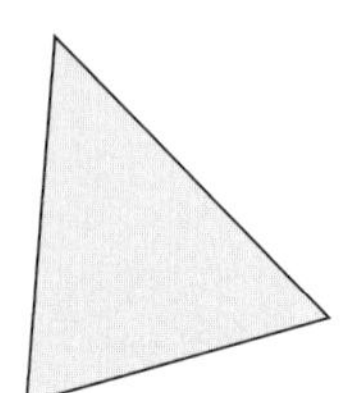

A right triangle has one 90° angle.

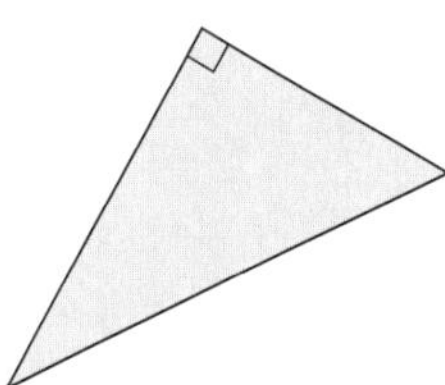

An obtuse triangle has one angle greater than 90°.

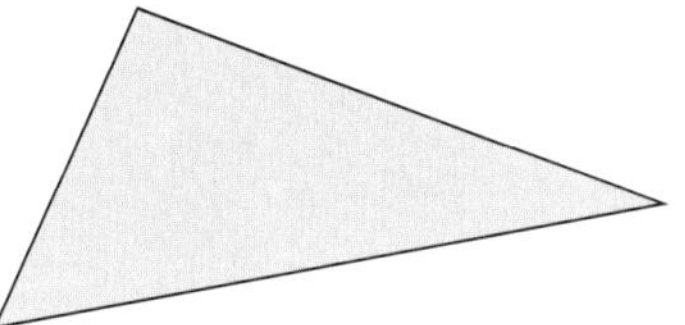

Use square dot paper or isometric dot paper.

1. Draw an isosceles triangle.
Is it acute, obtuse, or right? How do you know?

2. Draw an obtuse triangle.
Is it equilateral, scalene, or isosceles? How do you know?

3. Can you draw an obtuse isosceles triangle?
If you can, draw it.
If you cannot draw the triangle, say why it cannot be drawn.

4. Can you draw a right equilateral triangle?
If you can, draw it.
If you cannot draw the triangle, say why it cannot be drawn.

Constructing a Triangle

Here are two ways to construct a triangle, using a ruler, compass, and protractor.

Example 1

Construct △ABC with AB = 4 cm, BC = 6 cm, and CA = 7 cm.

Solution

You will need a ruler and compass.
Step 1 Sketch the triangle.

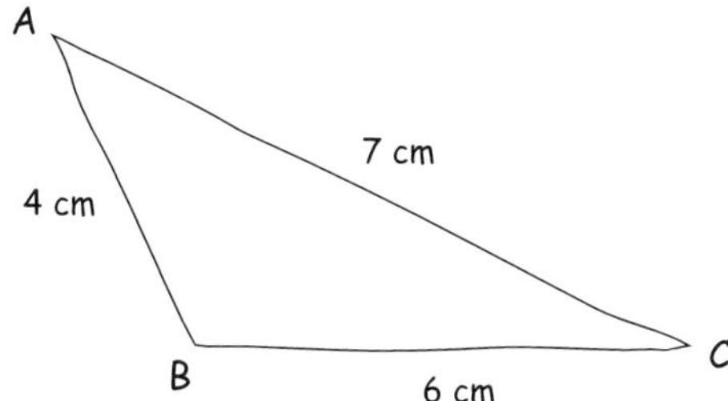

Step 2 Construct the triangle:
Use a ruler to draw side BC = 6 cm.
With the compass point and pencil 7 cm apart,
put the compass point on C and draw an arc.
All points on this arc are 7 cm from C.
With the compass point and pencil 4 cm apart,
put the compass point on B and draw an arc.
All points on this arc are 4 cm from B.
Make sure the arc intersects the first arc you drew.
Mark a point where the arcs intersect.
This point is 7 cm from C and 4 cm from B.
Label the point A. Join AB and AC. Label each side with its length.

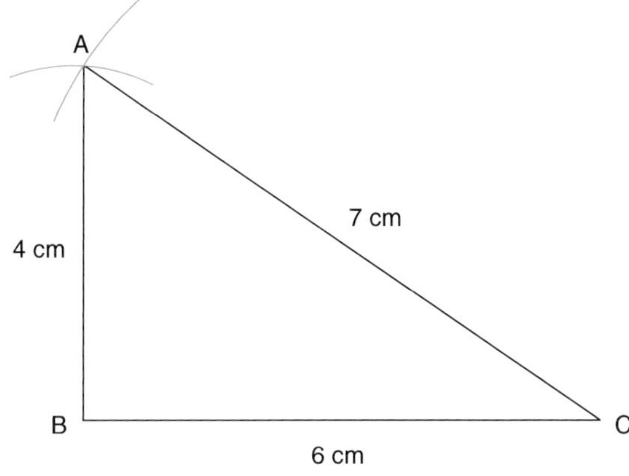

Example 2

Construct $\triangle BCD$ with $BC = 6$ cm, $\angle B = 110°$, and $\angle C = 30°$.

Solution

You will need a ruler and protractor.

Step 1 Sketch the triangle.

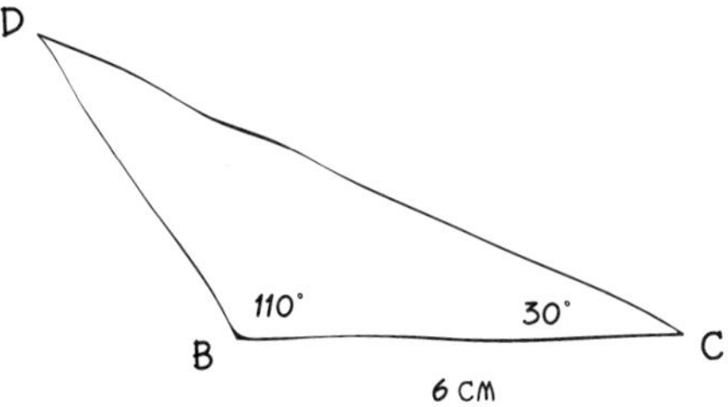

Step 2 Construct the triangle:

Use a ruler to draw side $BC = 6$ cm.

Use a protractor to make an angle of 110° at B.

Use a protractor to make an angle of 30° at C.

Label point D where the arms of the angles intersect.

Label the known side and angles.

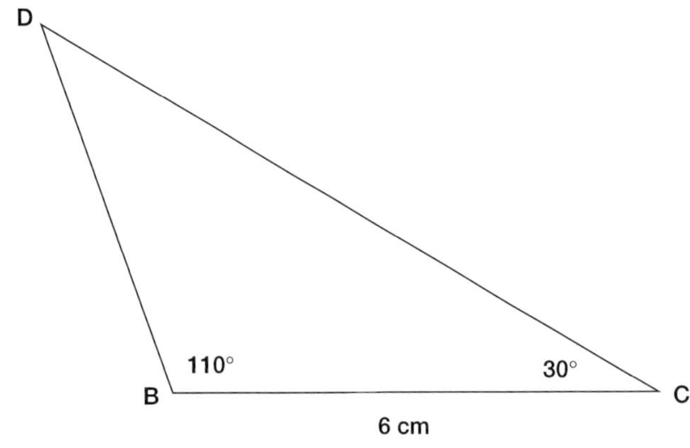

✓ **Check**

5. Construct each triangle.

a) $\triangle CDE$ with $CD = 4$ cm, $DE = 7$ cm, $CE = 9$ cm

b) $\triangle DEF$ with $DE = 7$ cm, $\angle D = 80°$, $\angle E = 30°$

Plotting Points on a Coordinate Grid

When we draw a horizontal axis and a vertical axis on grid paper, we have a coordinate grid.
The axes intersect at the origin, O.

We label each axis with numbers, beginning with 0 at the origin.

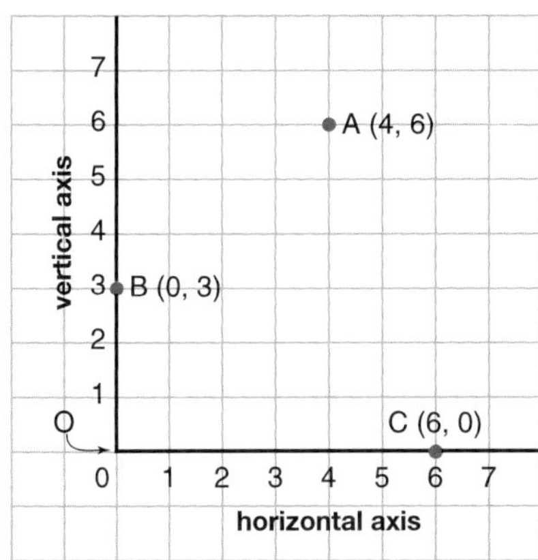

A point on a grid is described by its coordinates.

Point A has coordinates (4, 6).
To plot point A, start at 4 on the horizontal axis, then move up 6 spaces.
Mark a point. This is point A.

Point B has coordinates (0, 3).
To plot point B, start at 0, then move up 3 spaces. Point B is on the vertical axis.

Point C has coordinates (6, 0).
To plot point C, mark a point at 6 on the horizontal axis.

✓ Check

6. On grid paper, draw a coordinate grid.
Plot each point on the grid.
A(5, 7), B(3, 8), C(10, 4), D(9, 1), E(0, 8), F(5, 0)

7. **a)** Where are all the points with horizontal coordinate 0?
b) Where are all the points with vertical coordinate 0?

7.1 Classifying Figures

Focus Identify, describe, and classify geometric figures.

Look around the classroom.
Name the different figures you see.
Which figure is most common?

Explore

Work with a group.
You will need a ruler and a protractor.
Your teacher will give you a large copy of these figures.

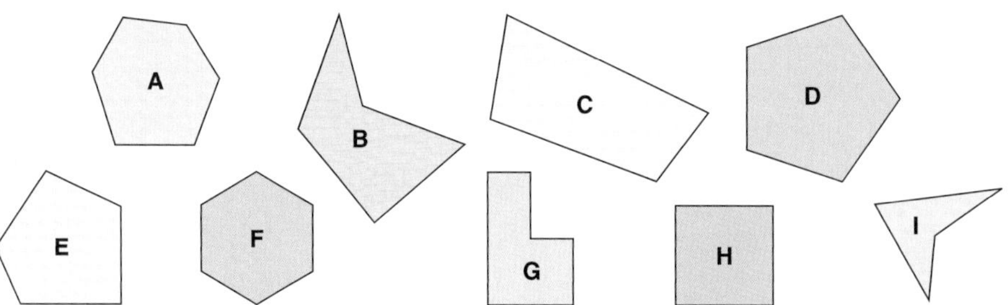

➢ Identify each figure.
Describe it.

➢ Choose two figures.
How many different ways can you compare them?

➢ Choose three figures. How are they the same?
How are they different?

Reflect & Share

Share your results with another group of classmates.
Work together to classify the figures in different ways.

Connect

A polygon is a closed figure with sides that are line segments.
Exactly 2 sides meet at a vertex.
The sides intersect only at the vertices.

This figure is a polygon.

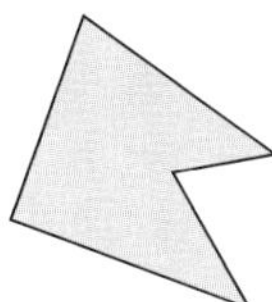

These figures are *not* polygons.

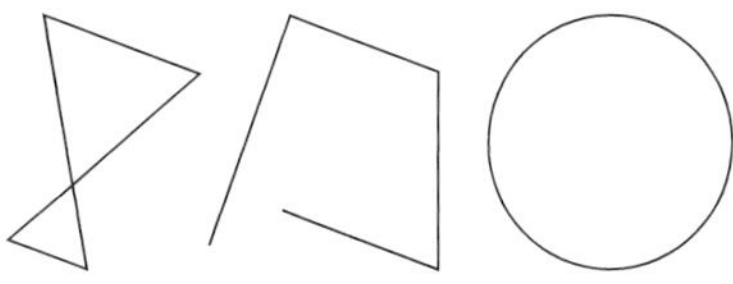

A regular polygon has line symmetry and rotational symmetry.

Recall that matching arcs or symbols in angles show that the angles are equal.

A regular polygon has all sides equal and all angles equal.
These polygons are regular.

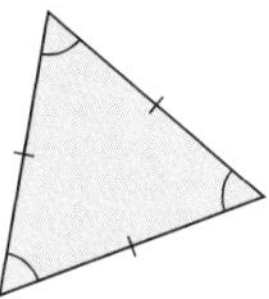
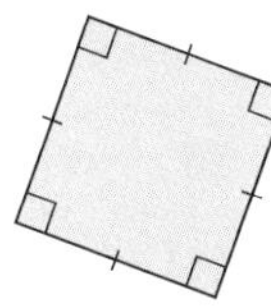
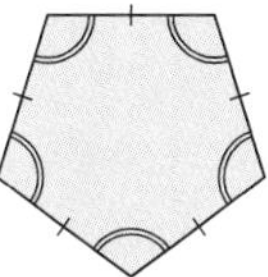
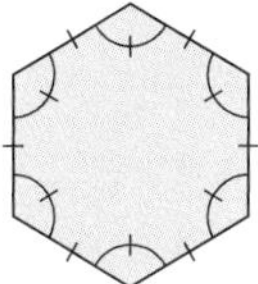
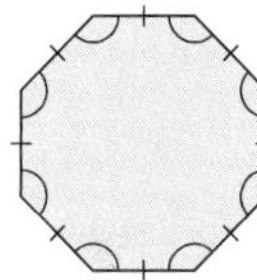

A **convex polygon** has all angles less than 180°.
These polygons are convex.

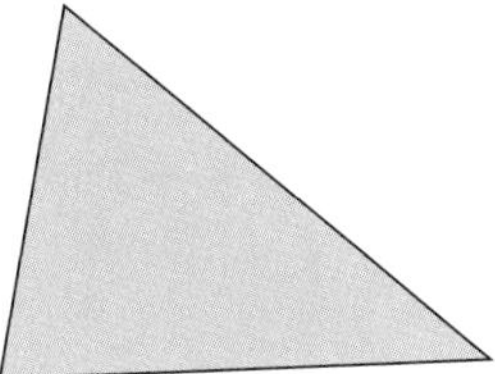
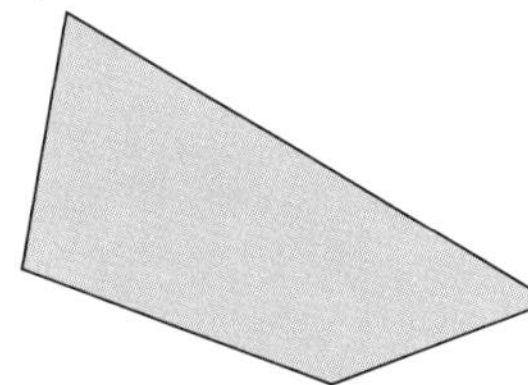
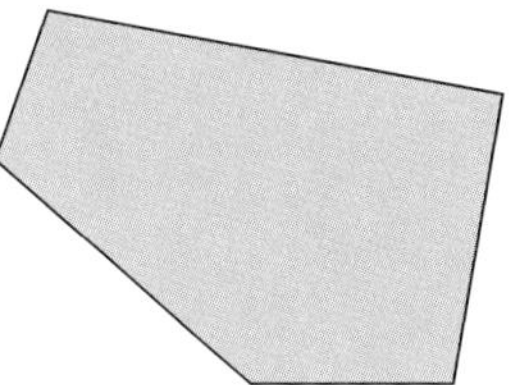

A **concave polygon** has at least one angle greater than 180°.
These polygons are concave.

An angle that is greater than 180° is a reflex angle.

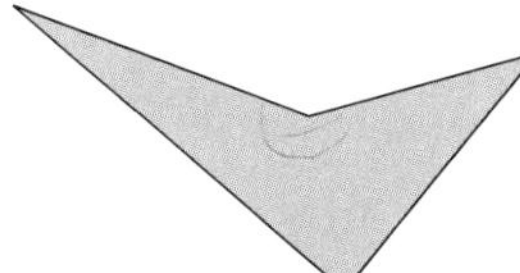
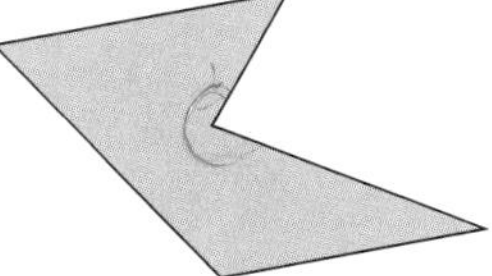
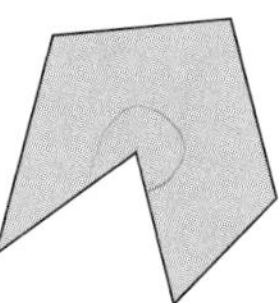

Example

Here is a regular hexagon.

a) How many lines of symmetry does it have?

b) What is the rotational symmetry?

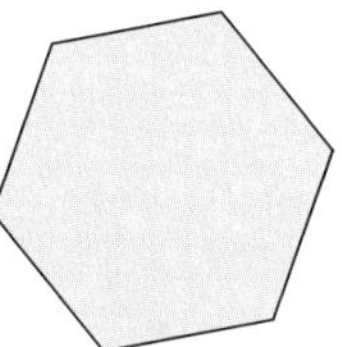

Solution

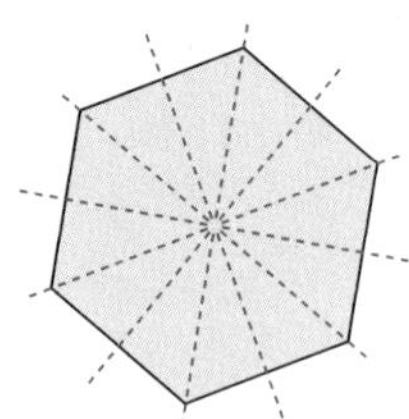

a) Trace the hexagon.
Fold the tracing paper so that one part of the hexagon coincides with the other.
The fold line is a line of symmetry.
Repeat the folding as many times as possible.

A regular hexagon has 6 lines of symmetry:
3 lines join opposite vertices, and 3 lines join the midpoints of opposite sides.

Label two corresponding vertices. Then you know when the tracing is back at the starting position.

b) Trace the hexagon. Place the tracing to coincide with the hexagon.
Rotate the tracing about its centre until the tracing coincides with the hexagon again.
Count how many times you can do this.

The tracing coincides with the hexagon 6 times.
So, a regular hexagon has rotational symmetry of order 6.

Practice

1. Explain why each figure is not a polygon.

a)

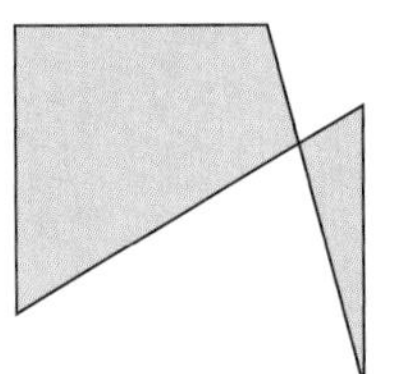

b)

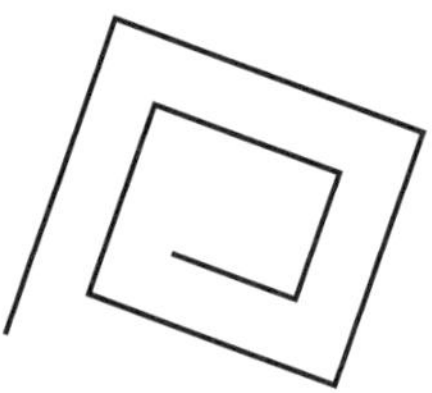

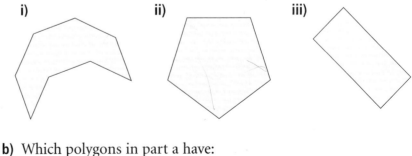

2. **a)** Is each polygon regular? How do you know?

i)

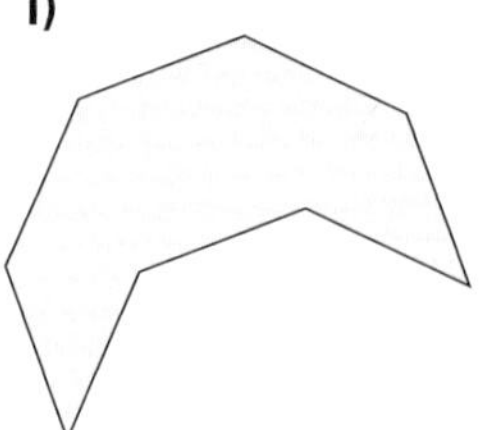

ii)

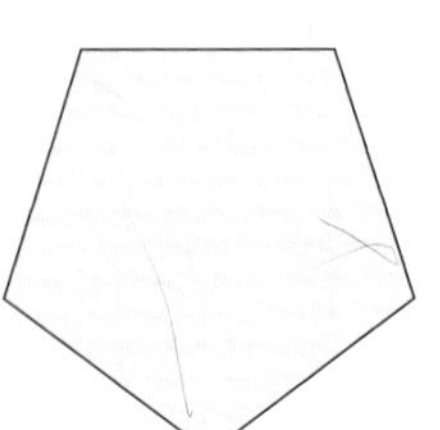

iii)

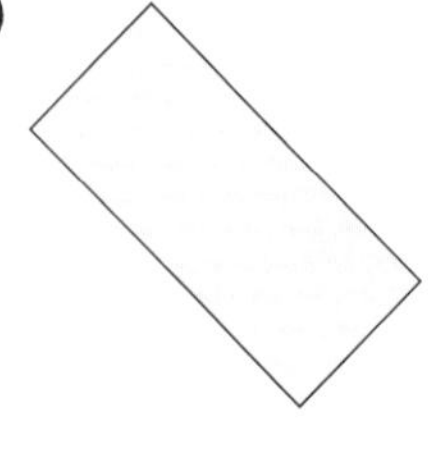

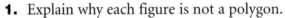

b) Which polygons in part a have:
i) line symmetry? **ii)** rotational symmetry?
How do you know?

3. Identify the figures in each flag.
Describe each figure as many ways as you can.
a) Congo **b)** Bosnia-Herzegovina **c)** Guyana **d)** Seychelles

4. Describe each figure. How are the figures the same? Different?

a)
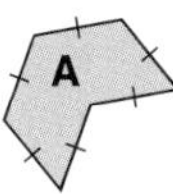

b)
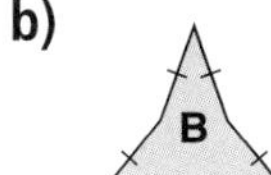

c)
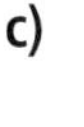
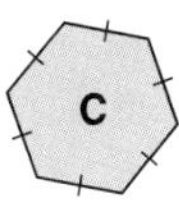

5. Match each polygon with its description below.

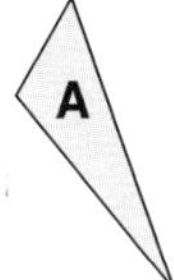

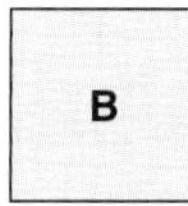

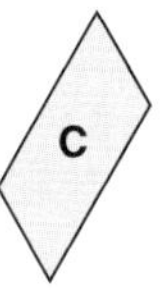

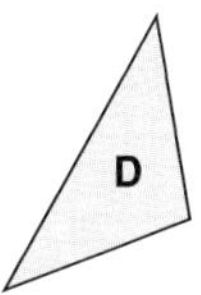

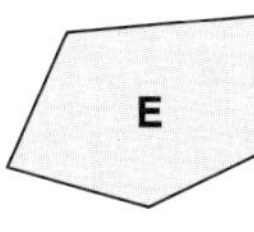

a) an isosceles triangle with an angle of 40°
b) a rhombus with a right angle
c) a pentagon with an angle of 120°
d) a parallelogram with an angle of 60°
e) an obtuse triangle with an angle of 110°

6. Use square dot paper or isometric dot paper.
Draw each polygon.
a) an isosceles triangle with a height of 4 units
b) a parallelogram with an angle of 45°
c) a trapezoid with a 90° angle and a 45° angle
d) a kite with exactly one right angle
e) a parallelogram with a 90° angle
f) a scalene obtuse triangle
g) an isosceles right triangle
h) a hexagon with exactly 3 right angles

7. Identify each polygon.
Describe it as many ways as you can.

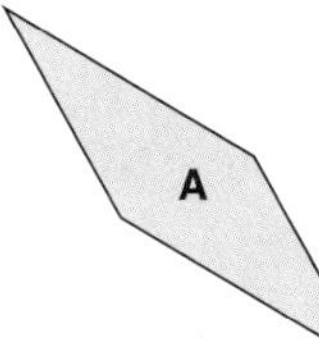

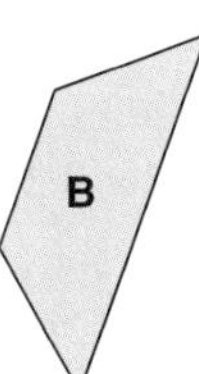

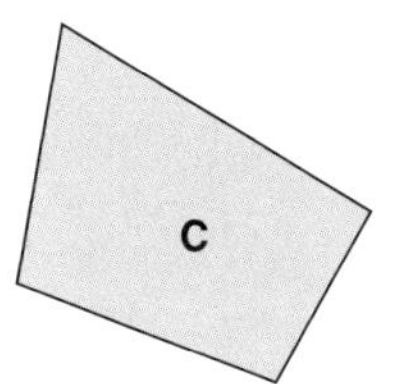

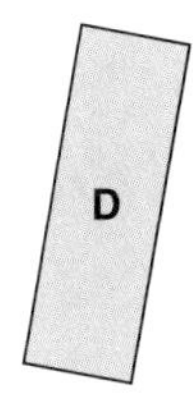

A quadrilateral is a polygon with 4 sides.

8. Use dot paper.

a) Draw a quadrilateral. Label it A.

b) Draw another quadrilateral that differs from quadrilateral A in only one way. Label it B.

c) Continue to draw quadrilaterals that differ in only one way. Label each one you draw. Change one side or angle each time. How many different quadrilaterals can you draw?

Number Strategies

Find the next 3 numbers in each pattern.

What is each pattern rule?

- 23, 28, 26, 31, 29,...
- 6, 9, 15, 27, 51,...
- 1, 3, 9, 27,...

9. Assessment Focus

The 3 points A, B, C are vertices of a polygon.
Copy the points on dot paper.

a) Find other vertices and sketch each figure.

i) a trapezoid with line symmetry

ii) a kite

iii) a parallelogram

iv) a pentagon

B

A

C

b) How many other figures can you make that have these points as 3 vertices? Identify each figure. Describe it as many ways as you can.

10. The lengths of three sides of a quadrilateral are 5 cm, 5 cm, and 8 cm.

a) Sketch and name the different quadrilaterals possible.

b) Suppose one angle is 90°. Which quadrilaterals are possible now? Justify your answer.

Math Link

Your World

The Department of Highways uses different figures for road signs. Which road signs use each of these figures: pentagon, octagon, square, circle, rectangle, triangle?

Reflect

Choose 3 different polygons. Sketch each polygon as many different ways as you can. Describe each polygon.

7.2 Congruent Figures

Focus Identify the conditions for congruence.

Explore

Work on your own.
You will need a ruler, protractor, and compass.
For each set of measurements given, how many different triangles can you draw?

➢ Construct a triangle with sides of length 5 cm, 7 cm, and 9 cm.
➢ Construct a triangle with two sides of length 9 cm and 5 cm, and one angle of 30°.
➢ Construct a triangle with one side of length 5 cm and two angles of 40° and 60°.

Reflect & Share

Compare your triangles with those of several classmates.

➢ How many different triangles can you draw in each case?
  - when you know 3 sides
  - when you know 2 sides and 1 angle
  - when you know 1 side and 2 angles
➢ What measurements do you need to know to be able to draw exactly one triangle?

Connect

➢ When 3 sides of a triangle are given, only one triangle can be drawn. So, if we know that two triangles have the same 3 sides, those triangles must be congruent.

Congruent figures have the same size and shape. These triangles are drawn to scale.

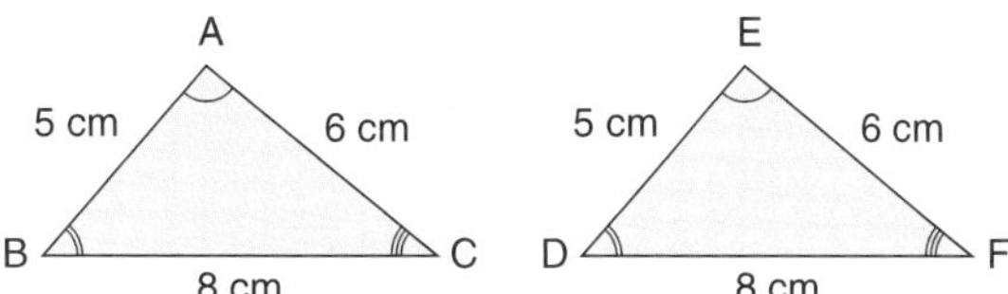

We say: Triangle ABC is congruent to triangle EDF.
We write: $\triangle ABC \cong \triangle EDF$

We list the corresponding vertices of the triangles in the same order.

△ABC and △EDF have:

corresponding sides equal	and	corresponding angles equal
AB = ED		∠A = ∠E
BC = DF		∠B = ∠D
AC = EF		∠C = ∠F

➢ When 2 sides and 1 angle of a triangle are given, there are two cases to consider.

- The given angle is between the 2 sides. Only one triangle can be drawn.

You may have to flip or rotate one triangle so both triangles face the same way.

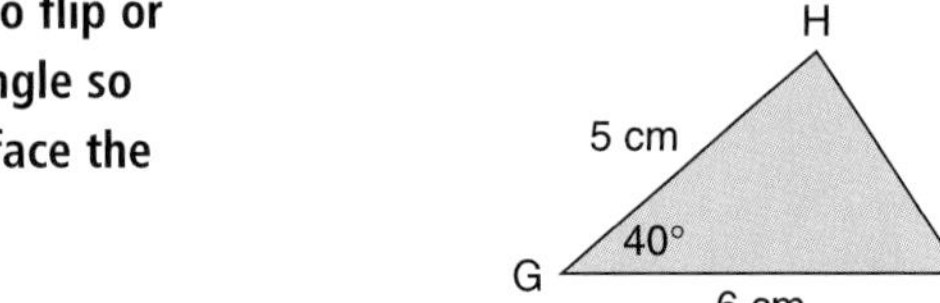

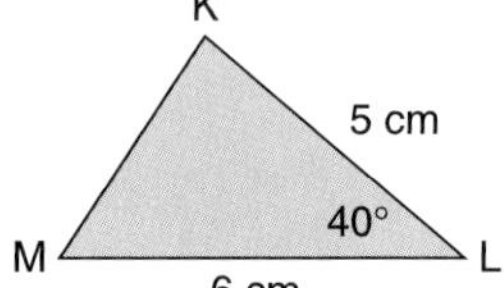

So, triangle GHJ is congruent to triangle LKM or △GHJ ≅ △LKM

- The given angle is *not* between the 2 sides. Sometimes more than one triangle can be drawn.

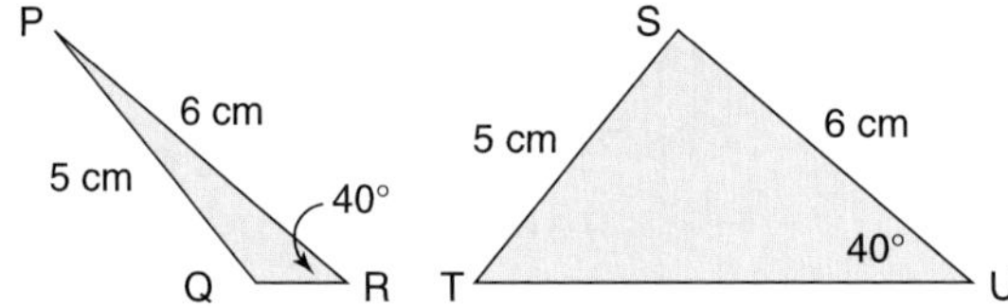

△PQR and △STU are *not* congruent.

➢ When 2 angles and the side between them are given, only one triangle can be drawn.

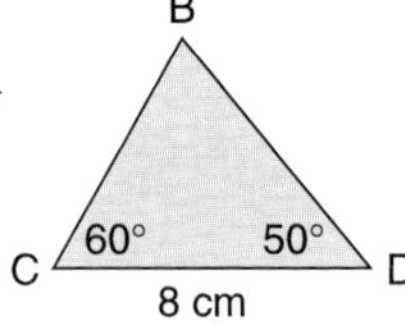

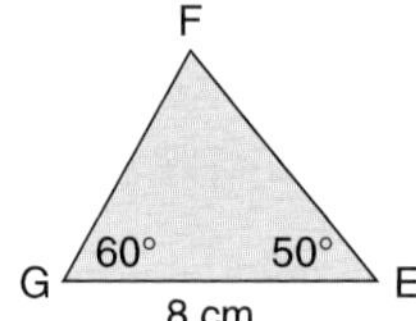

△BCD ≅ △FGE

Example

Are the figures in each pair congruent? How do you know?

a)

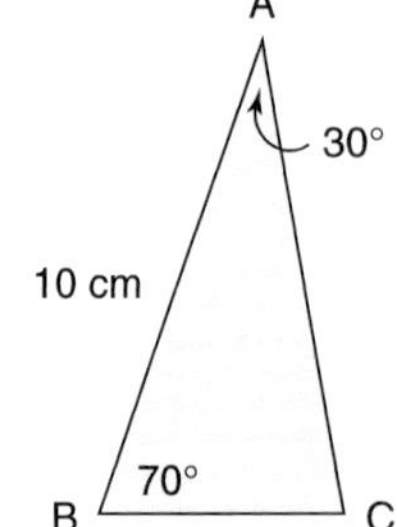

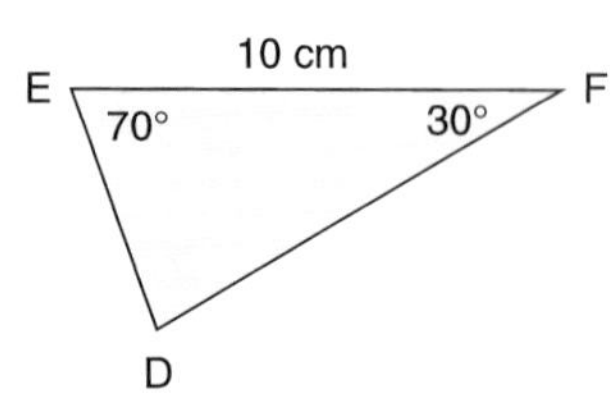

b)

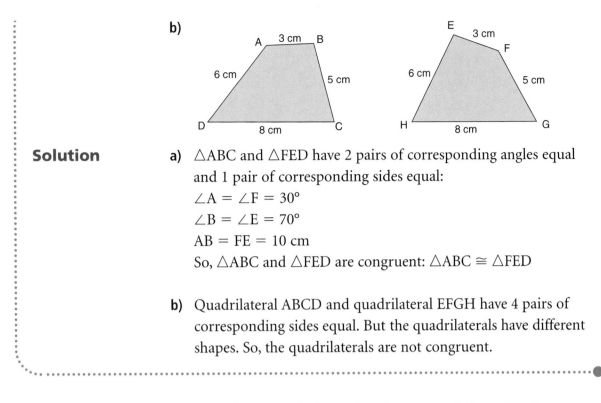

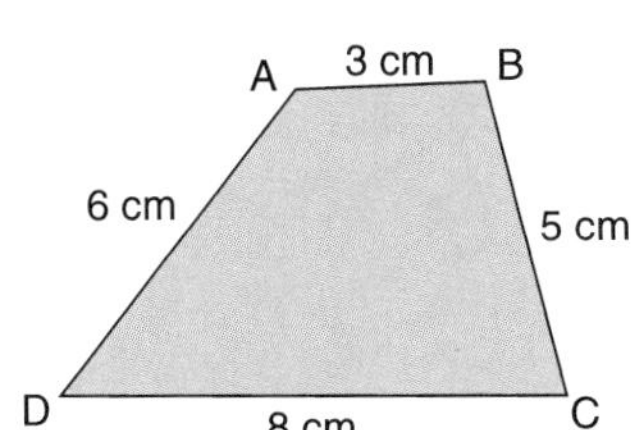

Solution

a) △ABC and △FED have 2 pairs of corresponding angles equal and 1 pair of corresponding sides equal:
∠A = ∠F = 30°
∠B = ∠E = 70°
AB = FE = 10 cm
So, △ABC and △FED are congruent: △ABC ≅ △FED

b) Quadrilateral ABCD and quadrilateral EFGH have 4 pairs of corresponding sides equal. But the quadrilaterals have different shapes. So, the quadrilaterals are not congruent.

Part b of the *Example* shows that for two quadrilaterals to be congruent, it is not sufficient that 4 pairs of corresponding sides are equal. We need to know that the corresponding angles are equal, too.

Practice

1. Look at the triangles below.
Find pairs of congruent triangles.
Explain why they are congruent.

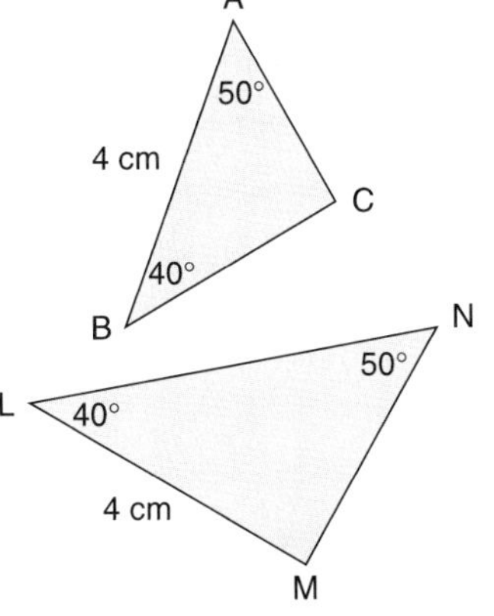

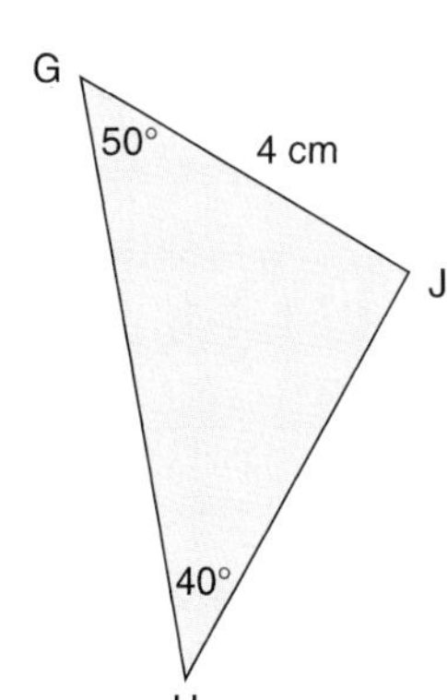

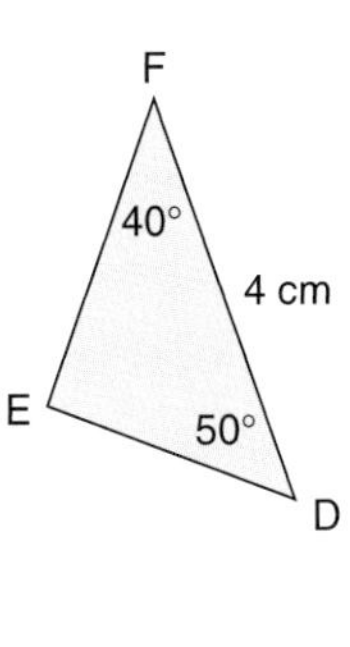

2. Are quadrilaterals ABCD and KLMN congruent?
How do you know?

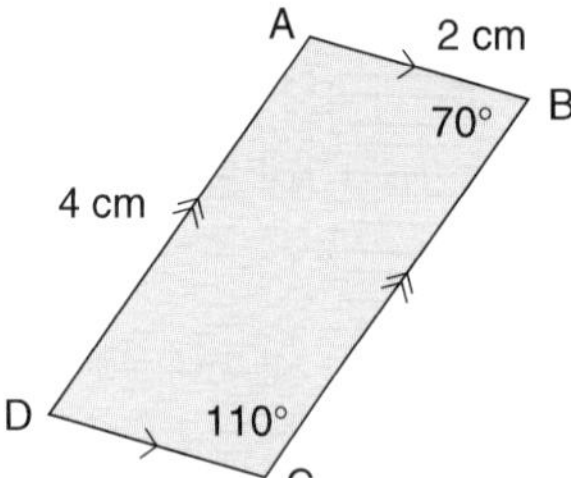

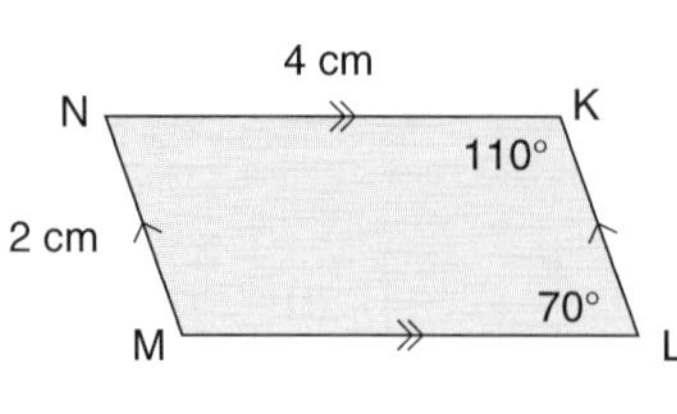

When you name congruent triangles, remember to list corresponding vertices in the same order.

3. In each figure below, name pairs of congruent triangles.
Explain how you know they are congruent.
Try to find more than one way to show the triangles are congruent.

a) ABCD is a kite.

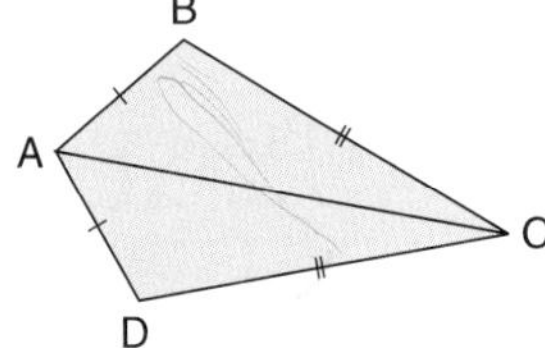

b) PQRS is a parallelogram.

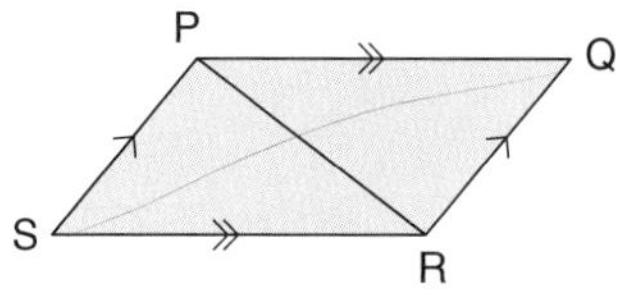

c) EFGH is a rhombus.

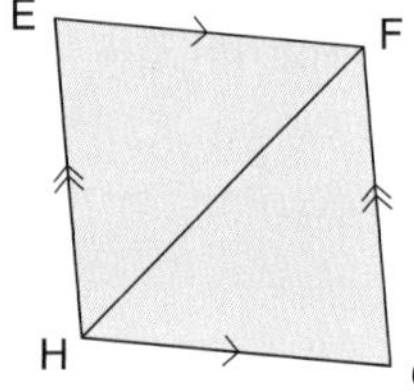

d) JKLM is a rectangle.

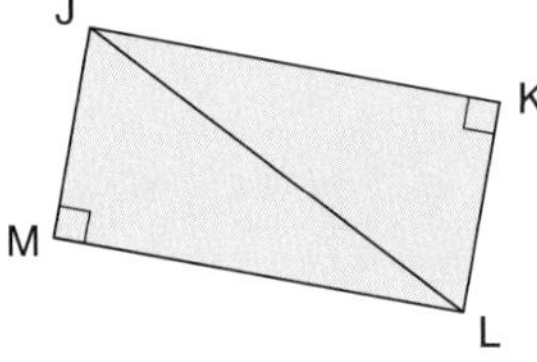

4. For each figure below:

a) Sketch the figure.

b) What are the fewest measurements you need to know to draw the figure?

c) How does your answer to part b help you identify congruent figures of this type?

i) parallelogram **ii)** rectangle **iii)** square

5. △ABC and △DEF have AB = DE = 6 cm and BC = EF = 7 cm.

a) Sketch the triangles.

b) What else do you need to know to tell if the triangles are congruent?

Mental Math

Which three factors of 24 have a sum of 20?

6. **Assessment Focus** Use dot paper.
   a) Draw two quadrilaterals with equal sides, but the quadrilaterals are not congruent.
      Explain why the quadrilaterals are not congruent.
   b) Use the 4 side lengths in part a. Draw two congruent quadrilaterals with these side lengths.
      Explain how you know the quadrilaterals are congruent.
   c) Explain how the quadrilaterals in parts a and b are different.

7. Alex called a carpet store.
   He wanted a piece of carpet to repair a damaged rug.
   Alex asked for a piece measuring 3 m by 4 m by 5 m by 6 m.
   Explain why the salesperson could not help Alex.

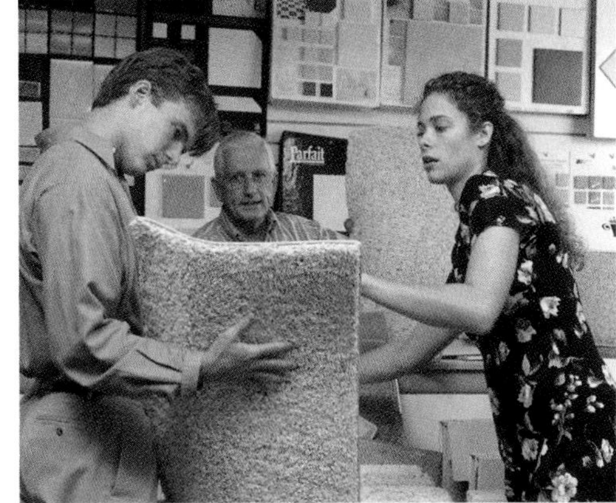

8. a) Are all isosceles triangles with two 50° angles congruent? Explain.
   b) Are all isosceles triangles with two 50° angles and exactly one side of length 10 cm congruent? Explain.

Take It Further

9. Construct a right triangle with one side 5 cm and the longest side 8 cm.
   a) Can you draw two different triangles with those measurements?
   b) If your answer to part a is yes, draw the triangles.
   c) If your answer to part a is no, explain how you know that only one triangle can be drawn with these measurements.

Reflect

Describe the different ways you can tell if two triangles are congruent.

Mid-Unit Review

LESSON

7.1 **1.** Identify each figure.

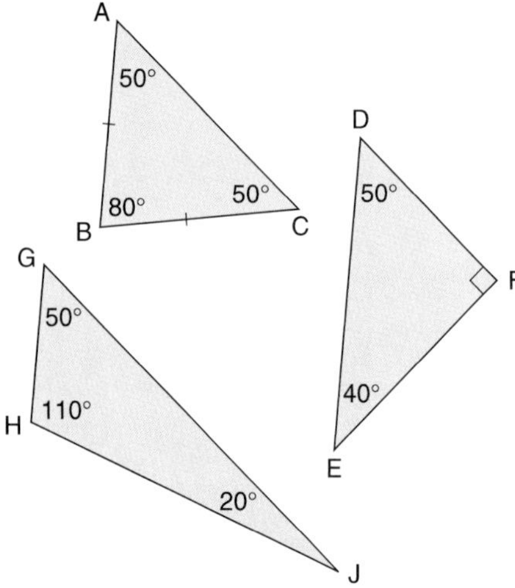

a) a scalene triangle with an angle of 50°

b) an isosceles triangle with an angle of 50°

c) a right triangle with an angle of 50°

d) an obtuse triangle with an angle of 50°

e) an acute triangle with an angle of 50°

7.1 **2.** Use dot paper.

7.2 **a)** Draw 2 congruent concave hexagons. How do you know the hexagons are congruent? How do you know they are concave?

b) Draw 2 congruent convex hexagons. How do you know the hexagons are convex? How do you know they are congruent?

7.2 **3.** Segment AB is one side of △ABC. Use dot paper.

a) Draw △ABC.

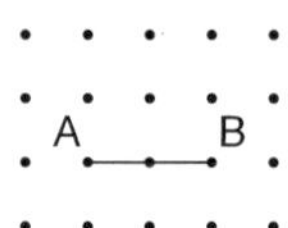

b) Draw a triangle congruent to △ABC. How do you know the triangles are congruent?

c) Draw a triangle that is *not* congruent to △ABC. How do you know the triangles are *not* congruent?

4. Use these figures.

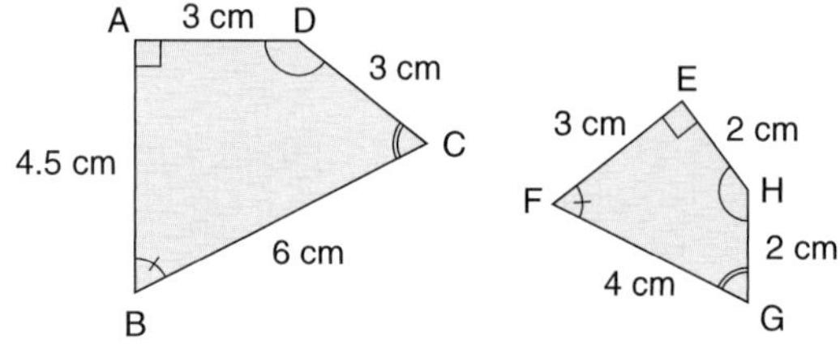

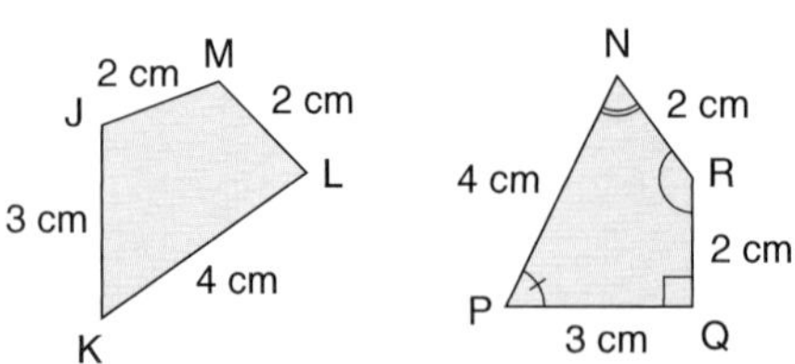

a) Identify 2 figures that are *not* congruent. How do you know they are not congruent?

b) Identify 2 congruent figures. How do you know they are congruent?

7.3 Transformations

Focus Recognize transformation images.

Explore

Work with a partner.
Your teacher will give you a large copy of these figures.

Use tracing paper and a Mira if they help.

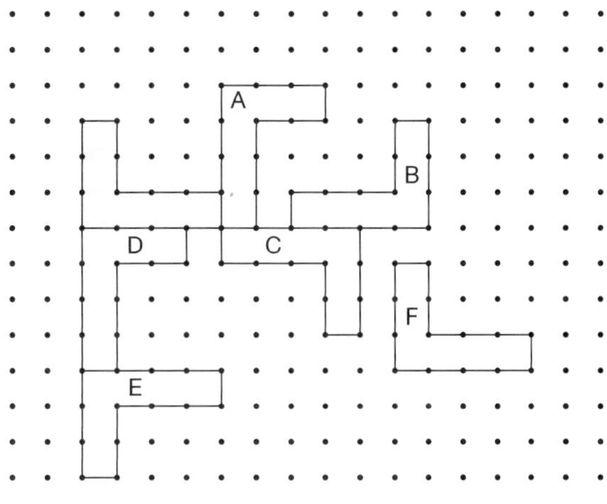

The shaded figure has been translated, rotated, and reflected.
Each labelled figure is the image after a transformation.
Identify the transformation that produced each image.
Explain how you know.

Reflect & Share

Discuss your strategies for identifying each transformation.
What is special about a reflection image? A translation image?
A rotation image?

Connect

We can show transformations on a grid.

Translation

The translation image and the shaded figure are congruent.

The shaded figure is translated 5 units right and 3 units up.
Its translation image is figure A.
The translation arrow shows the movement in a straight line.

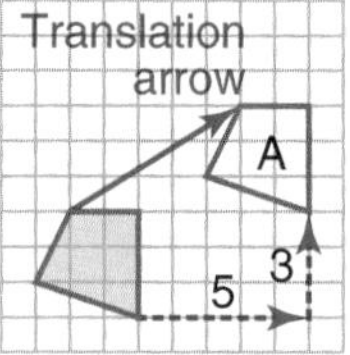

Reflection

The reflection image and the shaded figure are congruent.

The shaded figure is reflected in a horizontal line 1 unit below the figure. Its reflection image is figure B.

Mirror line
B

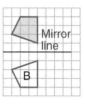

The figures have different orientations. That is, you flip one figure to make it coincide with the other figure.

Rotation

The rotation image and the shaded figure are congruent.

The shaded figure is rotated a $\frac{1}{4}$ turn clockwise. The turn centre is the vertex indicated.
The rotation image is figure C.

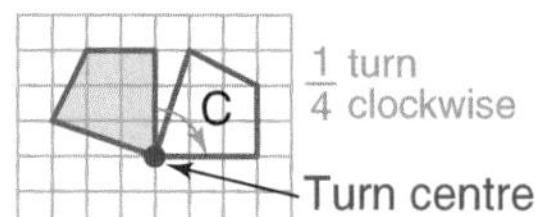

We get the same image if the shaded figure is rotated a $\frac{3}{4}$ turn counterclockwise about the turn centre.

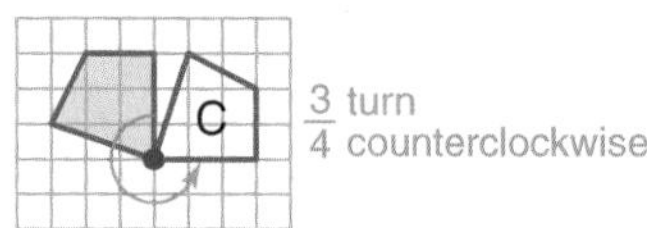

Here are the three images and the shaded figure on the same grid.

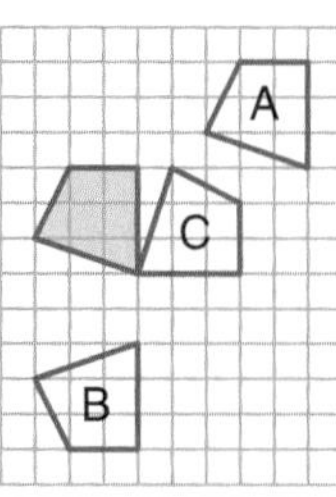

We can show transformations on a coordinate grid.

Example

Look at these rectangles.

Is one rectangle a transformation image of the other? Explain.

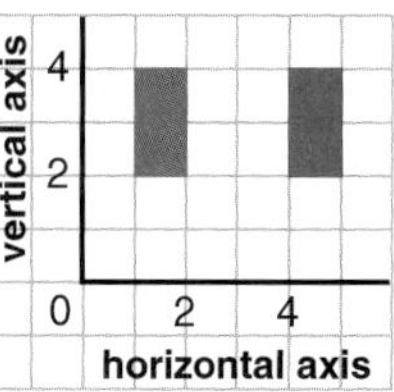

Solution

Let the blue rectangle be the original figure.
And let the red rectangle be the image.

Solution 1

The red rectangle is the image after a translation of 3 units right. The translation arrow shows the movement.

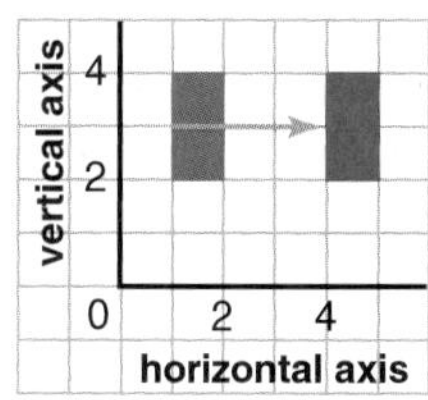

Solution 2

Use a Mira to verify the image.

The red rectangle is the image after a reflection in a vertical line through (3, 0) on the horizontal axis.

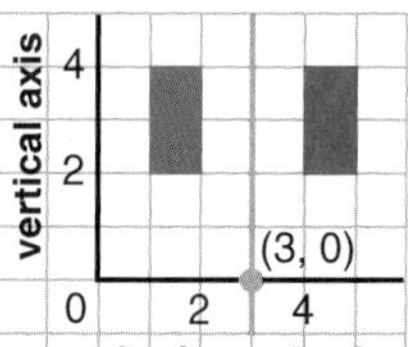

Solution 3

Use tracing paper to verify the image.

The red rectangle is the image after a rotation of a $\frac{1}{2}$ turn about the point with coordinates (3, 3).

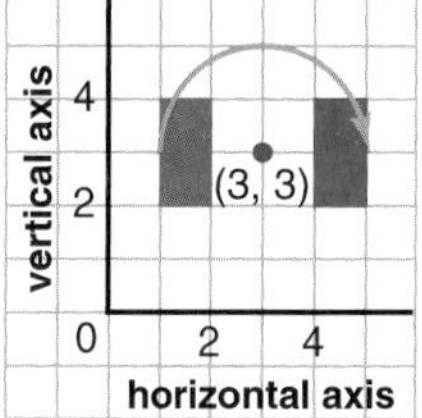

The *Example* shows that an image may be the result of any one of the 3 transformations.
It also shows a rotation about a turn centre that is not on the figure.

Practice

1. Use the figures below.

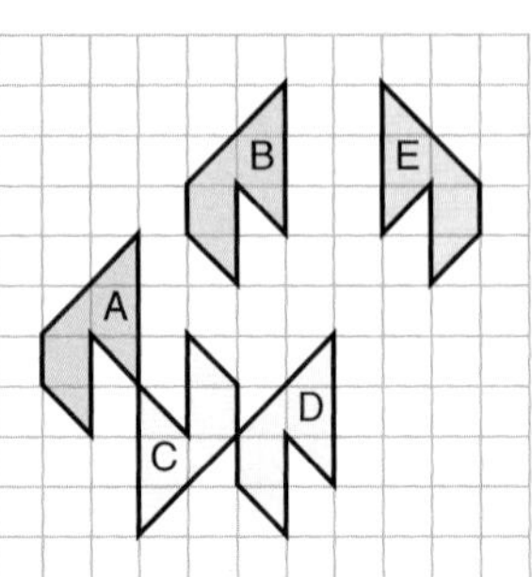

Identify the transformation for which:

a) Figure B is the image of Figure A.
b) Figure C is the image of Figure A.
c) Figure E is the image of Figure B.
d) Figure A is the image of Figure D.
e) Figure C is the image of Figure D.

Number Strategies

Add or subtract, as indicated.

- $\frac{5}{8} + \frac{7}{6}$
- $\frac{17}{10} - \frac{3}{4}$
- $\frac{11}{12} - \frac{2}{3}$
- $\frac{4}{5} + \frac{5}{6}$

2. Identify each transformation.

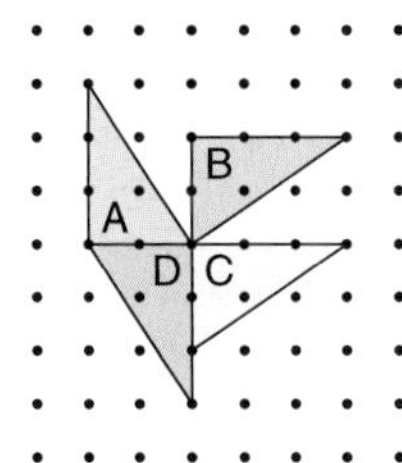

a) Figure A is the image of Figure B.
b) Figure B is the image of Figure C.
c) Figure C is the image of Figure D.
d) Figure D is the image of Figure A.

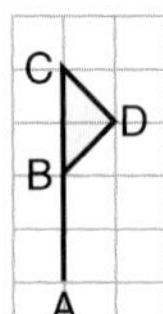

3. Draw this flag on a coordinate grid. The coordinates are A(11, 11), B(11, 13), C(11, 15), and D(12, 14).
Draw the image of the flag after each transformation.

a) a translation 3 units right
b) a translation 5 units down
c) a reflection in a vertical line through (9, 0)
d) a reflection in a horizontal line through (0, 8)
e) a rotation of a $\frac{1}{2}$ turn about point A
f) a rotation of a $\frac{1}{4}$ turn clockwise about point C

4. How many different ways can each figure be described as a transformation of another figure? Explain.

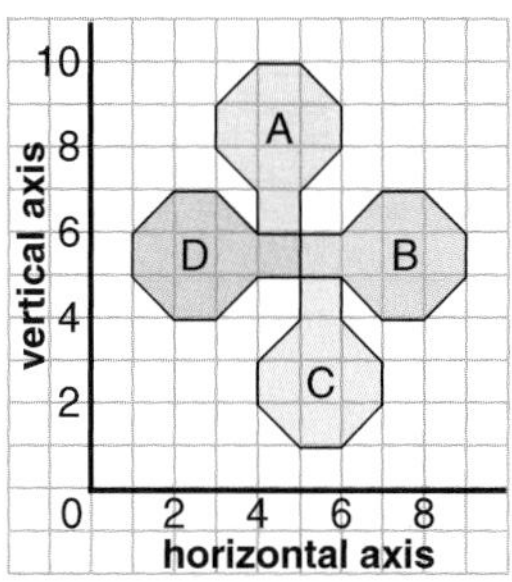

5. **a)** Which pairs of congruent figures do *not* represent a figure and its transformation image? How do you know?

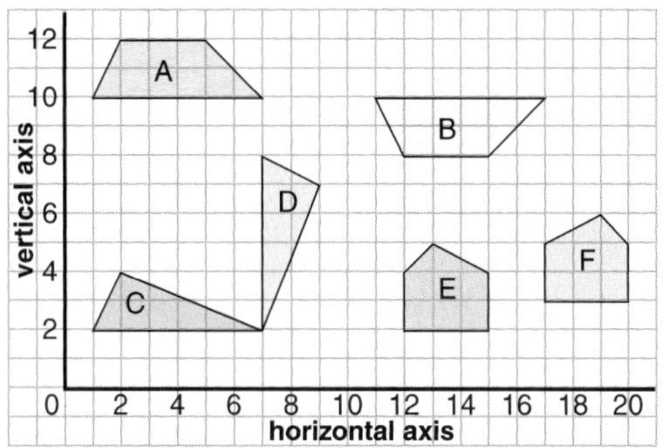

b) For each pair of congruent figures that do show a transformation, identify the transformation.

6. **Assessment Focus** Use grid paper.

In each case, describe the figure you drew.

a) Draw a figure for which a translation image is also a reflection image and a rotation image. Draw the translation image.

b) Draw a figure for which a translation image is also a reflection image, but *not* a rotation image. Draw the translation image.

c) Draw a figure for which a translation image is *not* a reflection image *nor* a rotation image. Draw the translation image.

Take It Further

7. Describe Figure A as a transformation image of Figure B as many different ways as possible.

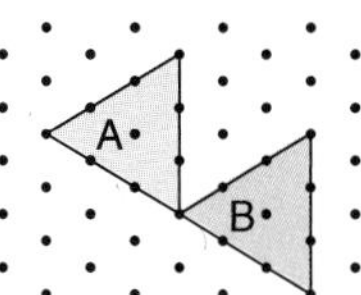

Reflect

When you see a figure and its transformation image on a grid, how do you identify the transformation?
Use diagrams in your explanation.

7.4 Tiling Patterns

Focus Construct and analyse tiling patterns.

Explore

Work on your own.
You will need index cards, a ruler, and scissors.

> You can rotate or flip the figure to try to make it fit.

➢ Draw a triangle on a card. Cut it out.
Use tracings of the triangle to cover a piece of paper.

➢ Draw a quadrilateral on a card. Cut it out.
Use tracings of the quadrilateral to cover a piece of paper.

➢ Draw a pentagon on a card. Cut it out.
Use tracings of the pentagon to cover a piece of paper.

Reflect & Share

Share your results with the class.

- Will congruent triangles cover a page and leave no gaps? Explain.
- Will congruent quadrilaterals cover a page and leave no gaps? Explain.
- Will congruent pentagons cover a page and leave no gaps? Explain.

How can you tell if congruent figures will cover a page and leave no gaps?

Connect

When congruent copies of a figure cover a page and leave no gaps, we say the figure **tiles the plane**.

➢ A triangle always tiles the plane.

> At any point where vertices meet, the angles add to 360°.

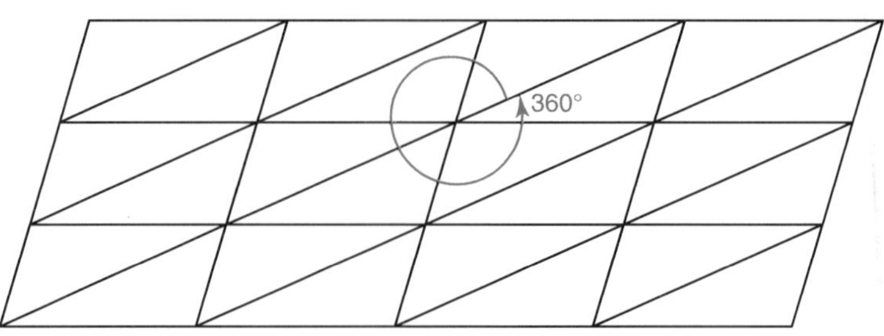

➢ A quadrilateral always tiles the plane.

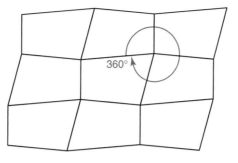

At any point where vertices meet, the angles add to 360°.

Example

Will a pentagon always tile the plane? Explain.

Solution

If we can find a pentagon that does *not* tile the plane, we can say that a pentagon does not always tile the plane.
Draw a regular pentagon.
Use tracing paper to repeat the pentagon to try to cover the page.

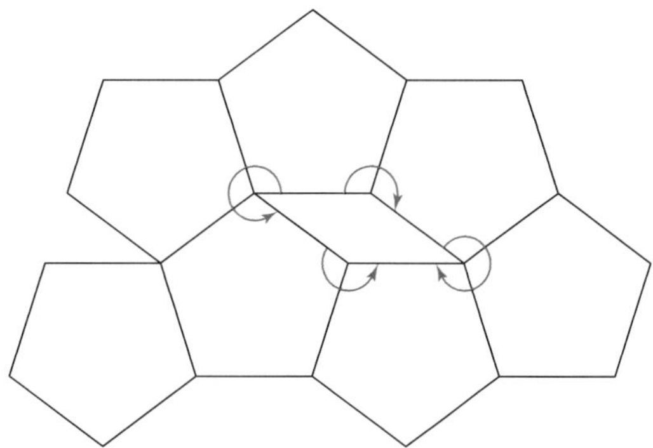

This pentagon does not cover the page.
It leaves gaps that are rhombuses.
Five vertices do not meet.
There are points where 3 vertices meet and the sum of the angles is less than 360°.
There are points where 2 vertices meet and the sum of the angles is less than 360°.
So, a pentagon does not always tile the plane.

In the *Practice* questions, you will investigate to find which other figures *do* tile the plane.

Practice

1. Use dot paper.
Draw a convex hexagon that is not regular.
Try to cover the dot paper with copies of this hexagon.
Does the hexagon tile the plane? Explain.

2. Use dot paper.
Draw a concave hexagon.
Try to cover the dot paper with copies of this hexagon.
Does the hexagon tile the plane? Explain.

3. Here is a regular octagon.

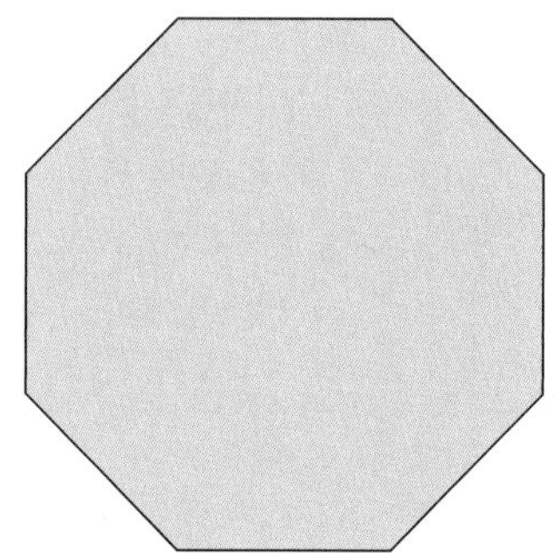

Trace this octagon.
Try to tile the plane.
What do you notice?

4. Look at the picture called *Reptiles,* drawn by M.C. Escher.

Which figure do you think Escher started with?
Explain how Escher's reptiles tile the plane.

Calculator Skills

Evaluate.

- $23.56 + 27.39 \times 4.35$
- $(23.56 + 27.39) \times 4.35$

Why are the answers different?

5. A floor tile is a regular hexagon.
What happens when you try to tile a rectangular floor with a regular hexagon?
Use isometric dot paper to find out.

6. Why do most tiling patterns in floors and patios use squares or rectangles?

7. **Assessment Focus**
Not all pentagons tile the plane. Use grid paper.

a) Find a pentagon that will tile the plane.
Describe the pentagon.
Explain how it tiles the plane.

b) How many different pentagons can you find that will tile the plane? Draw each pentagon and show how it tiles the plane.

c) Explain why some pentagons tile the plane, while others do not.

8. In question 3, you discovered that a regular octagon will not tile the plane.
Use grid paper. Find an octagon that will tile the plane.
Explain how it tiles the plane.

Take It Further

9. Think about "tiling" in nature. Which figures are used?

Reflect

How can you tell if a polygon will tile the plane?
Use examples in your explanation.

7.5 Using Transformations to Make Designs

Focus Create and analyse designs using transformations.

Explore

Work on your own.
You will need isometric dot paper.
Choose two or more of these Pattern Blocks.

Make a design to cover a page.
Copy your design on dot paper.
Label each figure in your design.
Explain your design in terms of transformation images.
That is, how do you rotate, translate, or reflect each Pattern Block to generate the design? Write your instructions carefully.

Reflect & Share

Trade instructions with a classmate.
Generate your classmate's pattern.
Check your version of the pattern with your classmate's.
How do they compare?

Connect

In *Section 7.4*, you investigated tiling patterns.
You used congruent copies of one figure.
You discovered that not all octagons tile the plane.
But an octagon and a square can tile the plane,
as shown in the *Example* that follows.

Example

Use transformations to describe how to construct this design.

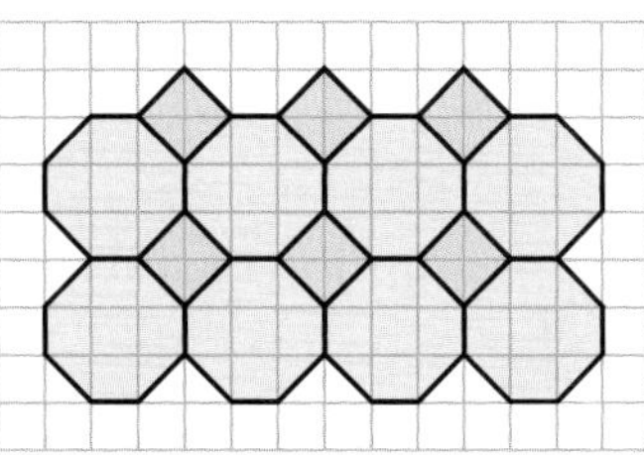

Solution

Label the figures in the design, as shown.

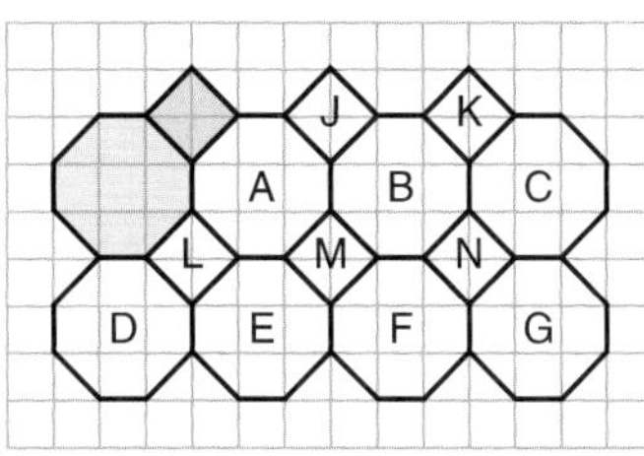

Start with the shaded octagon.

Step 1 To get octagon A, rotate the shaded octagon a $\frac{1}{2}$ turn about a turn centre that is at the midpoint of the right side.

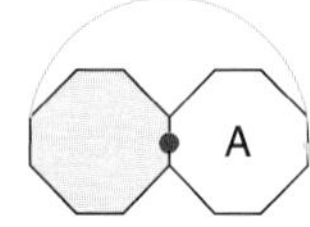

Repeat a similar rotation to get figure B from figure A.

Step 2 To get octagon D, rotate the shaded octagon a $\frac{1}{2}$ turn about a turn centre that is at the midpoint of the bottom side.

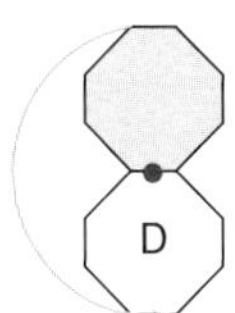

Repeat a similar rotation to get octagon E from octagon A.

Look at the shaded square.

Step 3 To get square J, rotate the shaded square a $\frac{1}{2}$ turn about the midpoint of the top side of octagon A.

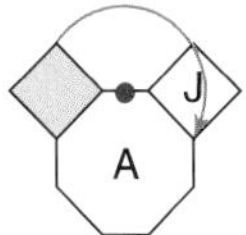

Repeat a similar rotation to get square K from square J.

Step 4 To get square L, rotate the shaded square a $\frac{1}{2}$ turn about the midpoint of the left side of octagon A.

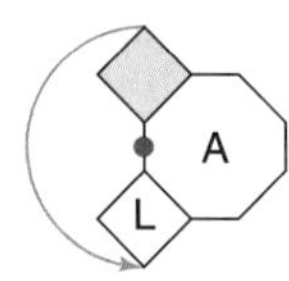

Repeat a similar rotation to get square M from square J.

Practice

1. Here is the design from the *Example*.

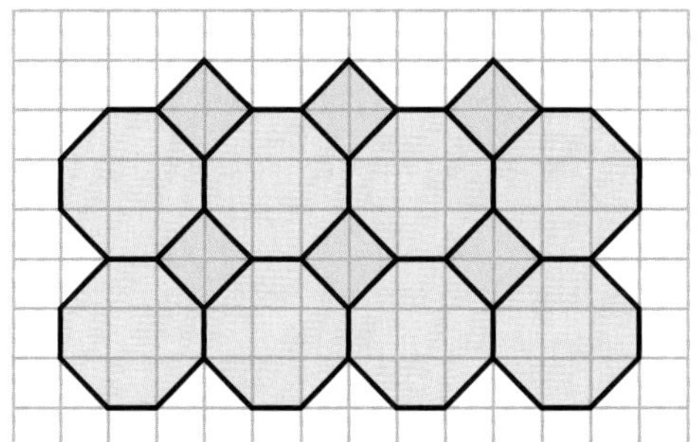

a) Use translations to describe how to construct this design.
b) Use reflections to describe how to construct this design.

2. Use this figure and transformations to create a design on grid paper.

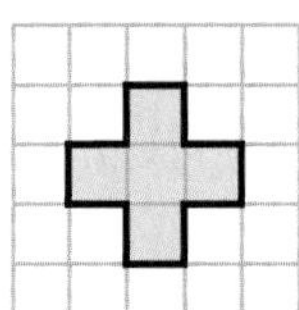

Describe the design in terms of transformations.

3. Use isometric paper. Use a parallelogram and an equilateral triangle to make a design.
Use transformations to describe the design.

4. Draw a figure. Use transformations of the figure to make a border design for a photo frame.
Draw the design. Describe how you made it.

Number Strategies

Which number is the least?

- the sum of all the factors of 30
- the sum of all the factors of 46
- the product of all the factors of 67

5. The Alhambra is a walled city and fortress in Granada, Spain. It was built in the 14th century. Here is part of one of its many tiling patterns.

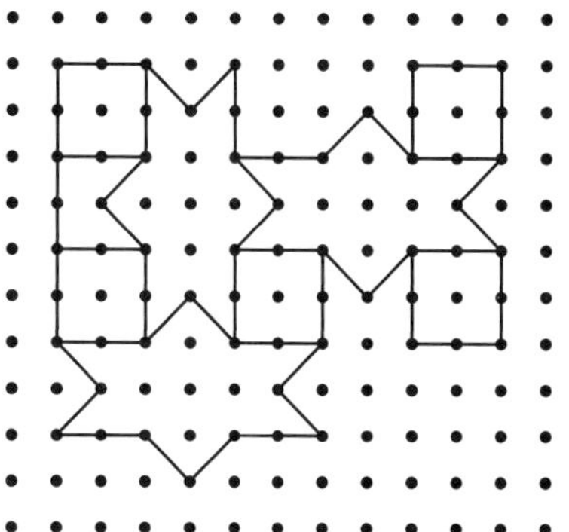

Copy this pattern on dot paper.
Continue the pattern to cover the page.
Use transformations to describe the pattern.

6. **Assessment Focus**
Use dot paper or grid paper.
Create a design that uses 2 or more figures that together tile the plane.
Colour your design.
Use transformations to describe your design.
Try to describe your design as many ways as you can.

7. Here is a flooring pattern.

Use a copy of this pattern.
Use transformations to describe the patterns in one square.

Reflect

When you use transformations to describe a design, how do you decide which transformation to use?
Include a design in your explanation.

Using a Computer to Transform Figures

Focus Use technology to create and analyse designs.

Software, such as *The Geometer's Sketchpad*, can be used to transform figures.
Follow these steps:

1. Open *The Geometer's Sketchpad.*
From the File menu, choose **New Sketch**.

To make a "grid paper" screen:

2. From the **Edit** menu, click on **Preferences**.
Select the **Units** tab.
Check that the Distance Units are cm.
Click **OK**.

3. From the **Graph** menu, choose **Define Coordinate System**.
The screen has grid lines and two numbered axes.

4. Click on each axis and the two red dots.
The axes and the dots are highlighted.
From the **Display** menu, choose **Hide Objects**.
The axes and dots disappear.
The screen appears like a piece of grid paper.

5. From the **Graph** menu, choose **Snap Points**.

Translating a Figure

6. To create a quadrilateral:
From the **Toolbox**, choose ╱.
Click and drag to construct a quadrilateral.

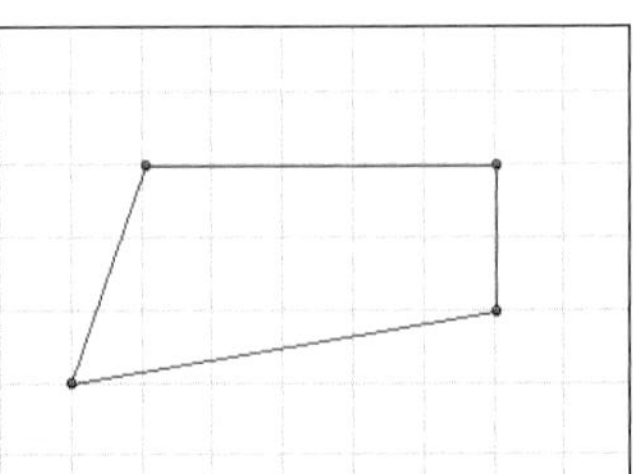

7. To translate the quadrilateral:
From the **Toolbox**, choose ↖.
Click each side of the quadrilateral to select it.
The quadrilateral is highlighted.

8. From the **Transform** menu, choose **Translate.**
Under **Translation Vector:**, choose **Rectangular.**
Under **Horizontal:**, choose **Fixed Distance.**
Enter 2.0 cm for the Horizontal distance.
Under **Vertical:**, choose **Fixed Distance.**
Enter 2.0 cm for the Vertical distance (below left).
Click **Translate** to get the quadrilateral and its image after a translation 2 right, 2 up (below right).

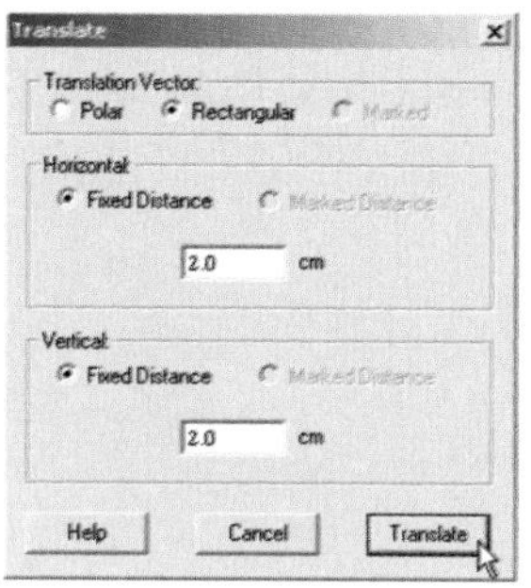

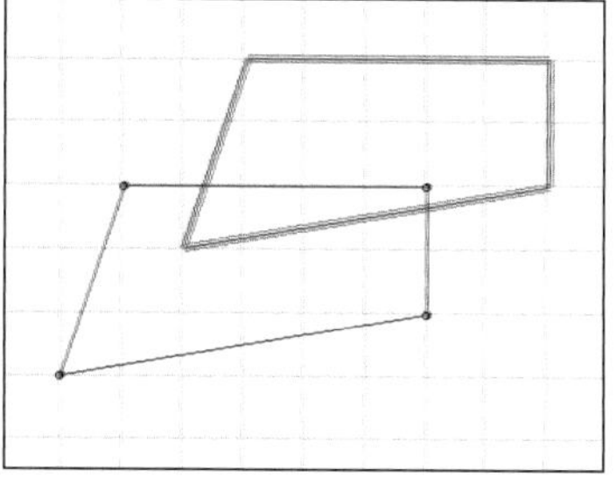

9. Drag any vertex or side of the original figure.
See what happens to the translation image.

10. From the **Edit** menu, choose **Undo Translate Point.**
The screen shows the original quadrilateral and translation image.
To print the quadrilateral and its translation image, from the **File** menu, choose **Print.**

11. Repeat *Steps 7* to *10* using different horizontal and vertical distances.

Rotating a Figure

12. From the **File** menu, choose **New Sketch.**
Follow *Steps 2* to *5* to make a "grid paper" screen.

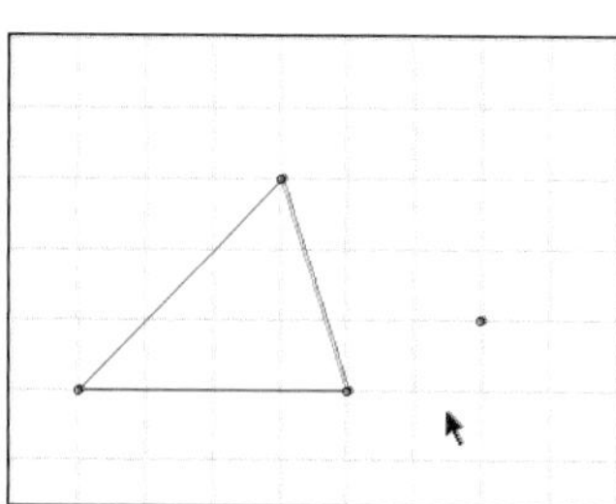

13. To create a triangle:
From the **Toolbox**, choose .
Click and drag to construct a triangle.

14. To rotate the triangle:
From the **Toolbox**, choose .
Click to place a point near the triangle.

15. Click to select the point.
From the **Transform** menu, choose **Mark Center**.
This is the turn centre for your rotation.

16. From the **Toolbox**, choose [selection arrow tool icon].
Click to select each side of the triangle.
The triangle is highlighted.

17. From the **Transform** menu, choose **Rotate**.
Under **Rotate By:**, choose **Fixed Angle**.
Enter 90 degrees. Click **Rotate** to show the triangle and its image after a rotation of 90° counterclockwise.

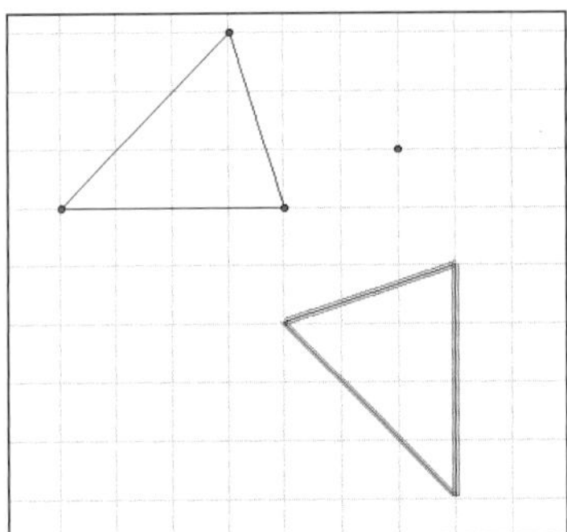

18. Drag any vertex or side of the original figure.
See what happens to the rotation image.

19. From the **Edit** menu, choose **Undo Translate Point**.
The screen shows the original triangle and rotation image.

20. Repeat *Steps 16* to *19* using a different number of degrees of rotation. Print the figure and its rotation image.

Reflecting a Figure

21. Repeat *Step 12*.

22. To create a polygon:
From the **Toolbox**, choose [straightedge tool icon].
Click and drag to construct a polygon.

23. To reflect the polygon:
With the Straightedge Tool still selected, draw a vertical line near your polygon. The line is highlighted.

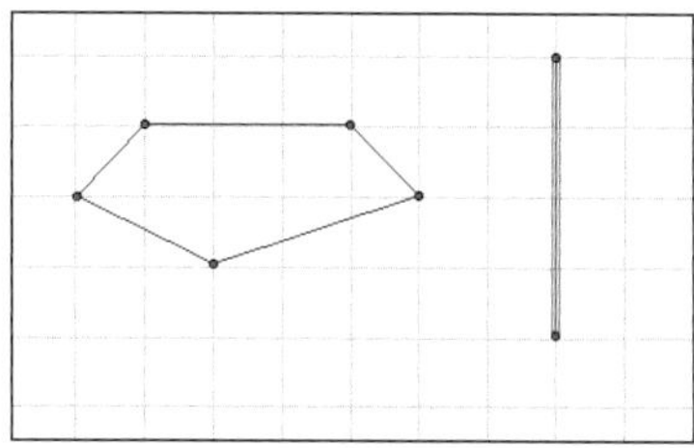

24. From the **Transform** menu, choose **Mark Mirror.**
    The line is a mirror line.

25. From the **Toolbox,** choose .
    Click to select each side of the polygon.
    The polygon is highlighted.

26. From the **Transform** menu, choose **Reflect**.
    The polygon and its reflection image are shown.

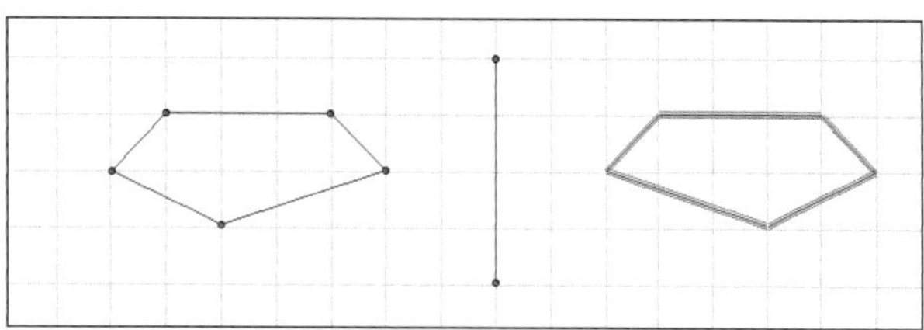

27. Drag any vertex or side of the original figure.
    See what happens to the reflection image.

28. Drag either end point from the mirror line.
    See what happens.

29. From the **Edit** menu, choose **Undo Translate Point**.
    Do this two times. The screen shows the original polygon and its reflection image.

30. Repeat *Steps 23* to *28* using a horizontal mirror line.
    Print the figure and its reflection image.

✓ Check

Use any or all of the transformations above to make a design that covers the screen.
Print your design.

Choosing a Strategy

1. A train is travelling at a rate of 1 km every 45 s.
At this rate, how far will the train travel in 1 h?

Remember to count squares of different sizes.

2. How many squares are in this rectangle?

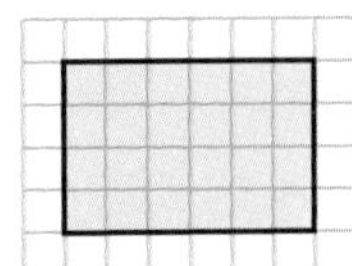

3. Use grid paper. Try to draw a quadrilateral with each number of lines of symmetry.
a) 0 **b)** 1 **c)** 2
d) 3 **e)** 4 **f)** 5
Which quadrilaterals could you not draw? Explain.

Strategies

- Make a table.
- Use a model.
- Draw a diagram.
- Solve a simpler problem.
- Work backward.
- Guess and check.
- Make an organized list.
- Use a pattern.
- Draw a graph.
- Use logical reasoning.

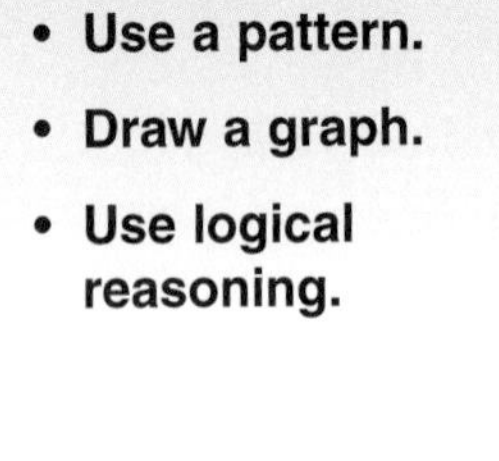

4. Use grid paper. Draw this figure:
It has at least 1 line of symmetry.
It has perimeter 24 units.
It has area 23 square units.

5. Copy the diagram below.
Write these numbers in the boxes: $\frac{1}{6}, \frac{1}{3}, \frac{1}{2}, \frac{2}{3}, \frac{5}{6}$, 1;
so the sum of the fractions along each side is :
a) $1\frac{1}{2}$ **b)** 2

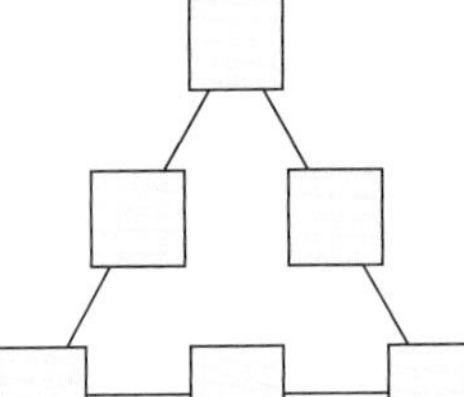

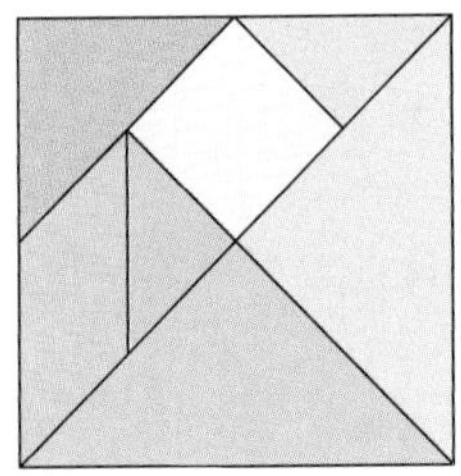

6. What fraction of the area of a tangram is triangles?

7. Write the next five terms in each pattern.
Describe each pattern rule.
a) A above the line, B C D below the line, E F above the line:

$$\frac{A \qquad\quad E\ F}{B\ C\ D}$$

b) 1, 5, 10, 25, …
c) O, T, T, F, F, S, S, …

Reading and Writing in Math

8. This rectangular prism is made with 12 different coloured cubes. The colours are black, white, red, orange, light green, dark green, light blue, dark blue, brown, yellow, pink, and purple.

Using linking cubes to build the prism.

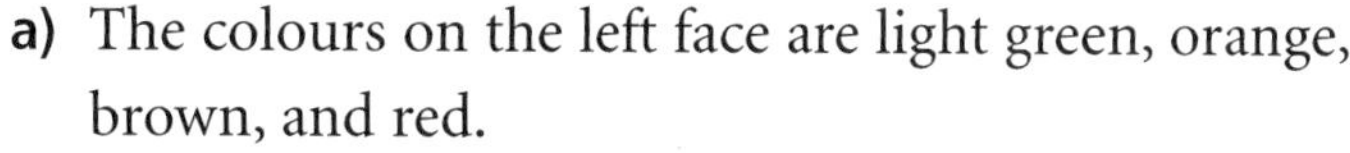

a) The colours on the left face are light green, orange, brown, and red.
   Draw and colour the back face of the prism.

Another congruent prism is made from the coloured cubes. The colours on the front face are: red, orange, dark green, light blue, black, and white.
The colours on the top face are: red, black, white, pink, purple, and yellow.
The colours on the right face side are: light blue, white, yellow, and brown.
The colours on the left face side are: red, dark green, pink, and dark blue.

b) Build the prism. Sketch the prism.
c) What colours are on the bottom face of the prism?
   How do you know?

9. In her fitness program Jessie runs on Mondays, Wednesdays, and Saturdays, and swims on Tuesdays and Fridays. Malcolm runs every third day and swims on the day after each run.
Jessie and Malcolm run together on Saturday July 6.
On what days and dates in July will they:
a) run together again?
b) swim together?

Office Space Planner

An office space planner plans the best use of the office space. He ensures that employees have a workplace that is functional and attractive. Systems furniture is a series of connected partitions, work surfaces, and cabinets. It is frequently used in offices. The planner uses a computer to design multiple 'standard' work areas. Each work area is designed to meet the needs of a group of employees with similar jobs. The work areas are also designed to 'fit' with other work areas of the same size and shape, and with work areas that have different sizes and shapes. It's all a bit of a puzzle! The space planner must solve the puzzle using geometry and an understanding of how people work and interact (ergonomics).

A workplace, where every work area or 'cubicle' is identical, is often seen as 'cell-like' or dehumanizing. Suppose you are an office planner. What might you do to make groups of work areas more appealing, and still make the best use of the available floor area?

Unit Review

Review any lesson with

What Do I Need to Know?

Conditions for Congruent Triangles

Two triangles are congruent if:

- three pairs of corresponding sides are equal

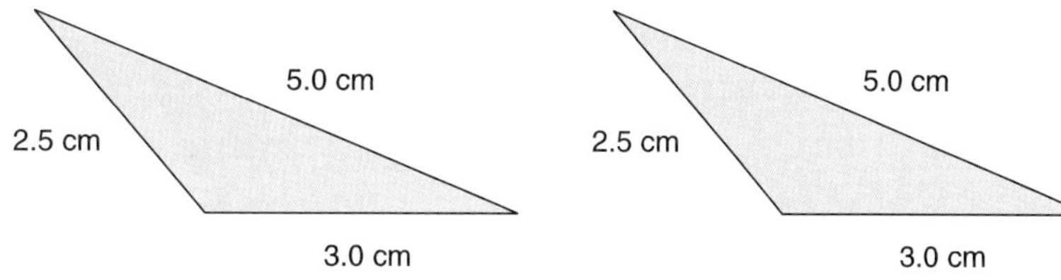

- two pairs of corresponding sides are equal and the corresponding angles between these sides are equal

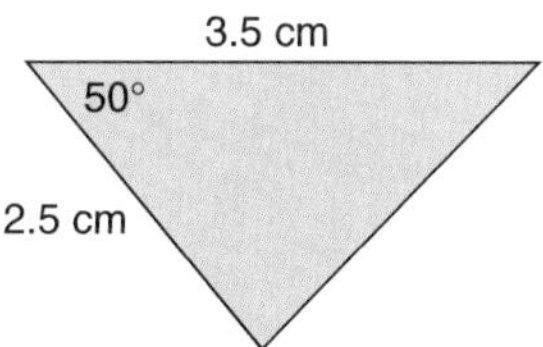

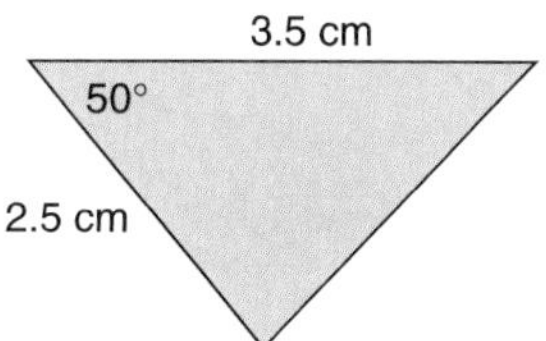

- two pairs of corresponding angles are equal and the corresponding sides between these angles are equal

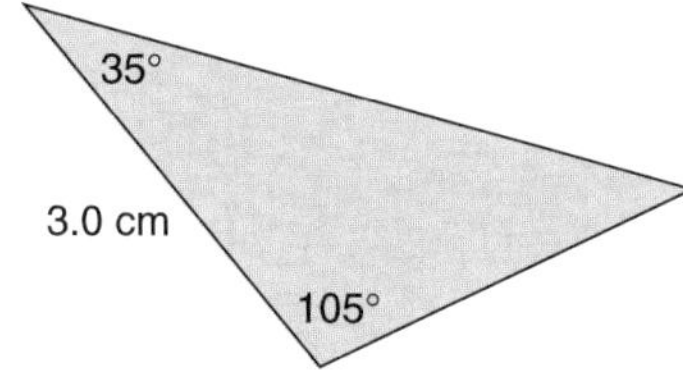

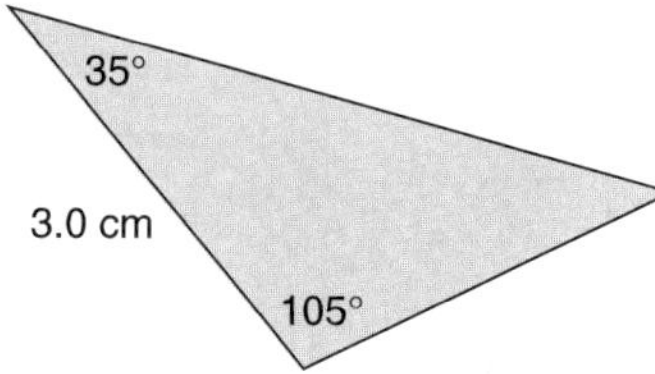

Conditions for Congruent Figures

For figures that are not triangles, two figures are congruent if corresponding sides are equal *and* corresponding angles are equal.

What Should I Be Able to Do?

For extra practice, go to page 444.

LESSON

7.1

1. Use grid paper or dot paper.
   Draw each figure.
   a) a concave hexagon
   b) a convex pentagon
   c) a concave quadrilateral
   d) a figure that is not a polygon
   e) a regular triangle
   Describe the attributes of each figure. Include angle measures.

2. Use grid paper or dot paper.
   Draw each figure.
   a) a hexagon with exactly 2 lines of symmetry
   b) a triangle with rotational symmetry of order 3
   c) a pentagon with exactly 3 acute angles
   d) a pentagon with exactly 3 obtuse angles
   Describe the attributes of each figure. Include angle measures.

7.2

3. Are the figures in each pair congruent? How do you know?
   a)

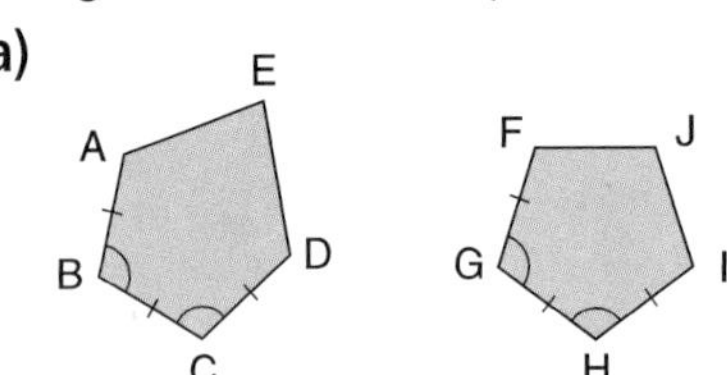

   b)

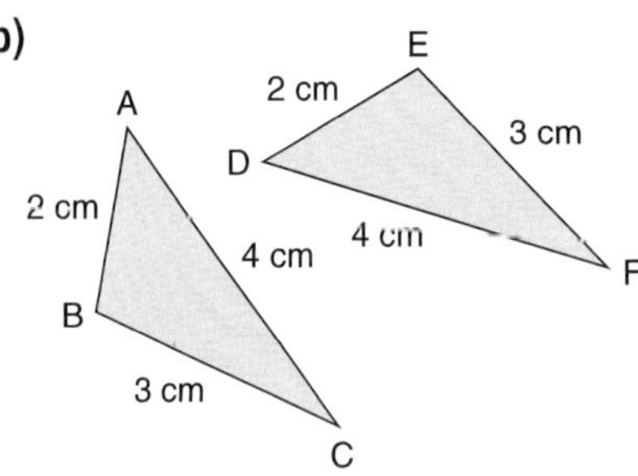

7.3

4. Plot these points on a coordinate grid:
   A(4, 6), B(4, 7), C(7, 9), and D(6, 6).
   Join the points to form a quadrilateral.
   The coordinates of the vertices of 3 images are given.
   Identify the transformation that produced each image.
   a) C(7, 9), E(5, 12), F(4, 12), G(4, 10)
   b) I(4, 16), J(6, 16), K(7, 13), L(4, 15)
   c) M(9, 4), N(8, 1), P(6, 1), Q(6, 2)

7.4

5. Copy this figure on grid paper.

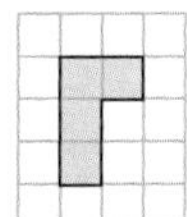

   How many different ways can you use the figure to tile the plane?
   Show each way you find.

7.5

6. Draw 2 different figures on grid paper that will together tile the plane.
   Use the figures to make a design.
   Colour one of each figure.
   Use transformations to explain how to create the design beginning with each coloured figure.

Practice Test

1. Use the figures below.

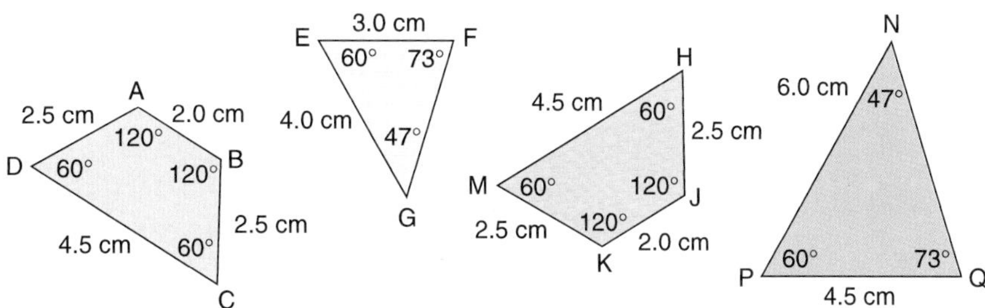

Identify:

a) two congruent figures, and explain how you know they are congruent

b) two figures that are *not* congruent, and explain how you know they are not congruent

c) a scalene triangle with a 60° angle

d) a quadrilateral with a 60° angle

2. Two triangles are congruent if they have 3 matching sides. Suppose two triangles have 3 matching angles. Are the triangles congruent? Justify your answer.

3. Three students looked at a figure and its transformation image.
Igal said the picture showed a translation.
Shaian said the picture showed a rotation.
Cherie said the picture showed a reflection.
All three students were correct. What might the picture be?
Draw a diagram to show your thinking.

4. Julie will use both of these tiles to cover her floor.

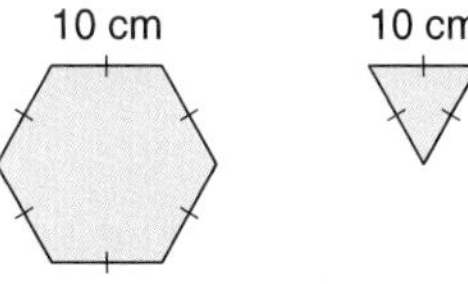

Use isometric paper.
Draw 2 different designs Julie could use.
For each design, use transformations to explain how to create the design.

Unit Problem Tessellations

When we tile the plane with congruent copies of one figure, we make a **tessellation.**

M.C. Escher was a famous Dutch artist.
He designed many different tessellations.

You will create two designs in the Escher style.
The first design is in the style of *Reptiles*, on page 268.

Part 1

Use square dot paper or grid paper.
Tile the plane with a figure of your choice.
Sketch a design on one figure.
Repeat the sketch until every figure in the plane has the design.
Use transformations to describe how to generate the design beginning with one tile.

Part 2

You could start with a rectangle, parallelogram, or regular hexagon, instead.

Start with a square. Draw congruent curves on 2 sides.
A curve that goes "in" on one side must go "out" on the other side.
Draw different congruent curves on the other 2 sides.

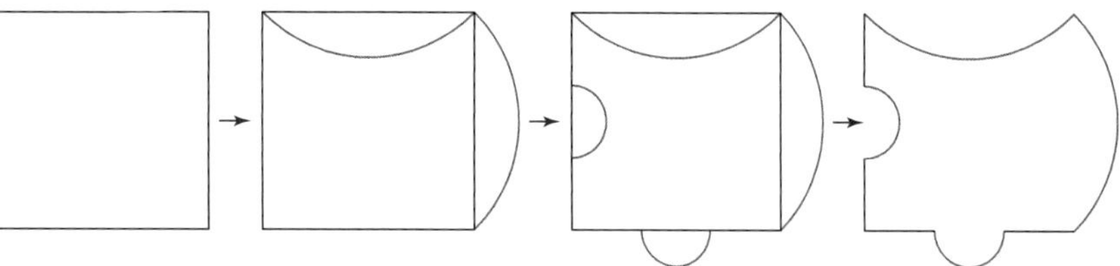

Trace the new figure on cardboard.
Cut out the figure.
Use it to tile the plane.

Add details to your tile so it represents an animal or an object of your choice.

Check List

Your work should show:

- ✓ the initial tile you created for each design
- ✓ the designs you created
- ✓ how you used transformations to create the designs
- ✓ the correct use of mathematical language

Reflect on the Unit

How are transformations related to congruent figures?
Include diagrams in your explanation.

Cross Strand Investigation

Pick's Theorem

Materials:
- 11 pin by 11 pin geoboard
- geobands
- square dot paper
- 0.5-cm grid paper

Work with a partner.

When a polygon is drawn on square dot paper, there are dots on the perimeter and dots inside.
Is there a relationship between the numbers of these dots?

As you complete this *Investigation*, include all your work in a report that you will hand in.

➢ Make a convex polygon on the geoboard.
Draw the polygon on square dot paper.
Count:
- the number of dots on the perimeter of the polygon
- the number of dots inside the polygon
Find the area of the polygon in square units.
Record your results in a table.

Polygon	Number of dots on the perimeter	Number of dots inside	Area in square units

➢ Repeat this process for 10 or more different polygons.
Include triangles, parallelograms, trapezoids, pentagons, hexagons, and so on.

➢ Choose two measurements: for example,
Number of dots on the perimeter and *Number of dots inside*.
Draw a scatter plot of the data.
What trends do you see in the graph? Explain.

- What patterns do you see in the table?
  How can you use the patterns to write an expression for the area of a polygon in terms of the number of dots inside the polygon and the number of dots on the perimeter?

- Use variables.
  Let the number of dots on the perimeter be p.
  Let the number of dots inside be i.
  Write a formula for the area, A, of a polygon in terms of p and i.
  This relationship is called **Pick's Theorem.**

Take It Further

- What happens to the area when the number of dots on the perimeter increases while the number of dots inside the polygon stays the same?
- What happens to the area when the number of dots inside the polygon increases while the number of dots on the perimeter stays the same?

UNIT 8

Working with Percents

Stores offer goods on sale to encourage you to spend your money.

What is the sale price of each item in the picture?
How did you calculate the sale price?
What do you need to add to find the price you pay?

What You'll Learn

- Relate decimals, fractions, and percents.
- Solve problems that involve fractions, decimals, and percents.
- Multiply decimals.
- Divide decimals.
- Draw circle graphs by hand.

Why It's Important

When you buy something, you pay sales tax. To be able to calculate the sales tax is useful. Then you know if you have enough money to buy the item.

Key Words

- percent
- percent circle

UNIT 8

Skills You'll Need

Writing a Fraction As a Decimal

To write a fraction as a decimal, try to write an equivalent fraction with denominator 100.
When we cannot write an equivalent fraction, we use a calculator to divide.

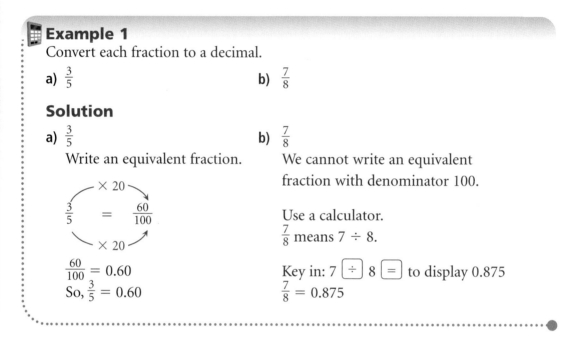

Example 1

Convert each fraction to a decimal.

a) $\frac{3}{5}$ b) $\frac{7}{8}$

Solution

a) $\frac{3}{5}$

Write an equivalent fraction.

$$\frac{3}{5} \overset{\times 20}{=} \frac{60}{100}$$

$\frac{60}{100} = 0.60$
So, $\frac{3}{5} = 0.60$

b) $\frac{7}{8}$

We cannot write an equivalent fraction with denominator 100.

Use a calculator.
$\frac{7}{8}$ means $7 \div 8$.

Key in: 7 [÷] 8 [=] to display 0.875
$\frac{7}{8} = 0.875$

Some conversions from fractions to decimals are worth remembering.
Try to remember these:

$\frac{1}{2} = 0.5$ $\frac{1}{4} = 0.25$ $\frac{1}{5} = 0.2$ $\frac{1}{8} = 0.125$ $\frac{1}{10} = 0.1$ $\frac{1}{100} = 0.01$

You can use these conversions to write other fractions as decimals.
For example, since $\frac{1}{10} = 0.1$, then $\frac{2}{10} = 0.2$, $\frac{3}{10} = 0.3$, and so on.

✓ Check

1. Write each fraction as a decimal. Use mental math.

a) $\frac{3}{4}$ b) $\frac{2}{5}$ c) $\frac{6}{10}$ d) $\frac{68}{100}$

2. Write each fraction as a decimal.

a) $\frac{5}{8}$ b) $\frac{3}{16}$ c) $\frac{3}{8}$ d) $\frac{7}{16}$

Percent

Percent means per hundred. One whole, or 1, is 100%.
So, 70% means $\frac{70}{100}$, 4% means $\frac{4}{100}$, and 100% means $\frac{100}{100}$, or 1.

Example 2

What percent of this hundredths chart is shaded each colour?

a) Red **b)** Blue **c)** Yellow

Solution

a) There are 11 red squares out of 100 squares.
That is: $\frac{11}{100} = 11\%$

b) There are 55 blue squares out of 100 squares.
That is: $\frac{55}{100} = 55\%$

c) There are 34 yellow squares out of 100 squares.
That is: $\frac{34}{100} = 34\%$

✓ Check

Use a hundred chart.

3. Shade:

a) 15% red **b)** 26% yellow **c)** 43% green **d)** 10% blue

4. What percent of the hundred chart in question 3 is not shaded?

8.1 Relating Fractions, Decimals, and Percents

Focus Relate percent to fractions and decimals.

We see uses of percent everywhere.

What do you know from looking at each picture?

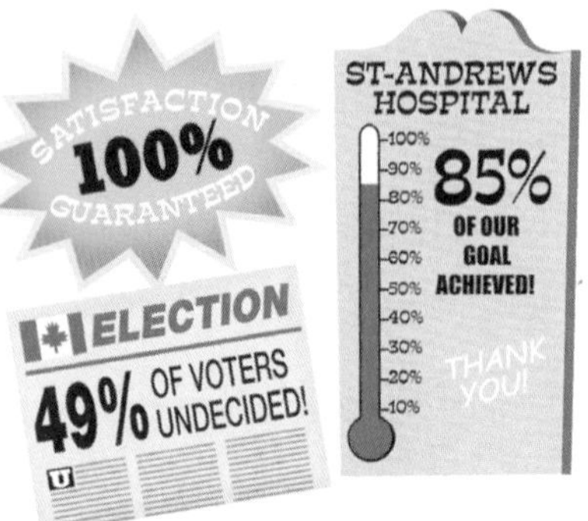

Explore

Work with a partner.
Your teacher will give you a large copy of this puzzle.
Describe each puzzle piece as a fraction, a decimal, and a percent of the whole puzzle.

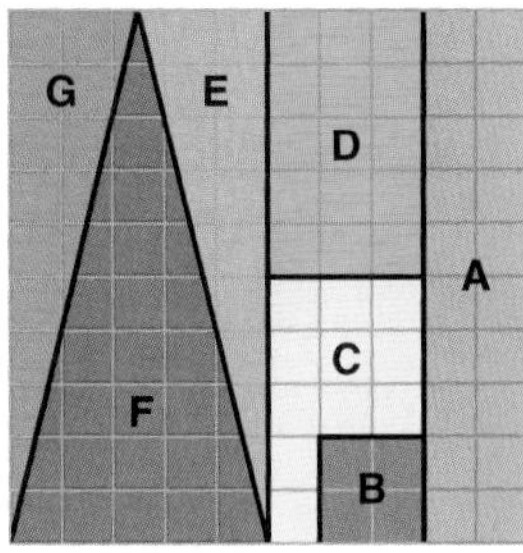

Reflect & Share

Compare your answers with those of another pair of classmates.
If the answers are different, how do you know which are correct?

Connect

➢ Since a percent can be written as a fraction, a percent can also be written as a decimal.
We can use number lines to illustrate the relationships.
For example:

$25\% = \frac{25}{100} = 0.25 \qquad 125\% = \frac{125}{100} = 1.25$

0   $\frac{25}{100}$, or $\frac{1}{4}$ $\frac{100}{100}$ $\frac{125}{100}$, or $\frac{5}{4}$

0   0.25   1.0   1.25

0   25%   100%   125%

➢ Conversely, a decimal can be written as a percent:

$0.15 = \frac{15}{100} = 15\%$ $\qquad$ $1.15 = \frac{115}{100} = 115\%$

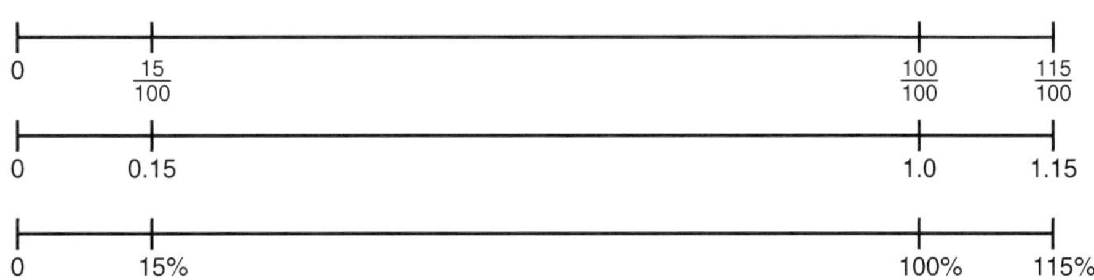

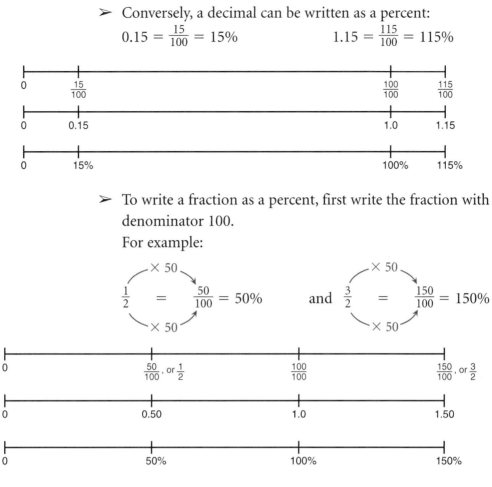

➢ To write a fraction as a percent, first write the fraction with denominator 100.

For example:

$\frac{1}{2} = \frac{50}{100} = 50\%$ (× 50 numerator and denominator) and $\frac{3}{2} = \frac{150}{100} = 150\%$ (× 50 numerator and denominator)

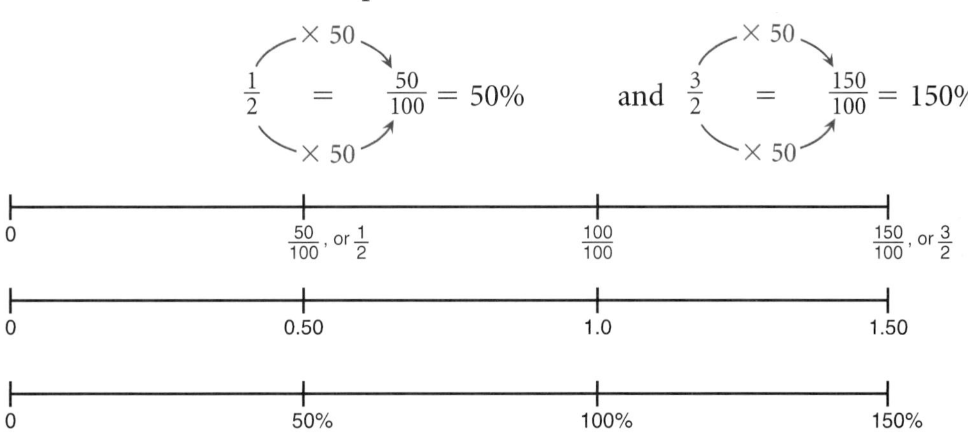

When a decimal has 3 digits after the decimal point, we can write it as a fraction with denominator 1000.

➢ Some fractions cannot be written with denominator 100.
Use a calculator to divide.

$$\frac{5}{8} = 0.625$$
$$= \frac{625}{1000} \quad \text{Divide numerator and denominator by 10.}$$
$$= \frac{62.5}{100}$$
$$= 62.5\%$$

Example

a) Write each percent as a fraction and as a decimal.

i) 75% **ii)** 9% **iii)** 130%

b) Write each fraction as a percent and as a decimal.

i) $\frac{2}{5}$ **ii)** $\frac{5}{2}$

Draw number lines to show how the numbers are related.

Solution

a) i) $75\% = \frac{75}{100} = 0.75$

ii) $9\% = \frac{9}{100} = 0.09$

iii) $130\% = \frac{130}{100} = 1.30$

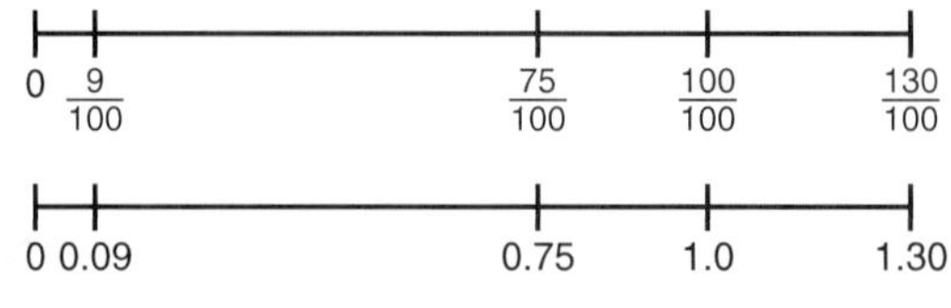

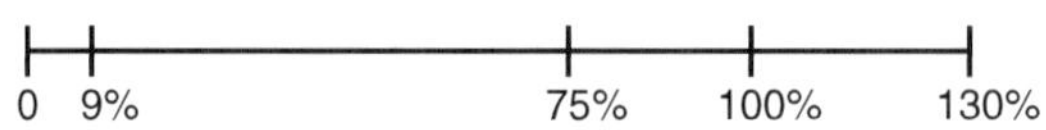

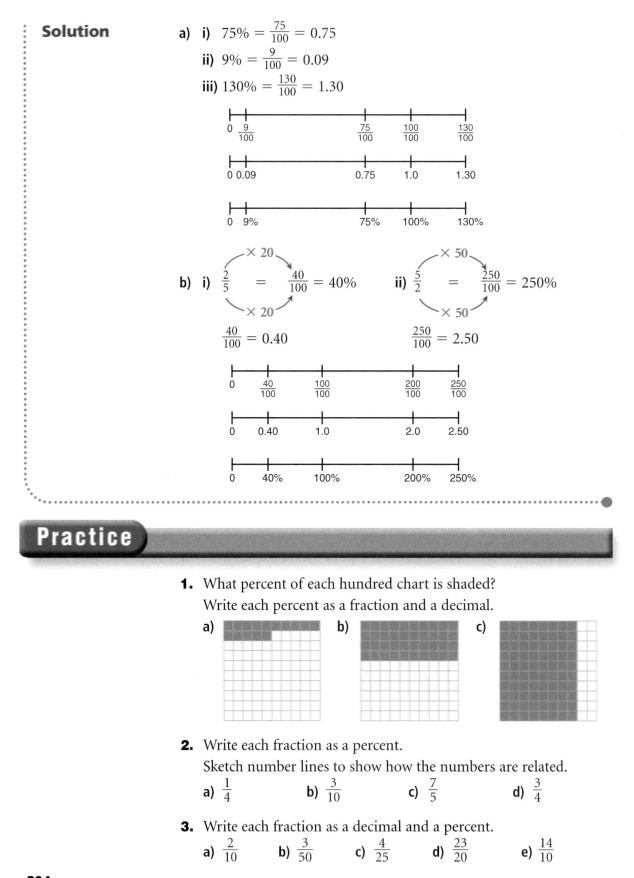

b) i) $\frac{2}{5} = \frac{40}{100} = 40\%$ (× 20 numerator and denominator)

$\frac{40}{100} = 0.40$

ii) $\frac{5}{2} = \frac{250}{100} = 250\%$ (× 50 numerator and denominator)

$\frac{250}{100} = 2.50$

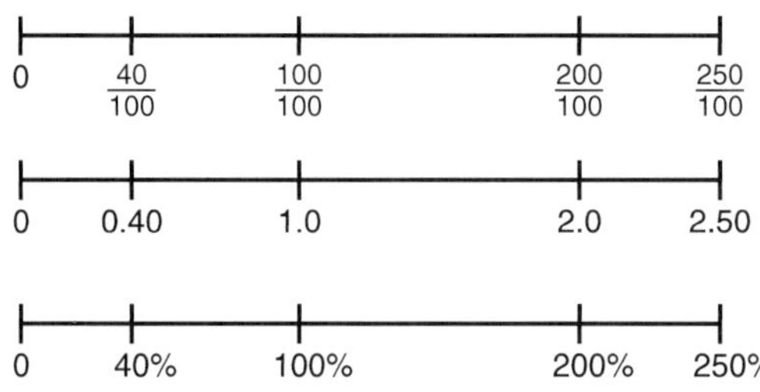

Practice

1. What percent of each hundred chart is shaded?
Write each percent as a fraction and a decimal.

a) 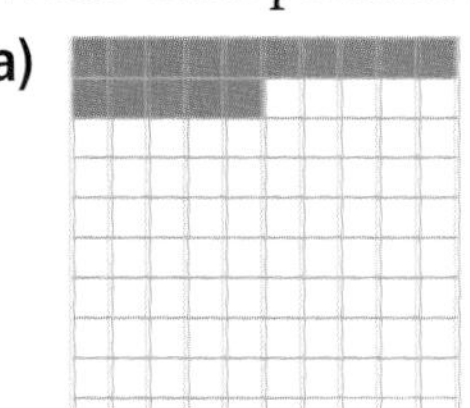 b) 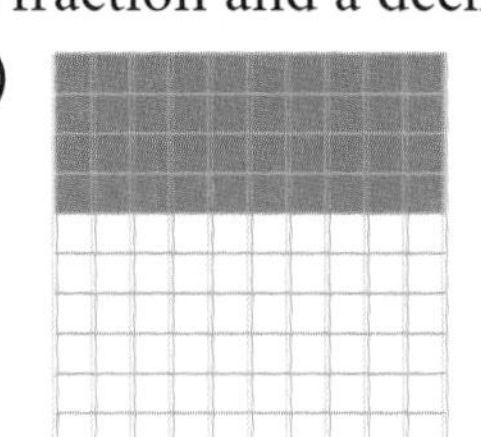 c) 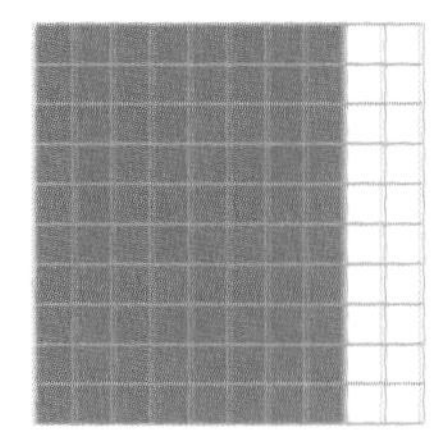

2. Write each fraction as a percent.
Sketch number lines to show how the numbers are related.

a) $\frac{1}{4}$ b) $\frac{3}{10}$ c) $\frac{7}{5}$ d) $\frac{3}{4}$

3. Write each fraction as a decimal and a percent.

a) $\frac{2}{10}$ b) $\frac{3}{50}$ c) $\frac{4}{25}$ d) $\frac{23}{20}$ e) $\frac{14}{10}$

4. Fred had 8 out of 10 on a test. Janet had 82% on the test.
Who did better? How do you know?

5. This equilateral triangle is 20% of a larger figure.
Use triangular grid paper.
Draw a figure that shows 100%.
Is there more than one answer? Explain.

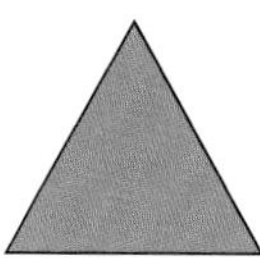

6. This orange square represents 25% of a larger figure.
Use 2-cm grid paper.
   a) Draw 50% of the larger figure.
   b) Draw 75% of the larger figure.
   c) Draw the larger figure.
   d) Draw 125% of the larger figure.

Number Strategies

How many:
- centimetres in 1 m?
- square centimetres in 1 m^2?
- cubic centimetres in 1 m^3?

Sketch a picture to show each relationship.

7. **Assessment Focus** You will need a sheet of paper and coloured pencils.
Divide the paper into these 4 sections.
   - 1 blue section that is $\frac{1}{2}$ the page
   - 1 red section that is 10% of the page
   - 1 yellow section that is 25% of the page
   - 1 green section to fill the remaining space

   Explain how you did this.
What percent of the page is the green section?
How do you know?

8. What does it mean when someone states, "She gave it 110%"?
How can this comment be explained using math?

9. Suppose each pattern is continued on a hundred chart.
The numbers in each pattern are coloured red. For each pattern, what percent of the numbers on the chart are red?
Explain your strategy for each pattern.
   a) 4, 8, 12, 16, 20, …
   b) 1, 3, 5, 7, …
   c) 2, 4, 8, 16, …
   d) 1, 3, 7, 13, …

Reflect

Suppose you know your mark out of 20 for an English test.
How could you write the mark as a percent?

Game

Showdown

HOW TO PLAY THE GAME:

1. Cut out the cards, then shuffle them. Deal all the cards. Each player stacks his cards face down in a pile.
2. Players turn over the first card in their piles, then compare the numbers. The player whose card shows the greater number wins and takes both cards. Both cards are placed in a "captured pile" next to the winner's original pile. See *Step 6* when there is a tie.
3. Play continues until all cards are turned up.
4. Each player then shuffles his captured pile of cards and play continues.
5. The game ends when one player has no cards.
6. **Showdown** If there is a tie between two cards, a showdown occurs. Each player takes the next two cards from his pile and places them face down on top of the original card. A third card is then turned over by each player, and these cards are compared. The player whose card shows the greater number takes all cards involved in the showdown. If there is a tie, another showdown occurs until the tie is broken.

Note: If a player is unable to place cards in a showdown because the player has only one card, the player's last card is the turnover card.

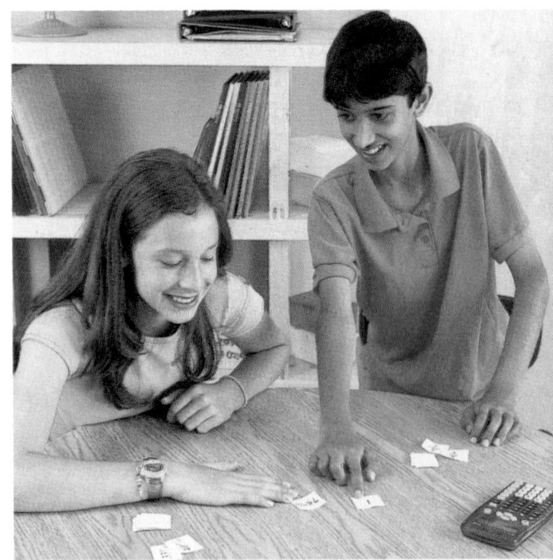

YOU WILL NEED

2 sheets of SHOWDOWN playing cards (48 cards); scissors; a calculator

NUMBER OF PLAYERS

2

GOAL OF THE GAME

To have all the cards when the game ends

What strategies did you use to find which number was greater?

8.2 Estimating and Calculating Percents

Focus Use mental math and estimation.

Explore

Work with a partner.
Look at the surface of your desk.

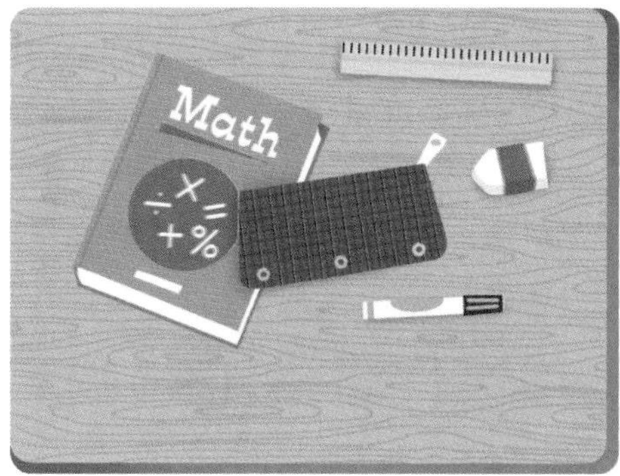

There is probably a textbook on it, and maybe a pencil case, an eraser, or a ruler.

How much of the surface is covered?
How much of the surface is not covered?

Use a calculator and a ruler.
Estimate the percent of your desk's surface that is covered and the percent that is not. Show your work.

Reflect & Share

Compare your results with those of another pair of classmates.
Discuss the strategies you used to find the percent of surface not covered.

Connect

Here is a sketch of a yard.

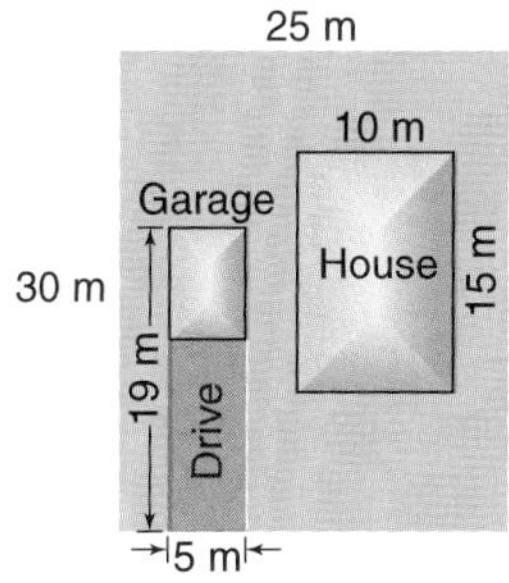

Round 245 to 250 to get a "friendly" number. Both 250 and 750 have 250 as a common factor.

➢ To find the percent of the yard that is covered by the house, garage, and drive, calculate the area covered by
- the house: 15 m × 10 m = 150 m^2
- the garage and the drive: 19 m × 5 m = 95 m^2

Total area covered is: 150 m^2 + 95 m^2 = 245 m^2
The area of the yard is: 30 m × 25 m = 750 m^2
The fraction of the yard that is covered is: $\frac{245}{750}$
For an estimate of the fraction, round 245 to 250.
The fraction of the yard that is covered is about $\frac{250}{750} = \frac{1}{3}$.
$\frac{1}{3}$ is about 30%.
So, about 30% of the yard is covered by the house, garage, and drive.

➢ To find the percent of the yard made up of garden and grass:
The yard is 100%.
Subtract: 100% − 30% = 70%
So, about 70% of the yard is made up of garden and grass.
We can show these percents on a number line.

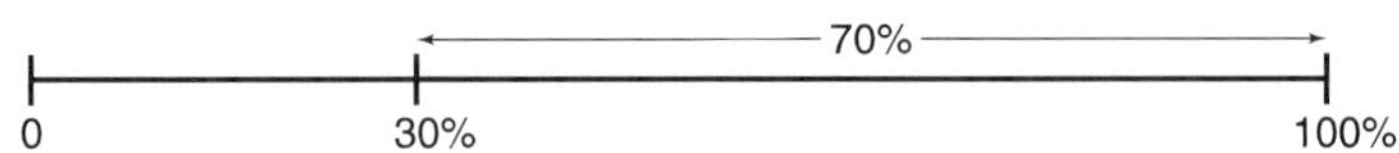

We can use mental math to estimate and calculate percent.

Example 1

There are 27 students in the Grade 7 class.
Five students are left-handed.

a) What is the fraction of students who are left-handed?

b) Estimate the percent of students who are left-handed.

Solution

a) The fraction of students who are left-handed is $\frac{5}{27}$.

b) *Method 1*

One whole or 100% is 27 students.
50% of 27 students is about 14 students.
25% of 27 students is about 7 students.
So, the percent of students who are left-handed is less than 25%.

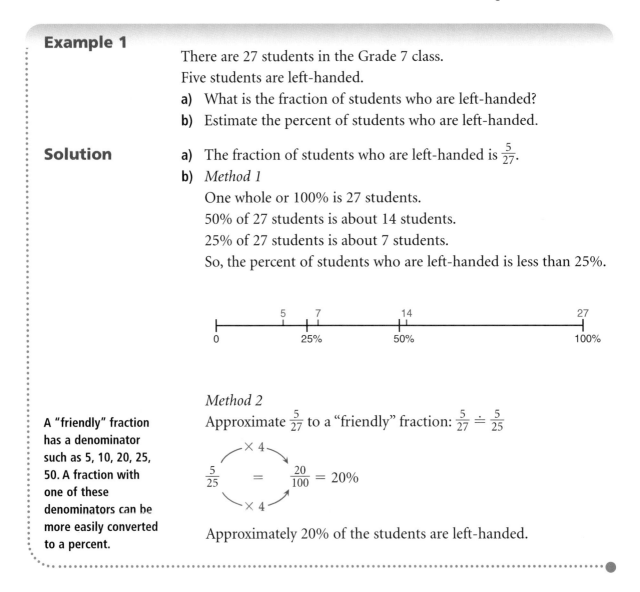

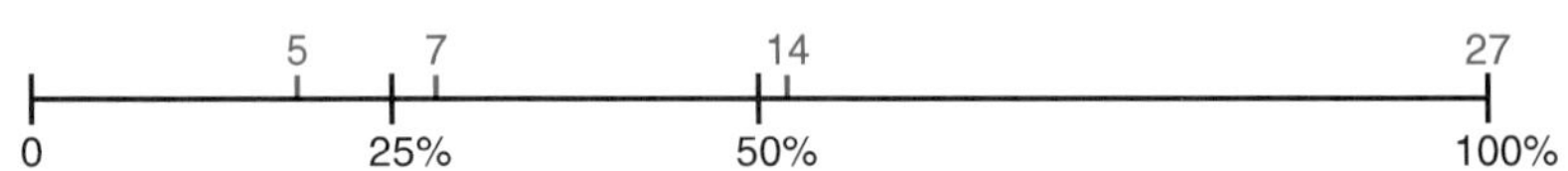

Method 2

Approximate $\frac{5}{27}$ to a "friendly" fraction: $\frac{5}{27} \doteq \frac{5}{25}$

$$\frac{5}{25} \overset{\times 4}{=} \frac{20}{100} = 20\%$$

Approximately 20% of the students are left-handed.

A "friendly" fraction has a denominator such as 5, 10, 20, 25, 50. A fraction with one of these denominators can be more easily converted to a percent.

Example 2

A pair of pants costs \$39.99.
The sales tax is 15%.
Estimate the cost of the pants.

Solution

Round \$39.99 to \$40.
To find 15%, find 10% and 5%.
10% of \$40 = $0.1 \times$ \$40 = \$4
5% is $\frac{1}{2}$ of 10%.
So, 5% of \$40 = $\frac{1}{2}$ of \$4 = \$2
So, the sales tax is \$4 + \$2 = \$6.
The cost of the pants is about \$40 + \$6 = \$46.
We can show these percents on a number line.

Mental math strategy:
A quick way to find 10% is to move the decimal point 1 place to the left:
10% of 40. = 4.0

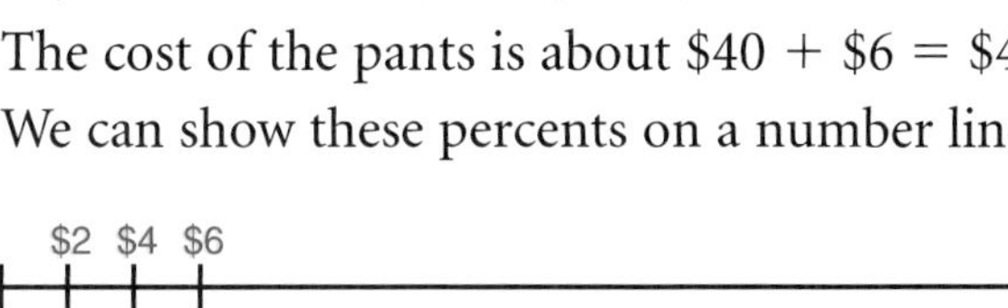

Practice

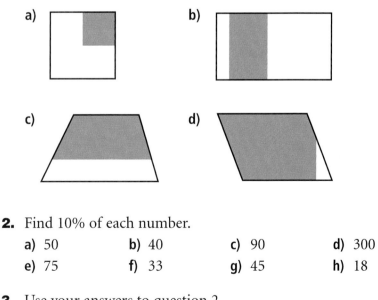

1. Estimate the percent of each figure that is shaded.

a) 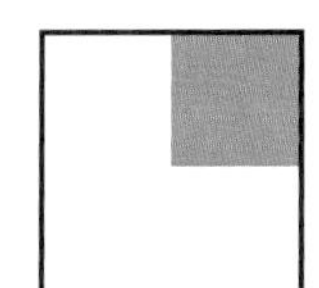

b) 

c) 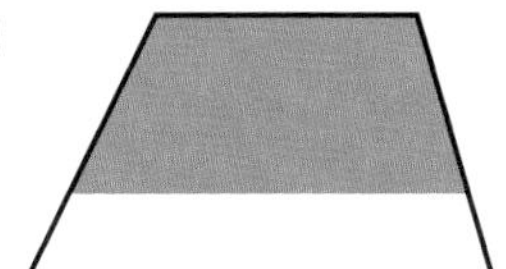

d) 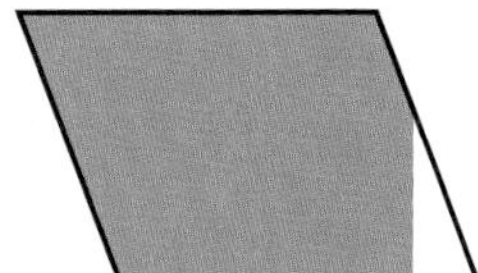

2. Find 10% of each number.

a) 50 **b)** 40 **c)** 90 **d)** 300
e) 75 **f)** 33 **g)** 45 **h)** 18

3. Use your answers to question 2.
Find 5% of each number in question 2.

4. Use your answers to questions 2 and 3.
Find 15% of each number in question 2.

5. This strip is 12 cm long.

Find the length of:

a) 25% of the strip **b)** 10% of the strip
c) 20% of the strip **d)** 150% of the strip

Sketch number lines to illustrate your answers.

Mental Math

How many squares are there on an 8 by 8 checkerboard?

Remember to count squares of all sizes.

6. A pair of shoes costs $65. The sales tax is 15%. Explain how to find the cost of the shoes using two different methods.

7. Estimate.

a) 49% of 150 **b)** 31% of 40
c) 149% of 60 **d)** 98% of 54
e) 90% of 44 **f)** 61% of 88
g) 2% of 200 **h)** 5% of 81

8. Scott estimated that 22% of 160 is approximately 30.
Do you agree with his estimate? Explain.
Sketch number lines to support your answer.

9. There were 341 pine trees and spruce trees in a woodlot.
One hundred twenty-two trees were pine.

a) What fraction of the trees were spruce?
b) Estimate the percent of spruce trees.

10. In a parking lot, there are 45 North American cars and 21 foreign cars.

a) What fraction of the cars are foreign?
b) Estimate the percent of cars that are foreign.
c) Estimate the percent of cars that are not foreign.

11. **Assessment Focus** Look at the front and back cover of this textbook, including the spine. Explain how you might estimate the percent of the book cover that is illustrated.
Show all your steps. Provide numbers to support your answer.

12. About 8% of Canada is covered by fresh water.
The area of Canada is approximately 9 970 000 km^2.

a) Estimate the area of Canada covered by fresh water.

b) About how much of Canada is not covered by fresh water?

13. About 23% of Canada is covered by tundra.
Use the data in question 12.
Estimate the area of tundra in Canada.

14. Raji's bedroom floor has an area of 12 m^2. She estimates that her bed, desk, and bookshelf cover approximately 7.5 m^2 of floor space.

a) What fraction of the floor space is not covered?

b) What percent of the floor space is not covered?

Sketch number lines to illustrate your answers.

Take It Further

15. Edward estimates he has travelled approximately 80 km.
The total length of Edward's trip is 430 km.
About what percent does Edward still have left to go?

Reflect

Which percents can you find by using mental math or estimation?
Give an example of how to find each percent you name.

Math Link

Your World

Percents are printed on the side of a cereal box to indicate the nutritional value of the contents. The percents relate to every 30-g serving (about 1 cup). Suppose there is a 10% sugar content. Then, in a 30-g serving, there are 3 g of sugar per cup of cereal. Next time you look for a box of your favourite cereal, check out the percents of sugar and fat. Compare them to another brand of cereal. Would your family doctor or dentist approve of your choice? Explain.

8.3 Multiplying to Find Percents

Focus Multiply decimals with hundredths.

Explore

Work with a partner.

How could you find how much you save on an item that originally cost $48.00?
Find several ways to solve this problem.

Reflect & Share

Compare strategies with another pair of classmates.
Which strategy would you use if the sale was 45% off? Explain.

Connect

A paperback novel originally cost $7.99.
It is on sale at 15% off.
To find how much you save, calculate 15% of $7.99.

$15\% = \frac{15}{100} = 0.15$

So, 15% of $7.99 $= \frac{15}{100}$ of 7.99
$= 0.15 \times 7.99$

Recall, from Unit 4, how we multiply two decimals with tenths.
We use the same method to multiply two decimals with hundredths.
To multiply: 0.15 × 7.99, multiply without the decimal points.
Then insert the decimal point in the answer by estimation or by counting decimal places.

$$\begin{array}{r} 799 \\ \times\ 15 \\ \hline 3995 \\ 7990 \\ \hline 11985 \end{array}$$

There is a total of 4 decimal places in the question; so, there will be 4 decimal places in the answer.

Estimate:
15% is about 20%, which is $\frac{1}{5}$.
$7.99 is about $10.00.

So, 0.15×7.99 is about $\frac{1}{5}$ of 10, which is 2.
So, $0.15 \times 7.99 = 1.1985$
Round to 2 decimal places.
1.1985 is 1.20, to 2 decimal places.
You save \$1.20 by buying the book on sale.
We can show this on a number line.

Example

A park has an area of 52.6 km^2.
Sixty-five percent of the park is forest.
The rest of the park is lakes.
What is the area of the lakes?

Solution

65% of the park is forest.
So, 100% − 65%, or 35% of the park is lakes.
The area of the lakes is: 35% of 52.6
$35\% = \frac{35}{100} = 0.35$
So, 35% of $52.6 = 0.35 \times 52.6$
Multiply: 526×35

$$\begin{array}{r} 526 \\ \times\ 35 \\ \hline 2630 \\ 15780 \\ \hline 18410 \end{array}$$

Since the area of the park is given to 1 decimal place, we round the answer to 1 decimal place.

Estimate:
35% of 52.60 is about 50% of 50, which is 25.
So, $0.35 \times 52.6 = 18.41$
35% of 52.6 km^2 is 18.41 km^2.
The area of the lakes is about 18.4 km^2.

Practice

1. Calculate.
   a) 10% of 27.3 b) 20% of 48.4 c) 1% of 30.6 d) 120% of 81.2

2. Find.
   a) 18% of 36 b) 24% of 67 c) 98% of 28 d) 67% of 112

3. Find each percent of $59.99.
   a) 25% b) 75% c) 30% d) 70% e) 80% f) 90%

4. The regular price of a radio is $60.00. Find the sale price when the radio is on sale for:
   a) 25% off b) 30% off c) 40% off

5. Find the cost of each item on sale.
   Each item has a 15% sales tax added to the sale price.
   a) coat: 55% off $90 b) shoes: 45% off $40

6. **Assessment Focus**
   a) Calculate each percent of 52.3.
      How can you do this by completing only one multiplication?
      i) 2% ii) 20% iii) 200%
   b) Make up a similar example. Choose a number and 3 related percents. Show how you only need to multiply once to find all the percents of the number.

7. How is calculating 25% of $15.00 the same as calculating 15% of $25.00? How are the calculations different? Sketch number lines to illustrate your answer.

8. A garage floor is rectangular.
   Its length is 9.0 m and its width is 5.1 m.
   The length and width of a Toyota Corolla are 4.5 m and 1.7 m.
   What percent of the garage floor is occupied by the car?

Number Strategies

Use Pattern Blocks.

Suppose the red block represents 1 whole.

What does each block represent?

- the blue block
- the green block
- the yellow block

Reflect

Choose a percent. Choose an amount of money.
Calculate the percent of the money. Show your work.

Mid-Unit Review

LESSON

8.1 **1.** Write each fraction as a decimal and as a percent. Sketch number lines to illustrate.
a) $\frac{4}{5}$ **b)** $\frac{3}{25}$ **c)** $\frac{118}{50}$ **d)** $\frac{7}{20}$

2. Write each fraction as a decimal and as a percent. Sketch number lines to illustrate.
a) $\frac{27}{20}$ **b)** $\frac{14}{25}$ **c)** $\frac{15}{8}$ **d)** $\frac{7}{16}$

3. This right isosceles triangle is 20% of a larger figure.

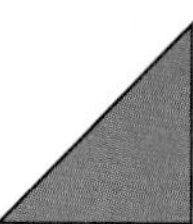

Draw a figure that represents 100%.

8.2 **4.** Estimate the percent of each figure that is shaded.

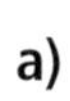

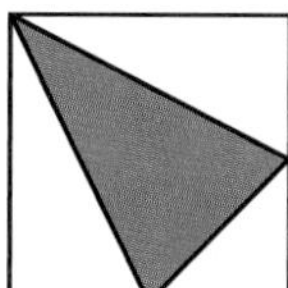

b)

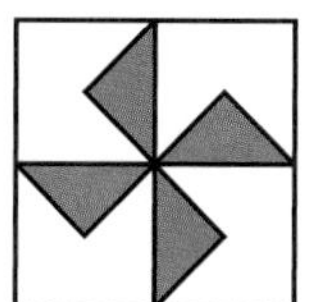

5. In a piggy bank, there were 21 pennies, 32 nickels, and 13 dimes.
a) What fraction of the coins were nickels?
b) Estimate the percent of coins that were nickels.
c) How much money was in the piggy bank?
d) Estimate the percent of money that was in dimes.

6. Find 10% of each number.
a) 28 **b)** 66 **c)** 35 **d)** 180

7. Use the results of question 6. Find 60% of each number in question 6.

8. Use estimation. Find an approximate percent for each fraction.
a) $\frac{14}{17}$ **b)** $\frac{21}{30}$ **c)** $\frac{118}{60}$ **d)** $\frac{172}{80}$ **e)** $\frac{2}{21}$

9. Estimate.
a) 14% of 98 **b)** 61% of 52
c) 76% of 202 **d)** 98% of 134

8.3 **10. a)** Find:
i) 5% of $1.00
ii) 30% of $1.00
iii) 130% of $1.00
iv) 20% of $1.00
b) Sketch a number line to illustrate your answers to part a.

11. Toni wants to buy a shirt. The original price is $85.00, but it is on sale for 30% off.
Toni will pay 15% sales tax. How much will the shirt cost?

12. How is calculating 85% of $40.00 the same as calculating 40% of $85.00? How are the calculations different? Sketch number lines to illustrate your answers.

8.4 Drawing Circle Graphs

Focus Use circle graphs to display data and solve problems.

You have drawn a circle graph using a computer.
Now that you can calculate percents,
you can draw a circle graph by hand.
This is a **percent circle**.
The circle is divided into
100 congruent sectors.
Each sector is 1% of
the whole circle.
You can draw a circle graph
on a percent circle.

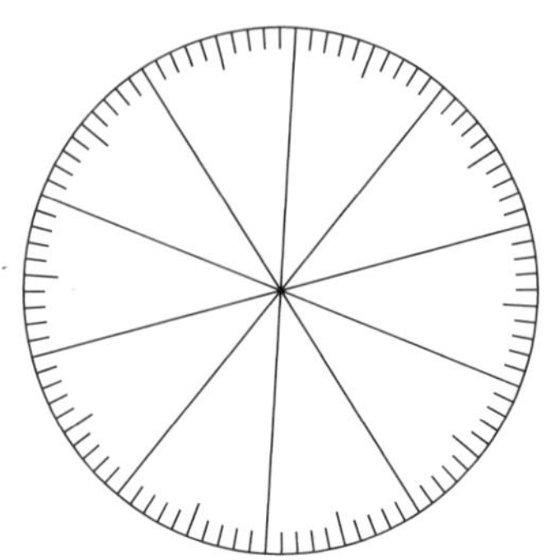

Explore

Work with a partner.
Your teacher will give you a percent circle.
Everyone in the class writes on the board the number of siblings he or she has.
Copy this table.
Record the data.

0 Siblings	1 Sibling	2 Siblings	More than 2 Siblings

Use the percent circle.
Draw a circle graph to display the data.
Write 2 questions you can answer by looking at the graph.

Reflect & Share

Trade questions with another pair of classmates.
Use your graph to answer your classmates' questions.
Compare graphs. If they are different, try to find out why.
How did you use fractions and percents to draw a circle graph?

Connect

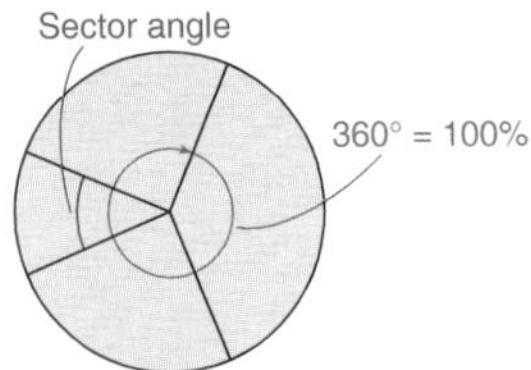

Recall that a circle graph shows how parts of a set of data compare with the whole set.
Each sector of a circle graph represents a percent of the whole circle.
The whole circle represents 100% and has a central angle of 360°.

This table shows the 2003 top 10 Ladies' Professional Golf Association (LPGA) money winners' place of birth.

Asia	Australia	Europe	North America
Kung	Teske	Sorenstam	Daniel
Pak			Inkster
Park			Jones
Han			Ochoa

To draw a circle graph to show what percent of the top 10 were born in each place, follow these steps.

Step 1
Write the number of players born in each place as a fraction of 10, then as a percent.

Asia: $\frac{4}{10} = 0.4 = \frac{40}{100} = 40\%$ Australia: $\frac{1}{10} = 0.1 = \frac{10}{100} = 10\%$

Europe: $\frac{1}{10} = 0.1 = \frac{10}{100} = 10\%$ North America: $\frac{4}{10} = 0.4 = \frac{40}{100} = 40\%$

The area of the circle represents all the golfers.
All the sector angles add to 360°.

Step 2
To find the sector angle for each place of birth, multiply each decimal by 360°.
Round to the nearest degree, when necessary.
Asia 40%: $0.40 \times 360° = 144°$
Australia 10%: $0.10 \times 360° = 36°$
Europe 10%: same as Australia, so 36°
North America 40%: same as Asia, so 144°

To check, add the angles. The sum should be 360°.

$$\begin{array}{r} 144° \\ 36° \\ 36° \\ +\ 144° \\ \hline 360° \end{array}$$

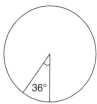

Step 3
Construct a circle.
Use a protractor to construct each sector angle.
Start with the smallest angle. Draw a radius.
Measure 36°.

Start the next sector where the previous sector finished.
Label each sector with its name and percent.
Write a title for the graph.

Top 10 LPGA Winners' Place of Birth

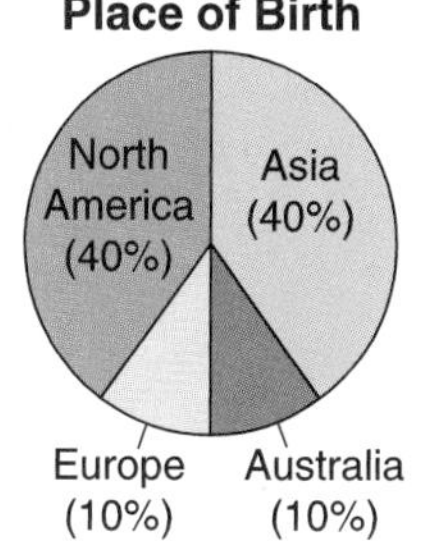

Example 1

This circle graph shows the world's gold production.

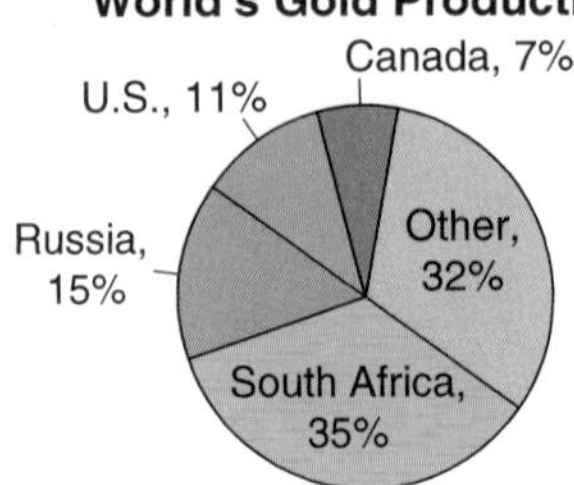

In 2002, the world's gold production was approximately 2300 t.
About how much gold would have been produced in each country?

a) Canada **b)** South Africa

Solution

a) 7% is produced in Canada.

Mass of gold $= 7\% \times 2300$
$= 0.07 \times 2300$
$= 161$

About 161 t would have been produced in Canada.

b) 35% is produced in South Africa.

Mass of gold $= 35\% \times 2300$
$= 0.35 \times 2300$
$= 805$

About 805 t would have been produced in South Africa.

Example 2

These four oceans have an area of approximately 337 million km^2.

a) Draw a circle graph to represent the data in the table.

b) Find the area of the largest ocean.

Ocean	Percent of Total Area
Atlantic	25
Arctic	3
Indian	22
Pacific	50

Solution

a) Each area is written as a percent of the total area of the oceans.
The area of the circle represents the total area of the oceans.
To find the sector angle for each ocean,
multiply each percent by 360°.

Atlantic: 25% of 360° $= 0.25 \times 360°$
$= 90°$

Arctic: 3% of 360° $= 0.03 \times 360°$
$= 10.8°$
$\doteq 11°$

Round each angle to the nearest degree, when necessary.

Indian: 22% of 360° $= 0.22 \times 360°$
$= 79.2°$
$\doteq 79°$

Pacific: 50% of 360° $= 0.50 \times 360°$
$= 180°$

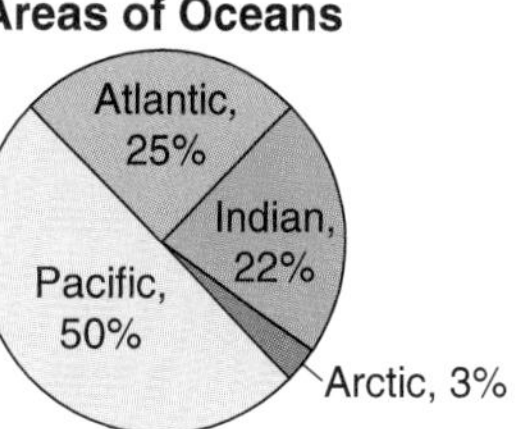

Construct a circle.
Use a protractor to construct each sector angle.
Label each sector with its name and percent.
Write a title for the graph.

b) The largest ocean is the Pacific Ocean.
Its area is:
50% of 337 000 000 km^2 $= 0.50 \times 337\ 000\ 000$ km^2
$= 168\ 500\ 000$ km^2
The largest ocean has an area about 168 500 000 km^2.

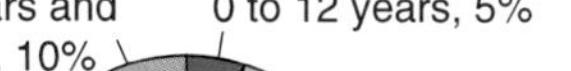

Practice

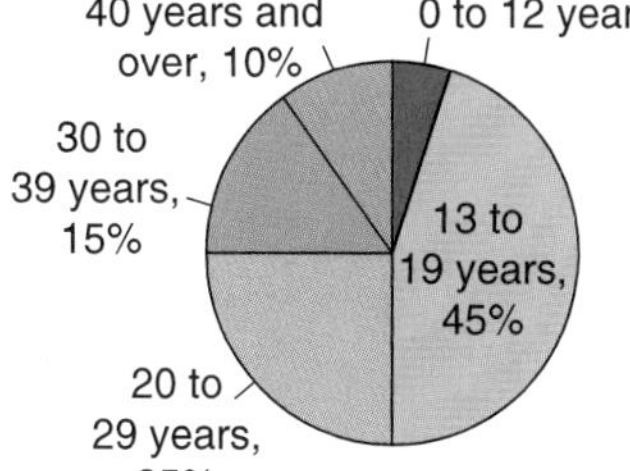

1. This circle graph shows the ages of viewers of a TV show. One week, approximately 250 000 viewers tuned in. How many viewers were in each age group?

a) 13 to 19 **b)** 20 to 29 **c)** 40 and over

2. a) Can the data in each table below be displayed in a circle graph? Explain.

i)

Canadians, Educational Attainment, 2001	
0 to 8 years of elementary school	10%
Some secondary school	17%
Graduated from high school	20%
Some post secondary education	9%
Post-secondary certificate or diploma	28%
University degree	16%

ii)

Canadian Households with These Appliances, 2000	
Automobiles	64%
Cell phone	42%
Dishwasher	51%
Internet	42%

b) For the data that could not be displayed in a circle graph, state what type of graph you would use to display it.

3. The table shows the number of Grade 7 students with each eye colour at Northern Public School.

Eye Colour	Number of Students
Blue	11
Brown	24
Green	9
Grey	6

a) Calculate the percent of students with each eye colour.
b) Draw a circle graph to represent the data.

4. In a telephone survey, 400 people voted for their favourite radio station.

Radio Station	Votes
MAJIC99	88
EASY2	?
ROCK1	120
HITS2	100

a) How many people chose EASY2?
b) Write the number of people who voted for each station as a percent of the total number surveyed.
c) Draw a circle graph to display the results of the survey.

Calculator Skills

How many times can you multiply 2 by itself until the product gets too great for your calculator display? Write the greatest product as a power of 2.

5. **Assessment Focus** Choose some labels from canned food, cereal boxes, or other foods.
a) List the nutritional information on each label.
b) Calculate the mass of each nutrient as a percent of the total mass.
c) Draw a circle graph to display the percent of each nutrient. Show your work.

Take It Further

6. This circle graph shows the percent of Earth's land occupied by each continent. The area of North America is approximately 220 million km^2. Use the percents in the circle graph. Find the approximate area of each of the other continents.

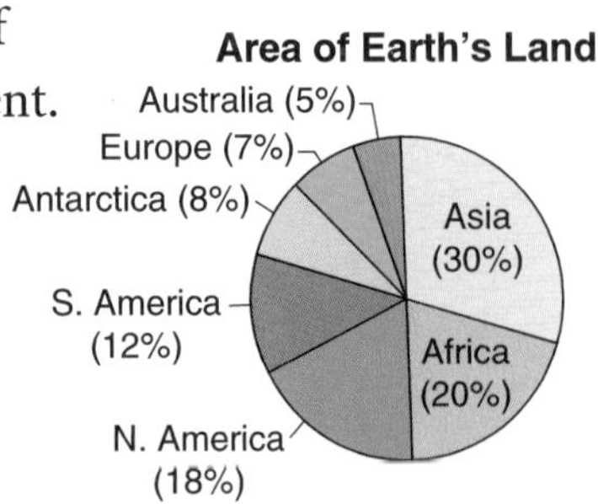

Reflect

What do you need to know about percents to be able to draw a circle graph? Include an example in your answer.

8.5 Dividing to Find Percents

Focus Divide decimals with hundredths.

Explore

Work with a partner.

Suppose you pay $15.00 for a shirt.
How could you find out what the original price was?
Draw a diagram to model this problem.
Show several strategies for solving the problem.

Reflect & Share

Compare your strategies with those of another pair of classmates.
Which strategies can you use to find the original price if you paid 35% of the original price? Explain.

Connect

Jenny wanted to know her brother Alan's mass.
Alan told Jenny that 15% of his mass is 6.75 kg.

Jenny knows what 15% is.
She wants to find 100%.

15% is 6.75.
So, 1% is: $\frac{6.75}{15}$
Use long division: $6.75 \div 15$
1% is 0.45.
So, 100% is: $0.45 \times 100 = 45$
Alan's mass is 45 kg.

$$\begin{array}{r} 0.45 \\ 15\overline{)6.75} \\ \underline{6\,0} \\ 75 \\ \underline{75} \\ 0 \end{array}$$

Example

This sign appeared in a shop window.

SALE
YOU PAY
65%
OF THE
LIST
PRICE!

Eric pays \$58.50 for a jacket.
What is the list price of the jacket?

Solution

Use a calculator or long division to find $\frac{\$58.50}{65}$.

65% of the list price is \$58.50.
So, 1% of the list price is: $\frac{\$58.50}{65} = \$0.90$

And, 100% is: $\$0.90 \times 100 = \$90.00$
The list price of the jacket is \$90.00.

Practice

1. 25% is 1.25 m.
   a) What is 50%? **b)** What is 100%?
   Sketch a number line to show your answer.

2. 35% is 4.2 kg.
   a) What is 1%? **b)** What is 100%?
   Sketch a number line to show your answer.

3. 45% is 13.5 cm.
   a) What is 1%? **b)** What is 100%?
   Sketch a number line to show your answer.

4. The principal reported that 75% of the total number of families attended the school's Fun Fair. Three hundred sixty families went to the fair. How many families have children at the school?

5. A hockey team played 30 games. It won 60% of the games. How many games did the team lose?

6. Grace has read 30% of a book. She has read 72 pages. How many pages are in the book?

Number Strategies

Add or subtract.

- $\frac{3}{5} + \frac{3}{6}$
- $\frac{4}{5} - \frac{1}{2}$
- $\frac{3}{4} + \frac{4}{3}$
- $\frac{5}{6} - \frac{1}{4}$

7. Paco ate 25% of a 16-slice pizza and placed the rest in the fridge. Santos ate 25% of the leftovers.

a) How many pieces were left?

b) What percent of the original pizza remained?

8. This year, 40 more children joined the local soccer club than last year. This is a 10% increase. How many students played in the club last year?

9. Assessment Focus Anika wants to buy a blouse.
The original price is $75.00. It is on sale for 30% off.
Anika will pay 15% sales tax.

a) How much will the blouse cost?

b) Does it make any difference to the cost in each situation?

i) The 30% is taken off before the 15% tax is added.

ii) The 15% tax is added before the 30% is taken off.

Explain. Draw number lines to show your thinking.

10. Write your own problem that involves working with percents. Solve your problem. Show your work.

Take It Further

11. A pair of shoes in a clearance store went through a series of reductions.
The regular price was $125. The shoes were reduced by 20%.
Three weeks later, the shoes were reduced by a further 20%.
Later in the year, the shoes were advertised for sale at $\frac{3}{4}$ off the ticket price.
Sean wants to buy the shoes. He has to pay 15% sales tax.

a) Sean has $40.00. Can Sean buy the shoes? Explain.

b) If your answer to part a is yes, how much change does Sean get?

Sketch number lines to illustrate your work.

12. A box was $\frac{3}{4}$ full. The box fell on the floor.
Thirty marbles fell out. This was 20% of the marbles that were in the box. How many marbles were in a full box?

Reflect

How does a good understanding of percents help you outside the classroom? Give an example.

Choosing a Strategy

Strategies

- Make a table.
- Use a model.
- Draw a diagram.
- Solve a simpler problem.
- Work backward.
- Guess and check.
- Make an organized list.
- Use a pattern.
- Draw a graph.
- Use logical reasoning.

Use a calculator when you need to.

1. Write 720 as the product of consecutive whole numbers. Find all the possible ways.

2. A digital clock shows this time. Seven minutes past 7 is a palindromic time.

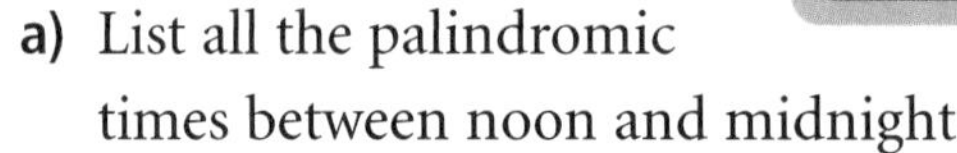

a) List all the palindromic times between noon and midnight.

b) What is the shortest time between two palindromic times?

3. I am a perfect square less than 400. The sum of my digits is also a perfect square. Which number could I be? Find all possible numbers.

4. The trail around Lake Pender is 20 km long. How long do you think it would take you to walk around the lake? Explain.

5. Jack's heart rate is 72 beats/min. How long will it take for Jack's heart to beat one million times?

6. A 4-cm cube is painted red on the top and bottom faces, blue on the front and back faces, and green on the side faces. The cube is cut into 1-cm cubes. How many of the small cubes will have:

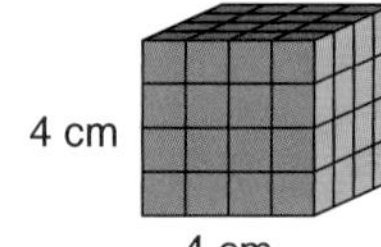

a) 3 colours of paint?
b) 2 colours?
c) 1 colour?
d) no paint?

7. Use dot paper. Draw a quadrilateral with at least two sides equal. How many different quadrilaterals can you draw?

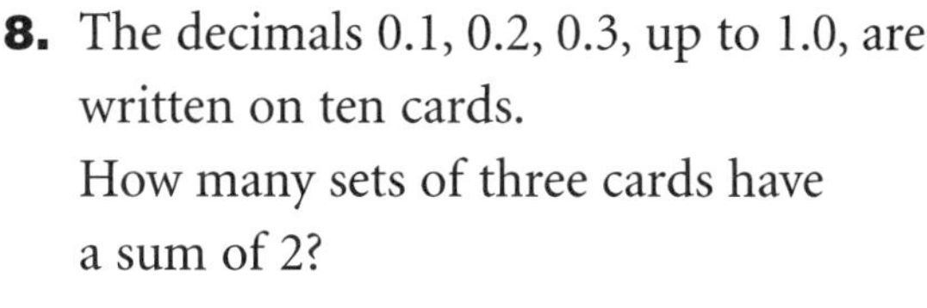

8. The decimals 0.1, 0.2, 0.3, up to 1.0, are written on ten cards.
How many sets of three cards have a sum of 2?

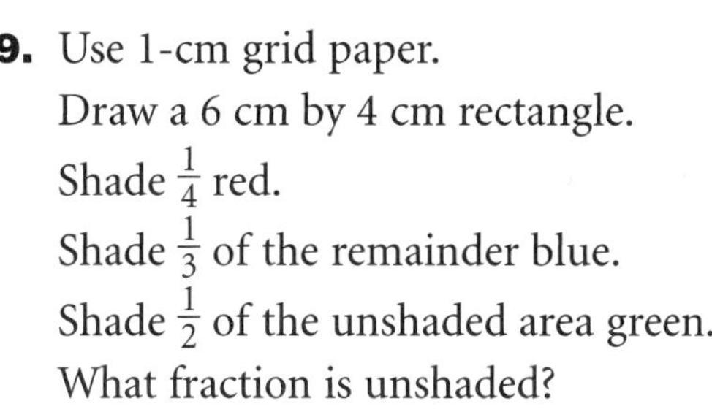

9. Use 1-cm grid paper.
Draw a 6 cm by 4 cm rectangle.
Shade $\frac{1}{4}$ red.
Shade $\frac{1}{3}$ of the remainder blue.
Shade $\frac{1}{2}$ of the unshaded area green.
What fraction is unshaded?

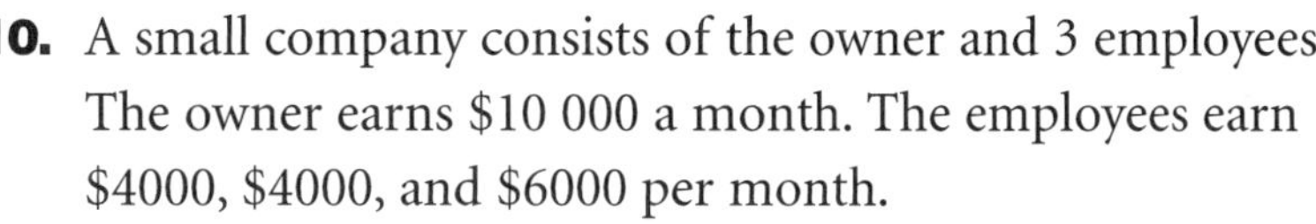

10. A small company consists of the owner and 3 employees.
The owner earns \$10 000 a month. The employees earn \$4000, \$4000, and \$6000 per month.

a) The employees ask the owner for a pay raise.
Should they use the mean, median or mode salary when they present their case? Explain.

b) Should the owner use the mean, median or mode when she explains she cannot give the employees a raise? Explain.

11. The area of a rectangular field is 3496 m^2.
Its perimeter is 260 m.
What are the dimensions of the field?

12. This figure comprises a square and two halves of a congruent square.

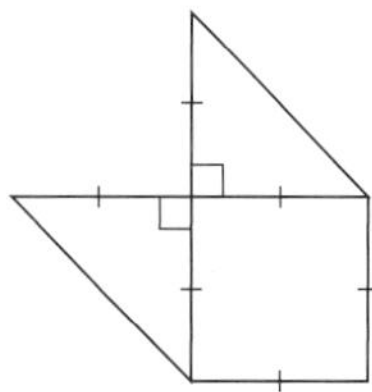

Arrange the parts of the figure to produce each new figure.
a) a rectangle **b)** a parallelogram **c)** a trapezoid **d)** a triangle
Sketch your answers.

Sports Trainer

Sports trainers use scientific research and scientific techniques to maximize an athlete's performance. An athlete may be measured for percent body fat, or percent of either fast- or slow-twitch muscle fibre.

A trainer may recommend the athlete eat pre-event meals that contain a certain percent of carbohydrate, or choose a "sports drink" that contains a high percent of certain minerals. The trainer creates and monitors exercise routines. These enable the athlete to attain a certain percent of maximum heart rate, speed, or power.

Most sports drinks contain minerals. Research shows that the most effective sports drink has a magnesium to calcium ratio of 1:2. The body absorbs about 87% of magnesium in a drink, and about 44% of calcium in a drink. One sports drink lists 100 mg of calcium per scoop. About how much magnesium is there in 1 scoop?

Unit Review

Review any lesson with

What Do I Need to Know?

✓ Here are some fractions, decimals, and percents you should know.

$1 = 1.0 = 100\%$

$\frac{1}{2} = 0.5 = 50\%$

$\frac{1}{4} = 0.25 = 25\%$

$\frac{1}{5} = 0.2 = 20\%$

$\frac{1}{10} = 0.1 = 10\%$

$\frac{1}{100} = 0.01 = 1\%$

What Should I Be Able to Do?

For extra practice, go to page 445.

LESSON

8.1

1. Write each fraction as a decimal and as a percent.

a) $\frac{8}{20}$ **b)** $\frac{14}{5}$ **c)** $\frac{14}{25}$

d) $\frac{7}{10}$ **e)** $\frac{9}{8}$ **f)** $\frac{17}{10}$

2. Write each number two other ways.

a) 0.18 **b)** 0.3

c) 80% **d)** $\frac{3}{8}$

3. This rectangle is 40% of a larger figure.

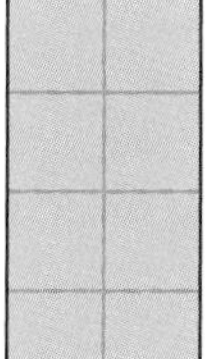

Use grid paper.

a) Draw a figure that shows 100%.

b) Draw a figure that shows 120%.

8.2

4. Estimate.

a) 39% of 250 **b)** 41% of 89

c) 19% of 60 **d)** 91% of 46

e) 97% of 64 **f)** 59% of 98

g) 3% of 300 **h)** 4% of 92

5. A DVD costs $29.99.
The sales tax is 15%.
Estimate the cost of the DVD.

8.3

6. There are 35 students in a Grade 7 class. On one day, 20% of the students were at a sports meet. How many students were in class?

7. The regular price of a DVD player is $120.00. What is the sale price in each case?

a) 25% off **b)** 30% off

c) 40% off **d)** 50% off

e) 60% off **f)** 45% off

8. The regular price for a mountain bike is $640.00.
It is on sale for 30% off.
The sales tax is 15%.

a) Jamie bought the bike at the regular price.
What did it cost her?

b) Sam bought the bike on sale.
How much did Sam save?

8.4 **9.** This circle graph shows the surface area of the Great Lakes.

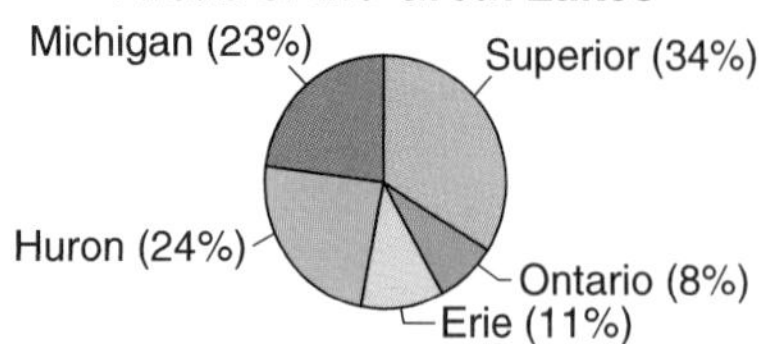

a) Which lake has a surface area about $\frac{1}{4}$ of the total area?

b) Explain why Lake Superior has that name.

c) The total area of the Great Lakes is about 244 000 km^2. Find the surface area of Lake Erie.

10. These tables show energy resources and electricity generation in Canada.

Primary Energy Resources in Canada, 2001	
Coal	11%
Hydro-electric	27%
Natural gas	24%
Nuclear	6%
Oil	32%

Electricity Generation by Fuel Type, 2001	
Coal	18%
Hydro-electric	61%
Natural gas	4%
Nuclear	13%
Oil	4%

a) Draw a circle graph to display the data in each table.

b) What do you know from looking at the two graphs?

11. Here are 25 players on the Toronto Maple Leafs roster for the 2003/2004 season.
The table shows each player's place of birth.

USSR	Canada	Europe	U.S.
Antropov	Belak	Berg	Fitzgerald
Mogilny	Belfour	Kaberle	Johnson
	Berehowsky	Nolan	Kidd
	Domi	Pilar	Klee
	Marchment	Ponikarovsky	
	McCabe	Reichel	
	Nieuwendyk	Renberg	
	Perrott	Sundin	
	Roberts		
	Stajan		
	Tucker		

a) Draw a circle graph to show what percent of the team was born in each place.

b) What if a U.S.-born player was traded for a USSR-born player? How would the graph change?

8.5 **12.** Eighty percent of Areyana's height is 140 cm. How tall is Areyana? Draw a number line to illustrate your answer.

13. At Lakehead Elementary School, 280 students participate in a walk for charity.
That is 70% of the students in the school. How many students attend the school?

Practice Test

1. How can 25% of one item be different from 25% of another? Explain.

2. The strip below is 25% of a longer strip.
   a) What is the length of a strip that is 80% of the longer strip?
   b) Draw the longer strip.

3. Find.
   a) 600% of 40
   b) 60% of 40
   c) 6% of 40

   What patterns do you see in the answers?

4. The regular price of a pair of shoes is $75.00.
   The shoes are on sale for 25% off.
   The sales tax is 15%.
   a) What is the sale price of the pair of shoes?
   b) What do the shoes cost, with sales tax?

Type of Land Cover in Canada

Type	Percent of Total Area
Forest and taiga	45
Tundra	23
Wetlands	12
Fresh water	8
Cropland and rangeland	8
Ice and snow	3
Human use	1

5. The table shows the type of land cover in Canada, as a percent of the total area.
   a) Draw a circle graph to display these data.
   b) Did you need to know the area of Canada to draw the circle graph? Explain.

6. This spring, 26 dogs were adopted from the local animal shelter.
   This is 130% of the number of dogs that were adopted last spring.
   How many dogs were adopted last spring?
   Draw a number line to illustrate your answer.

Unit Problem At the Shopping Mall

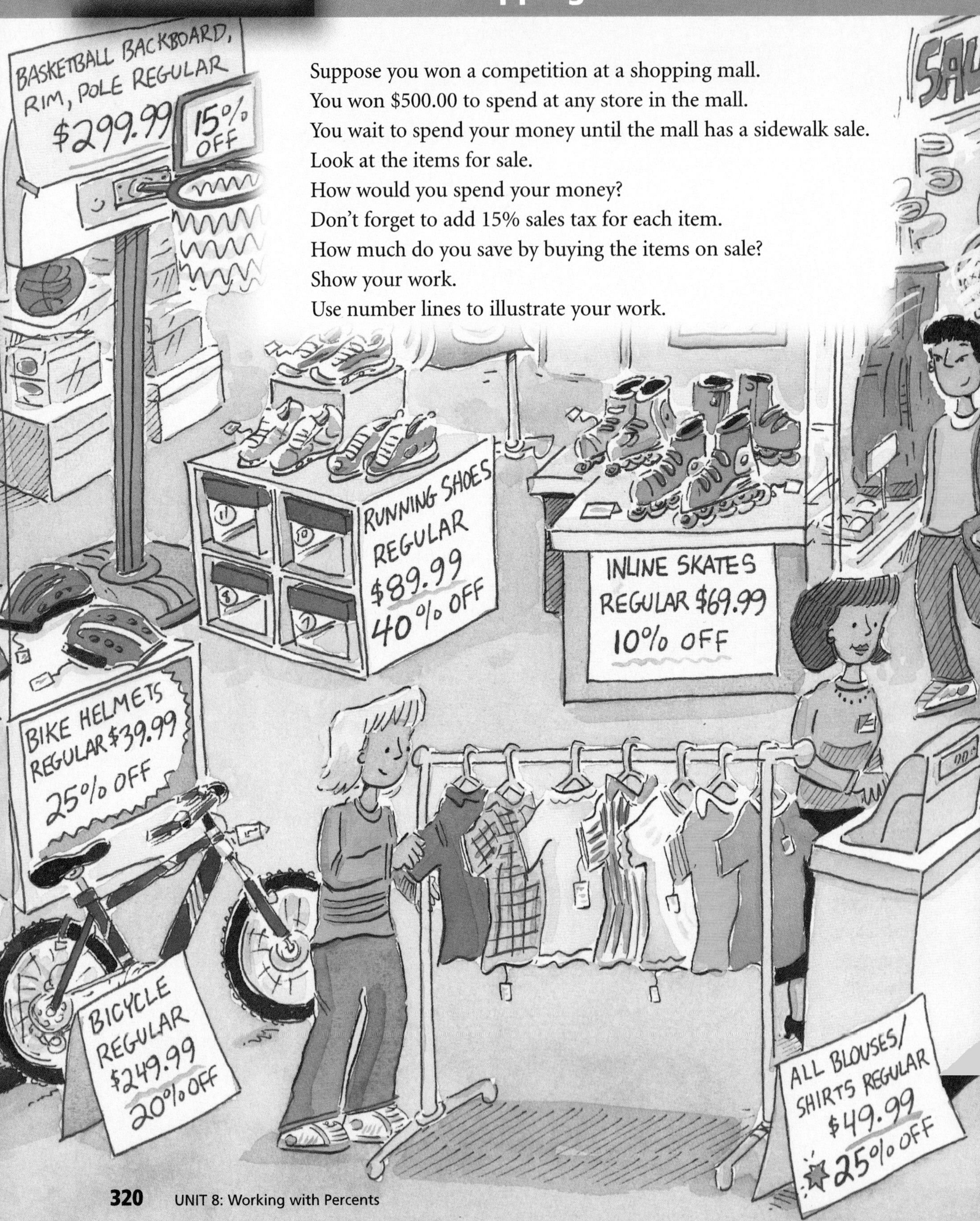

Suppose you won a competition at a shopping mall.
You won $500.00 to spend at any store in the mall.
You wait to spend your money until the mall has a sidewalk sale.
Look at the items for sale.
How would you spend your money?
Don't forget to add 15% sales tax for each item.
How much do you save by buying the items on sale?
Show your work.
Use number lines to illustrate your work.

Check List

Your work should show:

- ✓ a list of the items you bought and what you paid for each one
- ✓ a number line to illustrate each calculation
- ✓ how much you saved by buying the items on sale
- ✓ how you calculated the sales tax

Reflect on the Unit

What have you learned about percents and how they are used?

Units 1–8 Cumulative Review

UNIT

1 **1.** Use grid paper.
Draw a picture that shows a square root of each number.
a) 49 **b)** 16 **c)** 144

2 **2.** To make a pot of tea for 4 people, you need 3 tea bags.
a) How many tea bags are needed for each number of people?
i) 8 **ii)** 12 **iii)** 16 **iv)** 20
b) How many tea bags are needed for 6 people? Explain.

3 **3.** Students in a Grade 7 class are filling shoe boxes with toys for children in other countries. A shoe box measures 30 cm by 18 cm by 16 cm.
a) Find the volume of a shoe box.
The students fill 24 shoe boxes. Eight shoe boxes are packed into a larger box.
b) What could the dimensions of this larger box be?
c) What are the most likely dimensions of the larger box? Justify your choice.

4 **4. a)** Multiply: 3.6×2.4
b) Which other pair of factors has the same product as the product in part a?
How many different pairs of factors can you find?
Explain your work.

5 **5.** To celebrate his birthday, Justin and his friends played miniature golf. Here are their scores: 29, 33, 37, 24, 41, 38, 48, 26, 36, 33, 40, 29, 36, 22, 31, 38, 42, 35, 33
a) Draw a stem-and-leaf plot.
It was a par 36 course. This means that a good golfer takes 36 strokes to complete the course.
b) How many scores were under par? At par? Over par?
c) What was the range of the scores?
d) Calculate the mean, median, and mode scores.

6. Some Grade 7 students were surveyed about the average number of hours they spend reading each week, and their overall English mark out of 100. Here are the data:

Time (h)	Mark	Time (h)	Mark
0	55	0	60
0.5	65	0.5	62
1	70	1	84
1	68	1.5	75
1.5	78	2	83
2	85	2	77
2	88	2	81
2.5	91	2.5	79
2.5	80	3	90

a) Draw a scatter plot. What trends do you see?
b) Do you think a student will get a better English mark if he reads more? Explain.

UNIT

6 **7.** A parallelogram has base 2.4 cm and height 3.9 cm.

a) What is the area of the parallelogram?

b) What is the area of a triangle with the same base and height as the parallelogram?

8. Find the area and perimeter of this trapezoid.

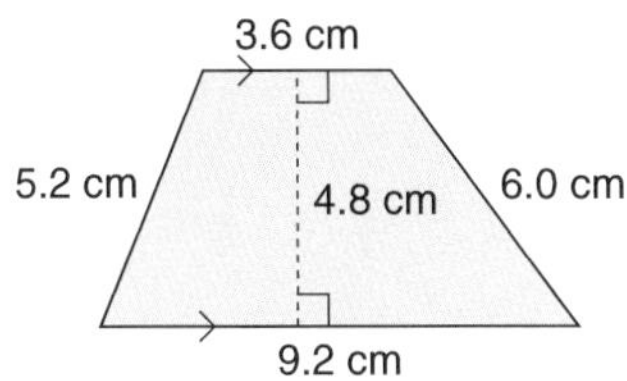

9. Find the area and perimeter of this figure.

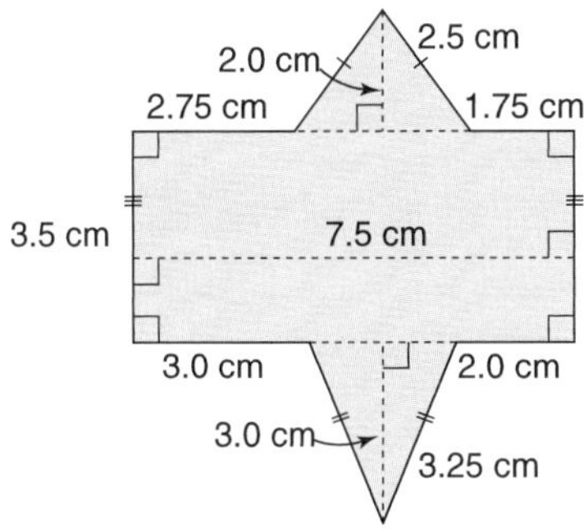

7 **10.** Use dot paper.
Draw two congruent figures.
Trade figures with a classmate.
Explain how you know your classmate's figures are congruent.

11. These quadrilaterals are congruent.

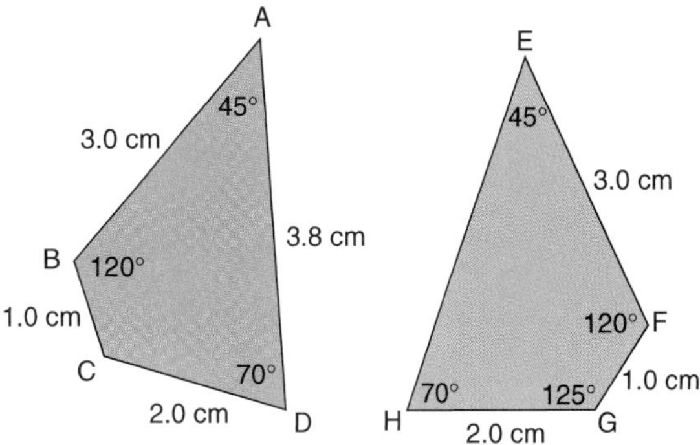

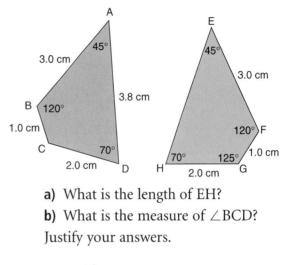

a) What is the length of EH?

b) What is the measure of ∠BCD?

Justify your answers.

12. Use grid paper.

a) Choose a figure that tiles the plane.
Create a design with your figure.

b) Choose one figure as Figure A.
Describe the position of another figure as a transformation image of Figure A.
Do this for 5 different figures.

8 **13.** The regular price of a scooter is $89.99. The scooter is on sale for 20% off.

a) What is the sale price of the scooter?

b) There is 15% sales tax. What would a person pay for the scooter?

14. How is calculating 30% of $70 the same as calculating 70% of $30?
Sketch number lines to illustrate your answer.

UNIT 9 Integers

Canada has 6 time zones.

- What time is it where you are now?
- You want to call a friend in Newfoundland. What time is it there?
- In the province or territory farthest from you, what might students be doing now?

What other questions can you ask about this map?

What You'll Learn

- Use integers to describe real-life situations.
- Model integers with coloured tiles.
- Compare and order integers.
- Add integers.
- Subtract integers.

Why It's Important

- We use integers to compare temperatures with the temperature at which water freezes.
- Integers extend the whole number work from earlier grades.

Key Words

- positive number
- negative number
- integer
- positive integer
- negative integer
- opposite integers
- zero pair

UNIT 9

Skills You'll Need

Mental Math Strategies for Addition and Subtraction

Example

Add or subtract.
Use mental math.

a) 38 + 17 **b)** 111 − 64

Solution

a) 38 + 17

Make a friendly number. Subtract from one number and add to the other.

So, 38 + 17 = 38 + 2 + 17 − 2

= 40 + 15

= 55

Subtract 2 from 17. Add 2 to 38.

b) 111 − 64

Subtract the ones, then subtract the tens.

Subtract 4: 111 − 4 = 107

Then subtract 60: 107 − 60 = 47

So, 111 − 64 = 47

Count back by 1s to subtract 4.

✓ Check

Use mental math.

1. Add or subtract. What strategy did you use?

a) 22 + 88 **b)** 69 − 29 **c)** 93 + 38 **d)** 132 − 85

2. In a magic square every row, column, and diagonal has the same sum.
Copy and complete each magic square. Explain how you did it.

a)

	1	6
	5	7
4		2

b)

17	10	
	14	
13	18	

9.1 What Is an Integer?

Focus Use real-world applications of integers.

We measure temperature in degrees Celsius.
The highest temperature in Prince George, BC, on April 27, 2004, was 12°C.
12 is a **positive number.**
12°C is the difference between the temperature of the air and the temperature at which water freezes, 0°C.

We may not be able to use a positive number to express a difference.
For example, the temperature inside a freezer is 4°C less than the freezing point of water. We represent this difference as –4°C.

–4 is a **negative number.**
We say "negative 4."

When we talk about temperatures below zero, we say "minus 4," rather than "negative 4."

Explore

Work with a partner.
Use a positive or a negative number to represent each situation.

- eight degrees above zero
- ten degrees below zero
- parking three levels below ground level
- two points ahead in a soccer game
- a loss of sixteen dollars
- taking four steps backward

Reflect & Share

Compare your answers with those of another pair of classmates.
For each situation, how did you decide whether to use a positive number or a negative number?

Connect

Mental Math

Use any math operation. Use the numbers around the circle. Write as many ways as you can to make the number in the circle.

Positive and negative whole numbers are called **integers**.
We put + in front of a number to indicate it is a **positive integer**.

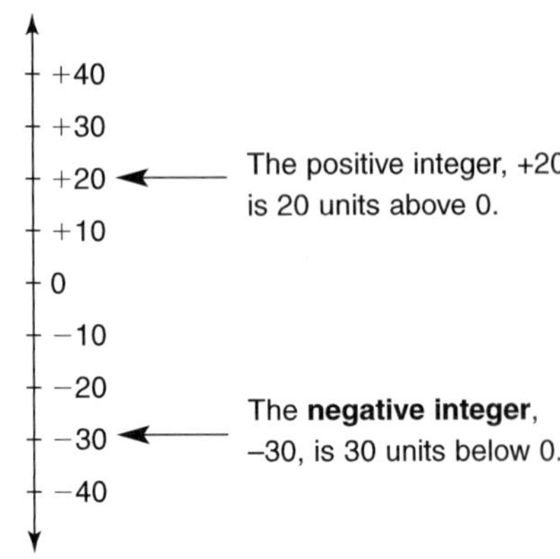

We can show integers on a number line.
The number line may be vertical, like a thermometer.

A number line may be horizontal.

−40 −30 −20 −10 0 +10 +20 +30 +40

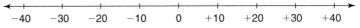

Opposite integers are the same distance from 0 but are on opposite sides of 0.
For example, +2 and −2 are opposite integers.
They are the same distance from 0 and are on opposite sides of 0.

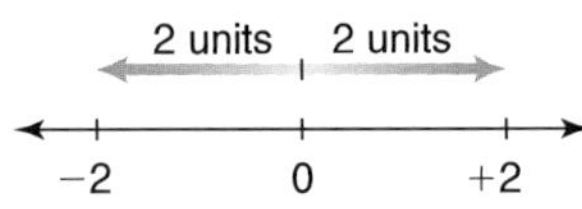

+4 and −4 are also opposite integers, as are +21 and −21.

Practice

1. Mark each integer on a number line.
a) +1 **b)** −5 **c)** −2 **d)** +9

2. Write the opposite of each integer.
a) +3 **b)** −1 **c)** −8000 **d)** +10

3. Use a positive or negative integer to represent each situation.
a) thirty-five degrees Celsius below zero in Yellowknife
b) a weather balloon 28 000 m above Earth's surface
c) diving 35 m below the ocean's surface
d) earning $500

Use question 3 as a model.

4. Use each integer below to describe a situation.
a) +4 **b)** −5 **c)** +120 **d)** −8500

5. Describe two situations in which you might use negative and positive integers. Write integers for your situations.

6. **Assessment Focus** Statistics Canada reported these data about Canada's population.

Years	Births	Deaths	Immigrants	Emigrants
1961-66	2 249 000	731 000	539 000	280 000
1996-2001	1 704 000	1 095 000	1 051 000	270 000

a) Which numbers can be represented by positive integers? Negative integers? Explain.
b) For each column of data in the table, find the difference in the numbers. Write the difference as a positive or negative integer. Explain your choice of integer.
c) Choose one time period. Use a number line and integers to explain the relationship between births and deaths.
d) Choose one time period. Use integers to explain the relationships between immigrants and emigrants.

Take It Further

7. Changes in stock prices on the Stock Exchange are written as positive or negative integers.
   a) Express each change as an integer.
      i) The value of Apple Computers increased $2.
      ii) Palm Tech dropped from $25 to $22.
      iii) MDS started the day at $13 and ended the day at $12.
      iv) Steve bought Global stock at $10 and sold it for $15.
   b) Look at the two stock prices in part a, ii. How are the prices related?
   c) Look at the two stock prices in part a, iv. How are the prices related?
   d) How can an integer be used to show the relationship between two prices of a stock? Explain.

Find the price of a stock in the financial section of a newspaper. Follow the price every day for one month. How are integers used to show how the stock price changes?

Reflect

Suppose you read a situation that can be described with integers. What clues do you look for to help you decide whether to use a positive or negative integer? Use examples in your explanation.

9.2 Comparing and Ordering Integers

Focus Use a number line to order and compare integers.

Elevation is the height above or below sea level. Elevation influences climate and how people live. For example, crops will not grow at elevations above 5300 m.

Explore

Work with a partner.
You will need an atlas or Internet access.
Here are some examples of extreme elevations around the world:

Vinson Massif, Antarctica	4897 m above sea level
Dead Sea, Israel/Jordan	411 m below sea level
Bottom of Great Slave Lake	458 m below sea level
Mt. Nowshak, Afghanistan	7485 m above sea level
Challenger Deep, Pacific Ocean	10 924 m below sea level

Research to find at least 4 more extreme elevations in Canada.
Two should be above sea level, and two should be below sea level.
Order *all* the elevations from least to greatest.

Reflect & Share

What strategies did you use to order the elevations?
What other ways could you display these data to show the different elevations?

Connect

We use the symbols $>$ and $<$ to show order.
The symbol points to the lesser number.

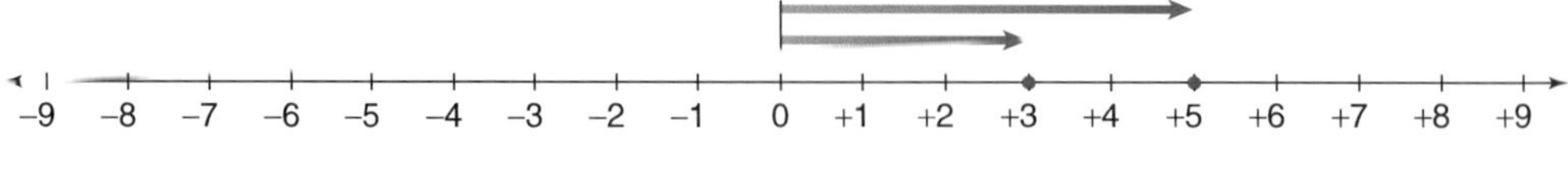

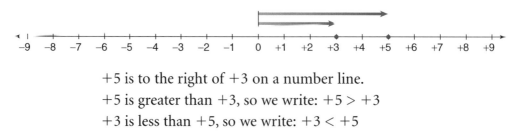

+5 is to the right of +3 on a number line.
+5 is greater than +3, so we write: $+5 > +3$
+3 is less than +5, so we write: $+3 < +5$

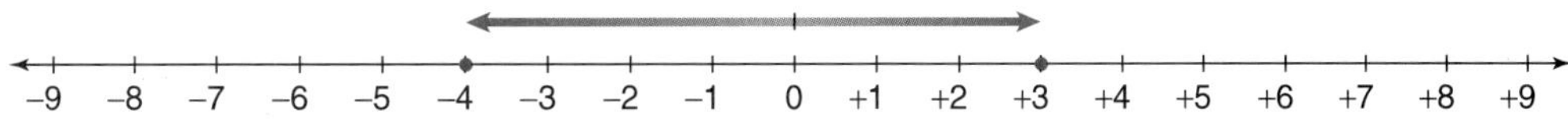

+3 is to the right of −4 on a number line.
+3 is greater than −4, so we write: +3 > −4
−4 is less than +3, so we write: −4 < +3

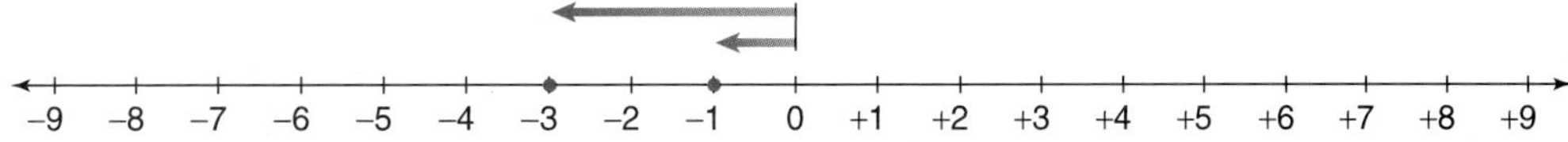

−3 is to the left of −1 on a number line.
−3 is less than −1, so we write: −3 < −1
−1 is greater than −3, so we write: −1 > −3

Example

For the integers 0, +1, −2, +3, −5:

a) Use a number line to order the integers from least to greatest.

b) Write the opposite of each integer.
Show the opposites on a number line.

c) Order the opposites from least to greatest.

Solution

a) Mark each integer on a number line.

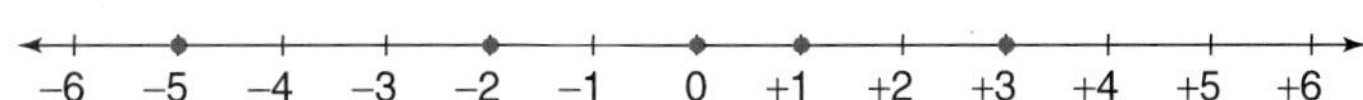

The integers increase from left to right.
So, the integers from least to greatest: −5, −2, 0, +1, +3

b) The opposite of an integer is its mirror image reflected in a vertical line drawn through 0 on a number line.
The opposite of −5 is +5. The opposite of −2 is +2.
Since 0 is the reference point, 0 is its own opposite.
The opposite of +1 is −1. The opposite of +3 is −3.

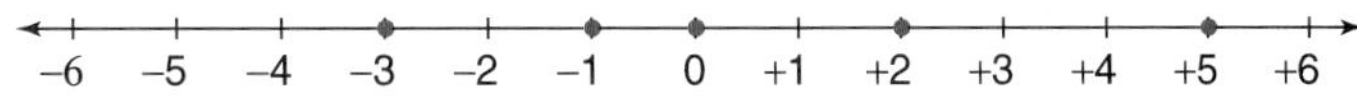

c) So, the opposite integers from least to greatest: –3, –1, 0, +2, +5

Practice

1. Copy each number line. Fill in the missing integers.

a) 

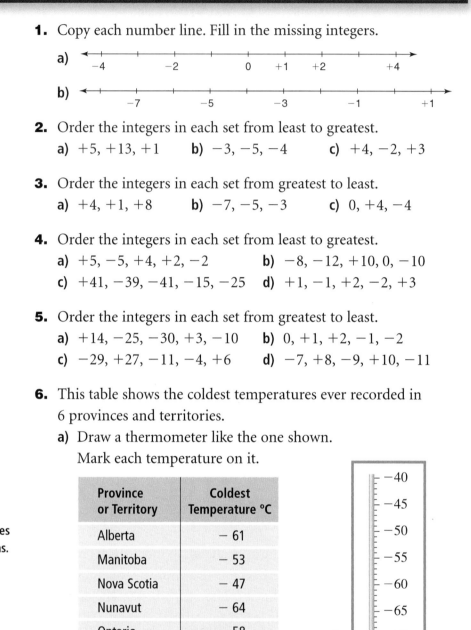

b) −7 −5 −3 −1 +1

2. Order the integers in each set from least to greatest.
a) +5, +13, +1 b) −3, −5, −4 c) +4, −2, +3

3. Order the integers in each set from greatest to least.
a) +4, +1, +8 b) −7, −5, −3 c) 0, +4, −4

4. Order the integers in each set from least to greatest.
a) +5, −5, +4, +2, −2 b) −8, −12, +10, 0, −10
c) +41, −39, −41, −15, −25 d) +1, −1, +2, −2, +3

5. Order the integers in each set from greatest to least.
a) +14, −25, −30, +3, −10 b) 0, +1, +2, −1, −2
c) −29, +27, −11, −4, +6 d) −7, +8, −9, +10, −11

6. This table shows the coldest temperatures ever recorded in 6 provinces and territories.
a) Draw a thermometer like the one shown.
Mark each temperature on it.

A real thermometer does not show negative signs. We include them for better understanding.

Province or Territory	Coldest Temperature °C
Alberta	− 61
Manitoba	− 53
Nova Scotia	− 47
Nunavut	− 64
Ontario	− 58
Quebec	− 54

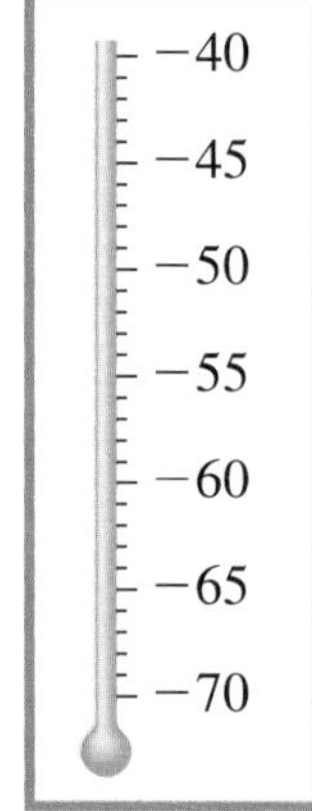

b) Order the temperatures in part a from least to greatest.
How can you use your thermometer to do this?

7. Copy and complete by placing $<$ or $>$ between the integers.
Use a number line if it helps.
a) +5 □ +10 b) −5 □ −10 c) −6 □ 0
d) −5 □ −4 e) +100 □ −101 f) −80 □ −40

Calculator Skills

Tina bought 6 packages of markers for her friends. Each package cost $4.95. The cashier charged 15% tax. Tina left the store with $13.42. How much money did Tina start with?

8. Assessment Focus

Look at the integers in the box.

	$+4$	
-8		-5
	$+9$	
0		$+8$

a) Which integers are:

i) greater than 0?

ii) between -3 and $+3$?

iii) greater than -10 and less than -5?

iv) less than $+1$?

b) What other questions can you ask about these integers? Write down your questions and answer them.

9. On January 18, 2002, the temperature in Charlottetown, Prince Edward Island, was -21°C; in Sydney, Nova Scotia, it was -23°C; in Point Lepreau, New Brunswick, it was -22°C. Which place was the warmest? Coldest? How do you know?

Take It Further

10. a) Draw a number line from -6 to $+6$. Find the integer that is:

i) halfway between -6 and $+6$

ii) halfway between -5 and $+1$

iii) halfway between -5 and -1

iv) 1 less than $+3$

v) 3 more than -4

vi) 4 less than -1

b) Explain why the answer for part a, ii is different from the answer for part a, iii.

c) -3 is halfway between two integers on a number line. Draw a number line and mark the two integers on it.

11. One day, the temperature in Wabash Lake, Newfoundland, was -41°C; in Pelly Bay, Nunavut, it was -51°C. The temperature in Churchill, Manitoba, was halfway between these temperatures. What was the temperature in Churchill?

12. Copy each pattern. Extend the pattern for 3 more terms. Describe each pattern in words.

a) $-5, -3, -1, +1, \ldots$

b) $+7, +4, +1, -2, \ldots$

c) $-20, -18, -16, -14, \ldots$

d) $-5, -10, -15, -20, \ldots$

Reflect

When two integers have different signs, how can you tell which is greater? When two integers have the same sign, how can you tell which is greater?

9.3 Representing Integers

Focus Use coloured tiles to represent integers.

We can use coloured tiles to represent integers.

One yellow tile can represent +1.

One red tile can represent −1.

A red tile and a yellow tile combine to model 0: −1, +1 } We call this a **zero pair.**

Explore

Work with a partner.
You will need coloured tiles.
How many different ways can you use coloured tiles to model each number?

➢ 0, +1, +2, +3, +4
➢ −1, −3, −5, −6

Draw a picture to show the tiles you used for each way you found.

Reflect & Share

Compare your models with those of another pair of classmates.
Look at all the models that represent one integer.
How do you know that all the models represent that integer?

Connect

We can model any integer in many ways.

Each set of tiles below models +5.

Each pair of 1 yellow tile and 1 red tile makes a zero pair. The pair models 0.

•

• 

• 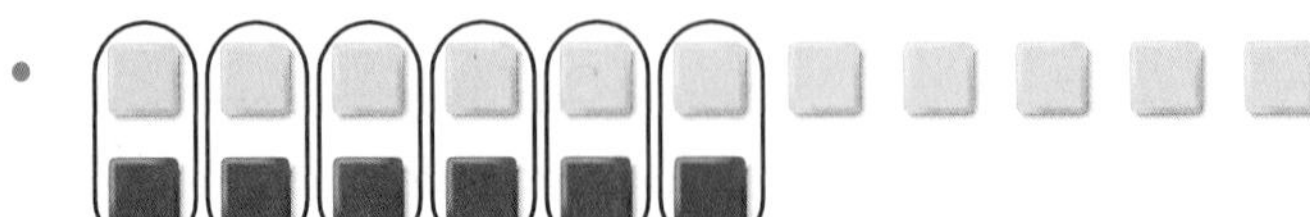

Example

Use coloured tiles to model −4 three different ways.

Solution

Start with 4 red tiles to model −4.
Add different numbers of zero pairs.
Each set of tiles below models −4.

Adding 4 zero pairs does not change the value.

- 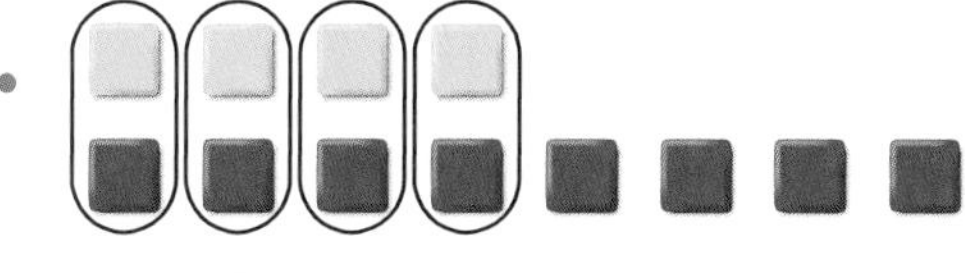

Adding 2 zero pairs does not change the value.

- 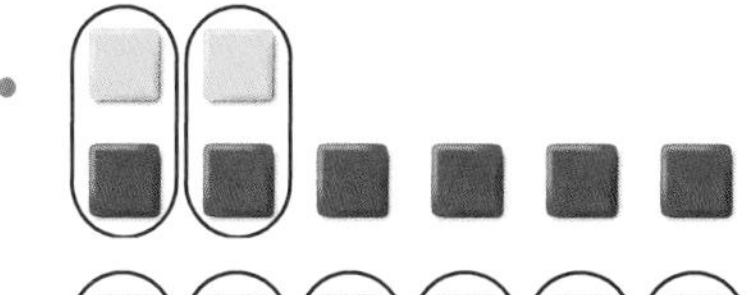

Adding 7 zero pairs does not change the value.

- 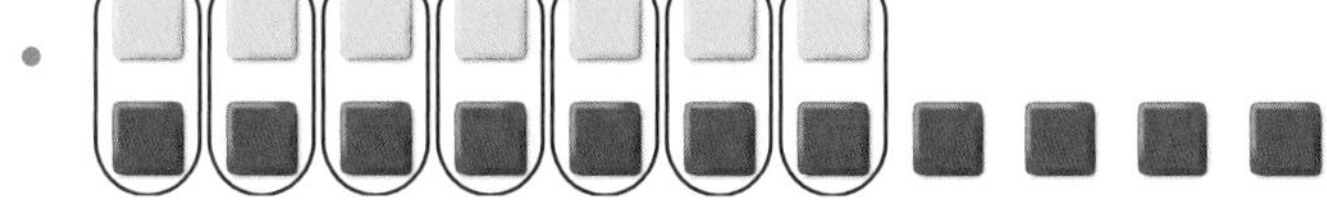

Practice

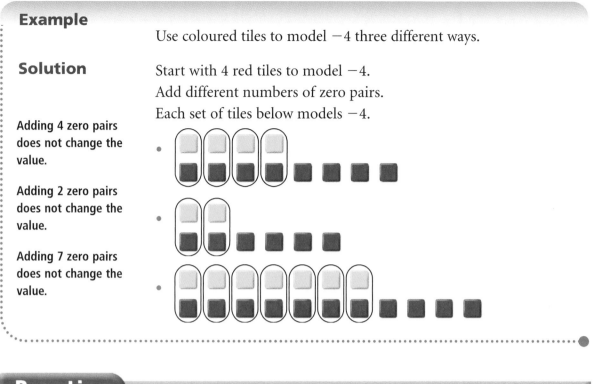

1. Write the integer modelled by each set of tiles.

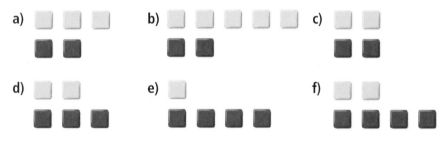

a) 

b) 

c) 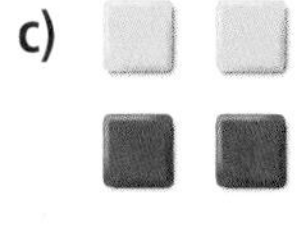

d) 

e) 

f) 

2. Use yellow and red tiles to model each integer. Draw the tiles.

a) −6 **b)** +7 **c)** +6 **d)** −2
e) +9 **f)** −4 **g)** 0 **h)** +10

3. Work with a partner. Place 10 yellow and 10 red tiles in a bag.

a) Pull out a handful of tiles. Tell the integer that the tiles model.

b) Have your partner tell what other set of tiles could model this integer.

Mental Math

Sarah ran a marathon in 3 h and 41 min. The race started at 7:45 a.m. At what time did Sarah finish?

4. **Assessment Focus**
   a) Choose an integer between -9 and $+6$.
      Use coloured tiles to model the integer.
   b) How many more ways can you find to model the integer?
      Create a table to order your work.
   c) What patterns can you find in your table?
   d) Explain how the patterns in your table can help you model an integer between -90 and $+60$.

5. a) Suppose you have 10 yellow tiles.
      How many red tiles would you need to model $+2$?
      How do you know?
   b) Suppose you have 100 yellow tiles.
      How many red tiles would you need to model $+2$?
      How do you know?

Math Link

Sports

In golf, a hole is given a value called **par**.
Par is the number of strokes a good golfer takes to reach the hole.
A score of $+2$ means a golfer took 2 strokes more than par, or 2 strokes over par.
A score of -1 means a golfer took 1 stroke fewer than par, or 1 stroke under par.
Some scores have special names.
A score of $+1$ is a bogey.
A score of -1 is a birdie.
A score of -2 is an eagle.

In a golf tournament, the golfer with the fewest strokes wins the game.

Reflect

Explain how it is possible to use different sets of red and yellow tiles to model the same integer.

9.4 Adding Integers with Tiles

Focus Use coloured tiles to add integers.

Recall that when you add two numbers,
such as 5 + 3,
you combine 5 counters with
3 counters to obtain 8 counters.

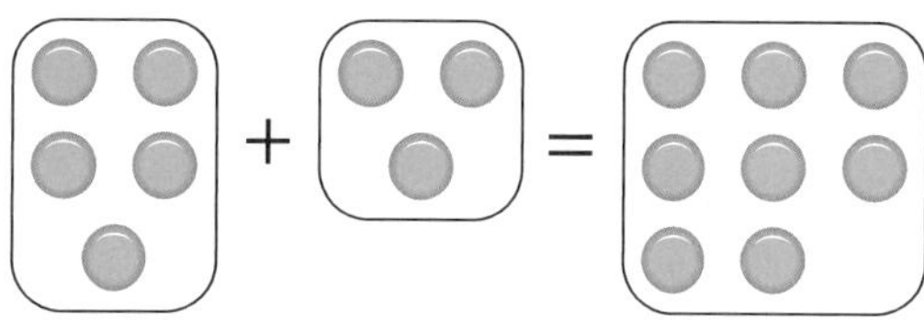

You can add two integers in a similar way.
You know that +1 and −1 combine to make a zero pair.
We can combine coloured tiles to add integers.

Explore

Work with a partner.
You will need coloured tiles.

- Choose two different positive integers.
  Add the integers.
  Draw a picture of the tiles you used.
  Write the addition equation.
- Repeat the activity for a positive integer and a negative integer.
- Repeat the activity for two different negative integers.

Reflect & Share

Share your equations with another pair of classmates.
How did you use the tiles to find a sum of integers?
How can you predict the sign of the sum?

Connect

- To add two positive integers: (+5) + (+4)
  Model each integer with tiles.

  +5: ▢ ▢ ▢ ▢ ▢

  +4: ▢ ▢ ▢ ▢

This is an addition equation. →

Combine the tiles. There are 9 yellow tiles.
They model +9.
So, $(+5) + (+4) = +9$

➢ To add a negative integer and a positive integer: $(-6) + (+9)$
Model each integer with tiles. Circle zero pairs.

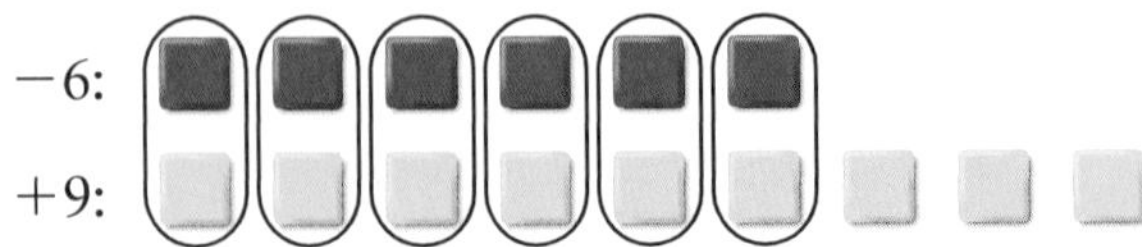

There are 6 zero pairs.
There are 3 yellow tiles left.
They model +3.
So, $(-6) + (+9) = +3$

➢ To add two negative integers: $(-3) + (-7)$
Model each integer with tiles.

Combine the tiles. There are 10 red tiles.
They model –10.
So, $(-3) + (-7) = -10$

Example

Add. $(+6) + (-5) + (-4)$

Solution

$(+6) + (-5) + (-4)$
Model each integer with tiles.
Circle zero pairs.

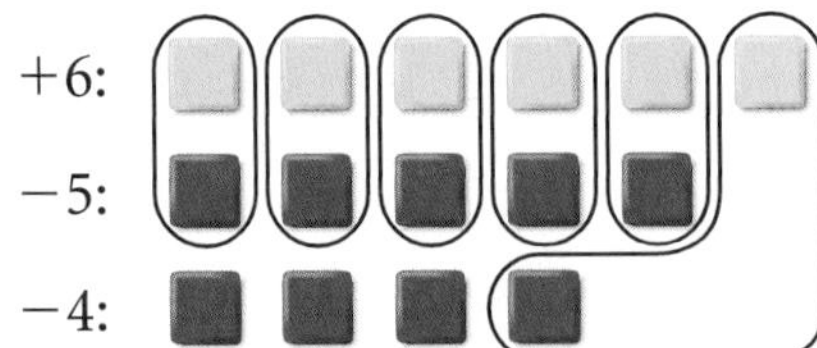

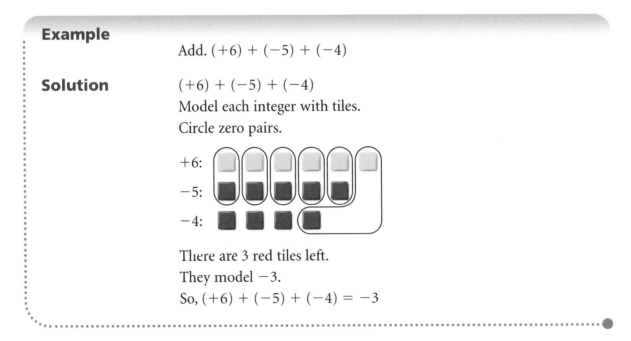

There are 3 red tiles left.
They model −3.
So, $(+6) + (-5) + (-4) = -3$

Practice

Use coloured tiles.

1. What sum does each set of tiles model?
   Write the addition equation.

   a) 

   b) 

   c) 

   d) 

   e) 

   f) 

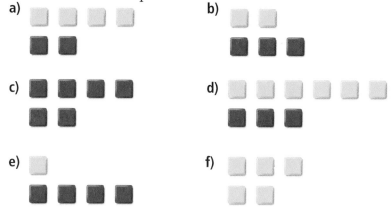

2. What sum does each set of tiles model?
   How do you know you are correct?
   a) 3 yellow tiles and 2 red tiles
   b) 3 yellow tiles and 4 red tiles
   c) 2 red tiles and 2 yellow tiles

3. Use coloured tiles to represent each sum. Find each sum.
   Sketch the tiles you used.
   a) $(+2) + (-2)$ b) $(-4) + (+4)$ c) $(+5) + (-5)$

4. Add. Sketch coloured tiles to show how you did it.
   a) $(+2) + (+3)$ b) $(-3) + (+4)$ c) $(-4) + (-1)$
   d) $(+1) + (-1)$ e) $(-3) + (-4)$ f) $(+5) + (-2)$

5. Add.
   a) $(+4) + (+3)$ b) $(-7) + (+5)$ c) $(-4) + (-5)$
   d) $(+8) + (-1)$ e) $(-10) + (-6)$ f) $(+4) + (-13)$

6. Represent each sentence with integers, then find each sum.
   a) The temperature is -3°C and rises 4 degrees Celsius.
   b) Ravinder earned \$5 and spent \$3.

7. Write 3 integer addition problems.
   Trade problems with a classmate.
   Solve your classmate's problems with coloured tiles.

Number Strategies

About what fraction of the large square is shaded in each diagram?

a) 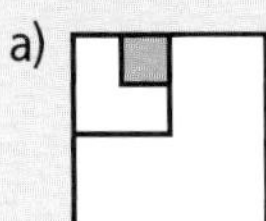

b) 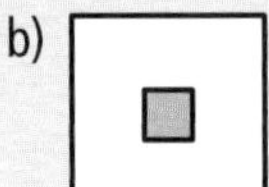

c) 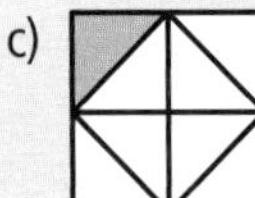

8. Add. Sketch coloured tiles to show how you did it.

a) $(+1) + (+2) + (+3)$ **b)** $(+2) + (-1) + (+3)$

c) $(-3) + (-1) + (-1)$ **d)** $(+4) + (-3) + (+1)$

e) $(-4) + (+1) + (-2)$ **f)** $(-5) + (-3) + (-2)$

9. Copy and complete.

a) $(+5) + \square = +8$ **b)** $\square + (-3) = -4$ **c)** $(+3) + \square = +1$

d) $(-5) + \square = -3$ **e)** $(+2) + \square = +1$ **f)** $\square + (-6) = 0$

10. Assessment Focus

a) Add: $(+3) + (-7)$

b) Suppose you add the integers in the opposite order: $(-7) + (+3)$. Does the sum change?
Use coloured tile drawings and words to explain the result.

c) How is $(-3) + (+7)$ different from $(+3) + (-7)$? Explain.

11. In a magic square every row, column, and diagonal has the same sum. Copy and complete each magic square. How did you do it?

a)

+3		+1
	0	
−1		

b)

−1		+1
	−2	
		−3

Take It Further

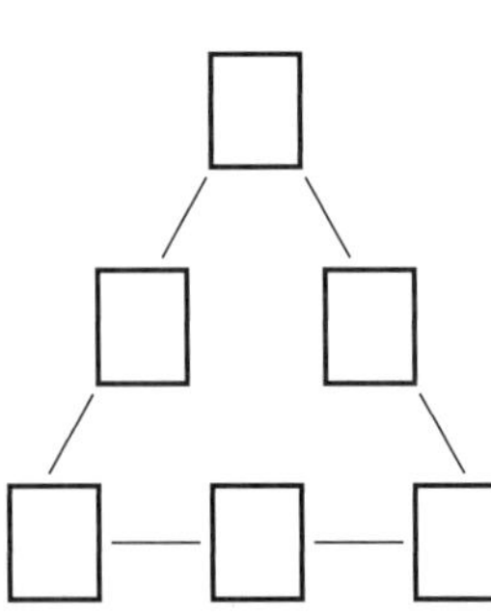

12. Add.

a) $(+4) + (+1) + (+1) + (+1)$

b) $(-3) + (+2) + (-1) + (+1)$

c) $(+3) + (-2) + (-1) + (-1)$

13. Copy the triangle at the left.
Place the numbers $-6, -5, -4, -3, -2, -1$ in the triangle so the sums of the sides are the same.
Explain how you solved the problem.

Reflect

Explain how to add two integers when the integers have:
- the same signs
- opposite signs

9.5 Adding Integers

Focus Add integers using number lines and patterns.

We can show the addition of whole numbers on a number line.

$4 + 2 = 6$

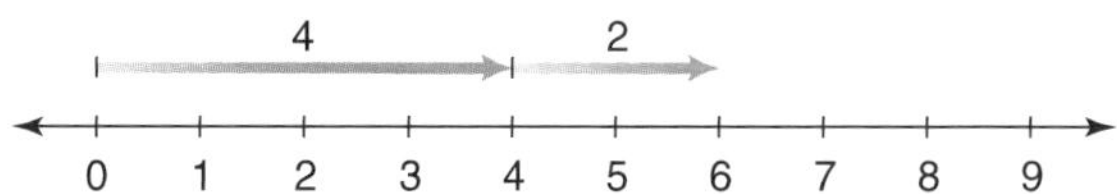

We can also show the addition of integers on a number line.

Explore

Work with a partner.
You will need copies of this number line.

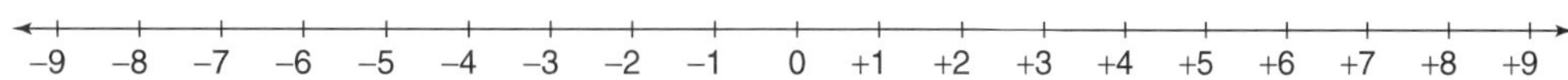

➢ Choose two different positive integers.
Use a number line to add them.
Write the addition equation.

➢ Repeat the activity for a positive integer and a negative integer.

➢ Repeat the activity for two different negative integers.

Reflect & Share

Trade your addition problems with another pair of classmates.
Answer your classmates' problems.
Compare answers.
If the answers do not agree, decide who is correct. Explain.

Connect

➢ To add a positive integer, move right (in the positive direction).

Start at -2.
Move 3 units right.

$(-2) + (+3)$

$(-2) + (+3) = +1$

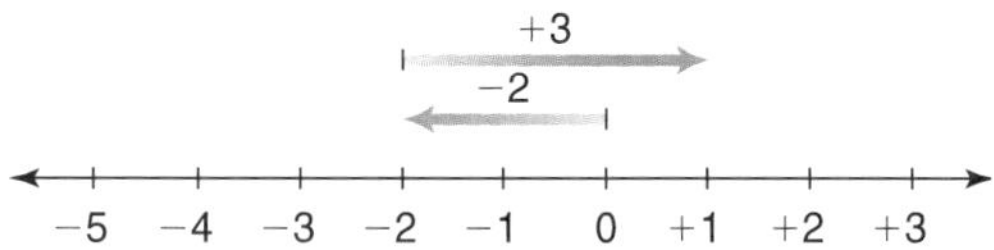

Start at -2.
Move 3 units left.

➢ To add a negative integer, move left (in the negative direction).

$(-2) + (-3)$

$(-2) + (-3) = -5$

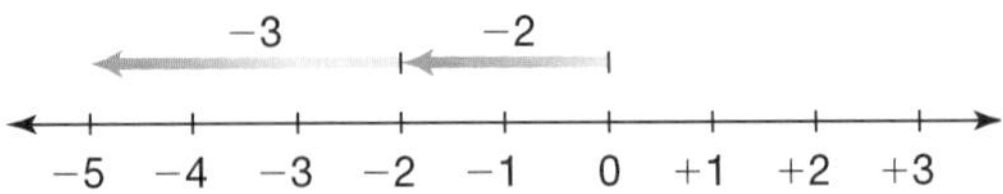

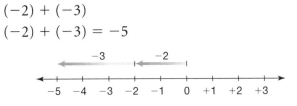

We can use patterning to add integers.

Example 1

Add. $(+5) + (-2)$

Solution

$(+5) + (-2)$

Think of a pattern. Start with facts you know.

Continue the pattern until you reach the fact you want.

$(+5) + (+2) = +7$

$(+5) + (+1) = +6$

$(+5) + (0) = +5$

$(+5) + (-1) = +4$

$(+5) + (-2) = +3$

Example 2

Sandra and Joe buy and sell CDs at a flea market.
In August, they bought 14 CDs for \$5 each.
They sold 6 CDs for \$9 each.

a) Did Sandra and Joe make money or lose money in August?

b) How much money did they make or lose?

Solution

Expenses: $14 \times \$5 = \$70$ Income: $6 \times \$9 = \$54$

a) Since the expenses are greater than the income, Sandra and Joe lost money in August.

b) Draw a number line.

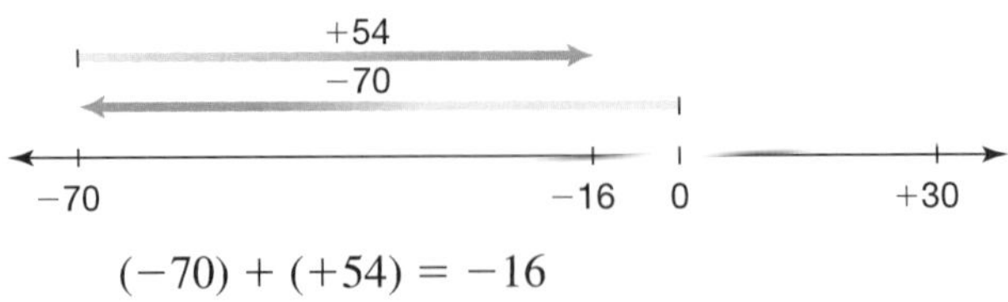

$(-70) + (+54) = -16$

In August, Sandra and Joe lost \$16.

Practice

Use a number line when it helps.

1. Add.

a) $(+1) + (+3)$ **b)** $(-1) + (+3)$

c) $(-3) + (+1)$ **d)** $(-1) + (-3)$

2. Find each sum. Use a pattern when you can.

a) $(+4) + (+2)$ **b)** $(+5) + (-3)$

c) $(-4) + (-2)$ **d)** $(-8) + (+2)$

3. a) Reverse the order of the integers in question 2, then add.

b) Compare your answers to the answers in question 2. What do you notice?

c) Make a general statement about your observations.

4. Look at these thermometers. Find each temperature after:

a) it falls 4°C **b)** it falls 7°C **c)** it rises 6°C

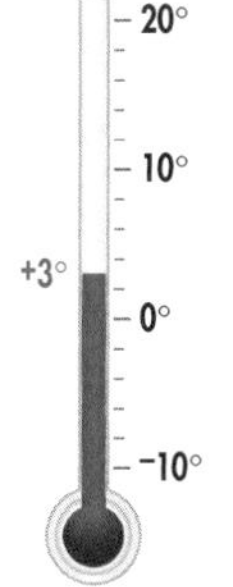

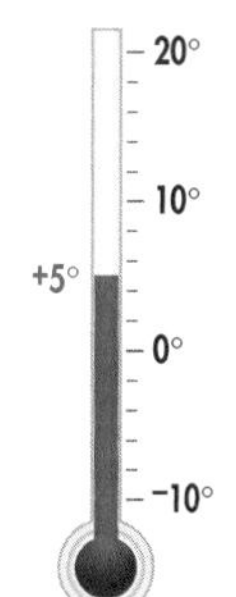

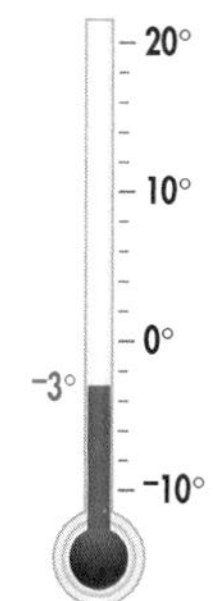

5. a) The temperature rises 7°C, then drops 2°C. What is the overall change in temperature?

b) Adrian loses \$4, then earns \$8. Did Adrian gain or lose overall?

c) The value of a stock went up \$3, then down \$2. What was the final change in the value of the stock?

6. Add.

a) $(+12) + (+3)$ **b)** $(+13) + (-7)$

c) $(-5) + (-10)$ **d)** $(-5) + (+8)$

e) $(-8) + (-7)$ **f)** $(+4) + (-10)$

7. Add.
   a) $(+30) + (+10)$
   b) $(+20) + (-10)$
   c) $(-35) + (-5)$
   d) $(-15) + (+18)$
   e) $(-82) + (+79)$
   f) $(-58) + (-22)$

Mental Math

Which expression does not belong? Why?

$12 \times 4 \times 50$
$25 \times 10 \times 10$
24×100
$99 \times 20 + 420$
80×30
$90 \times 30 - 300$

8. **Assessment Focus** Use an example to explain why each statement is true.
   Use a number line to support your explanations.
   a) The sum of two opposite integers is 0.
   b) The sum of two positive integers is always positive.
   c) The sum of two negative integers is always negative.
   d) The sum of a negative integer and a positive integer is sometimes negative and sometimes positive.

9. Add.
   a) $(+4) + (+3) + (-6)$
   b) $(-2) + (-4) + (+1)$
   c) $(-5) + (+3) + (-4)$
   d) $(+6) + (-8) + (+2)$
   e) $(+12) + (-3) + (-2)$
   f) $(-5) + (-8) + (-10)$

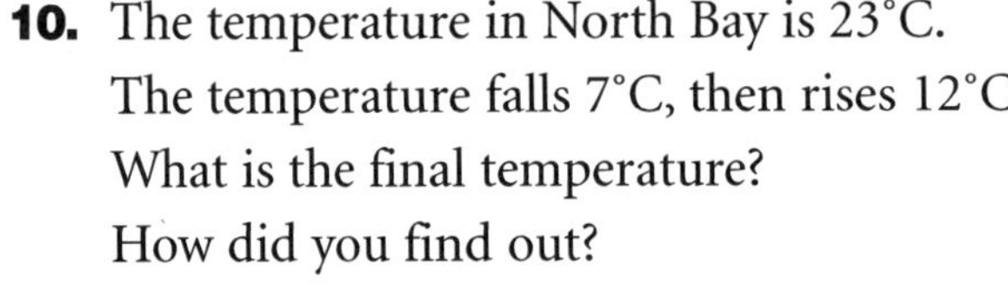

10. The temperature in North Bay is 23°C.
    The temperature falls 7°C, then rises 12°C.
    What is the final temperature?
    How did you find out?
    Which model did you use?

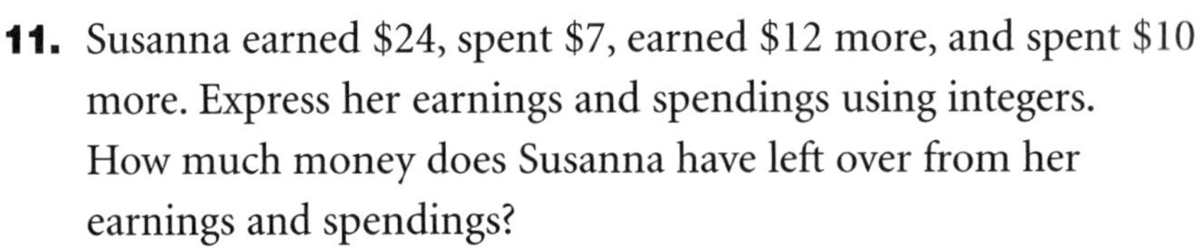

11. Susanna earned \$24, spent \$7, earned \$12 more, and spent \$10 more. Express her earnings and spendings using integers.
    How much money does Susanna have left over from her earnings and spendings?

Take It Further

12. Copy and complete.
    a) $(+10) + \square = +25$
    b) $(-10) + \square = -25$
    c) $(+20) + \square = +15$
    d) $(-20) + \square = -15$
    e) $(+35) + \square = +17$
    f) $(-35) + \square = -17$

Reflect

You have used three models to add integers.
Which model do you prefer? Why?

Mid-Unit Review

LESSON

9.1 **1.** Draw a number line. Show each integer on the number line: $+3, -2, -5, 0$

2. Use an integer to represent each situation.
- **a)** 12°C below zero
- **b)** a golf score of 3 strokes above par
- **c)** 10 m above sea level
- **d)** a drop of $2 in the price of a stock
- **e)** $25 earned
- **f)** a mountain elevation of 1500 m

9.2 **3.** Order these integers from least to greatest.
- **a)** $+4, -3, -2, +1, -4$
- **b)** $+18, +50, 0, -50, -17$

9.3 **4.** Use red and yellow tiles to model each integer two different ways. Draw the tiles.
- **a)** -5 **b)** 0
- **c)** $+8$ **d)** -1
- **e)** $+3$ **f)** -7

9.4 **5.** Use coloured tiles to add. Draw pictures of the tiles you used.
- **a)** $(+4) + (-1)$
- **b)** $(-3) + (-2)$
- **c)** $(-5) + (+1)$
- **d)** $(+6) + (+3)$
- **e)** $(-4) + (-8)$
- **f)** $(+4) + (+8)$

9.5 **6.** Use a number line to add.
- **a)** $(+3) + (+2)$ **b)** $(-5) + (-1)$
- **c)** $(-10) + (+8)$ **d)** $(+6) + (-5)$
- **e)** $(-8) + (+8)$ **f)** $(-5) + (+12)$

7. Use patterns to add.
- **a)** $(+6) + (-3)$ **b)** $(-2) + (+8)$
- **c)** $(+5) + (-9)$ **d)** $(-4) + (+9)$

8. Add.
- **a)** $(+4) + (+1) + (-2)$
- **b)** $(-3) + (-1) + (-4)$
- **c)** $(-5) + (+1) + (+3)$
- **d)** $(+6) + (-5) + (-8)$

9. a) Puja earned $50, was given $10, and spent $20. How much did Puja then have?

- **b)** The temperature starts at +5°C, goes up 2°C, then drops 10°C. What is the final temperature?
- **c)** The population of a city was 124 000, then it dropped by 4000 people. What was the population then?

10. a) Add. $(+4) + (-5)$
- **b)** Find another pair of integers that has the same sum as part a. Do this 3 times.

9.6 Subtracting Integers with Tiles

Focus Use coloured tiles to subtract integers.

To add integers, we combine groups of tiles.
To subtract integers, we do the reverse:
we "take away" tiles from a group.

Recall that equal numbers of red and yellow tiles model 0.
For example, $(-5) + (+5) = 0$

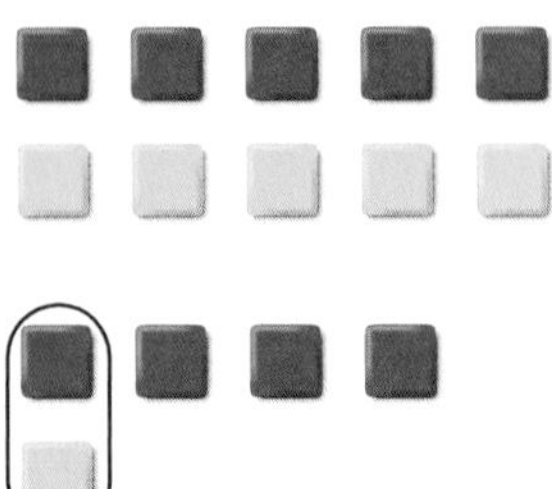

Adding 0 to a set of tiles does not change its value.
For example, $(-3) + 0 = -3$

Explore

Work with a partner.
You will need coloured tiles.
Use tiles to subtract. Sketch the tiles you used in each case.

- $(+5) - (+3)$
- $(+5) - (-3)$
- $(-3) - (+5)$
- $(-3) - (-5)$

Reflect & Share

Compare your results with those of another pair of classmates.
Did they draw the same sets of tiles? Explain.
When you subtracted, how did you know how many tiles to use to model each integer?

Connect

To use tiles to subtract integers, we model the first integer, then take away the number of tiles indicated by the second integer.

We can use tiles to subtract: $(+5) - (+9)$

Model +5.

There are not enough tiles to take away $+9$.
To take away $+9$, we need 4 more yellow tiles.

We add zero pairs without changing the value.
Add 4 yellow tiles and 4 red tiles. They represent 0.

By adding 0, the integer the tiles represent has not changed.
Now take away the 9 yellow tiles.

Since 4 red tiles remain, we write: $(+5) - (+9) = -4$

Example

Use tiles to subtract.

a) $(-2) - (-6)$ **b)** $(-6) - (+2)$ **c)** $(+2) - (-6)$

Solution

a) $(-2) - (-6)$

Model -2.

There are not enough tiles to take away -6.
To take away -6, we need 4 more red tiles.

We add zero pairs without changing the value.
Add 4 red tiles and 4 yellow tiles.

Now take away 6 red tiles.

Since 4 yellow tiles remain, we write: $(-2) - (-6) = +4$

b) $(-6) - (+2)$

Model -6.

There are no yellow tiles to take.
We need 2 yellow tiles to take away.

We add zero pairs.
Add 2 yellow tiles and 2 red tiles.

Now take away 2 yellow tiles.

Since 8 red tiles remain, we write: $(-6) - (+2) = -8$

c) $(+2) - (-6)$

Model $+2$.

There are no red tiles to take.
We need 6 red tiles to take away.

We add zero pairs.
Add 6 red tiles and 6 yellow tiles.

Now take away 6 red tiles.

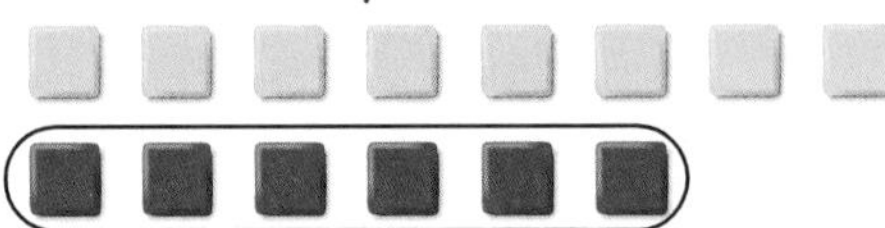

Since 8 yellow tiles remain, we write: $(+2) - (-6) = +8$

Notice the results in the *Example*, parts b and c.
When we reverse the order in which we subtract two integers, the answer is the opposite integer.

$(-6) - (+2) = -8$

$(+2) - (-6) = +8$

Practice

1. Use tiles to subtract. Draw pictures of the tiles you used.
   a) $(+7) - (+4)$ b) $(-2) - (-2)$ c) $(-9) - (-6)$
   d) $(+4) - (+2)$ e) $(-8) - (-1)$ f) $(+3) - (+3)$

2. Use tiles to subtract.
   a) $(-1) - (-4)$ b) $(+3) - (+8)$ c) $(-4) - (-11)$
   d) $(+7) - (+8)$ e) $(-4) - (-6)$ f) $(+1) - (+10)$

3. Subtract.
   a) $(-4) - (-1)$ b) $(+8) - (+3)$ c) $(-11) - (-4)$
   d) $(+8) - (+7)$ e) $(-6) - (-4)$ f) $(+10) - (+1)$

4. Subtract.
   a) $(+4) - (-7)$ b) $(-2) - (+8)$ c) $(-9) - (+5)$
   d) $(+6) - (-8)$ e) $(-3) - (+6)$ f) $(-5) - (+7)$

5. Subtract.
   a) $(+4) - (+5)$ b) $(-3) - (+5)$ c) $(-4) - (+3)$
   d) $(-1) - (-8)$ e) $(+8) - (-2)$ f) $(+4) - (-7)$

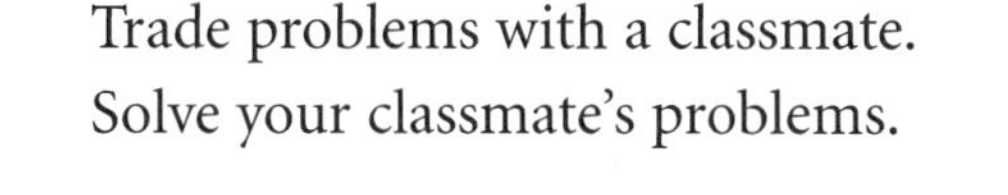

6. Write 3 integer subtraction problems.
   Trade problems with a classmate.
   Solve your classmate's problems.

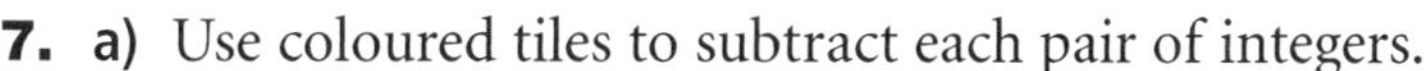

7. a) Use coloured tiles to subtract each pair of integers.
      i) $(+3) - (+1)$ and $(+1) - (+3)$
      ii) $(-3) - (-2)$ and $(-2) - (-3)$
   b) What do you notice about each pair of problems in part a?

8. $(+5) - (-2) = +7$
   Predict the value of $(-2) - (+5)$.
   Explain the reasoning for your choice.

9. **Assessment Focus** Use integers.
   Write a subtraction problem that would give each answer.
   How many problems can you write each time?
   a) $+2$ b) -3 c) $+5$ d) -6

Calculator Skills

Assume the ÷ key on your calculator does not work.

Find two ways to use your calculator to divide: 888 ÷ 24

10. Here is a magic square:

0	+5	−2
−1	+1	+3
+4	−3	+2

a) Subtract +4 from each entry.
Is it still a magic square? Why?

b) Subtract −1 from each entry.
Is it still a magic square? Why?

c) Make up your own magic square.

Take It Further

11. a) Find two integers with a sum of −1 and a difference of +5.

b) Create and solve a similar integer problem.

12. Evaluate.

a) $(+4) + (+1) - (+3)$

b) $(+1) - (+2) - (-1)$

c) $(-3) - (+1) + (+4)$

d) $(-2) - (-4) + (-1)$

e) $(+2) - (+1) - (+4)$

f) $(+1) - (+2) + (+1)$

13. Copy and complete.

a) $(+4) - \square = +3$

b) $(+3) - \square = -1$

c) $\square - (+1) = +4$

14. Which expression in each pair has the greater value?
Explain your reasoning.

a) i) $(+3) - (-1)$ ii) $(-3) - (+1)$

b) i) $(-4) - (-5)$ ii) $(+4) - (+5)$

Reflect

Here are 4 types of subtraction problems:

- (negative integer) – (negative integer)
- (negative integer) – (positive integer)
- (positive integer) – (positive integer)
- (positive integer) – (negative integer)

Write a problem for each type of subtraction.
Show how you use tiles to solve each problem.

9.7 Subtracting Integers

Focus Subtract integers using number lines and patterns.

Just as we can show addition of whole numbers on a number line, we can show subtraction of whole numbers on a number line.

$7 - 5 = 2$

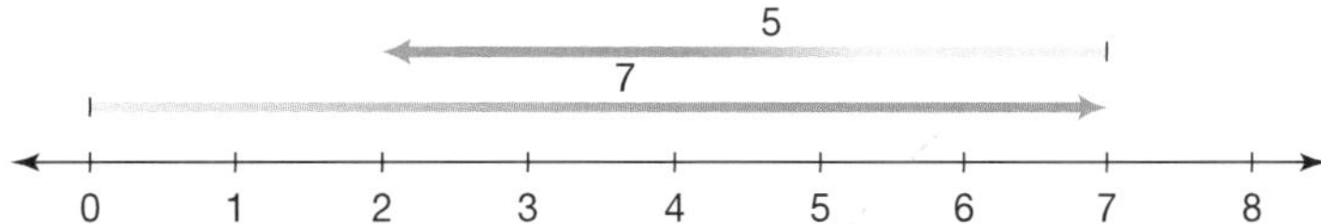

Explore

Work with a partner.

You will need copies of this number line.

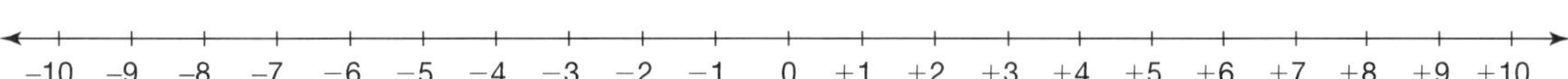

➢ Use the number line to subtract.

$(+6) - (-4)$ $\quad$ $(-3) - (+5)$

$(-5) - (-4)$ $\quad$ $(+7) - (+10)$

Check your answers using coloured tiles.

➢ Subtract. / Add.

Subtract.	Add.
$(+7) - (+2)$	$(+7) + (-2)$
$(-7) - (-2)$	$(-7) + (+2)$
$(+7) - (-2)$	$(+7) + (+2)$
$(-7) - (+2)$	$(-7) + (-2)$

What do you notice about the answers in each row?
What patterns do you see in each subtraction and addition?
Check your pattern using other integers.

Reflect & Share

Compare your answers with those of another pair of classmates.
How can you use addition to subtract two integers?

Connect

➢ To subtract two whole numbers, such as 5 – 2, we think, "What do we add to 2 to get 5?"
We add 3 to 2 to get 5; so, 5 – 2 = 3

We can do the same to subtract two integers.
For example, to subtract: $(+5) - (-2)$
Think: "What do we add to -2 to get $+5$?"

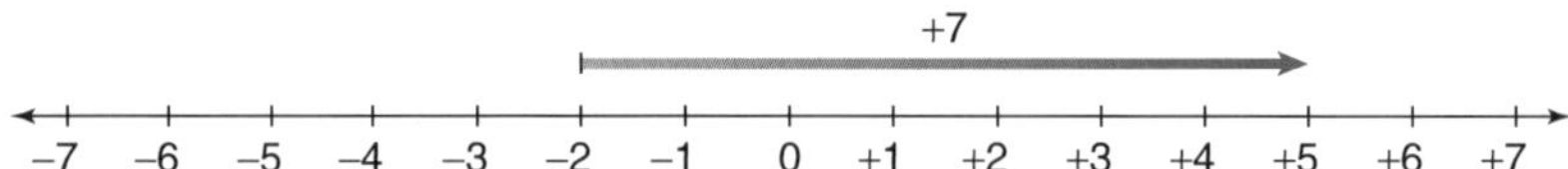

We add $+7$ to -2 to get $+5$; so, $(+5) - (-2) = +7$
We also know that $(+5) + (+2) = +7$.
We can look at other subtraction equations and related addition equations.

$(+9) - (+4) = +5$	$(+9) + (-4) = +5$
$(-9) - (-4) = -5$	$(-9) + (+4) = -5$
$(-9) - (+4) = -13$	$(-9) + (-4) = -13$
$(+9) - (-4) = +13$	$(+9) + (+4) = +13$

In each case, the result of subtracting an integer is the same as adding the opposite integer.
For example,

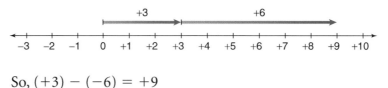

$(-9) - (+4) = -13$ $\qquad$ $(-9) + (-4) = -13$

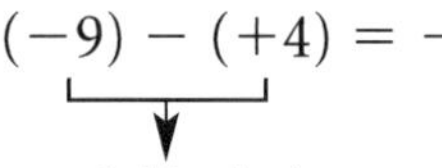

Subtract +4. $\qquad$ Add –4.

➢ To subtract an integer, we add the opposite integer.
For example, to subtract: $(+3) - (-6)$
Add the opposite: $(+3) + (+6)$

The opposite of –6 is +6.

+3 +6
−3 −2 −1 0 +1 +2 +3 +4 +5 +6 +7 +8 +9 +10

So, $(+3) - (-6) = +9$

Example 1

Use a number line to subtract.

a) $(+2) - (+9)$ **b)** $(+2) - (-9)$

Solution

a) To subtract: $(+2) - (+9)$
Add the opposite: $(+2) + (-9)$
Use a number line.
$(+2) + (-9) = -7$

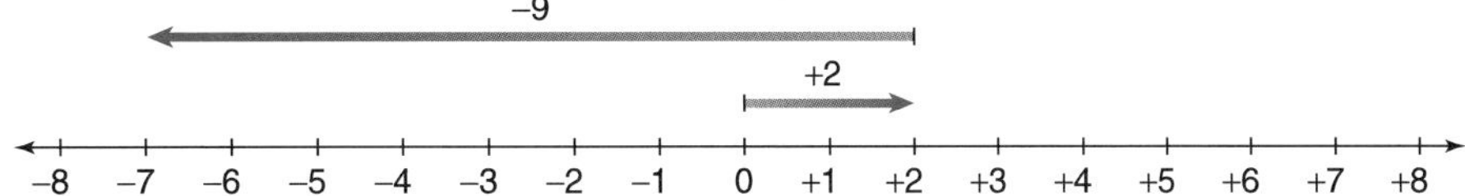

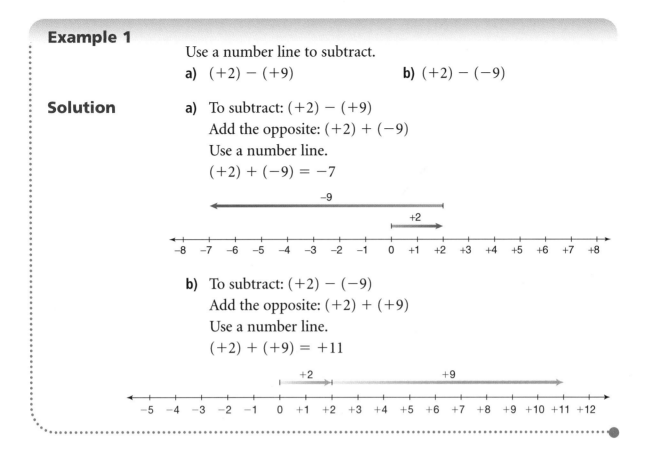

b) To subtract: $(+2) - (-9)$
Add the opposite: $(+2) + (+9)$
Use a number line.
$(+2) + (+9) = +11$

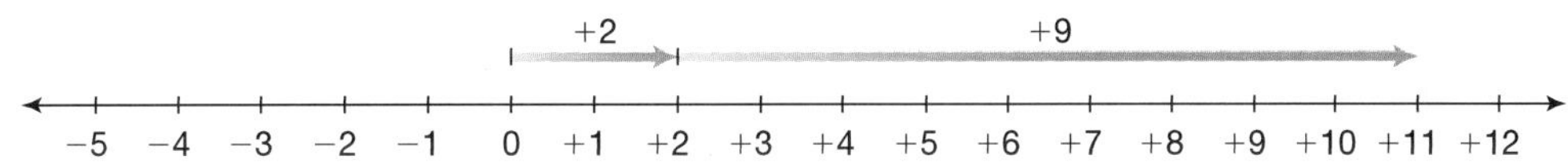

Example 2

On April 27, 2004, the highest temperature in Windsor was +5°C and the highest temperature in Yellowknife was −2°C.
What is the difference in temperature? Interpret the answer.

Solution

The difference between +5 and −2 can be written in two ways:

$(+5) - (-2)$
Add the opposite: $(+5) + (+2)$
$(+5) + (+2) = +7$
The difference in temperature is +7°C.
The temperature in Windsor is 7°C greater than the temperature in Yellowknife.

$(-2) - (+5)$
Add the opposite: $(-2) + (-5)$
$(-2) + (-5) = -7$
The difference in temperature is −7°C.
The temperature in Yellowknife is 7°C less than the temperature in Windsor.

Practice

1. Rewrite using addition.
   a) $(+6) - (+4)$ b) $(-5) - (+4)$ c) $(-2) - (-3)$
   d) $(+4) - (-2)$ e) $(+1) - (+1)$ f) $(+1) - (-1)$

2. Use a number line to subtract.
   Use coloured tiles to check your answers.
   a) $(+2) - (+1)$ b) $(+4) - (-3)$ c) $(-4) - (-1)$
   d) $(-5) - (+2)$ e) $(-2) - (-6)$ f) $(-3) - (-7)$

3. a) Reverse the order of the integers in question 2, then subtract.
   b) How are the answers different from those in question 2? Explain.

4. Use a number line to subtract.
   a) $(+10) - (+5)$ b) $(+7) - (-3)$ c) $(-8) - (+6)$
   d) $(-10) - (+5)$ e) $(-4) - (+4)$ f) $(-4) - (-4)$

5. Find the difference between:
   a) a temperature of +3°C and −5°C
   b) a temperature of −15°C and −10°C
   c) an elevation of 5 m above sea level and one of 2 m below sea level
   d) a golf score of 1 below par and one of 3 below par

6. The table shows the average afternoon temperatures in January and April for four Canadian cities.
   Find the difference between the temperatures in April and January for each city. Show your work.

	City	January Temperature	April Temperature
a)	Calgary	−4°C	+13°C
b)	Iqaluit	−22°C	−10°C
c)	Toronto	−3°C	+12°C
d)	Victoria	+7°C	+13°C

Calculator Skills

Find each answer.

- $15 \times (32 + 41)$
- $198 - 104 \div 13$
- $14 \times 15 - 16 \times 9$

7. Use patterns to subtract.

a) Subtract: $(+2) - (+5)$
Start the pattern with $(+6) - (+5) = +1$.

b) Subtract: $(+7) - (-3)$
Start the pattern with $(+7) - (+4) = +3$.

c) Subtract: $(-3) - (+7)$
Start the pattern with $(+8) - (+7) = +1$.

8. **Assessment Focus**

a) Subtract: $(-6) - (+11)$

b) Suppose we subtract the integers in the opposite order:
$(+11) - (-6)$
How does the answer compare with the answer in part a?
Use number lines or patterns to explain.

c) How is $(+6) - (-11)$ different from $(-6) - (+11)$?
Explain.

9. This table shows the mean daily maximum temperatures in degrees Celsius for Rankin Inlet for each month.

Jan.	Feb.	Mar.	Apr.	May	June	July	Aug.	Sept.	Oct.	Nov.	Dec.
−28	−28	−23	−12	−2	+8	+16	+14	+6	−3	−16	−24

a) What is the median?

b) What is the range?

c) What is the mode?

10. Evaluate.

a) $(+4) - (+2) - (+1)$

b) $(-2) - (+1) - (-4)$

c) $(-1) + (-2) - (+1)$

d) $(+5) - (+1) + (-2)$

e) $(+10) - (+3) - (-5)$

f) $(-7) - (+1) + (-3)$

11. Show three ways that +4 can be written as the difference of two integers.

Reflect

Choose two integers: one positive, one negative.
Add the integers. Subtract the integers.
Explain how the subtraction of two integers is related to addition.

Choosing a Strategy

Strategies

- Make a table.
- Use a model.
- Draw a diagram.
- Solve a simpler problem.
- Work backward.
- Guess and check.
- Make an organized list.
- Use a pattern.
- Draw a graph.
- Use logical reasoning.

1. A textbook is opened at random. The product of the page numbers is 23 256. What is the number on the left hand page?

2. Ms. Pantuso has a bag of candies that she wants to share equally among the students in her class.
On Monday, all 20 students were present. If she had shared the candies, she would have had 7 candies left over.
On Tuesday, two boys were absent. If she had shared the candies, she would again have had 7 left over.
On Wednesday, the two boys were still absent and one girl was absent. Ms. Pantuso shared all the candies among the students with none left over.

a) What was the least number of candies Ms. Pantuso could have had?

b) How many candies did each student receive?

3. Briony wants to print copies of her new brochure.
The local print shop charges 15¢ a copy for the first 25 copies, 12¢ a copy for the next 50 copies, and 8¢ a copy for any additional copies.
How much would Briony pay for each number of copies?

a) 60 copies **b)** 240 copies

4. What is the greatest number of 5 cm by 3 cm rectangles that can be cut from a 20 cm by 10 cm sheet of cardboard?

5. Mr. Anders estimates it will take him 4 h to build a wall.
His assistant would take 6 h to build the wall.

a) What fraction of the wall could each person build in one hour?

b) Suppose they worked together. What fraction could they build in one hour?

c) How long would it take them to build the wall?

6. The mean of five numbers is 13.
The mode is 16.
The median is 14.
Write two sets of numbers that satisfy these conditions.

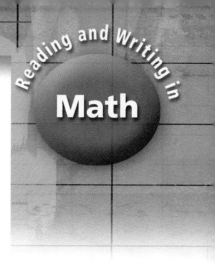

7. A rectangular prism has a square base, and a volume of 36 cm^3.
What are the possible whole number dimensions of the prism?

8. Copy this figure on grid paper.
Add one square to make the figure symmetrical. How many solutions can you find?

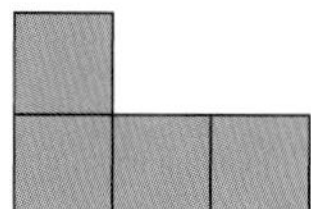

9. Eight students wrote a math test. Their mean mark was 54%.
Another student wrote the test and scored 99%.
What is the mean mark for the nine students?

10. Write 45 as the sum of consecutive integers.
How many solutions can you find?

11. a) The product of two whole numbers is 1000.
No number contains a zero.
What are the numbers?
How many different answers can you find?

b) The product of three whole numbers is 1000.
No number contains a zero.
What are the numbers?
How many different answers can you find?

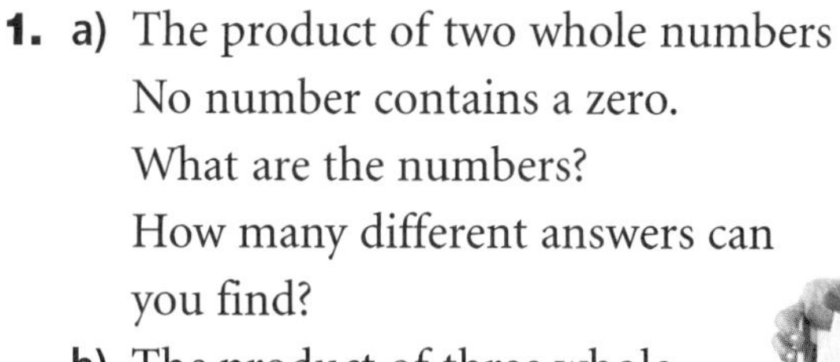

12. A book contains 124 pages numbered from 1 to 124.
How many times does the digit 7 appear?

Historian

The modern historian does a lot of 'detective' work, especially when reading old documents or journals that describe timelines. Adding or subtracting days, months, or years from a known date is a regular part of the work. The historian must deal with modern timekeeping conventions, such as Common Era (CE) and Before Common Era (BCE). But he must also know that, throughout history, different societies had different ways of describing time. Often it was simply recorded as a period of time before or after another significant date or event.

Suppose you read this entry in an 18th century explorer's journal dated May 21:

A fortnight is 2 weeks.

"We have been following this river for a fortnight. Three days into our journey we came upon a great waterfall blocking our path and had to portage around it. But the river has been calm since."

How would you be able to calculate what date the waterfall was discovered?

Suppose you knew that Augustus Caesar died in 14 CE at the age of 77. Can you calculate the year of his birth? Explain.

Unit Review

Review any lesson with

What Do I Need to Know?

✓ Integer Models

- You can use a number line to show integers.

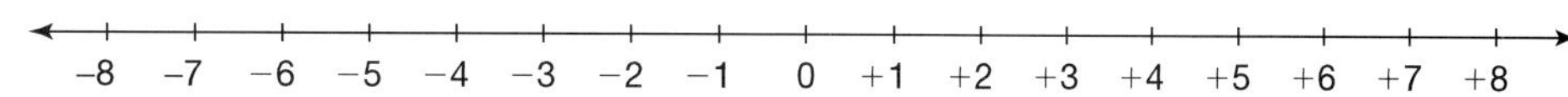

Negative numbers are to the left of 0. Positive numbers are to the right of 0.

- Coloured tiles model integers.

✓ Adding Integers

- You can use tiles to add integers.
$(-7) + (+2) = -5$

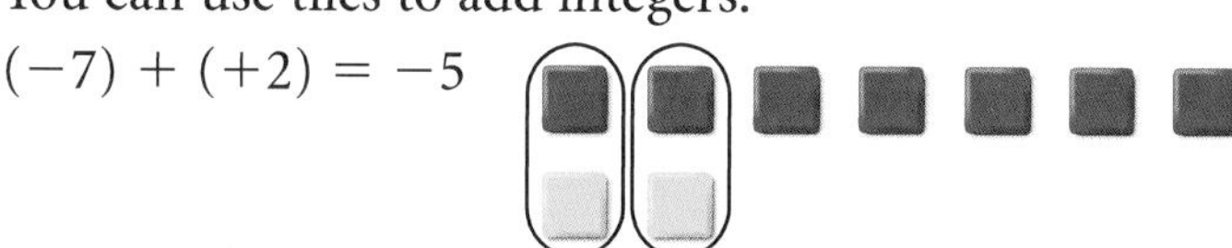

- You can use a number line to add integers.
$(+6) + (-3) = +3$

−3
+6

−8 −7 −6 −5 −4 −3 −2 −1 0 +1 +2 +3 +4 +5 +6 +7 +8

✓ Subtracting Integers

- You can use tiles to subtract integers: $(+3) - (-7)$
We need enough red tiles to take away 7 of them.
Model +3:

Since there are not enough tiles to take away −7, add 7 yellow tiles and 7 red tiles. Now take away 7 red tiles. There are 10 yellow tiles left.

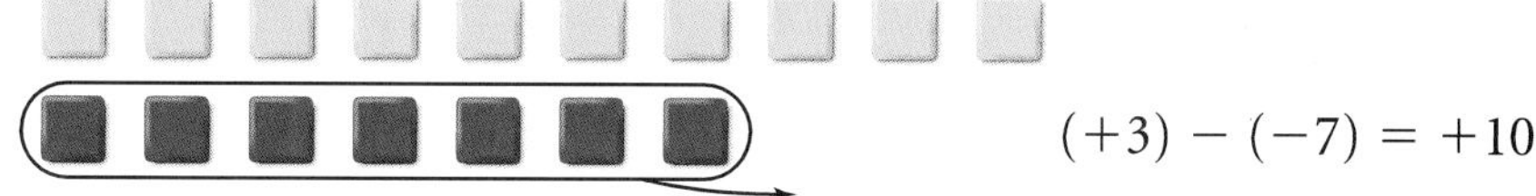

$(+3) - (-7) = +10$

- You can also subtract by adding the opposite:
$(-5) - (-8) = -5 + (+8)$
$= +3$

What Should I Be Able to Do?

For extra practice, go to page 446.

LESSON

9.1 **1.** Draw a number line. Mark each integer on the number line: +3, −5, +1, −2

2. Use an integer to represent each situation.

a) a golf score of 2 strokes under par

b) 250 m below sea level

c) 32°C

d) a loss of $125

e) an increase of $3 in the monthly cost of cable television

9.2 **3.** Order these integers from least to greatest: +200, −55, +150, −3, −54

9.4 9.6 **4.** Use tiles to add or subtract.

a) (−1) + (+3)

b) (+3) + (−4)

c) (−2) − (+3)

d) (−1) − (−3)

9.5 9.7 **5.** Use a number line to add or subtract.

a) (−1) + (+3)

b) (+6) + (−4)

c) (−4) − (+6)

d) (−5) − (−3)

6. When you add two positive integers, their sum is always a positive integer. When you subtract two positive integers, is their difference always a positive integer? Explain.

7. At midnight in North Bay, the temperature was −5°C. During the next 24 h, the temperature rose 12°C, then dropped 9°C. What was the final temperature? Show your work.

9.6 9.7 **8.** Use tiles or a number line to subtract.

a) (+4) − (+1)

b) (+5) − (−1)

c) (+2) − (−2)

d) (−4) − (+1)

e) (−6) − (−2)

f) (−10) − (−5)

g) (−4) − (−2)

9. Use tiles or a number line. Find the difference between:

a) a temperature of +5°C and −7°C

b) an elevation of −100 m and +50 m

c) a golf score of 1 over par and 2 under par

10. Subtract.

a) (+3) − (+1)

b) (−5) − (−2)

c) (+100) − (+60)

d) (−100) − (+60)

11. **a)** Find 5 pairs of integers with a sum of −6.

b) Find 5 pairs of integers with a difference of −3.

Practice Test

1. We measure time in hours.
   Suppose 12 noon is represented by the integer 0.
   a) Which integer represents 1 p.m. the same day?
   b) Which integer represents 10 a.m. the same day?
   c) Which integer represents 12 midnight the same day?
   d) Which integer represents 10 p.m. the previous day?

2. Order all the integers in question 1 from least to greatest.

3. Evaluate.
   a) $(+5) + (-8)$ b) $(-3) - (+7)$ c) $(-9) + (-1)$
   d) $(-4) + (+10)$ e) $(-6) - (-2)$ f) $(+12) - (-11)$

4. Without calculating the sum, how can you tell if the sum of two integers will be:
   a) zero? b) negative? c) positive?
   Include examples in your explanations.

5. Here is a different type of dartboard.

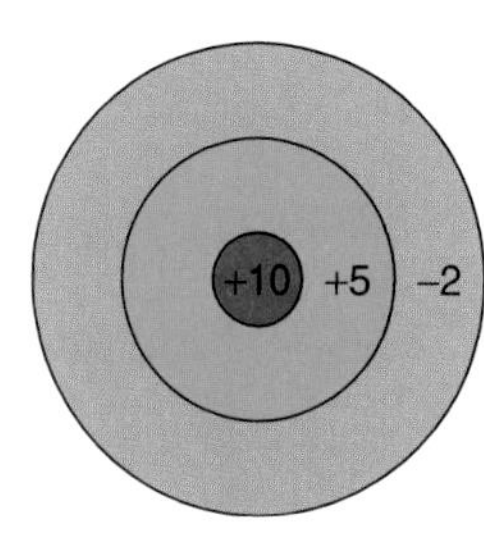

   A player throws 3 darts at the board. His score is the sum of the integers in the areas his darts land.
   Assume all 3 darts hit the board.
   a) How many different scores are possible?
   b) Find each score.

6. The lowest temperature possible is approximately –273°C.
   The temperature at which water boils is 100°C.
   What is the difference in these temperatures?

Unit Problem What Time Is It?

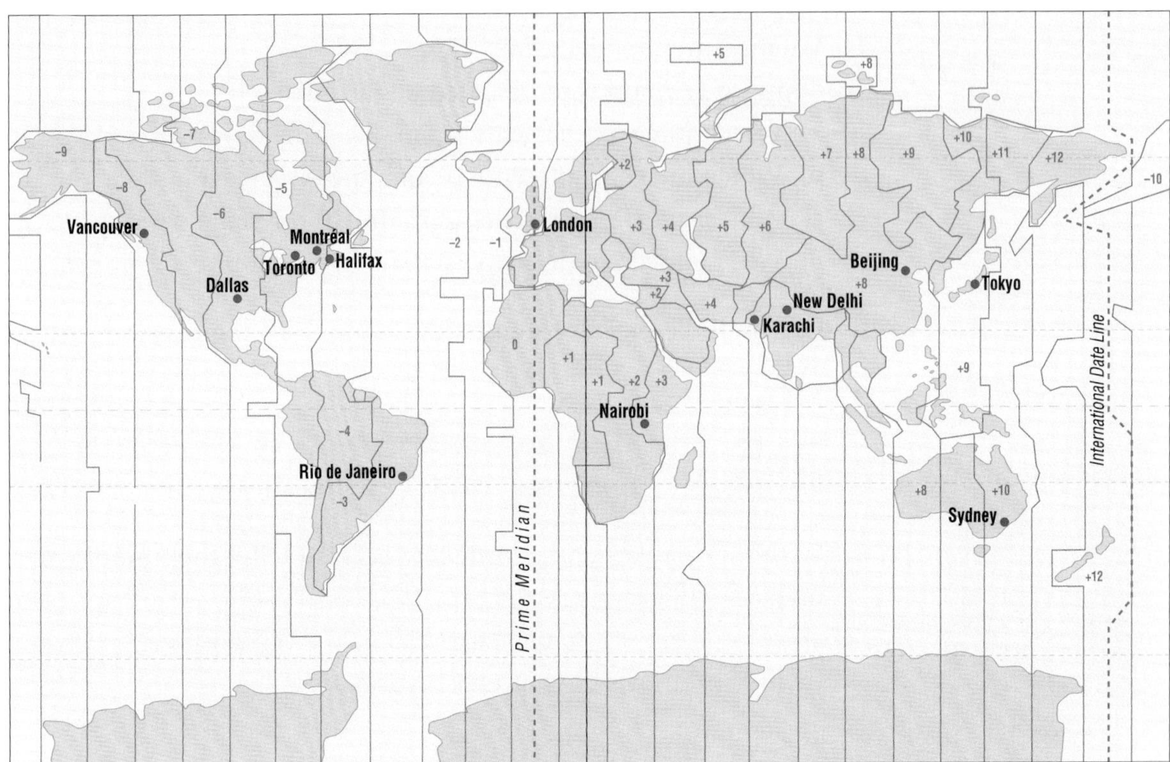

The map shows the world's time zones. Greenwich, in London, England, is the reference point, or the zero for the time zones. Its time is called UTC, or Coordinated Universal Time. London, England, is also in this time zone.
The positive and negative integers on the map show the changes in time from UTC.

The 2008 Summer Olympics will be held in Beijing, China.

1. The local start times of some Olympic events are given. If family members want to watch these events live, in Sudbury (the same time zone as Toronto), what time should they "tune in"?

a) 200-m backstroke at 2:00 p.m.

b) 100-m dash at 7:00 p.m.

c) gymnastics at 11:00 p.m.

d) middleweight boxing at 8:00 a.m.

2. An event is broadcast live in Montreal at 9:00 p.m.
What time is it taking place in Beijing?

3. Two pen pals plan to meet in Beijing for the Olympics.
Atsuko lives in Tokyo, Japan.
She can get a direct flight to Beijing that takes 4 h.
Paula lives in Sydney, Australia, and her direct flight takes 13 h.
What time does each girl leave her country to arrive in Beijing at 6 p.m., Beijing time?

4. Olympic funding depends on money from North American television networks. What problems will the organizers of the Beijing Olympics encounter when they plan the times for events?

5. Make up your own problem about the time zone map.
Solve your problem.

Show your work. Show how you can use integers to solve each problem.

Check List

Your work should show:

- ✓ how you used integers to solve each problem
- ✓ the strategies you used to add and subtract integers
- ✓ correct calculations
- ✓ a clear explanation of how integers relate to time zones

Reflect on the Unit

Choose a positive integer and a negative integer.
How many different ways can you add them? Subtract them?
Show your work.
If you used number lines, patterns, or coloured tiles, draw pictures to show how you used them.

UNIT

10 Patterning and Algebra

Students in a grade 7 class were raising money for charity. Some students had a "bowl-a-thon."

This table shows the money that one student raised for different bowling times.

Time (h)	Money Raised ($)
1	8
2	16
3	24
4	32
5	40
6	48

- What patterns do you see in the table?
- Suppose you drew a graph of the data. What might the graph look like?

What You'll Learn

- Describe, extend, and explain patterns.
- Use patterns to make predictions.
- Show patterns as graphs.
- Write and evaluate algebraic expressions.
- Read and write equations.
- Solve equations.

Why It's Important

- Extending a pattern is a useful problem-solving strategy.
- Using algebra is an efficient way to describe a pattern.

Key Words

- ordered pairs
- algebraic expression
- evaluate
- equation
- solve an equation

UNIT 10

Skills You'll Need

Order of Operations

Recall this order of operations.

Brackets	Perform operations inside the brackets.
Divide and multiply	Do in order from left to right.
Add and subtract	Do in order from left to right.

Example

Simplify.

a) $6 + 3 \times 4$ **b)** $(5 + 3) \div 2$ **c)** $18 \div 3 \times 2$

Solution

a) $6 + 3 \times 4 = 6 + 12$ Multiply first.
$= 18$ Then add.

b) $(5 + 3) \div 2 = 8 \div 2$ Add in brackets first.
$= 4$ Then divide.

c) $18 \div 3 \times 2 = 6 \times 2$ Divide first.
$= 12$ Then multiply.

✓ Check

1. Simplify.

a) $5 \times 7 + 2$ **b)** $5 \times (7 + 2)$ **c)** $13 + 2 \times 8$

d) $13 + 2 - 8$ **e)** $13 + 8 \div 2$ **f)** $13 - 8 \div 2$

g) $12 \div 4 + 2$ **h)** $12 \div (4 + 2)$ **i)** $12 + 4 \div 2$

2. a) Simplify.

i) $3 + 4 \times 2 + 5$ **ii)** $3 \times 4 + 2 \times 5$ **iii)** $3 \times (4 + 2) \times 5$

iv) $3 \times (4 + 2) + 5$ **v)** $3 \times 4 \times 2 + 5$ **vi)** $3 + 4 + 2 \times 5$

b) All the expressions in part a have the same numbers and the same operations. Why are the answers different?

Graphing on a Coordinate Grid

(3, 2) is an **ordered pair**. It tells the position of a point on a grid.
In an ordered pair, the first number is the horizontal distance from the origin, O.
The second number is the vertical distance from the origin.
We use a letter to label a point.
To plot point A(3, 2), start at 3 on the horizontal axis, then move up 2.
To plot point B(1, 4), start at 1 on the horizontal axis, then move up 4.

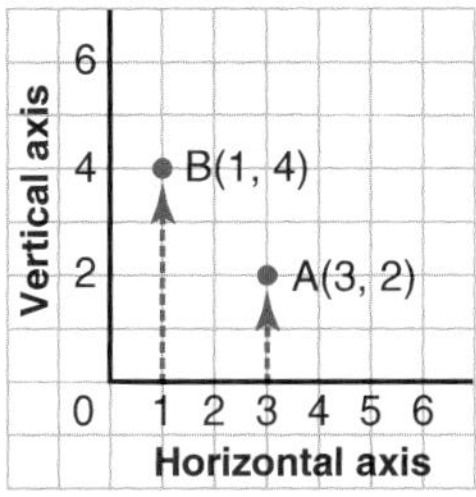

The numbers in an ordered pair are also called the coordinates of a point.

3. Write the ordered pair for each point on the grid.

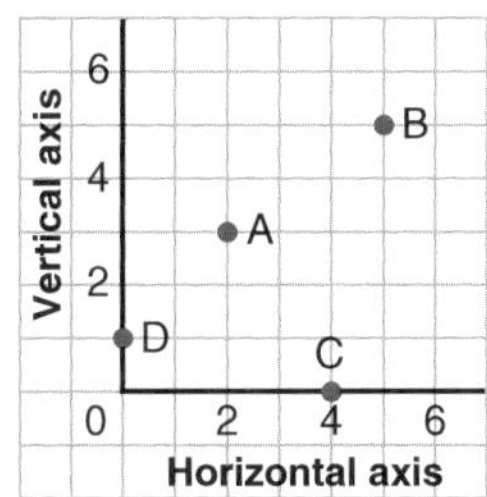

4. On graph paper, draw a grid.
Plot and label these points:
A(2, 9), B(5, 3), C(8, 8), D(0, 10)

5. The graph shows the money earned for the time worked.

a) How much money was earned in 4 h?

b) How long will it take to earn $12.00?

c) What is the hourly rate of pay?

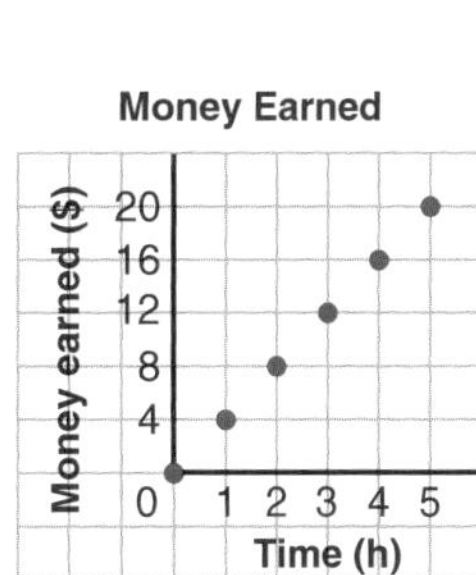

10.1 Number Patterns

Focus Extend patterns and use them to make predictions.

Explore

Work with a partner.

➢ Suppose this pattern continues.

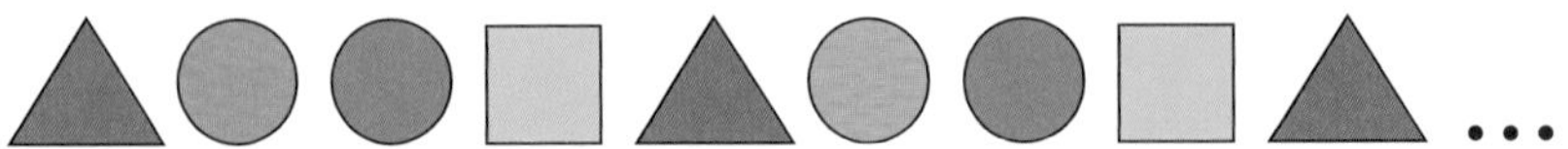

Describe the pattern.
What is the next figure in the pattern?
What is the 17th figure?
How can you find out without drawing 17 figures?

➢ Suppose this pattern continues.

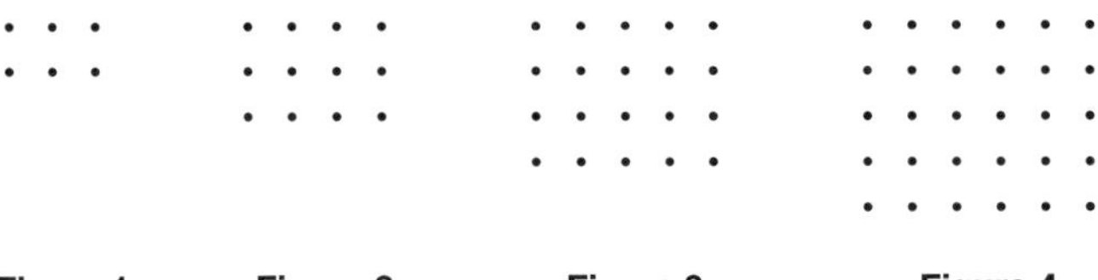

Figure 1 Figure 2 Figure 3 Figure 4

Describe the pattern.
What is the next figure in the pattern?
How many dots will there be in the 15th figure?
How can you find out without drawing 15 figures?

Reflect & Share

How are the two patterns the same?
How are they different?
Compare your answers with those of another pair of classmates.
Did you use the same strategies to answer the questions? Explain.

Connect

Here is a pattern of triangles.

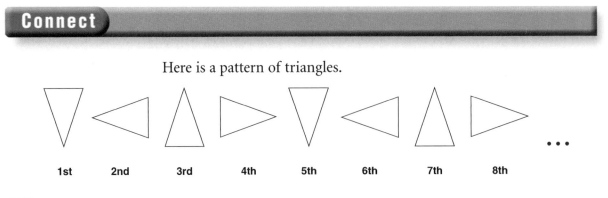

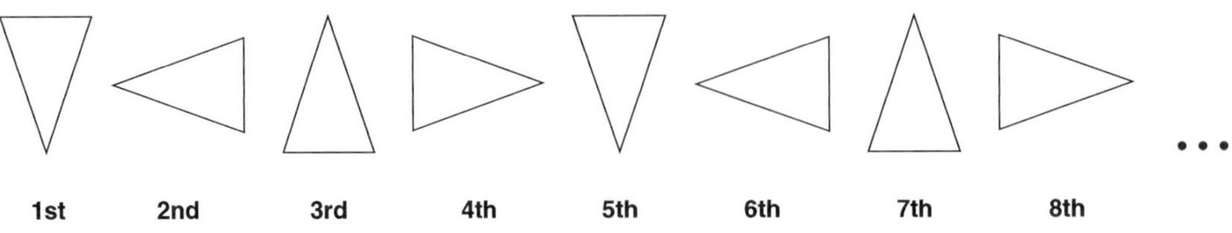

The pattern is made up of different positions of an isosceles triangle.
To get the next term each time, rotate the triangle a $\frac{1}{4}$ turn clockwise about its centre.
The core of the pattern is 4 triangles.
The 5th term is the same as the 1st term.
The 6th term is the same as the 2nd term, and so on.
To find any term in the pattern, we find which of the first 4 terms it matches.
Think of multiples of 4: 4, 8, 12, 16, 20, 24, 28, …
All the 4th, 8th, 12th, 16th, 20th, 24th, 28th, … terms have the triangle pointing to the right.

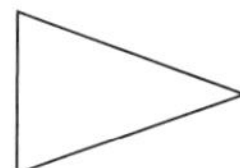

To find the 99th term, we find the closest multiple of 4.
100 is a multiple of 4, so the 100th term is the same as the 4th term.
The 99th term will be the same as the 3rd term:

The 99th term is the triangle pointing up.

We can use the same ideas to make predictions with number patterns.

Example

Each pattern continues.

i) Describe each pattern.
ii) Write the next 3 terms.
iii) Find the 50th term.

a) 4, 7, 10, 13, … **b)** 1, 4, 9, 16, …

Solution

a) 4, 7, 10, 13, …

i) The pattern begins with 4.
To get the next term, add 3 each time.

ii) The next 3 terms are: $13 + 3 = 16$
$16 + 3 = 19$
$19 + 3 = 22$

The next 3 terms are 16, 19, 22.

iii) Since the terms increase by 3 each time, compare the pattern with multiples of 3.

Pattern: 4, 7, 10, 13, 16, 19, 22, …

Multiples of 3: 3, 6, 9, 12, 15, 18, 21, …

Each term in the pattern is 1 more than a multiple of 3.

So, the terms in the pattern are multiples of 3, plus 1.

The 1st term: $1 \times 3 + 1 = 4$

The 2nd term: $2 \times 3 + 1 = 7$

The 3rd term: $3 \times 3 + 1 = 10$

The 4th term: $4 \times 3 + 1 = 13$, and so on

⋮ ⋮

The 50th term: $50 \times 3 + 1 = 151$

The 50th term is 151.

b) 1, 4, 9, 16, …

i) The pattern begins with 1.

To get the 2nd term, add 3.

To get the 3rd term, add 5.

To get the 4th term, add 7.

To get each successive term, increase the number you add by 2 each time.

ii) The next 3 terms are: $16 + 9 = 25$

$25 + 11 = 36$

$36 + 13 = 49$

The next 3 terms are 25, 36, 49.

Recall that a perfect square is the product of a number and itself.

iii) To use the same method to get the 50th term, we would need to know the 49th term and what to add.

So, we look at the pattern a different way.

The pattern is: 1, 4, 9, 16, 25, 36, 49, …

These are the perfect squares: $1^2, 2^2, 3^2, 4^2, 5^2, 6^2, 7^2, \ldots$

So, the 50th term is: $50^2 = 2500$

The 50th term is 2500.

Practice

1. This pattern continues.

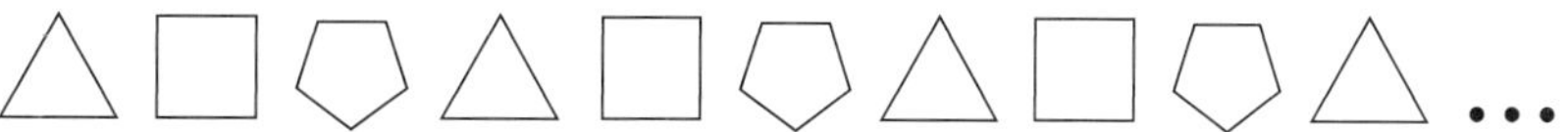

a) Describe the pattern.

b) Sketch the next 3 terms.

c) Sketch the 29th term and the 49th term.

2. This pattern continues.

 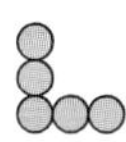 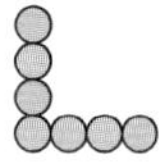 ...

a) Describe the pattern.

b) Sketch the next 3 terms.

c) Describe the 18th term and the 38th term.
Sketch them if you can.

3. For each pattern:

i) Describe the pattern.

ii) Write the next 3 terms.

iii) Find the 40th term. Explain how you found it.

a) 6, 9, 12, 15, ... b) 6, 10, 14, 18, ... c) 6, 11, 16, 21, ...

4. There is a pattern in the patterns in question 3.
Write the first 5 terms of the next pattern. Justify your answer.

5. For each pattern:

i) Describe the pattern.

ii) Write the next 3 terms.

iii) Find the 20th term.

a) 2, 4, 8, 16, ... b) 3, 6, 12, 24, ...

6. Look at the patterns below.
How are they the same? How are they different?

i) Write the next 3 terms for each pattern.

ii) Write the 20th term in each pattern.

a) 2, 5, 10, 17, 26, ... b) 0, 3, 8, 15, 24, ...

Mental Math

Estimate each product.
Order the products from least to greatest.

- 24.8 × 3.2
- 35.23 × 2.89
- 13.21 × 5.78
- 5.5 × 15.5

What strategies did you use?

7. This pattern continues.

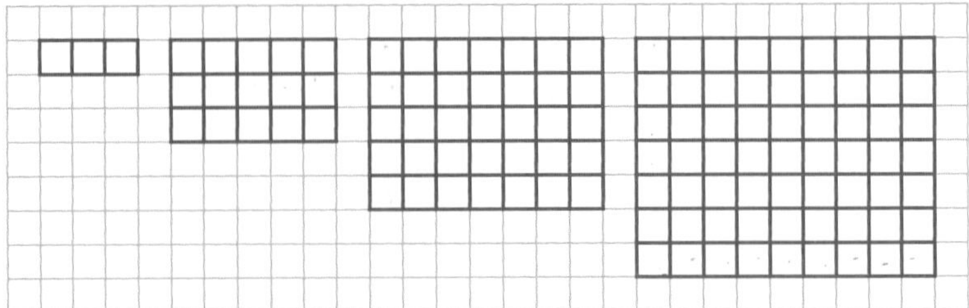

a) Describe the pattern.
b) Sketch the next 3 terms.
c) Describe the 17th term and the 37th term.
Sketch them if you can.

8. **Assessment Focus** Create two different number patterns.
Each pattern must contain the numbers 12 and 32.
Describe each pattern in words.
Write the next 4 terms in each pattern.

Take It Further

9. a) Describe this pattern. The pattern continues.
b) How many squares would be in the 10th figure?
c) What are the perimeters of the 4th figure and 5th figure?
d) What is the perimeter of the 10th figure?
e) How many squares are there in the figure with perimeter 72?
f) Could you make one of the figures using exactly 27 small squares? Explain.

Use a geoboard and geoband if they help.

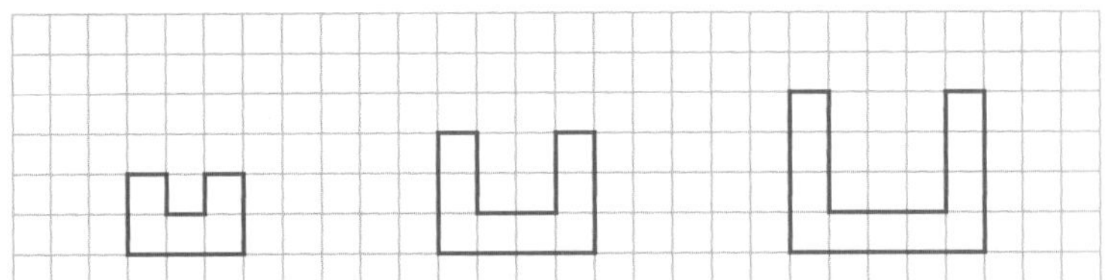

10. Create two different number patterns that contain the numbers 16, 20, and 25. Write the first 5 terms in each pattern.

Reflect

Describe how you identify a number pattern.
Use two different examples from this lesson.

10.2 Graphing Patterns

Focus Use a table and a graph to describe a pattern.

Explore

Work with a partner.
You will need grid paper.
One CD costs $10.

➢ Copy and complete this table.
Find the cost for up to 10 CDs.

➢ Graph the data in the table.

Number of CDs	Cost ($)
0	
2	
4	
6	
8	
10	

Reflect & Share

Describe the patterns in the table.
How are these patterns shown in the graph?

Connect

We can use a table and a graph to illustrate number patterns.
Recall this pattern from *Section 10.1, Example, page 369.*

Term 1: 4
Term 2: 7
Term 3: 10
Term 4: 13
Term 5: 16
Term 6: 19

We write these terms in a table.

Term Number	Term Value
1	4
2	7
3	10
4	13
5	16
6	19

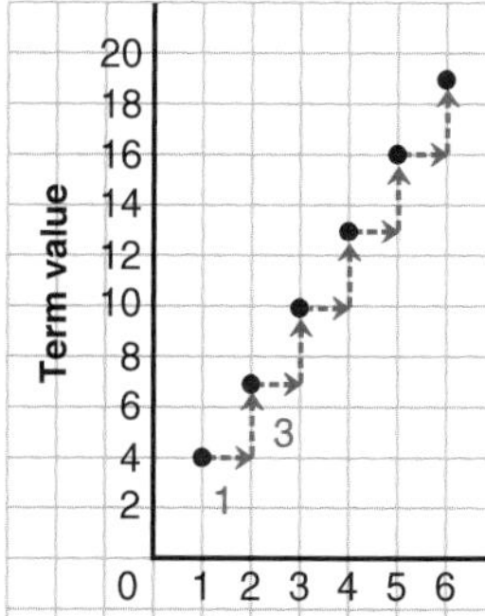

We plot these data on a graph.
The *Term number* is plotted on the horizontal axis.
The *Term value* is plotted on the vertical axis.

The graph is a set of points that lie on a straight line.
To get from one point to the next, move 1 unit right and 3 units up.
Moving 1 unit right is the same as adding 1 in the first column to get the next term number.
Moving 3 units up is the same as adding 3 in the second column to get the next term value.

We can use a table related to an Input/Output machine to make a pattern.

Example 1

a) Complete the table for this pattern:
Multiply each number by 2, then add 3.

b) Graph the pattern.
Explain how the graph shows the pattern.

Input	Output
1	
2	
3	
4	
5	

Solution

Input	Output
1	5
2	7
3	9
4	11
5	13

a) Multiply each Input number by 2, then add 3.
$1 \times 2 + 3 = 5$
$2 \times 2 + 3 = 7$
$3 \times 2 + 3 = 9$
$4 \times 2 + 3 = 11$
$5 \times 2 + 3 = 13$

b) The points lie on a straight line.
To get from one point to the next, move 1 unit right and 2 units up.
Moving 1 unit right is the same as adding 1 to an Input number to get the next Input number.
Moving 2 units up is the same as adding 2 to an Output number to get the next Output number.

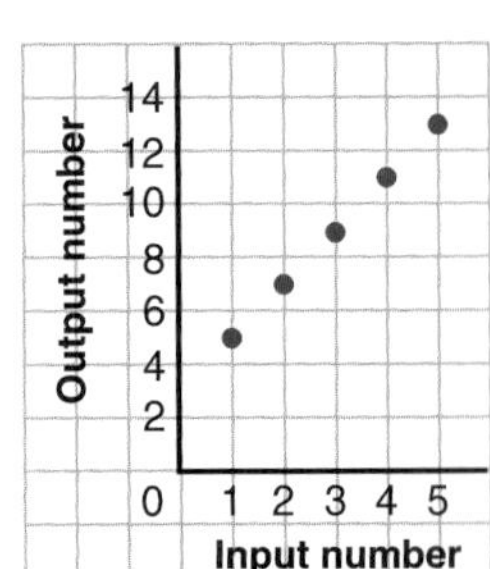

Example 2

a) Describe the patterns in this table.

b) Use the patterns to extend the table 3 more rows.

c) Graph the table in part b. Explain how the graph shows the patterns.

Input	Output
1	10
2	9
3	8
4	7
5	6

Solution

a) The numbers in the Input column start at 1 and increase by 1 each time.
The numbers in the Output column start at 10 and decrease by 1 each time.
The sum of matching Input and Output numbers is 11.

b) The next 3 Input numbers are 6, 7, 8.
The next 3 Output numbers are 5, 4, 3.

Input	Output
1	10
2	9
3	8
4	7
5	6
6	5
7	4
8	3

c) The graph is a set of points that lie on a straight line.

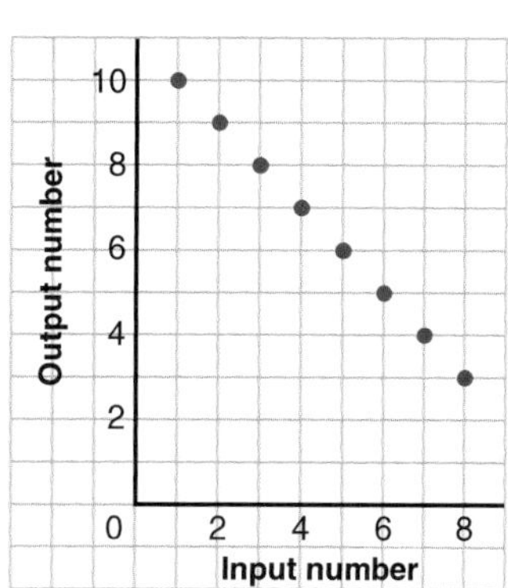

The line goes down to the right.
As the Input numbers increase from 1 to 8, the Output numbers decrease from 10 to 3.

Practice

Input	Output
1	
2	
3	
4	
5	

1. Copy and complete this table for each pattern.

a) Multiply each Input number by 3.
b) Add 2 to each Input number.
c) Multiply each Input number by 3, then add 2.
d) Add 2 to each Input number, then multiply by 3.

2. Copy and complete this table for each pattern.

a) Divide each Input number by 10.
b) Subtract 3 from each Input number.
c) Divide each Input number by 10, then subtract 3.

Input	Output
100	
80	
60	
40	
20	

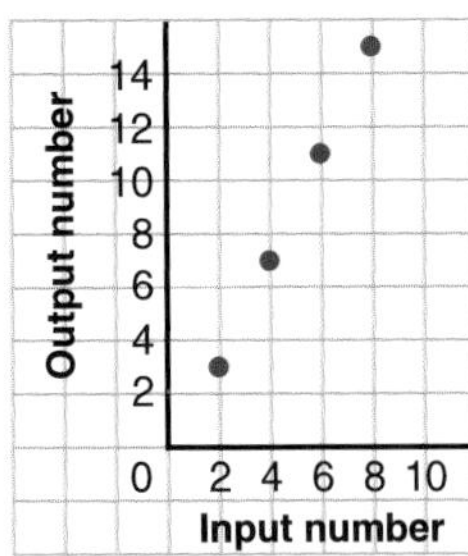

3. Look at this graph.
   a) Make an Input/Output table for the graph.
   b) What patterns do you see in the table?
   c) Extend the table 3 more rows. Explain how you did this.

4. The students at a school sell pins at a school fair to raise money for charity.
   The students charge $1.50 per pin.
   a) Copy and complete this table.
   b) Graph the data in the table in part a.
   c) Suppose you know how many pins were sold.
      How can you find how much money was collected:
      i) by using the table?   ii) by using the graph?

Number of Pins	Money Collected
10	
20	
30	
40	
50	
60	

5. For each table:
   i) Describe the pattern in the Output column.
   ii) How can you find an Output number when you know an Input number?
   iii) Write the next 3 rows in each table.

a)

Input	Output
2	6
4	8
6	10
8	12
10	14

b)

Input	Output
2	6
4	12
6	18
8	24
10	30

c)

Input	Output
2	6
4	10
6	14
8	18
10	22

6. **Assessment Focus** Mr. Francis is planning a school picnic.
   a) Mr. Francis estimates he needs 2 sandwiches for each student, plus 3 extras. Make a table for the number of sandwiches needed for 5, 10, 15, 20, 25, 30 students.
   b) Mr. Francis estimates he needs 1 drink for each student, plus 5 extras. Make a table for the number of drinks needed for up to 30 students.
   c) Draw graphs for the tables in parts a and b.
      Explain how each graph shows the patterns in the tables.

Take It Further

7. a) Copy this pattern on grid paper.
Extend the pattern to show the next 2 figures.

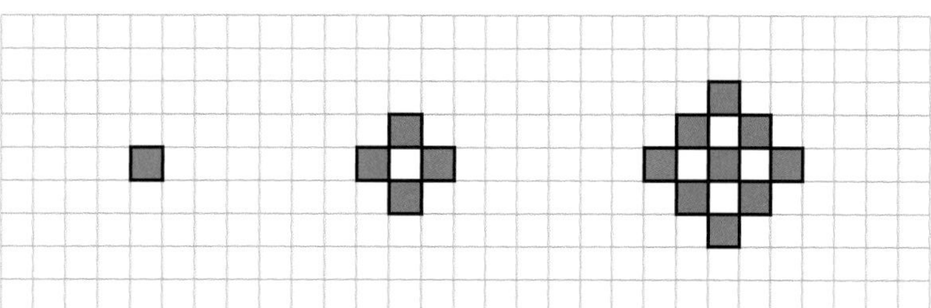

b) Copy and complete this table for the first 5 figures.

Figure Number	Number of Blue Squares

c) Draw a graph to show the data in the table.

d) How is this graph different from other graphs you have drawn?

e) How could you use the graph or the table to find the number of blue squares in the 9th figure?

Calculator Skills

Three numbers have a product of 24.5. One number is 0.25. What might the other two numbers be?

Reflect

Explain how a pattern in words can be represented by a table and a graph.
Use an example in your explanation.

Math Link

History

The word "algebra" comes from the Arabic word "al-jabr." This word appeared in the title of one of the earliest algebra texts, written around the year 825 by al-Khwarizmi. He lived in what is now Uzbekistan.

10.3 Variables in Expressions

Focus Use a variable to represent a set of numbers.

Explore

Work with a partner.
Tehya won some money in a competition.
She has two choices as to how she gets paid.
Choice 1: \$20 per week for one year
Choice 2: \$400 cash now plus \$12 per week for one year

Which method would pay Tehya more money? Explain.
For what reason might Tehya choose the method that pays less?

Reflect & Share

Work with another pair of classmates.
For each choice, write a rule you can use to calculate the total money Tehya has received at any time during the year.

Connect

Recall how we used variables in the formulas for the area and perimeter of a rectangle.

Area: $A = bh$
Perimeter: $P = 2(b + h)$

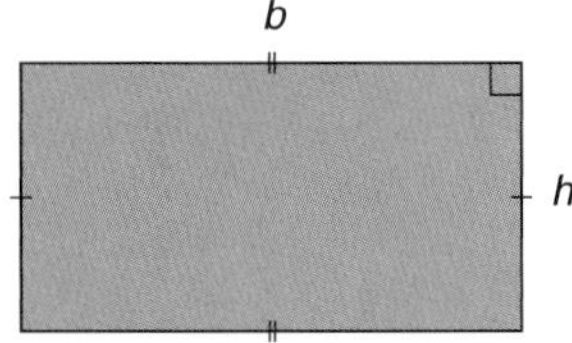

In these formulas, b represents the length of the base and h represents the height.

We can also use a variable to represent a number in an expression.
For example, we know there are 100 cm in 1 m.
There are 2×100 cm in 2 m.
There are 3×100 cm in 3 m.
To write an expression for the number of centimetres in any number of metres, we say there are $n \times 100$ cm in n metres.
n is a variable.
n represents any number we choose.

We can choose any letter as a variable.
The letters n and x are frequently used.
The expression $n \times 100$ is written $100n$.
$100n$ is an **algebraic expression.**

Variables are written in italics so they are not confused with units of measurement.

Here are some other algebraic expressions, and their meanings.
In each case, n represents the number.

- Three more than a number: $3 + n$ or $n + 3$
- Seven times a number: $7n$
- 8 less than a number: $n - 8$
- Twenty divided by a number: $\frac{20}{n}$

Example 1

A car travels at an average speed of 50 km/h.
How far will the car travel in: **a)** 3 h? **b)** t hours?

Solution

$t \times 50$ is equal to $50 \times t$, which is written $50t$.

In 1 h, the car travels 50 km.

a) In 3 h, the car travels: 3×50 km $= 150$ km

b) In t hours, the car travels: $t \times 50$ km $= 50t$ kilometres

Example 2

Write an algebraic expression for each statement.

a) the amount of money earned at $5/h

b) the perimeter of a square

c) eight more than three times a number

d) double a number and subtract 5

Solution

We often choose a letter to remind us what the variable represents.
***t* for time**
***s* for side length**
***n* for number**

For each statement, choose a variable to represent the number.

a) Let t hours represent the time worked.
Then, the amount earned is $5 \times t$, or $5t$ dollars.

b) Let s centimetres represent the side length of the square.
Then, the perimeter in centimetres is $4 \times s$, or $4s$ centimetres.

c) Let n represent the number.
Three times the number: $3n$
Then add 8: $3n + 8$

d) Let x represent the number.
Double the number means 2 times the number: $2x$
Then subtract 5: $2x - 5$

Practice

If you use x as a variable, write it so it is not confused with a multiplication sign, ×.

1. Write an algebraic expression for each statement.
   a) six more than a number
   b) a number multiplied by eight
   c) a number decreased by six
   d) a number divided by four

2. A person earns $4/h baby-sitting.
   Find the money earned for each time.
   a) 5 h   b) 8 h   c) t hours

3. Find the area of a rectangle for each length and width.
   a) length: 8 cm; width: 6 cm
   b) length: 10 cm; width: 5 cm
   c) length: l centimetres; width: w centimetres

4. A person walks at an average speed of 5 km/h.
   Find the distance walked in each time.
   a) 2 h   b) 5 h   c) t hours

Remember that the fraction bar indicates division.

5. Write each algebraic expression in words.
   Use the words "a number" in place of the variable.
   a) $n + 8$ b) $6a$ c) $\frac{p}{5}$
   d) $k - 11$ e) $27 - n$ f) x^2

6. Write an algebraic expression for each statement.
   a) Double a number and add three.
   b) Subtract five from a number, then multiply by two.
   c) Subtract one-half of a number from 17.
   d) Divide a number by seven, then add six.
   e) A number is subtracted from twenty-eight.
   f) Twenty-eight is subtracted from a number.

7. a) Write each expression in words.
      i) $(40 - 3)r$ ii) $40 - 3r$
   b) How are the expressions and statements in part a similar? Different?

Number Strategies

The regular price of a pair of running shoes is $74.99. What is the sale price in each case?

- 50% off
- 25% off
- 30% off
- 70% off

8. a) Write an algebraic expression for each statement.

i) three more than a number

ii) a number added to three

iii) three less than a number

iv) a number subtracted from three

b) How are the expressions in part a alike?
How are they different? Explain.

9. Write each expression in words.

a) $6h + 5$ b) $\frac{(n-3)}{4}$ c) $\frac{t}{4} + 12$

d) $3(x - 3)$ e) $32 - \frac{w}{5}$ f) $\frac{w}{5} - 32$

10. **Assessment Focus**

a) Use the cards below to make an algebraic expression for each statement. Write the expression.

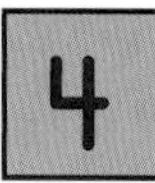

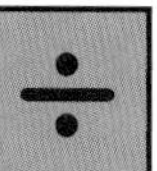

i) nine times a number subtract 4

ii) the sum of four times a number and nine

iii) a number plus five

iv) nine more than one-quarter of a number

b) Create two more expressions using the cards.
Write each expression in words.

Show your work.

11. A pizza with cheese and tomato toppings costs $8.00.
There is a cost of $1 for each extra topping.
Write an algebraic expression for the cost of a pizza with *e* extra toppings.

Reflect

Why do we write algebraic expressions? How are they useful?

Mid-Unit Review

LESSON

10.1 **1.** For each pattern:

i) Describe the pattern.
ii) Write the next 3 terms.
iii) Find the 10th term.

a) 5, 8, 11, 14, …
b) 14, 25, 36, 47, …
c) 1, 8, 27, 64, …
d) 1, 3, 7, 15, 31, …

2. a) Describe this pattern.

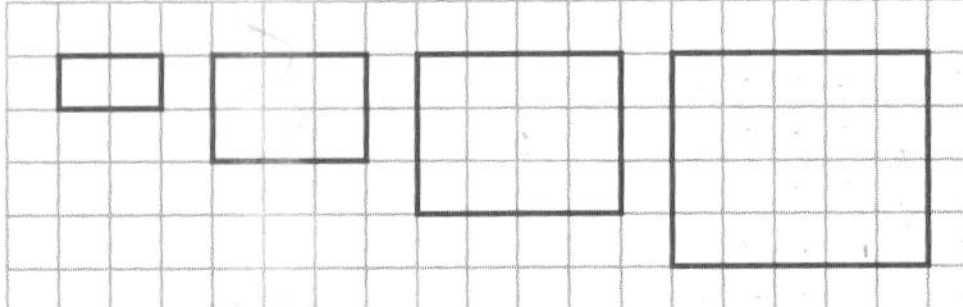

The pattern continues.

b) Write the dimensions of the next 2 rectangles.
c) Write the areas of the first 5 rectangles.
d) What are the dimensions and area of the 19th rectangle?
e) Which rectangle has area 110 square units?

10.2 **3.** a) Complete the table in the next column for this pattern: Multiply each term by 4, then subtract 1.

b) Graph the pattern. Explain how the graph shows the pattern.

Input	Output
1	
2	
3	
4	
5	
6	

4. a) Describe the pattern in the Output column.

b) How can you find an output number when you know an input number?

Input	Output
1	8
2	11
3	14
4	17
5	20
6	23

c) Write the next 3 rows in the table.
d) Graph the table. Explain how the graph shows the pattern.

10.3 **5.** Write an algebraic expression for each statement.

a) eleven more than a number
b) four less than a number
c) a number divided by three
d) a number multiplied by nine
e) the sum of five times a number, and 2
f) seventeen more than two times a number

6. Write each expression in words. Use the words "a number" in place of each variable.

a) $n + 3$ b) $21 - h$ c) $9n$ d) $\frac{a}{4}$

10.4 Evaluating Algebraic Expressions

Focus Substitute a number for a variable in an algebraic expression.

Explore

Work with a partner.
Ms. Prasad plans to hold a party for a group of her friends.
The cost of renting a room is \$25.
The cost of food is \$3 per person.
Which algebraic expression gives the total cost, in dollars, of the party for n people?

$3 + 25n$ $\quad$ $28n$ $\quad$ $28 + n$ $\quad$ $25 + 3n$

Check your answer by finding the cost for 10 people.

Reflect & Share

Compare your answer with that of another pair of classmates.
How did you decide which expression was correct?
How does the expression change in each of the following cases?

- The cost of food doubles.
- The rent of the room doubles.

Connect

When we replace a variable with a number, we substitute a number for the variable.

When we replace a variable with a number in an algebraic expression, we **evaluate** the expression. That is, we find the value of the expression for a particular value of the variable.

Recall the work you did in *Unit 6 Measuring Perimeter and Area.*
You substituted numbers for variables in the formulas for area and perimeter.
We use the same method to evaluate algebraic expressions.

Example

Write each algebraic expression in words.
Then evaluate for the value of the variable given.

a) $5k + 2$ for $k = 3$ $\qquad$ **b)** $\frac{(x - 3)}{5}$ for $x = 13$

Solution

5*k* means $5 \times k$.

a) $5k + 2$ means 5 times a number, then add 2.
Replace k with 3 in the expression $5k + 2$.
Use the order of operations.

$5k + 2 = 5 \times 3 + 2$ Multiply first.
$= 15 + 2$ Add.
$= 17$

b) $\frac{(x-3)}{5}$ means subtract 3 from a number, then divide by 5.
Replace x with 13.

$\frac{(x-3)}{5} = \frac{(13-3)}{5}$ Do the operation in brackets first.
$= \frac{10}{5}$ Divide.
$= 2$

Recall that a variable is a symbol that can represent a set of numbers. If we substitute consecutive numbers in an algebraic expression, we get a pattern.
Use the algebraic expression $3n + 2$.
Substitute $n = 1, 2, 3, 4$, and 5.

When $n = 1$, $3n + 2 = 3(1) + 2$
$= 3 + 2$
$= 5$

When $n = 2$, $3n + 2 = 3(2) + 2$
$= 6 + 2$
$= 8$

When $n = 3$, $3n + 2 = 3(3) + 2$
$= 9 + 2$
$= 11$

When $n = 4$, $3n + 2 = 3(4) + 2$
$= 12 + 2$
$= 14$

When $n = 5$, $3n + 2 = 3(5) + 2$
$= 15 + 2$
$= 17$

Use the values of n as the Input.
Use the values of $3n + 2$ as the Output.
Then, write the patterns in a table.
To get each Output number, multiply the Input number by 3, then add 2.

Input n	Output $3n + 2$
1	5
2	8
3	11
4	14
5	17

Practice

Mental Math

Find each sum.

- (–2) + (+10)
- (–6) + (–9)
- (+8) + (–7)
- (+11) + (+7)

1. Evaluate each expression by replacing x with 4.

a) $x + 5$ b) $3x$ c) $2x - 1$
d) $\frac{x}{2}$ e) $3x + 1$ f) $20 - 2x$

2. Evaluate each expression by replacing z with 7.

a) $z + 12$ b) $10 - z$ c) $\frac{(z+5)}{2}$
d) $3(z - 1)$ e) $35 - 2z$ f) $3 + \frac{z}{7}$

3. Write each algebraic expression in words.
Then, evaluate the expression for $n = 3$.

a) $n - 1$ b) $5n + 2$ c) $\frac{n}{3} + 5$
d) $n + 1$ e) $2(n + 9)$ f) $\frac{(n + 7)}{2}$

4. Copy and complete each table. Explain how to get an Output number when you know the Input number.

a)

Input x	Output $2x$
1	
2	
3	
4	
5	

b)

Input m	Output $10 - m$
1	
2	
3	
4	
5	

c)

Input p	Output $3p + 4$
1	
2	
3	
4	
5	

5. Jason works at a local fish and chips restaurant.
He earns \$7/h during the week, and \$9/h on the weekend.

a) Jason works 8 h during the week and 12 h on the weekend. Write an expression for his earnings.

b) Jason works x hours during the week, and 5 h on the weekend. Write an algebraic expression for his earnings.

c) Jason needs \$115 to buy sports equipment.
He worked 5 h on the weekend.
How many hours does Jason need to work during the week to have the money he needs?

6. **Assessment Focus** Kouroche is organising an overnight camping trip. The cost of renting a cabin is $20. The cost of food is $9 per person.
   a) How much will the trip cost if 5 people go? 10 people go?
   b) Write an algebraic expression for the cost of the trip if p people go.
   c) Suppose the cost of food doubles. Write an expression for the total cost of the trip for p people.
   d) Suppose the cost of the cabin doubles. Write an expression for the total cost of the trip for p people.
   e) Explain why using the variable p is helpful.

7. A value of n is substituted in each expression to get the number in the box. Find each value of n.

a) $5n$	30	b) $3n - 1$	11
c) $4n + 7$	15	d) $5n - 4$	11
e) $4 + 6n$	40	f) $\frac{n}{8} + 1$	5

Take It Further

8. Each table shows patterns. Write an algebraic expression to describe how each Output relates to the Input.

a)

Input x	Output
1	3
2	6
3	9
4	12

b)

Input x	Output
1	1
2	4
3	7
4	10

c)

Input x	Output
5	2
10	7
15	12
20	17

9. Find a value for p and a value for q so that $p - 3q$ has a value of 1. How many different ways can you do this? Explain.

Reflect

Explain why it is important to use the order of operations when evaluating an algebraic expression. Use an example to explain.

10.5 Reading and Writing Equations

Focus Translate statements into equations.

Explore

Work with a partner.

- Write an algebraic expression for these statements:
  Think of a number.
  Multiply it by 3.
  Add 4.
- The answer is 13. What is the original number?

Reflect & Share

Compare your answer with that of another pair of classmates.
If you found different values for the original number, who is correct?
Can both of you be correct?
How can you check?

Connect

When we write an algebraic expression as being equal to a number, we have an **equation**.
For example, we have an algebraic expression $3x + 2$.
When we write $3x + 2 = 11$, we have an equation.
An equation is a statement that two expressions are equal.

Here is another example.
Zena bought 3 CDs.
All 3 CDs had the same price.
The total cost was \$36.
What was the cost of 1 CD?

We can write an equation for this situation.
Let p dollars represent the cost of 1 CD.
Then $3p = 36$ is an equation that represents this situation.

Example 1

Mark thinks of a number.
He multiplies the number by 2, then adds 15.
The answer is 35. Write an equation for the problem.

Solution

Let n represent the number Mark thinks of.
Multiply the number by 2: $2n$
Then add 15: $2n + 15$
The equation is: $2n + 15 = 35$

Example 2

Write an equation for each sentence.

a) Three more than a number is 15.
b) Five less than a number is 7.
c) A number subtracted from 5 is 1.
d) A number divided by 3 is 10.

Solution

a) Three more than a number is 15.
Let x represent the number.
Three more than x: $x + 3$
The equation is: $x + 3 = 15$

b) Five less than a number is 7.
Let x represent the number.
Five less than x: $x - 5$
The equation is: $x - 5 = 7$

c) A number subtracted from 5 is 1.
Let x represent the number.
x subtracted from 5: $5 - x$
The equation is: $5 - x = 1$

d) A number divided by 3 is 10.
Let x represent the number.
x divided by 3: $\frac{x}{3}$
The equation is: $\frac{x}{3} = 10$

Practice

1. Write an equation for each sentence.
   a) Eight more than a number is 12.
   b) Three times a number is 12.
   c) Eight less than a number is 12.

Mental Math

Find each difference.

- (–7) – (–3)
- (–6) – (+5)
- (+2) – (–5)
- (+5) – (+9)

2. Write a sentence for each equation.
   a) $12 + n = 19$ b) $3n = 18$ c) $12 - n = 5$ d) $\frac{n}{2} = 6$

3. Write an equation for each sentence.
   a) Five added to two times a number is 35.
   b) Eight plus one-half a number is 24.
   c) Six subtracted from three times a number is 11.

4. Write each equation in words.
   a) $5x - 7 = 37$ b) $\frac{x}{3} + 4 = 9$ c) $17 - 2x = 3$

5. Match each equation with the correct sentence.
   a) $n + 4 = 8$ A. Four less than a number is 8.
   b) $4n = 8$ B. Four more than four times a number equals 8.
   c) $4n - 4 = 8$ C. The sum of four and a number is 8.
   d) $n - 4 = 8$ D. Four less than four times a number equals 8.
   e) $4 + 4n = 8$ E. The product of four and a number is 8.

6. Alona thinks of a number. She divides the number by 4, then adds 10. The answer is 14. Write an equation for the problem.

7. **Assessment Focus** Write an equation for each sentence.
   a) Bhavin's age 7 years from now will be 20.
   b) Five times the number of students is 295.
   c) The perimeter of a rectangle with length 15 cm and width *w* centimetres is 38 cm.
   d) The cost of 2 tickets at *x* dollars each and 5 tickets at $4 each is $44.

   Which equation was the most difficult to write? Explain.

Reflect

Describe the difference between an equation and an expression. Give an example of each.

10.6 Solving Equations

Focus Solve equations by inspection and by systematic trial.

Explore

Work with a partner.
On the way home from school, 3 students get off the bus at the first stop. Seven get off at the next stop. Five get off at the next stop. Ten get off at the next stop. There are now 2 students left on the bus.
How many students were on the bus when it left the school?
How many different ways can you solve the problem?

Reflect & Share

Discuss your strategies for finding the answer with another pair of classmates.
Did you use an equation? Did you use reasoning?
Did you draw a picture? Explain.

Connect

Recall the equation about the cost of 1 CD, from *Section 10.5 Reading and Writing Equations,* page 387.
The equation is $3p = 36$, where p is the cost of 1 CD.
When we use the equation to find the value of p,
we **solve the equation.**

Here are 2 ways to solve this equation.

Method 1: By Systematic Trial
$3p = 36$
We choose a value for p and substitute.
When $p = 10$, $3p = 30$
30 is too small, so choose a greater value of p.

When $p = 20$, $3p = 60$
60 is too large, so choose a lesser value of p.

When $p = 15$, $3p = 45$
45 is too large, so choose a lesser value of p.

When $p = 12$, $3p = 36$
This is correct.
The cost of 1 CD is \$12.

Method 2: By Inspection
$3p = 36$
We find a number which, when multiplied by 3, has product 36.
We know that $3 \times 12 = 36$; so, $p = 12$.
The cost of 1 CD is \$12.

We say that the value $p = 12$ makes the equation $3p = 36$ true.
A value $p = 10$ would not make the equation true because 3×10 does not equal 36.
The value $p = 12$ is the only solution to the equation.
That is, there is only one value of p that makes the equation true.

Example 1

Solve by inspection.

a) $x + 7 = 10$
b) $\frac{24}{n} = 6$
c) $40 - y = 30$
d) $9z + 2 = 38$

Solution

a) $x + 7 = 10$
Which number added to 7 gives 10?
We know that $3 + 7 = 10$; so, $x = 3$.

b) $\frac{24}{n} = 6$
This means $24 \div n = 6$.
Which number divided into 24 gives 6?
We know that $24 \div 4 = 6$; so, $n = 4$.

c) $40 - y = 30$
Which number subtracted from 40 gives 30?
We know that $40 - 10 = 30$; so, $y = 10$.

d) $9z + 2 = 38$
9 times which number, plus 2, gives 38?
We know $36 + 2 = 38$
So, 9 times which number is 36?
We know that $9 \times 4 = 36$; so, $z = 4$.

Example 2

Solve by systematic trial.

a) $2a - 28 = 136$

b) $\frac{y}{4} = 220$

Solution

a) $2a - 28 = 136$

When the numbers are large, use a calculator.

Try $a = 50$; then, $2 \times 50 - 28 = 72$

72 is too small, so choose a greater value of a.

Try $a = 100$; then, $2 \times 100 - 28 = 172$

172 is too big, so choose a lesser value of a.

Try $a = 75$; then, $2 \times 75 - 28 = 122$

122 is too small, so choose a greater value of a.

Try $a = 80$; then, $2 \times 80 - 28 = 132$

132 is too small, but it is close to the value we want.

Try $a = 82$; then, $2 \times 82 - 28 = 136$

This is correct.

$a = 82$ is the solution.

b) $\frac{y}{4} = 220$

Use a calculator. We know the number is much greater than 220, because the number is divided by 4 to get 220.

Try $y = 1000$; then, $\frac{1000}{4} = 250$ This is too big.

Try $y = 900$; then, $\frac{900}{4} = 225$ This is closer, but still too big.

Try $y = 850$; then, $\frac{850}{4} = 212.5$ This is too small.

Try $y = 880$; then, $\frac{880}{4} = 220$ This is correct.

$y = 880$ is the solution.

We can write, then solve, an equation to solve a problem.

Example 3

Kiera shared 420 hockey cards equally among her friends.

Each friend had 105 cards.

a) Write an equation that describes this situation.

b) Solve the equation to find how many friends shared the cards.

Solution

a) Let h represent the number of friends who shared the cards.
Then, each friend had $\frac{420}{h}$ cards.
Also, each friend had 105 cards.
So, the equation is: $\frac{420}{h} = 105$

b) Solve $\frac{420}{h} = 105$ by inspection.
Think: $420 \div h = 105$
Which number divides into 420 to give the quotient 105?
We know $400 \div 4 = 100$; so, try $h = 4$.
$420 \div 4 = 105$
So, the solution is $h = 4$.
Four friends shared the cards.

Practice

1. Solve each equation.
   a) $x + 3 = 12$
   b) $y + 9 = 9$
   c) $10 + 2z = 20$
   d) $17 + 3c = 26$

2. Solve each equation.
   a) $x - 4 = 3$
   b) $10 - n = 10$
   c) $2z - 7 = 1$
   d) $13 - 4k = 5$

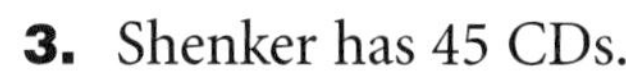

3. Shenker has 45 CDs.
   He gives 10 CDs to his brother.
   a) Write an equation you can solve to find how many CDs Shenker has left.
   b) Solve the equation.

4. Solve by inspection.
   a) $x + 4 = 15$
   b) $2k - 13 = 3$
   c) $3y = 24$
   d) $\frac{z}{9} = 2$

5. Solve by systematic trial.
   a) $n + 5 = 33$
   b) $8z = 88$
   c) $43 - 3y = 16$
   d) $\frac{x}{7} = 4$

Mental Math

Estimate.

- $\frac{1}{4}$ of 22
- $\frac{2}{5}$ of 36
- $\frac{2}{3}$ of 91
- $\frac{3}{8}$ of 79

6. The perimeter of a square is 156 cm.
   a) Write an equation you can solve to find the side length of the square.
   b) Solve the equation.

7. The side length of a regular hexagon is 9 cm.
   a) Write an equation you can solve to find the perimeter of the hexagon.
   b) Solve the equation.

8. Use questions 6 and 7 as a guide.
   a) Write your own problem about side length and perimeter of a figure.
   b) Write an equation you can use to solve the problem.
   c) Solve the equation.

9. Eli has 130 comic books.
He gives 10 to his sister, then shares the rest equally among his friends.
Each friend has 24 comic books.
   a) Write an equation you can solve to find how many friends were given comics.
   b) Solve the equation.

10. Find the value of n that makes each equation true.

a) $3n = 27$	b) $2n + 3 = 27$
c) $2n - 3 = 27$	d) $\frac{n}{3} = 27$
e) $\frac{n}{2} + 3 = 27$	f) $\frac{3n}{2} = 27$

11. Assessment Focus Write a problem that can be described by each equation. Solve each equation.
Which equation was the most difficult to solve? Explain.

a) $2x - 1 = 5$	b) $4y = 24$
c) $\frac{z}{38} = 57$	d) $5x + 5 = 30$
e) $\frac{25}{y} = 5$	f) $52 - 4 = 4x$

Reflect

How does knowing your number facts help you solve an equation by inspection? Give examples in your explanation.

The World of Work

Clothes Buyer

When you buy a pair of jeans, do you ever wonder who bought the jeans for the store to sell to you? The clothes buyer balances all kinds of purchasing variables (purchase price, quantity discounts, foreign exchange, shipping, and taxes) as well as selling variables (profit margin, the effect of price on sales, regional variations) to make the best purchase decision. If he buys too much stock, or at the wrong price, the company could end up selling the clothes at a loss. If the buyer buys too little, he misses out on sales, and customers go elsewhere. The buyer may use a spreadsheet. He can try different "what if" scenarios by changing either the variables or the formulas in the spreadsheet.

A buyer knows that the sales of an item (thousands of units per month) peak a few months after arrival and then slow down over time. However, sales of seasonal or trendy items peak almost immediately, remain steady for a couple of months, and then drop off quickly. What might graphs that show these two sales trends look like?

Choosing a Strategy

Strategies

- Make a table.
- Use a model.
- Draw a diagram.
- Solve a simpler problem.
- Work backward.
- Guess and check.
- Make an organized list.
- Use a pattern.
- Draw a graph.
- Use logical reasoning.

1. There are 2 schools. Each school has 3 buildings. Each building has 4 floors. Each floor has 5 classrooms. Each classroom has 6 rows of desks. Each row has 7 desks.
How many desks are there in the two schools?

2. **a)** Write the next three terms in this pattern: 1, 4, 3, 6, 5, 8, 7, …
b) What is the pattern rule?
c) Write the 21st and the 50th terms. Explain how you did this.

3. Here is a pattern of tiles.

a) Make a table to show the numbers of red and blue tiles in each term.
This pattern continues.
b) How many red tiles will there be in the 20th term?
c) How many blue tiles will there be in the 100th term?
d) What will be the total number of tiles in the 30th term?
e) How many red tiles will be in the term that has 48 blue tiles? How do you know?

4. A can that contains 5 red balls and 3 green balls has a mass of 43 g.
When the can contains 3 red balls and 5 green balls, the mass is 37 g.
When the can contains 1 red ball and 1 green ball, the mass is 19 g.
What is the mass of the can and each ball?

5. Marisha and Irfan have money to spend at the carnival.
If Marisha gives Irfan $5, each person will have the same amount of money. If, instead, Irfan gives Marisha $5, Marisha will have twice as much as Irfan.
How much money does each person have?

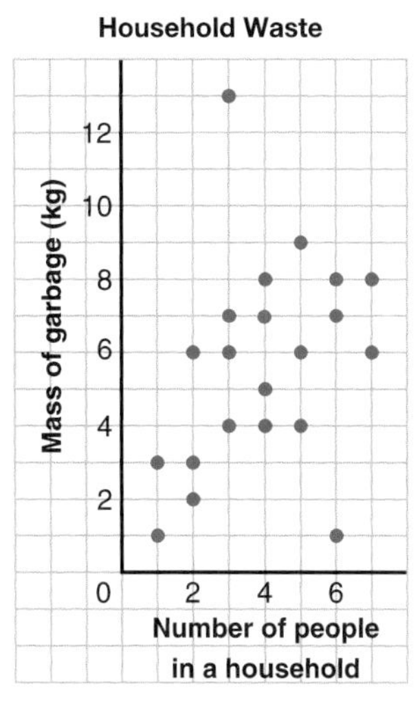

6. The graph shows the garbage put out by 21 households in one week.
   a) How does the mass of garbage relate to the number of people in the household?
   b) Give three possible reasons why one household has 13 kg of garbage.
   c) Give three possible reasons why one household has 1 kg of garbage.

7. For a school trip, the charge for using the school bus is $50. The cost of food is $10 per student.
   a) Copy and complete this table for up to 10 students.

Number of students	1	2	3	4	5
Total cost of trip ($)					

   b) What is the total cost for each number of students?
      i) 12 ii) 15 iii) 20
   c) Each person pays a fair share. What is the cost per person when each number of students goes on the trip?
      i) 5 ii) 10 iii) 15

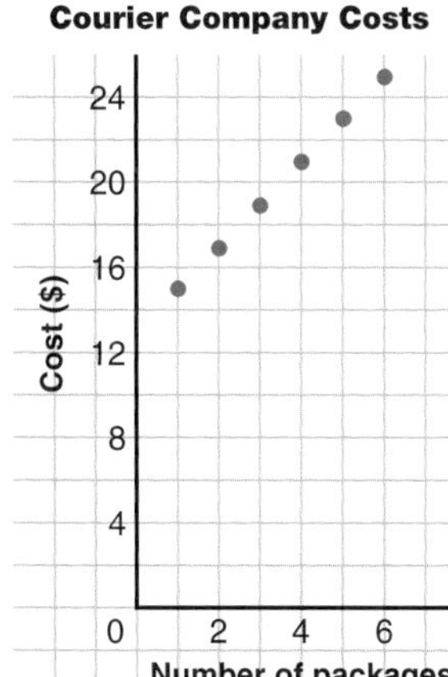

8. The graph shows the price charged by a local courier company to collect and deliver packages.
   a) What is the cost to have 6 packages collected and delivered?
   b) Extend the pattern in the graph. What is the cost to have 8 packages collected and delivered?
   c) Why does it cost $15 to collect and deliver one package, but only $17 to collect and deliver 2 packages?

9. I am a 3-digit number.
   My hundreds digit is the square of my ones digit.
   My tens digit is the product of my hundreds digit and my ones digit.
   a) What number, or numbers, could I be?
   b) What do you notice about your answer(s)?

Unit Review

Review any lesson with

What Do I Need to Know?

✓ A variable is a letter or symbol that represents a number, or a set of numbers.
A variable can be used to write an expression:
"3 more than a number" is $3 + n$.
A variable can be used to write an equation:
"4 more than a number equals 11" is $4 + n = 11$.

✓ We can solve equations by:
- inspection
- systematic trial

What Should I Be Able to Do?

For extra practice, go to page 447.

LESSON

10.1 **1.** For each pattern:
   i) Describe the pattern.
   ii) Write the next 3 terms.
   iii) Find the 20th term.
   Explain how you did this.

   a) 5, 12, 19, 26, …
   b) 3, 9, 27, 81, …
   c) 96, 93, 90, 87, …
   d) 10, 21, 32, 43, …
   e) 9, 13, 17, 21, …

2. Your favourite aunt gives you 1¢ on April 1, 2¢ on April 2, 4¢ on April 3. She continues doubling the daily amount until April 12.
   a) How much will you get on April 12?
   b) What is the total amount you will receive?

3. **a)** Describe this pattern:
   2, 5, 11, 23, 47, …
   b) Write the next 3 terms.
   c) Write a similar pattern.
   Use a different start number.

4. This pattern continues.

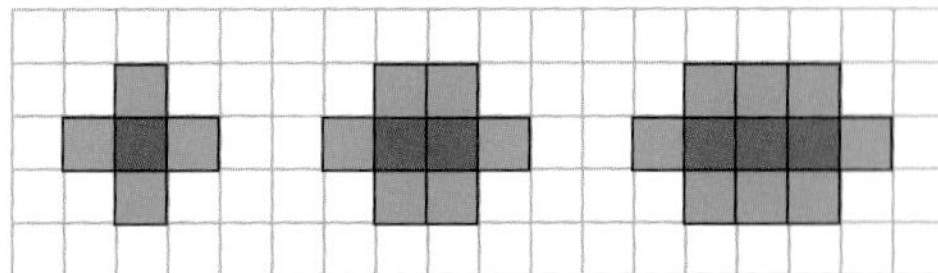

   a) Describe the pattern.
   b) Sketch the next 3 figures.
   c) Describe the 12th figure and the 22nd figure.
   Sketch them if you can.

LESSON

10.2

5. Copy and complete this table for each pattern.

Input	Output
4	
6	
8	
10	
12	

a) Add 3 to each Input number.
b) Multiply each Input number by 2.
c) Subtract 3 from each Input number.
d) Divide each Input number by 2.
e) Divide each Input number by 2, then add 3.
f) Multiply each Input number by 2, then subtract 3.

6. Look at this graph.

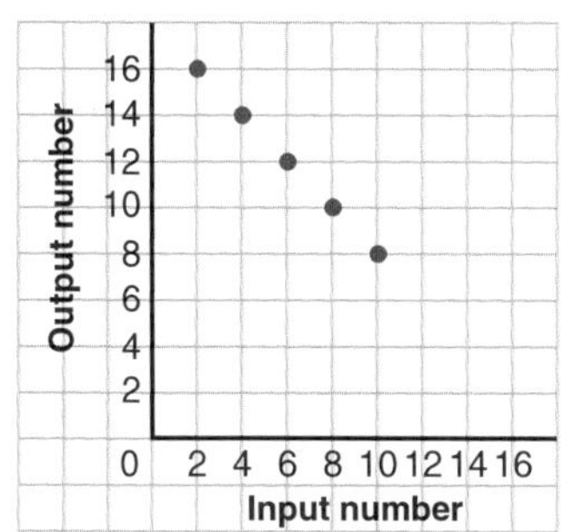

a) Make an Input/Output table for the graph.
b) What patterns do you see in the table?
c) Extend the table 3 more rows. Explain how you did this.
d) What happens if you try to extend the table further?

7. a) Describe the patterns in this table.
b) Use the patterns to extend the table 3 more rows.

Input	Output
5	1
15	3
25	5
35	7
45	9
55	11

10.3 8. Write an algebraic expression for each statement.
a) twenty more than a number
b) one less than a number
c) a number increased by ten
d) a number multiplied by thirteen

9. Write each algebraic expression in words.
a) $n + 4$
b) $25 - h$
c) $\frac{a}{5}$
d) $5 - 2n$

10.4 10. Evaluate each expression for $x = 3$.
a) $x + 8$
b) $9x$
c) $2x - 1$
d) $\frac{x}{2}$
e) $10x + 4$
f) $9 - 3x$

11. A value of n is substituted in each expression to get the number in the box. Find each value of n.
a) $5n$ 40
b) $6n - 1$ 11
c) $2n + 8$ 16
d) $3n - 4$ 14

LESSON

12. One pair of running shoes costs $70.

a) What is the cost of 3 pairs? 7 pairs?

b) What is the cost of r pairs of running shoes?

c) Write an algebraic expression for the number of pairs of shoes you could buy for d dollars.

10.5 13. Write each equation in words.

a) $x + 3 = 17$

b) $3y = 24$

c) $\frac{x}{4} = 5$

d) $3y - 4 = 20$

e) $7 + 4x = 35$

14. Write a problem that can be represented by each equation.

a) $x + 5 = 21$

b) $5n - 2 = 28$

15. Write an equation for each sentence.

a) Six times the number of people in the room is 258.

b) The area of a rectangle with length 6 cm and width w centimetres is 36 cm^2.

c) One-half of a number is 6.

16. Write a problem that can be represented by each equation.

a) $x + 2 = 23$

b) $4 - x = 12$

c) $5x = 35$

d) $\frac{x}{9} = 5$

17. Write an equation to find the length of one side of an equilateral triangle with perimeter 24 cm.

10.6 18. Solve each equation.

a) $12 = 3n$

b) $21 - n = 18$

c) $\frac{27}{n} = 9$

d) $\frac{n}{9} = 27$

e) $n - 21 = 30$

f) $3n + 2 = 11$

19. Solve each equation.

a) $17 - 3n = 2$

b) $17 + 3n = 47$

c) $3n - 17 = 4$

d) $\frac{n}{17} = 25$

20. At Queen Mary School, 98 students walk to school. There are 250 students in the school.

a) Write an equation you can solve to find how many students do not walk to school.

b) Solve the equation.

21. At Sir Robert Borden School, twice as many students take the bus as walk to school. Seventy-four students walk to school.

a) Write an equation you can solve to find how many students take the bus.

b) Solve the equation.

Practice Test

Input	Output
1	
2	
3	
4	
5	

1. a) Copy and complete the table for this pattern:
Multiply each number by 5, then subtract 3.

b) Graph the pattern.
Explain how the graph shows the pattern.

c) Extend the table 3 more rows.
Plot the point for each row on the graph.

d) How can you find the Output number when the Input number is 47?

e) How can you find the Input number when the Output number is 47?

f) Can the Input number be 100? Explain.

g) Can the Output number be 100? Explain.

2. Angelina wins money in a competition.
She is given the choice as to how she is paid.
Choice 1: Get \$1 the 1st day, \$2 the 2nd day, \$4 the 3rd day, \$8 the 4th day, and so on.
This pattern continues for 3 weeks.
Choice 2: Get \$1 000 000 today.

a) With which method of payment will Angelina get more money?

b) How did you use patterns to solve this problem?

c) After how many days will the money Angelina gets from Choice 1 be approximately \$1 000 000?

3. Here are 5 algebraic expressions: $2 + 3n$, $2n + 3$, $3n - 2$, $\frac{2n}{2}$, $\frac{3n}{2}$
Are there any values of n that will produce the same number when substituted in two or more of the expressions?
Investigate to find out. Show your work.

4. Solve each equation by systematic trial or by inspection.

a) $3x + 90 = 147$ **b)** $\frac{84}{h} = 12$

c) $\frac{26}{y} + 3 = 16$ **d)** $147 - 3x = 90$

Explain your choice of method in each case. Show your work.

Unit Problem Fund Raising

Two students raised money for charity in a bike-a-thon. The route was from Timmins to Kapuskasing, a distance of 165 km.

Part 1

Ingrid cycled at an average speed of 15 km/h.
How far does Ingrid travel in 1 h? 2 h? 3 h? 4 h? 5 h?
Record the results in a table.

Time (h)					
Distance (km)					

Graph the data in the table.
Graph *Time* horizontally and *Distance* vertically.

Write an algebraic expression for the distance Ingrid travels in t hours.
Use the expression to find how far Ingrid travels in 7 h.
How could you check your answer?

Write an equation to represent Ingrid travelling 135 km in t hours.
Solve the equation.
What have you found out?

Part 2

Liam cycled at an average speed of 20 km/h.
Repeat *Part 1* for Liam.

Part 3

How are the graphs for Ingrid and Liam alike?
How are they different?

Part 4

Ingrid's sponsors paid her $25 per kilometre.
Liam's sponsors paid him $20 per kilometre.
Make a table to show how much money each student raised for every 10 km cycled.

Distance (km)	Money Raised by Ingrid ($)	Money Raised by Liam ($)
10		
20		
30		

How much money did Ingrid raise if she cycled *d* kilometres?
How much money did Liam raise if he cycled *d* kilometres?

Liam and Ingrid raised equal amounts of money.
How far might each person have cycled? Explain.

Check List

Your work should show:

- ✓ all tables and graphs, clearly labelled
- ✓ the equations you wrote and how you solved them
- ✓ how you know your answers are correct
- ✓ explanations of what you found out

Reflect on the Unit

How are number patterns related to algebra?
How are algebraic expressions related to equations?
Give examples in your explanation.

UNIT 11

Probability

Many games involve probability and chance. One game uses this spinner or a number cube labelled 1 to 6.

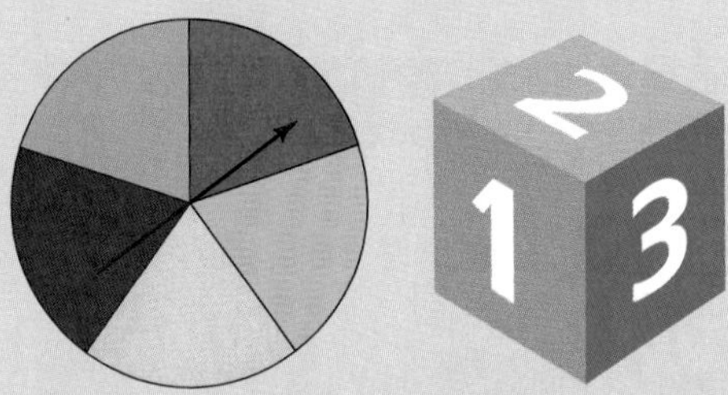

You can choose to spin the pointer or roll the number cube. You win if the pointer lands on red. You win if you roll a 6. Are you more likely to win if you spin the pointer or roll the number cube? Explain.

What You'll Learn

- Use the language of probability.
- Conduct simple experiments.
- List the possible outcomes of experiments by using tree diagrams, modelling, and lists.
- Identify possible outcomes and favourable outcomes.
- State the probability of an outcome.
- Understand how probability can relate to sports and games of chance.
- Use probability to solve problems.

Why It's Important

In the media, you hear and read statements about the probability of everyday events, such as living to be 100 or winning the lottery.
To make sense of these statements, you need to understand probability.

Key Words

- probability
- outcome
- tree diagram
- relative frequency
- experimental probability
- theoretical probability

UNIT 11

Skills You'll Need

Converting Fractions and Decimals to Percents

Percent (%) means "per hundred" or out of one hundred.

Example

Express each fraction as a decimal, then as a percent.

a) $\frac{9}{50}$ **b)** $\frac{1}{4}$ **c)** $\frac{5}{8}$ **d)** $\frac{7}{16}$

Solution

To convert a fraction to a decimal, try to write an equivalent fraction with denominator 100.

a) $\frac{9}{50} = \frac{18}{100}$ (× 2 numerator and denominator)

$\frac{18}{100} = 0.18$, or 18%

b) $\frac{1}{4} = \frac{25}{100}$ (× 25 numerator and denominator)

$\frac{25}{100} = 0.25$, or 25%

When you cannot write an equivalent fraction, use a calculator to divide.

c) $\frac{5}{8} = 5 \div 8$
$= 0.625$
$= 62.5\%$

d) $\frac{7}{16} = 7 \div 16$
$= 0.4375$
$= 43.75\%$

✓ Check

1. Express each decimal as a percent.

a) 0.1 **b)** 0.01 **c)** 0.24 **d)** 0.05

2. Express each fraction as a decimal, then as a percent.

a) $\frac{7}{10}$ **b)** $\frac{3}{5}$ **c)** $\frac{9}{25}$ **d)** $\frac{3}{4}$

3. Express each fraction as a decimal, then as a percent.

a) $\frac{7}{40}$ **b)** $\frac{3}{8}$ **c)** $\frac{13}{16}$ **d)** $\frac{51}{200}$

11.1 Listing Outcomes

Focus Investigate outcomes of experiments.

When you roll a number cube, the outcomes are equally likely.
For a spinner with sectors of equal areas, when the pointer is spun, the outcomes are equally likely.

Explore

Work with a partner. You will need a number cube labelled 1 to 6, and a spinner similar to the one shown below.

List the possible outcomes of rolling the number cube and spinning the pointer.
How many outcomes include rolling a 4?
How many outcomes include landing on red?
How many outcomes have an even number on the cube and the pointer landing on blue?

Reflect & Share

Compare the strategy you used to find the outcomes with that of another pair of classmates.
Was one strategy more efficient than another? Explain.

Connect

An outcome is the possible result of an experiment or an action.
When a coin is tossed, the possible outcomes are heads or tails.
To show the possible outcomes for an experiment that has two or more actions, we can use a **tree diagram**.

When 2 coins are tossed, the outcomes for each coin are heads (H) or tails (T).
List the outcomes of the first coin toss.
For each outcome, list the outcomes of the second coin toss.
Then list the outcomes for the coins tossed together.

1st Coin	2nd Coin	Outcomes
H	H	HH
	T	HT
T	H	TH
	T	TT

There are 4 possible outcomes: HH, HT, TH, TT

Example

Farah tosses a coin and spins the pointer on this spinner.

a) Draw a tree diagram to show the possible outcomes.
b) List all the possible outcomes.
c) How many outcomes include the pointer landing on pink?
d) How many outcomes include tails?

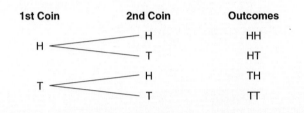

Solution

a) The sectors on the spinner have equal areas, so the outcomes are equally likely.
The possible outcomes for the spinner are: pink (P), yellow (Y), or blue (B).
For each colour, the possible outcomes for tossing the coin are: heads (H) or tails (T)

Spinner	Coin	Outcomes
P	H	PH
	T	PT
Y	H	YH
	T	YT
B	H	BH
	T	BT

b) The outcomes are: pink/heads, pink/tails, yellow/heads, yellow/tails, blue/heads, blue/tails
c) There are two outcomes with the colour pink: pink/heads, pink/tails
d) There are three outcomes with tails: pink/tails, yellow/tails, blue/tails

Practice

1. List the possible outcomes in each case.
   a) spinning the pointer

   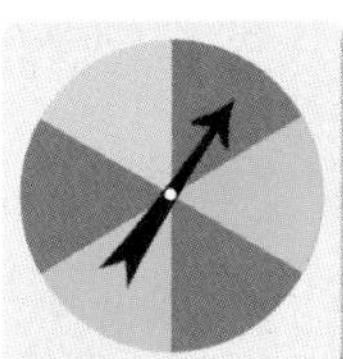

   b) rolling a number cube labelled 1 to 6

2. List the possible outcomes in each case.
   a) the colour of a traffic light when you reach it
   b) the gender of a baby who is born
   c) the points scored in a hockey game
   d) the suit of a card pulled from a deck of playing cards

3. The Scenic Railroad sells tickets for trips on Saturdays and Sundays. All-day and half-day trips are available. There are adult, child, and senior fares. Draw a tree diagram to show the possible ticket types.

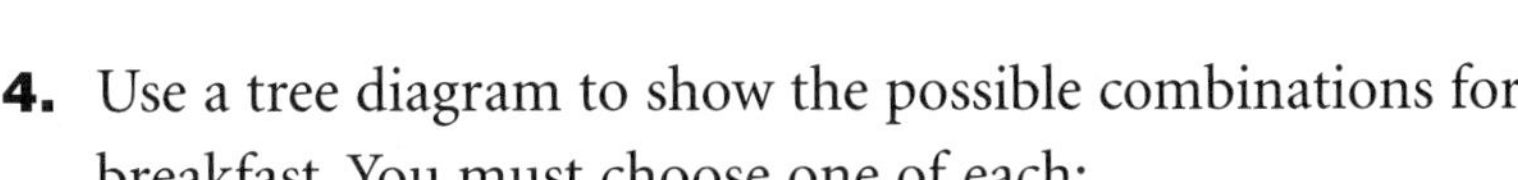

4. Use a tree diagram to show the possible combinations for breakfast. You must choose one of each:
   - eggs or fruit
   - toast, pancakes, or cereal
   - milk or juice

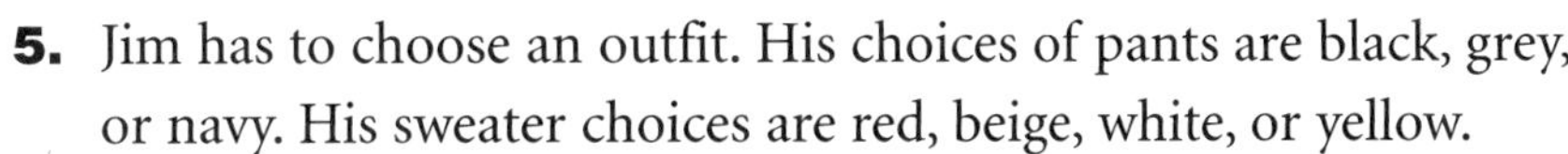

5. Jim has to choose an outfit. His choices of pants are black, grey, or navy. His sweater choices are red, beige, white, or yellow.
   a) Draw a tree diagram to display all the possible outfits.
   b) How many outfits have either black pants or a white sweater?
   c) How many outfits do not have black pants or do not have a white sweater?
   d) How many outfits have a black sweater?

Mental Math

Simplify.

- $(-3) + (+5)$
- $(-3) + (-5)$
- $(+3) + (-5)$
- $(+3) - (+5)$

6. A deli offers 2 soups, 4 salads, 5 sandwiches, and 3 beverages. How many choices are there for a customer who wants each of the following meals?
   a) a salad and a beverage
   b) soup, a sandwich, and a beverage
   c) soup, a salad, and a beverage
   d) a sandwich or salad, and a soup

7. Assessment Focus

a) Copy and complete this table.
Show the sums when two number cubes are rolled.

When one cube shows 1 and the other cube shows 4, then the sum is 5.

Sum of Numbers on Two Cubes

Number on Cube	1	2	3	4	5	6
1	2	3	4	5	6	7
2						
3						
4						
5						
6						

b) How many different outcomes are there for the sum of the numbers on the cubes?
c) In how many ways can the sum be 6?
d) In how many ways can the sum be 9?
e) In how many ways can the sum be 2 or 12?
f) Why do you think 7 is a lucky number?
g) Draw a tree diagram to show these results. Why do you think a table was used instead of a tree diagram?

Show your work.

Take It Further

8. A lock combination comprises the four digits from 1 to 4 in any order.
How many possible combinations are there in each case?
a) The digits cannot repeat within the code.
b) The digits can repeat within the code.

Reflect

Explain why a tree diagram is helpful to list the outcomes of an experiment.

11.2 Experimental Probability

Focus Determine probability from experiments.

Explore

Work with a partner.
You will need a coin.
When you toss a coin, which outcome do you think is more likely?
Do you think the outcomes are equally likely? Explain.

Outcome	Tally	Frequency
Heads		
Tails		

➢ Toss the coin 50 times.
How many times do you think you will get heads?
Record the results in a table.

➢ Write the number of heads as a fraction of the total number of tosses.
Write the number of tails as a fraction of the total number of tosses.
Add the fractions. What do you notice?

Reflect & Share

How do the results compare with your prediction?
Combine your results with those of another pair of classmates.
This is same as tossing the coin 100 times.
Write the new fractions for 100 tosses.
Add the fractions. What do you notice?

Connect

The **relative frequency** is the number of times an outcome occurs divided by the total number of times the experiment is conducted.

$$\text{Relative frequency} = \frac{\text{Number of times an outcome occurs}}{\text{Number of times experiment is conducted}}$$

The relative frequency may be written as a fraction, a decimal, or a percent. Relative frequency is also called **experimental probability**.

When a thumbtack is dropped, it can land with its point up or on its side.
Here are the results of 100 drops:

Outcome	Frequency
Point up	46
On its side	54

$$\text{Relative frequency of Point up} = \frac{\text{Number of times Point up}}{\text{Total number of drops}}$$
$$= \frac{46}{100}\text{, or } 0.46$$

$$\text{Relative frequency of On its side} = \frac{\text{Number of times On its side}}{\text{Total number of drops}}$$
$$= \frac{54}{100}\text{, or } 0.54$$

Outcome	Frequency	Relative Frequency
Point up	46	0.46
On its side	54	0.54

The sum of the relative frequencies for an experiment is 1.
That is, $\frac{46}{100} + \frac{54}{100} = 0.46 + 0.54$
$= 1$

Example

The number of times a player goes up to bat is referred to as the player's "at bats."
This table shows the number of at bats and hits for some of the greatest players in the Baseball Hall of Fame.

In baseball, a "batting average" is a relative frequency.

a) Calculate the batting average for each player.
b) Order the players from greatest to least batting average.

Players in Baseball Hall of Fame		
Player	**At Bats**	**Hits**
Aaron	12 364	3771
Cobb	11 429	4191
Gehrig	8 001	2721
Jackson	9 864	2584
Mantle	8 102	2415
Mays	10 881	3283

Solution

a) To calculate each player's batting average, divide the number of hits by the number of at bats.
Round each batting average to 3 decimal places.

Use a calculator to write each fraction as a decimal.

$\text{Aaron} = \frac{3771}{12\,364} \doteq 0.305$ $\text{Cobb} = \frac{4191}{11\,429} \doteq 0.367$

$\text{Gehrig} = \frac{2721}{8001} \doteq 0.340$ $\text{Jackson} = \frac{2584}{9864} \doteq 0.262$

$\text{Mantle} = \frac{2415}{8102} \doteq 0.298$ $\text{Mays} = \frac{3283}{10\,881} \doteq 0.302$

b) The batting averages, from greatest to least, are:
0.367, 0.340, 0.305, 0.302, 0.298, 0.262
The players, from greatest to least batting average, are:
Cobb, Gehrig, Aaron, Mays, Mantle, and Jackson

Practice

Name	At Bats	Hits
Yang Hsi	58	26
Aki	41	20
David	54	23
Yuk Yee	36	11
Eli	49	18
Aponi	42	15
Leah	46	22
Devadas	45	17

1. This table shows data for a baseball team.
Find the batting average of each player.
Round each answer to 3 decimal places.

2. Write each relative frequency as a decimal to 3 decimal places.
  a) A telemarketer made 200 phone calls and 35 new customers signed up. What is the relative frequency of getting a customer? Not getting a customer?
  b) A quality controller tested 175 light bulbs and found 5 defective. What is the relative frequency of finding a defective bulb? Finding a good bulb?

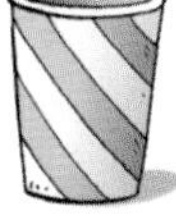

3. A paper cup is tossed.
The cup lands with the top up 27 times, the top down 32 times, and on its side 41 times.
  a) What are the possible outcomes of tossing a paper cup?
  b) Are the outcomes equally likely? Explain.
  c) State the relative frequency of each outcome.

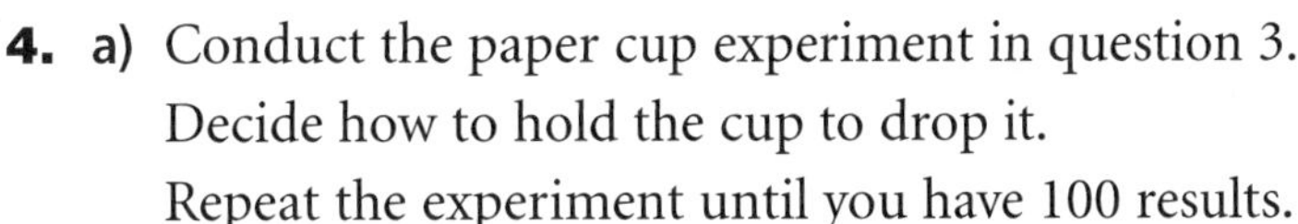

4. a) Conduct the paper cup experiment in question 3.
Decide how to hold the cup to drop it.
Repeat the experiment until you have 100 results.
  b) Compare your results with those from question 3.
Are the numbers different? Explain.

5. Use 3 red counters and 3 yellow counters.
You may place some or all of the counters in a bag.
You then pick a counter without looking.
How many different ways can you place the counters in the bag so you are more likely to pick a red counter than a yellow counter? Explain.

6. Copy and continue the table to show all months of the year. Have each student write her or his month of birth on the board. Find the number of students who were born in each month.
a) Complete the table.

Month	Tally	Frequency	Relative Frequency
January			
February			
March			

b) What is the relative frequency for birthdays in the same month as yours?
c) Find the sum of the relative frequencies. Explain why this sum makes sense.

Number Strategies

Find each percent.
- 10% of $325.00
- 15% of $114.00
- 20% of $99.99
- 25% of $500.00

7. **Assessment Focus** A regular octahedron has faces labelled 1 to 8. Two of these octahedra are rolled. The numbers on the faces the octahedra land on are added. Work with a partner. Use the regular octahedra you made in Unit 3. Label the faces of each octahedron from 1 to 8.

Conduct an experiment to find the relative frequency of getting a sum of 7 when two regular octahedra are rolled.
a) Report your results.
b) How are the results affected if you conduct the experiment 10 times? 50 times? 100 times? Explain.

Reflect

Suppose you know the relative frequency of one outcome of an experiment.
How can you use that to predict the likelihood of that outcome occurring if you conduct the experiment again?
Use an example to explain.

Mid-Unit Review

LESSON

11.1 **1.** Jenna plays a video game on her computer. Each time she plays, she can choose an easy, intermediate, or challenging level of difficulty. She can also choose 1 or 2 players. Use a tree diagram to show the possible game choices.

2. Use a tree diagram to show the possible lunch choices.

LUNCH SPECIAL
1 side dish • 1 main dish • 1 drink

SIDE DISH	MAIN DISH	DRINK
Egg roll	Sweet and sour chicken	Low-fat milk
Soup	Chop suey	Juice
Fried rice	Broccoli beef	Pop

11.2 **3.** Write each relative frequency as a decimal.

a) An air traffic controller's records show 512 planes landed one day. Seventeen planes were 727s. What is the relative frequency of a 727 landing?

b) A cashier served 58 customers in one shift. Thirty-two customers paid cash. What is the relative frequency of a customer paying cash?

c) Qam spun a pointer on a spinner 95 times. The pointer landed on purple 63 times. What is the relative frequency of landing on purple?

4. You will need 4 cubes: 2 of one colour, 2 of another colour; and a bag. Place the cubes in the bag. Pick 2 cubes without looking. Design and conduct an experiment to find the relative frequency of choosing 2 matching cubes.

5. A number cube is labelled 1 to 6.

a) What are the possible outcomes when this cube is rolled?

b) Are these outcomes equally likely? Explain.

c) Design and conduct an experiment to find the relative frequency of each outcome.

d) Do the results confirm your prediction in part b? Explain.

e) How does your answer to part d depend on the number of times you roll the number cube? Explain.

6. There are 3 blue counters and 3 green counters in a bag. You may add to the bag or remove from the bag, as listed below. You put:

a) 1 red counter in the bag

b) 1 more green counter in the bag

c) 2 blue counters in the bag

You then pick a counter without looking. Which of the actions above would make it more likely that you would pick a green counter? Explain.

11.3 Theoretical Probability

Focus Explore and apply theoretical probability.

Explore

Work in a group.
A carnival game has a bucket of different-coloured balls.
Each player is asked to predict the colour of the ball he or she will select.
The player then selects a ball, without looking.
If the guess is correct, the player wins a prize.
After each draw, the ball is returned to the bucket.

Use linking cubes.
Put 4 red, 3 blue, 2 yellow, and 1 green cube in a bag.
Suppose you take 1 cube without looking.
Predict the probability that you will pick each colour.
Play the game 50 times.
What is the experimental probability for picking each colour?
How does each predicted probability compare with the experimental probability?

Reflect & Share

Combine your results with those of another group of students.
How does each experimental probability compare with the predicted probability now?

Connect

Recall that when the outcomes of an experiment are equally likely, the probability of any outcome is:

$$\text{Probability} = \frac{\text{Number of favourable outcomes}}{\text{Number of possible outcomes}}$$

This is called the **theoretical probability**, but we usually say "probability."
You find the probability by analysing the possible outcomes rather than by experimenting.

When you pick an object without looking, the object is picked at random.

Twenty counters were put in a bag:
7 green, 6 black, 5 orange, and 2 purple
You take one counter from the bag without looking.
There are 4 outcomes: green, black, orange, and purple
Suppose the favourable outcome is black.
Then, the probability of picking a black counter is: $\frac{6}{20} = 0.3$

Suppose the favourable outcome is green.
Then, the probability of picking a green counter is: $\frac{7}{20} = 0.35$

Note that the outcomes are not equally likely.

We can predict the possible number of times an outcome will occur by multiplying the probability by the number of repetitions.
Suppose we pick a counter at random 54 times.
Then, the predicted number of times a black counter is picked is:
$0.3 \times 54 = 16.2$
We would expect to pick a black counter about 16 times.
However, we may never pick a black counter, or we might always pick a black counter.

Example

Suppose you roll a number cube 100 times. Predict how many times:

a) a 1 will show
b) a 5 will show
c) a 1 or a 5 will show
d) a 1 or a 5 will not show

How are the answers to parts c and d related?

Solution

When a number cube is rolled, there are six possible outcomes.
The outcomes are equally likely.

a) The probability of rolling a 1 is $\frac{1}{6}$.
So, the predicted number of times a 1 will show in 100 rolls is:
$\frac{1}{6} \times 100 = \frac{100}{6} \doteq 17$

b) The probability of rolling a 5 is also $\frac{1}{6}$.
So, the predicted number of times a 5 will show is also about 17.

c) The probability of rolling a 1 or a 5 is $\frac{2}{6}$, or $\frac{1}{3}$.
So, the predicted number of times a 1 or a 5 will show is:
$\frac{1}{3} \times 100 = \frac{100}{3} \doteq 33$

d) For a 1 and a 5 not to show, a 2, 3, 4, or 6 shows.
The probability of rolling a 2, 3, 4, or 6 is $\frac{4}{6}$, or $\frac{2}{3}$.
So, the predicted number of times a 1 or a 5 does not show is:
$\frac{2}{3} \times 100 = \frac{200}{3} \doteq 67$

The predicted number of times a 1 or a 5 shows and the predicted number of times a 1 or a 5 does not show are:
$33 + 67 = 100$
An outcome occurs or it does not occur. So,

Predicted number of times an outcome occurs	+	Predicted number of times the outcome does not occur	=	Number of times the experiment is conducted

In the *Example* part c, in 100 rolls, a 1 or a 5 will show about 33 times. This does not mean that a 1 or a 5 will show *exactly* 33 times, but the number of times will likely be close to 33.

The more times an experiment is conducted, the closer the experimental probability is to the theoretical probability.

Practice

1. A bag contains these granola bars: 12 apple, 14 banana, 18 raisin, and 10 regular. You pick one bar at random. Find the probability of choosing:

a) a banana granola bar **b)** an apple granola bar

When you see the word "probability" in a sentence, it means theoretical probability.

2. There are 8 names in a hat.
You pick one name without looking. Find each probability.

a) A three-letter name will be picked.
b) A five-letter name will be picked.
c) Laura will be picked.
d) Jorge will not be picked.

Number Strategies

Simplify.

- $\frac{5}{8} + \frac{3}{4}$
- $\frac{4}{5} - \frac{2}{3}$
- $1\frac{3}{10} + 2\frac{1}{2}$
- $\frac{2}{3} + \frac{2}{5} + \frac{3}{10}$

3. Is each statement true or false? Explain.

a) If you toss a coin 10 times, you will never get 10 heads.

b) If you toss a coin 10 times, you will always get exactly 5 heads.

c) If you toss a coin many times, the number of heads should be approximately $\frac{1}{2}$ the number of tosses.

4. The pointer on this spinner is spun 100 times.
Is each statement true or false? Justify your answer.

a) The pointer will land on *Win* about 33 times.

b) The pointer will land on *Win*, *Lose*, and *Tie* an equal number of times.

c) The pointer will land on *Lose* exactly 33 times.

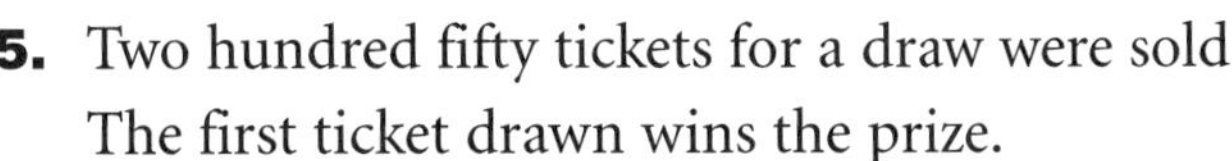

5. Two hundred fifty tickets for a draw were sold.
The first ticket drawn wins the prize.

a) Joe purchased 1 ticket. What is the probability Joe will win?

b) Maria purchased 10 tickets.
What is the probability Maria will win?

c) Ivan purchased 25 tickets.
What is the probability Ivan will *not* win?

6. Assessment Focus

a) Construct a spinner with red, yellow, blue, and green sectors, so the following probabilities are true.

- The probability of landing on red is $\frac{1}{4}$.
- The probability of landing on yellow is $\frac{1}{2}$.
- The probability of landing on blue is $\frac{1}{6}$.
- The probability of landing on green is $\frac{1}{12}$.

Explain how you drew your spinner.

b) In 200 trials, about how many times would the pointer land on each colour?

c) Suppose the spinner had been constructed so the probability of landing on yellow was $\frac{1}{4}$.
What effect would this have on the probability of landing on each other colour? Explain.

Reflect

How are theoretical probability and experimental probability similar? Different?
Use an example to explain.

11.4 Applications of Probability

Focus Solve probability problems.

Explore

Work with a partner.
You will play the *Sum and Product* game.
You will need 4 blank cards and a bag.
Write the numbers from 1 to 4 on the cards.
Place the cards in the bag.
Each person picks a card.
Both of you find the sum and the product of the two numbers.
One of you is Player A, the other is Player B.
If the sum is less than or equal to the product, Player A gets a point.
If the sum is greater than the product, Player B gets a point.

- Who is likely to win? Explain your reasoning.
- Play the game several times; you choose how many times. Who won?
- How does your prediction of the winner compare with your result?

Reflect & Share

Compare your results with those of another pair of classmates.
Work together to come up with an explanation of who is more likely to win.

Connect

- Probability can be expressed as a fraction, a decimal, or a percent. When probability is expressed as a percent, we use the word "chance."
  For example, the weather forecast is a 40% chance of rain today.
  This means that the probability of rain is: $\frac{40}{100} = 0.4$
- When an outcome is certain, the probability of it occurring is 1. For example, when we toss a coin, the probability of it landing heads or tails is 1.
  When an outcome is impossible, the probability of it occurring is 0. For example, when we roll a number cube labelled 1 to 6, the probability of a 7 showing is 0.

Example

Flick This is an Ultimate Frisbee team.
The team plays 3 games against 3 other teams.
All 4 teams have equal chances of winning.

a) What is the chance that Flick This will win all three of its games?
b) What is the chance that Flick This will win exactly one game?
c) What is the chance that Flick This will win at least two games?

Solution

For any game, the possible outcomes are win (W) or lose (L). These outcomes are equally likely. Draw a tree diagram to list the possible results of 3 games for Flick This.

1st Game	2nd Game	3rd Game	Outcomes
W	W	W	WWW
		L	WWL
	L	W	WLW
		L	WLL
L	W	W	LWW
		L	LWL
	L	W	LLW
		L	LLL

There are 8 possible outcomes.

a) There is 1 outcome in which Flick This wins all three games: WWW
So, the probability of 3 wins is: $\frac{1}{8} = 0.125$
So, the chance of winning 3 games is 12.5%.

The word "exactly" is included because "winning one game" might be interpreted as winning one or more games.

b) There are 3 outcomes in which Flick This wins exactly one game: WLL, LWL, LLW
So, the probability of winning exactly 1 game is: $\frac{3}{8} = 0.375$
So, the chance of winning exactly 1 game is 37.5%.

c) There are 4 outcomes in which Flick This wins at least two games: WWW, WWL, WLW, LWW
So, the probability of winning at least 2 games is: $\frac{4}{8} = \frac{1}{2} = 0.5$
So, the chance of winning at least 2 games is 50%.

Practice

1. The 1st, 2nd, and 3rd place winners of a contest can be female or male. This tree diagram shows the possible outcomes of the contest.

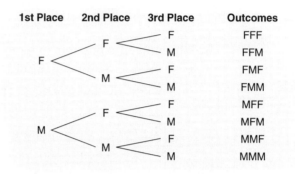

1st Place	2nd Place	3rd Place	Outcomes
F	F	F	FFF
		M	FFM
	M	F	FMF
		M	FMM
M	F	F	MFF
		M	MFM
	M	F	MMF
		M	MMM

a) How many possible outcomes are there?
b) What is the probability that all the winners are female?
c) What is the probability that none of the winners is male?
d) How are the answers to parts b and c related? Explain.

2. On this spinner, the pointer is spun once.
The colour is recorded.
The pointer is spun a second time.
The colour is recorded.
a) Suppose you win if you spin the same colour on both spins.
What are your chances of winning?
b) Suppose you win if you spin two different colours.
What are your chances of winning?

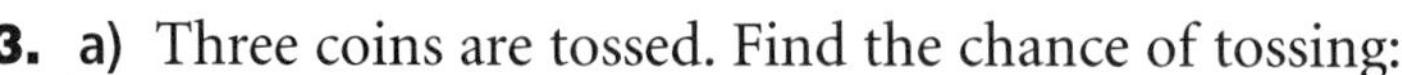

3. a) Three coins are tossed. Find the chance of tossing:
i) one heads and two tails ii) exactly two heads
iii) at least two tails iv) no heads
b) Why do we need the words "at least" in part a, iii?
What if these words were left out?
How would the answer change?
c) Why do we need the word "exactly" in part a, ii? What if this word was left out? How would the answer change?

4. At a carnival, the game with the least chance of winning often has the greatest prize. Explain why this might be.

5. There are four children in a family.
What is the chance of each event?
a) There are two boys and two girls.
b) There is at least one girl.
c) All four children are of the same gender.

6. **Assessment Focus** The school cafeteria has this lunch menu.
A student chooses a sandwich and a vegetable. Assume the choice is random.
a) Find the probability of each possible combination.
b) Suppose 3 desserts were added to the menu. Each student chooses a sandwich, a vegetable, and a dessert.
How would the probabilities of possible combinations change?
Use examples to explain your thinking.

Lunch Menu

Sandwich	**Vegetable**
Grilled Cheese	Broccoli
Chicken	Carrots
Tuna	

Take It Further

7. At the school carnival, there is a game with two spinners.

Spinner A

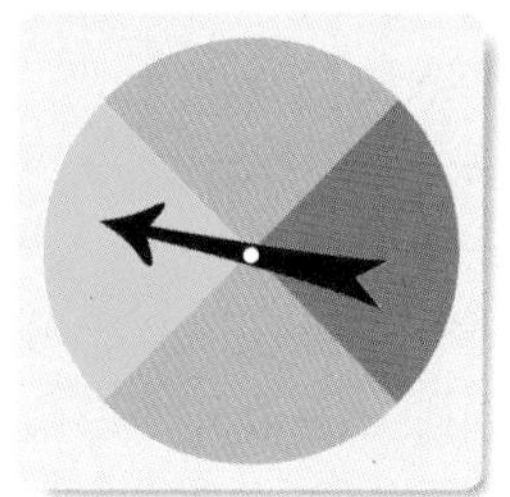

Spinner B

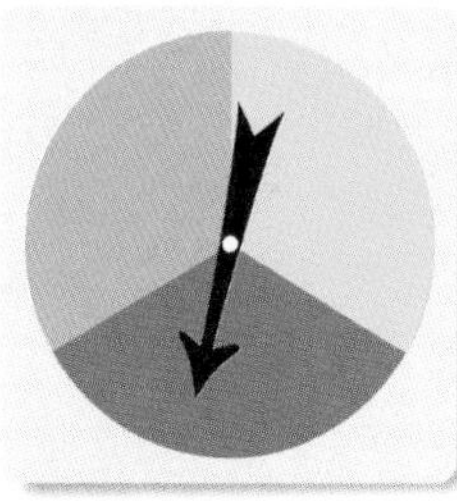

You get two spins.
You may spin the pointer on each spinner once, or spin the pointer on one spinner twice.
If you get pink on one spin and yellow on another spin (the order does not matter), you win.
To have the greatest chance of winning, what should you do?
Explain.

Calculator Skills

Which three consecutive prime numbers have a product of 7429 and a sum of 59?

Reflect

How is probability related to chance?
Use an example in your explanation.

Choosing a Strategy

Strategies

- Make a table.
- Use a model.
- Draw a diagram.
- Solve a simpler problem.
- Work backward.
- Guess and check.
- Make an organized list.
- Use a pattern.
- Draw a graph.
- Use logical reasoning.

1. For her birthday, Janine was given a row of 25 pennies.
   Her father replaced every second coin with a nickel.
   Her mother replaced every third coin with a dime.
   Her brother replaced every fourth coin with a quarter.
   Her uncle replaced every fifth coin with a loonie.
   How much did Janine get on her birthday?

2. Arif has a part-time job.
   He was offered \$96 per week or \$4.50/h.
   Which is the better deal? Explain.

3. a) The perimeter of a rectangle is 36 cm.
   What is the maximum possible area of the rectangle?
   b) The sum of the length, width, and height of a rectangular prism is 18 cm.
   What is the maximum possible volume of the prism?

4. What fraction of this figure is shaded?

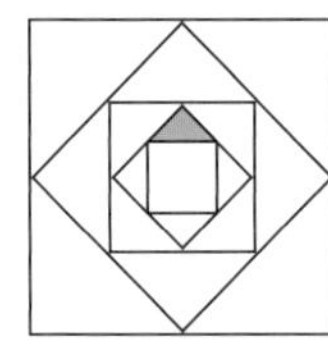

5. Divide the square at the left into four congruent figures.
   Record each way you find on dot paper.
   Find at least ten different ways to do this.

6. Running shoes cost \$79.99. They are on sale for 20% off.
   The sales tax of 15% has to be added.
   Which would you choose? Explain.
   a) Take the 20% off the price, then add the 15% sales tax.
   b) Add the 15% sales tax, then take off the 20%.

7. The Magic Money Box doubles any amount of money placed in it, then adds \$1 to it.
   Yesterday I placed a sum of money in the box and got a new amount.
   Today I put the new amount in the box and got \$75 out.
   How much did I put in the box yesterday?

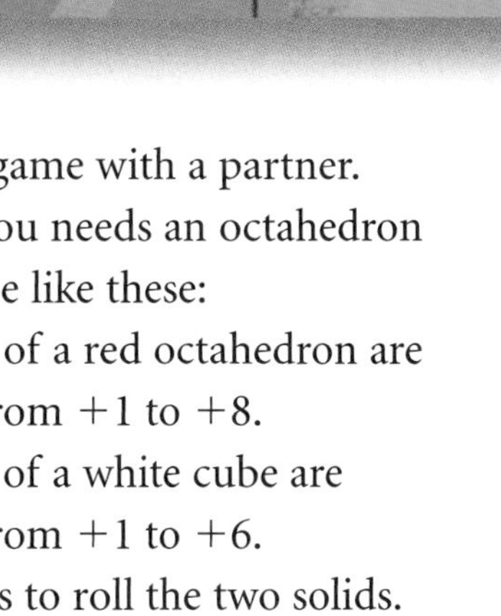

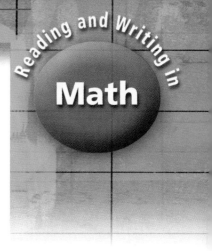

8. Play this game with a partner.
Each of you needs an octahedron and a cube like these:
The faces of a red octahedron are labelled from +1 to +8.
The faces of a white cube are labelled from +1 to +6.
Take turns to roll the two solids.
Subtract the red number from the white number.
The person with the lesser number scores a point.
The first person to reach 20 points is the winner.

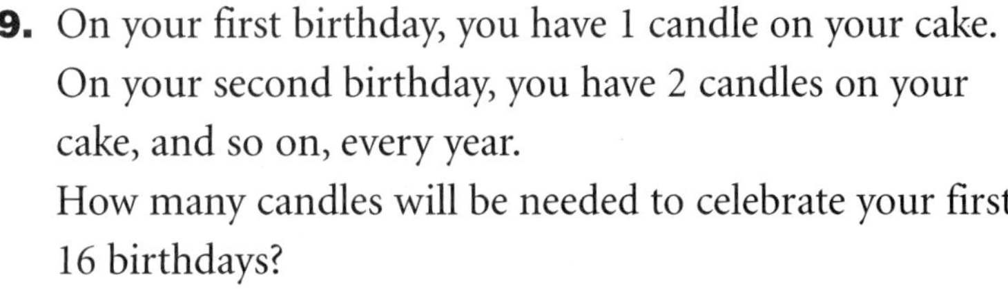

9. On your first birthday, you have 1 candle on your cake.
On your second birthday, you have 2 candles on your cake, and so on, every year.
How many candles will be needed to celebrate your first 16 birthdays?

10. A radio station plays an average of 16 songs every hour.
One-half the songs are pop, one-quarter are jazz, one-eighth are country, and the rest are classical.
One show is 3 h long. The songs are played at random.

a) How many classical songs would be played?

b) What is the probability that the first song played is jazz?

11. An octahedron has eight faces labelled 1 to 8.
A cube has six faces labelled 1 to 6.

a) Both solids are rolled. What is the probability that the sum of the numbers is 8?

b) Both solids are rolled. What is the probability that the sum of the numbers is a prime number?

Game

Empty the Rectangles

YOU WILL NEED

2 number cubes labelled 1 to 6; 12 counters

NUMBER OF PLAYERS

2

GOAL OF THE GAME

To remove all counters from all rectangles

What strategies can you use to improve your chances of winning this game?

HOW TO PLAY THE GAME:

1. Each player draws 6 rectangles on a piece of paper.

Label each rectangle from 0 to 5.

2. Each player places her 6 counters in any or all of the rectangles.
You can place 1 counter in each rectangle, or 2 counters in each of 3 rectangles, or even 6 counters in 1 rectangle.

3. Take turns to roll the number cubes.
Find the difference of the numbers.
You remove counters from the rectangle labelled with that number.
For example, if you roll a 6 and a 4, then $6 - 4 = 2$; so, remove all counters from rectangle 2.

4. The winner is the first person to have no counters left in any rectangle.

Sports

You know that a batting average of 0.300 means that a player has an average of 3 hits in 10 at bats. Research other examples of relative frequency in sport. Write what you find out.

Unit Review

Review any lesson with

What Do I Need to Know?

☑ Relative frequency $= \dfrac{\text{Number of times an outcome occurs}}{\text{Number of times experiment is conducted}}$

☑ Theoretical probability $= \dfrac{\text{Number of favourable outcomes}}{\text{Number of possible outcomes}}$

What Should I Be Able to Do?

For extra practice, go to page 448.

LESSON

11.1

1. a) Use a tree diagram to show the possible combinations for a breakfast. You can choose:
- a banana, an orange, or an apple
- carrots, celery, or cucumber, and
- yogurt or cheese

b) How many outcomes have a banana and cheese?

c) How many outcomes have an orange, celery, or a yogurt?

d) How many outcomes do not have an apple?

2. Four coins are tossed.

a) List all the possible outcomes.

b) How many outcomes have exactly 1 head?

c) How many outcomes have exactly 2 tails?

d) How many outcomes have at least 3 tails?

11.2

3. A biologist tested a new vaccine. She found that in 500 trials, the test was successful 450 times.

a) What is the relative frequency that the vaccine is successful?

b) Suppose the vaccine is used on 15 000 people. How many successes can be expected?

4. The owner of a shop recorded customer sales for one week.

Gender	Purchase	No Purchase	Total
Male	125	65	190
Female	154	46	200

Determine the relative frequency of each outcome.

a) A customer is male.

b) A customer is female.

c) A customer makes a purchase.

d) A male does not make a purchase.

e) A female makes a purchase.

5. Is each statement true or false? Explain.

a) When a coin is tossed 100 times, it will never show tails 100 times.

b) When a coin is tossed 100 times, it is unlikely to show heads 100 times.

c) When a coin is tossed 100 times, it will show tails exactly 50 times.

d) The more often a coin is tossed, the more likely that $\frac{1}{2}$ the results will be tails.

11.3 **6.** In a game show, each contestant spins the wheel once to win the money shown.

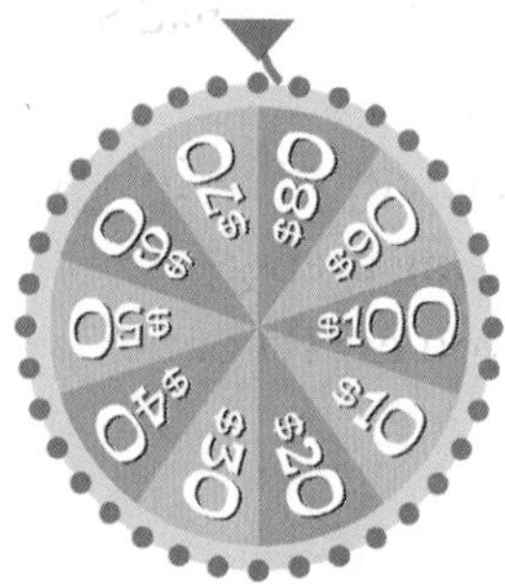

a) Are the probabilities of winning the amounts equally likely? Explain.

b) What is the probability of winning $100?

c) What is the probability of winning less than $50?

d) What is the probability of winning from $30 to $70?

7. Twenty cards are numbered from 1 to 20. The cards are shuffled. A card is drawn. Find the probability that the card has:

a) an odd number

b) a multiple of 4

c) a number that is not a perfect square

d) a prime number

11.4 **8.** Each of the numbers 1 to 15 is written on a separate card. The cards are shuffled and placed in a pile face down. A card is picked from the pile. Its number is recorded. The card is returned to the pile. In 99 trials, about how many times would you expect each outcome?

a) a 6

b) a multiple of 3

c) a number less than 10

d) an even number

9. What is the chance of each outcome?

a) tossing 2 coins and getting:

i) 2 heads

ii) 1 tail and 2 heads

b) tossing 3 coins and getting:

i) 1 head and 2 tails

ii) at least 1 tail

10. An electronic game has three coloured sectors. A colour lights up at random, followed by a colour lighting up at random again. What is the chance the two consecutive colours are the same?

Practice Test

1. A theatre shows movies on Saturday and Sunday.
There are matinee and evening shows.
There are adult, child, and senior rates.
Draw a tree diagram to show the possible ticket types.

2. A number cube is labelled 1 to 6.
The cube is rolled 60 times.
Predict how many times each outcome will occur.
Explain each answer.

a) 1 is rolled.
b) An even number is rolled.
c) A number greater than 3 is rolled.
d) 9 is rolled.

3. a) In Sarah's first 30 times at bat, she had 9 hits.
What is Sarah's batting average?
b) In Sarah's next game, she had 3 hits in 4 times at bat.
What is Sarah's new batting average?
c) How many hits would you expect Sarah to have in 90 times at bat? Explain your reasoning.

4. A number cube is labelled 1 to 6.
Suppose you roll a number cube twice.
Is it more likely you will get a 3 then a 5, or a 3 then a 3?
Explain your reasoning.

5. In the game "rock, paper, scissors," 2 players make hand signs.
Players can make a hand sign for rock, paper, or scissors.
On the count of 3, players show their hand signs.
Suppose the players choose their signs at random.
In 75 games, how many times would you expect to see both players showing rock?

Unit Problem Games of Chance

Part 1

Emma and Jonah created a spinner game called Match/No-Match.
Two people play the game.
A player spins the pointer twice.

If the pointer lands on the same colour (a match), the player scores.
If the pointer lands on different colours (a no-match), the opponent scores.

Jonah and Emma reasoned that, since there are two matching combinations (red/red and green/green), a player should score only 1 point for a match, and the opponent should score 2 points for a no-match.

Play the Match/No-Match game. Take at least 50 turns each.

Use the results to find the relative frequency of a match and of a no-match.

List the possible outcomes of a turn (two spins).
Find the theoretical probability of a match and a no-match.

Do you think the players have equal chances of winning? Explain.

Part 2

Design a game using spinners, number cubes, coins, or any other materials.
The game should use two different items.

Play the game.

Do the players have equal chances of winning? Explain.
Calculate some probabilities related to your game.
Show your work.

Check List

Your work should show:

- ✓ all calculations of frequency or probability, in detail
- ✓ diagrams, tables, or lists to show possible outcomes and results of each game
- ✓ an explanation of players' chances of winning each game
- ✓ correct use of the language of probability

Reflect on the Unit

Give at least two examples of how you use probability in everyday life.

Cross Strand Investigation

A Population Simulation

Materials:

- a paper cup
- 30 to 40 two-sided counters
- 0.5-cm grid paper

Work with a partner.

An animal population changes from year to year depending on the rates of birth and death, and on the movement of the animals.
A **simulation** is a model of a real situation. You will use a simulation to investigate how an animal population might decline.
As you complete this *Investigation*, include your completed table, graph, and written answers to the questions. You will hand these in.

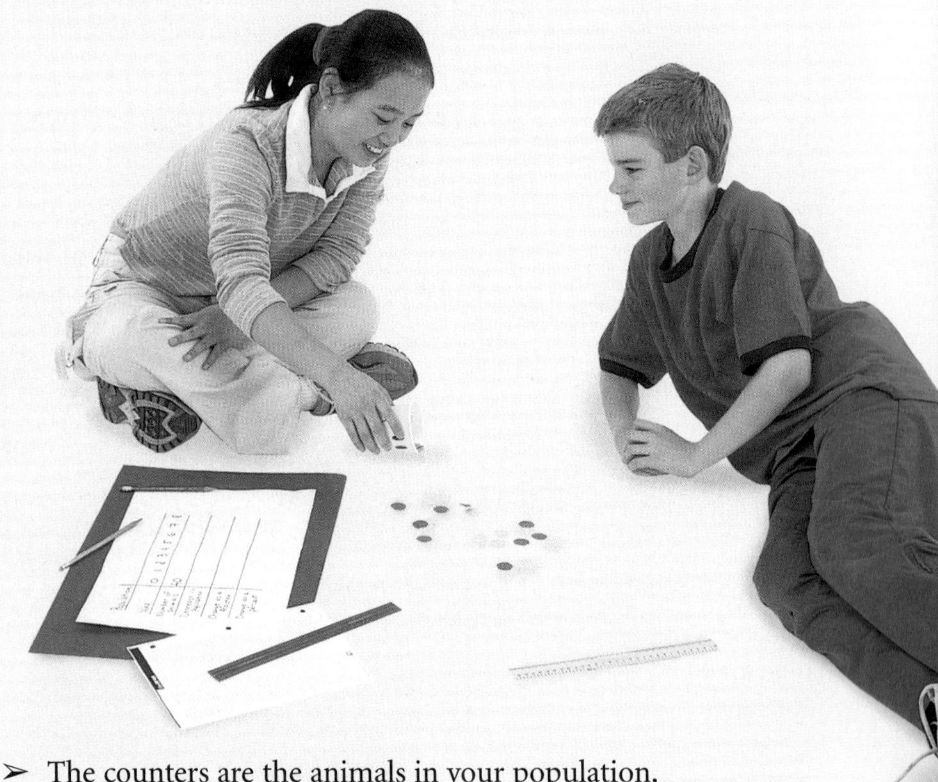

- The counters are the animals in your population.
  Count the number of animals.
  Record that number for Year 0 in the *Population* table.
- Put the counters in the cup.
  Choose which colour will be "face up."
  Pour the counters from the cup.
  Counters that land face up represent animals that died or moved away during the first year. Set them aside.
  Count the number of animals left.

Record that number as the population for Year 1.
Calculate and record the decrease in population.
Write the decrease as a fraction of the previous year's population.
Write the fraction as a percent.

- Place the counters representing live animals back in the cup.
  Repeat the experiment for Year 2.
  Record the data for Year 2 in the table.
- Continue the simulation. Record your data for up to 8 years, or until you run out of animals.
- Graph the population data.
  Plot *Year* horizontally and *Number of Animals* vertically.
  Explain your choice of graph.
  What trends do you see in the graph?

Population									
Year	**0**	**1**	**2**	**3**	**4**	**5**	**6**	**7**	**8**
Number of animals									
Decrease in population									
Change as a fraction									
Change as a percent									

- Describe the patterns you see in the table. Approximately what fraction and percent of the population remain from year to year?
- Use the patterns to predict the population for Year 9.
- How long does it take the population of animals to decrease to one-half its original size?
- What would happen to a population if there were no births to add to the population each year?

Take It Further

- Suppose you repeated this experiment, beginning with more animals. Would you see the same pattern? Explain.
  Combine your data with data of other students to find out.
- Which environmental factors may cause an animal population to change?

Cumulative Review

UNIT

1 **1.** Write the first 5 multiples of each number.

a) 6 b) 9 c) 12

2. Write all the factors of each number.

a) 36 b) 57 c) 75

2 **3.** There are two patchwork quilts.
In quilt A, the ratio of red squares to green squares is 5:7.
In quilt B, the ratio of red squares to green squares is 4:5.
The quilts are the same size.
Which quilt has more red squares?
Use grid paper to show your answer.

3 **4.** a) Write the formula for the surface area of a cube, with edge length *c* units.

b) Write the formula for the surface area of a rectangular prism with dimensions *l* units by *w* units by *h* units.

c) How can you get the formula for the surface area of a cube from the formula for the surface area of a rectangular prism? Use pictures in your explanation.

4 **5.** Add or subtract.

a) $2\frac{3}{4} - 1\frac{1}{3}$

b) $3\frac{1}{3} + 2\frac{3}{5}$

c) $3\frac{4}{5} - 2\frac{1}{10}$

d) $\frac{3}{10} + 1\frac{1}{2}$

e) $\frac{3}{8} + \frac{7}{4} + \frac{7}{2}$

f) $\frac{9}{10} + \frac{1}{2} + \frac{6}{5}$

6. Divide. Round the quotient to the nearest tenth where necessary.

a) $7.22 \div 1.9$

b) $7.22 \div 2.1$

c) $8.97 \div 2.3$

d) $8.98 \div 2.4$

5 **7.** a) The people who run the cafeteria survey students about their favourite foods.
How might the survey results affect the menu?

b) A local hair salon collects data on the number of clients who would like hair appointments on Sundays.
How might these data affect the days the salon is open?

8. Annette's practice times for a downhill ski run, in seconds, are:
122, 137, 118, 119, 124, 118, 120, 118

a) Find the mean time.

b) Find the median time.

c) Find the mode time.

d) Which measure of central tendency best represents the times? Explain.

e) What is the range?

f) What time must Annette get in her next run so the median is 120 s? Explain.

g) What time must Annette get in her next run so the mean is 121 s? Is this possible? Explain.

UNIT

9. a) What does this table show?

Toronto Blue Jays' Average Game Attendance	
Year	**Average Attendance**
1991	47 966
1992	49 402
1993	49 732
1994	50 098
1995	39 257
1996	31 600
1997	31 967
1998	30 300
1999	26 710
2000	21 058
2001	23 690
2002	20 209
2003	22 215

b) Do you think the average is the mean, the median, or the mode? Explain your choice.

c) Draw a line graph to display these data.

d) What trends does the graph show? Find out what happened to change the trend.

e) Draw a graph to display the data each way.

i) The marketing department wants attendance to look as great as possible.

ii) The shareholders want to show that the attendance is too low.

f) Explain how each graph in part e shows what was intended.

6 **10.** Find the area of each figure.

a)

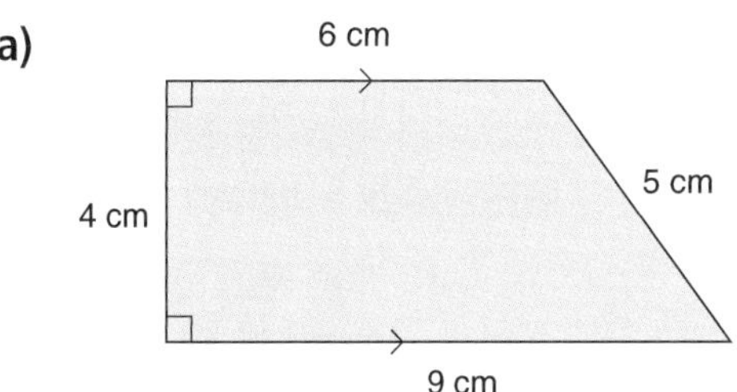

b)

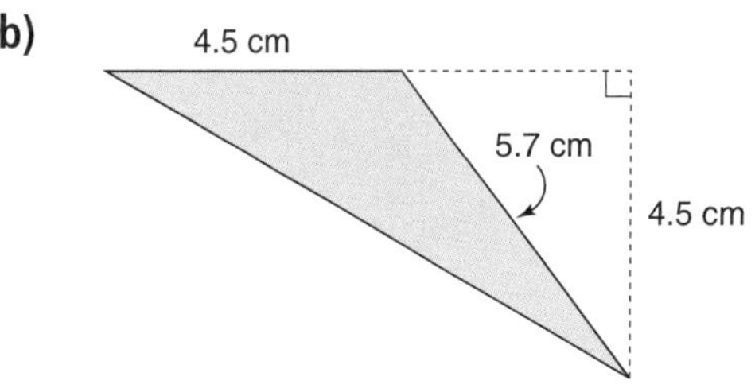

c)

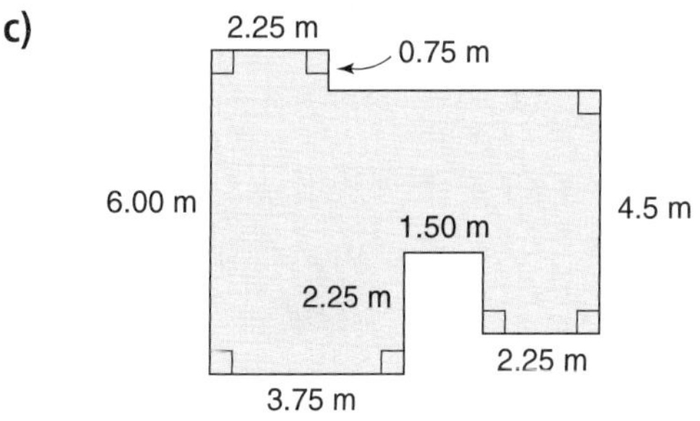

d)

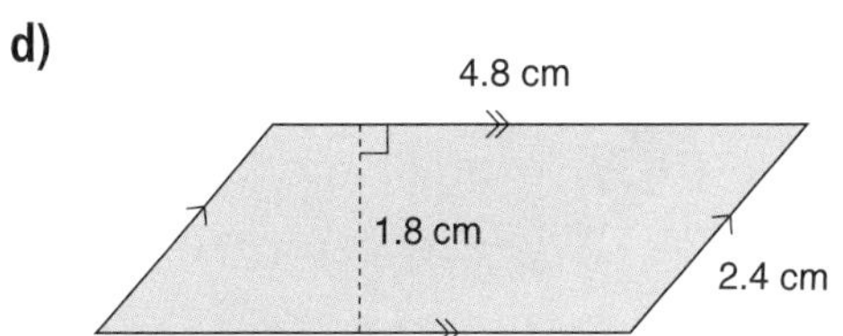

UNIT

11. If you can, find the perimeter of each figure in question 10. For which figures can you not find the perimeter? Explain.

7 **12.** a) Plot these points on a grid: A(3, 2), B(4, 5), C(7, 5), and D(8, 4). Join the points to draw figure ABCD.
b) Translate the figure in part a.
c) Rotate the figure in part a.
d) Reflect the figure in part a.
Trade grids with a classmate. Identify each of your classmate's transformations.

8 **13.** A sweater is on sale for 25% off the regular price. The sale price is $37.50. What was the regular price? Sketch a number line to illustrate the answer.

14. A theatre has 840 seats. For one performance, the theatre was 75% full.
a) How many people were in the theatre?
b) By the end of the performance, 30 people had left. How many people were in the theatre then?
c) Ninety percent of the remaining audience stood to give the performers a standing ovation. How many people were still sitting?

9 **15.** Order these integers from least to greatest.
$+5, -6, -8, +2, 0, -5, -1$

16. Add or subtract. Use coloured tiles or number lines.
a) $(+5) + (-9)$
b) $(-1) + (-5)$
c) $(+2) - (-8)$
d) $(-9) - (-3)$

17. A rock climber climbed 3 m, was lowered 1 m, then climbed 5 m more.
a) How high did she climb?
b) The total height of the climb is 10 m. How much farther does she have to climb?
Use coloured tiles if they help.

18. The temperature at 6 a.m. is -10°C. During the day, the temperature rises 17°C. What is the new temperature?

10 **19.** Write each algebraic expression in words.
a) $2 - 3x$
b) $3x - 2$
c) $35 - y$
d) $y + 35$
e) $2(x + 2)$
f) $\frac{z}{5} + 10$

20. Write each statement as an algebraic expression.
a) a number divided by twelve
b) one-twelfth of a number
c) eleven added to five times a number

21. Students are fund raising by washing cars.
The students charge $6.00 per car.

a) Copy and complete this table.

Numbers of Cars	Money Collected ($)
5	
10	
15	
20	
25	
30	

b) Graph the data in the table in part a.

c) What patterns do you see in the table? How could you extend each pattern?

d) Suppose you know how many cars were washed. How can you find how much money was collected in each case?

i) by using the table

ii) by using the graph

e) Suppose 27 cars were washed. How much money was collected?
How many different ways can you find the answer? Explain.

22. Solve each equation.

a) $2x + 3 = 15$

b) $\frac{x}{3} = 15$

c) $\frac{15}{x} = 3$

d) $2x - 3 = 15$

23. Evan had $852.00.
He shared the money equally with his brother and sister.

a) Write an equation you can solve to find out how much money each person got.

b) Solve the equation.

11 **24.** **a)** What are the possible outcomes when 3 coins are tossed?

b) What is the probability of each outcome?

c) Design and conduct an experiment to find the relative frequency of each outcome.

d) Write each relative frequency as a decimal.

e) How do the probabilities and relative frequencies compare?
Is this what you expect? Explain.

25. Each letter of the word PROBABILITY is written on a card.
The cards are placed in a box.
Suppose you pick a card, at random, record the letter, then replace the card.
In 55 trials, about how many times would you expect each outcome?

a) a P **b)** a B **c)** a vowel **d)** an X

26. Anca rolls two number cubes labelled 3 to 8. She adds the numbers that show on the cubes.
List the possible outcomes.
Use a tree diagram if it helps.

Extra Practice

1. Jean bought DVDs that cost \$23, \$18, \$29, \$52, and \$24, including tax. How much did he spend?

2. Canada has 891 163 km^2 of water. One hundred fifty-eight thousand three hundred sixty-four square kilometres of this water is in Ontario. How much water is in the rest of Canada?

3. An auditorium has 1456 seats. There are 28 seats in each row. How many rows are there?

4. One pair of running shoes costs \$99. How much would 99 pairs cost? How can you find out using mental math?

5. The average Canadian walks and runs about 193 000 km in a lifetime.

a) About how far is this per year? Per week?

b) Do you think the estimates in part a are reasonable? Explain.

6. Find the factors of each number.

a) 36 b) 56 c) 96

7. Write the first 10 multiples of each number.

a) 12 b) 15 c) 20

8. Find the greatest common factor of each pair of numbers.

a) 18, 42 b) 60, 33
c) 25, 75 d) 48, 84

9. Find the square of each number.

a) 7 b) 17
c) 27 d) 37

10. Find the lowest common multiple of each pair of numbers.

a) 18, 8 b) 24, 10
c) 36, 15 d) 42, 24

11. Find a square root of each number. Use grid paper. Draw a diagram to show each square root.

a) 81 b) 144
c) 225 d) 400

12. a) Find the area of a square with side length 14 cm.

b) What is the perimeter of the square?

13. a) Find the side length of a square with area 900 m^2.

b) What is the perimeter of the square?

14. Find the perimeter of a square with area 169 cm^2.

15. What is the volume of a cube with edge length 15 cm? How can you use exponents to find out?

16. Write in exponent form.

a) $4 \times 4 \times 4 \times 4 \times 4$

b) $12 \times 12 \times 12 \times 12$

17. a) Evaluate.

i) $5 \times 9 + 5$

ii) $56 \times 9 + 6$

iii) $567 \times 9 + 7$

b) Predict the answer for $5678 \times 9 + 8$. Use a calculator to check.

1. a) Draw a diagram to show the ratio 6:7.
   b) Draw a diagram to show the ratio 2:7.

2. Write each ratio in simplest form.
   a) 22:11 b) 21:12
   c) 25:15 d) 14:56

3. Write three ratios equivalent to each ratio. Show your work in tables.
   a) 5:7 b) 36:10
   c) 9:4 d) 32:44

4. Use these diagrams.

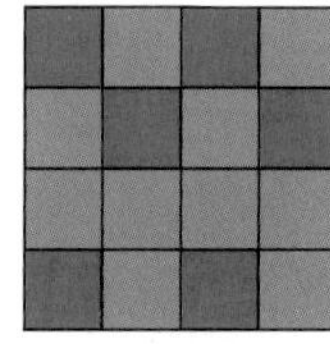

Figure A

Figure B

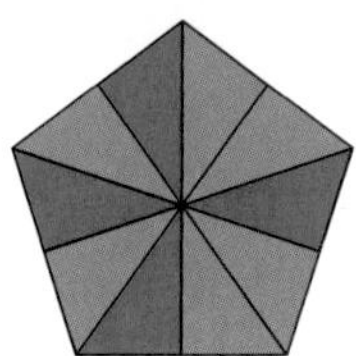

Figure C

Which diagram shows each red to blue ratio?
   a) 2:1 b) 2:3 c) 3:5

5. Arlene is 12 years old.
   Her brother is 4 years old.
   a) What is the ratio of their ages?
   b) What will the ratio be in one year?
   c) How old will Arlene and her brother be when the ratio of their ages is 2:1?

6. Two buckets contain equal numbers of Pattern Blocks. In Bucket A, the ratio of triangles to squares is 1:3. In Bucket B, the ratio of triangles to squares is 3:4.
   a) Which bucket contains more triangles? More squares? How do you know?
   b) What is the ratio of the number of triangles in Bucket A to the number of squares in Bucket B?

7. In a hockey club storeroom, the ratio of sticks to helmets is 5:3.
   a) There are 12 helmets.
      How many sticks are there?
   b) One new stick is added. What is the new ratio of sticks to helmets?

8. On a school trip, the ratio of boys to girls is 4 to 5.
   The ratio of girls to adults is 7 to 2.
   a) What is the ratio of boys and girls to adults?
   b) One hundred forty-six people went on the trip. How many were girls?

9. Find a pair of numbers between 30 and 50 that have a ratio of 6:5. How many different pairs can you find?

10. A spice mixture contains 5 g of coriander, 3 g of cumin, and 2 g of peppercorns.
    a) What is the ratio of the mass of each spice to the total mass?
    b) How much of each spice is needed to make 1 kg of spice mixture?

1. Use 3 linking cubes.
   Use square dot paper.
   a) Make an object.
      Draw the front, back, side, and top views of the object.
   b) How many different objects can you make with 3 linking cubes?
      Make each additional object.
      Draw its front, back, side, and top views.

2. Find each object in the classroom.
   Sketch its front, back, top, and side views.
   a) bookcase b) table c) pencil

3. Draw a pictorial diagram of each solid.
   a)

   b)

   c)

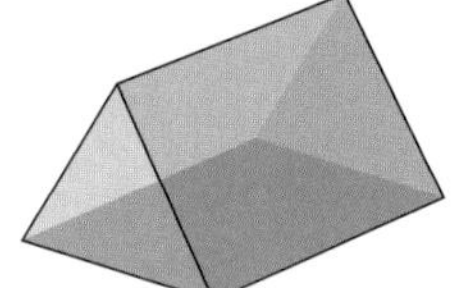

   d)

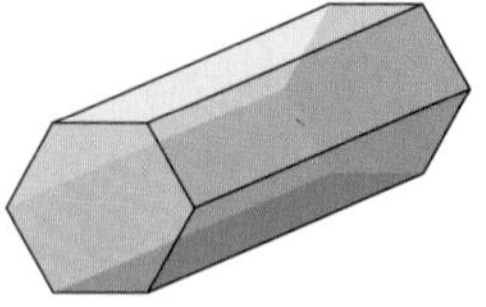

4. a) Draw the cube in question 3 on isometric dot paper.
   b) Draw the rectangular prism in question 3 on isometric dot paper.

5. Use 4 linking cubes.
   Make an object that is not a rectangular prism.
   Draw the object on isometric dot paper.

6. Use formulas.
   a) Find the area and perimeter of a rectangle with base 12.5 cm and height 3.6 cm.
   b) Find the area and perimeter of a square with side length 5.6 m.

7. Use formulas.
   a) Find the surface area of a rectangular prism with length 6 cm, height 7 cm, and width 4 cm.
   b) Find the volume of the prism in part a.
   c) Find the surface area of a cube with edge length 1.8 cm.
   d) Find the volume of the cube in part c.

8. Anthony is wrapping a birthday gift in a box that measures 30 cm by 20 cm by 8 cm.
   a) What is the surface area of the box?
   b) How much wrapping paper is needed if allowance is made for overlap? Sketch a diagram to illustrate your answer.

9. A shed has the shape of a rectangular prism. It is 2 m high, 3 m wide, and 4 m long. The walls and doors are to be painted inside and out. The roof, ceilings, and floor are to be painted. The shed has two windows; each measures 1 m by 1 m. What is the area that will be painted?

1. Write in simplest form.
   a) $\frac{18}{12}$ b) $\frac{12}{27}$ c) $\frac{6}{9}$ d) $\frac{8}{4}$

2. Draw a diagram to show how to write each improper fraction as a mixed number.
   a) $\frac{5}{3}$ b) $\frac{7}{5}$ c) $\frac{14}{4}$ d) $\frac{22}{6}$

3. Use a calculator.
   Write each fraction as a decimal.
   a) $\frac{17}{18}$ b) $\frac{13}{4}$ c) $\frac{3}{5}$ d) $\frac{7}{3}$

4. Use fraction strips and number lines to add.
   a) $\frac{2}{3} + \frac{3}{2}$ b) $\frac{1}{4} + \frac{7}{8}$
   c) $\frac{3}{5} + \frac{2}{10}$ d) $\frac{5}{3} + \frac{1}{12}$

5. The sum: $\frac{2}{3} + \frac{1}{5}$ is $\frac{13}{15}$.
   Use this result to add these fractions.
   a) $1\frac{2}{3} + 1\frac{1}{5}$ b) $3\frac{2}{3} + \frac{1}{5}$
   c) $\frac{1}{3} + \frac{1}{5} + \frac{1}{3}$ d) $\frac{1}{5} + 1\frac{2}{3}$

6. Use fraction strips and number lines to subtract.
   a) $\frac{7}{8} - \frac{1}{2}$ b) $\frac{7}{6} - \frac{2}{4}$
   c) $1 - \frac{5}{8}$ d) $\frac{11}{6} - \frac{2}{3}$

7. Add.
   a) $\frac{1}{5} + \frac{3}{8}$ b) $\frac{5}{4} + \frac{1}{6}$
   c) $\frac{4}{3} + \frac{1}{5}$ d) $\frac{7}{6} + \frac{1}{8}$

8. Subtract.
   a) $\frac{7}{4} - \frac{4}{3}$ b) $\frac{6}{5} - \frac{5}{6}$
   c) $\frac{3}{5} - \frac{2}{4}$ d) $\frac{7}{8} - \frac{4}{5}$

9. Add.
   a) $\frac{2}{3} + \frac{1}{2} + \frac{3}{4}$ b) $\frac{2}{5} + \frac{3}{10} + \frac{5}{2}$
   c) $\frac{4}{9} + \frac{5}{6} + \frac{1}{3}$ d) $\frac{3}{2} + \frac{1}{6} + \frac{4}{5}$

10. Write each sum as a multiplication question.
    a) $\frac{3}{5} + \frac{3}{5} + \frac{3}{5} + \frac{3}{5} + \frac{3}{5}$
    b) $\frac{7}{4} + \frac{7}{4} + \frac{7}{4}$

11. Find each sum in question 10.

12. Multiply.
    Draw a diagram to show each answer.
    a) $\frac{2}{8} \times 5$ b) $\frac{11}{6} \times 3$
    c) $4 \times \frac{7}{2}$ d) $6 \times \frac{1}{8}$

13. Multiply.
    Draw a picture on grid paper to show the product.
    a) 2.3×3.4 b) 1.8×2.2
    c) 4.1×3.7 d) 1.7×2.9

14. Divide.
    a) $3.5 \div 1.4$ b) $18.2 \div 5.2$
    c) $10.08 \div 3.6$ d) $6.75 \div 4.5$

15. Find the area of a rectangular vegetable plot with length 10.8 m and width 5.2 m.

16. A rectangular quilt has area 3.15 m^2.
    The quilt is 2.1 m long.
    What is its width?

17. One kilogram of grapes cost $5.89.
    a) How much do 2.4 kg cost?
    b) How much change is there from a $20-bill?

18. Evaluate.
    a) $3.5 + 2.4 \times 1.7 - 3.8$
    b) $15.3 - 8.75 \div 2.5 \times 1.2$

1. This graph was produced with a spreadsheet program.

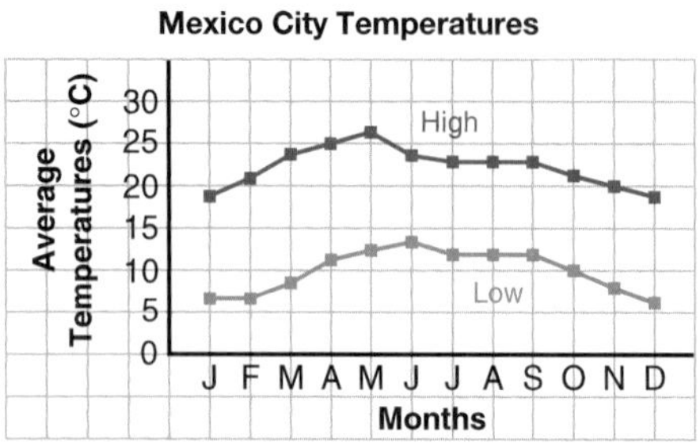

Mexico City Temperatures

Average Temperatures (°C)
30
25
20
15
10
5
0
High
Low
J F M A M J J A S O N D
Months

a) What is the approximate high temperature in May? In June?
b) Estimate the difference between the average high and the average low temperatures in October.
c) During which months does the average high temperature increase? When does the average low temperature increase?
d) Write one question for which each following statement is the answer.
   i) The highest temperature is about 26°C.
   ii) The lowest temperature is about 13°C.

2. The table shows the approximate areas of some countries.

Country	Area (km²)
Austria	84 000
Costa Rica	51 000
Denmark	43 000
Greece	132 000
Japan	378 000
Italy	301 000
Spain	195 000

a) Draw a bar graph. Explain why a line graph would not be appropriate.
b) Use your graph. Estimate the difference between the areas of Greece and Italy.
c) Use the table. Estimate the difference between the areas of Greece and Italy.
d) Look at a map of Europe. Are your answers for parts b and c reasonable?
e) Estimate the sum of the areas of Austria, Denmark, and Spain. Explain how you estimated the sum.

3. Here are the heights in centimetres of some 12-year-old students.
125, 152, 134, 141, 153, 127, 168, 154, 139, 147, 132, 137, 163, 133
a) Draw a stem-and-leaf plot.
b) What is the median height?
c) What is the mode? The mean?

4. The median shoe size of eight 12-year-old boys is $6\frac{1}{2}$. What might the shoe sizes be? Explain your answer.

5. Here are the times, in minutes and seconds, for 28 swimmers who raced in the 200-m backstroke:
2:25, 3:01, 1:45, 3:15, 2:30, 2:54, 3:10, 1:59, 2:25, 3:10, 3:09, 2:43, 2:18, 3:04, 2:53, 2:28, 3:14, 2:37, 3:03, 2:39, 2:27, 2:43, 3:09, 2:54, 3:11, 2:38, 2:42, 2:57
a) Draw a stem-and-leaf plot.
b) What is the range?
c) Which stem has the most leaves? What does this mean?
d) What is the median time?
e) What is the mode time?

1. **a)** On 0.5-cm grid paper, draw 3 different parallelograms with base 5.5 cm and height 8.5 cm.
b) What is the area of each parallelogram in part a?

2. On 0.5-cm grid paper, draw 3 different parallelograms with area 24 cm^2. What is the base and height of each parallelogram?

3. Use a formula.
Find the area of a parallelogram with base 11.3 cm and height 5.7 cm.

4. The window below consists of 5 pieces of glass. Each piece that is a parallelogram has a base of 1.6 m. What is the area of one parallelogram?

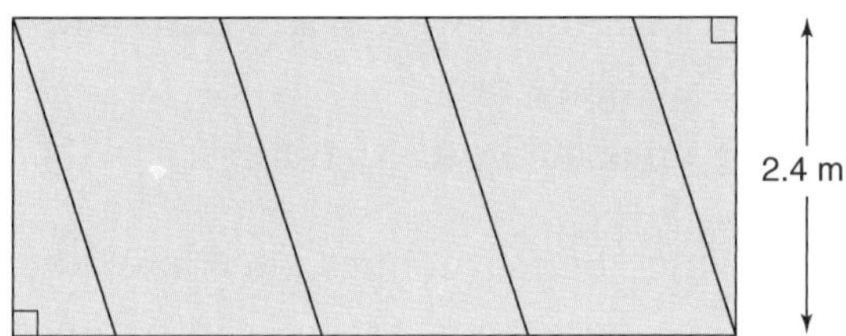

5. The base of each triangle in the window above is 0.8 m.
a) What is the area of one triangle?
b) What is the area of the window? Explain how you found the area.

6. **a)** On 0.5 cm-grid paper, draw 3 different triangles with base 4.5 cm and height 7.5 cm.
b) What is the area of each triangle in part a?

7. On 0.5-cm grid paper, draw 3 different triangles with area 12 cm^2.
a) What is the base and height of each triangle?
b) How are the triangles in part a related to the parallelograms in question 2?

8. Use a formula.
Find the area of a triangle with base 4.3 cm and height 2.6 cm.

9. **a)** Find the area of the shaded region in the square below.

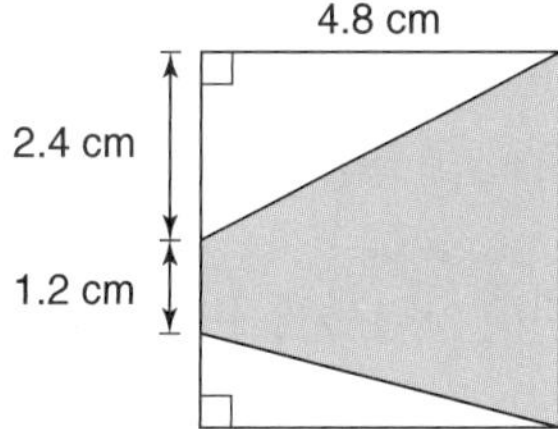

b) How many different ways can you find the area? Explain each way.
c) Estimate the perimeter of the shaded region in part a.
d) Can you calculate the perimeter of the shaded region in part a? Explain.

10. Calculate the perimeter and area of this figure.

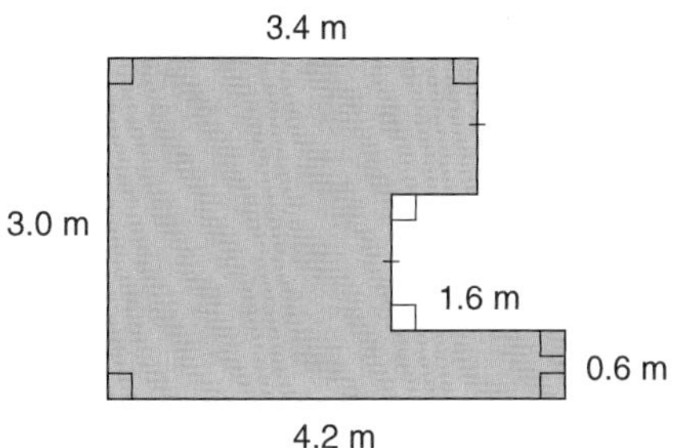

Use these figures for questions 1 to 5.

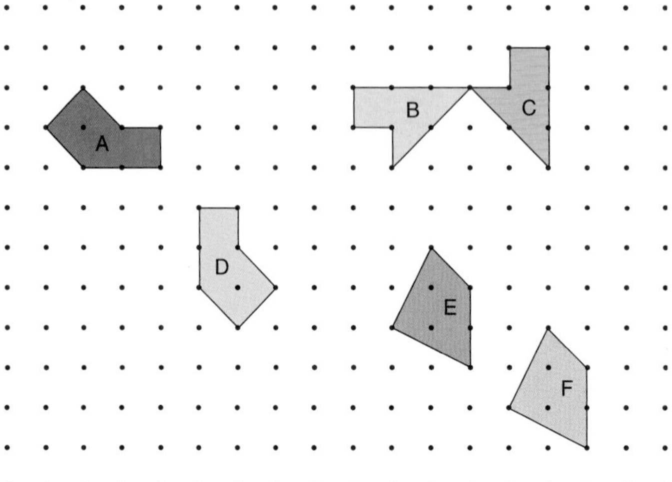

1. Classify each figure.
Describe its attributes.

2. Identify pairs of congruent figures. Explain how you know the figures are congruent.

3. Identify the transformation that each pair of congruent figures represents.

4. a) Use one figure from each pair. Try to tile the plane with each figure. Identify the figures that tile the plane.

b) For each figure that does not tile the plane:
- Find another figure that combines with the figure to tile the plane.
- Tile the plane with the two figures combined.

5. Use one tiling pattern from question 4. Use one of each type of figures. Explain how you can use transformations to tile the plane.

6. Use square dot paper or isometric dot paper. Draw each polygon.

a) an equilateral triangle with side length 3 units

b) a rhombus with base 4 units and an angle of 60°

c) an acute isosceles triangle

7. Which figures in question 6 have line symmetry? Draw the lines of symmetry on the figures.

8. Plot these points on a grid:
A(10, 8), B(10, 10), C(12, 12), D(13, 9)
Join the points to make a quadrilateral. Draw the image of the quadrilateral after each transformation.

a) a translation 3 units right and 4 units up

b) a reflection in a vertical line through (7, 0)

c) a rotation of a $\frac{1}{4}$ turn clockwise about A

1. Estimate what percent of each figure is shaded. Explain your strategy.

a) 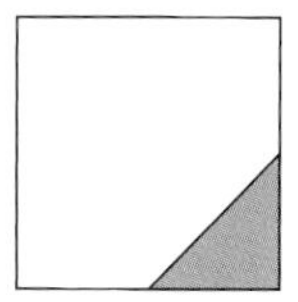

b) 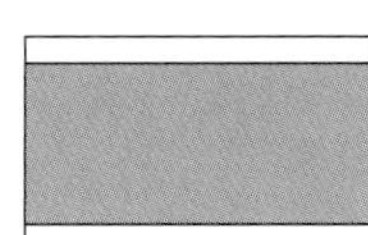

c) 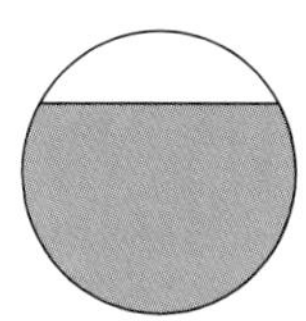

d) 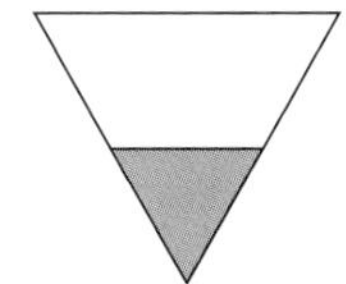

2. Write each fraction as a percent, then as a decimal.

a) $\frac{3}{4}$ b) $\frac{3}{2}$ c) $\frac{3}{5}$ d) $\frac{3}{20}$

3. Find each percent.

a) 10% of $200 b) 1% of $85
c) 10% of $60 d) 1% of $187
e) 10% of $55 f) 10% of $140
g) 1% of $5 h) 15% of $10

4. Find each percent. Explain your strategy.

a) 2% of $100
b) 4% of $300
c) 2% of $700
d) 3% of $800
e) 5% of $3000
f) 9% of $500
g) 4% of $100
h) 5% of $1000

5. Leigh drove 1470 km from Smith Falls, ON to Thunder Bay, ON. She stopped 370 km from Smith Falls. About what percent of her trip had she completed when she stopped?

6. Calculate the 15% sales tax and the total cost of each item.

a) a bicycle that costs $349.99
b) a CD that costs $17.98

7. This year 27 students will graduate from Central School. This is 15% of the school's population. What is the population of the school?

8. The depth of deep sea trenches is measured from sea level. The Tonga Trench in the South Pacific is 10 800 m deep. Yap Trench in the West Pacific is 79% of the depth of the Tonga Trench. How deep is the Yap Trench, to the nearest 10 m?

9. This graph shows how much time is spent in one day watching different types of TV programs.

TV Programs

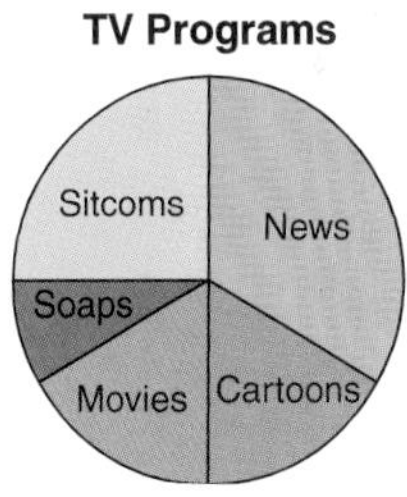

a) Which type of program is watched for the greatest amount of time?
b) Which two types of programs are watched for approximately the same amount of time?
c) Estimate the fraction of time spent watching sitcoms.
d) Suppose TV is watched for 1000 days. Estimate how much time is spent watching sitcoms.

1. Use an integer to describe each situation.
   a) The water level of Lake Superior rises 5 cm after low tide.
   b) The lowest recorded temperature is 89°C below 0°C recorded at Vostok, Antarctica, in 1983.
   c) A submarine river known as the Cromwell current flows below the surface of the Pacific ocean at depths up to 400 m.
   d) Mount Manaslu in Nepal has a height of 8156 m.

2. Use an integer to describe each situation.
   a) The time is 9 s before take-off.
   b) You earned $25 since yesterday.
   c) The average temperature close to the South Pole is 50°C below 0°C.

3. Sketch a number line. Show the integer that is 3 less than +2.

4. Replace each □ with < or > to make a true statement.
   a) −3 □ +5 b) −2 □ −4
   c) +1 □ 0 d) +8 □ −10

5. Order the integers from least to greatest.
   0, −2, +4, −15, +1, −1, +5

6. Write the integer that is out of order.
   a) −5, −2, +1, +17, +13
   b) −34, −7, +3, +7, −12
   c) −11, +11, +13, −13, +27
   d) −4, −3, +2, −1, 0

7. Add.
   a) (+6) + (+9) b) (−4) + (−7)
   c) (−8) + (−6) d) (−11) + (+5)
   e) (+7) + (−8) f) (−9) + (−12)
   g) (+13) + (−3) h) (−5) + (−8)

8. Subtract.
   a) (−14) − (+7) b) (+12) − (+9)
   c) (+16) − (−4) d) (−11) − (−8)
   e) (+22) − (+3) f) (+14) − (−7)
   g) (−19) − (−11) h) (+18) − (−3)

9. Add.
   Write the addition equation.
   a) (+4) + (+2) b) (−2) + (+3)
   c) (−3) + (−2) d) (+5) + (−6)
   e) (−23) + (+4) f) (−19) + (−3)
   g) (+13) + (−2) h) (+9) + (+13)

10. Subtract.
    Write the subtraction equation.
    a) (+5) − (+3) b) (+3) − (−4)
    c) (−5) − (+3) d) (−7) − (−4)
    e) (+13) − (−12) f) (−22) − (+32)
    g) (−23) − (−23) h) (−7) − (+10)

11. On December 11, the predicted high and low temperatures in Kenora, ON, were −1°C and −9°C.
    a) Which is the high temperature and which is the low temperature?
    b) What is the difference in temperatures?

12. Add or subtract as indicated.
    a) (+6) + (+6) b) (+6) + (−6)
    c) (−6) + (+6) d) (−6) + (−6)
    e) (+6) − (+6) f) (+6) − (−6)
    g) (−6) − (+6) h) (−6) − (−6)

Unit 10

1. Each pattern continues.
For each pattern:
i) Describe the pattern.
ii) Write the next 3 terms.
iii) Find the 15th term.
Explain how you found it.
a) 2, 5, 8, 11, 14, …
b) 1, 3, 6, 8, 11, …
c) 1, 3, 6, 10, 15, …
d) 3, 6, 11, 18, 27, …

2. a) Copy and complete this table for this pattern:
Multiply each Input number by 4, then subtract 1.

Input	Output
1	
2	
3	
4	
5	

b) Extend the table 3 more rows.
c) What patterns do you see in the table?
d) Graph the data.
e) Explain how the graph shows the patterns in the table.

3. Write each algebraic expression in words.
a) $x + 2$ b) $5 - y$ c) $3p$ d) $\frac{z}{2}$

4. Write an algebraic expression for each statement.
a) four more than two times a number
b) four less than two times a number
c) a number divided by four
d) two less than four times a number

5. Evaluate each expression by replacing n with 3.
a) $4 + n$ b) $4 - n$ c) $4 + \frac{3}{n}$
d) $4 - \frac{6}{n}$ e) $\frac{(n + 5)}{4}$ f) $\frac{(n - 1)}{2}$

6. Write an equation for each sentence.
a) Three more than a number is 18.
b) The sum of 6 and a number is 71.
c) A number divided by 5 is 14.
d) The product of 4 and a number is 64.

7. Write each equation in words.
a) $3p = 9$ b) $\frac{15}{n} = 3$
c) $r - 6 = 13$ d) $24n = 552$

8. Write an equation you can solve to answer each question.
a) Ray scored 14 points in the game. Tung scored 8 more points than Ray. How many points did Tung score?
b) Nema has 4 times as many hockey cards as Tamar. Tamar has 156 cards. How many cards does Nema have?
c) Adriel cycled 80 km less than Alona cycled. Alona cycled 218 km. How far did Adriel cycle?

9. Solve by inspection.
a) $n + 5 = 30$ b) $n - 5 = 30$
c) $5n = 30$ d) $\frac{n}{5} = 30$
e) $\frac{30}{n} = 5$ f) $5n + 10 = 30$

10. Solve by systematic trial.
a) $3x + 5 = 26$ b) $3x - 5 = 25$
c) $24 - 3x = 6$ d) $24 + 3x = 66$
e) $\frac{x}{13} = 19$ f) $\frac{414}{x} = 18$

1. The 12 face cards (J, Q, K) from a deck of cards are placed in a bag. One card is taken from the bag at random. The pointer on this spinner is spun.

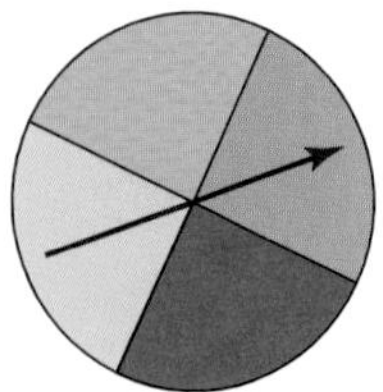

a) List the possible outcome of taking a card and spinning the pointer.
b) How many outcomes include taking the Jack of spades?
c) How many outcomes include landing on a green sector?

2. You will need a deck of playing cards.
a) Make a table with these headings.

Outcome	Tally	Frequency	Relative Frequency

b) A card is picked at random from the deck. Assume the suit does not matter. List the possible outcomes in the *Outcome* column.
c) Are the outcomes in part b equally likely? Explain.
d) Pick a card at random from the deck. Record it in the *Tally* column. Return the card to the deck. Return this experiment until you have 50 results. Complete the *Frequency* column.
e) Calculate and record the relative frequencies.
f) Do the results confirm your answer in part c? Explain.

3. A number cube is labelled 1 to 6. The number cube is rolled 150 times. Predict the number of times:
a) a 1 will show
b) a multiple of 3 will show
c) a number less than 4 will show

4. A box contains 3 red, 2 green, and 4 white candies. Carmen picked one candy at random, found it was white, and ate it. She picked a second candy at random, found it was red, and ate it. Carmen picked a third candy at random. Which colour is it most likely to be? Explain.

5. In the game SCRABBLE, there are 100 tiles. Two tiles are blank. Here is the number of tiles for each letter: A, 9; B: 2; C: 2; D: 4; E: 12; F: 2; G: 3; H: 2; I: 9, J: 1; K: 1; L: 4; M: 2; N: 6; O: 8; P: 2; Q: 1; R: 6; S: 4; T: 6; U: 4; V: 2; W: 2; X: 1; Y: 2; Z: 1.
The 100 tiles are placed in a bag. One tile is picked at random.
a) Which letter has the greatest probability of being picked?
b) What is the probability of picking a blank?
c) Which letter has the least probability of being picked?
d) Which letters have the same probability of being picked? What are these probabilities?
e) Does any letter have a 0% chance of being picked? Explain.

Take It Further

1. Find 2 consecutive prime numbers whose product is 899.

2. Use four 6s to make 42.

3. Use 25 coins to make $1.

4. Move one number from one box to another box so the sums of the numbers in the boxes will then be equal.

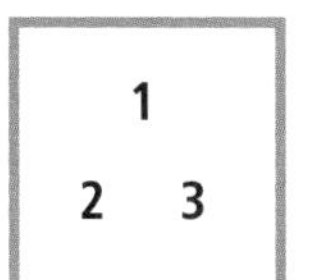

4
5 6

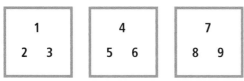

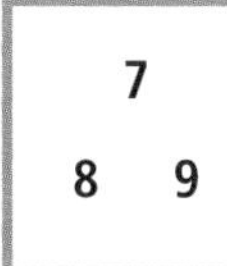

5. Use the digits 0, 1, 2, 3, 4, 5, 6, 7, 8, 9 to make a true equation.
$(\square + \square - \square + \square - \square + \square) \times$
$(\square - \square + \square - \square) = 0$

6. Lloyd gave $\frac{1}{2}$ his hockey cards to Jenny. He then gave $\frac{2}{3}$ of his remaining cards to Jerome. Lloyd ended up with 10 cards. How many cards did he start with?

7. Find 4 consecutive odd numbers that add to 120.

8. Leave the numerals in the order shown below. Place only + and − signs to make a true equation.
1 2 3 4 5 6 7 8 9 0 = 100

9. Use five 5s to make 30.

10. Use 3 five times to make 31.

11. Copy this figure on grid paper. How many rectangles are there in the figure?

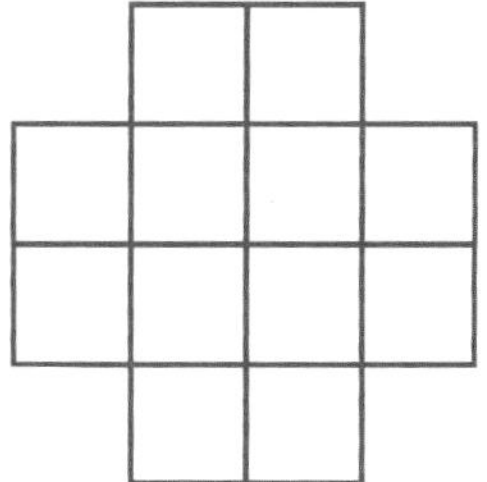

12. Use the digits 0, 1, 2, 3, 4, 5, 6, 7, 8, 9 to make a true equation.
$\square\square + \square\square + \square + \square\square + \square + \square + \square$
$= 99$

13. Use square dot paper.
Outline a square array of 25 dots.
Move only up and to the right.
How many paths can you take from A to B?

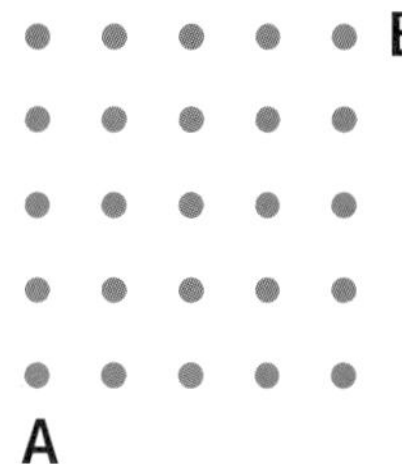

14. Use seven 4s to make 100.

15. Without using a calculator, find the sum of the whole numbers from 1 to 100, inclusive.
Try to find a quick way to do this.
Explain your thinking.

16. Twenty-four players enter a singles tennis tournament. How many matches must be played to find a winner?

Take It Further

17. Copy this diagram. How can you remove 6 line segments from this figure to get 2 triangles?

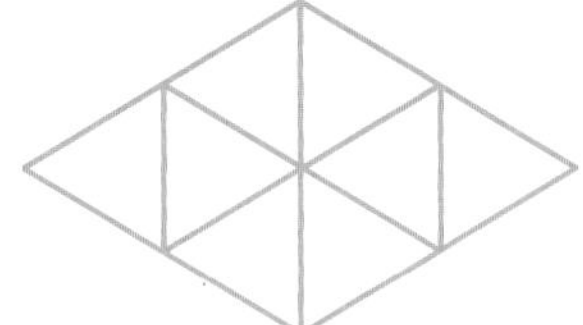

18. Two organisms are placed in a container. Their numbers double every 24 h. At the end of 14 days, the container is full. When was it half full?

19. The number 2 is special because $2 + 2 = 4$ and $2 \times 2 = 4$. Find another pair of numbers whose sum equals their product. Don't use 0. The numbers may be different.

20. The sum of the digits of a 2-digit number is 5. When the digits are reversed, the new number is 9 less than the original number. What was the original number?

21. Ali started a job on Monday, June 1. He was paid 1¢ the first day, 2¢ the second day, 4¢ the third day, and so on. His earnings doubled each day. He worked Monday to Friday all through June. How much did he earn altogether?

22. Suppose you have a 5-L container and an 8-L container. You need exactly 2 L of water in one of the containers. How can you do this?

23. Joanne had a bag of potatoes. When she counted them by 2s, she had 1 left over. When she counted them by 3s, there were 2 left over.
When she counted them by 4s, there were 3 left over.
When she counted them by 5s, there were none left over.
How many potatoes were in the bag?

24. Ms. Jones built a fence around her square vegetable garden.
Each side had 10 fence posts.
How many fence posts did she use?

25. Choose a digit. Use 3 of these digits to make 30. Try to find more than one way to do this.

26. Use counters to make this triangle. How can you move 3 of the counters to make the triangle point down instead of up?

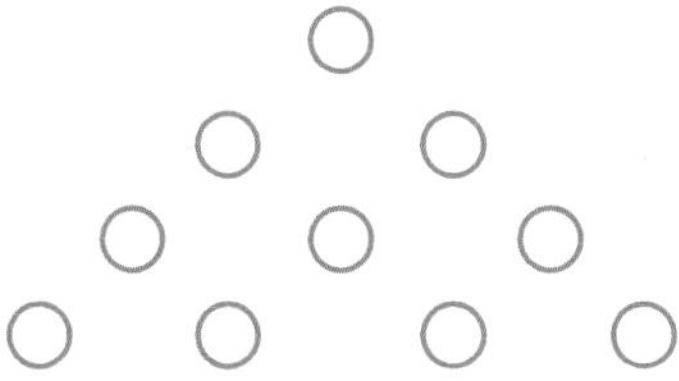

27. A kettle leaked 2 drops the first day, 4 drops the second day, and 8 drops the third day. It continues to leak following this pattern. When will the 500th drop leak?

28. The mass of a bag of stone chips is 20 kg plus half a bag of stone chips. What is the mass of a bag and a half of stone chips?

Illustrated Glossary

acute angle: an angle measuring less than 90°

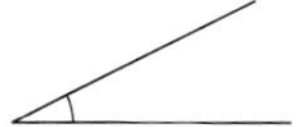

acute triangle: a triangle with three acute angles

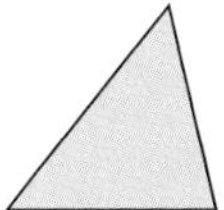

algebraic expression: a mathematical expression containing a variable: for example, $6x - 4$ is an algebraic expression

angle: the figure formed by two rays from the same endpoint

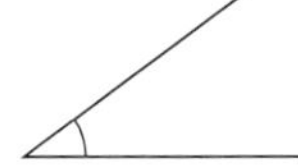

approximate: a number close to the exact value of an expression; the symbol $\doteq$ means "is approximately equal to"

area: the number of square units needed to cover a region

array: an arrangement in rows and columns

assumption: something that is accepted as true, but has not been proved

average: a single number that represents a set of numbers; see *mean*, *median*, and *mode*

bar graph: a graph that displays data by using horizontal or vertical bars (see page 175)

bar notation: the use of a horizontal bar over a decimal digit to indicate that it repeats; for example, $1.\overline{3}$ means 1.333 333 …

base: the side of a polygon or the face of a solid from which the height is measured; the factor repeated in a power

bias: an emphasis on characteristics that are not typical of the entire population

capacity: the amount a container can hold

circle graph: a diagram that uses parts of a circle to display data (see page 307)

common denominator: a number that is a multiple of each of the given denominators; for example, 12 is a common denominator for the fractions $\frac{1}{3}, \frac{5}{4}, \frac{7}{12}$

common factor: a number that is a factor of each of the given numbers; for example, 3 is a common factor of 15, 9, and 21

composite number: a number with three or more factors; for example, 8 is a composite number because its factors are 1, 2, 4, and 8

concave polygon: has at least one angle greater than 180°

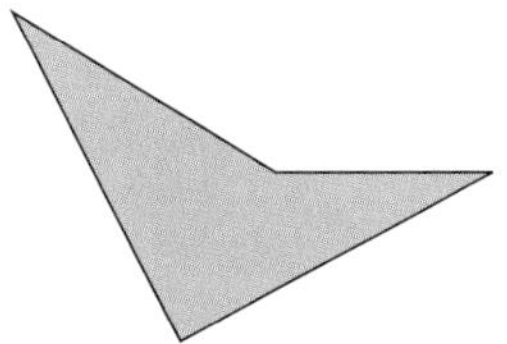

cone: a solid formed by a region and all line segments joining points on the boundary of the region to a point not in the region

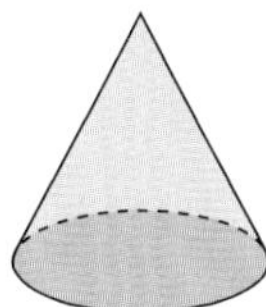

congruent: figures that have the same size and shape, but not necessarily the same orientation

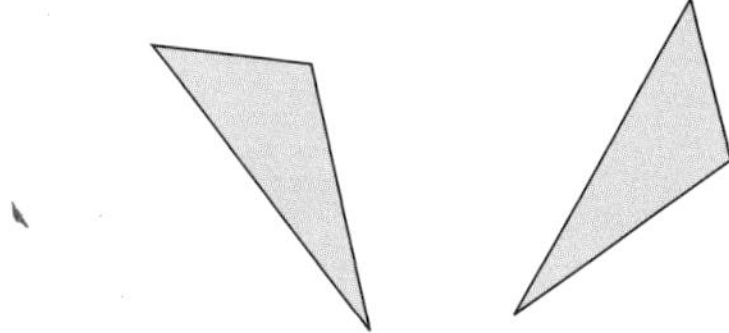

consecutive numbers: integers that come one after the other without any integers missing; for example, 34, 35, 36 are consecutive numbers, so are $-2, -1, 0$, and 1

convex polygon: has all angles less than 180°

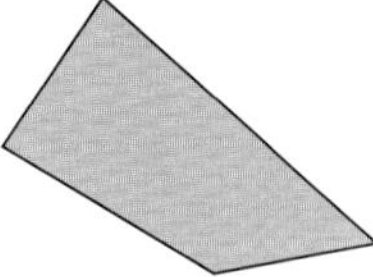

coordinate axes: the horizontal and vertical axes on a grid

coordinate grid: a two-dimensional surface on which a coordinate system has been set up

coordinates: the numbers in an ordered pair that locate a point on the grid

cube: a solid with six congruent square faces

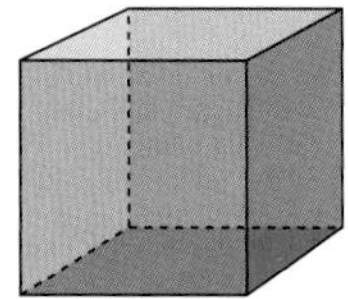

cube number: a power with exponent 3; for example, 8 is a cube number because $8 = 2^3$

cubic units: units that measure volume

cylinder: a solid with two parallel, congruent, circular bases

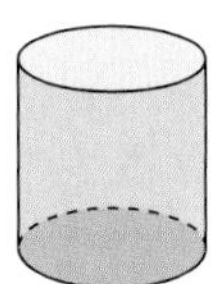

data: facts or information

database: an organized collection of facts or information, often stored on a computer

denominator: the term below the line in a fraction

diagonal: a line segment that joins two vertices of a figure, but is not a side

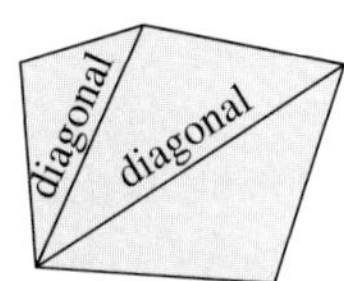

digit: any of the symbols used to write numerals; for example, in the base-ten system the digits are 0, 1, 2, 3, 4, 5, 6, 7, 8, and 9

dimensions: measurements, such as length, width, and height

dodecahedron: a polyhedron with 12 faces

equation: a mathematical statement that two expressions are equal

equilateral triangle: a triangle with three equal sides

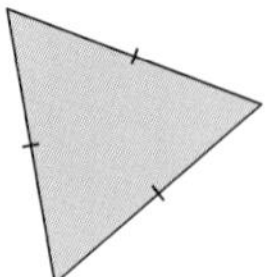

equivalent: having the same value; for example, $\frac{2}{3}$ and $\frac{6}{9}$ are equivalent fractions; 2:3 and 6:9 are equivalent ratios

estimate: a reasoned guess that is close to the actual value, without calculating it exactly

evaluate: to substitute a value for each variable in an expression, then simplify; to find the answer

even number: a number that has 2 as a factor; for example, 2, 4, 6

event: any set of outcomes of an experiment

experimental probability: the probability of an event calculated from experimental results; another name for the *relative frequency* of an outcome

exponent: a number, shown in a smaller size and raised, that tells how many times the number before it is used as a factor; for example, 2 is the exponent in 6^2

expression: a mathematical phrase made up of numbers and/or variables connected by operations

factor: to factor means to write as a product; for example, $20 = 2 \times 2 \times 5$

formula: a rule that is expressed as an equation

fraction: an indicated quotient of two quantities

fraction strips: strips of paper used to model fractions (see page 121)

frequency: the number of times a particular number occurs in a set of data

frustum: part of a cone or pyramid that remains when a cut is made parallel to the base, and the top of the cone or pyramid is removed (see page 90)

greatest common factor (GCF): the greatest number that divides into each number in a set; for example, 5 is the greatest common factor of 10 and 15

hectare: a unit of area that is equal to 10 000 m^2

hexagon: a six-sided polygon

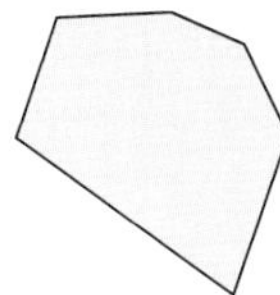

horizontal axis: the horizontal number line on a coordinate grid

icosahedron: a polyhedron with 20 faces

image: the figure that results from a transformation

improper fraction: a fraction with the numerator greater than the denominator; for example, both $\frac{6}{5}$ and $\frac{5}{3}$ are improper fractions

integers: the set of numbers ... $-3, -2, -1, 0, +1, +2, +3, \ldots$

intersecting lines: lines that meet or cross; lines that have one point in common

isometric view: a representation of an object as it would appear in three dimensions

isosceles acute triangle: a triangle with two equal sides and all angles less than 90°

isosceles obtuse triangle: a triangle with two equal sides and one angle greater than 90°

isosceles right triangle: a triangle with two equal sides and a 90° angle

isosceles triangle: a triangle with two equal sides

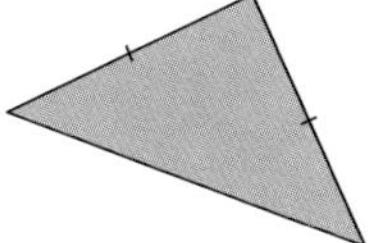

kite: a quadrilateral with two pairs of equal adjacent sides

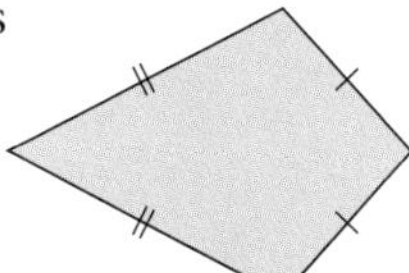

line graph: a graph that displays data by using points joined by line segments (see page 189)

line segment: the part of a line between two points on the line

line symmetry: a figure has line symmetry when it can be divided into 2 congruent parts, so that one part coincides with the other part when the figure is folded at the line of symmetry; for example, line *l* is the line of symmetry for figure ABCD

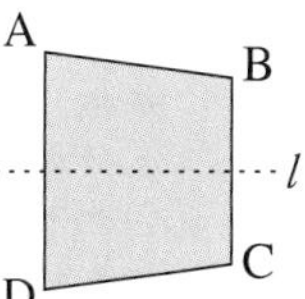

lowest common multiple (LCM): the lowest multiple that is the same for two numbers; for example, the lowest common multiple of 12 and 21 is 84

magic square: an array of numbers in which the sum of the numbers in any row, column, or diagonal is always the same (see page 326)

magic sum: the sum of the numbers in a row, column, or diagonal of a magic square

mass: the amount of matter in an object

mean: the sum of a set of numbers divided by the number of numbers in the set

median: the middle number when data are arranged in numerical order; if there is an even number of data, the median is the mean of the two middle numbers

midpoint: the point that divides a line segment into two equal parts

mixed number: a number consisting of a whole number and a fraction; for example, $1\frac{1}{18}$ is a mixed number

mode: the number that occurs most often in a set of numbers

multiple: the product of a given number and a natural number; for example, some multiples of 8 are 8, 16, 24,...

natural numbers: the set of numbers 1, 2, 3, 4, 5,...

negative number: a number less than 0

numerator: the term above the line in a fraction

obtuse angle: an angle greater than 90° and less than 180°

obtuse triangle: a triangle with one angle greater than 90°

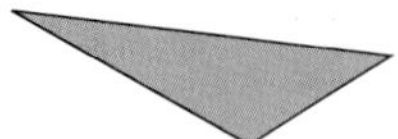

octagon: an eight-sided polygon

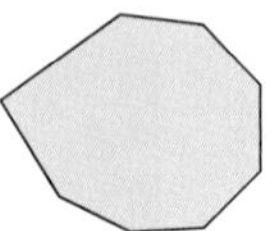

octahedron: a polyhedron with 8 faces

odd number: a number that does not have 2 as a factor; for example, 1, 3, 7

operation: a mathematical process or action such as addition, subtraction, multiplication, or division

opposite integers: two integers with a sum of 0; for example, +3 and −3 are opposite integers

order of operations: the rules that are followed when simplifying or evaluating an expression

outcome: a possible result of an experiment or a possible answer to a survey question

parallel lines: lines on the same flat surface that do not intersect

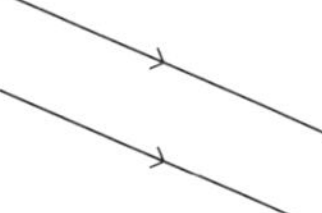

parallelogram: a quadrilateral with both pairs of opposite sides parallel

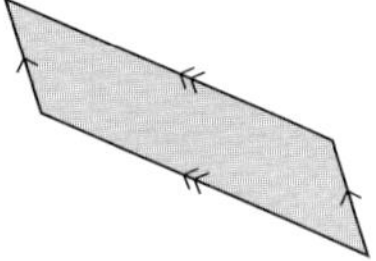

pentagon: a five-sided polygon

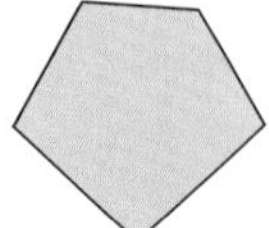

per capita: for each person

percent: the number of parts per 100; the numerator of a fraction with denominator 100

perfect cube: a number that is the cube of a whole number; for example, 64 is a perfect cube because $64 = 4^3$

perfect square: a number that is the square of a whole number; for example, 16 is a perfect square because $16 = 4^2$

perimeter: the distance around a closed figure

perpendicular lines: intersect at 90°

pictograph: a graph that uses a symbol to represent a certain number, and repetitions of the symbol illustrate the data (see page 176)

pictorial diagram: shows the shape of an object in two dimensions

polygon: a closed figure that consists of line segments; for example, triangles and quadrilaterals are polygons

polyhedron (*plural,* polyhedra): a solid with faces that are polygons

population: the set of all things or people being considered

positive number: a number greater than 0

power: an expression of a product of equal factors; for example, $4 \times 4 \times 4$ can be expressed as 4^3; 4 is the base and 3 is the exponent

prediction: a statement of what you think will happen

primary data: data collected by oneself; first-hand

prime number: a whole number with exactly two factors, itself and 1; for example, 2, 3, 5, 7, 11, 29, 31, and 43

prism: a solid that has two congruent and parallel faces (the *bases*), and other faces that are parallelograms

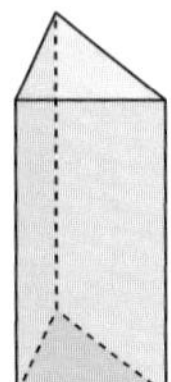

probability: the likelihood of a particular outcome; the number of times a particular outcome occurs, written as a fraction of the total number of outcomes

product: the result when two or more numbers are multiplied

pyramid: a solid that has one face that is a polygon (the *base*), and other faces that are triangles with a common vertex

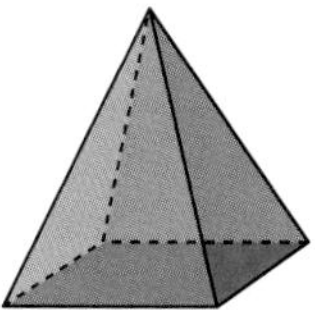

quadrilateral: a four-sided polygon

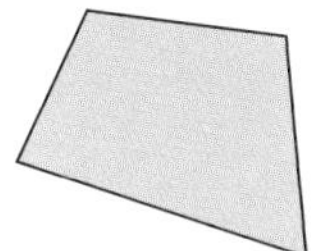

quotient: the result when one number is divided by another

range: the difference between the greatest and least numbers in a set of data

rate: a certain quantity or amount of one thing considered in relation to a unit of another thing

ratio: a comparison of two or more quantities with the same unit

rectangle: a quadrilateral that has four right angles

rectangular prism: a prism that has rectangular faces

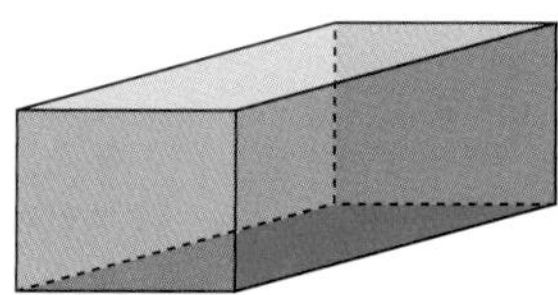

rectangular pyramid: a pyramid with a rectangular base

reflection: a transformation that is illustrated by a figure and its image in a mirror line

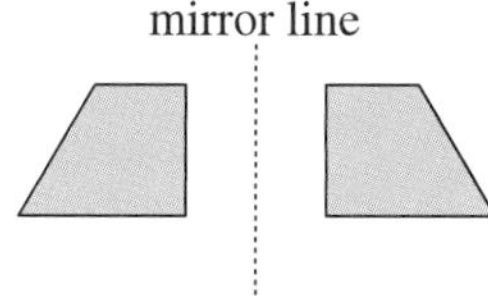

reflex angle: an angle between 180° and 360°

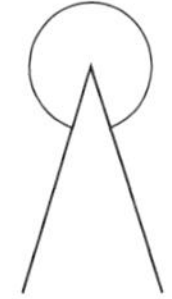

regular dodecahedron: a regular polyhedron with 12 congruent faces; each face is a regular pentagon (see page 90)

regular hexagon: a polygon that has six equal sides and six equal angles

regular icosahedron: a regular polyhedron with 20 congruent faces; each face is an equilateral triangle (see page 90)

regular octagon: a polygon that has eight equal sides and eight equal angles

regular octahedron: a regular polyhedron with 8 congruent faces; each face is an equilateral triangle (see page 90)

regular polygon: a polygon that has all sides equal and all angles equal

regular polyhedron: a solid with faces that are congruent regular polygons, with the same number of edges meeting at each vertex (see page 76)

related denominators: two fractions where the denominator of one fraction is a factor of the other; their lowest common denominator is the greater of the two denominators

relative frequency: the number of times a particular outcome occurred, written as a fraction of the total number of times the experiment was conducted

repeating decimal: a decimal with a repeating pattern in the digits that follow the decimal point; it is written with a bar above the repeating digits; for example, $\frac{1}{11} = 0.\overline{09}$

rhombus: a parallelogram with four equal sides

right angle: a 90° angle

right triangle: a triangle that has one right angle

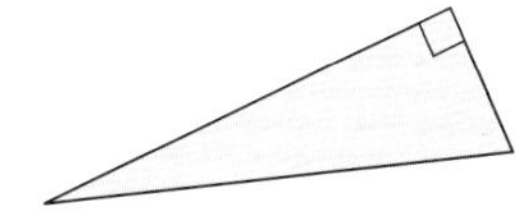

rotation: a transformation in which a figure is turned about a fixed point

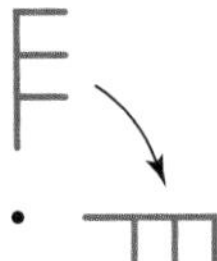

rotational symmetry: a figure that coincides with itself in less than one full turn is said to have rotational symmetry; for example, a square has rotational symmetry of order 4 about its centre O

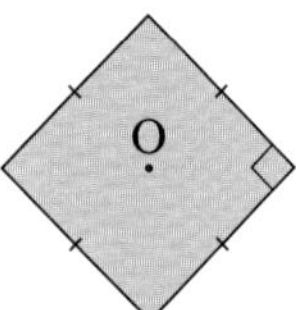

sample/sampling: a representative portion of a population

scale: the ratio of the distance between two points on a map, model, or diagram to the distance between the actual locations; the numbers on the axes of a graph

scalene triangle: a triangle with all sides different

scatter plot: a graph of data that is a set of points

secondary data: data not collected by oneself, but by others; data found from the library, or the Internet

similar figures: figures with the same shape, but not necessarily the same size

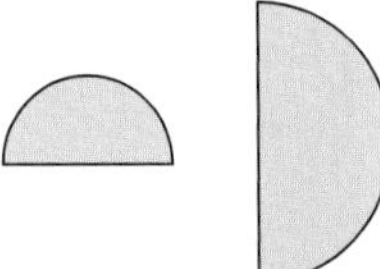

simplest form: a ratio with terms that have no common factors, other than 1; a fraction with numerator and denominator that have no common factors, other than 1

spreadsheet: a computer-generated arrangement of data in rows and columns, where a change in one value results in appropriate calculated changes in the other values

square: a rectangle with four equal sides

square number: the product of a number multiplied by itself; for example, 25 is the square of 5

square root: a number which, when multiplied by itself, results in a given number; for example, 5 is a square root of 25

statistics: the branch of mathematics that deals with the collection, organization, and interpretation of data

stem-and-leaf plot: an arrangement of data; for two-digit numbers, the tens digits are shown as the "stems" and the ones digits as the "leaves" (see page 179)

straight angle: an angle measuring 180°

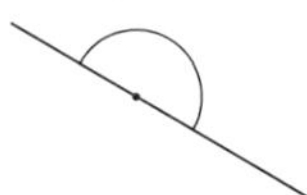

straightedge: a strip of wood, metal, or plastic with a straight edge, but no markings

surface area: the total area of the surface of an object

symmetrical: possessing symmetry; see *line symmetry* and *rotational symmetry*

term: of a fraction is the numerator or the denominator of the fraction

terminating decimal: a decimal with a certain number of digits after the decimal point; for example, $\frac{1}{8} = 0.125$

tessellation: a tiling pattern

tetrahedron: a solid with four triangular faces; a triangular pyramid

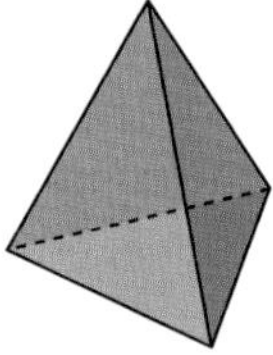

theoretical probability: the number of favourable outcomes written as a fraction of the total number of possible outcomes

three-dimensional: having length, width, and depth or height

transformation: a translation, rotation, or reflection

translation: a transformation that moves a point or a figure in a straight line to another position on the same flat surface

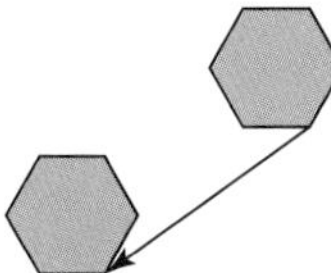

trapezoid: a quadrilateral that has at least one pair of parallel sides

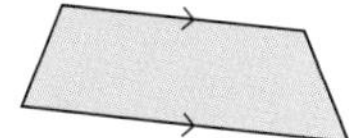

tree diagram: a diagram that resembles the roots or branches of a tree, used to count outcomes (see page 408)

triangle: a three-sided polygon

two-dimensional: having length and width, but no thickness, height, or depth

unit fraction: a fraction that has a numerator of 1

unit price: the price of one item, or the price of a particular mass or volume of an item

unit rate: the quantity associated with a single unit of another quantity; for example, 6 m in 1 s is a unit rate; it is written as 6 m/s

unrelated denominators: two fractions where the denominators have no common factors; their lowest common denominator is the product of the two denominators

variable: a letter or symbol representing a quantity that can vary

vertex (*plural,* **vertices):** the corner of a figure or a solid

vertical axis: the vertical number line on a coordinate grid

volume: the amount of space occupied by an object

whole numbers: the set of numbers 0, 1, 2, 3,…

zero pair: two opposite numbers whose sum is equal to zero

Index

Acknowledgments

The publisher wishes to thank the following sources for photographs, illustrations, and other materials used in this book. Care has been taken to determine and locate ownership of copyright material in this text. We will gladly receive information enabling us to rectify any errors or omissions in credits.

Photography

Cover: Gail Shumway/Getty Images
pp. 2–3 Ian Crysler; p. 4 (top) Photodisc; p. 4 (bottom) G.K. & Vikki Hart/Photodisc; p. 5 (top) Photodisc; p. 5 (bottom) David Thompson/Life File; p. 10 Canadian Press/Ryan Remiorz; p. 12 Corel Collection *Insects*; p. 13 Canadian Press/Harold Barkley; p. 23 Ray Boudreau; p.26 C Squared Studios/Photodisc/Getty Images; p. 27 Michael Newman/PhotoEdit Inc.; p. 28 Stefano Bianchetti/CORBIS/MAGMA; p. 32 © Comstock Images www.comstock.com; p. 39 Ray Boudreau; p. 40 Dorling Kindersley Media Library; p. 41 (top to bottom) Dorling Kindersley Media Library; John Warden/Index Stock; Photodisc/Getty Images; Don Mason/CORBIS/MAGMA; p. 52 Canadian Press/Don Denton; p. 53 Ian Crysler; p. 61 Anna Zuckerman–Vdovenko/PhotoEdit Inc.; p. 62 Ray Boudreau; p. 67 Ray Boudreau; p. 68 Canadian Press/*The London Free Press*/Christian Laforce; p. 69 Corel Collection *Classic Aviation*; p. 70 Corbis Royalty–Free/MAGMA; p. 72 (left) Ian Crysler; p. 72 (centre) Corel Collection *Working Animals*; p. 72 (right) Corel Collection *Mammals*; pp. 74–75 Gatorade® Bill Aron/PhotoEdit Inc.; CD case Photodisc; Timberland® shoes Cindy Charles/PhotoEdit Inc.; all others Ian Crysler; p. 78 Ray Boudreau; p. 80 Ray Boudreau; p.81 (left) Dadang Tri/Reuters/CORBIS/MAGMA; p. 81 (centre) James Shaffer/PhotoEdit Inc.; p. 81 (right) Corel Collection *Canoeing Adventure*; p. 82 Ray Boudreau; p. 84 Ray Boudreau; p. 85 Ray Boudreau; p. 86 Ray Boudreau; p. 87 (left) Ray McVay/Photodisc/Getty Images; p. 87 (centre) Ian Crysler; p. 87 (right) David Toase/Photodisc; p. 88 James Shaffer/PhotoEdit Inc.; p. 92 Jules Frazier; p. 93 (left column top to bottom) Ray McVay/Photodisc/Getty Images; Davies and Star/Getty Images; C Squared Studios/Photodisc/Getty Images; Ray Boudreau; p. 93 (right column, left) © Comstock Images www.comstock.com; (right) Dorling Kindersley Media Library; p. 97 Ray Boudreau; p. 101 Ray Boudreau; p. 104 Ray Boudreau; p. 106 Ray Boudreau; p. 107 (top) Ray Boudreau; p. 107 (centre) Dorling Kindersley Media Library; p. 107 (bottom) Cretas Images; p. 110 Spenser Grant/PhotoEdit Inc.; p. 111 Ray Boudreau; p. 112 Ian Crysler; p.

123 Ian Crysler; p. 127 Myrleen Ferguson/PhotoEdit Inc.; p. 131 Ray Boudreau; p. 132 Ray Boudreau; p. 135 Michael Newman/PhotoEdit Inc.; p. 136 Ray Boudreau; p. 139 Ray Boudreau; p. 144 Ray Boudreau; p. 153 Photodisc/Getty Images; p. 155 Stone Skyold/PhotoEdit Inc.; p. 156 Ray Boudreau; p. 157 Ray Boudreau; p. 162 Ray Boudreau; p. 166 Tom Stewart/CORBIS/MAGMA; p. 167 (top left) Tony Freeman/PhotoEdit Inc.; p. 167 (top right) Photodisc/Getty Images; p. 167 (bottom) Rudy von Briel/PhotoEdit Inc.; p. 174 (top) Ray Boudreau; p. 174 (bottom) Corel Collection *Birds*; p. 177 Ed Kashi/CORBIS/MAGMA; p. 179 Ray Boudreau; p. 183 Canadian Press/Jacques Boissinot; p. 185 Bettmann/CORBIS/MAGMA; p. 186 Mary Kate Denney/PhotoEdit Inc.; p. 188 D. Berry/Photo Link; p. 197 Digital Vision; p. 206 Ray Boudreau; p. 207 Ray Boudreau; p. 213 Ray Boudreau; p. 214 (top) © Comstock Images www.comstock.com; p. 214 (bottom) Dorling Kindersley Media Library; p. 215 (bottom) H. Wiensenhofer/Photo Link; p. 215 (top) royalty free; p. 217 Ray Boudreau; p. 231 Photo Researchers; p. 238 Ray Boudreau; p. 242 Robert Landou/CORBIS/MAGMA; p. 243 Ray Boudreau; pp. 244–245 Cathy Mellon Resources/PhotoEdit Inc.; p. 254 Corel Collections *Highway and Street Signs*; p. 255 Ian Crysler; p. 259 Tomas del Amo/Index Stock; p. 261 Ian Crysler; p. 268 M.C. Escher's Reptiles © 2004 The M.C. Escher Company–Baarn, Holland. All Rights Reserved; p. 269 Word&Image; p. 270 Ian Crysler; p. 273 Philip and Karen Smith/Photodisc/Getty Images; p. 276 © Comstock Images www.comstock.com; p. 279 Ian Crysler; p. 280 Mark Richards/PhotoEdit Inc.; p. 284 M.C. Escher's Fish © 2004 The M.C. Escher Company–Baarn, Holland. All Rights Reserved; p. 285 Ian Crysler; p. 287 Ian Crysler; pp. 288–289 royalty free; p. 296 Ian Crysler; p. 300 (top) Philippe Columbi/Photodisc/Getty Images; p. 300 (bottom) Damir Frkovic/Masterfile; p. 307 Canadian Press/Kevin Frayer; p. 310 Corbis Royalty–Free/MAGMA; p. 312 Canadian Press/Peterborough Examiner/Clifford Skarstedt; p. 314 Ian Crysler; p. 315 Ian Crysler; p. 316 Canadian Press/Aaron Harris; p. 324 (top) Bill Tice/MaxxImages; p. 324 (bottom) Tom Kitchin/Firstlight.ca; p. 325 Tom Bean/CORBIS/MAGMA; p. 327 Ron Watts/firstlight.ca; p. 329 Courtesy of Pier 21, National Historic Site; p. 333 J.Kobalenko/firstlight.ca; p. 334 Ray Boudreau; p. 336 Ryan McVey/Photodisc/Getty Images; p. 337 Ian Crysler; p. 343 © Digital Vision; p. 352 Ray Boudreau; p. 354 Corel Collections *Toronto*; p. 355 J. de Visser/Ivy Images; p. 356 © Stockbyte; p. 357 Ray Boudreau; p. 358 (bottom) Bettmann/CORBIS/MAGMA; p. 358 (inset) Erich Lessing/Art Resource, N.Y.; p. 363 Corel Collection *China and Tibet*; pp. 364–365 (left) Canadian Press/*Peterborough Examiner*/Clifford Skarstedt; (right top) Canadian Press/Calgary Herald/Dean Bicknell; (centre) Ray Boudreau; (bottom) David Young-Wolff; p. 376 SW Productions/Index Stock; p. 377 Ludovic Malsant/CORBIS/MAGMA; p. 380 Michael Newman/PhotoEdit Inc.; p. 381

Photodisc/Getty Images; p. 383 © Dinodia; p. 385 Canadian Press/Carl Patzel; p. 390 Michael Newman/PhotoEdit Inc.; p. 393 David Young–Wolff/PhotoEdit Inc.; p. 395 (bottom) Rob Melnychuk/Getty Images; p. 395 (inset) David Young–Wolff/PhotoEdit Inc.; p. 396 Gary Connor/PhotoEdit Inc.; p. 402 Ian Crysler; p. 403 (top) Tony Freeman/PhotoEdit Inc.; p. 403 (inset) James Schaffer/PhotoEdit Inc.; p. 404 (top) © Comstock Images www.comstock.com; p. 404 (centre) Tim Hall/Photodisc/Getty Images; p. 404 (bottom) David Young–Wolff; p. 404 (background) Dorling Kindersley Media Library; p. 405 (top) Photodisc/Getty Images; p. 405 (bottom) Michael Newman/PhotoEdit Inc., p. 405 (background) Johnathan A. Nourok; p. 409 David Zimmerman/CORBIS/MAGMA; p. 411 Ian Crysler; p. 414 Ian Crysler; p. 416 Ian Crysler; p. 417 Ian Crysler; p. 420 Ian Crysler; p. 422 Dennis MacDonald/PhotoEdit Inc.; p. 425 Ian Crysler; p. 426 Ian Crysler; p. 430 Ian Crysler; p. 432 Ian Crysler

Illustrations

Steve Attoe
Pierre Bethiaume
Steve MacEachern
Paul McCusker
Pronk&Associates
Michel Rabagliate
Craig Terlson

Answers

Unit 1 Patterns in Whole Numbers, page 4

Skills You'll Need, page 7

1.a) 40 **b)** 40 **c)** 80 **d)** 360

2.a) 300 **b)** 800 **c)** 600 **d)** 2400

3.a) 30 **b)** 5000 **c)** 1310 **d)** 6300

4. For example: When we multiply by 10, each number gets 10 times as great. Each digit in the number moves 1 place to the left in a place-value chart. We use 0 as a place holder.

5.a) 3600 **b)** 10 800 **c)** 132 000

6.a) 21 **b)** 17 **c)** 18
d) 26 **e)** 70 **f)** 15
g) 18 **h)** 50 **i)** 5

7.a) 53 **b)** 290 **c)** 425
d) 98 100 **e)** 2079 **f)** 496

8. b: 492, and c: 12 345

9. For example: 864, 1212, 2451, 10 548

10. a: 870

11.a) 1, 2, 3, 4, 5, 6, 10 **b)** 1, 7

1.1 Numbers All Around Us, page 12

1.a) 115 **b)** 208 **c)** 861 **d)** 73
e) 124 **f)** 336 **g)** 6500 **h)** 1050
i) 2075 **j)** 78 **k)** 181 **l)** 35

2.a) 6952 **b)** 7113 **c)** 3336
d) 2898 **e)** 31 **f)** 403

3. For example:
a) About 190; 100 + 90 = 190
b) About 100; 120 – 20 = 100
c) About 630; 70 × 9 = 630
d) About 6; 420 ÷ 70 = 6

4.a) Eight hundred fifteen million thirty-six thousand dollars.
b) For example, estimate:
$1 000 000 000 – $800 000 000 = $200 000 000
Exact answer: $184 964 000

5. 140 000 sandwiches

6. About 65 000 000 cm; 650 000 m; 650 km

7.a) 3600 bagels **b)** $1440.00

8. 220 h

9. For example:
a) About 1280; low **b)** About 3200; low
c) About 4; low **d)** About 2; low

10. For example: Last week, Sunil worked Monday, Tuesday, Wednesday, and Saturday. How much money did Sunil earn last week? Answer: $126

11. About 210 mm of rain fell in 2 days. About how much rain will fall in 3 days? What assumptions did you make? Answer: About 315 mm; I assumed rain continued falling at the same rate for 3 days.

12.a) No. The numbers are approximate.
b) 2 373 800 **c)** 593 450
d) About 5 times as many
e) For example: Approximately how many times as many people live in PEI and Nova Scotia as live in Newfoundland and Labrador? Answer: Approximately 2 times as many.

13.a) 4 and 6 **b)** 11 and 7 **c)** For example: 38 and 36
Part c has more than one answer.

1.2 Factors and Multiples, page 16

1. For example:
a) 5, 10, 15, 20 **b)** 14, 21, 28, 42 **c)** 48, 56, 80, 88

2.a) 1, 2, 3, 6, 9, 18 **b)** 1, 2, 4, 5, 10, 20
c) 1, 2, 4, 7, 14, 28 **d)** 1, 2, 3, 4, 6, 9, 12, 18, 36
e) 1, 37 **f)** 1, 3, 5, 9, 15, 45

3.a) 1, 2, 5, 10, 25, 50 **b)** 1, 3, 17, 51
c) 1, 67 **d)** 1, 3, 5, 15, 25, 75
e) 1, 2, 3, 4, 6, 7, 12, 14, 21, 28, 42, 84
f) 1, 2, 3, 4, 5, 6, 8, 10, 12, 15, 20, 24, 30, 40, 60, 120

4.a) Composite; 18 has more than 2 factors.
b) Prime; 13 has only 2 factors: itself and 1.
c) Composite; 9 has more than 2 factors.
d) Prime; 19 has only 2 factors: itself and 1.
e) Prime; 61 has only 2 factors: itself and 1.
f) Prime; 2 has only 2 factors: itself and 1.

5.a) 5 **b)** 4 **c)** 5 **d)** 3 **e)** 3

6.a) 12 **b)** 10 **c)** 36 **d)** 50 **e)** 54

7.a) Yes **b)** Yes

8.a) 1 or 3 **b)** 1, 2, 3, or 6

9. In 12 days

10. For example: 4 and 16 are "near-perfect" because the sum of all its factors, except itself, is one less than the number. 32 is also "near-perfect."

1.3 Squares and Square Roots, page 21

1.a) 64 **b)** 256 **c)** 1 **d)** 841

2.a) 16 **b)** 289 **c)** 169 **d)** 2704

3.a) i) 1 **ii)** 100 **iii)** 10 000 **iv)** 1 000 000
b) i) 100 000 000 **ii)** 1 000 000 000 000

4.a) 4 **b)** 2 **c)** 30 **d)** 12

5.a) 10 m **b)** 8 cm **c)** 9 m

6.a) $\sqrt{9}$, 4, $\sqrt{36}$, 36 **b)** $\sqrt{100}$, 15, 19, $\sqrt{400}$

7. 8, 9, 10, 11, 12, 13, 14

8. 1, 4, 9, 16, 25, 36, 49, 64, 81, 100, 121, 144, 169, 196, 225, 256, 289, 324, 361, 400

9.a) 12 m **b)** 48 m **c)** 20

10. 5 m

Unit 1 Mid-Unit Review, page 22

1.a) About 1 220 000; I rounded to the nearest ten thousand.

b) 135 880; but, since the numbers of Smiths and Jones change with every birth and death, we can never know the exact number.

c) For example: Approximately how many more adults have the surnames Jones and Williams than Smith? Answer: (400 000 + 280 000) – 540 000 = 140 000

2. $90

3.a) 1, 5, 7, 35 **b)** 1, 2, 3, 4, 6, 8, 12, 24

4. For example:

a) 2, 3 **b)** 5, 2 **c)** 7, 2

d) 5, 3 **e)** 3, 9 **f)** 7, 3

5. 6, 12, 18, 30, 36, 42 are in the loop with multiples of 6; 8, 16, 32, 40, 56, 64 are in the loop with multiples of 8; 24 and 48 are in the overlapping part of the loops.

6.a) 3 **b)** 30

7.a) 7 has only 2 factors: 1 and itself.

b) 8 has more than 2 factors.

8. No, because no even numbers are prime (except for 2).

9. 9 m

10.a) 7 **b)** 64 **c)** 10 **d)** 81

11. $8^2 + 6^2 = 64 + 36 = 100$

12. $100 = 10^2 = \sqrt{10\,000}$

13. Since $1 \times 1 = 1$ and $1^2 = 1$, then $\sqrt{1} = \sqrt{1^2} = 1$

1.4 Exponents, page 25

1.a) 2 **b)** 3 **c)** 7 **d)** 10 **e)** 6 **f)** 8

2.a) 5 **b)** 2 **c)** 1 **d)** 5 **e)** 10 **f)** 4

3.a) $2 \times 2 \times 2 \times 2$ **b)** $10 \times 10 \times 10$ **c)** $6 \times 6 \times 6 \times 6 \times 6$

d) 4×4 **e)** 2 **f)** $5 \times 5 \times 5 \times 5$

4.a) 3^4 **b)** 2^3 **c)** 5^6 **d)** 10^3 **e)** 79^2 **f)** 2^8

5.a) $5^2 = 25$ **b)** $3^4 = 81$ **c)** $10^5 = 100\,000$

d) $2^3 = 8$ **e)** $9^3 = 729$ **f)** $2^7 = 128$

6.a) 16 **b)** 1000 **c)** 243

d) 343 **e)** 256 **f)** 4

7.a) 10^2 **b)** 10^4 **c)** 10^5 **d)** 10^1 **e)** 10^3 **f)** 10^6

The exponent equals the number of zeros when the number is written in standard form.

8.a) 2^2 **b)** 2^4 **c)** 2^6 **d)** 2^8 **e)** 2^5 **f)** 2^1

9.a) $2^3 < 3^2$; $8 < 9$ **b)** $2^5 > 5^2$; $32 > 25$

c) $3^4 > 4^3$; $81 > 64$ **d)** $5^4 < 4^5$; $625 < 1024$

10. 5^2, 3^4, 6^3, 3^5

11.a) 531 441 **b)** 343 **c)** 15 625

d) 65 536 **e)** 43 046 721 **f)** 8 388 608

12.a) i) $16 = 2^4 = 4^2 = 16^1$ **ii)** $81 = 3^4 = 9^2 = 81^1$

iii) $64 = 2^6 = 4^3 = 8^2 = 64^1$

b) For example: $256 = 2^8 = 4^4 = 16^2 = 256^1$; $729 = 3^6 = 9^3 = 27^2 = 729^1$

13.a) For example: 8^2 **b)** 5^2 units squared

c) 9^3 units cubed

1.5 Number Patterns, page 30

1.a) 15, 17, 19 **b)** 625, 3125, 15 625

c) 16, 19, 22 **d)** 10 000, 100 000, 1 000 000

e) 16, 15, 14 **f)** 71, 69, 67

2.a) 13, 18, 24 **b)** 25, 36, 49

c) 141, 151, 161

d) 12 345, 123 456, 1 234 567

e) 256, 1024, 4096 **f)** 16, 8, 4

3.a) Start at 200. Subtract 1. Add 2. Increase the number by 1 each time you add or subtract. 202, 197, 203

b) Start at 4. Add 3. Increase the number added by 2 each time. 28, 39, 52

c) Start at 100. Subtract 1. Increase the number subtracted by 1 each time. 90, 85, 79

d) Start at 2. Add 4. Increase the number added by 2 each time. 30, 42, 56

e) Start at 50. Subtract 2. Increase the number subtracted by 2 each time. 30, 20, 8

f) Start at 2. Multiply by 3 to get the next term. 162, 486, 1458

4. For example: 23, 24, 27, 32, …
Start at 23. Add 1. Increase the number added by 2 each time. 39, 48, 59

5. 1089; 10 989; 109 989…; 10 999 999 989
2178; 21 978; 219 978…; 21 999 999 978
3267; 32 967; 329 967…; 32 999 999 967
⋮ ⋮ ⋮ ⋮
9801; 98 901; 989 901…; 98 999 999 901

6.a) 10, 15, 21 **b)** 1, 3, 6, 10, 15, 21

c) 28, 36; start at 1. Add 2. Increase the number added by 1 each time.

d) 4, 9, 16, 25, 36, 49, 64; these are perfect squares. 81, 100, 121

e) 2, 3, 4, 5, 6, 7, 8; each number is 1 greater than the previous number. 9, 10, 11

7.a) 64, 125, 216 **b)** 343, 512, 729; this is 7^3, 8^3, 9^3

8.a) 2, 4, 8, 16, 32, 64, 128, 256, 512, 1024

b) 2, 4, 8, 6 repeated

c) Every fourth term has the units digit 6.
2^{40} is the fortieth term and 40 is divisible by 4, so its units digit is 6.

d) For example: In the first 10 powers of 3, the units digit follows the pattern 3, 9, 7, 1, repeated. Every fourth term has the units digit 1, so, 3^{64} would have the units digit 1.

9. For example:
a) 1, 2, 4, 8, 16, 32, … Multiply each term by 2.
b) 1, 4, 9, 16, 25, 36, 49, … Start at 1. Add 1. Square each number added.
c) 5, 25, 125, 625, 3125, … Multiply each term by 5.

Reading and Writing in Math: Using Different Strategies, page 33

1. 45 m
2. 144
3. Twenty-five 1 by 1 squares; sixteen 2 by 2 squares; nine 3 by 3 squares; four 4 by 4 squares; one 5 by 5 square.

Unit 1 Unit Review, page 35

1.a) 12 542 b) 1000 c) 420
d) 3375 e) 1372 f) 78
2.a) 132 002
b) For example: How many more points did Kareem Abdul-Jabbar score than Michael Jordan?
Answer: 9110
3.a) For example: 99 + 100 + 101; 58 + 59 + 60 + 61 + 62
b) For example: The number of terms is equal to 300 divided by the middle term. The sum of the outside terms is double the middle term.
c) Yes; unless the number is prime.
4.a) 45 min, assuming he did not stop, and he maintained the same speed.
b) In a 5-weekend month, Tana will make $275, assuming she babysits the same amount of time at the same rate each weekend.
5. $2328
6.a) 1, 2, 3, 4, 6, 9, 12, 18, 36 b) 1, 2, 5, 10, 25, 50
c) 1, 3, 5, 15, 25, 75 d) 1, 7, 11, 77
7.a) 9, 18, 27, 36, 45, 54, 63, 72, 81, 90
b) 7, 14, 21, 28, 35, 42, 49, 56, 63, 70
c) 12, 24, 36, 48, 60, 72, 84, 96, 108, 120
d) 15, 30, 45, 60, 75, 90, 105, 120, 135, 150
8.a) 6 b) 180
9. One. Two is the only even prime number. All other even numbers have more than two factors.
10.a) 11 b) 13 c) 15
11.a) 5 b) 10 c) 9
12.a) 49 cm^2 b) 289 cm^2 c) 8649 m^2
13. 36 m
14. 25
15.a) 3^4; 3; 4; $3 \times 3 \times 3 \times 3$; 81
b) 2^5; 2; 5; $2 \times 2 \times 2 \times 2 \times 2$; 32
c) 10^7; 10; 7; $10 \times 10 \times 10 \times 10 \times 10 \times 10 \times 10$; 10 000 000
d) 5^4; 5; 4; $5 \times 5 \times 5 \times 5$; 625
e) 4^4; 4; 4; $4 \times 4 \times 4 \times 4$; 256
16.a) 10 000 g b) 10^4
17. 4^4, 5^3, 3^4, 2^6
18.a) i) 11, 12, 14 ii) 16, 32, 64
iii) 25, 36, 49 iv) 13, 18, 24
b) i) Start at 3. Add 2. Add 1. Continue to alternate the number added.
ii) Start at 1. Multiply by 2 to get the next term.
iii) Start at 1. Add 3. Increase the number added by 2 each time.
iv) Start at 3. Add 1. Increase the number added by 1 each time.
19.a) $1^2 + 2^2 = 5$; $2^2 + 3^2 = 13$; $3^2 + 4^2 = 25$; $4^2 + 5^2 = 41$
b) $5^2 + 6^2 = 61$; $6^2 + 7^2 = 85$
c) Start at 5. Add 8. Increase the number added by 4 each time.
20.a) $1^2 + 2^2 + 3^2 + 4^2 + 5^2 = 55$;
$1^2 + 2^2 + 3^2 + 4^2 + 5^2 + 6^2 = 91$
b) For example: The difference between consecutive terms is equal to a square number.

Unit 1 Practice Test, page 37

1. For example:
a) 1970 b) 45 c) 30 000
2. 3950
3. 4, 8, 12, 16, 24, 48 are in the loop for factors of 48;
9, 18 are in the loop for factors of 18.
1, 2, 3, 6 are in the overlapping part of the loops.
GCF = 6
4. 30, 60, 90, 120, 150, 180
5. 78
6. Once, the 21st day
7.a) $\sqrt{25}$, 5^2, 3^3, 2^5, 10^2
b) 2^3, 3^2, 17, $\sqrt{400}$, $10 \times 10 \times 10$
8. 64 cm^2
9.a) 15, 21, 28; start at 1. Add 2. Increase the number added by 1 each time.
b) 29, 31, 33; start at 23. Add 2 to get each new term.
c) 36, 25, 16; start at 100. Subtract 19. Decrease the number subtracted by 2 each time.
10.a) $1^2 + 3^2 + 5^2 = 35$ b) $6^2 - 1^2 = 35$
c) $4^2 + 19 = 35$

Unit 1 Unit Problem: Fibonacci Numbers, page 38

1.a) 6, 8; 7, 13
b) 1, 1, 2, 3, 5, 8, 13
A term is equal to the sum of the two preceding terms.
2.b) The Fibonacci numbers are the numbers of bees in each generation going back: 1, 1, 2, 3, 5, 8, 13, 21
3. 1, 1, 2, 3, 5, 8, 13, 21, 34, 55, 89, 144, 233, 377, 610
a) Even **b)** 3 **c)** 5
4. 5, 13, 34; they match every second term of the Fibonacci numbers, beginning at the fifth term. 89, 233

Unit 2 Ratio and Rate, page 40

Skills You'll Need, page 42

1.a) 15 **b)** 9 **c)** 14 **d)** 6
2.a) 4, 8, 12, 16, 20, 24 **b)** 7, 14, 21, 28, 35, 42
c) 9, 18, 27, 36, 45, 54 **d)** 12, 24, 36, 48, 60, 72
3.a) 36 **b)** 70 **c)** 80
4.a) 180 **b)** 12 **c)** 60
5.a) 12.8 m **b)** 0.68 km **c)** 2.454 kg **d)** 1.987 L
e) 820 cm **f)** 1250 m **g)** 450 g **h)** 2300 mL

2.1 What is a Ratio?, page 47

1.a) 3:15 **b)** 1:15 **c)** 7:4
2.a) Green to red counters is 9:7
b) Girls to boys is 8:3
c) Fiction to non-fiction books is 2:5
3. 5:7
4. For example:
a) 8:15 **b)** 15:8 **c)** 8:23 **d)** 6:21
5. For example:
a) red:green = 3:5; cats:total pets = 3:5
b) apples:bananas = 7:1
6. No. The ratio of shells for Jeff to Maria is 2:3. Jeff got $\frac{2}{5}$ of the shells and Maria got $\frac{3}{5}$.
7.a) **i)** 8:3 **ii)** 5:1 **iii)** 3:5 **iv)** 8:25
b) **i)** 5:3 **ii)** 3:1 **iii)** 3:3 **iv)** 4:16
8.a) 11 cups **b)** 3:2; 2:3
c) 5:11 **d)** 2:2, 2:3; 4:10
e) For example: If 2 cups of pecans are added to the salad, what is the ratio of pecans to oranges and apples? Answer: 2:5
9.a) For example: Red circles to red squares and red triangles is 3:5; red figures to green figures and blue figures is 8:3; triangles to circles is 5:3; green figures to blue figures is 2:1
b) Change 1 red circle to a green square. Then, red figures to green figures is 7:3; circles to triangles is 2:5.

2.2 Equivalent Ratios, page 52

1.a) For example: 6:8, 9:12, 30:40
b) For example: 7:2, 28:8, 70:20
2.a) 5:4 **b)** 1:3 **c)** 3:1 **d)** 1:2
3. 2:3 = 6:9; 9:12 = 3:4; 8:5 = 16:10; 1:2 = 3:6
4.a) For example: 30 non-fiction books and 10 fiction books
b) Many answers are possible.
5. 30 cm by 15 cm
6. For example: 5 red counters, 6 blue counters, and 8 green counters; or 10 red counters, 12 blue counters, and 16 green counters

2.3 Comparing Ratios, page 55

1. A
2.a) 70 pictures **b)** The box with ratio 3:2
3. Madhu; Alison made 54 of 117 shots and Madhu made 65 of 117 shots; 65 > 54
4.a) 5 cans of white paint mixed with 7 cans of blue paint
b) 3 cans of white paint mixed with 4 cans of blue paint
5.a) A 2:1; B 3:2
b) Add 1 can of concentrate to B.
6.a) Ms. Arbuckle's class; 2 more
b) No
7. Amin's party

Unit 2 Mid-Unit Review, page 57

1.a) 7:4 **b)** 3:2 **c)** 7:16 **d)** 3:11
2.a) **i)** 2:3 **ii)** 5:3 **iii)** 5:10 or 1:2
b) **i)** 1:2 **ii)** 4:2 or 2:1 **iii)** 4:7
3.a) 7:4 **b)** 3:4 **c)** 3:11
4.a) For example: 10:6, 50:30, 55:33
b) For example: 18:72, 30:120, 600:2400
5.a) **i)** 1:3 **ii)** 3:1 **iii)** 3:8
b) **i)** purple to blue **ii)** yellow to red, purple to green
6.a) 12 girls **b)** 3:2
7.a) Stronger **b)** Weaker

2.4 Applications of Ratios, page 60

1.a)

8	10
4	5
12	15
6	7.5

b) 1:3 **c)** 7.5 L **d)** 6 L
e) 20 cans orange concentrate, 10 cans cranberry concentrate, and 30 cans water
2.a) 1:50 **b)** 176 cm **c)** 13.5 m
3.a) 1:20 **b)** 7 cm **c)** 0.6 m **d)** 0.1 m
4. No. The units must be the same when writing ratios of measurement.
5.a) 63 g **b)** 10 L

6.a) His father **b)** 80 m **c)** 20 m

2.5 What Is a Rate?, page 64

1.a) 60 words/min **b)** 25 m/min **c)** 20 pages/h
2.a) 15 km/h **b)** 36 km/h **c)** 600 km/h
3. 120 beats/min
4.a) \$0.48/m **b)** \$2.40 **c)** 25 m
5.a) 25 km **b)** 25 km/h
6.a) \$50.00 **b)** £12
7. 8 min/km
8.a) **i)** 7 min/km **ii)** 8 min/km **iii)** 8.5 min/km
b) For example: 8.8 min/km; 6 h 27 min

Unit 2 Unit Review, page 69

1.a) 10:9 **b)** 19:4 **c)** 4:19
2. For example: Red to yellow is 2:9, green to blue is 2:3, red and green to blue is 1:1, blue to yellow is 2:3
3. For example: Divide each number by 5, 5:2; multiply each number by 2, 50:20
4. 24 cm by 16 cm
5. Ms. Beveridge's class
6.a) 2:45 or 1:22.5 **b)** 320 cm **c)** 13.5 m
7.a) 9 **b)** 12 red, 8 white
8.a) 40 km/h **b)** 250 m/min **c)** \$8/h
9.a) Lion **b)** 11:9 lion to zebra

Unit 2 Practice Test, page 71

1.a) **i)** 9:1 **ii)** 1:2 **iii)** 5:6
b) 27
2.a) Tigers; they have 21 wins for 12 losses. The Leos have 20 wins for 12 losses.
b) Leos; they would have 10 wins for 5 losses. The Tigers would have 7 wins for 5 losses.
3.a) 160 cm **b)** 1.25 m
4.a) Car A 5 m/s, Car B 4.5 m/s **b)** 2 m
5. No. For example: If both tests were out of 60, Trevor's mark would be $\frac{40}{60}$ and Anne's mark would be $\frac{45}{60}$. Anne's mark is higher.

Unit 2 Unit Problem: Who's the Smartest?, page 72

1. Human 40:1; monkey 70:1; camel 800:1
For example: Humans are the smartest because they have a greater brain mass to body mass ratio.
2. Human 10:1; monkey 6:1; camel 40:3
For example: Monkeys are the smartest because they have a greater brain length to body length ratio.
3. 0.5 cm long; 30 cm long

Unit 3 Geometry and Measurement, page 74

Skills You'll Need, page 76

1.a) For example: All of them have a base, faces, edges, and vertices. They have different shapes.
b) For example: Pentagonal prism—barn; triangular prism—Toblerone chocolate bar; square pyramid—pyramid in Egypt; hexagonal pyramid—top of church tower; cube—sugar cube; tetrahedron—juice pack

3.1 Sketching Views of Solids, page 79

1.a) Front view; adult and child
b) Top or bottom view; airplane
c) Side view; person in a wheelchair
2. J: Top or bottom view of D
K: Top or bottom view of E
L: Side view of B; side and back view of C; back view of E; side and back view of D
M: Side view of E
N: Side, front, and back view of A; front and back and top view of B
P: Top or bottom view of A
Q: Front and side view of D; front and top and side view of C; side view of B; front view of E
8.a) No. For example: A cube is the only prism with congruent faces, so all views are the same.
b) For example: A square pyramid or square prism
c) For example: A triangular prism
d) For example: A chair

3.2 Sketching Solids, page 86

6.c) \$31.80 **d)** Yes. Answers vary.
e) Answers vary.

3.3 Building Objects from Nets, page 91

1.a) Triangular prism
b) For example: The object has 2 congruent triangular faces, and 3 non-congruent rectangular faces. The 2 triangular faces are parallel.
2.a) Yes. For example: It is a solid with faces that are polygons.
3.a) Octa means eight, and an octahedron has eight sides.
b) It has 8 congruent triangular faces. It is regular because all the faces are congruent.
4.a) For example: A pyramid with a trapezoid base; it has 2 triangular congruent faces, 2 triangular non-congruent faces, and 1 trapezoid base.

b) For example: A pyramid with a parallelogram base; it has 2 pairs of congruent triangular faces and 1 parallelogram as a base.

Both of them are pyramids with 5 faces. Their bases are different.

5. The dodecahedron has 12 congruent faces that are regular pentagons.

6. A soccer ball is made up of pentagons and hexagons. Each hexagon is attached to 3 hexagons and 3 pentagons.

7.a) The bases are 2 congruent pentagons. The faces are 5 congruent rectangles.

b) A pentagonal prism.

8. For example: All of them are polyhedra.

Unit 3 Mid-Unit Review, page 93

4. For example: 5 different views; there might be a hidden cube that you would not see on isometric dot paper.

5. A pentagonal prism; 2 congruent pentagons that are parallel, 2 pairs of congruent rectangular faces, and 1 non-congruent rectangular face.

6.a) For example: Cube; rectangular prism

b) For example: Triangular prism; square pyramid

3.4 Using Variables in Measurement Formulas, page 96

1.a) 20 cm **b)** 36 cm **c)** 8 cm **d)** 32 cm

2.a) 18 cm^2 **b)** 22 cm^2

3.a) i) $b = 3; h = 2$ **ii)** $b = 5; h = 4$ **iii)** $b = 2; h = 2$

b) For example: b and h can be replaced by any value, but the formula for the area stays the same.

c) b and h have the same value.

4.a) $A = 48$ cm^2; $P = 32$ cm

b) $A = 31.5$ cm^2; $P = 27$ cm

5.a) $P = 11.2$ cm; $A = 7.84$ cm^2

b) $P = 12.4$ cm; $A = 9.61$ cm^2

6. The perimeter is equal to two times the base plus two times the height. The formulas are the same, because they show that all 4 side lengths are added.

3.5 Surface Area of a Rectangular Prism, page 99

1.a) 160 cm^2 **b)** 216 cm^2 **c)** 82 cm^2

2. $SA = 72$ cm^2

3.a) 76 cm^2 **b)** 135 cm^2 **c)** 133.6 cm^2

4.a) 6 $units^2$

b) The surface area is multiplied by 4.

c) The surface area is multiplied by 9.

d) 96 $units^2$; it is 6 times the square of the edge length.

5.b) For example: The surface area is $\frac{1}{4}$ of the original surface area. The length and width of each face is halved, so the area of each face is $\frac{1}{4}$ of the original area.

6.a) 4 cans of paint

b) For example: There are no windows, and the inside of the door is painted.

7. For example: When each length is doubled, the surface area quadruples. When each length is halved, the surface area is reduced to $\frac{1}{4}$ of its original value.

8.a) 832 cm^2 **b)** 436 cm^2 **c)** 1580 cm^2

9.a) 9 cm^2 **b)** 3 cm

10.a) 400-g box: $SA = 1954$ cm^2; 750-g box: $SA = 2610$ cm^2

b) Ratio of surface areas is 10:13; ratio of masses is 1:2

c) No. Answers vary.

11. 2 m by 2 m by 5 m

12. 3 cm by 4 cm by 6 cm

3.6 Volume of a Rectangular Prism, page 102

1.a) $A = 40$ cm^2; $V = 120$ cm^3

b) $A = 81$ cm^2; $V = 729$ cm^3

c) $A = 200$ cm^2; $V = 6000$ cm^3

2.a) 67.5 cm^3 **b)** 96 cm^3 **c)** 25.2 cm^3

3. 36 cm by 1 cm by 1 cm; 18 cm by 2 cm by 1 cm; 12 cm by 3 cm by 1 cm; 9 cm by 4 cm by 1 cm; 9 cm by 2 cm by 2 cm; 6 cm by 6 cm by 1 cm; 6 cm by 3 cm by 2 cm; 4 cm by 3 cm by 3 cm

4.a) 1260 cm^3 **b)** 42 cm^3

c) For example: 3 rows of 10, or 10 rows of 3

d) For example: 2 cm by 7 cm by 3 cm

5.a) The volume is doubled.

b) The volume is quadrupled.

c) The volume is multiplied by 8.

6. For example: The volume doubles if you double one of the lengths. The total surface area does not double.

7.a), b) 1 prism: 2, 3, 5, 7, 11, 13, 17, 19 cubes;
2 prisms: 4, 6, 9, 10, 14, 15 cubes;
3 prisms: 8 cubes;
4 prisms: 12, 16, 18, 20 cubes

c) For example: Any prime number will make exactly 1 rectangular prism.

8.a) For example: 6 cm by 2 cm by 2 cm; 12 cm by 2 cm by 1 cm; 4 cm by 3 cm by 2 cm

b) For example: Greatest surface area = 76 cm^2; least surface area = 52 cm^2

c) For example: 24 cm by 1 cm by 1 cm; $SA = 98$ cm^2

d) For example: 4 cm by 2 cm by 3 cm; $SA = 52$ cm^2

Unit 3 Unit Review, page 107

2.a) i) Top view: a railway

ii) Side view: a fish and a line with a hook

3.a) For example: It has 8 faces.

b) For example: It is made up of hexagons and triangles.

4.a) 49 cm^2 **b)** 36 m^2

5.a) $SA = 6c^2$ **b)** 96 cm^2

6.a) 268 m **b)** $805; 23 bundles are needed.

7.a) $SA = 72$ m^2; $V = 36$ m^3 **b)** $SA = 114$ cm^2; $V = 72$ cm^3

c) $SA = 15\,000$ cm^2; $V = 125\,000$ cm^3

8.a) 11 rolls of wallpaper, 1 can of paint

b) For example: There are no windows, and the inside of the door will be painted.

9. The cube has edge length 6 units.

10. 28 m by 1 m by 1 m, $SA = 114$ m^2;
14 m by 2 m by 1 m, $SA = 88$ m^2;
7 m by 4 m by 1 m, $SA = 78$ m^2;
7 m by 2 m by 2 m, $SA = 64$ m^2

12.a) $h = 3$ m; 1 m by 6 m by 3 m

b) $h = 4$ cm; 5 cm by 3 cm by 4 cm

13. For example: 10 cm

Unit 3 Practice Test, page 109

2.a) It has an equilateral triangle base with 3 congruent trapezoid faces, and an equilateral triangle top.
Name: truncated tetrahedron (frustum)

3.a) $SA = 776$ m^2, $V = 1344$ m^3

4.b) $V = s^3 = 343$ cm^3; $SA = 6s^3 = 294$ cm^2

5.b) Area of material = 12.6 m^2, $V = 2.7$ m^3;
Area of material = 13.8 m^2, $V = 2.64$ m^3

c) For example: The second design, because the volumes are almost the same, but the second design uses less material.

6. For example: A pentagonal pyramid

Unit 4 Fractions and Decimals, page 114

Skills You'll Need, page 116

1.a) 1 **b)** $\frac{5}{6}$ **c)** $\frac{5}{3}$ **d)** $\frac{3}{2}$

2.a) $\frac{1}{2}$ **b)** $\frac{1}{2}$ **c)** $\frac{5}{6}$ **d)** $\frac{1}{6}$

3.a) 0.5 **b)** 9.8 **c)** 12.4 **d)** 3.26 **e)** 0.72
f) 0.06 **g)** 0.056 **h)** 0.276 **i)** 0.008

4.a) 15.8 **b)** 7.61 **c)** 125.88 **d)** 3.72
e) 1276.38 **f)** 123.913 **g)** 16.45 **h)** 833.82

5.a) 3.1, 3.79, 4.116, 4.12, 7.32

b) 0.62, 0.65, 2.591, 4.15, 4.4

c) 1.25, 1.43, 2.55, 2.81, 3.62

d) 1.752, 1.8, 2.67, 3.669, 3.68

4.1 Combining Fractions, page 122

1.a) $\frac{2}{3}$ **b)** $\frac{3}{4}$ **c)** $\frac{5}{8}$ **d)** $\frac{5}{6}$

2.a) **i)** $\frac{2}{5}$ **ii)** 1 **iii)** $\frac{7}{10}$ **iv)** $\frac{3}{4}$

b) Since the denominator stays the same, just add the numerators.

3.a) $\frac{3}{10}$ **b)** $\frac{5}{6}$ **c)** $\frac{1}{2}$ **d)** $\frac{3}{8}$

4.a) $\frac{7}{8}$ **b)** $\frac{5}{6}$ **c)** $\frac{6}{10}$ or $\frac{3}{5}$ **d)** 1

5. For example: $\frac{3}{10} + \frac{7}{10} = 1$; $\frac{5}{10} + \frac{1}{2} = 1$; $\frac{1}{3} + \frac{2}{3} = 1$

6.a) Meena ate $\frac{1}{8}$.
Her brother ate $\frac{2}{8}$ and her mother ate $\frac{3}{8}$.

b) Her brother's fraction can also be written as $\frac{1}{4}$.

c) $\frac{6}{8}\left(\text{or } \frac{3}{4}\right)$ of the pizza was eaten, and $\frac{2}{8}\left(\text{or } \frac{1}{4}\right)$ was left over.

7.a) 7 **b)** 2 **c)** 8

8. For example: $\frac{1}{6} + \frac{4}{6} = \frac{5}{6}$; $\frac{2}{3} + \frac{1}{6} = \frac{5}{6}$; $\frac{1}{2} + \frac{2}{6} = \frac{5}{6}$

4.2 Adding Fractions Using Models, page 126

1.a) $\frac{3}{4}, \frac{9}{12}$ **b)** $\frac{4}{12}, \frac{1}{3}$

2.a) $\frac{5}{4}$ **b)** $\frac{17}{10}$ **c)** $\frac{7}{5}$ **d)** $\frac{14}{8}$ or $\frac{7}{4}$

3. For example: $\frac{1}{2} + \frac{2}{2} = \frac{3}{2}$; $\frac{1}{6} + \frac{4}{3} = \frac{3}{2}$; $\frac{1}{4} + \frac{5}{4} = \frac{3}{2}$

4.a) $\frac{11}{8}$ **b)** $\frac{13}{10}$ **c)** $\frac{5}{4}$ **d)** $\frac{9}{6}$ or $\frac{3}{2}$

5.a) $\frac{9}{8}$ **b)** $\frac{6}{4}$ or $\frac{3}{2}$ **c)** $\frac{10}{6}$ or $\frac{5}{3}$ **d)** $\frac{14}{10}$ or $\frac{7}{5}$

6.a) One denominator is a multiple of the other.

b) The common denominator is one of the two denominators.

7.a) $\frac{7}{6}$ **b)** $\frac{9}{10}$ **c)** $\frac{13}{12}$ **d)** $\frac{16}{10}$ or $\frac{8}{5}$

8.a) The product of the 2 denominators tells the number line to use.

b) Each denominator is not a multiple or a factor of the other.

c) The product of the unrelated denominators gives the common denominator, and the number line to use.

9. $\frac{1}{2} + \frac{1}{3} + \frac{3}{4} = \frac{19}{12}$ or $1\frac{7}{12}$

10. Yes. $\frac{1}{2} + \frac{1}{4} + \frac{3}{8} + \frac{5}{8} = \frac{14}{8} < 2$

11.a) For example: $\frac{1}{2} + \frac{3}{4}$; $\frac{1}{3} + \frac{5}{6}$; $\frac{3}{4} + \frac{5}{6}$ **b)** $\frac{5}{6} + \frac{1}{4} = \frac{13}{12}$ or $1\frac{1}{12}$

12. There is $\frac{13}{8}$ of the chocolate left.

13. The pitcher holds 2 cups.

14.a) twenty-fourths **b)** fifteenths
c) twentieths **d)** twelfths

4.3 Adding Fractions, page 130

1.a) $\frac{5}{6}$ **b)** $\frac{8}{15}$ **c)** $\frac{9}{20}$ **d)** $\frac{11}{30}$

2.a) 1 **b)** 8 **c)** 2 **d)** 20

3.a) $\frac{13}{10}$ or $1\frac{3}{10}$ **b)** $\frac{13}{12}$ or $1\frac{1}{12}$ **c)** $\frac{22}{15}$ or $1\frac{7}{15}$ **d)** $\frac{17}{12}$ or $1\frac{5}{12}$

4.a) $\frac{8}{9}$ **b)** $\frac{7}{12}$ **c)** $\frac{7}{8}$ **d)** $\frac{13}{8}$ or $1\frac{5}{8}$

5.a) $\frac{13}{12}$ or $1\frac{1}{12}$ **b)** $\frac{11}{18}$ **c)** $\frac{41}{30}$ or $1\frac{11}{30}$ **d)** $\frac{21}{20}$ or $1\frac{1}{20}$

6. $\frac{3}{16}$

7. $\frac{3}{4} + \frac{4}{5}$; $\frac{31}{20} > \frac{9}{6}$

8.a) $\frac{13}{8}$ or $1\frac{5}{8}$ **b)** $\frac{43}{20}$ or $2\frac{3}{20}$ **c)** $\frac{35}{18}$ or $1\frac{17}{18}$

9.a) $3\frac{2}{3}$ **b)** $4\frac{5}{6}$ **c)** $6\frac{13}{24}$

10. $9\frac{5}{12}$

11. Statement b is true. The sum of the fractions must be less than or equal to 1 whole.

12. For example: $\frac{1}{2}+\frac{1}{5}+\frac{3}{10}=1$

13. 1

4.4 Subtracting Fractions Using Models, page 134

1.a) $\frac{1}{4}$ **b)** $\frac{3}{5}$ **c)** $\frac{1}{3}$ **d)** $\frac{1}{4}$

2.a) Subtract the numerators while keeping the same denominator.

b) For example: $\frac{3}{10}-\frac{2}{10}=\frac{1}{10}$; $\frac{7}{9}-\frac{5}{9}=\frac{2}{9}$; $\frac{5}{6}-\frac{4}{6}=\frac{1}{6}$

3.a) $\frac{5}{6}-\frac{1}{3}=\frac{3}{6}=\frac{1}{2}$ **b)** $\frac{5}{4}-\frac{1}{2}=\frac{3}{4}$ **c)** $\frac{11}{8}-\frac{3}{4}=\frac{5}{8}$

4.a) $\frac{1}{8}$ **b)** $\frac{1}{6}$ **c)** $\frac{3}{4}$ **d)** $\frac{1}{10}$

5.a) $\frac{1}{4}$ **b)** $\frac{3}{8}$ **c)** $\frac{1}{2}$ **d)** $\frac{1}{3}$

6. Aaron has $\frac{1}{6}$ cup of raisins left.

7.a) $\frac{5}{12}$ **b)** $\frac{7}{6}$ or $1\frac{1}{6}$ **c)** $\frac{3}{10}$ **d)** $\frac{7}{6}$ or $1\frac{1}{6}$

8.a) $\frac{5}{8}$ **b)** $\frac{5}{6}$ **c)** $\frac{3}{10}$ **d)** $\frac{5}{6}$

9.a) $\frac{3}{2}$ or $1\frac{1}{2}$ **b)** $\frac{2}{5}$ **c)** $\frac{3}{4}$ **d)** $\frac{1}{3}$

10. No; he needs $\frac{1}{12}$ cup more.

11.a) $\frac{1}{2}$ **b)** $\frac{4}{5}$ **c)** 5, 3

12.a) More; she used $\frac{5}{8}$ of a tank.

b) She used $\frac{1}{8}$ more.

13.a) Part iii

b) For example: By using estimation, or number lines

4.5 Subtracting Fractions, page 137

1.a) $\frac{2}{5}$ **b)** $\frac{1}{3}$ **c)** $\frac{1}{3}$ **d)** $\frac{2}{7}$

2.a) $\frac{1}{8}$ **b)** $\frac{1}{9}$ **c)** $\frac{11}{10}$ or $1\frac{1}{10}$ **d)** $\frac{5}{6}$

3.a) $\frac{11}{18}$ **b)** $\frac{1}{3}$ **c)** $\frac{3}{8}$ **d)** $\frac{13}{30}$

4.a) $\frac{1}{12}$ **b)** $\frac{7}{4}$ or $1\frac{3}{4}$ **c)** $\frac{2}{15}$ **d)** $\frac{9}{20}$

5.a) $\frac{1}{6}$ **b)** $\frac{11}{12}$ **c)** 2 **d)** $\frac{1}{12}$

6.a) $4\frac{3}{7}$ **b)** $1\frac{5}{18}$ **c)** $2\frac{1}{10}$ **d)** $2\frac{1}{10}$

7.a) Terri; she bikes $3\frac{3}{4}$ h the next Saturday, and Sam only bikes $3\frac{1}{2}$ h.

b) Terri bikes $\frac{1}{4}$ h longer than Sam.

c) How to add and subtract fractions

8. The recipe uses $\frac{1}{12}$ cup more walnuts.

9. For example: $\frac{5}{4}-\frac{1}{2}=\frac{3}{4}$; $\frac{8}{4}-\frac{5}{4}=\frac{3}{4}$; $\frac{4}{4}-\frac{1}{4}=\frac{3}{4}$

10. The other fraction is between $\frac{1}{2}$ and $\frac{3}{4}$.

Unit 4 Mid-Unit Review, page 140

1.a) $\frac{5}{6}$ **b)** $\frac{5}{6}$ **c)** $\frac{3}{4}$ **d)** $\frac{4}{5}$

2.a) $1\frac{13}{10}$ or $2\frac{3}{10}$ **b)** $7\frac{13}{10}$ or $8\frac{3}{10}$

3.a) $\frac{7}{5}$ or $1\frac{2}{5}$ **b)** $\frac{7}{6}$ or $1\frac{1}{6}$ **c)** $\frac{4}{3}$ or $1\frac{1}{3}$ **d)** $\frac{11}{6}$ or $1\frac{5}{6}$

4.a) $\frac{19}{12}$ or $1\frac{7}{12}$ **b)** $\frac{13}{6}$ or $2\frac{1}{6}$ **c)** $\frac{11}{10}$ or $1\frac{1}{10}$ **d)** $\frac{25}{18}$ or $1\frac{7}{18}$

5.a) $\frac{11}{5}$ or $2\frac{1}{5}$ **b)** $\frac{13}{8}$ or $1\frac{5}{8}$ **c)** $\frac{25}{18}$ or $1\frac{7}{18}$

6.a) $5\frac{2}{3}$ **b)** $3\frac{7}{12}$ **c)** $5\frac{1}{8}$

7.a) $\frac{1}{8}$ **b)** $\frac{9}{10}$ **c)** $\frac{1}{2}$ **d)** $\frac{7}{6}$ or $1\frac{1}{6}$

8. Samantha's; $\frac{7}{8}>\frac{4}{5}$

9.a) $\frac{11}{12}$ **b)** $\frac{1}{12}$

10.a) $\frac{13}{10}$ or $1\frac{3}{10}$ **b)** $\frac{1}{2}$ **c)** $\frac{13}{12}$ or $1\frac{1}{12}$ **d)** $\frac{7}{10}$

11.a) $\frac{5}{4}$ or $1\frac{1}{4}$ **b)** $\frac{3}{8}$

12.a) $1\frac{1}{4}$ **b)** $1\frac{1}{4}$

4.6 Exploring Repeated Addition, page 142

1.a) $3\times\frac{1}{4}$ **b)** $5\times\frac{2}{7}$ **c)** $4\times\frac{3}{10}$

2.a) $\frac{1}{8}+\frac{1}{8}+\frac{1}{8}+\frac{1}{8}+\frac{1}{8}$ **b)** $\frac{2}{5}+\frac{2}{5}+\frac{2}{5}$

c) $\frac{5}{12}+\frac{5}{12}+\frac{5}{12}+\frac{5}{12}$

3.a) $\frac{12}{7}$ **b)** $\frac{5}{12}$ **c)** $\frac{20}{15}$ or $\frac{4}{3}$

d) 9 **e)** $\frac{14}{5}$ **f)** $\frac{9}{2}$

4.a) $\frac{12}{5}$ **b)** $\frac{35}{10}$ or $\frac{7}{2}$ **c)** 5

d) $\frac{5}{2}$ **e)** 7 **f)** 6

5. 16 h

6.a) **i)** $\frac{12}{10}$ or $\frac{6}{5}$ **ii)** $\frac{12}{10}$ or $\frac{6}{5}$

b) The whole number in one question is the numerator in the other question.
For example: $2\times\frac{3}{12}=\frac{6}{12}=\frac{1}{2}$; $3\times\frac{2}{12}=\frac{6}{12}=\frac{1}{2}$

7. $\frac{9}{4}$ cups

8. b) For example: A set of 5 objects divided in half.

9. It will take Jacob and Henry $3\frac{3}{4}$ h to fill all the shelves.

Technology: Fractions to Decimals, page 144

1.a) Terminating decimals: $\frac{1}{4}, \frac{1}{5}, \frac{1}{8}, \frac{1}{10}, \frac{1}{16}, \frac{1}{20}$

Repeating decimals: $\frac{1}{3}, \frac{1}{6}, \frac{1}{7}, \frac{1}{9}, \frac{1}{11}, \frac{1}{12}, \frac{1}{13}, \frac{1}{14}, \frac{1}{15}, \frac{1}{17}, \frac{1}{18}, \frac{1}{19}$

b) The decimal for $\frac{2}{6}$ is two times the decimal for $\frac{1}{6}$, and so on.

2. $0.\overline{1}$; $0.\overline{01}$; $0.\overline{001}$

3.a) $0.\overline{3}$; 0.3333333… > 0.3 **b)** $\frac{1}{9}$; 0.1111111… > 0.11

4.7 Multiplying Decimals, page 147

1.a) $1.7\times1.5=2.55$ **b)** $2.3\times1.3=2.99$

2.a) 3.9 **b)** 3.92 **c)** 4.32

3.a) 0.92 **b)** 1.14 **c)** 0.56

4.a) 86.4 **b)** 86.4 **c)** 8.64

5.a) 15.54 **b)** 2.67 **c)** 0.54

6. 76 km

7. 161.65 m^2

8.a) i) 11.34 ii) 2.94 iii) 0.40

b) The number of decimal places in the product is equal to the sum of the decimal places in the numbers that are multiplied.

9. For example: 0.1×3.6; 0.2×1.8; 0.3×1.2

10.a) 2.52 b) 7.46 c) 35.22

11. The area is 9.18 m^2.

12.a) i) 25.44 ii) 2.88 iii) 0.24

b) The number of decimal places in the product is equal to the sum of the decimal places in the numbers that are multiplied.

13. When you multiply 2 decimals with tenths, you get a decimal with hundredths, and so on.

4.8 Dividing Decimals, page 151

1.a) 18 b) 1.9 c) 21 d) 2.5 e) 3

2.a) 1.7 b) 31.5 c) 17.4 d) 12

3.a) 29 b) 3.2 c) $17.1\overline{6}$

4.a) 18.2 b) 23.4 c) 3.2

5.a) 66.3 b) 6.4 c) 11.3

6.a) 18.25 b) 1.5 c) 115.4

7. For example: $0.024 \div 0.2$; $0.036 \div 0.3$; $0.048 \div 0.4$

8.a) No b) Yes, 0.5 m more

9. 21.5 m

10.a) 338.57 b) 0.338 57 c) 3.3857 d) 33.857

11. 0.125 g yeast, 2.5 g salt, 2 kg flour, 85 g cardamom, 1.875 L milk, 7.5 g butter, 0.4 kg sugar

12. 6.25 days

4.9 Order of Operations with Decimals, page 155

1.a) 31.4 b) 3 c) 6.2

2.a) 13.6 b) 8.1 c) 8.7

d) 146.6 e) 43.3 f) 1499.75

3.a) 32.75 b) 168.885 c) 42.2

d) 19.991 73 e) 41.3 f) 62.56

4.a) 10.7 b) 69.4 c) 30.68 d) 5

5.a) 242.2 b) 667.5

6. The mean time is 15.6 min.

7. 105.2

Unit 4 Unit Review, page 158

1.a) $\frac{2}{5}$ b) $\frac{1}{2}$ c) equal d) $\frac{7}{2}$

2.a) $\frac{5}{6}$ b) 1 c) $\frac{3}{4}$ d) $\frac{7}{10}$

3. For example: $\frac{3}{8}+\frac{2}{8}=\frac{5}{8}$; $\frac{1}{2}+\frac{1}{8}=\frac{5}{8}$; $\frac{1}{4}+\frac{6}{16}=\frac{5}{8}$

4.a) $\frac{3}{2}$ b) $\frac{5}{4}$ c) $\frac{7}{5}$ d) $\frac{5}{4}$

5.a) $\frac{7}{10}$ b) $\frac{3}{10}$

6.a) $\frac{11}{15}$ b) $\frac{7}{8}$ c) $\frac{29}{30}$ d) $\frac{17}{20}$

7.a) $\frac{37}{30}$ or $1\frac{7}{30}$ b) $\frac{13}{20}$ c) $\frac{17}{15}$ or $1\frac{2}{15}$ d) $\frac{25}{24}$ or $1\frac{1}{24}$

8.a) $8\frac{2}{3}$ b) $3\frac{7}{12}$ c) $5\frac{1}{2}$ d) $7\frac{13}{20}$

9.a) $\frac{43}{24}$ or $1\frac{19}{24}$ b) $\frac{97}{30}$ or $3\frac{7}{30}$ c) $\frac{83}{40}$ or $2\frac{3}{40}$

10.a) $\frac{1}{6}$ b) $\frac{3}{10}$ c) $\frac{5}{8}$ d) $\frac{1}{2}$

11. For example: $\frac{3}{4}-\frac{1}{2}=\frac{1}{4}$; $\frac{1}{2}-\frac{1}{4}=\frac{1}{4}$; $\frac{6}{8}-\frac{1}{2}=\frac{1}{4}$

12.a) Ali b) $\frac{1}{12}$

13.a) $\frac{1}{2}$ b) $\frac{3}{2}$ or $1\frac{1}{2}$ c) $\frac{27}{20}$ or $1\frac{7}{20}$ d) $\frac{19}{12}$ or $1\frac{7}{12}$

14.a) $1\frac{5}{8}$ b) $2\frac{2}{15}$ c) $6\frac{1}{6}$ d) $\frac{11}{20}$

15.a) $\frac{7}{4}$ b) 3 c) $\frac{21}{5}$ or $4\frac{1}{5}$ d) 4

16.a) Sasha has $\frac{1}{2}$ of the tomatoes left.

b) Sasha has 8 tomatoes left.

17. Orit has 8 hours left in her day.

18. 5.32 m^2

19.a) 7 bottles b) 0.3 L

20.a) Delia earns $112.50 in a week. b) $56.25

21. 13.6 km

22.a) 7 b) 50.4 c) 3.5

23.a) 13.26 b) 9.8

Unit 4 Practice Test, page 161

1.a) $\frac{13}{8}$ or $1\frac{5}{8}$ b) $\frac{9}{10}$ c) $\frac{1}{4}$ d) $\frac{29}{18}$ or $1\frac{11}{18}$

2.a) For example: $\frac{1}{5}+\frac{2}{5}=\frac{3}{5}$; $\frac{1}{10}+\frac{1}{2}=\frac{3}{5}$; $\frac{1}{3}+\frac{4}{15}=\frac{3}{5}$

b) For example: $\frac{4}{5}-\frac{3}{5}=\frac{1}{5}$; $\frac{7}{10}-\frac{1}{2}=\frac{1}{5}$; $\frac{4}{3}-\frac{17}{15}=\frac{1}{5}$

3.a) $4\frac{7}{40}$ b) $6\frac{11}{12}$

4. All the jobs will take $7\frac{3}{4}$ h to complete. Including lunch and travel time, she'll need more than 8 h.

5.a) i) $\frac{9}{2}$ ii) $\frac{14}{3}$ iii) 7

b) i) 4.5 ii) $4.\overline{6}$ iii) 7.0

c) 4.5, $4.\overline{6}$, 7.0

6.a) 7 bags of fertilizer b) $108.50

7. 102.875

Unit 4 Unit Problem: Publishing a Book, page 162

1. $3\frac{7}{8}$ pages

4. 4; there will be room for one $\frac{1}{8}$-page advertisement.

6. $2810

7.a) $3.88 b) $5.54 c) 388 books

Cumulative Review, Units 1–4, page 164

1. 40

2.a) 1 m by 29 m, 2 m by 28 m, 3 m by 27 m, … 29 m by 1 m

b) 15 m by 15 m; a square has the greatest area.

3. For example:

a) $41 = 6^2 + 5$; $43 = 6^2 + 7$; $45 = 4^2 + 29$; $47 = 6^2 + 11$

b) For example, $47 = 4^2 + 31$

4.a) 9, 4, 1; start at 7^2, reduce the base by 1 each time.

b) 63, 127, 255; start at 3, double it and add 1 each time.

c) 7776, 46 656, 279 936; start at 6, multiply by 6 each time.

5.a) 1:2 b) 1:2 c) 1:5

6.a) Carla; by comparing equivalent ratios, Carla has the most hits: 45:60

b) Irina has the fewest hits: 36:60

7.a) 12 b) 9:15 or 3:5

8.a) Back view; letter b) Side view; picnic table

c) Front view; microwave oven

9.a) 28 cm^2 b) 119.5 cm^2 c) 0.54 m^2

11.a) $\frac{15}{8}$ or $1\frac{7}{8}$ b) $\frac{11}{12}$ c) $\frac{9}{10}$ d) $\frac{1}{2}$

12.a) Riley; $\frac{1}{10}$ more b) $\frac{3}{10}$

13.a) $\frac{20}{8}$ or $2\frac{1}{2}$ b) 3 c) $\frac{9}{10}$ d) $\frac{25}{4}$ or $6\frac{1}{4}$

14.a) 7.35 b) 0.96

15. 3.5 m

16.a) 8.45 b) 6.16 c) 8.6 d) 0.7

The answers are different for parts c and d because the order of operations is different.

Unit 5 Data Management, page 166

Skills You'll Need, page 168

1.a) Mean: 5.125; median: 5; mode: 5, 9

b) Mean: 28.$\bar{4}$; median: 24; mode: 21

c) Mean: 14.5; median: 15; mode: 16

d) Mean: 73; median: 74; mode: 76, 81

5.1 Collecting Data, page 170

1.a) Secondary data b) Primary data

c) Secondary data

2.a) Secondary data b) Primary data

c) Secondary data d) Primary data

3. For example: If the president of a company wants you to buy her product, she might use biased data to show that her company's product is better.

4.a) For example: "The school gets very hot in the summer. Should there be more air conditioners?"

b) "Should the school buy more air conditioners?"

5.a) Biased. For example: "Should children eat candy?"

b) Biased. For example: "Which do you think is more fun, snowboarding or skiing?"

6. For example: "What is your favourite style of shoe? What make of shoes do you prefer?"
The survey results would let the person know what makes and styles of shoes to stock.

7.a) For example: Watching television

b) For example: "What is your favourite pastime?"

d) For example: My prediction was incorrect. The favourite pastime is playing sports.

5.2 Recording Data, page 176

1.a) 8; 6; 5; 5; 10; 6 b) 40

c) Most popular: Toronto Maple Leafs; least popular: Montreal Canadiens and Ottawa Senators

3.a) For example: "What do you mainly use the Internet for?"

b) 360

c) The number of icons would increase; the number of icons would decrease.

e) For example: Yes; a bar graph is easier to read.

f) For example: "What do people use the Internet for the most?" Answer: Research.

4.a) There are two pieces of information for each category.

b) The female population is slightly less than the male population.

c) For example: PEI

d) The data are too small for the scale on the graph.

e) For example: No; the range is too large.

6.a) For example: "How do you spend your money each week?"

7.a) 0–2; 3–5; 6–8; 9–11; 12–14; 15–17; 18–20

b) Frequency: 11; 15; 15; 9; 2; 3; 4

5.3 Stem-and-Leaf Plots, page 182

1.a) The plot shows the hours worked by part-time staff at a video store in one month.

b) 33 c) 91 h; 139 h d) 48 h

e) 122 h f) 137 h

2.b) 54 kg; 28 kg c) 26 kg

d) 37 kg e) 35 kg

3. For example: Data that are arranged in intervals could not be shown in a stem-and-leaf plot.

5.a) For example: I cannot tell from the data alone; I would have to calculate the mean, median, and/or mode.

b) For example: With a stem-and-leaf plot, I could show that the median and mode are less than 50 g. The manufacturer's claim is not true.

Unit 5 Mid-Unit Review, page 184

1.a) Yes

b) For example: "Do we need a new hockey arena?"

2.c) For example: "What type of movie was the least popular?" Answer: Foreign.

d) For example: We know the type of movie rented the most and the least in one day. We know the total number of movies rented in one day.

4.b) 65 c) 2 d) 9 e) 75 f) 75

5.4 Line Graphs, page 191

1.a) For example: It shows Nathan's height from age 8 to age 16.

b) **i)** 125 cm **ii)** 150 cm **iii)** 180 cm

c) During year 12 to 13; during year 15 to 16. The steepest part of the graph shows when Nathan grew the most. The least steep part of the graph shows when Nathan grew the least.

d) For example: 185 cm **e)** For example: 185 cm

2.a) The table shows the average monthly rainfall in Vancouver and Ottawa.

c) For example: Vancouver: The graph shows a downward trend from January to July, then an upward trend from July to December.
Ottawa: The graph shows an upward trend from January to August, then a downward trend from August to December.

d) April and September. For example: At some point during these months, Ottawa and Vancouver had approximately the same rainfall.

e) Vancouver: 104.4 cm; Ottawa: 70.2 cm

4.a) It depends on the speed of the car and the wetness of the pavement.

c) For example: Because the data change over time.

d) They are both upward trends.

e) About 45 m **f)** About 45 km/h

g) For example: "A car takes 44 m to stop on wet pavement. How fast was it travelling?" The line graph fills in the information left out of the table.

5.a) i: Yearly sales. For example: The data change over time. You can also predict future sales.

c) For example: The graph generally shows an upward trend, so, annual sales have increased over time.

d) A bar graph would be suitable for part ii.

e) For example: Most of the shoes sold are sizes 7, 8, and 9. 2003 was the year the store sold the most shoes, and 1997 was the year the store sold the fewest shoes.

5.5 Applications of Mean, Median, and Mode, page 200

1.a) Mean ≐ 119.8 s; median = 119 s; mode = 118 s

b) For example: The mode best describes Ira's race time, because it is the time he gets most often.

c) 5 s

2.a) Math: Mean = 74.6; median = 75; no mode;
Spelling: Mean = 77.3; median = 81; mode = 81;
History: Mean = 74.4; median = 74; mode = 74

b) For example: The mean is the average of Caitlin's marks in each subject. The median gives the middle mark. The mode is the mark she gets most often in each subject.

c) All measures of central tendency show Spelling as Caitlin's best marks, and History as her worst marks.

3.a) Week 1: Mean = \$825; median = \$800; no mode
Week 2: Mean = \$825; median = \$775; no mode

b) Mean = \$825; median = \$787.5; mode = \$600

c) For example: The mean is the same for parts a and b. There is no mode in part a, only in part b.

d) For example: The median; half the tips are less than the median, and half the tips are greater than the median.

4.a) Median = 120 s; mode = 118 s **b)** 122 s

5. For example: 18, 24, 25, 26, 27; there are many different sets. The five numbers must have a sum of 120, and the middle number must be 25.

6.a) Part i; mean ≐ 395.3 g

b) Yes. For example: This shipment is acceptable because the mean mass is greater than 395 g.

7.a) Mean = 34, median = 33.5, mode = 30

b) **i)** When each number is increased by 10, the mean, median, and mode increase by 10.

ii) When each number is doubled, the mean, median, and mode are doubled.

5.6 Evaluating Data Analysis, page 204

1. For example: The graph on the right is misleading because the vertical scale starts at 100 instead of 0.

2.a) For example: The graph on the left, because the upward trend is steeper.

b) For example: The graph on the right, because the scale makes the profits seem smaller.

c) For example: \$126 million; I assumed that the upward trend would continue.

3. For example: In order to bias the results in someone's favour. A misleading graph can be drawn by not using a proper scale.

4.a) For example: Manufacturer A's trucks are much more dependable than B, C, and D.

b) B: 97.5; C: 96.5; D: 95.5

c) For example: No. The range of the data is only 3. There is only a 1% difference between adjacent manufacturers.

5.a) For example: The bars are low and close to the same size, so the expenses look low.

b) For example: The scale does not start at 0, and the difference in heights of the bars increases, so it looks like expenses are getting higher.

Unit 5 Unit Review, page 208

1. For example:

a) "What is your favourite summer activity?"

b) "In the summer, people like to swim to cool down. What is your favourite summer activity?"

2.a) The data show the average weekly earnings in 2001, for various jobs.

c) For example: A bar graph is easy to read, and we can compare earnings for different jobs. A circle graph could not be used because we're not looking at percents or parts of a whole. A line graph could not be used because the data are not measured over time.

d) Mining; Health Care; these jobs are represented by the tallest and shortest bars.

e) For example: Multiply the data by 52 to get average annual earnings. Then, divide the average annual earnings by 12 to get average monthly earnings.

f) For example: Mean.

3.a) 17; 10; 9; 4; 20 **b)** 60

c) Metro PD, because it is the least favourite.

d) Reality Shock, because it has the most viewers.

4.b) For example: The median and the mode. The boxes with the greatest and least mass, and the range of the data.

c) For example: No, the shipment will not be approved if the mean is used, since the mean mass of a box of raisins is less than 100 g.

d) 99.9 g **e)** 100.3 g

f) Yes; the mode is higher than 100 g. No; the median is less than 100 g.

5.b) For example: Calgary: Upward trend from February to June, downward trend from June to November. Charlottetown: Downward trend from January to April, and from May to July; upward trend from July to November.

c) No. Charlottetown gets more rain than Calgary year round; the 2 cities never get the same amount of rain in a given month.

d) Calgary: 40 cm; Charlottetown: 106 cm

e) Calgary: 2.05 cm; Charlottetown: 8.6 cm

f) For example: Charlottetown gets the most rain in November and the least rain in July. Calgary gets the most rain in June and the least rain in February.

6.a) Mode; the storeowner needs to know which size sweater sells the most.

b) Mean; this is the highest of the 3 values, and will get Robbie the most money.

c) Median; if Tina's score is greater than the median, she is in the top half of her class.

7.a) Mean **b)** Mode

Unit 5 Practice Test, page 211

1.a) For example: Primary data are data I collect. Secondary data come from another source.

b) **i)** Secondary data **ii)** Primary data

2.b) 1:30, or 90 s **c)** 2:54.5, or 2 min 54.5 s

d) Yes; 2:39, 2:47, 3:07, 3:11, 3:25

3.a) 94 **b)** 86 **c)** 85

4.a) For example: I used a bar graph because the data are not measured over time.

b) For example: The scale would change to allow for the greater number. Another bar would be added to the graph.

d) For example: The graph from part a, because it is easier to read.

Unit 6 Measuring Perimeter and Area, page 214

Skills You'll Need, page 216

1.a) $P = 30$ cm, $A = 36$ cm^2

b) $P = 26$ m, $A = 40$ m^2

c) $P = 18$ cm, $A = 20.25$ cm^2

d) $P = 8.4$ cm, $A = 3.6$ cm^2

6.1 Area of a Parallelogram, page 219

1.a) $b = 12$ cm, $h = 4$ cm **b)** $b = 10$ cm, $h = 12$ cm

c) $b = 4.0$ cm, $h = 8.8$ cm **d)** $b = 8.0$ cm, $h = 4.4$ cm

2.a) 48 cm^2 **b)** 120 cm^2 **c)** 35.2 cm^2 **d)** 35.2 cm^2

3.b) **i)** 15 cm^2 **ii)** 24.5 cm^2

The areas are the same, but the parallelograms have different shapes.

5.a) 24 cm^2 **b)** 12 cm **c)** 8 cm

d) For example: 1 cm by 48 cm, 2 cm by 24 cm, 3 cm by 16 cm, 4 cm by 12 cm, 6 cm by 8 cm, 8 cm by 6 cm, 12 cm by 4 cm, 16 cm by 3 cm, 24 cm by 2 cm, 48 cm by 1 cm

6.a) 5 cm **b)** 14 cm **c)** 7 cm

7.a) For example: 8 **b)** For example: 12

c) For example: 4

8. No. For example: The area of A is equal to the area of B.

9.a) The two triangles are congruent.

b) 60 cm^2

c) 30 cm^2; the area of each triangle is one-half the area of the parallelogram.

10.a) 95.04 m^2 **b)** 132 m^2

c) For example: Subtract the area of the patio from the sum of the areas of the patio and gardens.
Area of the gardens = 36.96 m^2

6.2 Area of a Triangle, page 222

1.a) $b = 7$ m, $h = 3$ m **b)** $b = 3$ cm, $h = 5$ cm
c) $b = 6$ m, $h = 8$ m **d)** $b = 4$ cm, $h = 7$ cm
2.a) 10.5 m^2 **b)** 7.5 cm^2 **c)** 24 m^2 **d)** 14 cm^2
3.b) **i)** 6 cm^2 **ii)** 24.375 cm^2
The areas are the same for the 3 different triangles in parts i and ii.
5.b) **i)** For example: By doubling the height or the base, the area of the triangle doubles.
ii) For example: By halving the height or the base, the area of the triangle is halved.
6.b) 12 cm^2
For example: All the triangles have different side lengths.
7.a) 10 cm **b)** 8 cm **c)** 3 cm **d)** 5 cm
8. For example: I double the area, then divide by the base.
9.a) 8.55 m^2 **b)** 2 cans
10.a) 92.98 m^2 **b)** 33 sheets; $823.35

Unit 6 Mid-Unit Review, page 225

1.a) $P = 15$ m, $A = 12.5$ m^2 **b)** $P = 13.6$ m, $A = 11.56$ m^2
2.a) 7 cm^2 **b)** 9.2 cm^2 **c)** 3 cm^2
3.a) 2700 cm^2 **b)** For example: $b = 60$ cm, $h = 90$ cm
c) For example: $b = 30$ cm, $h = 45$ cm
4.a) 12 cm^2 **b)** 3.5 cm^2 **c)** 2.2 m^2
5. $1265.63, or $1375 if the contractor rounds to the next square metre of concrete.

6.3 Area and Perimeter of a Trapezoid, page 228

1.a) 15 cm^2 **b)** 12 cm^2 **c)** 16 cm^2
2.a) 65 cm^2 **b)** 38 cm^2
3.a) 5 cm^2 **b)** $A \doteq 58.6$ cm^2
4.a) $A = 156$ cm^2, $P = 54$ cm **b)** $A = 816$ m^2, $P = 124$ m
5.a) **i)** 33.6 cm^2 **ii)** 66 m^2
b) **i)** No; there is not enough information.
ii) Yes; $P = 36$ m
6.a) Flowers: $A = 5.2$ m^2; vegetables: $A = 3.965$ m^2; herbs: $A = 2.535$ m^2
b) $A = 11.7$ m^2; find the sum of the three areas in part a, or find the area of the rectangle.
8.a) For example: Divide the area of the parallelogram by 2 to find the area of each trapezoid.
9.a) 510 cm^2 **d)** Larger
10. For example:
Area of a trapezoid $= \frac{1}{2}(\textit{base 1} + \textit{base 2}) \times h$

6.4 Measuring Irregular Figures, page 236

1. 24 m^2
2.a) 31 m^2 **b)** 27 m^2
3.a) Answers vary. **b)** $A = 42.56$ m^2, $P = 37.6$ m
4.b) $A = 2200$ m^2, $P = 220$ m
c) For example: Count the squares on the grid and multiply by 100 to get the area; count the sides of the squares and multiply by 10 to get the perimeter.
5.b) 135 m^2
c) No. For example: The areas of the garden and the backyard never change, so you are always subtracting the same numbers.
6.b) All the perimeters are the same; $P = 26$ m
c) For example: You cannot make an L-shaped pool with area 30 m^2 and arm width 5 m. You end up with a rectangle.

Unit 6 Unit Review, page 240

1.a) 6.8 cm^2 **b)** 2.94 cm^2 **c)** 3.125 cm^2 **d)** 5.98 cm^2
2.a) 186 cm^2 **b)** 1125 cm^2
3.a) 64 cm **b)** 145 cm
4. For example: The height of the trapezoid is about 10 cm.
5.a) $P = 37.2$ cm, $A = 52.28$ cm^2
b) $P = 48$ m, $A = 155.52$ m^2
6.a) 1105.5 m^2 **b)** $10 756.50

Unit 6 Practice Test, page 241

1.a) $A = 63$ cm^2, $P = 34$ cm **b)** $A = 9$ cm^2, $P = 25.5$ cm
c) $A = 8.1$ cm^2, $P = 13.9$ cm
d) $A = 27$ cm^2, $P = 26$ cm
2.a) Area is doubled. **b)** Area is halved.
c) Area stays the same.
4.a) 25.5 cm^2 **b)** 36 cm

Unit 7 Geometry, page 244

Skills You'll Need, page 246

3. Yes.
4. No. An equilateral triangle always has three equal angles of 60°. A right triangle has one angle of 90°.
7.a) On the vertical axis **b)** On the horizontal axis

7.1 Classifying Figures, page 252

1.a) For example: A polygon has sides that intersect only at the vertices. The sides of this figure don't only intersect at the vertices.
b) For example: A polygon is a closed figure. This is not a closed figure.
2.a) **i)** No. Not all the angles are equal.
ii) Yes. All the sides and all the angles are equal.
iii) No. Not all the sides are equal.
b) **i)** All of the polygons in part a have line symmetry.

ii) Figures ii and iii in part a have rotational symmetry.

3. For example:

a) Parallelogram **b)** Isosceles triangle

c) Concave polygon

d) Obtuse triangles, scalene triangles

4.a) Concave polygon **b)** Concave polygon

c) Regular polygon

In every figure, all the sides are equal. Only figure c has equal angles.

5.a) D **b)** B **c)** E **d)** C **e)** A

7. For example: A: Parallelogram, convex polygon, quadrilateral; B: trapezoid, convex polygon, quadrilateral; C: quadrilateral, convex polygon; D: rectangle, parallelogram; E: kite, quadrilateral

9.b) For example: Many different figures. Quadrilaterals, trapezoids, parallelograms, concave polygons, convex polygons, obtuse triangles

10.a) For example: Rectangle, parallelogram, trapezoid, kite, quadrilateral

b) For example: All the quadrilaterals in part a are possible.

7.2 Congruent Figures, page 257

1. $\Delta ABC \cong \Delta DFE$; $\angle A = \angle D = 50^{\circ}$; AB = DF = 4 cm; $\angle B = \angle F = 40^{\circ}$

2. Yes. Quadrilateral ABCD and quadrilateral LKNM have 4 pairs of corresponding sides equal, and 4 pairs of corresponding angles equal.

3. For example:

a) $\Delta ABC \cong \Delta ADC$; they have 3 pairs of corresponding sides equal.

b) $\Delta PQR \cong \Delta RSP$; they have 2 pairs of corresponding sides equal, and 1 pair of corresponding angles equal, between these sides.

c) $\Delta HEF \cong \Delta FGH$; they have 3 pairs of corresponding sides equal.

d) $\Delta JKL \cong \Delta LMJ$; they have 2 pairs of corresponding sides equal, and 1 pair of corresponding angles equal, between these sides.

4. For example:

b) i) one side length, one angle, height

ii) length and width **iii)** length of one side

c) For example: Congruent parallelograms have corresponding sides equal and corresponding angles equal. Congruent rectangles have equal bases and equal heights. Congruent squares have equal sides.

5.b) For example: We need to know the angle between the 2 sides, or the length of the third side.

6. For example:

a) The corresponding angles are not equal.

b) All the corresponding angles are equal, and all the corresponding sides are equal.

c) The quadrilaterals in part a have different angles than the quadrilaterals in part b.

7. For example: The salesperson needed to know the shape of the quadrilateral.

8.a) No; they can have different side lengths.

b) Yes; when 2 angles and the side between these angles are known, only 1 triangle can be drawn.

9.a) No

Unit 7 Mid-Unit Review, page 260

1.a) ΔDEF and ΔGHJ **b)** ΔABC **c)** ΔDEF

d) ΔGHJ **e)** ΔABC

2.a) For example: Corresponding sides are equal, and corresponding angles are equal. The hexagons are concave because one angle is greater than 180° in each hexagon.

b) For example: The hexagons are convex because all the angles are less than 180°. The hexagons are congruent because corresponding sides are equal and corresponding angles are equal.

3.b) For example: Corresponding angles are equal and corresponding sides are equal.

c) For example: Corresponding angles are not equal, and two corresponding sides are not equal.

4.a) For example: Quadrilaterals ABCD and JKLM are not congruent. They do not have equal corresponding sides or angles.

b) EFGH $\cong$ QPNR; all corresponding sides and all corresponding angles are equal.

7.3 Transformations, page 264

1. For example:

a) Figure A is translated 3 units right and 3 units up

b) Rotate Figure A one-half turn about its turn centre (where Figure A and Figure C touch).

c) Figure B is reflected in a vertical line 1 unit to the right (between Figure B and Figure E).

d) Figure D is translated 4 units left and 2 units up.

e) Rotate Figure D one-half turn about its turn centre (where Figure D and Figure C touch).

2. For example:

a) Rotate Figure B one-quarter turn counterclockwise about the point where Figures A and B meet.

b) Translate Figure C 2 units up.

c) Rotate Figure D one-quarter turn counterclockwise about the point where the vertices of Figure D and Figure C meet.

d) Rotate Figure A one-half turn about the midpoint of the base of Figure A.

4. For example: Rotate Figure A one-quarter turn counterclockwise about point (5, 6) to get Figure D. Reflect Figure A through a diagonal line going through points (5, 6) and (8, 9) to get Figure B.

5.a) Figures A and B do not represent a transformation, and Figures E and F do not represent a transformation.

b) Figure D is the image of Figure C after a rotation of one-quarter turn clockwise about the point (7, 2).

7. For example: Translate Figure B 3 units diagonally up to the left. Reflect Figure B in a diagonal line that runs through the point where Figure A and Figure B meet.

7.4 Tiling Patterns, page 268

1. For example: No, it does not tile the plane. It leaves gaps that are squares.

2. For example: Yes.

3. For example: It does not tile the plane. It leaves gaps that are squares.

4. For example: Escher started with a regular hexagon. At each vertex 3 hexagons meet, and the sum of the angles is 360°.

5. For example: Parts of the edges will not be covered by a full tile. Tiles will have to be cut to fit.

6. For example: Because squares and rectangles tile a larger square or rectangle, which is often the shape of a floor.

7.a) For example: Pentagons that tile the plane meet at vertices where the sum of the angles is 360°.

8. For example: There are no gaps between the octagons that tile the plane.

9. For example: Honeycombs are hexagons.

Reading and Writing in Math: Choosing a Strategy, page 278

1. 80 km

2. 50

3. Cannot draw d and f. For example: Quadrilaterals can have a maximum of 4 lines of symmetry, and triangles are the only polygons that can have 3.

5.a) For example: Top row: $\frac{1}{6}$; middle row: 1, $\frac{5}{6}$;

bottom row: $\frac{1}{3}, \frac{2}{3}, \frac{1}{2}$

b) For example: Top row: 1; middle row: $\frac{1}{6}, \frac{1}{3}$;

bottom row: $\frac{5}{6}, \frac{1}{2}, \frac{2}{3}$

6. $\frac{3}{4}$

7. For example:

a) $\frac{\text{HI K}}{\text{G J}}$; the letters that have curves are on the bottom.

b) 100, 200, 500, 1000, 2000; this represents currency in cents: penny, nickel, dime, quarter, loonie, toonie, \$5 bill, \$10 bill, \$20 bill.

c) E, N, T, E, T; the letters represent the first letter of each number: one, two, three, four, and so on.

8.a) Back face of the prism: Brown, light blue, dark green, red, purple, white

c) Dark green, orange, light blue, brown, dark blue, light green

9.a) Monday July 15, Wednesday July 24, Saturday July 27

b) Tuesday July 16, Friday July 19

Unit 7 Unit Review, page 282

1. For example:

a) Six-sided figure with one angle greater than 180°

b) Five-sided figure, with all angles less than 180°

c) Four-sided figure, with one angle greater than 180°

d) A figure that is not closed, or a circle

e) All sides are equal, all angles are equal.

2. For example:

a) Six-sided figure; convex polygon. 1 pair of 60° angles, 2 pairs of 150° angles.

b) A regular polygon. All sides are equal, all angles are equal, 60°.

c) Five-sided concave polygon. One angle is 240°. Three angles are less than 90°.

d) Five-sided convex polygon. Three angles are 120°, 2 angles are 90°.

3.a) No; not all pairs of corresponding sides are congruent.

b) Yes; all three pairs of corresponding sides are congruent.

4.a) One-quarter turn clockwise about point C.

b) Reflect Figure ABCD in a horizontal line through (0,11).

c) A translation 2 units right and 5 units down.

Unit 7 Practice Test, page 283

1.a) ABCD ≅ JKMH; corresponding pairs of angles and corresponding sides are equal.

b) ΔEFG and ΔPQN are not congruent; corresponding sides are not equal.

c) ΔEFG or ΔPQN **d)** ABCD or JKMH

2. For example: No. The side lengths could be different.

3. For example: Two squares.

Unit 8 Working with Percents, page 288

Skills You'll Need, page 290

1.a) 0.75 **b)** 0.4 **c)** 0.6 **d)** 0.68
2.a) 0.625 **b)** 0.1875 **c)** 0.375 **d)** 0.4375
4. 6%

8.1 Relating Fractions, Decimals, and Percents, page 294

1.a) 15%; $\frac{15}{100}$, 0.15 **b)** 40%; $\frac{40}{100}$, 0.40
c) 80%; $\frac{80}{100}$, 0.80
2.a) 25% **b)** 30% **c)** 140% **d)** 75%
3.a) 0.2, 20% **b)** 0.06, 6% **c)** 0.16, 16%
d) 1.15, 115% **e)** 1.4, 140%
4. Janet; 82% is greater than $\frac{8}{10}$, or 80%
5. For example: Yes; the 5 triangles can be arranged into different figures.
7. The green section is 15%.
8. For example: Giving 100% is like giving one whole. Giving 110% is giving more than one whole.
9.a) 25% **b)** 50% **c)** 6% **d)** 10%

8.2 Estimating and Calculating Percents, page 299

1. Estimates may vary. For example:
a) 25% **b)** 30% **c)** 60% **d)** 90%
2.a) 5 **b)** 4 **c)** 9 **d)** 30
e) 7.5 **f)** 3.3 **g)** 4.5 **h)** 1.8
3.a) 2.5 **b)** 2 **c)** 4.5 **d)** 15
e) 3.75 **f)** 1.65 **g)** 2.25 **h)** 0.9
4.a) 7.5 **b)** 6 **c)** 13.5 **d)** 45
e) 11.25 **f)** 4.95 **g)** 6.75 **h)** 2.7
5.a) 3 cm **b)** 1.2 cm **c)** 2.4 cm **d)** 18 cm
6. For example: Method 1: Find 15% of $65. Method 2: Find 10% of $65, then halve the amount to get 5% of $65, and add the two amounts to get 15% of $65. The cost of the shoes is $74.75.
7. For example:
a) 75 **b)** 12 **c)** 90 **d)** 53
e) 40 **f)** 53 **g)** 4 **h)** 4
8. For example: No. 10% of 160 is 16, so 20% of 160 is 32. This would be a closer estimate.
9.a) $\frac{219}{341}$ **b)** Approximately 60%
10.a) $\frac{21}{66}$ or $\frac{7}{22}$ **b)** Approximately 30%
c) Approximately 70%
12.a) Approximately 1 000 000 km^2
b) Approximately 9 000 000 km^2
13. Approximately 2 500 000 km^2
14.a) $\frac{4.5}{12}$ **b)** Approximately 40%
15. Approximately 80%

8.3 Multiplying to Find Percents, page 304

1.a) 2.73 **b)** 9.68 **c)** 0.306 **d)** 97.44
2.a) 6.48 **b)** 16.08 **c)** 27.44 **d)** 75.04
3.a) $15.00 **b)** $45.00 **c)** $18.00
d) $41.99 **e)** $47.99 **f)** $53.99
4.a) $45.00 **b)** $42.00 **c)** $36.00
5.a) $46.58 **b)** $25.30
6.a) **i)** 1.046 **ii)** 10.46 **iii)** 104.6
Keep moving the decimal point one place to the right.
7. For example: You get the same answer: $3.75
8. 16.7%

Unit 8 Mid-Unit Review, page 305

1.a) 0.8, 80% **b)** 0.12, 12%
c) 2.36, 236% **d)** 0.35, 35%
2.a) 1.35, 135% **b)** 0.56, 56%
c) 1.875, 187.5% **d)** 0.4375, 43.75%
4. For example:
a) 50% **b)** 33%
5.a) $\frac{32}{66}$ or $\frac{16}{33}$ **b)** Approximately 50%
c) $3.11 **d)** Approximately 40%
6.a) 2.8 **b)** 6.6 **c)** 3.5 **d)** 18
7.a) 16.8 **b)** 39.6 **c)** 21 **d)** 108
8. For example:
a) 80% **b)** 70% **c)** 200% **d)** 210% **e)** 10%
9. For example:
a) 14 **b)** 30 **c)** 150 **d)** 133
10.a) **i)** $0.05 **ii)** $0.30 **iii)** $1.30 **iv)** $0.20
11. $68.43
12. For example: You get the same answer: $34.00

8.4 Drawing Circle Graphs, page 309

1.a) 112 500 **b)** 62 500 **c)** 25 000
2.a) **i)** Yes; it adds up to 100%.
ii) No; it adds up to more than 100%.
b) **ii)** A bar graph.
3.a) Blue, 22%; brown, 48%; green, 18%; grey, 12%
4.a) 92
b) MAJIC99, 22%; EASY2, 23%; ROCK1, 30%; HITS2, 25%
6. Approximate area: Australia, 61 million km^2; Antarctica, 98 million km^2; Europe, 86 million km^2; South America, 147 million km^2; Asia, 367 million km^2; Africa, 244 million km^2

8.5 Dividing to Find Percents, page 312

1.a) 2.5 m **b)** 5 m
2.a) 0.12 kg **b)** 12 kg

3.a) 0.3 cm **b)** 30 cm

4. 480 families

5. 12 games

6. 240 pages

7.a) 9 pieces **b)** Approximately 56%

8. 400 students

9.a) $60.38 **b)** No.

11.a) Yes; the shoes cost $23.00, so $40.00 is enough.

b) $17.00

12. 200 marbles

Reading and Writing in Math: Choosing a Strategy, page 314

1. For example: 8 × 9 × 10; 1 × 2 × 3 × 4 × 5 × 6

2.a) 12:21, 1:01, 1:11, 1:21, 1:31, 1:41, 1:51, 2:02, 2:12, 2:22, 2:32, 2:42, 2:52, 3:03, 3:13, 3:23, 3:33, 3:43, 3:53, 4:04, 4:14, 4:24, 4:34, 4:44, 4:54, 5:05, 5:15, 5:25, 5:35, 5:45, 5:55, 6:06, 6:16, 6:26, 6:36, 6:46, 6:56, 7:07, 7:17, 7:27, 7:37, 7:47, 7:57, 8:08, 8:18, 8:28, 8:38, 8:48, 8:58, 9:09, 9:19, 9:29, 9:39, 9:49, 9:59, 10:01, 11:11

b) 2 minutes (between 9:59 and 10:01)

3. 36; 81; 100; 121; 144; 169; 196; 225; 324

4. For example: About 4 h, if I walk 5 km/h.

5. About 231.5 h

6.a) 8 **b)** 24 **c)** 24 **d)** 8

8. 8 sets

9. $\frac{1}{4}$

10.a) Mean, $6000 **b)** Mode, $4000

11. 38 m by 92 m

Unit 8 Unit Review, page 316

1.a) 0.4, 40% **b)** 2.8, 280% **c)** 0.56, 56%

d) 0.7, 70% **e)** 1.125, 112.5% **f)** 1.7, 170%

2. For example:

a) 18%, $\frac{9}{50}$ **b)** 30%, $\frac{3}{10}$

c) 0.8, $\frac{4}{5}$ **d)** 0.375, 37.5%

4. For example:

a) 100 **b)** 36 **c)** 12 **d)** 41

e) 62 **f)** 59 **g)** 9 **h)** 4

5. Approximately $34.50

6. 28 students

7.a) $90.00 **b)** $84.00 **c)** $72.00

d) $60.00 **e)** $48.00 **f)** $66.00

8.a) $736.00 **b)** $220.80

9.a) Lake Huron

b) For example: It has the greatest surface area.

c) 26 840 km^2

10.b) For example: I know that the greatest primary energy resource in Canada in 2001 was oil, and the least was nuclear. I know that hydro-electricity generated the most electricity in 2001, and oil and natural gas generated the least.

11.a) Canada, 44%; USSR, 8%; U.S., 16%; Europe, 32%

b) The U.S. section of the circle graph would change to 12%; the USSR section of the circle graph would change to 12%.

12. 175 cm

13. 400 students

Unit 8 Practice Test, page 319

1. For example: One item may cost a different amount than the other; or one item may be a different size than another.

2.a) 16 cm

b) The original strip is 20 cm long.

3.a) 240 **b)** 24 **c)** 2.4

4.a) $56.25 **b)** $64.69

5.b) No. For example: I only need to know the percents to draw the graph (as long as they add up to 100%).

6. 20 dogs

Cumulative Review, Units 1–8, page 322

2.a) **i)** 6 **ii)** 9 **iii)** 12 **iv)** 15

b) For example: 5 tea bags. You need $4\frac{1}{2}$ tea bags, but you can't break a tea bag in half.

3.a) 8640 cm^3

b) For example: 60 cm by 36 cm by 32 cm

c) 60 cm by 36 cm by 32 cm; this box has the smaller surface area.

4.a) 8.64

b) For example: Many different pairs of factors are possible. 0.1 × 86.4, 0.2 × 43.2, 0.3 × 28.8, and so on.

5.b) 10 under par; 2 at par; 7 over par

c) 26

d) Mean ≐ 34, median = 35, mode = 33

6.a) For example: There is an upward trend from left to right.

b) For example: Yes. The graph shows that students who read 1.5 hours or more per week do better than students who read less than 1.5 hours per week.

7.a) 9.36 cm^2 **b)** 4.68 cm^2

8. A = 30.72 cm^2, P = 24 cm

9. A = 33 cm^2, P = 28 cm

10. For example: Corresponding side lengths and corresponding angles are equal.

11.a) 3.8 cm **b)** 125°

13.a) $71.99 **b)** $82.79

14. For example: The operations are the same, since order does not matter in multiplication, and both have a product of $21.

Unit 9 Integers, page 324

Skills You'll Need, page 326

1.a) 110 **b)** 40 **c)** 131 **d)** 47

2.a) First row: 8, 1, 6; second row: 3, 5, 7; third row: 4, 9, 2. The magic sum is 15.

b) First row: 17, 10, 15; second row: 12, 14, 16; third row: 13, 18, 11. The magic sum is 42.

9.1 What Is an Integer?, page 328

2.a) –3 **b)** +1 **c)** +8000 **d)** –10

3.a) –35°C **b)** +28 000 m **c)** –35 m **d)** +$500

4. For example:

a) The temperature in Hamilton increased 4°C.

b) George owes Stan $5.00.

c) Maya walked 120 steps forward.

d) The shipwreck is 8500 m below sea level.

5. For example: To describe the weather: A high of +7°C and a low of –2°C.
To describe altitude in relation to sea level: +400 m above sea level, –3000 m below sea level.

6.a) Positive integers: Births, Immigration
For example: These numbers represent an increase in population.
Negative integers: Deaths, Emigration
For example: These numbers represent a decrease in population.

b) Births: –545 000; deaths: +364 000; immigration: +512 000; emigration: –10 000

c) For example: Births are an increase in population (above or to the right of 0 on the number line).
Deaths are a decrease in population (below or to the left of 0 on the number line).

d) For example: Immigration is an increase in population (above or to the right of 0 on the number line).
Emigration is a decrease in population (below or to the left of 0 on the number line).

7.a) **i)** +$2 **ii)** –$3 **c)** –$1 **d)** +$5

b) For example: The final price is $3 less than the initial price.

c) For example: The final price is $5 more than the initial price.

d) For example: A negative integer represents a decrease in price; a positive integer represents an increase in price.

9.2 Comparing and Ordering Integers, page 332

1.a) Missing integers: –3, –1, +3

b) Missing integers: –8, –6, –4, –2, 0

2.a) +1, +5, +13 **b)** –5, –4, –3 **c)** –2, +3, +4

3.a) +8, +4, +1 **b)** –3, –5, –7 **c)** +4, 0, –4

4.a) –5, –2, +2, +4, +5 **b)** –12, –10, –8, 0, +10

c) –41, –39, –25, –15, +41 **d)** –2, –1, +1, +2, +3

5. a) +14, +3, –10, –25, –30 **b)** +2, +1, 0, –1, –2

c) +27, +6, –4, –11, –29 **d)** +10, +8, –7, –9, –11

6.b) –64, –61, –58, –54, –53, –47
For example: I wrote the temperatures on the thermometer in order from bottom to top.

7.a) +5 < +10 **b)** –5 > –10 **c)** –6 < 0

d) –5 < –4 **e)** +100 > –101 **f)** –80 < –40

8.a) **i)** +4, +8, +9 **ii)** 0 **iii)** –8 **iv)** –8, –5, 0

b) For example: Which integers are less than –4?
Answer: –5, –8

9. Warmest: Charlottetown, Prince Edward Island, because –21°C is the greatest integer. Coldest: Sydney, Nova Scotia, because –23°C is the least integer.

10.a) **i)** 0 **ii)** –2 **iii)** –3
iv) +2 **v)** –1 **vi)** –5

b) For example: The distance between –5 and +1 is 6 units; half of 6 units is 3 units; 3 units to the right of –5 is –2. The distance between –5 and –1 is 4 units; half of 4 units is 2 units; 2 units to the right of –5 is –3.

c) For example: –3 is halfway between –8 and +2.

11. –46°C

12.a) –5, –3, –1, +1, +3, +5, +7
Start at –5. Move 2 to the right to get the next term.

b) +7, +4, +1, –2, –5, –8, –11
Start at +7. Move 3 to the left to get the next term.

c) –20, –18, –16, –14, –12, –10, –8
Start at –20. Move 2 to the right to get the next term.

d) –5, –10, –15, –20, –25, –30, –35
Start at –5. Move 5 to the left to get the next term.

9.3 Representing Integers, page 335

1.a) +1 **b)** +3 **c)** 0 **d)** –1 **e)** –3 **f)** –2

4.a) For example: +3

b) For example: 3 yellow tiles, 0 red tiles; 4 yellow tiles, 1 red tile; and so on. Many answers are possible.

c) For example: There are always 3 more yellow tiles than red tiles.

d) For example: To model +30: Start with 30 yellow tiles and 0 red tiles. Increase each number of yellow and red tiles by 1.

5.a) 8 red tiles; (+10) + (–8) = +2

b) 98 red tiles; (+100) + (–98) = +2

9.4 Adding Integers with Tiles, page 339

1.a) (+4) + (–2) = +2 **b)** (+2) + (–3) = –1
c) (–4) + (–2) = –6 **d)** (+6) + (–3) = +3
e) (+1) + (–4) = –3 **f)** (+3) + (+2) = +5

2.a) (+3) + (–2) = +1 **b)** (+3) + (–4) = –1
c) (–2) + (+2) = 0

3.a) 0 **b)** 0 **c)** 0

4.a) +5 **b)** +1 **c)** –5 **d)** 0 **e)** –7 **f)** +3

5.a) +7 **b)** –2 **c)** –9 **d)** +7 **e)** –16 **f)** –9

6.a) (–3) + (+4) = +1 **b)** (+5) + (–3) = +2

7. For example: (–5) + (–3) = –8; (–7) + (+2) = –5; (–4) + (+8) = +4

8.a) +6 **b)** +4 **c)** –5 **d)** +2 **e)** –5 **f)** –10

9.a) (+5) + (+3) = +8 **b)** (–1) + (–3) = –4
c) (+3) + (–2) = +1 **d)** (–5) + (+2) = –3
e) (+2) + (–1) = +1 **f)** (+6) + (–6) = 0

10.a) –4
b) No; the sum is still –4. For example: Order does not matter when adding; the integers have not changed sign.
c) (–3) + (+7) = +4, (+3) + (–7) = –4; the integers have changed sign.

11.a) First row: +3, –4, +1; second row: –2, 0, +2; third row: –1, +4, –3. The magic sum is 0.
b) First row: –1, –6, +1; second row: 0, –2, –4; third row: –5, +2, –3. The magic sum is –6.

12.a) +7 **b)** –1 **c)** –1

13. For example: First row: –3; second row: –4, –5; third row: –2, –6, –1. The vertices are consecutive numbers and the middle integers are consecutive.

9.5 Adding Integers, page 343

1.a) +4 **b)** +2 **c)** –2 **d)** –4

2.a) +6 **b)** +2 **c)** –6 **d)** –6

3.a) +6; +2; –6; –6 **b)** The answers are the same.
c) For example: Order does not matter when adding integers.

4.a) –1°C **b)** –2°C **c)** +3°C

5.a) +5°C **b)** Gain **c)** +$1

6.a) +15 **b)** +6 **c)** –15 **d)** +3 **e)** –15 **f)** –6

7.a) +40 **b)** +10 **c)** –40 **d)** +3 **e)** –3 **f)** –80

8.a) For example: Opposite integers are the same distance from 0, so their sum equals 0.
b) For example: To add positive integers, move to the right on a number line. The numbers to the right of 0 are always positive, so the sum is always positive.
c) For example: To add negative integers, move to the left on a number line. The numbers to the left of 0 are always negative, so the sum is always negative.
d) For example: If the greater integer in the sum is negative, the answer is negative. If the greater integer in the sum is positive, the answer is positive.

9.a) +1 **b)** –5 **c)** –6 **d)** 0 **e)** +7 **f)** –23

10. 28°C; (+23) + (–7) + (+12) = +28

11. (+24) + (–7) + (+12) + (–10) = +19; Susanna has $19 left.

12.a) (+10) + (+15) = +25 **b)** (–10) + (–15) = –25
c) (+20) + (–5) = +15 **d)** (–20) + (+5) = –15
e) (+35) + (–18) = +17 **f)** (–35) + (+18) = –17

Unit 9 Mid-Unit Review, page 345

2.a) –12 **b)** +3 **c)** +10 **d)** –2 **e)** +25 **f)** +1500

3.a) –4, –3, –2, +1, +4 **b)** –50, –17, 0, +18, +50

5.a) +3 **b)** –5 **c)** –4 **d)** +9 **e)** –12 **f)** +12

6.a) +5 **b)** –6 **c)** –2 **d)** +1 **e)** 0 **f)** +7

7.a) +3 **b)** +6 **c)** –4 **d)** +5

8.a) +3 **b)** –8 **c)** –1 **d)** –7

9.a) $40 **b)** –3°C **c)** 120 000

10.a) –1
b) For example: (+7) + (–8), (–6) + (+5), (–10) + (+9)

9.6 Subtracting Integers with Tiles, page 349

1.a) +3 **b)** 0 **c)** –3 **d)** +2 **e)** –7 **f)** 0

2.a) +3 **b)** –5 **c)** +7 **d)** –1 **e)** +2 **f)** –9

3.a) –3 **b)** +5 **c)** –7 **d)** +1 **e)** –2 **f)** +9

4.a) +11 **b)** –10 **c)** –14 **d)** +14 **e)** –9 **f)** –12

5.a) –1 **b)** –8 **c)** –7 **d)** +7 **e)** +10 **f)** +11

6. For example: (–5) – (–8) = +3; (+6) – (–4) = +10; (–9) – (+3) = –12

7.a) **i)** +2 and –2 **ii)** –1 and +1
b) For example: The answers are opposite integers. Order matters when you subtract.

8. For example: –7; the integers are the same but in a different order, so the answer should be the opposite integer.

9. Many answers are possible. For example:
a) (–3) – (–5) **b)** (+6) – (+9)
c) (+7) – (+2) **d)** (–4) – (+2)

10.a) Yes, because each row, column, and diagonal equal the same number (–9).
b) Yes, because each row, column, and diagonal equal the same number (+6).
c) For example: First row: –5, 0, –7; second row: –6, –4, –2; third row: –1, –8, –3

11.a) +2 and –3

b) For example: Find 2 integers with a sum of –7 and a difference of +3. –2, –5

12.a) +2 **b)** 0 **c)** 0 **d)** +1 **e)** –3 **f)** 0

13.a) (+4) – (+1) = +3 **b)** (+3) – (+4) = –1

c) (+5) – (+1) = +4

14.a) i; because + 4 > –4 **b)** i; because +1 > –1

9.7 Subtracting Integers, page 354

1.a) (+6) + (–4) **b)** (–5) + (–4) **c)** (–2) + (+3)

d) (+4) + (+2) **e)** (+1) + (–1) **f)** (+1) + (+1)

2.a) +1 **b)** +7 **c)** –3 **d)** –7 **e)** +4 **f)** +4

3.a) –1; –7; +3; +7; –4; –4

b) For example: The answers are opposite integers. Order matters when subtracting.

4.a) +5 **b)** +10 **c)** –14 **d)** –15 **e)** –8 **f)** 0

5.a) –8°C **b)** +5°C **c)** –7 m **d)** –2

6.a) +17°C or –17°C **b)** +12°C or –12°C

c) +15°C or –15°C **d)** +6°C or –6°C

7.a) –3 **b)** +10 **c)** –10

8.a) –17 **b)** +17; it is the opposite integer.

c) For example: (+6) – (–11) = (+6) + (+11) = +17; the sum of two positive integers is a positive integer. (–6) – (+11) = (–6) + (–11) = –17; the sum of two negative integers is a negative integer.

9.a) –7.5°C **b)** 44°C **c)** –28°C

10.a) +1 **b)** +1 **c)** –4 **d)** +2 **e)** +12 **f)** –11

11. For example: (+9) – (+5) = +4; (–3) – (–7) = +4; (+2) – (–2) = +4

Reading and Writing in Math: Choosing a Strategy, page 356

1. 152

2.a) 187 **b)** 11

3.a) $7.95 **b)** $22.95

4. 12

5.a) Mr. Anders: $\frac{1}{4}$; his assistant: $\frac{1}{6}$

b) $\frac{5}{12}$ **c)** 2 hrs 24 min

6. For example: 6, 13, 14, 16, 16; 9, 10, 14, 16, 16

7. 1 cm by 1 cm by 36 cm; 2 cm by 2 cm by 9 cm; 3 cm by 3 cm by 4 cm; 6 cm by 6 cm by 1 cm

8. For example: 4 ways, using line symmetry and rotational symmetry.

9. 59%

10. There are many solutions. For example: 22 + 23, 14 + 15 + 16, 7 + 8 + 9 + 10 + 11, and so on.

11.a) 8 × 125; one answer

b) 1 × 8 × 125; 2 × 4 × 125; 8 × 5 × 25

12. 22 times

Unit 9 Unit Review, page 360

2.a) –2 **b)** –250 m **c)** +32°C **d)** –$125 **e)** +$3

3. –55, –54, –3, +150, +200

4.a) +2 **b)** –1 **c)** –5 **d)** 2

5.a) +2 **b)** +2 **c)** –10 **d)** –2

6. No. For example: If the first integer is greater than the second, then the difference is positive. If the first integer is less than the second, then the difference is negative.

7. (–5°C) + (+12°C) + (–9°C) = –2°C

8.a) +3 **b)** +6 **c)** +4 **d)** –5

e) –4 **f)** –5 **g)** –2

9.a) +12°C or –12°C **b)** –150 m or +150 m **c)** +3 or –3

10.a) +2 **b)** –3 **c)** +40 **d)** –160

11.a) For example: (–3) + (–3); (–9) + (+3); (–7) + (+1); (+6) + (–12); (–6) + 0

b) For example: (+5) – (+8); (+2) – (+5); (–2) – (+1); (–5) – (–2); (–11) – (–8)

Unit 9 Practice Test, page 361

1.a) +1 **b)** –2 **c)** –12 **d)** –14

2. –14, –12, –2, +1

3.a) –3 **b)** –10 **c)** –10 **d)** +6 **e)** –4 **f)** +23

4. For example:

a) When the integers are the same, but with opposite signs: (+3) + (–3) = 0

b) When both integers are negative: (–7) + (–8) = –15

c) When both integers are positive: (+9) + (+11) = +20

5.a) 10

b) +30, +25, +20, +18, +15, +13, +8, +6, +1, –6

6. +373°C or –373°C

Unit 9 Unit Problem: What Time Is It?, page 362

1.a) 1:00 a.m. **b)** 6:00 a.m. **c)** 10:00 a.m. **d)** 7:00 p.m.

2. 10:00 a.m.

3. Atsuko leaves at 3:00 p.m. and Paula leaves at 7:00 a.m.

Unit 10 Patterning and Algebra, page 364

Skills You'll Need, page 366

1.a) 37 **b)** 45 **c)** 29 **d)** 7 **e)** 17

f) 9 **g)** 5 **h)** 2 **i)** 14

2.a) i) 16 **ii)** 22 **iii)** 90

iv) 23 **v)** 29 **vi)** 17

b) For example: The indicated operations are in different positions in the expressions.

3. A(2, 3); B(5, 5); C(4, 0); D(0, 1)

5.a) $16 **b)** 3 h **c)** $4/h

10.1 Number Patterns, page 371

1.a) For example: The first term is a triangle, the second term is a square, and the third term is a pentagon. These three terms repeat.

b) Square, pentagon, triangle

c) 29th term: square; 49th term: triangle

2.a) For example: Three circles are arranged in an "L" shape. A circle is added to the vertical arm and the horizontal arm each time.

b) 18th term: 19 circles along the vertical arm, 19 circles along the horizontal arm; 38th term: 39 circles along the vertical arm, 39 circles along the horizontal arm

3.a) i) Each term in the pattern is a multiple of 3. The 1st term is the 2nd multiple of 3. The 2nd term is the 3rd multiple of 3.

ii) 18, 21, 24

iii) The 40th term is the 41st multiple of 3: $3 \times 41 = 123$

b) i) Start at 6. Add 4 each time. **ii)** 22, 26, 30

iii) The 40th term is $6 + 4 \times 39 = 162$

c) i) Start at 6. Add 5 each time. **ii)** 26, 31, 36

iii) The 40th term is $6 + 5 \times 39 = 201$

4. 6, 12, 18, 24, 30, …
Part a increases by 3, part b increases by 4, part c increases by 5. The next pattern increases by 6.

5.a) i) Start at 2. Multiply by 2 each time.

ii) 32, 64, 128 **iii)** 1 048 576

b) i) Start at 3. Multiply by 2 each time.

ii) 48, 96, 192 **iii)** 1 572 864

6. For example: In both patterns, start by adding 3, then keep adding consecutive odd numbers each time. The starting number for each pattern is different.

a) i) 37, 50, 65 **ii)** 401

b) i) 35, 48, 63 **ii)** 399

7.a) For example: Start with 1 row of 3 squares. The length and width of the rectangle increases by 2 units each time.

c) 17th term: 33×35; 37th term: 73×75

8. For example: 12, 16, 20, 24, 28, 32; start at 12. Add 4 each time. Next 4 terms: 36, 40, 44, 48
2, 12, 22, 32; start at 2. Add 10 each time.
Next 4 terms: 42, 52 62, 72

9.a) For example: A "U" shape made of squares. Start with 5 squares. Add 3 each time.

b) 32 **c)** 30; 36 **d)** 66 **e)** 35

f) No; 27 does not fit the pattern.

10. For example: 11, 13, 16, 20, 25; 16, 17, 20, 25, 32

10.2 Graphing Patterns, page 375

1.a) Output: 3; 6; 9; 12; 15 **b)** Output: 3; 4; 5; 6; 7

c) Output: 5; 8; 11; 14; 17 **d)** Output: 9; 12; 15; 18; 21

2.a) Output: 10; 8; 6; 4; 2 **b)** Output: 97; 77; 57; 37; 17

c) Output: 7; 5; 3; 1; –1

3.a) Input: 2; 4; 6; 8; Output: 3; 7; 11; 15

b) When the Input increases by 2, the Output increases by 4.

c) Input: 10; 12; 14; Output: 19; 23; 27
Increase the Input by 2 and the Output by 4.

4.a) Money collected: \$15; \$30; \$45; \$60; \$75; \$90

c) i) For example: Find the number of pins in the left column, and find the money collected along the same row in the right column.

ii) For example: Find the number of pins along the horizontal axis. Move vertically until you reach a point on the graph. Then move left to read the money collected on the vertical axis.

5.a) i) Start at 6. Add 2 each time.

ii) Add 4 to the Input number.

iii) Input: 12; 14; 16; Output: 16; 18; 20

b) i) Start at 6. Add 6 each time.

ii) Multiply the Input number by 3.

iii) Input: 12; 14; 16; Output: 36; 42; 48

c) i) Start at 6. Add 4 each time.

ii) Multiply the Input number by 2, then add 2.

iii) Input: 12; 14; 16; Output: 26; 30; 34

6.a) Number of students: 5; 10; 15; 20; 25; 30
Number of sandwiches: 13; 23; 33; 43; 53; 63

b) Number of students: 5; 10; 15; 20; 25; 30
Number of drinks: 10; 15; 20; 25; 30; 35

c) For example: For the graph in part a: To get from one point to the next, move 5 squares right and 10 squares up. Moving 5 squares right is the same as adding 5 to the Input number to get the next Input number. Moving 10 squares up is the same as adding 10 to the Output number to get the next Output number, and so on.

7.b) Figure Number: 1; 2; 3; 4; 5
Blue Squares: 1; 4; 9; 16; 25

d) For example: The dots appear to lie along a curve. The dots for other graphs appear to lie along a line.

e) For example: If you use the table, the number of blue squares is the figure number squared.

10.3 Variables in Expressions, page 380

1.a) $n + 6$ **b)** $8n$ **c)** $n - 6$ **d)** $\frac{n}{4}$

2.a) \$20 **b)** \$32 **c)** \$$4t$

3.a) 48 cm^2 **b)** 50 cm^2 **c)** $l \times w$ cm^2

4.a) 10 km **b)** 25 km **c)** $5t$ km

5. For example:

a) Eight more than a number

b) A number multiplied by six
c) A number divided by five
d) A number decreased by eleven
e) Twenty-seven decreased by a number
f) A number squared

6.a) $2n + 3$ **b)** $(n - 5) \times 2$ **c)** $17 - \frac{n}{2}$
d) $\frac{n}{7} + 6$ **e)** $28 - n$ **f)** $n - 28$

7. For example:
a) i) Subtract three from forty, then multiply by a number.
ii) A number is multiplied by three and then subtracted from forty.
b) They have the same numbers and use the same variable, but different terms are multiplied and subtracted.

8.a) i) $n + 3$ **ii)** $3 + n$ **iii)** $n - 3$ **iv)** $3 - n$
b) For example: All expressions all involve a number and three, but the order and the operations are different.

9. For example:
a) Six times a number, then add five
b) One-quarter of three less than a number
c) Twelve added to one-quarter of a number
d) Three times the difference of a number and three
e) One-fifth of a number subtracted from thirty-two
f) Thirty-two subtracted from one-fifth of a number

10.a) i) $9n - 4$ **ii)** $4n + 9$ **iii)** $n + 9 - 4$ **iv)** $n \div 4 + 9$
b) For example: The sum of nine times a number and four: $9n + 4$; five less than a number: $n + 4 - 9$

11. The cost of a pizza with e extra toppings is \$8.00 + \$1e

Unit 10 Mid-Unit Review, page 382

1.a) i) Start at 5. Add 3 each time.
ii) 17, 20, 23 **iii)** 32
b) i) Start at 14. Add 11 each time.
ii) 58, 69, 80 **iii)** 113
c) i) The cubes of whole numbers
ii) 125, 216, 343 **iii)** 1000
d) i) Start at 1. Multiply by 2, then add 1 each time.
ii) 63, 127, 255 **iii)** 1023

2.a) For example: Start with a rectangle with width 1 unit and length 2 units. The width and length increase by 1 unit each time.
b) 5×6; 6×7 **c)** 2, 6, 12, 20, 30
d) 19×20; area = 380
e) The 10th rectangle: 10×11

3.a) Output: 3; 7; 11; 15; 19; 23
b) For example: To get from one point to the next, move 1 square right and 4 squares up. Moving 1 square right is the same as adding 1 to the Input number to get the next Input number. Moving 4 squares up is the same as adding 4 to the Output number to get the next Output number.

4.a) Start at 8. Add 3 each time.
b) Multiply the Input number by 3, then add 5.
c) Input: 7; 8; 9; Output: 26; 29; 32
d) For example: To get from one point to the next, move 1 square right and 3 squares up. Moving 1 square right is the same as adding 1 to the Input number to get the next Input number. Moving 3 squares up is the same as adding 3 to the Output number to get the next Output number.

5.a) $n + 11$ **b)** $n - 4$ **c)** $\frac{n}{3}$
d) $9n$ **e)** $5n + 2$ **f)** $2n + 17$

6. For example:
a) The sum of a number and three
b) A number subtracted from twenty-one
c) Nine times a number
d) One-quarter of a number

10.4 Evaluating Algebraic Expressions, page 385

1.a) 9 **b)** 12 **c)** 7 **d)** 2 **e)** 13 **f)** 12
2.a) 19 **b)** 3 **c)** 6 **d)** 18 **e)** 21 **f)** 4

3. For example:
a) A number decreased by one; 2
b) The sum of five times a number and two; 17
c) The sum of one-third of a number and five; 6
d) One added to a number; 4
e) Two times the sum of a number and nine; 24
f) One-half of the sum of a number and seven; 5

4.a) Output = two times each Input number: 2; 4; 6; 8; 10
b) Output = ten minus the Input number: 9; 8; 7; 6; 5
c) Output = the sum of three times the Input number and four: 7; 10; 13; 16; 19

5.a) In dollars: $7 \times 8 + 9 \times 12$ **b)** In dollars: $7x + 9 \times 5$
c) 10 h

6.a) \$65; \$110 **b)** $9p + 20$
c) $18p + 20$ **d)** $9p + 40$
e) For example: The algebraic expressions for the different charges can be easily written, and p is the first letter in "people".

7.a) 6 **b)** 4 **c)** 2 **d)** 3 **e)** 6 **f)** 32

8.a) Output = $3x$ **b)** Output = $3x - 2$
c) Output = $x - 3$

9. For example: $p = 4$, $q = 1$
There are many different ways to do this. The value of p has to be one more than three times the value of q.

10.5 Reading and Writing Equations, page 389

1.a) $n + 8 = 12$ **b)** $3n = 12$ **c)** $n - 8 = 12$

2. For example:

a) The sum of twelve and a number is nineteen.

b) Three times a number is eighteen.

c) Twelve decreased by a number is five.

d) One-half of a number is six.

3.a) $2n + 5 = 35$ **b)** $8 + \frac{n}{2} = 24$ **c)** $3n - 6 = 11$

4. For example:

a) Seven subtracted from five times a number is thirty-seven.

b) Four added to one-third of a number is nine.

c) Seventeen decreased by two times a number is three.

5.a) C **b)** E **c)** D **d)** A **e)** B

6. $\frac{n}{4} + 10 = 14$

7.a) $b + 7 = 20$ **b)** $5n = 295$

c) $2w + 30 = 38$ **d)** $2x + 20 = 44$

10.6 Solving Equations, page 393

1.a) $x = 9$ **b)** $y = 0$ **c)** $z = 5$ **d)** $c = 3$

2.a) $x = 7$ **b)** $n = 0$ **c)** $z = 4$ **d)** $k = 2$

3.a) $n = 45 - 10$ **b)** $n = 35$

4.a) $x = 11$ **b)** $k = 8$ **c)** $y = 8$ **d)** $z = 18$

5.a) $n = 28$ **b)** $z = 11$ **c)** $y = 9$ **d)** $x = 28$

6.a) $4s = 156$ **b)** $s = 39$ cm

7.a) $p = 6 \times 9$ **b)** $p = 54$ cm

8. For example:

a) The length of a rectangle is 12 cm and the perimeter is 30 cm. What is the width of the rectangle?

b) $24 + 2w = 30$ **c)** $w = 3$ cm

9.a) For example: $10 + 24x = 130$ **b)** $x = 5$

10.a) $n = 9$ **b)** $n = 12$ **c)** $n = 15$

d) $n = 81$ **e)** $n = 48$ **f)** $n = 18$

11. For example:

a) Sheila bought two tickets, and got $1 off. She paid a total of $5. What is the regular price of a ticket? $x = 3$

b) The perimeter of a square is 24 cm. What is the side length? $y = 6$

c) When a group of people is divided into 38 equal groups, there are 57 groups. How many people are there in total? $z = 2166$

d) Eli has 5 groups of comic books. When he buys 5 more comics, he has 30 in all. How many comics are in each group? $x = 5$

e) When 25 bananas are divided equally amongst some friends, each friend gets 5 bananas. How many friends are there? $y = 5$

f) Four cards are removed from a deck of 52 cards. Each of the 4 players are dealt the rest of the cards. How many cards do they each get? $x = 12$

Reading and Writing in Math: Choosing a Strategy, page 396

1. 5040

2.a) 10, 9, 12

b) Start at 1. Add 3 for the next term, then take away 1 for the next.

c) 21; 52

For example: Each odd term is equal to the term number; each even term is equal to the term number plus 2.

3.a) Term 1: 4 Blue, 1 Red; Term 2: 8 Blue, 4 Red; Term 3: 12 Blue, 9 Red

b) 20th term: 400 red tiles **c)** 100th term: 400 blue tiles

d) 30th term: a total of 1020 red and blue tiles

e) 144 red tiles; the number of blue tiles is the term number times 4; the number of red tiles is the term number squared.

4. Can: 12 g; red ball: 5 g; green ball: 2 g

5. Irfan: $25; Marisha: $35

6. For example:

a) The mass of garbage generally increases with the number of people in a household.

b) A household produces a lot of garbage, and doesn't recycle; the household produces heavier garbage; this week, the household threw out a really heavy item.

c) The people may have been away on vacation for part of the week; they didn't throw out any heavy items; they recycle and use a composter.

7.a) Total cost of trip: $60; $70; $80; $90; $100; $110; $120; $130; $140; $150

b) **i)** $170 **ii)** $200 **iii)** $250

c) **i)** $20 **ii)** $15 **iii)** $13.33

8.a) $25 **b)** $29

c) For example: We're paying for the cost of the trip. Carrying 2 packages instead of 1 doesn't make much difference.

9.a) 111 or 482

b) For example: The digits are either all even or all odd.

Unit 10 Unit Review, page 398

1.a) **i)** Start at 5. Add 7 each time.

ii) 33, 40, 47 **iii)** 138; 20th term $= 5 + 19 \times 7$

b) **i)** The pattern is consecutive powers of 3.

ii) 243, 729, 2187

iii) 3 486 784 401; 20th term $= 3^{20}$

c) i) Start at 96. Subtract 3 each time.
ii) 84, 81, 78 **iii)** 39; 20th term = $96 - 19 \times 3$
d) i) Start at 10. Add 11 each time.
ii) 54, 65, 76 **iii)** 219; 20th term: $10 + 19 \times 11$
e) i) Start at 9. Add 4 each time.
ii) 25, 29, 33 **iii)** 85; 20th term: $9 + 19 \times 4$

2.a) $20.48 **b)** $40.95

3.a) Start at 2. Double the number, then add 1 each time.
b) 95, 191, 383 **c)** For example: 5, 16, 49, 148

4.a) For example: Start with a purple square in the middle and a green square on all four sides. A purple square is added to the middle, and a green square is added to the top and bottom rows each time.
c) 12th figure: 12 purple squares in the middle, 1 green square on each end, 12 green squares on the top, 12 green squares on the bottom.
22nd figure: 22 purple squares in the middle, 1 green square on each end, 22 green squares on the top, 22 green squares on the bottom.

5.a) Output: 7; 9; 11; 13; 15 **b)** Output: 8; 12; 16; 20; 24
c) Output: 1; 3; 5; 7; 9 **d)** Output: 2; 3; 4; 5; 6
e) Output: 5; 6; 7; 8; 9 **f)** Output: 5; 9; 13; 17; 21

6.a) Input: 2; 4; 6; 8; 10; Output: 16; 14; 12; 10; 8
b) Input: Start at 2. Add 2 each time.
Output: Start at 16. Subtract 2 each time.
c) Input: 12; 14; 16; Output: 6; 4; 2
Add 2 to the Input each time; subtract 2 from the Output each time.
d) The Output will become negative.

7.a) Input: Start at 5. Increase by 10 each time.
Output: Start at 1. Increase by 2 each time.
b) Input: 65; 75; 85; Output: 13; 15; 17

8.a) $n + 20$ **b)** $n - 1$ **c)** $n + 10$ **d)** $13n$

9. For example:
a) Four more than a number
b) A number subtracted from 25
c) One-fifth of a number
d) Five decreased by two times a number

10.a) 11 **b)** 27 **c)** 5 **d)** 1.5 **e)** 34 **f)** 0

11.a) 8 **b)** 2 **c)** 4 **d)** 6

12.a) $210; $490 **b)** $70*r* **c)** $\frac{d}{70}$

13. For example:
a) The sum of a number and three is seventeen.
b) Three times a number is 24.
c) A number divided by four is five.
d) Three times a number, decreased by four, is 20.
e) Seven plus four times a number is 35.

14. For example:
a) The sum of the pennies in my pocket and five is 21. How many pennies are in my pocket?
b) If you buy 5 tickets to a play, you get a $2 discount. You then pay a total of $28. How much are the tickets at regular price?

15.a) $6n = 258$ **b)** $6w = 36$ **c)** $\frac{n}{2} = 6$

16. For example:
a) A number plus 2 is 23.
b) Four decreased by a number is 12.
c) Five times a number is 35.
d) One-ninth of a number is 5.

17. $3l = 24$

18.a) $n = 4$ **b)** $n = 3$ **c)** $n = 3$
d) $n = 243$ **e)** $n = 51$ **f)** $n = 3$

19.a) $n = 5$ **b)** $n = 10$ **c)** $n = 7$ **d)** $n = 425$

20.a) $n = 250 - 98$ **b)** $n = 152$

21.a) $b = 2w$, $w = 74$ **b)** $b = 148$

Unit 10 Practice Test, page 401

1.a) Output: 2; 7; 12; 17; 22
c) Input: 6; 7; 8; Output: 27; 32; 37
d) Output = $47 \times 5 - 3$ **e)** Add 3, divide by 5
f) Yes, because the Input number goes up by 1 each time.
g) No, because the Output number ends in a 2 or a 7.

2.a) Choice 1
b) For example: The pattern is a power of 2.
c) After 20 days

3. For example: Yes; $n = 0$, $n = 1$

4.a) 19 **b)** 7 **c)** 2 **d)** 19

Unit 10 Unit Problem: Fund Raising, page 402

Part 1

Time (h): 1; 2; 3; 4; 5; Distance (km): 15; 30; 45; 60; 75
Distance = $15t$. In 7 h, distance = $15 \times 7 = 105$ km
$15t = 135$, $t = 9$ h

Part 2

Time (h): 1; 2; 3; 4; 5; Distance (km): 20; 40; 60; 80; 100
Distance = $20t$. In 7 h, distance = $20 \times 7 = 140$ km
$20t = 135$, $t = 6.75$ h

Part 3

For example: Both of the graphs increase over time; they are linear. Liam's is steeper and goes up by 20.

Part 4

Distance (km): 10; 20; 30; 40; 50
Money raised by Ingrid ($): 250; 500; 750; 1000; 1250
Money raised by Liam ($): 200; 400; 600; 800; 1000
Ingrid raises $25*d*; Liam raises $20*d*
To raise equal amounts of money, Ingrid cycles 40 km, and Liam cycles 50 km.

Unit 11 Probability, page 404

Skills You'll Need, page 406

1.a) 10% **b)** 1% **c)** 24% **d)** 5%
2.a) 0.7, 70% **b)** 0.6, 60% **c)** 0.36, 36% **d)** 0.75, 75%
3.a) 0.175, 17.5% **b)** 0.375, 37.5%
c) 0.8125, 81.25% **d)** 0.255, 25.5%

11.1 Listing Outcomes, page 409

1.a) Red, green, yellow **b)** 1, 2, 3, 4, 5, 6
2.a) Red, yellow, green **b)** Boy, girl
c) 0, 1, 2
d) Hearts, diamonds, clubs, spades
3. Saturday, all day, adult; Saturday, all day, child; Saturday, all day, senior; Saturday, half day, adult; Saturday, half day, child; Saturday, half day, senior; Sunday, all day, adult; Sunday, all day, child; Sunday, all day, senior; Sunday, half day, adult; Sunday, half day, child; Sunday, half day, senior
4. Eggs, toast, milk; eggs, toast, juice; eggs, pancakes, milk; eggs, pancakes, juice; eggs, cereal, milk; eggs, cereal, juice; fruit, toast, milk; fruit, toast, juice; fruit, pancakes, milk; fruit, pancakes, juice; fruit, cereal, milk; fruit, cereal, juice
5.a) Black, red; black, beige; black, white; black, yellow; grey, red; grey, beige; grey, white; grey, yellow; navy, red; navy, beige; navy, white; navy, yellow
b) 6 **c)** 6 **d)** 0
6.a) 12 **b)** 30 **c)** 24 **d)** 18
7.b) 11 **c)** 5 **d)** 4 **e)** 2
f) It occurs the most often.
g) For example: The table is easier to read. The tree diagram doesn't show the sums.
8.a) 24 **b)** 256

11.2 Experimental Probability, page 413

1. Yang Hsi: 0.448; Aki: 0.488; David: 0.426; Yuk Yee: 0.306; Eli: 0.367; Aponi: 0.357; Leah: 0.478; Devadas: 0.378
2.a) 0.175; 0.825 **b)** 0.029; 0.971
3.a) Top up, top down, on its side
b) For example: No, the shape of the cup makes it more likely to land on its side.
c) Top up: 0.27; top down: 0.32; side: 0.41
5. 6 ways; 1 red, 0 yellow; 2 red, 0 yellow; 3 red, 0 yellow; 2 red, 1 yellow; 3 red, 1 yellow; 3 red, 2 yellow
6.c) For example: The sum of the relative frequencies should be 1.
7.b) For example: The relative frequency is approximately the same for each set of results.

Unit 11 Mid-Unit Review, page 415

1. Easy, 1 player; easy, 2 players; intermediate, 1 player; intermediate, 2 players; challenging, 1 player; challenging, 2 players
2. Egg roll, chicken, milk; egg roll, chicken, juice; egg roll, chicken, pop; egg roll, chop suey, milk; egg roll, chop suey, juice; egg roll, chop suey, pop; egg roll, broccoli beef, milk; egg roll, broccoli beef, juice; egg roll, broccoli beef, pop; soup, chicken, milk; soup, chicken, juice; soup, chicken, pop; soup, chop suey, milk; soup, chop suey, juice; soup, chop suey, pop; soup, broccoli beef, milk; soup, broccoli beef, juice; soup, broccoli beef, pop; fried rice, chicken, milk; fried rice, chicken, juice; fried rice, chicken, pop; fried rice, chop suey, milk; fried rice, chop suey, juice; fried rice, chop suey, pop; fried rice, broccoli beef, milk; fried rice, broccoli beef, juice; fried rice, broccoli beef, pop
3.a) 0.033 **b)** 0.552 **c)** 0.663
4. 0.333
5.a) 1, 2, 3, 4, 5, 6 **b)** Yes, they each occur once.
d) For example: Yes.
e) For example: The relative frequency is approximately the same for each set of results.
6. Part b; adding green counters increases the probability of picking green.

11.3 Theoretical Probability, page 418

1.a) About 0.26 **b)** About 0.22
2.a) 0.5 **b)** 0.5 **c)** 0.125 **d)** 0.875
3.a) False; it could happen, but it is unlikely.
b) False; you will not always get exactly this outcome.
c) True; the more you toss a coin, the more likely this outcome will occur.
4.a) True; *Win* covers $\frac{1}{3}$ of the spinner.
b) False; 100 is not divisible by 3, so an equal number of times is not possible.
c) False; this outcome will not always occur. The experimental results may be different from the theoretical results.
5.a) 0.004 **b)** 0.04 **c)** 0.9
6.a) For example: I divided 360 by each denominator to find the angle in degrees for each sector of the spinner.
b) Red: 50; yellow, 100; blue: 33; green; 17
c) For example: The probability of landing on each other colour would increase, because the sum of the fractions must equal 1 whole. If one decreases, one or more of the others increases.

11.4 Applications of Probability, page 422

1.a) 8 **b)** 0.125 **c)** 0.125

d) They are the same; if all the winners are female, none of the winners can be male, which is the answer to part c.

2.a) 25% **b)** 75%

3.a) i) 37.5% **ii)** 37.5% **iii)** 50% **iv)** 12.5%

b) For example: "At least" includes 2 tails and 3 tails. If these words were left out, 3 tails would not be included, and the probability of getting tails would be lower.

c) For example: "Exactly" means 3 heads are not included. If this word was left out, this could mean 2 heads or 3 heads, and the probability would change.

4. For example: People are not likely to win, so the carnival owners can afford to be generous with the prize.

5.a) 37.5% **b)** 93.75% **c)** 12.5%

6.a) $\frac{1}{6}$

b) For example: There would be 18 different combinations. Each combination would have a probability of $\frac{1}{18}$.

7. Spin the pointer on each spinner once. Spin the pointer on spinner A twice. Both are equally likely: 25%.

Reading and Writing in Math: Choosing a Strategy, page 424

1. $6.97

2. For example: It depends on the number of hours worked. If he works less than 22 h, $96 per week is a better deal. If he works 22 h or more, $4.50/h is better.

3.a) 81 cm^2 **b)** 216 cm^3

4. For example: $\frac{1}{32}$

6. a and b are the same; the final price is $73.59 in both cases.

7. $18

9. 136

10.a) 6 **b)** 0.25

11.a) 0.125 **b)** About 0.396

Unit 11 Unit Review, page 427

1.a) Banana, carrots, yogurt; banana, carrots, cheese; banana, celery, yogurt; banana, celery, cheese; banana, cucumber, yogurt; banana, cucumber, cheese; orange, carrots, yogurt; orange, carrots, cheese; orange, celery, yogurt; orange, celery, cheese; orange, cucumber, yogurt; orange, cucumber, cheese; apple, carrots, yogurt; apple, carrots, cheese; apple, celery, yogurt; apple, celery, cheese; apple, cucumber, yogurt; apple, cucumber, cheese

b) 3 **c)** 14 **d)** 12

2.a) HHHH, HHHT, HHTH, HTHH, THHH, HHTT, HTHT, HTTH, THHT, THTH, TTHH, HTTT, THTT, TTHT, TTTH, TTTT

b) 4 **c)** 6 **d)** 5

3.a) 0.9 **b)** 13 500

4.a) 0.487 **b)** 0.513 **c)** 0.715

d) 0.342 **e)** 0.77

5.a) False; it is very unlikely, but it could happen.

b) True; it is very unlikely.

c) False; this outcome will not always occur in practice.

d) True; with a greater number of trials, the experimental and theoretical probabilities are likely to be close.

6.a) Yes; the circle is divided into 10 equal parts.

b) 0.1 **c)** 0.4 **d)** 0.5

7.a) 0.5 **b)** 0.25 **c)** 0.8 **d)** 0.4

8.a) 7 times **b)** 33 times **c)** 59 times **d)** 46 times

9.a) i) 25% **ii)** 0%

b) i) 37.5% **ii)** 87.5%

10. About 33%

Unit 11 Practice Test, page 429

1. Saturday, matinee, adult; Saturday, matinee, child; Saturday, matinee, senior; Saturday, evening, adult; Saturday, evening, child; Saturday, evening, senior; Sunday, matinee, adult; Sunday, matinee, child; Sunday, matinee, senior; Sunday, evening, adult; Sunday, evening, child; Sunday, evening, senior

2.a) 10 times; it is likely to appear once every 6 rolls.

b) 30 times; one-half the numbers are even.

c) 30 times; one-half the numbers are greater than 3.

d) 0 times; 9 is not a number on the cube.

3.a) 0.3 **b)** 0.353

c) For example: 27, if her batting average stays at 0.3.

4. Equally likely; for example: The probabilities are the same.

5. About 8 times

Cumulative Review, Units 1–11, page 434

1.a) 6, 12, 18, 24, 30 **b)** 9, 18, 27, 36, 45

c) 12, 24, 36, 48, 60

2.a) 1, 2, 3, 4, 6, 9, 12, 18, 36

b) 1, 3, 19, 57 **c)** 1, 3, 5, 15, 25, 75

3. Quilt B

4.a) $SA = 6c^2$ **b)** $SA = 2lw + 2lh + 2wh$

c) For example: Substitute c for l, w, and h.

5.a) $1\frac{5}{12}$ **b)** $5\frac{14}{15}$ **c)** $1\frac{7}{10}$

d) $1\frac{4}{5}$ **e)** $\frac{45}{8}$ or $5\frac{5}{8}$ **f)** $\frac{26}{10}$ or $2\frac{3}{5}$

6.a) 3.8 **b)** 3.4 **c)** 3.9 **d)** 3.7

7.a) For example: The cafeteria staff may change the menu based on students' favourite foods.

b) For example: If many customers would like Sunday appointments, the salon might stay open on Sundays.

8.a) 122 s **b)** 119.5 s **c)** 118

d) For example: The median. **e)** 19s

f) 120 s, or any time above 120 s **g)** 113 s

9.a) For example: It shows the average attendance at the Blue Jays' games in Toronto from 1991 to 2003.

b) For example: The mean.

d) For example: The data show a downward trend as time goes on. Attendance was high around the years the Jays won the World Series.

f) For example: The graph in part i minimizes the downward trend. The graph in part ii makes the downward trend seem larger.

10.a) 30 cm^2 **b)** 10.125 cm^2

c) 36 m^2 **d)** 8.64 cm^2

11.a) 24 cm

b) Cannot find; missing side length

c) 30 m **d)** 14.4 cm

13. $50.00

14.a) 630 **b)** 600 **c)** 60

15. –8, –6, –5, –1, 0, +2, +5

16.a) –4 **b)** –6 **c)** +10 **d)** –6

17.a) 7 m **b)** 3 m

18. +7°C

19. For example:

a) Two decreased by three times a number

b) Three times a number minus two

c) Thirty-five decreased by a number

d) The sum of a number and 35

e) Two times the sum of a number and two

f) The sum of one-fifth of a number and ten

20.a) $\frac{n}{12}$ **b)** $\frac{n}{12}$ **c)** $5n + 11$

21.a) Money collected ($): 30; 60; 90; 120; 150; 180

c) For example: When the number of cars increases by 5, the cost increases by $30.

d) **i)** Find the row with that value in it.

ii) Find the number of cars along the horizontal axis, and read the cost along the vertical axis.

e) $162; 3 ways. A table, a graph, or by multiplying.

22.a) $x = 6$ **b)** $x = 45$ **c)** $x = 5$ **d)** $x = 9$

23.a) $3p = 852.00$ **b)** $p = \$284.00$

24.a) HHH, HHT, HTH, HTT, THH, THT, TTH, TTT

b) 3 heads: $\frac{1}{8}$; 2 heads, 1 tail: $\frac{3}{8}$; 1 head, 2 tails: $\frac{3}{8}$; 3 tails: $\frac{1}{8}$

e) For example: The more times I conduct the experiment, the closer the relative frequency is likely to be to the calculated probability.

25.a) 5 **b)** 10

c) 20 (or 25, if you include Y as a vowel)

d) 0

26. 6, 7, 8, 9, 10, 11, 12, 13, 14, 15, 16

Extra Practice

Unit 1, page 438

1. $146

2. 732 799 km^2

3. 52

4. $9801

5.a) For example: Assuming the average Canadian lives 80 years, about 2400 km/year, and about 46 km/week.

6.a) 1, 2, 3, 6, 12, 18, 36 **b)** 1, 2, 4, 7, 8, 14, 28, 56

c) 1, 2, 4, 6, 8, 12, 16, 24, 48, 96

7.a) 12, 24, 36, 48, 60, 72, 84, 96, 108, 120

b) 15, 30, 45, 60, 75, 90, 105, 120, 135, 150

c) 20, 40, 60, 80, 100, 120, 140, 160, 180, 200

8.a) 6 **b)** 3 **c)** 25 **d)** 12

9.a) 49 **b)** 289 **c)** 729 **d)** 1369

10.a) 72 **b)** 120 **c)** 180 **d)** 168

11.a) 9 **b)** 12 **c)** 15 **d)** 20

12.a) 196 cm^2 **b)** 56 cm

13.a) 30 m **b)** 120 m

14. 52 cm

15. 1350 cm^3

16.a) 4^5 **b)** 12^4

17.a) **i)** 50 **ii)** 510 **iii)** 5110

b) 51 110

Unit 2, page 439

1.a) For example: 6 red squares, 7 blue squares

b) For example: 2 triangles, 7 circles

2.a) 2:1 **b)** 7:4 **c)** 5:3 **d)** 1:4

3. For example:

a) 10:14, 15:21, 20:28 **b)** 18:5, 72:20, 108:30

c) 18:8, 27:12, 36:16 **d)** 8:11, 16:22, 64:88

4.a) Figure B **b)** Figure C **c)** Figure A

5.a) 3:1 **b)** 13:5

c) Arlene will be 16 years old. Her brother will be 8 years old.

6.a) Bucket B contains more triangles. Bucket A contains more squares.

b) 7:16

7.a) 20 sticks **b)** 7:4

8.a) 63:10 **b)** 70 girls

9. 48 and 40; 42 and 35

10.a) Coriander, 1:2; cumin, 3:10; peppercorns, 1:5

b) 500 g of coriander, 300 g of cumin, and 200 g of peppercorns

Unit 3, page 440

1.b) For example: Two different objects.

6.a) $A = 45$ cm^2; $P = 32.2$ cm **b)** $A = 31.36$ m^2; $P = 22.4$ m

7.a) $SA = 188$ cm^2 **b)** $V = 168$ cm^3

c) $SA = 19.44$ cm^2 **d)** $V = 5.832$ cm^3

8.a) 2000 cm^2

b) For example: 2488 cm^2, if there is 1 cm extra on each side.

9. 88 m^2

Unit 4, page 441

1.a) $\frac{3}{2}$ **b)** $\frac{4}{9}$ **c)** $\frac{2}{3}$ **d)** 2

2.a) 1 whole circle, and $\frac{2}{3}$ of another circle.

b) 1 whole circle, and $\frac{2}{5}$ of another circle.

c) 3 whole circles, and $\frac{1}{2}$ of another circle.

d) 3 whole circles, and $\frac{2}{3}$ of another circle.

3.a) $0.9\overline{4}$ **b)** 3.25 **c)** 0.6 **d)** $2.\overline{3}$

4.a) $\frac{13}{6}$ or $2\frac{1}{6}$ **b)** $\frac{9}{8}$ or $1\frac{1}{8}$ **c)** $\frac{8}{10}$ or $\frac{4}{5}$ **d)** $\frac{21}{12}$ or $1\frac{3}{4}$

5.a) $2\frac{13}{15}$ **b)** $3\frac{13}{15}$ **c)** $\frac{13}{15}$ **d)** $1\frac{13}{15}$

6.a) $\frac{3}{8}$ **b)** $\frac{8}{12}$ or $\frac{2}{3}$ **c)** $\frac{3}{8}$ **d)** $\frac{7}{6}$ or $1\frac{1}{6}$

7.a) $\frac{23}{40}$ **b)** $\frac{17}{12}$ or $1\frac{5}{12}$ **c)** $\frac{23}{15}$ or $1\frac{8}{15}$ **d)** $\frac{31}{24}$ or $1\frac{7}{24}$

8.a) $\frac{5}{12}$ **b)** $\frac{11}{30}$ **c)** $\frac{1}{10}$ **d)** $\frac{3}{40}$

9.a) $\frac{23}{12}$ or $1\frac{11}{12}$ **b)** $\frac{32}{10}$ or $3\frac{1}{5}$ **c)** $\frac{29}{18}$ or $1\frac{11}{18}$ **d)** $\frac{74}{30}$ or $2\frac{14}{30}$

10.a) $\frac{3}{5} \times 5$ **b)** $\frac{7}{4} \times 3$

11.a) 3 **b)** $\frac{21}{4}$

12.a) $\frac{5}{4}$ **b)** $\frac{11}{2}$ **c)** 14 **d)** $\frac{3}{4}$

13.a) 7.82 **b)** 3.96 **c)** 15.17 **d)** 4.93

14.a) 2.5 **b)** 3.5 **c)** 2.8 **d)** 1.5

15. 56.16 m^2

16. 1.5 m

17.a) $14.14 **b)** $5.86

18.a) 3.78 **b)** 11.1

Unit 5, page 442

1.a) 26°C; 24°C **b)** About 11°C

c) From January to May; from February to June

d) i) For example: What is the greatest average high temperature shown on the graph?

ii) For example: What is the lowest temperature between June and September?

2.a) The data are not measured over time.

b) About 170 000 km^2 **c)** About 169 000 km^2

e) About 320 000 km^2, round each area to the nearest ten thousand: 80 000 + 40 000 + 200 000 = 320 000 km^2.

3.a) 140 cm **c)** There is no mode.

d) 143.2 cm

4. For example: 5, 6, 6, 6, 7, 7, 7, 8; many shoe sizes are possible, as long as the mean of the 4th and 5th terms equals the median, $6\frac{1}{2}$.

5.b) 1 min 30 s

c) The stem for 2 minutes. For example: Most swimmers took between 2 and 3 minutes to complete the race.

d) 2:48 **e)** 2:25, 2:43, 2:54, 3:09, 3:10

Unit 6, page 443

1.b) 46.75 cm^2

2. For example: $b = 6$ cm, $h = 4$ cm; $b = 8$ cm, $h = 3$ cm; $b = 5$ cm, $h = 4.8$ cm

3. 64.41 cm^2

4. 3.84 m^2

5.a) 0.96 m^2

b) 13.44 m^2; add the areas of the two triangles and the areas of the three parallelograms.

6.b) 16.875 cm^2

7.a) For example: $b = 6$ cm, $h = 4$ cm; $b = 8$ cm, $h = 3$ cm; $b = 5$ cm, $h = 4.8$ cm

b) For example: They have the same base and height; each triangle is one-half the area of each parallelogram.

8. 5.59 cm^2

9.a) 14.4 cm^2

b) For example: Find the area of the trapezoid; find the area of the square and subtract the area of the two triangles.

c) About 16 cm

d) No; the lengths of all the sides of the trapezoid are not known.

10. $P = 16$ m; $A = 9.72$ m^2

Unit 7, page 444

1. For example: A and D: Hexagonal concave polygons, 4 right angles, one angle greater than 180°.
B and C: Pentagonal concave irregular polygons, 2 right angles, 2 angles less than 90°, 1 angle greater than 180°.
E and F: Quadrilateral convex irregular polygons, no parallel sides.

2. Figures A and D, E and F, B and C; the figures have the same size and shape.

3. Figure D is the image of Figure A, after a reflection in a diagonal between the 2 figures.
Figure C is the image of Figure B after a rotation of a $\frac{1}{4}$-turn clockwise about a point that is 2 points below the vertex where the 2 figures meet. Figure F is the image of Figure E after a translation of 3 units right and 2 units down.

4.a) Figures B, C, E, F tile the plane.

7. The equilateral triangle, the rhombus, and the acute isosceles triangle.

Unit 8, page 445

1.a) About 15% **b)** About 75%
b) About 80% **d)** About 25%
2.a) 75%, 0.75 **b)** 150%, 1.50
c) 60%, 0.60 **d)** 15%, 0.15
3.a) \$20 **b)** \$0.85 **c)** \$6.00 **d)** \$1.87
e) \$5.50 **f)** \$14.00 **g)** \$0.05 **h)** \$1.50
4.a) \$2.00 **b)** \$12.00 **c)** \$14.00 **d)** \$24.00
e) \$150.00 **f)** \$45.00 **g)** \$4.00 **h)** \$50.00
5. About 80%
6.a) Sales tax: \$52.50; total cost: \$402.49
b) Sales tax: \$2.70; total cost: \$20.68
7. 180 students
8. 8530 m
9.a) The News **b)** Movies and Cartoons
c) About $\frac{1}{4}$ **d)** About 250 days

Unit 9, page 446

1.a) +5 cm **b)** –89°C **c)** –400 m **d)** +8156 m
2.a) –9 s **b)** +\$25 **c)** –50°C
3. –1
4.a) $-3 < +5$ **b)** $-2 > -4$ **c)** $+1 > 0$ **d)** $+8 > -10$
5. –15, –2, –1, 0, +1, +4, +5
6.a) +17 **b)** –12 **c)** –13 **d)** +2
7.a) +15 **b)** –11 **c)** –14 **d)** –6
e) –1 **f)** –21 **g)** +10 **h)** –13
8.a) –21 **b)** +3 **c)** +20 **d)** –3
e) +19 **f)** +21 **g)** –8 **h)** +21
9.a) +6; (+4) + (+2) = +6 **b)** +1; (–2) + (+3) = +1
c) –5; (–3) + (–2) = –5 **d)** –1; (+5) + (–6) = –1
e) –19; (–23) + (+4) = –19 **f)** –22; (–19) + (–3) = –22
g) +11; (+13) + (–2) = +11 **h)** +22; (+9) + (+13) = +22
10.a) +2; (+5) – (+3) = +2 **b)** +7; (+3) – (–4) = +7
c) –8; (–5) – (+3) = –8 **d)** –3; (–7) – (–4) = –3
e) +25; (+13) – (–12) = +25 **f)** –54; (–22) – (+32) = –54
g) 0; (–23) – (–23) = 0 **h)** –17; (–7) – (+10) = –17
11.a) High temperature: –1°C, low temperature: –9°C
b) 8°C
12.a) +12 **b)** 0 **c)** 0 **d)** –12
e) 0 **f)** +12 **g)** –12 **h)** 0

Unit 10, page 447

1.a) i) Start at 2. Add 3 each time.
ii) 17, 20, 23 **iii)** 44
b) i) Start at 1. Alternate between adding 2 and adding 3 each time.
ii) 13, 16, 18 **iii)** 36
c) i) Start at 1. Add 2. Increase the number you add by 1 each time.
ii) 21, 28, 36 **iii)** 120
d) i) Start at 3. Add 3. Increase the number you add by 2 each time.
ii) 38, 51, 66 **iii)** 227
2.a) Output: 3; 7; 11; 15; 19 **b)** Output: 23; 27; 31
c) The Input number starts at 1 and increases by 1 each time. The Output number starts at 3, and increases by 4 each time.
e) For example: To get from one point to the next, move 1 square right and 4 squares up. Moving 1 square right is the same as adding 1 to the Input number to get the next Input number. Moving 4 squares up is the same as adding 4 to the Output number to get the next Output number.
3. For example:
a) A number plus two
b) Five decreased by a number
c) Three times a number **d)** A number divided by two
4.a) $2n + 4$ **b)** $2n - 4$ **c)** $\frac{n}{4}$ **d)** $4n - 2$
5.a) 7 **b)** 1 **c)** 5 **d)** 2 **e)** 2 **f)** 1
6.a) $n + 3 = 18$ **b)** $6 + n = 71$ **c)** $\frac{n}{5} = 14$ **d)** $4n = 64$
7. For example:
a) The product of 3 and a number is 9.
b) Fifteen divided by a number is 3.
c) A number decreased by 6 is 13.
d) The product of 24 and a number is 552.
8.a) For example: Let t represent the number of points Tung scored. $t = 14 + 8$; $t = 22$
b) For example: Let n represent the number of cards Nema has. $n = 4 \times 156$; $n = 624$
c) For example: Let a represent how far Adriel cycled, in kilometres. $a = 218 - 80$; $a = 138$
9.a) $n = 25$ **b)** $n = 35$ **c)** $n = 6$
d) $n = 150$ **e)** $n = 6$ **f)** $n = 4$
10.a) $x = 7$ **b)** $x = 10$ **c)** $x = 6$
d) $x = 14$ **e)** $x = 247$ **f)** $x = 23$

Unit 11, page 448

1.a) J♥G, J♥B, J♥R, J♥Y, J♦G, J♦B, J♦R, J♦Y, J♠G, J♠B, J♠R, J♠Y, J♣G, J♣B, J♣R, J♣Y, Q♥G, Q♥B, Q♥R, Q♥Y, Q♦G, Q♦B, Q♦R, Q♦Y, Q♠G, Q♠B, Q♠R, Q♠Y, Q♣G, Q♣B, Q♣R, Q♣Y, K♥G, K♥B, K♥R, K♥Y, K♦G, K♦B, K♦R, K♦Y, K♠G, K♠B, K♠R, K♠Y, K♣G, K♣B, K♣R, K♣Y
b) 4 **c)** 12
2.b) Outcome: Ace, 2, 3, 4, 5, 6, 7, 8, 9, 10, J, Q, K
c) Yes

3.a) 25 times **b)** 50 times **c)** 75 times

4. White; there are 7 candies left: 2R, 2G, 3W. The probability of it being white is $\frac{3}{7}$, and the probability of it being red or green is only $\frac{2}{7}$.

5.a) E **b)** $\frac{1}{50}$ **c)** J, K, Q, X, Z

d) J, K, Q, X, Z: $\frac{1}{100}$; B, C, F, H, M, P, V, W, Y: $\frac{1}{50}$; D, L, S, U: $\frac{1}{25}$; N, R, T: $\frac{3}{50}$; A, I: $\frac{9}{100}$

e) No; each letter is in the bag, so each letter has a probability of being picked.

Take It Further, page 449

1. 29, 31

2. $6 \times \left(\frac{6}{6} + 6\right)$

3. For example: 2 quarters, 3 dimes, 20 pennies

4. Move 9 from box 3 to box 1.

5. For example: $(7 + 0 - 3 + 6 - 5 + 4) \times (9 - 2 + 1 - 8) = 0$

6. 60 cards

7. 27, 29, 31, 33

8. For example: $1 - 2 + 3 - 4 + 5 + 6 - 7 + 8 + 90 = 100$

9. $\left(\frac{5}{5} \times 5\right) \times 5 + 5$

10. $33 - 3 + \frac{3}{3}$

11. 51

12. For example: $10 + 24 + 6 + 35 + 7 + 8 + 9 = 99$

13. 50

14. $\left(\frac{4}{4} + 4\right) \times \left(\frac{4}{4} + 4\right) \times 4$

15. 5050

16. 23 matches

17. Remove the 6 segments that make up the 2 inner triangles.

18. At the end of 13 days.

19. For example: 11 and 1.1, 3 and $\frac{3}{2}$, 4 and $\frac{4}{3}$

20. 32

21. $41 943.04

22. Fill the 5-L container, pour it into the 8-L container. Fill the 5-L container again, and pour it into the 8-L container until it's full. There will be 2 L of water left in the 5-L container.

23. 35 potatoes

24. 36 posts

25. For example: $5 + (5 \times 5)$ or $(6 \times 6) - 6$

26. Move the top counter down. Move the 2 counters at each end of the bottom row to each end of the second row from the top.

27. On day 8

28. 60 kg